T0295784

Economic Inequality and Poverty

Economic Inequality and Poverty

Facts, Methods, and Policies

NANAK KAKWANI
HYUN H. SON

OXFORD
UNIVERSITY PRESS

OXFORD
UNIVERSITY PRESS

Great Clarendon Street, Oxford, OX2 6DP,
United Kingdom

Oxford University Press is a department of the University of Oxford.
It furthers the University's objective of excellence in research, scholarship,
and education by publishing worldwide. Oxford is a registered trade mark of
Oxford University Press in the UK and in certain other countries

Impression: 1

Published in the United States of America by Oxford University Press
198 Madison Avenue, New York, NY 10016, United States of America

British Library Cataloguing in Publication Data
Data available

Library of Congress Control Number: 2021951057

ISBN 978–0–19–885284–1

DOI: 10.1093/oso/9780198852841.001.0001

Printed and bound by
CPI Group (UK) Ltd, Croydon, CR0 4YY

Contents

Preface

In 1980, Oxford University Press, New York published my book for the World Bank entitled *Economic Inequality and Poverty: Methods of Estimation and Policy Applications*. Amartya Sen, Nobel Laureate in Economics in 1998, reviewed the book for the World Bank. His comments were so complimentary that I was overwhelmed. I recall that one of his comments was, "Kakwani can publish this book by any publisher, but it would be good for the World Bank to publish it." After 38 years, I am again overwhelmed by the comments made by the three reviewers of this book for Oxford University Press. One of the reviewers pointed out, "There is, however, to the best of my knowledge, no textbook right now that offers, at both the theoretical and empirical level, an up-to-date version of income inequality and poverty analysis."

All three reviewers made very thoughtful comments. Although I could not accept all their recommendations, I was happy to take many of them. Furthermore, while drafting the proposal, I was conscientious about giving substantial empirical applications of all the techniques presented in the new book.

One of the reviewers correctly points out that the emphasis of the previous book was on statistical analysis. Since I wrote an earlier book, my research interest shifted substantially to evidence-based policy. However, the current book provides rigorous development of inequality and poverty methods over the last 50 years; it emphasizes economic applications, using actual country-level household surveys.

In the 1990s, polarization became a focus of research among economists because they were concerned about the shrinking of the middle class. The size of the middle class has important implications for economic growth and social welfare. The current book has developed new techniques linking the shrinking of the middle class and polarization.

Poverty, inequality, and growth (PIG) are three widely debated, interrelated issues among development economists. A substantial amount of research has been carried out on PIG relationships using cross-country regression models. However, conflicting conclusions from this research have also led to a deep division among researchers. This book extensively discusses the PIG relationships at the core of development economics. In addition, two substantive chapters, namely, "Economic Growth and Poverty" and "Pro-Poor Growth," have been added, providing new insights into the PIG relationships.

Poverty is traditionally measured in income space. However, a society's ultimate objective is to enhance people's well-being—a multidimensional concept. Thus, there are several dimensions of poverty. The current book has a chapter on multidimensional poverty, and it provides a critical evaluation of many unresolved issues in measuring multidimensional poverty, proposing some new techniques.

The earlier book made substantive contributions, proving many theorems and corollaries on relationships among individuals' or families' distribution of economic variables. These relationships play a crucial role in understanding many economic phenomena. This volume has explored many more economic applications of the theorems developed in the earlier book in a separate chapter. This volume provides a framework quantifying the distributional relations among economic variables. This framework should help readers discover new applications, leading to the advancement of evidence-based economic policies.

The relevance of the progressivity of taxation and social programs to policymaking depends on whether it helps assess its social welfare implications. The literature on taxation has not explored the social welfare implications of tax progressivity measures. This volume has four chapters on taxation and social welfare programs, providing their social welfare implications. They deal with measuring horizontal and vertical equity and tax discrimination. The techniques of evaluating social programs are developed in these chapters.

Over the past 50 years, economic inequality and poverty issues have become central to public debates. As a result, the literature measuring economic inequality and poverty has profoundly expanded. It has developed many new methodologies, but at the same time, it has also generated many unresolved controversies. This volume has attempted to resolve these controversies.

Prices play a crucial role in people's everyday lives. However, people have different economic circumstances and consumption patterns, so prices on living standards differ from one person to another. Thus, they can have a profound effect on inequality and poverty. This volume has included two chapters: one on the impact of prices on inequality and the other on poverty. These chapters provide a precise meaning to price indices comparing social welfare when consumers face continuously changing prices.

This enlarged book has taken about 10% of material from my earlier book, which means that 90% of the material in the book is new. The book provides a rigorous development of inequality and poverty measures and detailed country-level analysis and policies. It has utilized household surveys to illustrate the application of methods, showing how they can help draw evidence-based policy conclusions. The book has many technical derivations, but every equation has been explained in non-technical terms, and every concept has been given an intuitive explanation. There might not be any competing book in the market covering such a wide range of topics, focusing on empirical applications.

Hyun Son has collaborated with me on this book; without her contributions, it would not have been possible to complete this substantive volume.

Nanak Kakwani

List of Figures

List of Tables

List of Abbreviations

AGIC	absolute growth incidence curve
APEGR	absolute poverty equivalent growth rate
APGC	absolute poverty growth curve
BGAD	between-group absolute deprivation
BGRD	between-group relative deprivation
CHIP	Chinese Household Income Project
CV	compensation variation
EV	equivalent variation
FIES	Family Income and Expenditure Survey
HE	horizontal equity
IGTI	inequality–growth trade-off index
ILO	International Labour Organization
KIHASA	Korean Institute for Health and Social Affairs
LDPI	Laspeyres Democratic Price Index
LIS	Luxembourg Income Study
LMDPI	Laspeyres multiplicative democratic price index
LSPI	Laspeyres social price index
MCL	minimum cost of living
MDG	Millennium Development Goal
MDPI	multiplicative democratic price index
NBS	National Bureau of Statistics
PEGR	poverty equivalent growth rate
PIHS	Pakistan Integrated Household Survey
PIG	poverty, inequality, and growth
PIP	price index for the poor
P–L law	Pareto–Levy law
PPP	purchasing power parity
RGIC	relative growth incidence curve
RPEGR	relative poverty equivalent growth rate
RPGC	relative poverty growth curve
RSCP	relative social cost of poverty
SCP	social cost of poverty
SRR	social rate of return
SUL	social utility loss
TSCP	total social cost of poverty
TSPI	true social price index
UBI	universal basic income
UNDP	United Nations Development Programme
VE	vertical equity
VLSS	Vietnamese Living Standard Surveys
WDR	World Development Report
WGAD	with-group absolute deprivation
WGRD	within-group relative deprivation

1
Introduction

1.1 Scope and Limitations

In a closed economy, income is created in production with factors such as land, labor, capital, and entrepreneurship. Production takes place in thousands of firms and government organizations, and, at the same time, income is created and distributed to individuals. From this process, a pattern of income distribution emerges that is stable over time and space. This feature of income distribution has provoked several alternative theories explaining income generation.

This literature discusses two facets of income distribution: (a) the functional distribution, the share of the total national income that each factor of production receives, and (b) the size distribution of income or personal income distribution. The functional distribution of income deals with the division of income based on production factors, including land, labor, and capital. It deals with income distribution among individuals, households, other income units. Most of the economic literature on distribution has focused on the functional distribution of income. Recently, there has been growing interest in the size distribution of income. The present volume, however, concerns the size distribution of income.

The main reason for strong interest in the functional distribution of income had been that the classical economists believed that the focus on owners of factors of production was essential to enhance economic growth. Economic growth was considered critical for bettering people's lives. But now, it is increasingly realized that economic growth is necessary but not sufficient to enhance society's welfare. The size distribution of income is directly linked with the standard of living people enjoy. How much income people receive matters more to them than the amount of income they derive from the factors of production they own.

The size distribution of income generated by the production process results from the complex market forces. It can be called, for convenience, a primary income distribution. In contrast, a secondary income distribution ultimately occurs after redistribution due to various government policies in taxation, social security, and other interventions.

Alleviating income inequality and poverty are two central goals of economic development. Income inequality has been a source of worldwide upheaval, fueling social and political unrest. Addressing rising inequality has now become the top of the agenda of many governments and development organizations today. The widening

Economic Inequality and Poverty. Nanak Kakwani and Hyun Son, Oxford University Press.
© Nanak Kakwani and Hyun Son (2022). DOI: 10.1093/oso/9780198852841.003.0001

disparity between the top 1% and bottom 99% has become a serious political issue in countries like the United States. Because of increasing concerns about inequality, many governments have instituted redistribution policies through taxation and public programs. This volume has made significant contributions to analyzing governments' redistribution policies.

While there has been notable progress in reducing poverty in the past decades, poverty remains an unfinished agenda in many developing countries. The number of people living in extreme poverty worldwide has declined sharply but is still unacceptably high. The World Bank has proposed a new paradigm to reduce extreme poverty worldwide to less than 3% by 2030. Many governments have now adopted safety net programs to achieve a rapid poverty reduction, and this volume has provided a methodology to assess safety net programs.

This volume is about the measurement of inequality and poverty, both of which are derived from the size distribution of income. Since 1970, research on measuring economic inequality and poverty has accelerated. Inequality measures tend to be viewed as no more than statistical devices for measuring dispersion in income distributions. There is a growing consensus that these measures should be derived from social welfare functions that incorporate society's normative judgments. This volume provides detailed analyses of the linkages between social welfare functions and measures of income inequality. Similarly, the volume presents pioneering work on systematically analyzing the link between poverty measures and social welfare functions, which has yet to be explored in the literature.

This volume develops techniques to estimate income inequality and poverty using actual data collected from several sources. More importantly, the methods developed in the volume provide a swathe of policy applications, particularly in public finance, social policies, and labor markets.

Poverty, Inequality, and Growth (PIG) are three widely debated interrelated issues among development economists. A substantial amount of research has been carried out on PIG relationships using cross-country regression models. However, conflicting conclusions from this research have also led to a deep division among researchers. This volume provides an extensive discussion of the PIG relationships at the core of development economics.

This introductory chapter summarizes how income inequality and poverty measurements have evolved in the past 50 years. The remaining chapters attempt to include new developments and debates associated with inequality and poverty. The main focus of the volume is on applications of techniques to draw policy implications. It has utilized household surveys to illustrate the application of methods, showing how they can help draw policy conclusions.

However, the volume has excluded some essential topics, such as chronic poverty and vulnerability. Chronic poverty is an important topic because it introduces a distinction between the temporarily poor and the chronically poor. Vulnerability has become an essential topic in poverty analysis in recent years as information on the identification of poor households and individuals and those at risk of falling into poverty is crucial in designing strategies of poverty reduction. However, this volume has excluded this topic given insufficient empirical analysis. Notwithstanding, the book has covered essential inequality and poverty issues developed in the last 50 years.

1.2 Theories of Size Distribution of Income: A Brief Review

Various theories have been advanced to explain the distribution of income among individuals. In the literature, two leading schools of thought have emerged. The first may be called the statistical theoretical school, and such authors lead this as Gibrat (1931), Roy (1950), Champernowne (1952, 1953), Levy (1925), Aitchison and Brown (1954, 1957), and Rutherford (1955). These authors explained the generation of income with the help of specific stochastic processes. This research was inspired by Pareto (1897), who observed a certain regularity in the distribution of incomes in various countries and over time. He formulated his famous Pareto law of income distribution based on these regularities.[1] Chapter 2 has provided a short but exhaustive review of the stochastic income generation models proposed in the literature.

The most severe criticism of stochastic models is that they only explain the partial income generation process. As Mincer (1958) pointed out, these models shed no light on the economics of the income distribution process.

A significant conclusion emerging from the review in Chapter 2 is that none of the distribution functions offered by this literature fits well with the observed income distributions. Although many prominent scholars have contributed to developing stochastic income generation models, this literature has not found much practical application in development economics.

The second school of thought, which may be called the socio-economic school, seeks to explain income distribution utilizing economic and institutional factors, such as gender, age, occupation, education, geographical differences, and the distribution of wealth. Three groups of authors belong to this school. The first follows the human capital approach, based on the hypothesis of lifetime income maximization. Mincer initiated this approach in 1958, and it was subsequently developed by Becker (1962, 1967), Chiswick (1968, 1971, 1974), Husen (1968), and De Wolff and Van Slijpe (1972). This approach has also attracted some criticism, the most severe being that it deals mainly with the market's supply side, which provides labor of various levels of education.[2]

---

[1] For a survey of stochastic models, see Bjerke (1961).
[2] See Tinbergen (1975), p. 4. In addition, see Blinder (1974) for a consideration of other criticisms.

The second group of authors, concentrating on the demand side of the market, has been referred to as the education planning school by Tinbergen (1975) and is represented by such authors as Bowles (1969), Dougherty (1971, 1972), and Psacharopoulos and Hinchliffe (1972). This group holds that the demand for various labor is derived from the production process.

The third group of authors is the supply and demand school, pioneered by Tinbergen (1975). He considered income distribution a result of the supply and demand for different kinds of labor. His analysis applies not only to labor income but also to incomes from other factors of production.

Tinbergen (1975) has elegantly described these models, so it was unnecessary to discuss them in this volume.

1.3 Lorenz Curve and Its Variants

The measurement of inequality goes back more than 115 years. In 1905, the American statistician M. O. Lorenz undertook an empirical study to measure the concentration of wealth in the United States. He proposed a graphical device to describe the concentration of wealth. This simple two-dimensional curve is still widely used to represent and analyze income distribution. It is famously known as the Lorenz curve and appeared in almost all studies of income distributions subsequently undertaken. The curve does not provide a precise law of income generation, but this volume has revealed many applications in economic analysis.

Chapter 3 presents many statistical and mathematical properties of the Lorenz curve, which have many economic applications discussed in the volume. Thus, the Lorenz curve is not merely a graphical device used to describe distributions but a valuable tool for critically analyzing many economic situations.

The chapter makes a significant contribution to linking the skewness of the Lorenz curve with economic development. Kuznets (1953) hypothesized that as a country develops, the share of the middle-income group increases. Chapter 3 demonstrates that the Lorenz curve changes its shape as a country develops. The Lorenz curve is skewed toward (0, 0) or toward (1, 1). When the Lorenz curve of a country becomes skewed toward (1, 1), the share of its middle-income class increases.

Unfortunately, recent literature on the middle class has paid little attention to Kuznets' pioneering work, carried out more than 50 years ago. Hence, the chapter has developed an index of skewness derived from the new coordinate system proposed by Kakwani and Podder (1976). Based on this index, the empirical results for 50 developing and developed countries, presented in the chapter, provide overwhelming evidence of Kuznets' hypothesis of the linkage between the size of the middle class and economic development.

Finally, the chapter also proposes the Lorenz curve's variants, including relative and absolute deprivation and Bonferroni (1930) and Zenga (2007) curves. These curves have been used to determine how government cash transfers and taxes impact the relative deprivation suffered by the Australian population. The curves have also helped compare India's and China's relative and absolute inequality.

1.4 Social Welfare Ranking of Income Distribution

Enhancing social welfare is an essential development objective. Social welfare functions are used to assess how economic resources are utilized in identifying policies that work and those that do not. Chapter 4 is devoted to social welfare rankings of income distributions. Suppose a government has two alternative policies that give rise to income distributions A and B. The choice of policies must depend on which policy creates income distribution, with higher social welfare. This chapter has attempted to clarify the issues in measuring social welfare.

There are two distinct issues in measuring social welfare. First is determining individuals' economic welfare, informing which individual in society is better off or worse off than the other. The second is aggregating individuals' welfare for the whole society. The welfare literature has primarily focused on the second issue. Evaluation of government policies cannot be accomplished unless the economic welfare of all individuals in society is known. Chapter 4 briefly discusses both these issues. It shows that the determination of individuals' economic welfare is highly complex. Empirical studies use per capita income as a proxy for individual economic welfare. However, there is a need for extensive research on this issue.

The Lorenz curve became popular because it could visibly depict income inequality. For 65 years, empirical studies used the Lorenz curve as a visual graphic device. But all this changed when, in 1970, Atkinson published a pioneering paper that provided a linkage between the Lorenz curve and social welfare functions. Chapter 4 has extended Atkinson's (1970) theorem, providing four theorems that carefully explain the general requirements of the link between the Lorenz curve and social welfare functions.

The four theorems have identified the four kinds of dominance:

1. The Lorenz curve
2. The Bonferroni curve
3. Generalized Lorenz curve
4. Generalized Bonferroni curve.

Dominance 1 and 2 imply that one distribution is unambiguously more equally (or unequally) distributed than the other. While dominance 3 and 4 inform when one distribution is welfare superior to another.

The mean welfare of individuals measures the average standard of living of the society. The average standard of living and inequality in distribution are the two distinct aspects of social welfare linked by an exact relationship. The empirical illustration presented in the chapter shows that equality ordering could be different from welfare ordering.

That raises a crucial question of which ordering of the two should determine the relevant policies. Chapter 4 concludes that both orderings could be helpful in the choice of desirable policies. This chapter has also provided a linkage between welfare ranking and stochastic dominance, commonly used in decision-making problems under uncertainty.

1.5 Measures of Income Inequality

While the Lorenz preference provided only a partial ordering of distributions, inequality literature has offered numerous inequality measures to obtain the complete income distribution ranking. Many empirical studies have observed that various inequality measures provided conflicting rankings of countries. Atkinson (1970) argued that the differences in the rankings were so contradictory that no clear picture emerges of the relative degree of inequality in advanced and developing countries. The publication of this paper led to an expansion of research on inequality measures. This research also gave rise to innovations and controversies. Chapter 5 has attempted to cover most of the research on inequality measures undertaken in the last 50 years. Its emphasis has also been on the resolution of some of the controversies.

Because of conflicting results displayed by conventional inequality measures, choosing among alternative inequality measures became critical in the inequality literature. How should one know which inequality measures are most desirable for policy? The literature proposed axioms considered desirable for inequality measures to possess. Chapter 5 provides the most comprehensive set of axioms with ethical implications that could be the basis for evaluating alternative inequality measures. The chapter also offers many lemmas, providing practical methods for assessing inequality.

In his classic paper, Dalton (1920) advanced an attack on conventional inequality measures from a welfare standpoint, and, about 50 years later, many researchers pursued the attack; notable among them were Aigner and Heins (1967), Bentzel (1970), and Atkinson (1970). Their criticisms focus on the conventional measures, which are statistical devices that measure the relative dispersion of a frequency distribution devoid of any society's normative judgment.

Arguing that any inequality measure must incorporate society's preferences, Dalton proposed a measure based on the idea of proportional welfare loss resulting from income inequality. Atkinson criticized Dalton's measure because it is variant with respect to linear transformations of the utility function. His main concern was that Dalton's measure would require additional judgment about the parameters of the linear function. Therefore, he developed an alternative class of inequality measures by introducing the concept of "the equally distributed equivalent level of income" that produced inequality measures invariant to any linear transformation. Also,

Sen (1972, 1973), Allingham (1972), and Muellbauer (1975b) proposed alternative measures based on more general assumptions about social welfare than the measures considered by Dalton and Atkinson.

Atkinson's paper had been the most influential in linking inequality with social welfare functions. It provided a practical social welfare framework for measuring inequality. But this framework is restricted to utilitarian social welfare functions, and Chapter 5 extends this framework to a general class of social welfare functions. Using this framework, the chapter develops a family of inequality measures that give different weights to transfers at different income levels. It also derives a new inequality measure based on Bonferroni's (1930) social welfare function.

In 1967, Theil proposed two measures of inequality based on the notion of entropy in information theory. These measures gained popularity because they could be decomposed into between-group and within-group inequality. This decomposition was an exciting innovation among the applied economists because it could explain how much inequality is contributed by various social groups. It enables policymakers to target specific groups to reduce overall inequality.

The decomposability of inequality measures ensures subgroup consistency, implying an increase in inequality in one group; keeping group means and population shares constant does not decrease inequality. As a result, the Gini index came under severe criticism because it does not possess decomposability and subgroup consistent properties. Empiricists then began to utilize decomposable measures extensively. Consequently, the most utilized inequality measure, the Gini index, lost its popularity.

Chapter 5 argues that the literature had been unduly critical of the Gini index to measure inequality. The chapter makes a significant contribution, showing the Gini index can indeed be decomposed as the sum of between-group relative deprivation (BGRD) and within-group relative deprivation (WGRD). Because the Gini social welfare function is interdependent, it does not lend to within-group and between-group inequality decomposition while ignoring other groups' incomes. The critics ignored the interdependence property of the Gini index, and they concluded that the Gini index was not a good measure of inequality. This chapter has proposed a new axiom that satisfies subgroup consistency in relative deprivations, more relevant for an interdependent social welfare function.

In the 1970s and 1980s, academic researchers focused on inequality and poverty measures. In 1990, the focus shifted to measuring polarization. The research on this issue began because of concerns among some economists about the shrinking of the middle class. Foster and Wolfson (1992) wrote an outstanding paper linking polarization and the shrinking size of the middle class. This paper focused on bi-polarization, but in 1994, Esteban and Ray developed a general polarization framework for many social groups, called multi-group polarization. Chapter 5 analyzes both kinds of polarization and develops new measures of polarization. It illustrates the application of these measures to Brazilian data. The chapter also demonstrates that a falling middle class has accompanied the rising inequality in China.

1.6 Identification of the Poor

There are two distinct issues in measuring poverty, as Sen (1976) points out. The first is identifying the poor, and the second is constructing an aggregate poverty index that measures the degree of suffering by a society. The literature on poverty measurement has primarily focused on the second issue. Since Sen's (1976) seminal paper, a great deal of research has been carried out to develop numerous aggregate poverty measures.

More than a century ago, in 1901, Rowntree defined families in primary poverty as those with total earnings insufficient to maintain the "minimum necessities of merely physical efficiency." The poverty line is the level of income that is just sufficient to buy these so-called minimum necessities of life, and a family is poor if its income falls below that line. Thus, a poverty line is a practical tool to identify the poor.

It is necessary to emphasize that poverty indices cannot precisely reflect poverty in a society without an accurate estimate of a poverty line. Surprisingly, the literature has almost ignored the specification of poverty lines, except for Ravallion and Bidani (1994) and Ravallion (1998) papers. Chapter 6 is devoted to constructing the poverty line, which shows that the specification of poverty lines is complex, requiring intensive research.

Chapter 6 offers a new model for constructing a poverty line by defining society's minimum acceptable standard of living in monetary units. It uses consumer theory to generate food and non-food poverty lines. The food poverty line is the monetary expenditure required to meet the minimum caloric requirements of a healthy person. Therefore, the food poverty line is calculated by multiplying the minimum caloric requirement of an individual of given age and sex by the monetary cost of each calorie consumed.

The determination of minimum living standards is complex and requires subjective judgment. The chapter has proved a critical theorem linking the minimum living standard with the real caloric cost. This theorem demonstrates that if two persons meet their calorie requirements, the person who incurs a higher real calorie cost enjoys a higher standard of living. The more affluent individuals may not consume more calories, but they consume food rich in protein, which is more expensive than the cost per calorie consumed. The more impoverished individuals consume more carbohydrates, which has a lower calorie cost. The theorem emphasizes that both the number and cost of calories are critical to determining living standards.

The non-food poverty line is determined by calculating non-food spending consistent with the minimum living standard defined from the food poverty line. Thus, both food and non-food poverty lines are determined simultaneously, consistent with the consumer theory. Although the construction of poverty lines incurs value judgments, the new model developed in the chapter helps make such *ad hoc* assumptions more justifiable.

The methodology developed in the chapter is applied to construct poverty thresholds for data obtained from Pakistan. However, the poverty thresholds obtained from the model are country-specific and cannot compare poverty across countries. Therefore, this chapter also provides the construction of global poverty lines utilized to produce global poverty counts. The international comparisons of the poverty line require purchasing power parity (PPP) estimates, which is the currency conversion for comparing countries' living standards with different price levels.

The World Bank developed its initial international poverty line at the 2005 PPP, but in 2015 it released its new PPP conversions that sparked debate about how a new global poverty threshold should be established based on the 2011 PPP. Kakwani and Son (2016) proposed a new methodology of equivalent poverty lines to determine the international poverty line based on the 2011 PPP. The World Bank applied this methodology to arrive at the official global poverty line of $1.90. International development agencies and empiricists have now adopted this as the new global poverty line.

1.7 Aggregate Poverty Measures

Sen's seminal paper, published in 1976, opened the door for developing many aggregate poverty measures. According to Sen, the poor suffer a different degree of deprivation that an aggregate poverty measure must capture. He developed a poverty measure that incorporated three aspects of poverty: (i) the percentage of poor, (ii) the aggregate income gap, and (iii) the inequality among the poor. His poverty measure was a composite measure of poverty, combining these three distinct aspects of poverty.

He proposed an axiomatic approach to deriving his poverty measure that became a new mantra for measuring poverty. Chapter 7 provides an extensive development of the aggregate poverty measures. It also derives poverty social welfare functions that give positive weights to the poor (who have income less than or equal to the poverty line) and zero weights to the non-poor (who have income above the poverty line). All poverty measures proposed in the literature have an implicit poverty social welfare function based on this weighting method.

The poverty measures proposed in the literature are relative poverty measures, showing that poverty remains unchanged when the poverty line and everyone's income increase or decrease by the same proportion. Chapter 7 has developed absolute poverty measures that do not show any change in poverty when the poverty line and income are increased or decreased by the same absolute amount. These measures provide the total social cost of poverty in monetary units that society needs to eliminate poverty. They provide insights into how much governments should spend on alleviating or reducing poverty. Absolute poverty measures could become a helpful tool for policymakers engaged in poverty reduction policies.

The chapter introduces the two general poverty social welfare functions: (i) rank order social welfare functions and (ii) additive separable utilitarian social welfare functions. The rank order poverty social welfare functions are interdependent, meaning the welfare of an individual depends not only on her consumption or income but also on the consumption or income of others in society. These welfare functions capture the relative deprivation the poor suffer. In contrast, the additive utilitarian social welfare functions assert that an individual's welfare depends only on her consumption or income and is not affected by the consumption of others in society. These social welfare functions do not capture the relative deprivation suffered by society. The most popular class of Foster, Greer, and Thorbecke (1984) measures and their numerous variants are derived from the utilitarian poverty social welfare functions. Sen's (1976) poverty measure and its variants are derived from the rank order social welfare functions.

Because Sen's poverty measure and its variants are derived from interdependent poverty social welfare functions, they are not additively decomposable and thereby violate the poverty subgroup consistency. The poverty subgroup consistency property is intuitively appealing, implying the overall poverty level will fall if a subgroup experiences a poverty reduction, while the population shares and poverty in the rest of the subgroups remain unchanged. If it is violated, it has undesirable policy implications. The class of utilitarian poverty measures is additively decomposable and is subgroup consistent. Thus, the empirical analysts abandoned using Sen's poverty measure and its variants in favor of the additively decomposable poverty measures.

This chapter has restated this controversy, and it has illustrated the decomposability and subgroup consistency of Sen's poverty measure utilizing a Chinese empirical illustration. The chapter makes a vital contribution to examining Sen's poverty measure, finding that its variants are also decomposable and subgroup consistent.

The chapter concludes that poverty measures should be chosen in two categories, depending on whether one adopts highly restricted utilitarian or interdependent poverty social welfare functions.

1.8 Multidimensional Poverty

According to the 2000–2001 World Bank Development Report, "Poverty is the pronounced deprivation in well-being." This definition raises many questions: How is well-being defined? What are the elements necessary to ensure a decent level of well-being? These questions are not by any means easy to answer. The economic literature in the 1970s and 1980s advanced many approaches to describe well-being; vital among them are basic needs, economic growth, quality of life, utility, welfare, and happiness.

In society, some people enjoy a higher level of well-being than others. Multidimensional poverty exists when some sections of society are so deprived in some dimensions that they cannot function with the dignity. Some essential dimensions of poverty are: nutritionally deprived, suffering from ill-health not cared for, high mortality rates, lack of adequate shelter and clothing, and being illiterate, among others.

In many articles and books, Nobel Laureate Amartya Sen[3] developed the conceptual framework of well-being in functioning and capabilities. The functionings are directly related to the kind of life people lead, whereas capabilities are the opportunities people have to lead lives of their choice.

The United Nations Development Programme (UNDP) in 1990 created the Human Development Index, and then introduced the Millennium Development Goals in 2000 and the Sustainable Development Goals in 2015. Sen's (1985) seminal work on functionings and capabilities had been the most influential in developing the UNDP well-being indicators. Sen's conceptual framework of well-being led to a clear shift toward a multidimensional approach to poverty measurement.

There is now a widespread consensus that poverty is multifaceted, reflecting deprivation people suffer in many aspects of life. A person is multidimensionally poor if she does not possess basic capabilities. As Thorbecke (2008) points out, Sen's capabilities and functionings framework is the most comprehensive in capturing the concept of multidimensional poverty.

Chapter 8 in the volume carefully reviews the development of multidimensional poverty. Although the literature on multidimensional poverty has made considerable progress in identifying the poor and developing multifaceted poverty indices, too many unresolved issues remain to be considered. The chapter has provided a comprehensive discussion of many unresolved problems. The literature has developed many multidimensional measures, making many arbitrary assumptions that led to an arbitrary degree of poverty.

This chapter proposes an alternative analysis of multifaceted poverty requiring a lesser degree of arbitrariness. The inequity index developed in the chapter would be an indispensable tool in formulating public policies to reduce multidimensional poverty.

Chapter 8 presents an illustration of multidimensional poverty in Brazilian municipalities for 2010. The empirical estimates present the analysis of ill-being (not well-being) indicators divided into four broad dimensions: health, education, living conditions, and labor market activities. The ill-being indicators fall into a mixture of both output and outcome indicators. The chapter concludes that it would be meaningless to aggregate the output and outcome indicators into a composite poverty index. From the policy perspective, it is also more insightful to analyze poverty in various dimensions instead of constructing a composite index.

1.9 Relationships among the Distributions of Economic Variables

Relationships among the distributions of various economic variables are at the core of the economic analysis. For example, economic theory suggests a close relationship between family expenditure and income. Income provides families with entitlement to consumption, whereas expenditure is the actual consumption of the family. In 1960,

---

[3] Sen's (1985) book provides an excellent presentation of his ideas of functioning and capability.

an Indian statistician, P. C. Mahalanobis, proposed extending and generalizing the Lorenz curve to understand the consumer behavior patterns associated with different commodities. He generalized the Lorenz curve, calling it the concentration curve, to depict the distributions of commodities graphically. The Indian Planning Commission extensively utilized consumer behavior to formulate its five-year plans.

Kakwani (1977c) provided a more general and rigorous treatment of concentration curves to study the relations among the distributions of different economic variables. He proved many theorems and corollaries that led to numerous applications in economics. Chapter 9 provides a detailed discussion of concentration curves and related theorems. It reveals how concentration curves can help understand the relationships among economic variables. The chapter offers many new economic applications helpful in analyzing economic policies. Chapter 10 provides a detailed discussion of these applications.

The elasticity of one variable with respect to another is crucial in analyzing relationships among various economic phenomena. Econometric models are used to estimate these elasticities called point elasticity, defined at a particular point. However, many economic applications require aggregate elasticity for the whole population. Chapter 9 discusses a new concept of aggregate elasticity using concentration indices. These concentration indices can be readily estimated from household surveys, providing a practical method of estimating aggregate elasticity.

Chapter 10 provides numerous economic applications of aggregate elasticity, and Chapters 11–13 apply the notion of aggregate elasticity to analyze equity in taxations, deriving several tax progressivity measures.

Economists use social welfare functions to evaluate the allocation of resources to ascertain whether people are becoming better off or worse off. Social welfare is defined in income space. Chapter 9 introduces a generalized social welfare function to define it for any function $g(x)$, representing an economic variable. For example, suppose $g(x)$ denotes the well-being of a person with income x; one can derive a social well-being function as a function of average well-being and the concentration index of well-being. The concentration index of well-being measures the inequity in well-being, the positive (negative) value of which indicates that the non-poor (poor) enjoy higher (lower) well-being than the poor (non-poor). Chapter 10 provides applications of the concentration indices of a function to evaluate equity in many economic variables.

1.10 Application of Concentration Curves to Economic Analysis

Chapter 10 provides many economic applications of the theorems and corollaries developed in Chapter 9. These applications relate to analyzing the relationships among individuals' or families' distribution of economic variables. These relationships play a crucial role in understanding many economic phenomena. This chapter discusses some of the applications; others are considered in detail in subsequent chapters. The applications discussed in the chapter are supplemented by empirical analysis using the actual household surveys.

This chapter provides a framework for quantifying the distributional relations among economic variables. This framework will help readers discover new applications, leading to the advancement of evidence-based economic policies.

In his study of family budgets, Ernest Engel (1957) made empirical observations on families' expenditures on various commodities and their income. He arrived at his famous Engel law stating that the proportion of expenditure on food decreases as the families' standard of living rises. This law is regarded as universally valid and has been used when comparing the standard of living across countries. Many empirical studies have been carried out to estimate the Engel elasticity that revealed the consumption patterns of various socio-economic groups. The Indian Planning Commission has used Engel elasticity in developing its five-year plans. The elasticity also has a practical application in indirect taxation; if the indirect tax is levied on a necessary (luxury) commodity, the poor pay proportionally more (less) tax than the non-poor.

The estimation of Engel elasticity requires the specification of the Engel function. Econometric studies have explored both the linear and nonlinear forms of Engel curves. Chapter 10 has provided a novel method of estimating Engle elasticity using the idea of aggregate elasticity based on the concentration index developed in Chapter 9. This proposed elasticity index satisfies the adding up criterion, which says the weighted average of elasticities of all commodities must always equal one. This criterion is essential for estimating Engel elasticities for any expenditure system. The elasticities calculated from individually specified Engel curves seldom satisfy this criterion.

In Keynesian economics, the aggregate consumption function is the crucial relation, and this relation can be either linear or curvilinear. Chapter 10 draws some interesting conclusions about the relationship between consumption and income distributions. It also explores the impact of income tax and interest rates on consumption-income distributions.

In his seminal paper, Stiglitz (1969) proved that the distribution of wealth and income would tend to a state of complete equalization if the balanced growth were stable in such a model. He established his proposition by comparing wealth growth rates between an arbitrary pair of rich and poor income groups. Using concentration curves, Chapter 10 strengthens the Stiglitz proposition by proving that it is unambiguously valid for any inequality measure based on the Lorenz dominance.

Macroeconomists have a deep interest in understanding the relationship among employment, productivity, and economic growth. The aggregate employment elasticity of economic growth is a valuable tool to explore the relationship. There is sizable literature on estimating employment-growth elasticity using a cross-country employment and GDP data panel. In this regard, the International Labor Organization (ILO) has pioneered many studies on the econometric estimation of elasticity using cross-country regression models. Chapter 10 points out the many limitations of these studies and proposes a new method of analyzing employment–productivity relationships using the aggregate elasticity developed in Chapter 9. The chapter offers a decomposition, explaining the contribution of various labor market indicators to the aggregate elasticity. This methodology is applied to Brazilian household survey data.

Chapter 10 also develops a methodology to quantify the contributions of labor market indicators and non-labor income to the inequality in per capita household income. The empirical application to Brazil indicates that expanding jobs and hours of work contributed positively to inequality. But productivity increase made the most significant contribution to inequality. Many public debates emphasize creating productive jobs by increasing the productivity of workers. This policy results in a substantial rise in inequality. As this application concludes, policymakers need to consider the trade-offs between the two policy objectives

Households derive income from many sources, such as wages and salaries, business income, dividends from shares, property income, and government transfers. These income sources, called factor incomes, reveal the income structure in the economy. Chapter 10 analyzes each factor's income contribution to total per capita household income inequality. In some sense, this analysis links the size and functional distributions of income. The chapter further extends this idea to a dynamic decomposition to explain the trends in inequality over time. This decomposition applied to Ukraine reveals interesting policy insights into how the country underwent structural changes in its transition to a market economy.

The 2006 edition of the World Bank's annual flagship publication, the World Development Report, was devoted to analyzing inequity in opportunity, and this topic was new and generated vast interest among researchers. Roemer (1998) developed the conceptual framework of the inequalities in opportunity, which the World Bank adopted in its report. According to this conceptualization, the total inequality of income is partitioned into two components: (i) inequality caused by individual circumstances and (ii) inequality caused by individual efforts. The main idea of this theory is that inequality caused by individual circumstances is unjust, and that caused by efforts is just. The main message is that society must only concern itself with unjust inequality caused by individual circumstances. This approach has been criticized because it is difficult to distinguish between circumstances and efforts variables. There is no consensus on these variables, as seen in Kanbur and Wagstaff (2014) and Kakwani and Son (2016).

Chapter 10 views this issue differently. It defines inequity in opportunity as the inequity in access to essential services in education, health, clean water, electricity, and so on. It derives the inequity index of opportunity using the aggregate elasticity developed in Chapter 9; the larger is its value, the more inequitable is the opportunity. It applies the methodology to analyze inequity in education and health opportunities in Indonesia utilizing the National Socioeconomic Survey data.

The chapter concludes that overall, Indonesia's healthcare system is not equitable. The economic circumstances of individuals do matter in accessing healthcare. While Indonesia has recently performed well in enhancing its economic growth, inequities in healthcare provision remain.

1.11 Tax Progressivity and Redistributive Effect of Taxation

The tax literature emphasizes two fundamental principles: efficiency and equity. If a tax system distorts agents' behavior, it leads to a social welfare loss. Such distortions occur when agents minimize their tax, creating many distortions such as discouraging work or distorting prices. Efficiency is concerned with the loss of social welfare caused by distortions. On the other hand, equity focuses on how citizens share the tax burden, and on distributive justice, that is, taxes should be fair. Tax progressivity and redistributive effects of taxes are closely related to the fairness of taxes.

This volume has extensively dealt with equity in taxation in Chapters 11–13. However, it does not discuss issues relating to efficiency. The quantitative measurement of the impact of various distortions on social welfare is exceptionally complex, as shown by the optimum taxation literature. However, this literature has illuminated the basic structure of the problem and clarified several problematic issues. Still, it has not answered a fundamental question of how progressive income tax should be (Atkinson 1973).

In the taxation literature, horizontal equity (HE) and vertical equity (VE) are the two fundamental commands of social justice. The HE requires equal treatment of equals, and the VE requires unequal treatment of unequal. Unfortunately, the two commands are not precise enough to measure them quantitatively. For example, there may be few or no equals in the real world. Similarly, it is difficult to know to what degree the unequal should be treated unequally in the real world.

Kakwani and Lambert (1998) introduced a set of three equity axioms, which assist in measuring HE and VE using real-world data. Chapter 11 discusses these axioms and shows how one can utilize them to measure tax's progressivity and redistribution effect. The chapter distinguishes the concepts of tax progressivity and the redistribution effect of taxation.

Tax progressivity deals with an equity principle of taxation, suggesting that wealthier persons must pay more tax or higher tax rates than their poorer counterparts. On the other hand, the redistributive effect of taxation is an outcome of the equity principle. It measures the impact of taxes on income inequality; the progressive tax reduces inequality, while the regressive tax increases it, and the proportional tax does not affect inequality. Thus, while the two concepts are related, they are distinct.

A significant contribution of this chapter is that it provides quantitative estimates of losses of the redistributive effects of a tax system when it violates each of the equity axioms. Thus, the chapter provides new measures of inequities in taxation. These measures facilitate the international comparison of inequities across countries, and the chapter illustrates these comparisons in nine developed countries.

Chapter 11 also develops HE and VE measures and shows that redistributive tax impact is the sum of HE and VE. This decomposition shows that the violation of HE reduces the redistribution impact of taxes, while VE increases the redistributive effect of the tax.

Chapter 11 extends Kolm's (1976a, 1976b) pioneering idea of absolute inequality to define relative and absolute tax progressivity measures. Relative measures of progressivity remain unchanged if everyone's tax is increased or decreased by the same proportion. Similarly, absolute measures of progressivity remain unchanged when everyone's tax is increased or decreased by the same absolute amount. The chapter derives tax progressivity measures using the equity axioms of taxation.

Among several relative measures of tax progressivity proposed in the literature, the Kakwani index, proposed by Kakwani in 1977, is extensively used to analyze equity in taxation and government expenditures. The index is also applied to analyzing equity in access to health, education, and essential services. Chapter 11 develops the absolute Kakwani measure of tax progressivity, indicating the extent to which a tax system deviates from a situation where everyone pays the same amount of tax.

The HE requires no systematic discrimination against any social group in tax payment. Different social groups must pay taxes based on one tax code. If various social groups face different tax codes, the tax system is discriminatory. Kakwani and Lambert (1999) proved that systematic discrimination against any social group results in social welfare loss. The loss of social welfare in monetary units provides a valuable measure of horizontal inequity. This chapter revisits this study and offers helpful insights.

Many governments in developed countries offer relief packages to their population in response to the Coronavirus (COVID-19) pandemic. The relief packages aim to provide cash payments to people to maintain their minimum needs. However, governments may exclude specific groups from these transfers because of resource constraints. For instance, temporary residents, overseas students, and undocumented migrants may be excluded from the pandemic relief. This chapter provides a model to calculate the social welfare loss caused by excluding a social group from the government relief initiatives. It illustrates the loss of social welfare caused by discrimination.

Governments collect revenue from various taxes, such as personal income tax, company tax, estate gift duties, indirect taxes, and so on. Governments aim to design a tax system that yields the maximum revenue with minimum inequity in the tax system. To achieve this aim, a government needs to know the progressivity of various taxes and how much they contribute to the total tax system's progressivity. This chapter has discussed a tax progressivity decomposition to answer this question.

Economists have been arguing for ages that indirect taxes are regressive, and that is why they have preferred to rely on personal income taxes that are usually deemed progressive. The analysis presented in this chapter shows that the regressive taxes based on the relative measure can become progressive when using the absolute concept of tax progressivity. Hence, a crucial question arises as to what progressivity concept one should apply to analyze equity in taxation. The two ideas of progressivity have different value judgments, and it is not easy to provide a definitive answer to this question. A compromise will be to present the analysis to policymakers based on both ideas.

1.12 Normative Measures of Tax Progressivity and Redistributive Effects

Progressivity of taxation and government social programs are central to public debates. If tax progressivity measures have policy relevance, they must help assess the social welfare implications of taxation and government social welfare programs. Unfortunately, the literature on taxation has not explored the social welfare implications of tax progressivity measures until recently.

Kakwani and Son (2021) proposed a general social welfare framework. The social welfare framework argues that every tax progressivity measure has an implicit social welfare function that must be the basis for assessing their normative properties. Using their social welfare framework, they derived several tax progressivity measures proposed in the literature, as well as some additional tax progressivity measures. Chapter 12 thoroughly discusses the linkages between tax progressivity and social welfare functions. It also explores the social welfare implications of the relationship between tax progressivity and redistributive impacts of taxes.

Suppose the government collects the tax revenue of $1 per person. The government can invest such revenue in public goods or other government services such as education, health, and welfare programs. Many governments in developed countries offer relief packages to their population in response to the COVID-19 pandemic. However, as the saying goes, there is no such thing as a free lunch, which implies that someone must pay the cost of implementing a policy. When the government collects tax revenue, society must incur social welfare loss. For the government to break even, it must create a social rate of return from its investments equal to the social welfare loss caused by taxation. The government's primary objective must be to maximize the social rate of return from tax and government welfare programs.

Chapter 12 develops a decomposition, showing that the social welfare loss due to taxation can be decomposed into three contributions. First is the loss due to horizontal inequity, which occurs when the tax system does not treat all persons equally. The second is the loss when the tax system is proportional. The third is when the tax system is progressive or regressive. The progressive tax system contributes to the gain in social welfare, whereas the regressive tax system entails the loss in social welfare. This decomposition provides the empirical estimates of each contribution. Thus, it informs policymakers how much gains (losses) a society suffers when the tax system is proportional, progressive, or regressive.

The chapter emphasizes the administration cost of collecting tax revenue; the higher the administrative cost, the higher the social welfare loss from taxation. Thus, it concludes that any tax reform must consider three factors: (i) a tax system that is progressive; (ii) minimum administrative costs incurred in collecting taxes; and (iii) efficient investments of tax revenues to maximize the social rates of return.

Finally, the chapter offers an international comparison of tax progressivity and tax redistribution in nine developed countries. This comparison requires pre-tax income distributions obtained from the Luxembourg Income Study database for 2013. Gross household income is the total monetary and non-monetary current income, and disposable income is the gross income net of taxes and social security contributions. Thus taxes include both income tax and social security payments.

1.13 Negative Income Tax Plans

In his book *Capitalism and Freedom*, the Nobel Laureate economist Milton Friedman (1962) proposed a negative income tax plan. This concept gained momentum with this publication, and many prominent economists proposed alternative negative income tax plans, including Lampman (1964, 1971), Green (1966), Tobin (1965), Smith (1965), and Rolph (1967). These plans had a dual role: first, they generated revenue for the government to perform its regular operations; second, they provided safety net income to low-income families. The plans performed the dual role by extending income tax rates beyond zero to negative levels, and the cash transfers to families were viewed as a negative income tax.

Although the negative income tax plans gained substantial popularity, policymakers were concerned they might have severe consequences for work effort. Thus, between 1968 and 1982, the United States and Canada conducted a series of experiments to test the labor-supply effects of the plans. Unfortunately, these experiments did not prove helpful in understanding their impact on labor supply.

The proposed negative income tax plans have attractive features that consider the incomes of households and their needs based on their household composition. Thus, they can simultaneously play an essential role in reducing poverty and inequality. While no country ever adopted negative income tax plans, the United States has implemented the earned income tax credit, which works similarly and benefits millions of Americans.

Chapter 13 develops a general framework that incorporates all the literature's proposed negative income tax plans. This framework uses three parameters: marginal tax rate, the lump-sum subsidy given to each family, and tax credit per family member. In addition, this chapter evaluates the negative income plans using the two equity principles of taxation: progressivity and redistributive effects.

Chapter 11 discussed the two concepts of tax progressivity: absolute and relative. Chapter 13 derives both absolute and relative measures of progressivity for the general framework of negative income plans. It evaluates the various negative income plans by the elasticities of progressivity measures with respect to the three parameters of negative income tax plans.

Chapter 13 also explores the redistributive impact of negative tax plans, measuring the extent to which they reduce income inequality. If they increase inequality, such plans should be deemed anti-poor and not adopted. The chapter also distinguishes the relative and absolute measures of redistributive effects. It demonstrates that negative tax plans may increase income inequality under certain conditions. This finding is significant in the literature and can inform the design of negative income tax plans.

Evaluating alternative negative income tax plans combines family income and family size and composition. The relationship between income and family size and composition is not known a priori. For instance, it is not known a priori whether wealthier families have larger or smaller family sizes. Also, the relationship between family composition and family income is not known. Given these problems, the evaluation of negative income tax plans becomes complex. This chapter, however, has derived the conditions under which negative income plans are always progressive. It demonstrates that negative income tax plans will always be absolute progressive if family size decreases as family income increases. This means family members are more concentrated among the lower-income families. But, if the family size increases with the family income, it is impossible to conclude whether negative income tax plans are absolute progressive or regressive. This situation is at odds with the essential purpose of negative income tax plans to support the poor. However, this situation might be unlikely in practice because wealthier families tend to be smaller in size than their poorer counterparts.

Chapter 13 also provides an empirical assessment of alternative negative income tax plans using the 1964 income data from Current Population Reports of the United States Bureau of the Census. The empirical results show that Friedman's plan is the least progressive, whereas Smith's plan is the most progressive. In addition, the relative progressivity measure for the Rolph and Smith plans exceeds one, which indicates that a significant proportion of lower-income families are receiving cash transfers and not paying tax.

1.14 Social Welfare Programs

Social welfare or safety net programs have become an essential pillar of economic development policies, and such programs have increased many folds over the last two decades. Coady, Grosh, and Hoddinott (2004) have listed 85 programs in 36 developing countries. According to the World Bank report, "The State of Social Safety Nets 2015," almost 1.9 billion people are beneficiaries of safety net programs.

The primary objective of these programs is to reduce poverty and provide a safety net to people. They are means-tested and targeted at the poor or those who face a potential risk of falling into poverty. Chapter 14 is devoted to the evaluation methodologies of these programs, and it develops several targeting methods that assess the effectiveness of the programs in maximizing poverty reduction with minimum cost.

There are two distinct issues in designing targeted programs. First is identifying qualified beneficiaries who are most in need, and the second is deciding how much cash transfers should be given to them to meet their minimum basic needs. Thus, targeting efficiency is judged by two targeting methods: (i) beneficiary incidence and (ii) benefit incidence. This chapter provides a systematic development of targeting methods to help design social welfare policies.

When anyone invests in any project, their concern is how much the return rate from investment is. Using a similar idea, when the government invests in a social program, it should concern itself with the social rate of return created by the program. When a social program makes cash transfers to the population, it generates social welfare. Chapter 14 introduces the idea of the social rate of return (SRR), defined as the social welfare generated by a program as a proportion of the program's total cost. Because the social welfare function is concave or quasi-concave, an increase in SRR would mean that the program benefits the poor more than the non-poor. Conversely, a low or negative SRR signifies that the program does not achieve its intended objective of reducing poverty with minimum cost.

Every program incurs two costs: (i) transfer cost and (ii) administrative cost. The total program cost is the sum of these two costs. Targeting indicators proposed in the literature do not consider the cost of programs. It is essential to assess a program's efficiency based on how much operational cost it incurs and how much social welfare it generates. Since government resources are scarce, it is crucial to take account of program costs. The SRR can be the most attractive indicator for this purpose as it considers society's normative value judgments and the program costs. This chapter also provides the operationalization of the SRR using alternative classes of social welfare functions.

China's Minimum Living Standard Guarantee program (Dibao) is the world's most extensive social safety net program. The government first introduced the program in urban areas in the 1990s but extended it to rural areas in the early 2000s. As a result, the rural Dibao became more popular than the urban Dibao, covering 42.72 million individual beneficiaries. Kakwani, Li, Wang, and Zhu (2019) evaluated the program. This chapter provides a more extensive evaluation of China's rural Dibao program.

Given the limitations of accurately obtaining people's income or consumption, this chapter recommends using the proxy means test as a targeting framework. The basic idea of a proxy means test is to provide a decision rule to identify which households should or should not be included in the program. One can arrive at such a decision rule by a set of easily identifiable proxy variables at the household level. Local authorities can quickly implement this rule when identifying program beneficiaries.

Such a system will be an objective way of selecting program beneficiaries. Moreover, it should significantly improve targeting and reduce the cost of running the program, and that should help China achieve its goal of eradicating extreme poverty by 2020.

1.15 Social Price Indices and Inequality

The economy's output is ultimately consumed by people, who make their purchasing decisions based on market prices. So prices play a crucial role in people's everyday lives. However, they have different economic circumstances and consumption patterns, so the impact of prices on people's living standards differs from one person to another.

There is vast literature on the economic theory of price indices that quantify the impact on people's welfare. This theory has provided a precise meaning to price indices, relevant to making individuals' welfare comparisons when facing continuously changing consumer prices. Many economists have contributed to the development of the theoretical foundation of consumer price indices, including Hicks (1946), Pollak (1983, 1998), Diewert (1976, 1983, 1990a, 1990b, 1993, 1998), Samuelson and Swamy (1979), and Konüs (1924).

Most of the literature on the price index theory focuses on comparing the welfare of a single consumer in different price situations. The Laspeyres price index is the most widely used measure of the cost of living over time, with many countries adopting it as an essential price metric. The index measures the cost of living for an average consumer. However, the price index, defined for an average consumer, is insensitive to the impact of relative price changes on income inequality. Chapter 15 is devoted to measuring the effects of relative price changes on income inequality.

This chapter discusses social price indices derived from social welfare functions defined for many individuals in society. Such an index is called a social cost of living index, and it considers specific value judgments of society. The chapter discusses the general social expenditure function framework developed by Son and Kakwani (2006). It provides derivations of social price indices from two alternative classes of social welfare functions.

The first social welfare function class is utilitarian, which purports that every individual has the same utility function. Next, a class of social price indices is derived using a homothetic utility function proposed by Atkinson (1970). Finally, the chapter shows that Prais' (1959) democratic and plutocratic social price indices and Diewert's (1993) multiplicative democratic cost of a living index are particular cases of this general class of social price indices.

The second class of social cost of living indices is derived based on a class of Kakwani's social welfare functions proposed by Kakwani (1980b), which considers the interdependence of individual utilities.[4] These cost of living indices capture the idea of relative deprivation suffered by individuals with different income levels.

A significant contribution of this chapter is that it derives the explicit relationship between social price indices and aggregate inequality measures. The impact of relative price changes on the Gini index is derived as a particular case of this general relationship.

The methodology developed in the chapter is applied to estimate social price indices for Thailand and South Korea. Comparing the impact of relative prices on inequality between Thailand and South Korea is interesting because South Korea has maintained a more egalitarian income distribution than Thailand. This comparison indicates that

---

[4] Individual utility depends not only on his or her consumption but also on the consumption of others in the society. Sen's (1974a) social welfare function is a particular member of this class.

the usual Laspeyres price index can provide countries with high initial inequality biased inflation rates. In contrast, the Laspeyres index seems to provide reasonable inflation rates in counties with low initial inequality.

1.16 Impact of Prices on Poverty

Inflation is a perennial challenge that governments face. They pay enormous attention to controlling it. Central banks perform this task by managing interest rates when the inflation rate falls outside a narrow band. A country's macroeconomic policies primarily focus on the aggregate inflation rate. Most countries measure inflation rates using the Laspeyres price index, which uses the average budget shares as the weights. However, this index does not inform how the prices affect the poor and the most vulnerable society.

The Nobel prize laureate Kenneth Arrow (1958) noted that people with lower incomes have consumption patterns that differ from those with higher incomes. Therefore, if prices of necessities increase faster than those of luxuries, the poor will be more adversely affected than the non-poor. Thus, the impact of prices can likely significantly affect poverty. However, until recently, the literature has not dealt with measuring the effect of prices on poverty. Son and Kakwani (2008) were the first to develop the methodology to capture the impact of consumer prices on poverty.

Chapter 16 is devoted to quantifying the impact of prices on poverty. The effect depends on what poverty measure is used. This chapter's methodology uses the entire class of Foster, Greer, and Thorbecke (1984) poverty measures. The price effect is captured by employing the price elasticity of poverty. The chapter demonstrates that this elasticity can be decomposed into the sum of two components. The first component is the income effect, and the second component is the distribution effect. The distribution effect determines whether price changes are pro-poor or anti-poor.

The main contribution of this chapter is the derivation of a new price index for the poor (PIP). The weights used in this new index are derived from the price elasticity of poverty. Thus, there will be a monotonic relationship between the PIP and the poverty changes; the higher the index, the greater the increase in poverty due to price increases.[5]

How should governments determine tax rates on various goods and services? This chapter explores policies that have a bearing on the linkage between prices and poverty. Developing countries collect a significant amount of revenue from indirect taxes, and these rates have both direct and indirect impacts on the prices of goods and services. The government can determine these tax rates to have a minimum effect on poverty. The poverty elasticity with respect to prices and the pro-poor index developed in the chapter provides a valuable tool to determine tax rates.

---

[5] Note that this relationship will be the first-order approximation because in this study we ignore the substitution effect of price changes.

Government policies, directly and indirectly, impact the prices of various services it provides to its population. For instance, the government provides health, education, utilities, and transportation services. However, many governments tend to recover the cost by charging private users a price for various services. How should the government then determine the charges on multiple services? A social objective should be that such services are available to everyone irrespective of their economic circumstances. In other words, the poor should be able to afford the utilization of such services. This chapter has developed a pro-poor price index, which can help formulate government price policies with the most negligible adverse impact on the poor.

This chapter presents a case study of Brazil's price indices and their underlying inflation rates. The study uses the 2002–3 Brazilian Family Expenditure Survey, covering 48,470 households throughout the country. The empirical results show that Brazil's inflation has increased poverty during the 1999–2006 period.

National statistical offices regularly report inflation rates using the Laspeyres price index. This chapter recommends that these statistical offices regularly publish the PIP index alongside their regular Laspeyres price index. The difference between the PIP and Laspeyres price index informs the degree to which inflation contributes to poverty, and this information will help governments to formulate poverty alleviation policies.

1.17 Economic Growth and Poverty

Suppose a society seeks to eliminate or reduce poverty as rapidly as possible. In that case, the core question development economists often ask is whether economic growth is sufficient to achieve this social objective or whether public policies should directly target the poor.

The answer to these questions requires calculating the trade-offs between growth and inequality. The trade-offs could be better understood using the idea of growth and inequality elasticities of poverty. Economists have attempted to calculate these elasticities using the cross-country regression models. This chapter critically reviews these models to assess whether the literature answers the core question. Unfortunately, the literature on this issue has offered conflicting answers, making an informed policy difficult. This chapter offers reasons why the cross-country regression models cause conflicting answers.

This chapter makes many contributions. First, it addresses how economic growth should be measured, identifying three alternative definitions of economic growth. The most widely used definition is the gross domestic product (GDP) growth rate, measuring the rate of expansion of the real output, including services produced in the economy. The two other measures of economic growth are the per capita GDP and per capita income or consumption. The individuals' actual per capita consumption of goods and services usually measures the population's average standard of living. Poverty and inequality are measured either from per capita income or consumption. The chapter shows no one-to-one relationship between the average standard of living and economic growth measured by the GDP growth rate, implying that economic growth is insufficient to achieve a higher average standard of living.

The poverty and inequality literature interchangeably uses the three definitions of economic growth. Still, the chapter shows that their magnitudes differ across countries and regions in the world. Moreover, the literature does not guide which measure of economic growth should be used. The chapter argues that various studies have arrived at conflicting conclusions about the impact of economic growth on poverty because there is no consensus on which growth measure should be used.

This chapter follows the non-parametric approach that Kakwani (1993) pioneered to estimate the poverty elasticity for individual countries using household surveys. The chapter has derived the growth and inequality elasticities for several poverty measures calculated from individual countries' household surveys. This approach is promising for evidence-based policy analysis at the individual country level.

Economic growth increases the average standard of living, which reduces poverty. However, economic growth can also be accompanied by increasing inequality and rising poverty. Therefore, two factors impact poverty. The answer to the core question posed in the chapter depends on the trade-off between the two. Thus, the chapter develops the inequality–growth trade-off index. This index will be of value to policymakers in assessing how much they should focus on growth and how much they should focus on poverty reduction through poverty alleviation interventions.

Kakwani (2000) developed a discrete-time decomposition that explains the growth of poverty as the sum of the growth and inequality components. This decomposition quantifies the contributions of economic growth and change in inequality on growth in poverty. The chapter illuminates this decomposition, providing a valuable method to help governments decide whether to pursue economic growth first and foremost or focus on poverty alleviation policies that directly benefit the poor.

This chapter presents a case study for China to illustrate how much economic growth and inequality have played a role in its unprecedented poverty reduction. China's growth rate trend in poverty shows that economic growth has contributed to poverty reduction. Although inequality has increased poverty, it had a relatively much smaller impact.

If China wants to reduce poverty rapidly, this chapter suggests reducing its focus on economic growth and following the inequality-reduction strategy with a higher payoff than the growth-enhancing policies. The inequality-reducing policies must benefit the poor more than the non-poor, and the extremely poor must receive higher benefits than the poor. China's government must assess its social welfare programs to know why they favor the rich in distributing the program benefits.

1.18 Pro-Poor Growth and Poverty Reduction

In the 1950s and 1960s, the trickle-down effect of economic growth was the dominant development thinking. The belief was that economic growth was essential to reduce poverty. It was also believed that economic growth accelerates through investments made by the rich. Therefore, economic growth will be enhanced if the rich receive higher returns from their investments. Thus, the trickle-down paradigm asserted that economic growth must benefit the rich first, and then in the second round, the benefits trickle down to the poor when the rich start spending their gains. Accordingly, the trickle-down paradigm will diffuse benefits automatically to all segments of society.

The trickle-down paradigm can reduce poverty even if the poor receive only a tiny fraction of total growth benefits. While this process may reduce poverty, the rate of poverty reduction will be slow. In the late 1960s and 1970s, many economists became disillusioned with the trickle-down strategy, including Ahluwalia, Carter, and Chenery (1979) and Ahluwalia (1976). From 1970 onwards, the trickle-down paradigm was dead and buried.

The term pro-poor growth evolved in the late 1990s when the international development agencies began espousing it. Poverty reduction became a primary concern of their development strategy, spurring interest in pro-poor growth. Rapid and sustained poverty reduction required pro-poor growth. Economic growth always accompanies the redistribution of income across the population, and if economic growth redistributes income in favor of the poor, it can accelerate poverty reduction. Thus, the pro-poor growth generated a fair amount of policy and academic debate in the new millennium, by McCulloch and Baulch (1999), Kakwani and Pernia (2000), Dollar and Kraay (2002), Eastwood and Lipton (2001), Ravallion and Chen (2003), and Son (2004).

This debate did not lead to any consensus on defining or measuring pro-poor growth. Therefore, Chapter 18 provides a detailed discussion of pro-poor growth and its estimation.

The fundamental idea behind pro-poor growth is that it considers two factors: (i) the magnitude of the economic growth rate and (ii) the distribution of benefits of growth. Since these two factors impact poverty reduction, maximizing growth alone will not necessarily lead to a maximum poverty reduction. Chapter 18 elaborates on the idea of "poverty equivalent growth rate" (PEGR), proposed by Kakwani and Son (2008), which is the composite index of the two factors. The index is calculated for any chosen poverty measure. It also satisfies the essential requirement that it has a monotonic relationship with poverty reduction. Thus, maximizing the PEGR indices imply a maximum decrease in poverty. Therefore, if the goal of policymakers is to achieve rapid and sustainable poverty reduction, they should maximize the PEGR.

Stochastic dominance is a powerful tool used to rank the social welfare of income distributions. Using stochastic dominance, one can rank income distribution without specifying a social welfare function. This chapter has extended this idea of stochastic dominance to determine if a growth process is pro-poor or anti-poor without specifying any poverty line and a poverty measure.

Household income and expenditure surveys are the data sources used to calculate poverty measures. The chapter provides a method of calculating the PEGR utilizing the class of additive poverty measures, and this method can easily be applied to nonadditive poverty measures.

Finally, the chapter presents four Asian case studies: South Korea, Thailand, Vietnam, and China. In the late 1990s, the Asian crisis hit all Asian countries to varying degrees. The case studies analyze how these four Asian countries managed the crisis to protect the poor. The chapter concludes that government policies matter in mitigating the impact of external shocks.

1.19 Summarizing the Main Contributions of the Book

Over the past 50 years, economic inequality and poverty issues have become central to public debates. As a result, the literature measuring economic inequality and poverty has profoundly expanded. It has developed many new concepts and methods, but at the same time, it has also generated many unresolved controversies. This book has attempted to cover how income inequality and poverty measurements have evolved in the past 50 years. The main focus of the volume is on applications of techniques for measuring poverty and inequality in order to draw policy implications. It has utilized household surveys to illustrate the application of these methods and show how they can help draw evidence-based policy conclusions.

2

Income Distributions

2.1 Introduction

The shape of observed income distributions has attracted the attention of several scholars over the past hundred years. Pareto was one of the pioneers in finding regularities in income distributions in various countries and over time. He identified his now-famous Pareto income distribution law in 1897 using inductive reasoning based on these regularities. This law provided an exact relationship between income x and the number of people with income x or more. Pareto believed that this law was universally valid and applicable to the distribution of income in all countries at all times. However, subsequent empirical studies indicated that the Pareto law applies only to higher-income groups. Despite Pareto's assertions that the law was universally valid over the whole income range, this chapter demonstrates that the Pareto law is suitable to describe income distributions of only the richest 50% of the population.

These observations have led many authors to propose alternative probability laws that describe observed distribution over the whole income range. Many well-known economists believed that the shape of income distributions was stable over time and space. They attempted to explain the generation of income distribution by a stochastic process. This chapter provides a short but exhaustive review of the income generation models proposed in the literature, including those that satisfy the weak Pareto law, such as Champernowne's model of income generation and the Pareto–Levy law, and those that do not satisfy the weak Pareto law, such as lognormal distribution and the Gamma density function.

Finally, the chapter provides some concluding remarks that question the usefulness of the stochastic processes explaining the observed shape of income distribution functions.

2.2 Basic Concepts of Income Distribution Functions

This section discusses the basic concepts of income distribution functions. Suppose x represents the income of a unit, and there are n units that have been grouped into $(T+1)$ income classes: $(0 \text{ to } x_1), (x_1 \text{ to } x_2), \dots \dots \dots, (x_T \text{ to } x_{T+1})$. This can be conceptualized as a random experiment. Assume that a unit belongs to the $(t+1)^{th}$ income class if it gets t heads in the tossing of T coins. It follows that the probability of a unit

Economic Inequality and Poverty. Nanak Kakwani and Hyun Son, Oxford University Press.
© Nanak Kakwani and Hyun Son (2022). DOI: 10.1093/oso/9780198852841.003.0002

selected at random having income in the interval x_t and x_{t+1} is the number of combinations of T objects taken t at a time divided by the total number of combinations. This probability has been computed assuming that all experiment outcomes are equally likely. Each coin yields either heads or tails with equal probability; therefore, T coins will have 2^T possible outcomes. An event is the number of heads obtained in this experiment. It is not difficult to show that t heads will be received by tossing T coins in ^TC_t number of ways.

Suppose 1,000 income units are placed in four income classes (0 to 1,000), (1,000 to 2,000), (2,000 to 3,000), and (3,000 and over), with income limits for each class marked by appropriate units of money. Three coins will be tossed for each income unit, and depending on the number of heads obtained, the unit will be placed in one of the four income classes. Thus, if no head is obtained, the unit will be placed in the first income class; with one head, it will be placed in the second class, and so on. This process generates the following income distribution.

Income classes	Expected frequency
0–1,000	125
1,000–2,000	375
2,000–3,000	375
3,000–over	125
Total	1,000

This simple example is a random experiment describing a hypothetical income distribution. Each likely outcome of a random experiment is defined as a sample point, and the sample space denoted by Ω is the totality of all outcomes or sample points. An event is defined as a subset of the sample space, and the set of all events is defined as the event space, which may be denoted by A. In this experiment, the sample space consists of eight sample points, where the event space has four events.

A function can characterize any random experiment, say $f(x)$, a rule that transforms each point in one set of points into one and only one point in another set of points. The first collection of points is called the domain, and the second collection is the function's counter domain. A function $X(a)$, whose domain is the event space A and counter-domain is a set of real numbers, is called a random variable. An event that belongs to the event space A is denoted by a. Although the random variable $X(a)$ is a function, it is indicated by X for convenience.

Assuming that income X of a unit is a random variable whose domain is a set of real numbers varying from 0 to ∞, then the function $F(x)$ is defined as

$$F(x) = P(X \le x)$$

is called the probability distribution function, where P stands for probability. The function $F(x)$ is interpreted as the probability that a unit selected at random will have income less or equal to x. The essential properties of this function are as follows:

(a) $\lim_{x \to \infty} F(x) = 1$

(b) $\lim_{x \to 0} F(x) = 0$

(c) $F(x)$ is a monotone, non-decreasing function of x.

The function $F(x)$ has a domain $(0, \infty)$ and the counter domain $(0, 1)$. Furthermore, if $F(x)$ is continuous and has a continuous derivative at all values of x, then it follows that

$$\frac{dF(X)}{dX} = f(x)$$

where $f(X) \geq 0$. The fundamental theorem of integral calculus yields

$$F(x) - F(0) = \int_0^x f(X)\, dX,$$

which on using property (b), yields

$$F(x) = \int_0^x f(X)\, dx$$

The probability density function is denoted by $f(X)$. It is written in the usual differential notation

$$P(x \leq X \leq x + dx) = f(x),$$

which is the probability that the random variable X lies in an infinitely small interval $(x, x + dx)$.

$F(x)$ and $f(x)$ are essential statistics extensively utilized in this book. For a given $f(x)$, $F(x)$ is uniquely derived. The probability density function $f(x)$ can characterize every observed income distribution. Many density functions have been proposed in the literature to characterize observed income distribution. The following section provides a review of well-known density functions.

2.3 Normal Distribution

The normal distribution, most widely used to describe the probability behavior of random phenomena, was discovered in 1733 by De Moivre in connection with his work on the limiting form of the binomial distribution. His discovery, however, remained unnoticed for about 70 years but was then rediscovered by Gauss in 1809 and Laplace in 1812. Both arrived at the normal distribution function connected with their work on the theory of errors of observations. Thus, the distribution is also referred to as the Gaussian law.

A large number of distributions observed in reality are at least approximately normal, and the well-known central limit theorem provides a theoretical explanation of this empirical phenomenon. The theorem states that the sum of a large number of random variables follows a normal distribution under fairly general assumptions. The central limit theorem also implies that the arithmetic mean of a large number of independent variables is approximately normally distributed. This result holds even for individual functions of a more general character than the mean (Cramer 1946). This property has led to many statistical tests of significance used widely in statistics.

There had been a widespread belief that the shape of the observed income distributions is invariant over time and space. Therefore, many authors have attempted to explain income generation by a stochastic process. If income could be conceived as the result of the sum of a large number of random variables, one would expect that income would follow the normal distribution according to the central limit theorem. However, this conclusion may also follow from a different phenomenon. Suppose individual's intelligence determines income level; it could be assumed that income is normally distributed. In that case, one could expect that income is approximately normally distributed. But, in reality, this result does not hold.

The normal distribution is symmetric with a finite mean and variance. It is bell-shaped, which means that much of the probability mass is concentrated around the mean. But observed income distributions are always positively skewed with a long tail. Thus, the normal distribution cannot describe either the frequency distribution or income generation. Many researchers have attempted to determine income distribution functions that generate positively skewed income distributions. The following sections review alternative models of income generation that yield positively skewed distributions.

2.4 The Pareto Law

Pareto (1897) was the first to observe a certain regularity in income distribution in various countries and over time. Based on these regularities, he formulated his famous law of income distribution. He arrived at this law using inductive reasoning by observing income distributions from some countries over time.

The Pareto law of income distribution states that in all places and at all times, the distribution of income is given by the empirical formula

$$R(x) = \left(\frac{x}{x_0}\right)^{-\alpha} \quad \text{when } x > x_0 \qquad (2.4.1)$$

$$= 1 \qquad \text{when } x \leq x_0$$

$R(x) = 1-F(x)$ is the proportion of income units with income x or higher; α is called the Pareto parameter, whose value is clustered around 1.5–1.7.

The density function of the Pareto distribution is obtained by differentiating (2.4.1) with respect to x:

$$f(x) = \alpha x_0^\alpha x^{-1-\alpha} \quad \text{when } x \geq x_0 \qquad (2.4.2)$$
$$= 0 \quad \text{when } x < x_0.$$

The curve (2.4.1) can be transformed into the logarithm form:

$$\log(R(x)) = \alpha \log(x_0) - \alpha \log(x). \qquad (2.4.3)$$

Therefore, the graph of the Pareto function on the double logarithm will be a straight line with slope $-\alpha$. This curve implies that the elasticity of $R(x)$ with respect to x is $-\alpha$. In other words, if x increases by 1%, the proportion of units having income higher than x declines by α%. Therefore, the parameter α can be interpreted as the elasticity of the decreased number of units when moving to a higher-income class. This interpretation also suggests that the parameter α can be used to measure equality in income distribution; the higher its value, the more equal the income distribution.

Davis (1941), a US mathematician, asserted that α value substantially greater than 1.5 leads to revolution from the right, implying insufficient reward for special abilities. Similarly, a value significantly smaller than 1.5 inspires the proletarian revolution from the left. This sociological interpretation of the Pareto law is interesting, but serious concerns have been raised about the validity of the Pareto law.

The mean of the Pareto distribution is given by

$$E(x) = \alpha x_0^\alpha \int_{x_0}^{\infty} x^{-\alpha} dx,$$

which will be finite only if $\alpha>1$. If this condition is met, it follows that

$$E(x) = \frac{\alpha x_0}{(\alpha - 1)}.$$

This equation implies that the mean of the Pareto distribution is proportional to the initial income x_0.

The variance of the Pareto distribution is derived as equal to

$$V(x) = \frac{\alpha x_0^2}{(\alpha - 2)(\alpha - 1)^2},$$

which exists only if $\alpha>2$. As noted, the value of α is clustered around 1.5–1.7 but not greater than 2, which means that the variance of the estimated Pareto distribution will not exist.

The Pareto law that applies only to higher incomes can be theoretically shown by finding the first derivative of the density function in (2.4.2):

$$f'(x) = -\alpha(1+\alpha)x_0^{\alpha}x^{-2-\alpha},$$

which is negative for all positive values of α. The density function of the Pareto distribution decreases monotonically for all values of x greater than x_0. From this, it follows a conclusion that the Pareto Law can be valid only for that range of income for which the density function decreases. It is demonstrated below that the Pareto law is valid for an even shorter income range.

The elasticity of $R(x) = 1 - F(x)$ with respect x is given by

$$r(x) = \frac{xf(x)}{1 - F(x)} \qquad (2.4.4)$$

where $r(x) \geq 0$. Note that for the Pareto distribution, $r(x)$ is equal to α for all values of x. The first derivative of $r(x)$ from (2.4.4) is given by

$$r'(x) = \frac{r(x)}{x}\left[1 + \in(x) + r(x)\right] \qquad (2.4.5)$$

where $\in(x) = \frac{xf'(x)}{f(x)}$ is the elasticity of the probability density function $f(x)$ with respect to x.

Because the observed income distributions are unimodal, the elasticity $\in(x)$ will be positive up to the mode; then, it becomes negative. Equation (2.4.5) implies that $r'(x) > 0$ for $x \leq x^*$ where x^* satisfies

$$\in(x^*) = -1 - r(x^*), \qquad (2.4.6)$$

which proves that $r(x)$ is a monotonically increasing function of x up to the point x^*. Consequently, the Pareto distribution, for which $r(x)$ is always constant, cannot apply for income levels less than x^*. It is clear from (2.4.6) that $\in(x)$ is strictly negative. Because $\in(x)$ is positive for income below the mode and equals zero at the modal value, the point x^* must be strictly greater than the mode. This demonstrates that the Pareto distribution will be valid only for incomes strictly greater than the mode.

Theoretically, it is difficult to say how far beyond the mode the income level x^* will extend. However, because the observed income distributions are skewed toward the right with a long tail, the proportion of the population having income less than or equal to x^* could be almost invariably greater than 50%. That means that the Pareto distribution is suitable to describe income distributions of at most 50% of the population. In other words, the Pareto distribution is not valid for a population smaller than 50%. This result demonstrates that the Pareto law does not apply to the whole income range. Thus, the Pareto distribution is not suitable to characterize income distributions.

Many researchers have questioned the validity of the Pareto law, although Pareto claimed that the law was valid for income distributions in all countries and all times. Shirras (1935), after a detailed examination of income tax and supertax statistics, concluded: "There is indeed no Pareto law. It is the time that it should entirely be discarded in studies on income distribution."

2.5 Generation of Income Distribution: Champernowne's Model

The observed income distributions are skewed toward the right with a long tail; the shape is stable over time and space. This feature led many authors to think that a stochastic process might explain income generation. Gibrat (1931) was the first to advance this line of thought. He proposed the "law of proportionate effect," which generates a positively skewed distribution, which will be discussed briefly later in this chapter. First, however, this section provides a short account of a stochastic process suggested by Champernowne in 1953. His model demonstrates that, under suitable conditions, any initial income distribution will, over time, approach the Pareto distribution.

The model divides the income scale above a specific minimum income x_0 into an enumerably infinite number of income classes. The ith income class given by (x_{i-1} to x_i) satisfies the condition that $x_i = kx_{i-1}$ for $i=1, 2, ...,$ ∞, where k is a constant. This assumption implies that the endpoints of income classes are equidistant on a logarithm scale. The width of income classes on such a scale is $log(k)$. The income units move across these income classes from one discrete period to the next.

If $P_r(r, u)$ is the transitional probability that a unit belonging to class r at time t will move to class $r+u$ by time $t+1$, then

$$\sum_{u=-(r-1)}^{\infty} P_t\left(r, u\right) = 1,$$

which implies that an income unit in class r will be in one of the income classes $1, 2, ...,$ ∞ with probability equal to 1. Suppose $P_t(r)$ is the probability that at time t, a unit is in income class r, the income distribution $P_{t+1}(s)$ at the time $(t+1)$ will be given by

$$P_{t+1}\left(s\right) = \sum_{u=-\infty}^{s-1} P_t\left(s - u\right) P_t\left(s - u, u\right). \tag{2.5.1}$$

The model makes the following assumptions:

Assumption 2.1 *There is an heir to his income for every dying income receiver in the following year.*

This assumption implies that the number of incomes is constant in every period.

Assumption 2.2 *For every value of t and r, and for some fixed integer n*

$$P_t(r, u) = 0 \tag{2.5.2}$$

if u>1 or u < −n, and

$$P_t(r, u) = p_u > 0 \tag{2.5.3}$$

if − n ≤ u ≤ −r

Equation (2.5.2) implies that no income unit moves up by more than one or down by more than n income classes in a year. At the same time, equation (2.5.3) has two impli-cations. First, the transitional probabilities $P_t(r, u)$ are constant with respect to time; second, they are independent of income level r and determined entirely by u alone. Note that u is the number of income classes a unit moves in a single period. In other words, a transitional probability depends only on the number of income classes a unit moves in a single period. Because the income classes are equidistant on a logarithmic scale, any given proportionate income change is equiprobable at all income levels.

Assumption 2.3

$$\sum_{u=-n}^{1} u p_u < 0$$

This assumption means that in all units, initially in any one of the income classes $n+1, n+2, \ldots \ldots \ldots$, the expected number of income classes shifted during the follow-ing period is negative. This assumption is needed to prevent income from increasing indefinitely without stabilizing to an equilibrium distribution.

If $P^*(s)$ denotes the equilibrium distribution, the transitional equation (2.5.1) be-comes under Assumption 2.2:

$$P^*(s) = \sum_{u=-n}^{1} P^*(s - u) p_u \tag{2.5.4}$$

for all $s>1$. And

$$P^*(1) = \sum_{u=-n}^{0} P^*(1 - u) q_u$$

for $s=1$, where $q_u = \sum_{v=-n}^{u} p_v$. To determine $P^*(s)$, finding a nontrivial solution of equation (2.5.4) is necessary. For this purpose, substitute $P^*(s)=c\,Z$ into (2.5.4), which yields

$$g(Z) = \sum_{u=-n}^{1} p_u Z^{1-u} - Z = 0 \qquad (2.5.5)$$

where $g(Z)$ is a polynomial of degree $(n+1)$.

Descartes' rule of signs establishes that (2.5.5) has no more than two real positive roots. One root is unity. To determine the second root, calculate $g'(Z)$ from (2.5.5) at $Z=1$:

$$g'(1) = -\sum_{u=-n}^{1} u p_u,$$

which under assumption 2.3 is always positive. Because $g(0) = p_1 > 0$, $g(1) = 0$, and $g'(1) > 0$, the second real positive root must lie between 0 and 1. If this root is b, the equilibrium distribution will be given by

$$P^*(s) = c_1 b^s \qquad (2.5.6)$$

where $0 < b < 1$. The constant c_1 is determined to make probabilities sum to unity.

To establish the link between the equilibrium distribution (2.5.6) and the Pareto law, we calculate the probability

$$R(x_s) = \Pr(X \geq x_s) = \sum_{r=s}^{\infty} P^*(r) = c\sum_{r=s}^{\infty} b^r,$$

which is the sum of a geometric series, adding up

$$R(x_s) = \frac{c b^s}{(1-b)}. \qquad (2.5.7)$$

Note that this geometric series is convergent because b is positive and less than unity. Since income classes satisfy the condition that $x_i = k x_{t-1}$, it follows that

$$x_s = k^s x_0 \qquad (2.5.8)$$

where x_0 is the minimum income.

Transforming equations (2.5.7) and (2.5.8) into logarithms and eliminating s yields

$$\log R(x_s) = \gamma - \alpha \log x_s \qquad (2.5.9)$$

where

$$\alpha = -\frac{\log(b)}{\log(k)} \quad \text{and} \quad \gamma = \log\frac{c x_0^\alpha}{(1-b)}$$

where α is the Pareto parameter, and since $0 < b < 1$, α will always be positive. Thus, equation (2.5.9) shows that the logarithm of the probability of income exceeding x_s is a linear function of the logarithm of x_s, which is the Pareto law in its exact form.

Champernowne's model has generated the amazing result that any initial income distribution will, over time, approach the Pareto distribution. It is also surprising as the Pareto law's empirical evidence is not valid for the whole income range. The assumptions underlying the model are highly restricted. Champernowne relaxed some of the assumptions and proved that under more general conditions, the Pareto law ceases to be obeyed exactly. However, the law continues to apply asymptotically to the occupants of high-income groups. The following section discusses in greater detail this aspect of the Pareto law.

2.6 The Pareto–Levy Law

Extensive empirical work on observed income distributions confirmed that the Pareto law fits rather well toward the upper tail. This led Mandelbrot (1960) to introduce the weak Pareto law:

$$R(x) \text{ behaves like } \left(\frac{x}{x_0}\right)^{-\alpha}, \text{ as } x \to \infty,$$

which implies that

$$\lim_{x \to \infty} \frac{R(x)}{\left(\dfrac{x}{x_0}\right)^{-\alpha}} = 1 \tag{2.6.1}$$

For an unspecified value of the parameter α, the Pareto law defined in (2.4.2) is the strong Pareto law defined by Mandelbrot. When α assumes value 1.5, the Pareto law in (2.4.2) is the strongest Pareto law. Based on empirical evidence, the strong Pareto law is not strictly applicable. In contrast, there is little disagreement over the validity of the weak Pareto law.

Before introducing the Pareto–Levy law, it is essential to define stable probability law. Suppose the observed income X is equal to the sum of n independent random variables $X_1, X_2, \ldots \ldots \ldots, X_n$ such that all X_i follow the same probability distribution up to linear transformation, which assumes the existence of coefficient $a_i > 0$ so that all $a_i X_i + b_i$ follow the same distribution. If X has the same distribution as an individual X_i again up to the linear transformation, such a probability law is stable. Mathematically this can be written as

$$\left(a_1 X_1 + b_1\right) \oplus \left(a_2 X_2 + b_2\right) \oplus \cdots \cdots \cdots \left(a_n X_n + b_n\right) = aX + b \tag{2.6.2}$$

where a and b are two constants that always exist for whatever values a_i and b_i take, so that $a_i > 0$, and the sign $\oplus$ denotes the addition of random variables.

Equation (2.6.2) implies that the probability distribution of $(aX+b)$ is the same as that of individual random variables $(a_1 X_1 + b_1), (a_2 X_2 + b_2), \ldots \ldots \ldots, (a_n X_n + b_n)$.

If this idea is applied to incomes, income distribution remains the same, regardless of the number of components that constitute income. In this context, it is worth mentioning that, although the set of components comprising income generally differs from country to country, the shape of the observed income distribution in each country is the same.

The Gaussian law, a well-known normal distribution, is a stable probability law. Levy (1925) constructed a family of stable laws that are non-Gaussian and satisfy the weak Pareto law with the parameter α restricted to the range $0 < \alpha < 2$. Mandelbrot (1960) defined the Pareto–Levy (P–L) law as the class of stable probability laws that satisfy the weak Pareto law with α lying in the range $0 < \alpha < 2$.

Unfortunately, the density function of the P–L law cannot be expressed in a closed analytical form but is determined indirectly with a Laplace transform. The probability distribution function can, however, be defined for large x as

$$F(x) \sim 1 - x^{-\alpha}[u^*\Gamma(1-\alpha)]^\alpha$$

where $\Gamma(1-\alpha) = \int_0^\infty e^{-x}x^{-\alpha}dx$ is the gamma function, α is the Pareto parameter in the range $1 < \alpha < 2$, and u^* is a positive scalar parameter.

The P–L distribution has a finite mean and infinite variance. As long as α is not close to 2, the distribution rapidly becomes indistinguishable from a strong Pareto distribution for the same α. If α approaches 2, the P–L density will tend toward a Gaussian density. From this observation, Mandelbrot concluded that the P–L density is worth considering only if α is not too close to 2. The distribution has never been empirically tested, perhaps because of its complexity.

2.7 Family of Distribution Functions Satisfying the Weak Pareto Law

This section considers a family of income distribution functions that satisfy the weak Pareto law. The strong Pareto law asserts that the elasticity $r(x)$ defined in (2.4.4) is constant and equal to α, whereas the weak Pareto law implies that $lim_{x\to\infty}r(x) = \alpha$, meaning that $r(x)$ approaches α as x approaches infinity. Consider the following general form of $r(x)$:

$$r(x) = \frac{\alpha x^\beta}{c^\beta + x^\beta}. \tag{2.7.1}$$

Note that if $\beta > 0$ as x approaches infinity, $r(x)$ approaches α, which means that the weak Pareto law is satisfied by this specification of $r(x)$. Differentiating (2.7.1) with respect to x yields

$$r'(x) = \frac{\alpha\beta c^{\beta}x^{\beta}}{(c^{\beta} + x^{\beta})^{2}},$$

which is always positive if the parameters α, β, and c are strictly positive. Therefore, $r(x)$ is a monotonically increasing function of x.

Combining (2.4.4) and (2.7.1) gives the following first-order differential equation

$$\frac{dF(x)}{dx} = \frac{\alpha[1 - F(x)]x^{\beta-1}}{(c^{\beta} + x^{\beta})},$$

which on integration gives

$$[1 - F(x)] = k(c^{\beta} + x^{\beta})^{-\left(\frac{\alpha}{\beta}\right)} \tag{2.7.2}$$

where k is the constant of the integration. So $F(x)$ satisfies the conditions (a), (b), and (c) as stated at the beginning of this chapter. It should then follow that $\beta>0$ and $k=c^{\alpha}$. With these restrictions, notice that $F(x)=0$ for $x=0$, $F(x)$ approaches 1 as x approaches infinity. The density function corresponding to this function is obtained by differentiating (2.7.2) with respect to x as

$$f(x) = \alpha c^{\alpha}x^{\beta-1}(c^{\beta} + x^{\beta})^{-\left(\frac{\alpha}{\beta}\right)-1},$$

from which the jth moment of x yields

$$E(x^{j}) = \alpha c^{\alpha} \int_{0}^{\infty} x^{j+\beta-1}(c^{\beta} + x^{\beta})^{-\left(\frac{\alpha}{\beta}\right)-1} dx \tag{2.7.3}$$

where E denotes the expectation operator.

Transforming x into y using the relation $y = \left(\frac{x}{c}\right)^{\beta}$, the integral on the right-hand side of (2.7.3) reduces to the Beta distribution of the second kind. Thus, the jth moment of x is obtained as

$$E(x^{j}) = \frac{\alpha}{\beta} c^{j} B\left(\frac{j}{\beta} + 1, \frac{\alpha - j}{\beta}\right) \tag{2.7.4}$$

where $B(m, n)$ is the Beta distribution with parameters m and n, given $B(m, n) = \int_{0}^{1} x^{m-1}(1 - x)^{n-1} dx$. This integral converges only if $m>0$ and $n>0$, which from (2.7.4) implies that the jth moment of this distribution exists only if $j<\alpha$.

Empirically, the Pareto parameter α tends to have values in the range $1 < \alpha < 3$; thus, at the most first two moments of x can be derived from the parameters of this distribution. If α is restricted to the range $1 < \alpha < 2$, it yields the P–L range, the distribution of which will have a finite mean and infinite variance.

Burr (1942) first proposed the distribution function (2.7.2); later, in an unpublished paper presented at the 1958 meeting of the Econometric Society, Sargan applied it to income data.[1]

Three special cases of the family of distribution functions (2.7.2) are interesting. If $c=0$, the function (2.7.2) reduces to the Pareto distribution function as given in (2.4.1). If $\beta=1$, the function (2.7.2) becomes

$$1 - F(x) = k(c + x)^{-\alpha}, \tag{2.7.5}$$

which is called the Pareto distribution of the second kind. This function was suggested by Pareto himself but has rarely been applied to empirical data.

The third case is obtained by introducing $\beta=\alpha$ into the density function of (2.7.2). Thus, $f(x) = \alpha c^{\alpha} x^{\alpha-1} (c^{\alpha} + x^{\alpha})^{-2}$ which transforms into

$$dF(x) = \frac{e^{\varphi} d\varphi}{\left(1 + e^{\varphi}\right)} \tag{2.7.6}$$

using the transformation $\left(\frac{x}{c}\right)^{\alpha} = e^{\varphi}$. The distribution function (2.7.6) is the well-known sech square distribution widely used in bioassay problems. Fisk (1961b) proposed using this distribution for graduating income distributions. His investigation suggests that the sech square distribution may prove helpful in examining income distributions in populations that are homogeneous in at least one characteristic, such as occupation. He arrived at this distribution as the limiting case of the distribution functions proposed by Champernowne (1952).

2.8 Champernowne's Distribution

In 1937, Champernowne suggested a family of functions to graduate pre-tax income distributions.[2] Later in 1952, he provided further explanations of the properties of these functions. Of the three forms of the distribution function, he considered that only one provided a good fit with most of his studied income distributions.

---

[1] Singh and Maddala (1976) derived this distribution using an alternative approach of hazard rate or failure rate.
[2] Champernowne's PhD dissertation, submitted in 1937 to Cambridge University, was published in 1973 by Cambridge University Press as *Distribution of Income Between Persons*.

The general form of Champernowne's distribution is written as

$$\varphi(z) = \frac{n}{\cosh\{\alpha\gamma(z - z_0)\} + \lambda}$$

where $z = log(x)$ is called the income power, and $\varphi(z)$ is the density function of z. The parameters are n, λ, z_0 and λ; z_0 is the median income power.

The majority of the distribution studied by Champernowne gave a value of λ less than 1. In this case, the distribution function is given by

$$1 - F(x) = \frac{1}{\theta} tan^{-1} \frac{\sin \theta}{\cos\theta + \left(\frac{x}{x_0}\right)^{\alpha}},$$

where $\cos\theta$ and $z_0 = log x_0$. The parameters α and θ are restricted to the ranges $\alpha > 0$ and $0 \leq \theta < \pi$. These restrictions are required for $F(x)$ to be a single-valued and monotonically increasing function of x. Fisk (1961b) noted that moments of x exist up to order j where $j < \alpha$. Further, it can be seen that $r(x)$ approaches α as x approaches infinity for this distribution. Thus, the distribution satisfies the weak Pareto law, and α is the Pareto parameter. The parameter θ, however, has no simple interpretation. Fisk investigated the effect of θ on the shape of the distribution of x, concluding that the shape of the curve is relatively insensitive to changes in the value of θ over the range $0°$ and $45°$, where it will, therefore, be reasonable to put $\theta = 0$. He argued that for sections of the homogeneous population in one characteristic (for example, occupation), θ might be zero. It can be seen that as θ approaches zero, the Champernowne distribution approaches the sech square distribution. Thus, Fisk derived the sech square distribution as a limiting case of Champernowne's distribution.

2.9 Laws of Income Distribution Violating the Weak Pareto Law

So far, the distribution functions have the common property that, for large values of income, they can be approximated by Pareto law given in (2.4.1), satisfying the weak Pareto law. This section concerns the distribution functions that do not obey the weak Pareto law. In this class, the lognormal distribution is most widely used. Aitchison and Brown (1957) have given a detailed history of this distribution. Gibrat (1931) published an extensive study of this distribution and presented his proportionate effect that positively skewed distribution. A brief outline of this law follows.

Suppose an individual's income begins with X_0 and subsequently undergoes a series of random, independent, proportional changes $m_1, m_2, \ldots \ldots \ldots, m_t$, where m_i can be either negative or positive. After t periods during which these changes have taken place, her income becomes

$$X_t = X_0 (1 + m_1)(1 + m_2) \ldots \ldots \ldots (1 + m_t),$$

the logarithm of which will be

$$lnX_t = lnX_0 + \sum_{i=1}^{t} u_i \qquad (2.9.1)$$

where $u_i = ln(1 + m_i)$.

According to the central limit theorem, if u_i are mutually independent, the distribution of $ln(X_i)$ will tend toward normality as t becomes large, and the random variable X_t will then follow a lognormal distribution. Therefore, a random variable is lognormally distributed if its logarithm follows the normal probability law.

Kalecki (1945) criticized this simple stochastic process because the standard deviation of the logarithm of income increases continuously with time, which can be demonstrated by the property that the variance of a sum of mutually independent random variables is the sum of the variances. Thus (2.9.1) yields

$$Var(lnX_t) = \sum_{i=1}^{t} Var(u_i)$$

which shows that, with time, the variance of $ln X_t$ grows steadily. Because the tendency for such an increase is not observed in the real world, Kalecki (1945) suggested modifying this process by introducing a negative correlation between X_t and m_t, which ensures that the variance of $ln X_t$ does not grow steadily. Although a simple economic interpretation of this negative correlation is that the percentage increase in income is likely to be lower for the rich than for the poor, it is difficult to justify or refute this assumption without evidence.

The distribution of lognormal distribution is derived by assuming that $log(X)$ is normally distributed with a mean μ and variance σ^2. The distribution function $F(x)$ for the random variable X is, therefore, given by

$$F(x) = \int_0^x \frac{1}{X\sigma\sqrt{2\pi}} exp\{-\frac{1}{2\sigma^2}(logX - \mu)^2\}dX, \qquad X > 0 \qquad (2.9.2)$$

which is usually denoted by $\Lambda(x/\mu, \sigma^2)$.

Note that $r(x)$, defined in (2.4.4), for lognormal distribution approaches infinity as x approaches infinity, proving that lognormal distribution violates the weak Pareto law.

Lognormal distribution has many attractive properties. First, it is closely related to the normal distribution, which provides efficient estimation procedures and statistical inference. Second, the distribution provides a good fit with the middle-income ranges, covering about 60% of the population. Third, it produces a positively skewed distribution consistent with observed income data.

Although lognormal distribution has been used extensively in empirical work, it also has limitations. It fits poorly toward the tails; it overcorrects the positive skewness of the income distribution, which is demonstrated by the fact that the logarithm transform of observed income distributions exhibits negative skewness while lognormal distribution assumes symmetry. Moreover, the distribution is defined only over positive income levels. This limitation is of little consequence because the observations on negative or zero incomes are relatively few compared to the total observations.

Rutherford (1955) suggested an exciting extension of Gibrat's law of proportionate effect by introducing "birth" and "death" considerations into the model. He based his model on the following assumptions: (a) Newcomers enter the labor force at a constant rate, (b) the income distribution of the newcomers is lognormal, (c) mortality is unrelated to income power, and (d) the number of survivors declines exponentially with age. He deduced that the resulting income distribution would eventually approach the Gram–Charlier Type A distribution from these assumptions.[3] He also provided an experimental method of fitting this distribution. Still, his distribution did not offer a better approximation to observed income distributions than the distributions considered by Champernowne and Fisk.

There are still two other distribution functions that do not obey the weak Pareto law. The first is one suggested by Pareto himself, which has the probability distribution function:

$$F(x) = 1 - \frac{c^\alpha e^{-\beta x}}{(x+c)^\alpha} \qquad (2.9.3)$$

where α and β are two parameters. As defined in (2.4.4) for this distribution, $r(x)$ is given by

$$r(x) = \frac{x(\beta x + \beta c + \alpha)}{(x+c)},$$

which approaches infinity as x approaches infinity. It violates the weak Pareto law unless, of course, $\beta = 0$, in which case the function (2.9.3) reduces to the Pareto distribution of the second kind as given in (2.7.5). Pareto estimated β from the empirical distributions and found its value so small that he neglected it.[4]

The other distribution that does not satisfy the weak Pareto law is the Gamma density, fitted to income data by Amoroso (1925) and later proposed by Salem and Mount (1974). The Gamma density function is given by

$$f(x) = \frac{\lambda^\alpha x^{\alpha-1} e^{-\lambda x}}{\Gamma(\alpha)}$$

where $0 < x < \infty$ and α and λ are positive parameters, $\Gamma(\alpha)$ is the Gamma function; the parameter α indicates the degree of inequality, and the second parameter λ is a scale parameter.

---

[3] The Gram–Charlier series of Type A represents the expansion in orthopolinomials. For more details, see Cramer (1946), 222.
[4] See Hayakawa (1951).

Salem and Mount fitted the Gamma distribution to personal income data in the United States for 1960 and 1969. Their empirical results showed that the Gamma distribution fits the data better than the lognormal but is not entirely satisfactory; it exaggerates the skewness, although this tendency is even more marked in the lognormal fit.

2.10 Concluding Remarks

Economic growth generates additional goods and services in the economy, which the population consumes. The growth process also may create more jobs and opportunities. But all persons may not proportionally enjoy the consumption of goods and services produced. Income distribution is generated from a growth process that determines the standard of living enjoyed by society. It is, therefore, not surprising that many scholars were attracted to explaining the generation of income distributions observed in many countries and over time. A large body of empirical evidence in many countries showed remarkable regularity in observed income distributions. The income distributions are always positively skewed with a long tail.

These observations led many scholars to explain income generation by a stochastic process. This chapter has provided a short but exhaustive review of the income generation models proposed in the literature. A significant conclusion emerging from this review is that none of the distribution functions offered by this literature fits well with the observed income distributions. Thus, income generation is complex and cannot be explained by stochastic models. Although many prominent scholars have contributed to developing stochastic income generation models, this literature has not found much practical application in development economics.

A lognormal distribution is the only one that has seen some applications in analyzing economic problems. The distribution was extensively used in the 1950s and 1960s, when national statistical offices did not release unit-record data for household surveys, providing only grouped data. Data analysis was carried out using an income distribution model. The lognormal model is analytically simple, and its close relationship with normal distribution provides ready access to statistical inference. India's five-year plans extensively utilized the lognormal distribution to project outcomes of expected achievement. Now, household unit-record data are readily available, and with the development of user-friendly software, the lognormal distribution has become somewhat obsolete. Development indicators such as poverty and inequality measures representing the entire distribution are now directly and more accurately estimated from household surveys.

3

The Lorenz Curve and Its Variants

3.1 Introduction

The Lorenz curve is widely used as a graphical device to represent and analyze income distribution. It is defined as the relationship between the cumulative proportion of individuals and the cumulative proportion of income received when individuals are arranged in ascending order of their income. Lorenz proposed this curve in 1905 to compare and analyze inequalities in wealth in different countries during different epochs. The curve has been used principally as a convenient graphical device to represent the size distribution of income.

This chapter discusses numerous applications of the Lorenz curve, which suggests that the Lorenz curve is not just a graphical device to describe income and wealth distribution. It introduces the Lorenz curve in formal and rigorous terms, deriving many analytical results, which open up opportunities for many applications in economics relating to measuring and analyzing inequality in income.

The statistical literature has developed many distribution functions widely used in practical situations. The chapter derives the Lorenz curve from many such distribution functions. However, the Lorenz curve derived from these distribution functions does not provide a good fit with the observed income distributions. Kakwani and Podder (1973, 1976) and Kakwani (1981a) proposed an alternative approach that directly specifies a functional form of the Lorenz curve. These functional forms can be estimated from the observed income distributions. Once the Lorenz function is defined and calculated from actual data, the inequality measures can be derived as functions of the parameters of the Lorenz curve. The density function can also be obtained from the estimated equation of the Lorenz curve. The chapter discusses three alternative specifications of the Lorenz curve, and two fit exceptionally well with a broad range of income distributions observed in many countries and over many epochs.

This chapter proves many theoretical results on the symmetry of the Lorenz curve. If the Lorenz curve is not symmetric, it is skewed either toward (0, 0) or (1, 1). It is unlikely that an observed income will be found to be perfectly symmetric. In most situations, the empirical income distributions will be skewed toward (0, 0) or toward (1, 1). The chapter explores how economic development is related to the skewness of the Lorenz curve. It demonstrates that the skewness of the Lorenz curve is associated with the size of the middle-income class. Finally, a measure of the

Economic Inequality and Poverty. Nanak Kakwani and Hyun Son, Oxford University Press.
© Nanak Kakwani and Hyun Son (2022). DOI: 10.1093/oso/9780198852841.003.0003

skewness of the Lorenz curve is proposed that provides an alternative approach to test Kuznets' hypothesis regarding income shares of the low- and middle-income classes in developed and developing countries.

Inequality may be measured in both a relative and absolute sense. If inequality measures remain unchanged when each person receives the same proportion of income, such measures are called relative measures of inequality. The Lorenz curve measures relative inequality. Alternatively, Kolm (1976a, 1976b) has proposed absolute measures of inequality that do not show any change in inequality when the income of everyone is increased or decreased by the same amount. Such measures are called absolute measures of inequality. This chapter has proposed several absolute inequality curves that provide alternative approaches to ranking income distributions from the perspective of absolute inequality.

Finally, the chapter discusses the Lorenz curve's variants, including relative deprivation (proposed by Kakwani in 1984), and Bonferroni (1930) and Zenga (2007) curves. The relative deprivation curve has been used to determine how government cash transfers and taxes impact the relative deprivation suffered by the Australian population. The Lorenz, Bonferroni, and Zenga inequality curves have been used to compare India's and China's relative and absolute inequality.

3.2 Definition of the Lorenz Curve

The Lorenz curve is the relationship between the proportion of people with income less than or equal to a specific amount and the proportion of total income received by those people. To explain this idea, consider a hypothetical economy with five people whose incomes, arranged in ascending order, are 2, 3, 5, 6, and 8 with a total income of 24. The cumulative proportion of people whose incomes are less than or equal to 2, 3, 5, 6, and 8 is given by $p = 1/5, 2/5, 3/5, 4/5$, and $5/5$, and the cumulative proportion of their incomes is given by $L(p) = 2/24, 5/24, 10/24, 16/24$, and $24/24$.

The Lorenz curve is obtained by plotting p on the horizontal axis with $L(p)$ for the corresponding values on the vertical axis. This is a simple way of describing a Lorenz curve. However, this simple curve has numerous economic applications, as explored in this volume. The applications require formal derivations of the curve's properties, which are derived below.

Suppose income X of a unit is a random variable with the probability density function $f(X)$,[1] which gives the probability distribution function as

$$F(x) = \int_0^x f(X)\ dx, \qquad (3.2.1)$$

---

[1] The income X can be negative for some units but is assumed to be nonnegative here for notational convenience.

which is interpreted as the proportion of people having an income of less than or equal to x. $F(x)$ lies between 0 and 1. The properties of this function are discussed in Chapter 2.

Further, assume that the mean μ of the distribution exists, then the first-moment distribution function is defined as

$$F_1(x) = \frac{1}{\mu} \int_0^x X f(X) \, dx. \tag{3.2.2}$$

$F_1(x)$ is interpreted as the proportional share of the total income of the people having an income less or equal to x and varies from 0 to 1. If $f(X)$ is continuous, the derivative of $F_1(x)$ exists and is given by

$$\frac{dF_1(x)}{dx} = \frac{x f(x)}{\mu} \tag{3.2.3}$$

which implies that $F_1(x)$ is a monotonically non-decreasing function of x.

The Lorenz curve is the relationship between the variables $F(x)$ and $F_1(x)$ and is obtained by inverting functions (3.2.1) and (3.2.2) and eliminating x. Alternatively, the curve can be plotted by generating the values of $F(x)$ and $F_1(x)$ from (3.2.1) and (3.2.2) by considering the sufficient number of the values of x. The curve is represented in a unit square (Figure 3.1).

The ordinate and abscissa of the curve are $F_1(x)$ and $F(x)$, respectively. The derivative of $F(x)$ from (3.2.1) is given by

$$\frac{dF(x)}{dx} = f(x),$$

which on combining with (3.2.3) gives the slope of the Lorenz curve as

$$\frac{dF_1(x)}{dF(x)} = \frac{x}{\mu}, \tag{3.2.4}$$

which is positive for positive income. Similarly, the second derivative of the curve is obtained as

$$\frac{d^2 F_1(x)}{dF^2} = \frac{d}{dF(x)} \left(\frac{dF_1(x)}{dF(x)} \right) = \frac{1}{\mu f(x)} > 0, \tag{3.2.5}$$

which is also positive for $f(x) > 0$. These two derivatives imply that the slope of the Lorenz curve is positive and increases monotonically; in other words, the curve is increasing monotonically and is convex to the F-axes. From this, it follows that $F_1(x) \leq F(x)$ for all x. The straight line $F_1(x) = F(x)$ is called the egalitarian line when all income units receive the same income.

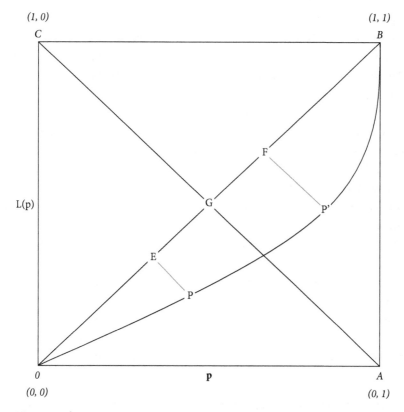

Fig. 3.1 The Lorenz curve

It will be helpful to introduce the following notation:

$$L(p) = F_1(x) \tag{3.2.6}$$

where

$$p = F(x) \tag{3.2.7}$$

so that $0 \leq p \leq 1$. The functional form $L(p)$, called the Lorenz function, obtained by eliminating x from (3.2.6) and (3.2.7), is interpreted as the proportion of total income received by the poorest pth proportion of the population. It satisfies the following conditions:

(a) If $p = 0$, $L(p) = 0$
(b) If $p = 1$, $L(p) = 1$
(c) $L'(p) = \dfrac{x}{\mu} \geq 0$ and $L''(p) = \dfrac{1}{\mu\, f(x)} > 0$
(d) $L(p) \leq p$ \hfill (3.2.8)

where $L'(p)$ and $L''(p)$ are the first and second derivatives of $L(p)$ with respect to p, respectively. These conditions imply that the Lorenz curve is represented in a unit square.

In Figure 3.1, the diagonal OB through the unit square is called the egalitarian line. The Lorenz curve lies below this line. When $L(p) = p$, the Lorenz curve coincides with the egalitarian, which means that each person receives the same income; that is the case of perfect equality. Then $p - L(p)$ measures the deviation of the Lorenz curve from the perfect equality and will be called the Lorenz inequality curve; the higher this curve, the greater the inequality will be.

In perfect income inequality, the Lorenz curve coincides with OA and AB, implying that only one person receives all the income in the society, the perfect inequality in society. As the curve shifts above the x-axis, the income distribution becomes more equal, achieving perfect equality when it coincides with the egalitarian line. If the government aims to achieve greater equality, it can use the Lorenz curve to rank government policies or programs.

Suppose two alternative government policies result in two different income distributions, X_1 and X_2. If the Lorenz curve of X_1 is above X_2 at all points, then the first policy is preferred over the second policy from an equity point of view. However, if the two Lorenz curves intersect, neither policy can be more equitable than the other. Thus, the Lorenz curve provides only a partial ranking of distribution. Still, it is a powerful tool and has been used widely as a convenient graphical device to describe income distribution and many other variables that affect people's well-being.

3.3 Lorenz Curve for Well-Known Distribution Functions

3.3.1 Pareto Distribution

The distribution function of the Pareto law as defined in (2.4.1) is given by

$$F(x) = 1 - \left(\frac{x}{x_0}\right)^{-\alpha}, \tag{3.3.1}$$

which is defined only for $x \geq x_0$.

If the mean of the Pareto distribution exists, using the density function given in (2.4.2), the first-moment distribution function can be written as

$$F_1(x) = \frac{1}{\mu} \int_0^x \alpha\, x_0^\alpha\, X^{-\alpha}\, dX \tag{3.3.2}$$

where $\mu = \frac{\alpha x_0}{(\alpha - 1)}$ is the mean of the Pareto distribution, which exists if the Pareto parameter $\alpha > 0$. On evaluating the integral (3.3.1), we obtain

$$F_1(x) = \frac{1}{\mu} \frac{\alpha x_0}{(\alpha - 1)} \left[1 - \left(\frac{x_0}{x}\right)^{\alpha - 1}\right], \tag{3.3.3}$$

from which it follows that $F_1(x)$ approaches 1 as x approaches infinity. If x varies from 0 to ∞, $F_1(x)$ lies between 0 and 1. Substituting (3.3.1) and (3.3.3) into (3.2.6) and (3.2.7), respectively, yields the equation of the Lorenz function as

$$L(p) = 1 - (1-p)^\delta \qquad (3.3.4)$$

where $\delta = (\alpha - 1)/\alpha$. The restriction $\alpha > 1$ implies that $0 < \delta < 1$. As α approaches infinity, δ approaches 1, in which $L(p) = p$ means that the Lorenz curve coincides with the egalitarian line. Hence, the underlying income distribution is perfectly equal; every income unit receives the same income. When $0 < \delta < 1$, $L(p) < p$, which implies that the underlying income distribution is unequal. Note that the degree of inequality depends on the magnitude of δ; the smaller the value, the more unequal the income distribution.

The Lorenz curve for the Pareto distribution depends only on one parameter, δ, which implies that the Lorenz curves for the Pareto distribution never intersect. However, there is robust empirical evidence that the Lorenz curves intersect in a significant number of situations. That is why the Lorenz curve provides only a partial ranking of inequality in income distributions. However, this partial ranking need not be considered a weakness of the Lorenz curve. Sen (1973) criticized complete ranking because the concept of inequality has different facets which may point in different directions. And, thus many times, a total ranking cannot be achieved.

Inequality measures have been devised to obtain the complete ranking of income distributions. These measures require value judgments, which should be evaluated based on social welfare functions. A detailed discussion of inequality measures is given in Chapter 5.

3.3.2 Family of Distribution Functions

The equation of the Lorenz function for the family of distribution functions discussed in Chapter 2 is derived below. The distribution function obtained in (2.7.2) yields

$$\left(\frac{x}{c}\right)^\beta = \left[(1-p)^{-\left(\frac{\beta}{\alpha}\right)} - 1\right]. \qquad (3.3.5)$$

The first-moment distribution function for this distribution is given by

$$F_1(x) = \frac{1}{\mu}\int_0^x \alpha c^\alpha X^\beta \left(c^\beta + X^\beta\right)^{-\left(\frac{\alpha}{\beta}\right)-1} dX \qquad (3.3.6)$$

where the mean μ is given by

$$\mu = \frac{\alpha}{\beta} cB\left(\frac{1}{\beta} + 1, \frac{\alpha - 1}{\beta}\right)$$

$B(m, n)$ is the Beta function with parameters m and n. The integral (3.3.6) is evaluated by substituting $y = \left(\frac{x}{c}\right)^{\beta}$, which gives

$$F_1(x) = B_z\left(\frac{1}{\beta} + 1, \frac{\alpha - 1}{\beta}\right) \tag{3.3.7}$$

where $z = \left(\frac{x}{c}\right)^{\beta}$, and $B_z(m, n)$ is the incomplete Beta distribution of the second kind and is defined by

$$B_z(m, n) = \frac{1}{B(m, n)} \int_0^z \frac{y^{m-1} dy}{(1 + y)^{m+n}}.$$

From (3.3.5) and (3.3.7), the equation of the Lorenz function is derived as

$$L(p) = B_z\left(\frac{1}{\beta} + 1, \frac{\alpha - 1}{\beta}\right) \tag{3.3.8}$$

where

$$z = \left[(1 - p)^{-\left(\frac{\beta}{\alpha}\right)} - 1\right] \tag{3.3.9}$$

The particular cases can now be considered. Substituting $\beta = 1$ into (3.3.8) gives

$$L(p) = 1 - \alpha(1 - p)^{\delta} + (\alpha - 1)(1 - p),$$

which is the Lorenz function for the Pareto distribution of the second kind. Similarly, the Lorenz function for the sech square distribution considered by Fisk (1961b) is obtained by substituting $\beta = \alpha$ into (3.3.8) and (3.3.9). In both cases, the Lorenz function reduces to one parameter function, which rules out the possibility of the intersection of the Lorenz curves.

3.3.3 Lognormal Distribution

The Lorenz function implied by lognormal distribution is now derived below. The probability distribution function for lognormal distribution is denoted by

$$F(x) = \Lambda(x/\mu, \sigma^2)$$

where

$$\Lambda(x/\mu, \sigma^2) = \int_0^x \frac{1}{X\sigma\sqrt{2\pi}} \exp\left\{-\frac{1}{2\sigma^2}(\ln X - \mu)^2\right\} dX \text{ for } x > 0 \tag{3.3.10}$$

The first-moment distribution function can be written as

$$F_1(x) = \frac{1}{\mu} \int_0^x X d\Lambda(X/\mu, \sigma^2) \qquad (3.3.11)$$

where $\mu = \exp\left(\mu + \frac{\sigma^2}{2}\right)$ is the mean of the lognormal distribution with parameters μ and σ^2. Using Theorem 2.6 in Aitchison and Brown (1957), equation (3.3.11) yields

$$F_1(x) = \Lambda(x/\mu + \sigma^2, \sigma^2) \qquad (3.3.12)$$

To derive the Lorenz function, define the relation

$$x = \varphi(t)$$

where $t = \frac{1}{\sqrt{2\pi}} \int_0^x \exp(-X^2/2) \, dX$ is the standard normal distribution function. Then if $p = \Lambda(x/\mu, \sigma^2)$, it follows that

$$\frac{\ln(x) - \mu}{\sigma} = \varphi(p) \qquad (3.3.13)$$

σ being the standard deviation of $\ln(x)$. Similarly, if $L(p) = F_1(x)$, equation (3.3.12) becomes

$$\frac{\ln(x) - \mu - \sigma^2}{\sigma} = \varphi(L(p)). \qquad (3.3.14)$$

Eliminating $\ln(x)$ from (3.3.13) and (3.3.14) gives the equation of the Lorenz function as

$$\varphi(L(p)) = \varphi(p) - \sigma, \qquad (3.3.15)$$

which depends only on one parameter, implying that the Lorenz curves underlying the lognormal distribution cannot intersect. As pointed out, there are a significant number of cases when the Lorenz curves of observed income distributions do intersect. Thus, lognormal distribution cannot describe the empirical income distributions in all situations. Moreover, lognormal distribution does not fit well at the lower and upper-income distributions.

Aitchison and Brown, in their classic book on lognormal distribution, published in 1957, stated their belief that the lognormal distribution is as fundamental as the normal distribution. It arises from a theory of elementary errors combined by a multiplicative process, just as the normal distribution arises from a theory of errors combined by the addition process. Thus, there is a close similarity between normal and lognormal distributions. Moreover, like a normal distribution, lognormal distribution has many practical applications. But as shown here, lognormal distribution does not help describe income distributions because it rules out the observed phenomenon of the intersection of the Lorenz curves. Moreover, it does not perform well at the lower and upper ends of the income distribution.

3.4 Direct Approaches to Specifying the Lorenz Curve

The previous section derived the Lorenz function from some well-known income distribution functions. However, as noted in Chapter 2, the income distribution functions proposed in the literature rarely provide a good fit with a wide range of observed income distributions. Therefore, Kakwani and Podder (1973, 1976) and Kakwani (1981a) proposed an alternative approach that directly specifies a functional form of the Lorenz curve. Once the Lorenz function is defined and estimated from actual data, the inequality measures can be derived as functions of the parameters of the equation. Also, the density function can also be obtained from the equation of the Lorenz curve.

Kakwani and Podder (1973) suggested the following functional form of the Lorenz curve:

$$L(p) = pe^{-\gamma(1-p)} \tag{3.4.1}$$

where $\gamma \geq 0$ is the parameter. If $\gamma > 0$, the curve lies below the egalitarian line; if $\gamma = 0$, the curve coincides with the egalitarian line. Differentiating (3.4.1) twice yields

$$L'(p) = e^{-\gamma(1-p)}(1 + \gamma p)$$

$$L''(p) = 2\gamma e^{-\gamma(1-p)}(2 + \gamma p).$$

Suppose $\gamma > 0$, both these derivatives are positive for all values of p in the interval 0 and 1. Thus, the curve (3.4.1) is sloping upward and increasing monotonically, thereby satisfying all the four conditions (a)–(d) given in (3.2.8).

Kakwani and Podder (1973) fitted the curve (3.4.1) to Australian data using the ordinary least square method to the transformed equation

$$ln(p) - lnL(p) = \gamma ln(1 - p)$$

But the empirical fit was unsatisfactory. Moreover, this curve specification depends on only one parameter, which rules out the possibility of intersecting Lorenz curves.

Following a similar approach, Kakwani and Podder (1976) proposed a new coordinate system for the Lorenz curve using the transformations:

$$\pi = \frac{p + L(p)}{\sqrt{2}} \text{ and } \eta = \frac{p - L(p)}{\sqrt{2}} \tag{3.4.2}$$

Because the Lorenz curve lies below the egalitarian line, $L(p) < p$. It implies that $\eta \geq 0$. Further, if income is always positive, (3.4.2) will mean that

$$\eta \leq \pi.$$

They proposed the following specification of the Lorenz curve:

$$\eta = a\pi^{\alpha}(\sqrt{2} - \pi)^{\beta} \tag{3.4.3}$$

where $a > 0$, $\alpha > 0$, and $\beta > 0$. The restriction $a > 0$ implies that $\eta \geq 0$ for all values of π in the range 0 to $\sqrt{2}$, indicating that the Lorenz curve lies below the egalitarian line. Further, restrictions $\alpha > 0$ and $\beta > 0$ mean that η takes value zero when $\pi = 0$ or $\pi = \sqrt{2}$.

The curve (3.4.3) can be estimated using the ordinary least square method to the transformed equation:

$$ln(\eta) = ln(a) + \alpha ln(\pi) + \beta ln(\sqrt{2} - \pi) \tag{3.4.4}$$

Kakwani and Podder (1976) suggested methods to improve the efficiency of the estimates by utilizing specific properties of the Lorenz curve. They also showed that once the parameters of (3.4.3) are estimated from the actual data using (3.4.4), the inequality and poverty measures can be derived as functions of the parameters of the equation. Also, one can calculate the density function, which may serve many vital purposes.

The empirical results indicate that this specification of the Lorenz curve provides an extremely good fit for the entire range of the observed income distributions. Jain (1975) fitted the same equation of the Lorenz curve to about 500 income distributions from about 70 countries for several years. Her study, widely quoted in the 1970s, indicated that the new system of coordinate systems provided a good fit with almost all income distributions used.

Kakwani (1981a) proposed a new functional form of the Lorenz curve, which he used for the estimation of a class of welfare measures:

$$L(p) = p - ap^{\alpha}(1 - p)^{\beta} \tag{3.4.5}$$

where a, α and β are assumed to be greater than zero. Note that $L(p) = 0$ for both $p = 0$ and $p = 1$. The sufficient conditions for $L(p)$ convex to the p axis are $0 < \alpha \leq$

1 and $0 < \beta \leq 1$. The Lorenz function parameters a, α, and β can be estimated by regressing $ln[p - L(p)]$ on $ln(p)$ and $ln(1 - p)$. The inequality and poverty measured can be derived as functions of the three parameters.

Kakwani (1993) applied this Lorenz function to Ivory Coast household expenditure data, obtaining the following regression

$$ln[p - L(p)] = -0.1798 + 0.9967L(p) + 0.5355[ln(1 - p)]$$

$$(.0039) \quad (.0021) \qquad (.0017)$$

where the figures in the bracket are the standard errors of the coefficient estimates, and the value of the coefficient of determination, R^2, was calculated to be 0.9929, an extremely high value given that 1,569 observations were used in its calculation. Comparing the actual values with the Lorenz curve $L(p)$ shows that this curve provides an extremely good fit over the entire income range.

It is essential to point out that the World Bank adopted the equation of this Lorenz curve in its interactive computational tool to replicate the calculations of poverty and inequality in developing countries. In addition, researchers worldwide use this tool to calculate the poverty measures for any given poverty line.

3.5 Some Useful Lemmas

The perpendicular distance between the Lorenz curve and the egalitarian line, $\varphi(p) = p - L(p)$, is equal to zero when $p = 0$ and $p = 1$. The first and second derivatives of $\varphi(p)$ are derived as

$$\varphi'(p) = 1 - L'(p)$$

$$\varphi''(p) = -L''(p)$$

which shows that $\varphi'(p)$ becomes 0 at the point where the Lorenz curve has a slope of 1 and the second derivative of $\varphi(p)$ is always negative. If p_μ is the point at which the Lorenz curve has the slope of unity, which from a standard optimization requirement in calculus implies that $\varphi(p)$ is maximum at $p = p_\mu$. Equation (3.2.8) means that the slope of the Lorenz curve is unity at the income level $x = \mu$. Thus, Lemma 3.1 follows.

Lemma 3.1 *The distance between the Lorenz curve and the egalitarian line is maximum at an income level $x = \mu$, μ being the mean income.*

Next, divide the population into two groups. All units with income less than the population mean income belonging to the first group and the rest belonging to the second group. If μ_1 and μ_2 denote the mean incomes of the first and second group, respectively, it follows that

$$L(p_\mu) = \frac{p_\mu \mu_1}{\mu}$$

$$1 - L(p_\mu) = \frac{(1 - p_\mu)\mu_2}{\mu} \qquad (3.5.1)$$

where the mean income of the whole population is given by $\mu = p_\mu \mu_1 + (1 - p_\mu)\mu_2$.

Suppose some income is transferred from the richer second group to the poorer first group so that both have the same mean income. In that case, the gain in the income of the first group as a proportion of the mean income of the whole population is $p_\mu(\mu - \mu_1)/\mu$, which from (3.5.1) simplifies to $p_\mu - L(p_\mu)$, the maximum distance between the Lorenz and egalitarian line leads to Lemma 3.2.

Lemma 3.2 *If the population is divided into two groups so that in the first (second) group all the people have income less (greater) than the population mean, the proportion of income that should be transferred from the second group to the first so that both have the same mean income is equal to the maximum distance between the Lorenz curve and the egalitarian line.*

This Lemma suggests that the maximum distance between the egalitarian line and the Lorenz curve, given by $\varphi(p_\mu) = p_\mu - L(p_\mu)$, where p_μ is the proportion of the population having income less than the mean income μ, can be a measure of income inequality.

3.6 Symmetric Lorenz Curve

The symmetry of the Lorenz curve is defined with respect to the diagonal drawn perpendicular to the egalitarian line. Suppose that in Figure 3.1, PE and P'F are the perpendiculars drawn on the egalitarian line from any two points P and P', respectively, on the Lorenz curve. If EG = GF, it follows that for asymmetric Lorenz curve, PE = P'F. If the Lorenz curve is not symmetric, it is skewed either toward (0, 0) or (1, 1). The curve is defined as skewed toward (0, 0) if P'F is greater than PE. Similarly, the curve is skewed toward (1, 1) if P'F is less than PE. The formal condition of symmetry is derived in Lemma 3.3.

Lemma 3.3 *The Lorenz curve $q = L(p)$ is symmetric if and only if*

$$1 - p = L(1 - q). \qquad (3.6.1)$$

Proof. If p is any point on the curve with coordinates (p, q), it can be seen from Figure 3.1 that OM = OL + LM and EL = EN + NL. Further, $OL = LE = \left(\frac{1}{\sqrt{2}}\right) OE$ and $EN = NP = \left(\frac{1}{\sqrt{2}}\right) PE$. Because OM = p and NL = PM = q, it follows that $p = \frac{1}{\sqrt{2}}(OE + PE)$ and $q = \frac{1}{\sqrt{2}}(OE - PE)$, which on solving for OE and PE, gives

$$OE = \frac{1}{\sqrt{2}}(p + q) \text{ and } PE = \frac{1}{\sqrt{2}}(p - q) \qquad (3.6.2)$$

Similarly, if p' is any other point on the Lorenz curve with coordinates (p', q'), then

$$OF = \frac{1}{\sqrt{2}}(p' + q') \text{ and } P'F = \frac{1}{\sqrt{2}}(p' - q') \qquad (3.6.3)$$

If the point p' is such that EG = GF, it follows that $OF = \sqrt{2} - OE$, which from (3.6.2) and (3.6.3) gives

$$p' + q' = 2 - p - q \qquad (3.6.4)$$

If the Lorenz curve is symmetric, it should satisfy PE = P'F, which on using (3.5.3) and (3.5.4) gives

$$p' - q' = p - q \qquad (3.6.5)$$

then solving for p' and q' from (3.5.5) and (3.5.6) gives

$$p' = 1 - q \text{ and } q' = 1 - p. \qquad (3.6.6)$$

Because (p', q') is a point on the Lorenz curve $q = L(p)$, the result given in (3.5.2) follows immediately from (3.6.6). This proves the necessary part of Lemma 3.3. Moreover, the sufficiency condition can be confirmed by showing that if P' is a point with coordinates $(1 - q)$ and $(1 - p)$, EG = GF and P'F = PE. This follows immediately from (3.6.2) and (3.6.3), which completes the proof of Lemma 3.3.

Lemma 3.3 implies that if (p, q) is any point on a Lorenz curve, the point $(1 - q, 1 - p)$ also lies on the same curve. This can be interpreted as if the bottom p percent of the population earns q percent of the total income; the top q percent makes p percent of the total income.

Differentiating (3.6.1) with respect to p gives

$$L'(1 - q)L'(p) = 1. \tag{3.6.7}$$

According to Lemma 3.1, $L'(p)$ equals unity at the point $p = p_\mu$, where p_μ is the value of p at which $x = \mu$. Thus equation (3.6.7) at point $p = p_\mu$ gives

$$L'(p_\mu) = 1 \text{ and } L'(1 - q_\mu) = 1$$

where $q_\mu = L(p_\mu)$. Since $L'(p) > 0$ for all p in the range $0 \leq p \leq 1$, $L'(p)$ is a monotonically increasing function of p. Thus, there cannot be two different values of p at which $L'(p) = 1$. From this, it immediately follows that $p_\mu = 1 - q_\mu$, which leads to Lemma 3.4.

Lemma 3.4 *If the Lorenz curve $q = L(p)$ is symmetric, then*

$$p_\mu + L(p_\mu) = 1. \tag{3.6.8}$$

This Lemma can only give the necessary condition, but it is not sufficient to say that the Lorenz curve will always be symmetric.

Lemma 3.5 provides an alternative condition of symmetry of the Lorenz curve in terms of the density function.

Lemma 3.5 *The necessary and sufficient condition for the Lorenz curve $q = L(p)$ to be symmetric is*

$$\frac{f\left(\frac{\mu^2}{x}\right)}{f(x)} = \left(\frac{x}{\mu}\right)^3 \tag{3.6.9}$$

for all x where $f(x)$ is the density function.[2]

Proof: The necessary and sufficient condition for the Lorenz curve $q = L(p)$ to be symmetric is provided in (3.6.1). Differentiating this equation with respect p yields (3.5.8), which on differentiating again yields

$$[L'(p)]^3 = \frac{L''(p)}{L''(1 - q)} \tag{3.6.10}$$

where use has been made of (3.6.7). If p corresponds to income level x and $p' = (1 - q)$ to income level x', the condition (c) in (3.2.8) yields

$$L'(p) = \frac{x}{\mu} \text{ and } L''(p) = \frac{1}{\mu f(x)} \tag{3.6.11}$$

---

[2] This lemma was suggested by Champernowne (1956), but he did not provide its proof.

$$L'(1 - q) = \frac{x'}{\mu} \text{ and } L''(1 - q) = \frac{1}{\mu \, f(x')}. \tag{3.6.12}$$

Substituting these equations into (3.5.8) gives

$$x' = \frac{\mu^2}{x} \tag{3.6.13}$$

which demonstrates that, if p corresponds to income level x, $p' = 1 - q$ corresponds to income level $\frac{\mu^2}{x}$. Combining (3.6.11) and (3.6.12) with (3.6.10) yields (3.5.10). This proves the necessary aspect of the condition in Lemma 3.5.

The sufficiency aspect of the Lemma is determined if equation (3.6.9) implies equation (3.6.1). Because the point $[p', L(p')]$ corresponds to the income level $\frac{\mu^2}{x}$, then

$$L'(p') = \frac{\mu}{x} \text{ and } L''(p') = \frac{1}{\mu f\left(\frac{\mu^2}{x}\right)} \tag{3.6.14}$$

Equations (3.6.11), (3.6.12), and (3.6.14) in conjunction with (3.6.9) yield

$$L'(p)L'(p') = 1 \tag{3.6.15}$$

$$L''(p') = L''(p)[L'(p')]^3. \tag{3.6.16}$$

Differentiating (3.6.14) with respect to p and using (3.6.16) gives

$$L'(p)\frac{dp'}{dp} = -1 \tag{3.6.17}$$

which on integration gives

$$L(p') = c - p \tag{3.6.18}$$

where c is the constant of integration.

Substituting (3.6.15) into (3.6.17) yields

$$\frac{dp'}{dp} = -L'(p),$$

which on integration becomes

$$p' = c_1 - L(p) \tag{3.6.19}$$

where c_1 is the constant of integration.

Equations (3.6.18) and (3.6.19) yield

$$L(c_1 - q) = c - p$$

$$L(c - q') = c_1 - p'$$

where $q' = L(p')$. Fulfilling the conditions that $q = 0$ when $p = 0$ and $q' = 0$ when $p' = 0$, these two equations become $L(c_1) = c$ and $L(c) = c_1$.

Both of which can be true if either $c = c_1 = 0$ or $c = c_1 = 1$. It is evident from (3.6.18) and (3.6.19) that c and c_1 cannot be both equal to zero; if they were p' and $L(p')$, they would be negative. Hence, $c = c_1 = 1$, from which it follows that $p' = 1 - q$ and $L(p') = 1 - p$. These two equations together lead to (3.6.1). Thus, the proof of Lemma 3.5 is complete.

Lemma 3.6 *The Lorenz curve for lognormal distribution is symmetric.*

The proof follows immediately from Lemma 3.5 if the lognormal density function in equation (3.6.9) is used.

3.7 Economic Development and Skewness of the Lorenz Curve

If the Lorenz curve is not symmetric, it is skewed either toward $(0, 0)$ or $(1, 1)$. It is unlikely that an observed income will be found to be symmetric. In most situations, the empirical income distributions will be skewed toward $(0, 0)$ or toward $(1, 1)$. This section explores how economic development is related to the skewness of the Lorenz curve.

Kuznets (1955) was a pioneer in observing income distribution patterns during a country's economic development. In his classic paper "Economic Growth and Income Inequality," he began investigating the linkage between economic growth and income distribution in 1955 (Kuznets 1955). In this paper, he examined income distribution in a cross-section of countries at different levels of development. Based on this empirical evidence, he hypothesized that "in the early phase of industrialization of the underdeveloped countries, income distribution will tend to widen before leveling forces become strong enough, first to stabilize and then reduce income inequalities." This hypothesis became popularly known as an inverted U-shaped pattern of income inequality; inequality first increased and then decreased with development.

Kuznets returned to the debate in 1963 with a plentiful supply of empirical evidence. He concluded that the shares of the upper-income groups are distinctly larger in developing countries than in developed countries. The top 5% of families or spending units in most developing countries receive 30% of the total income or more. In contrast, the shares in developed countries range from 20 to 25%. He further observed that the shares of the lower-income groups are either higher or insignificantly different in developing countries than in developed countries. Based on these observations, he concluded that the share of the middle-income group is smaller in developing countries than in developed countries.

This section provides an alternative approach based on the skewness of the Lorenz curve to test Kuznets' hypothesis regarding income shares in developed and developing countries. To that end, consider Figure 3.2, which contains two Lorenz curves corresponding to income distributions I and II. These curves are not symmetric with respect to the alternate diagonal AC. The Lorenz curve I is skewed toward (0, 0), whereas the Lorenz curve II is skewed toward (1, 1).

Compare the shares of the lower-income group (say, the bottom 20% population) under the two Lorenz curves. The income share of this group is larger with Lorenz curve I than with Lorenz curve II. Similarly, comparing the upper-income group's shares (say, the top 20% population) under the two income distributions indicates that with Lorenz curve I, this share is given by the length BG, and Lorenz curve II is given by length BH.

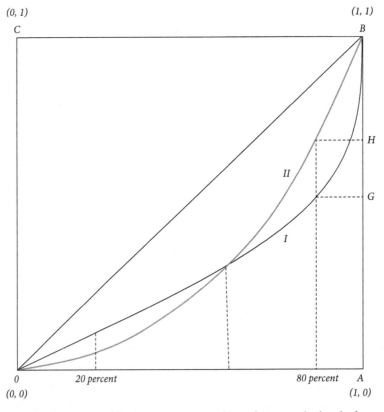

Fig. 3.2 Skewness of the Lorenz curve and its relation to the level of development

Therefore, the share of the upper-income group is larger with Lorenz curve I than with Lorenz curve II. The middle-income group has a smaller income share with Lorenz curve I, which is skewed toward (0,0), than with Lorenz curve II, which is skewed toward (1,1).

To recapitulate, Kuznets' hypothesis is that as a country develops, the share of the middle-income group increases. Thus, in the course of economic development, the Lorenz curve changes its shape concerning its skewness from (0, 0) toward (1, 1). Comparing two countries, one skewed toward (0, 0) will be less developed than the other skewed toward (1, 1). In the context of the present discussion, the Kuznets hypothesis will be established if the empirical results show that the Lorenz curve for developing countries is generally skewed toward (0, 0). In contrast, the Lorenz curve for developed countries is skewed toward (1, 1). Thus, the skewness of the Lorenz curve determines the level of economic development. This idea has not been explored in the economic development literature.

3.8 Intercountry Comparison of Skewness of Lorenz Curve

This section examines the degree of the skewness of the Lorenz curve for 50 countries at different stages of development indicated by their per capita income. The data are from a compilation by Jain (1975). These data on the size distribution of income were available in the form of a frequency distribution giving (a) the number of individuals in different income ranges and (b) the total income of each range. However, the income ranges varied from one source to another, and, therefore, the distributions were not comparable in their original form. To ensure comparability, the data were transformed into estimates of income shares accruing to different quintiles of the population by fitting the equation of the new coordinate system in (3.4.3). This specification of the Lorenz curve contains three parameters a, α, and β, estimated by the ordinary least-squares method after transforming (3.4.3) into logarithms. The estimated parameters could then determine the quintile shares for each country's income distribution. The quintile shares immediately provided the income shares of the bottom 40%, middle 40%, and top 20% of the population.

The coefficient of determination R^2, which is the correlation coefficient between the actual and estimated value of η, was estimated for the Lorenz curve of each income distribution. The estimated values of R^2 were found to be extremely high at over 0.99. Moreover, the actual and estimated values of η, though not reported here, were very close to at least two decimal places. From these observations, it may be concluded that the density function underlying the new coordinate system for the Lorenz curve provides an excellent fit to a wide range of income distributions observed in different countries.

The estimated parameters of the new coordinate system in (3.4.3) led to an estimate of the skewness of the Lorenz curve. The Lorenz curve is symmetric if $\alpha = \beta$, skewed toward (0, 0) if $\alpha > \beta$ and skewed toward (1, 1) if $\alpha < \beta$. Thus, α/β is a proposed measure of skewness of the Lorenz curve. The curve is skewed toward (0, 0) if α/β is greater than 1 and skewed toward (1, 1) if α/β is less than 1.

Table 3.1 presents the income shares of the bottom 40%, middle 40%, and top 20% of the population. The last column in the table gives values of the measure of skewness. The value of skewness measure is greater than unity for all developing countries except Barbados. On the other hand, the skewness index is less than unity for most developed countries except Greece and Spain. Thus, these results demonstrate that except for three countries, the Lorenz curves are skewed toward (0, 0) for all developing countries, whereas those in developed countries are skewed toward (1, 1). This observation overwhelmingly supports Kuznets' hypothesis that the income shares of the middle group are higher in developed countries than in developing countries.

The income shares of different groups show that the upper-income groups (top 20%) are distinctly higher in the developing countries than in the developed countries. These shares are, in general, larger in Latin American countries, with an average of 56.6%. The average is 53.9% in African countries, whereas, in Asian countries, it is 47.2%. The same group has the lowest average of 43.1% in developed countries. These observations support Kuznets' hypothesis of higher-income shares of the upper-income group in developing countries.

The shares of the bottom income group (bottom 40%) are not significantly different between the Asian and developed countries. However, the shares are considerably lower in African and Latin American countries. From these observations, it is difficult to determine whether the lower-income groups receive higher, lower, or equal shares in developing countries than developed countries.

The income shares of the middle-income groups between the 40th and 80th percentiles are larger in developed countries than in developing countries. This fact corresponds to the earlier observation that the Lorenz curves for developed countries are skewed toward (1, 1). Thus, an important conclusion emerging from this analysis is that as a country develops, the shares of middle-income groups increase.

Recent literature has extensively examined the role of the middle class in economic development. An emerging consensus among economists is that an increase in the middle-class size leads to greater overall prosperity. Recently, in some developed countries, the middle class has been shrinking. For instance, in the United States, the income share of households belonging to the middle class declined from 53% in 1967 to 43% in 2013 (Gebeloff and Searcey, 2015). Foster and Wolfson (2009) have attempted to explain the phenomenon of the shrinking middle class as caused by the increased polarization in society. The linkage between the disappearance of the middle class will be discussed in Chapter 5 of the book.

Kuznets advanced the relationship between the size of the middle class and economic development almost 60 years ago. The intercountry analysis of 50 countries presented above has provided overwhelming evidence of Kuznets' hypothesis of the linkage between the size of the middle class and economic development. Thus, it is somewhat surprising that the recent literature on the middle class has not mentioned Kuznets' pioneering work.

Table 3.1 Income shares and a measure of skewness of the Lorenz curve in 50 countries

	Income share of bottom 40%	Income share of middle 40%	Income share of top 20%	Skewness index α/β
Asia				
Indonesia	17.3	30.7	52.0	1.725
India	15.5	32.6	51.9	1.352
Pakistan	20.6	37.9	41.5	1.152
Malaysia	12.4	32.6	55.0	1.123
Sri Lanka	17.9	36.5	45.6	1.121
Hong Kong	15.6	35.4	49.0	1.118
South Korea	18.7	37.9	43.4	1.088
Taiwan	20.3	38.9	40.8	1.084
Philippines	11.9	34.1	54.0	1.020
Thailand	16.8	38.0	45.2	1.014
South Vietnam	19.2	39.5	41.3	1.010
Average	(16.9)	(35.8)	(47.2)	
Africa				
Madagascar	13.0	26.9	60.1	1.520
Ivory Coast	16.5	31.7	51.8	1.453
Dahomey	15.8	32.5	51.7	1.428
Malawi	15.0	32.1	52.9	1.277
Chad	19.3	35.9	44.8	1.253
Tanzania	13.5	30.8	55.7	1.25
Senegal	9.4	28.1	62.5	1.139
Uganda	16.6	36.8	46.6	1.071
Sierra Leone	7.2	30.0	62.8	1.031
Sudan	13.9	36.0	50.1	1.016
Average	(14.02)	(32.08)	(53.9)	
Latin America				
Argentina	16.6	32.5	50.9	1.321
Chile	13.0	31.2	55.8	1.203
Venezuela	8.2	26.4	65.4	1.146
Costa Rica	13.6	33.2	53.2	1.122
Colombia	10.1	29.8	60.1	1.088
Brazil	9.2	29.3	61.5	1.074
Mexico	11.2	31.9	56.9	1.081
Dominican Rep.	12.4	33.3	54.3	1.071
Panama	9.8	30.8	59.4	1.066
El Salvador	10.1	31.8	58.1	1.031
Ecuador	10.5	32.3	57.1	1.021
Barbados	14.7	38.4	46.9	0.960
Average	(11.6)	(31.7)	(56.6)	
Developed Countries				
United States	19.5	41.4	39.1	0.908
Sweden	16.0	39.5	43.3	0.918
Canada	19.0	41.0	40.0	0.924
Denmark	lB.3	39.7	44.0	0.932
Germany, Fed. Rep. of	18.9	40.8	40.3	0.930
Australia	20.0	41.1	38.9	0.933

Continued

	Income share of bottom 40%	Income share of middle 40%	Income share of top 20%	Skewness index α/β
Norway	17.1	41.9	41.0	0.838
France	10.0	35.3	54.7	0.939
Netherlands	13.7	37.0	49.3	0.987
Finland	11.7	37.9	50.4	0.899
New Zealand	16.7	41.3	42.0	0.867
United Kingdom	18.5	41.2	40.3	0.838
Japan	16.0	39.9	44.1	0.921
Greece	17.4	37.9	44.7	1.045
Hungary	23.7	42.7	33.6	0.839
Yugoslavia	18.4	40.2	41.4	0.955
Spain	16.5	38.0	45.5	1.019
Average	(17.0)	(39.8)	(43.1)	

3.9 Relative and Absolute Inequality

Inequality may be measured in both relative and absolute sense. If inequality measures remain unchanged when the same proportion alters each person's income, such measures are called relative inequality measures. The Lorenz curve measures relative inequality because the curve remains unchanged when all incomes are increased or decreased by the same proportion. The relative Lorenz inequality curve measures the deviation of the Lorenz curve from the egalitarian line:

$$\varphi_R = [p - L(p)] \tag{3.9.1}$$

where $L(p) = p$ is the egalitarian line. $\varphi_R = 0$ if $p = 0$ or $p = 1$. The curve increases first until $x = \mu$, and then it decreases. The higher the curve, the greater the relative inequality.

Alternatively, Kolm (1976a, 1976b) has proposed the absolute measures of inequality which do not show any change in inequality when the income of everyone is increased or decreased by the same amount. Such measures are called absolute or leftist measures of inequality.

According to Kolm, an equi-proportional increase in all incomes must increase absolute inequality because richer persons will enjoy a higher incremental rise in living standards than poorer ones.

Although inequality is commonly perceived as a relative concept, an absolute idea of inequality can also be attractive since government transfer policies are generally understood as absolute benefits going to the poor. A hypothetical example can intuitively explain the distinction between the two. For example, suppose there are two persons with incomes, $100 and $1,000, a policy that gives $15 to the poor and $100 to the rich will not be readily accepted as pro-poor even if the poor benefit proportionally

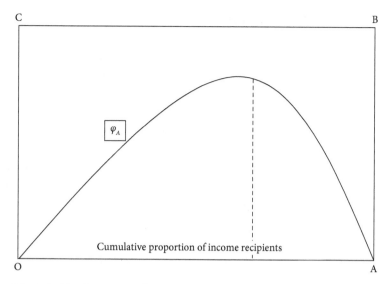

Fig. 3.3 Absolute inequality curve, φ_A

more than the non-poor. This policy has reduced relative inequality but increased absolute inequality. Most people will perceive the absolute concept of inequality as more appealing than the relative concept.

An absolute inequality curve can be proposed as given by

$$\varphi_A(p) = \mu[p - L(p)] \tag{3.9.2}$$

It is easy to show that $\varphi_A(p) = 0$ if $p = 0$ or $p = 1$. The curve increases first until $x = \mu$, and then it decreases. The higher the curve, the greater the absolute inequality.

It is easy to show that if the incomes of all persons are increased or decreased by the same amount, the curve does not change. In Figure 3.3, each point on the curve indicates the deviation of a person's income at the pth percentile in a situation where everyone received the same income. OA is the egalitarian line. If the curve coincides with the egalitarian line, each person gets the same income, perfect equality. The higher the absolute inequality curve, the greater the absolute inequality of income. The curve attains the maximum value at the point where $x = \mu$. A policy will be judged as absolute pro-poor (anti-poor) if $\varphi(p)$ shifts downward (upward).

The absolute inequality is measured in monetary units. So, the idea of absolute inequality seems intuitively attractive because it informs how much is the monetary cost of inequality to society or how much it will cost if society wants to eliminate or reduce absolute inequality. The main drawback of measuring inequality in money metric is that it can only be measured in real income discounted for inflation. In making an international comparison of inequality, the correct exchange rates would be required. This problem can be addressed using the purchasing power parity (PPP) exchange rates, which are now readily available for all countries over time.

3.10 Variants of the Lorenz Curve

The literature on inequality now provides some variants of the Lorenz curve, which have valuable interpretations of inequality. This section offers three such variants.

3.10.1 Relative Deprivation Curves

Since the concept of inequality is closely related to relative deprivation, it seems intuitively appealing to describe an income distribution in terms of relative deprivation suffered by individuals at different income levels. Thus, Kakwani (1984d) introduced a relative deprivation curve to represent and analyze income distribution. This curve is derived as follows.

Suppose the income x of an individual is a continuous random variable with mean income μ and density function $f(x)$. An individual with income x compares her income with all other individuals in society. She selects other individuals one by one at random and makes all possible comparisons. Assuming that she chooses an individual with income y and feels deprived, discovering her income x is lower than the income y of the person selected for comparison. Suppose the degree of deprivations suffered by her is measured by a function $u(x, y)$, then in all pairwise comparisons, her expected deprivation will be

$$E(deprivation) = \int_{x}^{\infty} g(x, y)f(y)dy \qquad (3.10.1)$$

The probability of selecting an individual with income y is $f(y)dy$ and $g(x, y) = 0$ if $y \leq x$, which implies that she feels no deprivation if her income is higher than the selected person's income. This assumption rules out the possibility of her feeling happy or guilty because she finds herself more prosperous.

The following restrictions are imposed on the deprivation function:

$$\frac{\partial g(x, y)}{\partial y} > 0 \text{ and } \frac{\partial g(x, y)}{\partial x} < 0 \qquad (3.10.2)$$

These restrictions are intuitively reasonable because the higher the income y relative to x, the greater the deprivation. To make this idea of deprivation empirically operational, it is necessary to specify the function $g(x, y)$. Specifying this function requires some value judgment because there can be many defensive alternative forms.

Kakwani (1984d) specified the following simple form:

$$\begin{aligned} g(x, y) &= (y - x) \quad if \, y > x \\ &= 0 \qquad\qquad if \, y \leq x \end{aligned} \qquad (3.10.3)$$

This implies that in any pairwise comparison, the deprivation suffered by an individual with a lower income equals the difference in incomes.

Substituting (3.10.3) into (3.10.1) results in the following expected deprivation suffered by a person with income x at the pth percentile:

$$E(deprivation|x_p) = \mu[1 - L(p)] - \mu L'(p)(1 - p). \tag{3.10.4}$$

This equation provides the absolute deprivation measured in monetary units suffered by an individual with income at the pth percentile.

The expected deprivation must be maximum when $p = 0$, obtained from (3.10.4) equal to μ. Thus, dividing (3.10.3) by μ gives the relative deprivation:

$$\varphi(p) = 1 - L(p) - L'(p)(1 - p) \tag{3.10.5}$$

where p varies from 0 to 1. $\varphi(p)$ is interpreted as the relative deprivation suffered by an individual at the pth percentile and satisfies the following conditions:

(a) If $p=0$, $\varphi(p) = 1$
(b) If $p=1$. $\varphi(p) = 0$
(c) $\varphi'(p) = - (1 - p)L''(p) < 0$.

Condition (c) implies that the relative deprivation decreases monotonically as p increases, following from the property that the second derivative of the Lorenz curve is always positive. At the egalitarian line, $L(p)=p$ for all p, that is, all persons in society have equal income; the deprivation curve coincides with the horizontal axis. Thus, the higher the curve, the greater the deprivation society suffers, implying higher inequality.

Table 3.2 presents the numerical values of the relative deprivation suffered by individuals at various percentiles based on the Australian data in 1975–76. The estimates are based on three income definitions. The market income is the income earned by individuals when government cash transfers are excluded and no personal income tax is deducted from the income. The gross income is the market income plus government cash transfers, and the disposable income is obtained after personal income tax is removed from the gross income.

Figure 3.4 presents the three deprivation curves, one for each income definition. None of these curves cross, indicating that taxes and government cash benefits reduce the relative deprivation at all percentiles. The curve based on gross income drops steeply compared to that found on market income up to about the 20th percentile, and then the difference between the two curves becomes gradually small until they meet at the 100th percentile. From this observation, it is concluded that government cash transfers play a crucial role in reducing the relative deprivation suffered by the bottom 20% of the population. The curve based on disposable income moves relatively

Table 3.2 Relative deprivation curves in Australia, 1975–76

Percentiles	Market income (Percent)	Gross income (Percent)	Disposable income (Percent)
10th	85.3	62.4	57.7
20th	61.2	51.9	48.2
30th	47.3	43.9	40.4
40th	40.1	34.5	33.1
50th	31.2	27.7	25.2
60th	23.7	21.8	20.0
70th	17.2	15.1	13.4
80th	12.2	11.5	10.3
90th	5.7	5.2	4.6
100th	0	0	0

close to that found on gross income. Although personal income tax reduces relative deprivation at all percentiles, the magnitudes of these reductions are small.

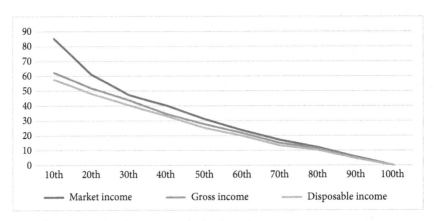

Fig. 3.4 Relative deprivation curves for three income concepts

3.10.2 Bonferroni Curve

The Lorenz curve describes income distributions by income share at different percentiles. Carl Emilio Bonferroni (1930) proposed a curve similar to the Lorenz curve based on the cumulative mean of the income distribution. If all individuals are ranked in ascending order of their income, the cumulative mean of incomes up to the pth percentile is given by

$$\mu_p = \frac{1}{p} \int_0^p x_p dp$$

where x_p is an individual's income at the pth percentile and $dp = f(x)dx$. Then the Bonferroni curve is defined as

$$B(p) = \frac{\mu_p}{\mu}$$ (3.10.6)

Note that for all non-negative incomes, $\mu_p = 0$ if $p = 0$ and $\mu_p = \mu$ if $p = 1$, which implies that $B(p)$ lies between 0 and 1.

The Lorenz curve $L(p)$ is defined as the income share of the bottom p proportion of the population and is given by $L(p) = \frac{p\mu_p}{\mu}$, which immediately yields the relationship between the Lorenz curve and the Bonferroni curve as

$$B(p) = \frac{L(p)}{p}$$ (3.10.7)

If all individuals receive the same income, the Lorenz curve coincides with the egalitarian line; $L(p)=p$, which on substituting in (3.10.7) gives $B(p)=1$ for all p. Thus, $B(p)=1$ for all p is the egalitarian line, when everyone receives the same income. The Bonferroni relative inequality curve is given by

$$B_R(p) = \frac{p - L(p)}{p},$$ (3.10.8)

which satisfies the following conditions:

$$\lim_{p \to 0} B_R(p) = 1 \ and \ B_R(p) = 0 \ if \ p = 1$$

and the curve decreases monotonically as p increases from 0 to 1.

Further, the higher the Bonferroni relative inequality curve, the more unequal the distribution. A distribution X will have greater relative inequality than Y if the Bonferroni relative inequality curve for X is higher than that for Y.

Suppose the two Bonferroni relative inequality curves intersect. In that case, one cannot infer whether distribution X is more or less inequitable than Y. To obtain a complete ranking of the income distributions, one needs to calculate the inequality measure derived from the Bonferroni curve, discussed in Chapter 5.

The absolute Bonferroni inequality curve is proposed as

$$B_A(p) = \frac{\mu(p - L(p))}{p} = \mu - \mu_p$$ (3.10.9)

When the same amount increases all incomes, the inequality curve does not change. It satisfies the following conditions

$$\lim_{p \to 0} B_A(p) = \mu \ and \ B_A(p) = 0 \ if \ p = 1$$

and the curve decreases monotonically when p increases from 0 to 1.

3.10.3 Zenga's Curve

Another variant of the Lorenz curve, proposed by Zenga (2007), is similar to the Bonferroni curve. The Bonferroni curve compares the cumulative mean income of the bottom p proportion of the population with the mean of the total population. However, Zenga's curve compares the cumulative mean income of the bottom p proportion of the population with the mean income of the top p proportion of the population.

The mean income of the top p proportion of the population is given by

$$\mu_{(1-p)} = \frac{1}{(1-p)} \int_p^1 x_p dp$$

so that

$$\mu = p\mu_p + (1-p)\mu_{(1-p)}.$$

The Zenga relative curve is defined as

$$Z(p) = \frac{\mu_p}{\mu_{(1-p)}} \tag{3.10.10}$$

The relationship between the Zenga curve and the Lorenz curve is given by

$$Z(p) = \frac{(1-p)L(p)}{p(1-L(p))}. \tag{3.10.11}$$

Substituting $L(p) = p$ gives $Z(p) = 1$ for all p, in which case everyone receives the same income, so there is perfect equality. $1 - Z(p)$ will be the Zenga relative inequality curve given by

$$Z_R(p) = \frac{p - L(p)}{p[1 - L(p)]}, \tag{3.10.12}$$

which satisfies the following condition

$$\lim_{p \to 0} Z_R(p) = 1 \text{ and } \lim_{p \to 1} Z_R(p) = 1.$$

The curve first decreases and then increases.

Zenga's absolute inequality curve is proposed as

$$Z_A(p) = \mu_{(1-p)} - \mu_P,$$

which is related to the Lorenz curve as

$$Z_A(p) = \frac{\mu(p - L(p))}{p[1 - L(p)]},$$ (3.10.13)

which satisfies the following conditions

$$\lim_{p \to 0} Z_A(p) = \mu \text{ and } \lim_{p \to 1} Z_A(p) = \mu.$$

Thus, the curve first decreases and then increases.

3.11 Comparison of Inequality: China versus India

This section makes an inequality comparison between India and China, utilizing the three inequality curves: the Lorenz, Bonferroni, and Zenga curves. The decile shares of income distributions of the two countries were downloaded from the World Bank Povcal Net program for 2015. The comparisons of relative inequality are depicted in Figures 3.5–3.7, while those of absolute inequality are presented in Figures 3.8–3.10.

These figures show that all three inequality curves, both relative and absolute, are uniformly higher for China than for India at all points. These observations conclude that relative and absolute concepts indicate that China has unambiguously higher inequality than India. The gap in absolute inequality between India and China is much more significant. The massive gap in absolute inequality occurs because China's real per capita income measured in the 2011 PPP is almost three times that of India. It is beyond the scope of this exercise to analyze why China has higher inequality than India.

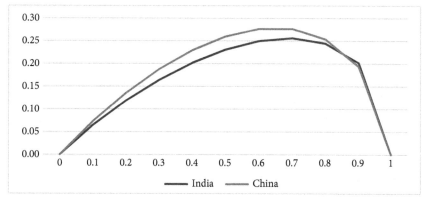

Fig. 3.5 India and China comparison of the relative Lorenz inequality curve

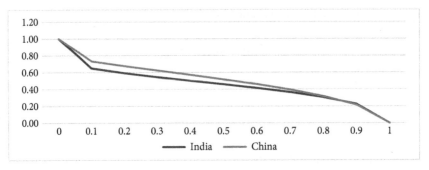

Fig. 3.6 India and China comparison of the relative Bonferroni inequality curve

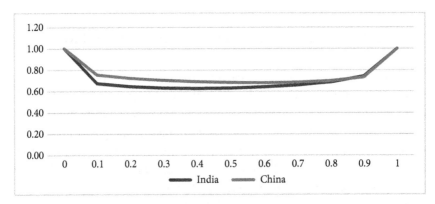

Fig. 3.7 India and China comparison of the relative Zenga inequality curve

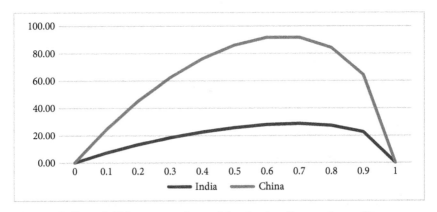

Fig. 3.8 India and China comparison of the absolute Lorenz inequality curve

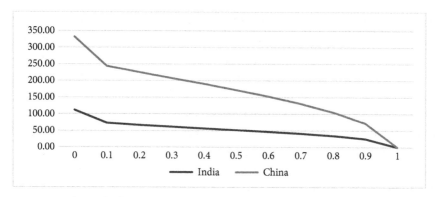

Fig. 3.9 India and China comparison of the absolute Bonferroni inequality curve

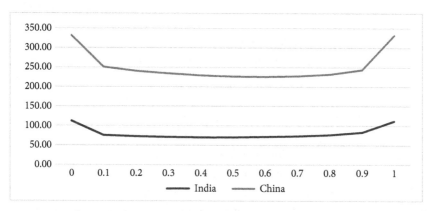

Fig. 3.10 India and China comparison of the absolute Zenga inequality curve

3.12 Concluding Remarks

M. O. Lorenz (1905) undertook an empirical study to measure the concentration of wealth in the United States. He published this study in the *Journal of the American Statistical Association*, where he proposed a graphical device to describe the concentration of wealth. This graphic device is a two-dimensional curve relating the cumulative proportion of individuals with the cumulative proportion of the wealth they own when individuals are arranged in ascending order of their wealth. Because of its simplicity, the curve became the most widely used graphical device to represent and analyze income distribution. It became famous as the Lorenz curve and appeared in almost all studies of income distributions subsequently undertaken.

This chapter has introduced the Lorenz curve in formal and rigorous terms. Many analytical results have been derived, which open up opportunities for many applications in economics relating to measuring and analyzing inequality in income. In addition, the chapter has demonstrated that the Lorenz curve is not just a graphical device to describe and represent income distribution, and it has many applications. For instance, it can be used as a criterion for ranking government policies or programs.

Suppose two alternative government policies result in two different income distributions, X_1 and X_2. If the Lorenz curve of X_1 is above X_2 at all points, then the first policy is preferred over the second policy from an equity point of view. However, if the two Lorenz curves intersect, neither policy can be more equitable than the other. Thus, the Lorenz curve provides only a partial ranking of distribution. However, this partial ranking need not be considered a weakness of the Lorenz curve. Since the concept of inequality has different facets, which may point in different directions. And thus, many times, a total ranking cannot be achieved.

Inequality measures have been devised to obtain the complete ranking of income distributions. These measures require value judgments, which should be evaluated based on social welfare functions. A detailed discussion of inequality measures is given in Chapter 5.

This chapter has derived the Lorenz curve for the well-known income distributions, discussed in Chapter 2. The Lorenz curves obtained from these distributions depend only on one parameter, implying that they do not intersect. However, the empirical evidence indicates many cases when the Lorenz curves of observed income distributions intersect. Thus, the well-known distributions proposed to explain income generation cannot describe the observed income distribution in all situations.

Given the limitations of the well-known distribution functions, this chapter has proposed an alternative approach that directly specifies a functional form of the Lorenz curve. Once the Lorenz function is defined and estimated from actual data, the inequality measures can be derived as functions of the parameters of the equation. The estimated Lorenz curve also lends to estimates of the density function.

The chapter has discussed three alternative functional forms of the Lorenz curve, two of which fit exceptionally well to a wide range of observed income distributions in developing and developed countries. The World Bank adopted one of the two specifications in its interactive computational tool to replicate the calculations of poverty and inequality in developing countries. Researchers worldwide use this tool to calculate the poverty measures for any given poverty line.

This chapter has also proved many analytical results on the symmetry of the Lorenz curve. If the Lorenz curve is not symmetric, it is skewed either toward $(0, 0)$ or $(1, 1)$. It is unlikely that an observed income will be found to be perfectly symmetric. In most situations, the empirical income distributions will be skewed toward $(0, 0)$ or toward $(1, 1)$.

The chapter has shown how the skewness of the Lorenz curve is related to economic development. In this regard, based on sizable empirical evidence, Kuznets hypothesized that as a country develops, the share of the middle-income group increases. This chapter has demonstrated that in the course of economic development, the Lorenz curve changes its shape concerning its skewness from $(0, 0)$ toward $(1, 1)$. When the Lorenz curve of a country becomes skewed toward $(1, 1)$, the share of its middle-income class increases.

The chapter has developed an index of skewness derived from the new coordinate system. If the index is greater than 1, the Lorenz curve is skewed toward $(0, 0)$. The empirical results for 50 developing and developed countries showed that the skewness index value was greater than 1 for all developing countries and less than 1 for all developed countries. These results have provided overwhelming evidence of the Kuznets hypothesis of the linkage between the size of the middle class and economic development. Unfortunately, the recent literature on the middle class has paid little attention to Kuznets' pioneering work, carried out almost 60 years ago.

This chapter has distinguished the relative and absolute inequality curves. The Lorenz curve measures relative inequality because the curve remains unchanged when all incomes are increased or decreased by the same proportion. Alternatively, the absolute inequality curve does not change when the income of everyone is increased or decreased by the same amount. Although inequality is commonly perceived as a relative concept, absolute inequality has an intuitive appeal. For example, it informs how much is the monetary cost of inequality to society or how much it will cost if society wants to eliminate or reduce inequality.

This chapter has proposed several absolute inequality curves that provide alternative approaches to ranking income distributions from the perspective of absolute inequality.

Finally, the chapter has offered three variants of the Lorenz curve: relative deprivation, Bonferroni, and Zenga curves. Since the concept of inequality is closely related to relative deprivation, it seems intuitively appealing to describe an income distribution in terms of relative deprivation suffered by individuals at different income levels. Accordingly, this chapter has derived a relative deprivations curve, which has been used to determine how the government cash transfers and taxes impact the relative deprivation suffered by the Australian population.

The chapter has also compared relative and absolute inequality between India and China, utilizing the Lorenz, Bonferroni, and Zenga inequality curves. From this comparison, the chapter has concluded that China has an unambiguously higher relative and absolute inequality of per capita consumption than India.

4

Welfare Ranking of Income Distributions

4.1 Introduction

This chapter concerns the welfare ranking of income distributions. A typical question in welfare economics is whether the welfare of society under a chosen policy A is higher or lower than under an alternative policy B. Policies have a different effect on individuals' economic welfare. A social welfare function explicitly specifies society's normative judgments on who should gain or lose from any policy. Thus, welfare ranking of income distributions is essential to know which policy will result in higher or lower social welfare.

There are two distinct issues in measuring social welfare. First is determining individuals' economic welfare, informing which individual in society is better off or worse off. The second is aggregating individuals' welfare for the whole society. Thus, a social welfare function is a rule of aggregating economic welfare of individuals. The welfare literature has primarily focused on the second issue, and this chapter briefly discusses both problems.

Because the Lorenz curve displays the deviation of each individual income from perfect equality, it captures, in a sense, the essence of inequality. The nearer the Lorenz curve to the egalitarian line, the more equal the income distribution. Consequently, the Lorenz curve could be used as a criterion for ranking income distributions.

Atkinson (1970), in his seminal paper, provided a linkage between the Lorenz curve and social welfare functions. He justified the Lorenz curve ranking in terms of social welfare by showing that the Lorenz curve ranking is identical to the ranking implied by social welfare provided the Lorenz curves do not intersect.

Atkinson's result assumes that the social welfare function equals the sum of individual utilities and that every individual has the same utility function. Still, this result is remarkable because one can rank the distributions without specifying the form of the utility function except that it is increasing and concave. His paper provided the welfare foundation of the Lorenz curve, attracting the attention of prominent economists. Dasgupta, Sen, and Starrett (1973) and Rothschild and Stiglitz (1973) demonstrated that the Atkinson theorem is more general and would hold for any symmetric quasi-concave social welfare function.

The Lorenz curve ranking has a limitation in that it depends on the assumption that the distributions compared must have the same mean income. If the distributions

Economic Inequality and Poverty. Nanak Kakwani and Hyun Son, Oxford University Press.
© Nanak Kakwani and Hyun Son (2022). DOI: 10.1093/oso/9780198852841.003.0004

have different means, the Lorenz curve may fail to provide a welfare ranking of distributions. Working independently, Shorrocks (1983) and Kakwani (1984c) extended the Lorenz partial ordering. They arrived at a criterion that would rank any two distributions with different means, the essential income distribution requirement. This criterion is called the generalized Lorenz curve dominance. This chapter develops this new ranking criterion for several alternative classes of social welfare functions.

The Lorenz criterion is not the only one used to rank distributions. Chapter 3 discussed the Bonferroni ranking criterion. This chapter develops the generalized Bonferroni criterion that provides the social welfare ranking of income distributions. This criterion holds for several alternative classes of social welfare functions.

4.2 Some Useful Definitions

Definition 4.1 The distribution $\tilde{x}$ is said to be Lorenz dominant $\tilde{y}$ if the Lorenz curve for $\tilde{x}$ lies above the Lorenz curve for $\tilde{y}$ at all points.

The above definition implies that the distribution $\tilde{x}$ is Lorenz dominant in the distribution $\tilde{y}$ if and only if

$$L_x(p) \geq L_y(p) \tag{4.2.1}$$

for all p in the interval $0 \leq p \leq 1$, where $L_x(p)$ and $L_y(p)$ are the Lorenz curves for the distributions $\tilde{x}$ and $\tilde{y}$, respectively.

Definition 4.2 The distribution $\tilde{x}$ is said to be the generalized Lorenz dominant to the distribution $\tilde{y}$ if and only if

$$\mu_x L_x(p) \geq \mu_y L_y(p), \tag{4.2.2}$$

where μ_x and μ_y are the means of distributions $\tilde{x}$ and $\tilde{y}$, respectively.

The definition of the Lorenz curve for a finite number of individuals, the distributions of which must be discrete, is as follows. If there are n individuals arranged in ascending order of their incomes, $x_1 \leq x_2, \ldots \ldots \ldots, \leq x_n$, the Lorenz curve's ordinate at $p=i/n$ for $i = 0, 1, 2, \ldots \ldots \ldots, n$ will be

$$L\left(\frac{i}{n}\right) = \frac{\sum_{k=1}^{i} x_k}{\sum_{k=1}^{n} x_k} \tag{4.2.3}$$

where $i \leq n$ and if all incomes are nonnegative $L(0)=0$.

If $\tilde{x}$ and $\tilde{y}$ are two ordered distributions,

$$x_1 \leq x_2, \ldots \ldots \ldots, \leq x_n \text{ and } y_1 \leq y_2 \ldots \ldots \ldots, y_n$$

Lorenz dominance in (4.2.1) is equivalent to

$$\frac{\sum_{k=1}^{i} x_k}{\sum_{k=1}^{n} x_k} \geq \frac{\sum_{k=1}^{i} y_k}{\sum_{k=1}^{n} y_k}$$

for all i. The generalized Lorenz dominance given in (4.2.2) is equivalent to

$$\sum_{k=1}^{i} x_k \geq \sum_{k=1}^{i} y_k$$

for all i. The Lorenz and generalized Lorenz dominance conditions will be identical if the two distributions have the same means.

Rothschild and Stiglitz (1973) proposed the following definition of regressive transfers.

Definition 4.3 Suppose $\tilde{x}$ is an ordered distribution and $\tilde{y}$ is another distribution obtained from $\tilde{x}$ by transferring income d from individual j to the richer k so that

(i) $y_j = x_j - d$
(ii) $y_k = x_k + d$
(iii) $y_i = x_i$

for all $i \neq j, k$, where $x_j \leq x_k$. Such a transfer is called a regressive transfer. $\tilde{y}$ differs from $\tilde{x}$ by a single regressive transfer. There can be a series of regressive transfers.

Definition 4.4 The function $g(\tilde{x})$ is concave if, only if,

$$\lambda g(\tilde{x}) + (1 - \lambda) g(\tilde{y}) \leq g[\lambda \tilde{x} + (1 - \lambda) \tilde{y}]$$

for any λ in the range $0 < \lambda < 1$ and any two vectors $\tilde{x}$ and $\tilde{y}$ in the domain of the function g.

Definition 4.5 The function $g(\tilde{x})$ is strictly concave if, only if,

$$\lambda g(\tilde{x}) + (1 - \lambda) g(\tilde{y}) < g[\lambda \tilde{x} + (1 - \lambda) \tilde{y}]$$

for any λ in the range $0 < \lambda < 1$ and for any two vectors $\tilde{x}$ and $\tilde{y}$ in the domain of the function g.

A strictly concave function is necessarily concave, but the converse may not be true. For example, a linear function is concave but not strictly concave.

Definition 4.6 The function $g(\tilde{x})$ is quasi-concave if, only if,

$$Minimum\ [g(\tilde{x}), g(\tilde{y})] \le g[\lambda\tilde{x} + (1-\lambda)\tilde{y}]$$

for any λ in the range $0<\lambda<1$ and for any two vectors $\tilde{x}$ and $\tilde{y}$ in the domain of the function g.

Note that quasi-concavity is a weaker condition than concavity. A concave function is always quasi-concave, but the converse may not be true.

4.3 Individual Welfare

The welfare of an individual is generally defined in terms of the utility an individual enjoys. It is more or less equated to pleasure or happiness. But how can one measure pleasure or happiness, which depends on an individual's state of mind. It is so subjective that it is impossible to quantify and produce a meaningful economic analysis tool. In his famous book, *Economics of Welfare,* Pigou (1920), regarded as the father of welfare economics, opted for a narrower but pragmatic approach to measuring individual welfare. He proposed to measure it by economic welfare, defined as that part of the welfare that can be measured in monetary units. This approach is now widely used to analyze the distribution of personal economic welfare.

In a market economy, individuals' welfare can be measured by their entitlement to the consumption of goods and services. Individuals get entitlement to consumption depending on how much income they have, and they exchange income for consumer goods at market prices. Thus, individuals' income in the reference period can be used as a composite measure of their entitlement. Although money income is widely used to measure economic welfare, it has many limitations.

An ideal welfare measure should incorporate all factors that contribute to economic welfare directly or indirectly. Household income or expenditure surveys are the primary sources of data on the income of households. Income is derived from several sources, such as wages and salaries, business income, government cash benefits, returns from investments, and in-kind transfers. These surveys do not provide enough information to consider all the relevant factors affecting economic welfare. As Sen (1973) points out, "to aspire, for ideal welfare measure which considers all the factors is a hopeless task because typical concepts of welfare tend to be extremely complicated when made operational." In this context, Kakwani (1986, 32) points out, "Even if all factors cannot be incorporated, due to data limitations, it is important to specify them and evaluate their effects on the distribution of economic welfare."

Income measures individuals' capability to enjoy the consumption of goods and services produced by the economy. The actual consumption of goods and services by individuals determines their standard of living. Individuals have discretion to decide how much they spend their income on expenditures in current and future periods. Generally, individuals smooth their consumption over time by borrowing or dissaving when they have low income and by saving when they have excess income. According to Friedman (1957), consumption is a better measure of individuals' permanent living standards.[1]

Poverty and inequality are estimated either by income or consumption expenditure. The nationally representative household surveys are the primary data sources on the income or consumption of households. Income or consumption expenditures of individuals are then derived from the information on the income or consumption of households collected from the surveys. In this regard, an assumption is made that households allocate their resources so that each individual belonging to the household enjoys the same level of welfare. However, this assumption cannot be readily validated because hardly any literature deals with household allocation mechanisms within households.

The economic welfare of households also depends on their needs. Since households differ in size, age composition, and other characteristics, they will have different needs. The problem of assessing individuals' needs is highly complex. A person's needs depend on many factors such as age, sex, occupation, health status, taste, and several other factors, many of which are not easily quantifiable. Attempts have been made in the literature to estimate consumer scales from household surveys that facilitate comparing the economic welfare of households with different needs.

There has been a sizable literature on this topic, including Rothbarth (1943), Nicholson (1949), Prais and Houthakker (1955), Forsyth (1960), Barten (1964), Singh and Nagar (1973), Muellbauer (1975a, 1975b, 1975c), Kakwani (1977f), and Deaton (1998). In this regard, Kakwani (1986, 31) has concluded that the various methods that have been developed to estimate consumer unit scales raise both theoretical and practical difficulties of one kind or another, and the only solution seems to be to use several alternative consumer unit scales that are intuitively justifiable.

In summing up, determining individuals' economic welfare is highly complex. Still, it is essential to measure it to assess which individual in society is better off or worse off. Moreover, an evaluation of any government policy cannot be accomplished unless the economic welfare of all individuals in society is known. Thus, it is essential to measure individuals' economic welfare, even if its measurement does not have the desired accuracy.[2]

4.4 Social Welfare Function

Social welfare relates to groups of individuals, a country, or a society within the state. A typical question in welfare economics is whether the welfare of society under a chosen policy A is higher or lower than an alternative policy B. A social welfare function is a rule of aggregating economic welfare of individuals. The primary purpose of using a social welfare function is to evaluate how economic resources are allocated in

---

[1] For an excellent discussion of individuals' welfare indicators, see Anand and Harris (1994).
[2] An excellent discussion of individual welfare is given in Deaton (1980, and Deaton and Zaidi (2002).

identifying which policies work and which do not. Policies have different effects on individuals' economic welfare. Some individuals might gain, while others lose from a policy. Thus, in any evaluation, normative judgments cannot be avoided. A social welfare function explicitly specifies normative judgments by assigning weights to different individuals.

Pareto (1897) proposed a general criterion for evaluating the economic allocation of resources. His rule states that any change in resource allocation improves the welfare of the society if it makes at least one person better off and no one worse off. A situation is called "Pareto optimal" if no alternative changes result in Pareto improvement. It means that an economy can achieve its optimality as long as nobody in the society can become better off without making anyone else worse off.

The Pareto criterion has a severe limitation. It implies that any given individual welfare distribution with fixed total economic welfare will always be considered Pareto optimal. Any change in welfare distribution that makes someone better off will make someone else worse off. It means that an economy can be Pareto optimal, even when some people are super-rich and rolling in luxury while others are almost starving, as long as the starving people cannot be made better off without making the super-rich worse off. Thus, the Pareto criterion fails to provide a framework for analyzing welfare distribution across individuals.

Bergson (1938), subsequently refined by Samuelson (1947), introduced the concept of a general social welfare function. In its most general form, the Bergson and Samuelson social welfare function is defined as a function of the economic welfare of all individuals in society. Under certain conditions, this social welfare function offers a legitimate framework for distributing welfare across individuals. A particular form of this general social welfare is the utilitarian welfare function used widely for policymaking. The following section discusses this function.

4.5 Utilitarian Social Welfare Function

Under the utilitarian approach, the objective of a society is to maximize the sum of individual utilities. Suppose a society comprises of n individuals who have economic welfare denoted by a vector

$$\tilde{x} \approx (x_1, x_2, \ldots \ldots \ldots, x_n).$$

Given this, one can construct a utility function of the ith individual as $u_i(\tilde{x})$, which summarizes the individual preferences. The ith person prefers $\tilde{x}$ to $\tilde{y}$ if and only if $u_i(\tilde{x}) > u_i(\tilde{y})$. The utilitarian social welfare function can then be written as

$$W = \sum_{i=1}^{n} u_i(\tilde{x}),$$

which is referred to as a Benthamite social welfare function. In this social welfare function, individual preferences are defined over the entire distribution of economic welfare $\tilde{x}$ rather than the economic welfare of the ith individual.

One could argue that individuals care only about their economic welfare rather than others.' In this case, the utility of the ith individual is given by $u_i(x_i)$; thus, the utilitarian social welfare function will be

$$W = \sum_{i=1}^{n} u_i(x_i).$$

In this social welfare function, every individual has a different utility with given economic welfare. It can be demonstrated that maximizing this utility function with a given level of total income does not equal economic welfare distribution. The optimal welfare distribution will be perfectly equal only if everyone in society has the same utility. If it is assumed that everyone in society has the same utility function, then the utilitarian social welfare function will be given by

$$E\left[u\left(\tilde{x}\right)\right] = \frac{1}{n}\sum_{i-1}^{n} u\left(x_i\right) \tag{4.4.1}$$

where E stands for expected value defined over the probability distribution of $\tilde{x}$. Assume that the distribution $\tilde{x}$ is characterized by the continuous random variable x that has density function $f(x)$, then the social welfare function in (4.5.1) is given by

$$E\left[u\left(\tilde{x}\right)\right] = \int_{0}^{\infty} u\left(x\right)f\left(x\right)dx \tag{4.5.2}$$

where economic welfare x is assumed to vary from zero to infinity. The utility function $u(x)$ has the following properties:

$$u'\left(x\right) > 0 \text{ and } u''\left(x\right) < 0$$

implying that the utility increases and the marginal utility decreases as x increases. The individual utility function is concave, which means that the social welfare function in (4.5.2) is also concave.

4.6 Atkinson's Theorem

As pointed out in Chapter 3, the Lorenz curve can rank income distribution from the equity perspective. Suppose there are two alternative government policies, which result in two different income distributions, $\tilde{x}$ and $\tilde{y}$. If the Lorenz curve of $\tilde{x}$ is above that of $\tilde{y}$ at all points, then from an equity point of view, the first policy is preferred over the second policy. However, if the two Lorenz curves intersect, neither policy can be more equitable than the other. Thus, the Lorenz curve provides only a partial ranking of distribution.

In his seminal paper published in 1970, Atkinson proved the remarkable theorem that linked the Lorenz curve ranking of income distributions with social welfare functions. He demonstrated that the ranking of income distributions according to the Lorenz curve criterion is identical to the ranking by social welfare. This theorem showed that the Lorenz curve is not just a graphical device representing income distributions, and it is closely related to social welfare, vital in evaluating government policies. The Lorenz curve can be directly computed from the observed income distributions and can be employed to conduct an evidence-based welfare analysis of resource allocation.

As discussed in Section 4.2, the distribution $\tilde{x}$ is said to be Lorenz dominant to the distribution $\tilde{y}$ if the Lorenz curve for $\tilde{x}$ lies at or above for the distribution $\tilde{y}$ at all points. The formal definition of Lorenz dominance was given in (4.2.1). Atkinson's theorem is then formally stated as follows:

Theorem 4.1 *If $\tilde{x}$ and $\tilde{y}$ are the two welfare distributions of individuals having the same mean, then the following statements are equivalent:*

(a) $L_x(p) \geq L_y(p)$ *for all p in the interval* $0 \leq p \leq 1$

(b) $E(u(\tilde{x})) \geq E(u(\tilde{y}))$

where $E(u(\tilde{x}))$ and $E(u(\tilde{y}))$ are the utilitarian social welfare as defined in (4.5.2) for distributions $\tilde{x}$ and $\tilde{y}$, respectively.

This theorem implies that if social welfare is the sum of the individual utilities, and if every individual has an identical utility function, the ranking of distributions according to the Lorenz curve criterion is identical to the ranking implied by this social welfare, provided the Lorenz curves do not intersect. In other words, there is a Lorenz dominance as stated in condition (a) in Definition 4.1. Thus, under the Lorenz dominance, one can judge between the distributions without knowing the form of the utility function, except that it is increasing and concave.

The Lorenz criterion is not the only one used to rank distributions. Chapter 3 discussed the Bonferroni ranking criterion defined in (3.10.3) as

$$B(p) = \frac{L(p)}{p}, \qquad\qquad (4.6.1)$$

which can be computed for any welfare distribution of individuals. Similar to the Lorenz dominance, one can define the Bonferroni dominance as stated below:

The distribution $\tilde{x}$ is said to be Bonferroni dominant to the distribution $\tilde{y}$ if the Bonferroni curve for $\tilde{x}$ lies at or above for the distribution $\tilde{y}$ at all points. Formally, this definition can be rewritten as

$$B_x(p) \geq B_y(p) \text{ for all } p \text{ in the interval } 0 \leq p \leq 1 \qquad\qquad (4.6.2)$$

where $B_x(p)$ and $B_y(p)$ denote the Bonferroni curves for distributions $\tilde{x}$ and $\tilde{y}$, respectively. Differentiating (4.6.2) gives

$$\frac{dB(p)}{dL(p)} = \frac{pL'(p) - L(p)}{p^2 L'(p)} = \frac{x_p - \tilde{x}_p}{px_p} > 0 \text{ for all } p \tag{4.6.3}$$

where x_p is the welfare level of an individual at the pth centile and $\tilde{x}_p$ is the mean welfare of the bottom p proportion of individuals when ranked by their welfare. It is easy to show that $x_p > \tilde{x}_p$ for all values of p, which implies that $\frac{dB(p)}{dL(p)} > 0 \text{ for all } p$, which also means that if any distribution is the Lorenz dominant, then it will also be Bonferroni dominant, satisfying (4.6.2). This leads to Theorem 4.2.

Theorem 4.2 *If $\tilde{x}$ and $\tilde{y}$ are the two welfare distributions of individuals having the same mean, then the following statements are equivalent:*

(a) $B_x(p) \geq B_y(p)$ *for all p in the interval $0 \leq p \leq 1$.*

(b) $E(u(\tilde{x})) \geq E(u(\tilde{y}))$

where $E(u(\tilde{x}))$ and $E(u(\tilde{y}))$ are the utilitarian social welfare as defined in (4.5.2) for distributions $\tilde{x}$ and $\tilde{y}$, respectively.

This theorem demonstrates that the ranking of distributions according to the Bonferroni curve criterion is identical to the ranking implied by the utilitarian social welfare in (4.5.2), provided the distributions have the same means and Bonferroni curves do not intersect. In other words, there is a Bonferroni dominance as stated in condition (a) in Theorem 4.2.

4.7 Generalized Lorenz Curve

Atkinson's theorem shows that the Lorenz curve is a powerful tool to judge the distributions from the welfare point of view, provided the distributions have the same means. If the distributions have different means, the Lorenz curve may fail to provide a welfare ranking of distributions. Consider an example of two distributions $\tilde{x}$ and $\tilde{y}$, which have means μ_x and μ_y, respectively. If distribution $\tilde{x}$ has a higher Lorenz curve than distribution $\tilde{y}$ at all points, then it can be unambiguously inferred that if $\mu_x > \mu_y$, distribution $\tilde{x}$ will have higher social welfare than distribution $\tilde{y}$. On the other hand, if $\mu_x < \mu_y$, the Lorenz curve can fail to make a normative statement about the two distributions. The same is true for the Bonferroni ranking as stated in Theorem 4.2.

The Lorenz curve (also the Bonferroni curve) makes the distributional judgment independently of the size of mean welfare, which, as Sen (1973) points out, "will make sense only if the relative ordering of welfare levels were strictly neural to the operation of multiplying everybody's income by a given number." Unfortunately, this requirement is rather extreme because multiplying everybody's income by a given positive number increases the economic welfare of everyone, which in turn increases social welfare. Sen, recognizing this limitation, concluded that "the problem of extending the Lorenz ordering to cases of variable mean income is quite a serious one and this—naturally enough—restricts the usefulness of this approach severely."

Kakwani (1984c) extended the Lorenz partial ordering and arrived at a criterion that would rank any two distributions with different means, which is the essential requirement of the observed income distributions.[3] The new ranking criterion is given by $L(\mu, L(p))$:

$$L(\mu, p) = \mu L(p) \qquad (4.5.1)$$

where μ is the mean welfare of individuals, and $L(p)$ is the Lorenz curve of the welfare distribution. This curve will be referred to as the generalized Lorenz curve. The ranking of distributions according to $L(\mu, p)$ is justified from the welfare point of view in terms of several alternative classes of social welfare functions. This chapter discusses the alternative social welfare functions that give the same ranking as the generalized Lorenz curve. The results presented in this chapter have been drawn mainly from Kakwani (1984c).

4.8 Welfare Ranking and Utilitarian Social Welfare Function

The relationship between the generalized Lorenz curve and the utilitarian social welfare function discussed in Section 4.4 is stated in Theorem 4.3.

Theorem 4.3 *If $\tilde{x}$ and $\tilde{y}$ are two distributions with means μ_x and μ_y, respectively, the following statements are equivalent:*

(a) $\mu_x L_x(p) \geq \mu_y L_y(p)$ for all p in the interval $0 \leq p \leq 1$
(b) $E[u(\tilde{x})] \geq E[u(\tilde{y})]$

where $L_x(p)$ and $L_y(p)$ are the Lorenz curves of the distributions $\tilde{x}$ and $\tilde{y}$, respectively, and the individual utility function u(x) is increasing and concave.

Proof: The following lemma, which is due to Hardy, Littlewood, and Polya (1929, 1934), will be used in proving this theorem.

Lemma 4.1 *Suppose m(x) and n(x) are increasing functions of x. Then the necessary and sufficient conditions for*

---

[3] Shorrocks (1983) working independently also arrived at the same criterion.

$$\int_a^b u\left(m\left(x\right)\right) dx \geq \int_a^b u\left(n\left(x\right)\right) dx$$

to be true for every increasing and concave u(x) is

$$\int_a^l m\left(x\right) dx \geq \int_a^l n\left(x\right) dx$$

for a ≤ l ≤ b, with equality for the extreme value of l.

The Lorenz curves always satisfy the following conditions (see Chapter 3):

$$x = \mu_x L'_x\left(p\right) \quad and \quad y = \mu_y L'_y\left(p\right) \tag{4.8.1}$$

where $L'_x\left(p\right)$ and $L'_y\left(p\right)$ are the first derivatives of $L_x\left(p\right)$ and $L_y\left(p\right)$, respectively, and p varies from 0 to 1. Because $dp=f(x)dx$ and Substituting (4.8.1) into (4.5.2) yields

$$E\left[u\left(\tilde{x}\right)\right] = \int_0^1 u\left[\mu_x L'_x\left(p\right)\right] dp$$

and

$$E\left[u\left(\tilde{y}\right)\right] = \int_0^1 u\left[\mu_y L'_y\left(p\right)\right] dp.$$

Since $\mu_x L'_x\left(p\right)$ and $\mu_y L'_y\left(p\right)$ are increasing functions of p because the second derivatives $L''_x\left(p\right)$ and $L''_y\left(p\right)$ are positive (see Chapter 3). Thus, the lemma provides the necessary and sufficient condition for

$$\left[u\left(\tilde{x}\right)\right] \geq E\left[u\left(\tilde{y}\right)\right]$$

to be true for every increasing and concave utility function u as

$$\int_0^l \mu_x L'_x\left(p\right) dp \geq \int_0^l \mu_y L'_y\left(p\right) dp \tag{4.8.2}$$

for $0 \leq l \leq 1$, with equality for extreme values of l. Evaluating the integrals (4.8.2) becomes

$$\mu_x L_x\left(p\right) \geq \mu_y L_y\left(p\right)$$

for all l in the interval $0 \leq l \leq 1$, the same condition (a) in Theorem 4.3. Thus, the proof of that theorem is complete.

The theorem is a generalization of Atkinson's theorem when the distributions have different means. However, the theorem is valid only when the generalized Lorenz curves do not intersect. Thus, the generalized Lorenz curve provides only the partial ranking of welfare distribution like the Lorenz curve. However, the empirical evidence of cross-country analysis presented by Kakwani (1984c) showed that the generalized Lorenz curves are less likely to cross than the Lorenz curve.

The theorem has many policy applications that require the welfare ranking of distributions. The generalized Lorenz curves can be readily computed from the observed income distributions. One can judge between the distributions with different means without knowing the form of the utility function because the theorem is valid for all utility functions $u(x)$, increasing and concaving.

If the distributions have the same means, the theorem leads to Atkinson's theorem stated in Theorem 4.1. Atkinson arrived at his theorem by exploiting the work on economically unrelated but similar problems of decision-making under uncertainty.[4] He also provided an alternative proof of his theorem. This section has proved his theorem as a particular case of the more general Theorem 4.3.

Similar to the generalized Lorenz curve, there also exists the generalized Bonferroni curve, which is given by

$$B(\mu, p) = \mu B(p) \tag{4.8.3}$$

The inequality proved in (4.6.4) implies the following inequality:

$$\frac{dB(\mu, p)}{dL(\mu, p)} > 0 \text{ for all } p \text{ in the range } 0 \leq p \leq 1.$$

That means that the ranking of distributions by the generalized Lorenz curve is the same as the generalized Bonferroni curve. This leads to Theorem 4.4.

Theorem 4.4 *If $\tilde{x}$ and $\tilde{y}$ are two distributions with means μ_x and μ_y, respectively, the following statements are equivalent:*

(c) $\mu_x B_x(p) \geq \mu_y B_y(p)$ for all p in the interval $0 \leq p \leq 1$
(d) $E[u(\tilde{x})] \geq E[u(\tilde{y})]$

where $B_x(p)$ and $B_y(p)$ are the Bonferroni curves of the distributions $\tilde{x}$ and $\tilde{y}$, respectively, and the individual utility function $u(x)$ is increasing and concave.

This theorem shows that the generalized Bonferroni curves also provide a welfare ranking of distributions. One can judge between any two distributions without specifying the utility function $u(x)$ form, except that it is increasing and concave.

---

[4] See Hadar and Russell (1969), Hanoch and Levy (1969), and Rothschild and Stiglitz (1970)

4.9 Some Implications of the Theorems

The four theorems presented in Sections 4.5 to 4.7 report the four kinds of dominance:

1. The Lorenz curve
2. The Bonferroni curve
3. Generalized Lorenz curve
4. Generalized Bonferroni curve.

Dominance 1 and 2 imply that one distribution is unambiguously more equally (or unequally) distributed than the other. On the other hand, dominance 3 and 4 indicate that one distribution always has higher social welfare. The mean welfare of individuals measures the average standard of living of the society. The average standard of living and inequality in distribution are the two distinct aspects of social welfare linked by an exact relationship. In this regard, Kaplow (2005) has raised an important question: If social welfare is the relevant metric to guide policy, why measure inequality? If there is a trade-off between the average standard of living and inequality, the inequality ordering will not be the same as the welfare ordering. For normative purposes, as Kaplow has argued, "direct measures of social welfare are superior in addressing the relevant policy questions." Following this reasoning, the generalized Lorenz and Bonferroni curves are more relevant orderings than those of the Lorenz and Bonferroni curves.

But, the question arises as to whether one should then wholly dispose of the measurement of inequality. The answer may be yes and no. The phenomenon of inequality has attracted much attention among development economists and international donor agencies. The widening disparity between the top 1% and the bottom 99% has recently become a contentious issue in the United States. Stiglitz (2012) has argued that "inequality comes at the expense of less stable and less efficient economic systems." The main message of several books published recently has been that high inequality is undesirable in society and requires appropriate policy actions (Atkinson 2015, Bourguignon 2015, Piketty 2014). High inequality also reduces the effectiveness of economic growth in increasing the average standard of living and reducing poverty. This literature suggests that the focus on inequality is unavoidable. However, Kaplow (2005) also points out that the growth process impacts the average standard of living and inequality, which are the two distinct aspects of social welfare. Thus, social welfare is a relevant measure of resource allocation. Therefore, the focus on social welfare is essential, but inequality should also play a vital role in policy debates about resource allocation.

The following implications are drawn from the theorems:

1. If the two distributions have the same Lorenz (Bonferroni) curves, the distributions with a higher mean will be welfare superior.

2. When the Lorenz (Bonferroni) curves intersect, one cannot unambiguously conclude that one distribution is more equal or unequal than the other. But, it may still be possible to infer that one distribution is welfare superior to the other. For example, consider the two hypothetical distributions:

$$\tilde{x}: \quad (2,3,5,6)$$

$$\tilde{y}: \quad (1,4,4,5)$$

Both the Lorenz and Bonferroni curves intersect: but the generalized Loren and Bonferroni curves for distribution $\tilde{x}$ dominant over the distribution $\tilde{y}$.

Thus, Theorems 4.1 and 4.2 imply that one cannot unambiguously conclude if any distribution is more equal or unequal than the other. However, it is possible to conclude unequivocally that the distribution $\tilde{x}$ is welfare superior to the distribution $\tilde{y}$.

3. Even if one distribution is more unequal than the other, it is still possible to conclude that the more unequal distribution is welfare superior. Consider the two distributions:

$$\tilde{x}: \quad (3,3,5,13)$$

$$\tilde{y}: \quad (2,4,4,4)$$

The Lorenz and Bonferroni curves for distribution $\tilde{x}$ are lower than that of the distribution $\tilde{y}$, but the generalized Lorenz and Bonferroni curves are higher. Thus, the distribution $\tilde{x}$ is more unequal than the distribution $\tilde{y}$ but still is welfare superior.

The four theorems 4.1 to 4.4 presented are based on the restrictive assumptions that the social welfare function is utilitarian; every individual has the same utility function, increasing and concaving. These restrictions are relaxed in the subsequent sections.

4.10 Abba Lerner's Probabilistic Social Welfare Functions

Since individuals have different tastes, the assumption of the same utility function for each person cannot be defended. This assumption is now relaxed. Suppose there are n individuals in society who have n different utility functions, $u_1(x), u_2(x), \ldots \ldots \ldots,$ $u_n(x)$. Each $u_i(x)$ is increasing and concave. Insufficient information is available as to which individual has which utility function. Lerner (1944) made the Bayesian assumption that every possibility is equally likely. Hence, the expected utility of an individual with income x is given by

$$\bar{u}(x) = \frac{1}{n}\sum_{i=1}^{n} u_i(x)$$

Every individual has the same expected utility, which is increasing and concave. Lerner's probabilistic social welfare function for the distributions $\tilde{x}$ and $\tilde{y}$ is defined as

$$E[\bar{u}(\tilde{x})] = \int_0^\infty \bar{u}(x)f(x)\,dx,$$

and

$$E[\bar{u}(\tilde{y})] = \int_0^\infty \bar{u}(y)g(y)\,dy,$$

respectively. It can be easily demonstrated that $\bar{u}(x)$ is increasing and concave. All the requirements of Lemma 4.1 due to Hardy, Littlewood, and Polya (1929) are satisfied. Thus, the proof of the four theorems follows.

The four theorems 4.1–4.4 do not need to assume that every individual has the same utility function. Still, it is necessary to assume that each has an equal probability of having any utility function.

4.11 A Further Generalization of the Theorems

To arrive at a stronger version of the theorems, a class of social welfare functions must be considered that are not necessarily utilitarian. Suppose there are n persons in the society, then a general social welfare function developed by Bergson (1938) and subsequently refined by Samuelson (1947) is defined as

$$W(\tilde{x}) = W(x_1, x_2, \ldots\ldots\ldots, x_n)$$

where $\tilde{x} = (x_1, x_2, \ldots\ldots\ldots, x_n)$ is the vector of individual welfare of n persons.
Theorem 4.5 can now be stated.

Theorem 4.5 *The following statements are equivalent:*

(a) $\mu_x L_x(p) \geq \mu_y L_y(p)$ *for all p in the interval* $0 \leq p \leq 1$
(b) $W(\tilde{x}) \geq W(\tilde{y})$

where $W(\tilde{x})$ is a non-decreasing, symmetric, and quasi-concave social welfare function.

The symmetry of the social welfare function requires that the social welfare function remains unchanged if two individuals interchange their welfare. This requirement is reasonable because it excludes the possibility of discrimination among individuals.

Proof: If $\tilde{x}$ and $\tilde{y}$ are two ordered distributions,

$$x_1 \leq x_2, \ldots \ldots \ldots, \leq x_n \text{ and } y_1 \leq y_2 \ldots \ldots \ldots y_n$$

The generalized Lorenz dominance stated in (a) implies that

$$\sum_{k-1}^{i} x_k \geq \sum_{k=1}^{i} y_k \qquad (4.11.1)$$

for all $i = 1, 2, \ldots \ldots \ldots, n$.

The following lemma, which is due to Rothschild and Stiglitz (1973), will be employed to prove Theorem 4.5.

Lemma 4.2 *If the distribution $\tilde{y}$ is obtained from the distribution $\tilde{x}$ by a sequence of regressive transfers, then*

$$W(\tilde{x}) \geq W(\tilde{y})$$

where $W(\tilde{x})$ is non-decreasing, symmetric, and quasi-concave.

The proof of Theorem 4.5 consists of demonstrating $(a) \rightarrow (b) \rightarrow (a)$. First, it will be shown that if (a) is true, then the distribution $\tilde{y}$ can be obtained by a sequence of regressive transfers from the distribution $\tilde{x}$. Condition (a) is equivalent to (4.11.1). Let k be the first integer so that $x_k > y_k$; this yields a new distribution $X(k)$ as follows. Transfer an amount $(x_k - y_k)$ from individual k to $(k+1)$, which lowers the welfare of the kth individual to y_k and raises the welfare of the $(k+1)$th individual by the same amount. The distribution $x(k)$ is then given by:

$$x_i(k) = y_i, \quad \text{for } i \leq k$$

$$x_{k+1}(k) = x_{k+1} + (x_k - y_k)$$

$$x_i(k) = x_i \quad \text{for } i > (k+1)$$

It is evident that the distribution $x(k)$ satisfies condition (4.10.1) and, therefore, is generalized Lorenz dominant to the distribution $\tilde{y}$ and that $x(k)$ agrees with $\tilde{y}$ in k places (one more than $\tilde{x}$). Applying the same procedure to $x(k)$ yields a new distribution $x(k+j)$, which is again the generalized Lorenz dominant to $\tilde{y}$ in $(k+j)$ places. When $j=(n-k)$, the distribution $\tilde{y}$ is obtained. Thus, $\tilde{y}$ can be obtained from $\tilde{x}$ by a sequence of less than n regressive transfers. Then Lemma 4.2 implies that $W(\tilde{x}) \geq W(\tilde{y})$, which proves $(a) \rightarrow (b)$.

The proof of the theorem will be complete if it is shown that $(b) \rightarrow (a)$ for any symmetric and quasi-concave social welfare function. Consider the social welfare function

$$W^i(\tilde{x}) = \sum_{k=1}^{i} x_k,$$

which is symmetric and quasi-concave. Thus

$$W^i(\tilde{x}) \geq w^i(\tilde{y})$$

implies that

$$\sum_{k=1}^{i} x_k \geq \sum_{k=1}^{i} y_k,$$

which is the condition of the generalized Lorenz dominance, as stated in (4.11.1). This completes the proof of Theorem 4.5.

Theorem 4.5 is a generalization of Theorem 4.3. It proves that the generalized Lorenz curve dominance leads to higher social welfare for a general class of Bergson–Samuelson social welfare functions, which are not necessarily utilitarian. This general class of functions has minimal non-decreasing, symmetric, and quasi-concave individual welfare requirements. It follows from this theorem that Theorems 4.1–4.3 are also valid for this general class of social welfare functions. Thus, the four kinds of dominance discussed in Section 4.8 lead to higher social welfare for this general class of social welfare functions.

4.12 Stochastic Dominance

The idea of stochastic dominance is commonly used in the problems of decision-making under uncertainty. It is concerned with choosing between two distributions: how would decision-makers choose between them when their preferences are unknown? Their criterion for making such decisions is to maximize an expected utility with minimal knowledge of their utility function.

Although the idea of stochastic dominance emerged from lotteries, several applications in microeconomics have been developed; for instance, the theory of labor supply under uncertainty, auction theory, optimal portfolio selection, and oligopoly theory.

Atkinson (1970) first pointed out how stochastic dominance could be applied to rank income distributions to maximize social welfare. He arrived at his remarkable theorem by exploiting the second-order dominance in decision-making theory under uncertainty.

4.12.1 First-Order Stochastic Dominance

Suppose $F_1(x)$ and $F_2(x)$ are the two cumulative distribution functions; the distribution $F_1(x)$ first-order stochastic dominates the distribution $F_2(x)$ if

(a) $F_1(x) \leq F_2(x)$ for all x.

It can be demonstrated that if (a) holds, the condition

(b) $\int_0^\infty u(x) f_1(x) \, dx \geq \int_0^\infty u(x) f_2(x) \, dx$

will always hold provided $u'(x) \geq 0$. Thus, the two conditions (a) and (b) are equivalents for any increasing utility function.

Suppose $u(x)$ is the utility function of a decision-maker. In that case, the first-order dominance implies that the decision-maker always prefers the distribution $F_1(x)$ to the distribution $F_2(x)$, regardless of what $u(x)$ is, as long as it is non-decreasing.

The utility theory also requires the utility function to be concave because the consumers are risk-averse. If the concavity requirement is imposed on the utility function, the dominance can be weakened, which leads to second-order dominance.

4.12.2 Second-Order Stochastic Dominance

The distribution $F_1(x)$ second-order stochastic dominates the distribution $F_2(x)$ if

(c) $\int_0^x F_1(t) \, dt \leq \int_0^x F_2(t) \, dt$ for all x

The second-order dominance is a weaker requirement than first-order dominance because first-order dominance implies second-order dominance, not vice versa. Nevertheless, it can be demonstrated that the second-order dominance in (c) is equivalent to the generalized Lorenz curve dominance in Theorem 4.3 in condition (a).

The stochastic dominance literature was focused only on utilitarian social welfare, under which everyone has the same utility function, which is non-decreasing and concave. This chapter has demonstrated that the generalized Lorenz curve dominance provides social welfare ranking of individual welfare distributions for several alternative classes of social welfare functions.

4.13 An Illustration Using Lao PDR Data

Lao PDR is located in the East-Asia region, growing rapidly in the 1990s. Like the governments of its neighbors, the government of Lao PDR gave high priority to economic growth. The government believed that promoting economic growth would enhance the welfare of the people. It accomplished this objective by emphasizing macroeconomic policies such as maintaining stable low inflation and promoting domestic and foreign investments. How did these policies impact inequality and social welfare? This section uses the four dominance conditions to answer this question. It utilizes the Lao Expenditure and Consumption Surveys conducted in 1992–93 and 1997–98.

Real GDP per capita in Lao PDR grew at an annual rate of 4.6% between 1992–93 and 1997–98. This impressive growth accompanied an increase in inequality. Figure 4.1 shows that the Lorenz curve shifted downwards at all points. Therefore, it is concluded that the inequality between 1992–93 and 1997–98 has increased unambiguously. The Bonferroni dominance curves presented in Figure 4.2 show a sharper increase in inequality in the period.

Figures 4.3 and 4.4 show that both the generalized Lorenz and Bonferroni curves have shifted upwards at all points. These curves conclude that social welfare measured by a general class of social welfare functions has increased unambiguously.

It was possible to arrive at conclusive results because the dominance conditions for Lao PDR between the two periods were met. But there is no guarantee that the curves will not cross in other situations. Kakwani (1984c), in an international comparison of 72 countries, concluded that the Lorenz curves crossed about 70% of all pairwise comparisons, meaning that it was possible to say in 30% of cases which of the two countries had higher or lower income inequality. The generalized Lorenz curves crossed in 20%

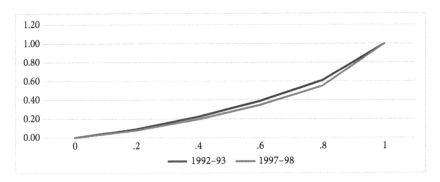

Fig. 4.1 Lorenz curve dominance

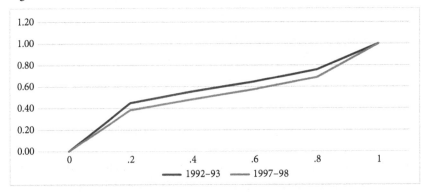

Fig. 4.2 Bonferroni curve dominance

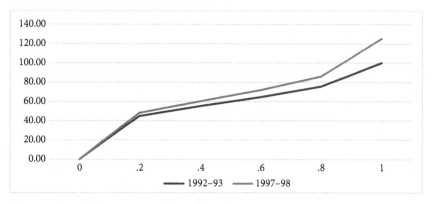

Fig. 4.3 Generalized Lorenz curve dominance

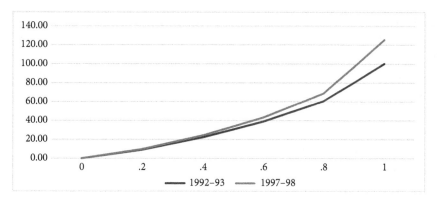

Fig. 4.4 Generalized Bonferroni curve dominance

of cases, meaning that in 80% of cases, it was possible to conclude which of the two countries had higher or lower social welfare. Thus, the overall conclusion emerging from this empirical study was that the generalized Lorenz curves are less likely to cross than the well-known Lorenz curves.

4.14 Concluding Remarks

In 1905, M. O. Lorenz proposed a simple diagram extensively used as a convenient graphical device to represent income distribution. It visibly depicts inequality, and it seemingly has no welfare foundation. For 65 years, empirical studies used the Lorenz curve as a visual graphic device. But all this changed when in 1970, Atkinson published a pioneering paper that provided a linkage between the Lorenz curve and social welfare functions. This chapter has discussed four theorems that carefully explain the general requirements of the link between the Lorenz curve and social welfare functions.

The four theorems have identified the four kinds of dominance:

1. The Lorenz curve
2. The Bonferroni curve

3. Generalized Lorenz curve
4. Generalized Bonferroni curve.

Dominance 1 and 2 imply that one distribution is unambiguously more equally (or unequally) distributed than the other. And dominance 3 and 4 inform when one distribution is welfare superior to another.

The mean welfare of individuals measures the average standard of living of the society. The average standard of living and inequality in distribution are the two distinct aspects of social welfare linked by an exact relationship. The empirical illustration presented in the chapter showed that equality ordering could be different from welfare ordering. That raises a crucial question of which ordering of the two should determine the relevant policies. Although this chapter has attempted to answer this question, it requires normative judgments, making it challenging to reach a consensus.

There are two distinct issues in measuring social welfare. First is determining individuals' economic welfare, informing which individual in society is better off or worse off. The second is aggregating individuals' welfare for the whole society. The welfare literature has primarily focused on the second issue. Evaluation of government policies cannot be accomplished unless the economic welfare of all individuals in society is known. A brief discussion of this issue in the chapter shows that determining individuals' economic welfare is highly complex. Thus, there is a need for extensive research on this issue.

5

Measurement of Income Inequality

5.1 Introduction

Whereas the Lorenz preference provides only a partial ordering of distributions, measures of income inequality have been devised to offer a complete ranking of income distributions. Of all these measures, the Gini index is the most widely used. Besides the Gini index, the empirical literature has frequently utilized the coefficient of variation, the relative mean deviation, and the standard deviation of logarithms of income. And in 1967, Theil proposed two new inequality measures derived from entropy in information theory. Economists have recognized that alternative inequality measures do not provide the same ranking of distributions.

Yntema (1933) was the first to demonstrate such conflicts in ranking. He conducted an empirical study of ten wealth and seven income distributions, and he concluded that there was little overall uniformity in the ranking of these distributions. In his study of three countries, Puerto Rico, Argentina, and Mexico, Weisskoff (1970) observed that the Gini index ranked Puerto Rico as the most equal, while the standard deviation of logarithms of income showed Mexico the most equal. When the coefficient of variation was used to measure inequality, Mexico's income distribution became more equal. In his highly influential paper, Atkinson (1970) argued that the differences in the ranking were so contradictory that no clear picture emerges of the relative degree of inequality in advanced and developing countries.

Because of conflicting results displayed by conventional inequality measures, choice among alternative inequality measures became critical in the inequality literature. Champernowne (1974) conducted a detailed simulation study to judge the relative merits of various inequality measures. He concluded that there could be no single "best" measure. The choice of a measure should depend on the particular aspect of inequality in which one is interested. Some measures are more suited to reflect specific characteristics of distribution than others.

How should one know which inequality measures are most desirable? Kakwani (1980a) proposed a set of inequality axioms desirable to assess income inequality. Since the publication of his book, some new desirable axioms have been presented in the literature.

This chapter provides the most comprehensive set of axioms. These axioms have ethical implications that can become the basis for evaluating alternative inequality measures. The chapter also offers many lemmas, providing practical methods

Economic Inequality and Poverty. Nanak Kakwani and Hyun Son, Oxford University Press.
© Nanak Kakwani and Hyun Son (2022). DOI: 10.1093/oso/9780198852841.003.0005

of assessing inequality. This approach is called an axiomatic approach to assessing inequality measures.

In his classic article, Dalton (1920) pioneered an attack on conventional inequality measures from a welfare standpoint, and, about 50 years later, Aigner and Heins (1967), Atkinson (1970), Bentzel (1970), and others pursued the attack. Their criticisms focus on the fact that these measures are statistical devices that measure the relative dispersion of a frequency distribution without reference to the normative notion of social welfare. Arguing that any inequality measure must incorporate society's preferences, Dalton proposed a measure based on the idea of proportional welfare loss resulting from income inequality. Atkinson criticized Dalton's measure because it is variant with respect to linear transformations of the utility function and proposed an alternative class of inequality measures by introducing "the equally distributed equivalent level of income." Also, Allingham (1972), Sen (1973), and Muellbauer (1975b) proposed alternative measures based on more general assumptions about social welfare than the measures considered by Dalton and Atkinson.

Because the inequality measures proposed by Dalton, Atkinson, and others rely heavily on the value judgments represented by the social welfare functions chosen, they are normative measures. The conventional measures, in contrast, are called positive measures because they do not make explicit use of any concept of social welfare. Sen (1973) argued that the distinction between the two kinds of measures is not a firm one and that every positive measure embodies an implicit social welfare function.

A series of papers by Atkinson (1970), Newbery (1970), Sheshinski (1972b), Dasgupta, Sen, and Starrett (1973), and Rothschild and Stiglitz (1973) discussed the social welfare properties of the Gini index. Atkinson's paper has been the most influential in linking inequality with social welfare functions, and it has provided a neat social welfare framework for measuring inequality. But this framework is restricted to utilitarian social welfare functions, and this chapter extends this framework to general social welfare functions.

The social welfare function implicit in the Gini index is interdependent, capturing the idea of relative deprivation as defined by Runciman (1966). This chapter also proposes a general social welfare function class that captures society's relative deprivation. These functions lead to a family of inequality measures that give different weights to transfers at different income levels in the distribution. The Gini index is a particular member of this family of inequality measures.

Theil (1967) proposed two inequality measures based on the notation of entropy in information theory. Entropy is a measure of disorder in thermodynamics. These measures gained popularity because of their decomposability property. The decomposability was an exciting innovation among applied economists because it could explain how much inequality is contributed by various social groups so that policymakers could target specific groups to reduce overall inequality. The decomposability of inequality measures ensures that subgroup consistency is always satisfied. The Gini index has been subjected to undue criticism because it does not possess a decomposability property.

Although decomposable inequality measures are extensively used in empirical work, no one has questioned their validity other than the Nobel Laureate economist Amartya Sen (2006). This chapter's social welfare framework does not lead to any decomposable inequality measures. If inequality measures have any policy relevance, they must be evaluated based on value judgments made explicit by a social welfare function. That raises a debatable question of whether one should accept decomposable inequality measures, satisfying the subgroup consistency, or the measures derived from some acceptable social welfare functions. This chapter addresses this issue using the notion of relative deprivation.

The measurement of polarization has recently attracted much attention in economics. In the 1970s and 1980s, academic research focused on inequality and poverty measures. In the 1990s, the focus shifted to measurements of polarization. The research on this issue began because of concerns among some economists about the shrinking of the middle class. Foster and Wolfson (1992) wrote an outstanding paper that links polarization and the shrinking size of the middle class. This paper gave rise to the concept of bi-polarization. Alternatively, Esteban and Ray (1994) developed a general framework of polarization for any number of social groups, which is called multi-group polarization. This chapter provides detailed discussions of both bi-polarization and multi-group polarization, deriving new measures of polarization.

5.2 Axioms of Inequality Comparison

If $x_1 \leq x_2 \leq \ldots\ldots\ldots \leq x_n$ is an ordered income distribution among n individuals denoted by a nonnegative vector $\widetilde{x} = (x_1, x_2, \ldots\ldots\ldots, x_n)$, a general inequality measure $\theta(\widetilde{x})$ is defined as a unique function of $x_1, x_2, \ldots\ldots\ldots, x_n$ satisfying specific desirable properties. These properties are presented below in the form of axioms, noting that these axioms may not be desirable in all situations. The purpose here is not to justify them but to provide a framework for comparing various inequality measures.

Axiom 5.1 (Symmetry)

$$\theta(\widetilde{x}) = \theta(\pi(\widetilde{x}))$$

where π is any permutation of $\widetilde{x}$.

The symmetry axiom requires that an inequality measure be invariant to any interpersonal permutation of incomes. That means that if any two individuals interchange their incomes, an inequality measure must remain unchanged. The axiom implies that it does not matter who is earning income. Thus, the axiom ensures impartiality between individuals; the inequality measure depends on the frequency distribution of income and not how particular individuals are ranked within the distribution.

Axiom 5.2 (Population Principle) *Inequality remains unaffected if a proportionate number of persons are added to all income levels.*

This axiom corresponds to Dalton's principle of proportionate additions of persons. It implies that if any two populations with the same income distribution $\tilde{x}$ are merged, inequality remains the same. The axiom means that the population size does not matter when inequality is compared in any two-income distribution. Thus, if an inequality measure has the same value, say for China with a population of 1.4 billion and a much smaller country, say for Bhutan with a population of less than a million, then both nations are regarded as equally equal or unequal. That is an essential property because it allows comparing inequality across countries with different populations.

Axiom 5.3 (Relative Principle) *If $\tilde{y} = \lambda\tilde{x}$ $(\lambda > 0)$, $\theta(\tilde{x}) = \theta(\tilde{y})$*
This axiom implies that the inequality measure should remain unaffected if the same proportion alters each income; therefore, the inequality measure is independent of the measurement scale.

Because the Lorenz curve is scale-independent, the inequality measures associated with it will always satisfy this axiom. The measures satisfying this axiom are called relative measures of inequality.

Axiom 5.4 *If the new distribution $\tilde{y}$ is obtained from $\tilde{x}$ by adding to incomes of all individuals a constant amount d, it follows that*
If $d > 0, \theta(\tilde{y}) < \theta(\tilde{x})$
If $d > 0, \theta(\tilde{y}) > \theta(\tilde{x})$
This axiom corresponds to Dalton's (1920) principle of equal additions to income, implying that equal additions to all income diminish inequality, and equal subtractions increase it. For example, the following lemma is related to this axiom.

Lemma 5.1 *If the new distribution $\tilde{y}$ is obtained from $\tilde{x}$ by adding to incomes of all individuals a constant amount d, the distribution $\tilde{y}$ is Lorenz superior (inferior) to the distribution $\tilde{x}$ if d is greater (less) than zero.*

For proof of this lemma, see Kakwani (1980a, 66).

Axiom 5.5 (Absolute Principle) *If $\tilde{y} = \tilde{x} + a$, where a is a constant, $\theta(\tilde{x}) = \theta(\tilde{y})$.*

According to Kolm (1976a, 1976b), this axiom implies that the inequality measure should remain unaffected if each income is increased or decreased by the same absolute amount. Inequality measures satisfying Axiom 5.5 are called absolute or leftist measures of inequality. As discussed in Chapter 3, inequality may be measured in relative or absolute terms. Suppose inequality measures remain unchanged when each person's income increases or decreases by the same proportion. Such measures are called relative or rightist measures of inequality. The Lorenz curve measures relative inequality because the curve remains unchanged when the incomes of all persons are increased or decreased by the same proportion.

An absolute inequality measure will always fulfill the property stated in Lemma 5.2.

Lemma 5.2 *If the income of everyone in society is increased (decreased) by the same proportion, the absolute measure of inequality will always increase (decrease).*

This lemma is intuitively apparent because an equal-proportional increase (decrease) in all incomes implies that the richer will enjoy a higher (lower) incremental improvement in their living standards than their poorer counterparts. This lemma has exciting implications for economic growth. If the benefits of economic growth are distributed in equal proportions, the relative inequality does not change, but the absolute inequality will increase.

Axiom 5.6 relates to the effect of transfers on inequality.

Axiom 5.6 (Transfer Principle) *If a transfer of income $d < h/2$ takes place from a person with income x to a person with lower income $x - h$, inequality is reduced.*

This axiom corresponds to Dalton's (1920) principle of transfers. The restriction $d < h/2$ ensures that transfer is not so large as to reverse the relative positions of two individuals. Any number of such transfers between any two consecutive individuals subject to this restriction will not alter the ranking of individuals. This process of transfer is called rank preserving transfer. If the transfer is equal to half of the difference between the two incomes, there will be a maximum reduction in inequality, that is, when $d = h/2$. This axiom must hold for both relative and absolute measures of inequality.

Axiom 5.7 (Transfer-Sensitivity Principle) *If a transfer of income $d < h/2$ takes place from a person with income x to a person with lower income $x - h$, then the magnitude of inequality reduction must be larger for smaller x.*

Axiom 5.7 is a stronger version of Axiom 5.6. It requires that inequality reduction be larger to income transfers at the lower- rather than upper-income distribution. Kakwani (1980a) proposed Axiom 5.7 in connection with the derivation of the class of poverty measures. Foster, Greer, and Thorbecke (1984) used this axiom to derive their famous FGT poverty measures class. Shorrocks and Foster (1987) revisited Axiom 5.6 in their discussion of inequality measures.

Axiom 5.6 requires that the inequality measures be sensitive to transfers at all income levels. The following lemma gives the condition that the transfer axiom is always satisfied.

Lemma 5.3 *Any inequality measure which is the arithmetic mean of a convex function satisfies Dalton's transfer principle.*

Proof: Let $\theta(\tilde{x}) = \theta(x_1, x_2, \ldots\ldots\ldots, x_n)$ be the inequality measure. If the partial derivative $\partial\theta/\partial x_i$ exists for all x_i, the change in inequality due to an infinitesimal transfer of income δ from individual i to individual j can be expressed as

$$d\theta = \partial\theta/\partial x_i\,(-\delta) + \partial\theta/\partial x_j\,(+\delta) \tag{5.2.1}$$

which, according to Axiom 5.6, should be negative for all $\delta > 0$, $x_i > x_j$ and $\delta < (x_i - x_j)/2$. Thus, Axiom 5.6 will be satisfied if

$$\frac{\partial\theta}{\partial x_i} - \frac{\partial\theta}{\partial x_j} > 0 \tag{5.2.2}$$

for all $x_i > x_j$. If the inequality measure is written as

$$\theta(\tilde{x}) = \sum_{i=1}^{n} V(x_i), \tag{5.2.3}$$

then condition (5.2.2) becomes

$$V'(x_i) - V'(x_j) \geq 0 \tag{5.2.4}$$

for all $x_i > x_j$, where $V'(x_i)$ is the first derivative of $V(x_i)$ with respect to x_i. Condition (5.2.4) will always be satisfied if the function $V(x_i)$ is convex for all i. This result proves Lemma 5.3.

Lemma 5.4 *If income is a continuous random variable, income inequality is expressed as*

$$\theta = \int_0^{\infty} V(x)f(x)\,dx \tag{5.2.5}$$

where f(x) is the density function of x and V(x) is a convex function of x. The relative sensitivity of inequality to an infinitesimal transfer of income from a person with income x to a person with income (x – h) depends on the magnitude of T(x) given by[1]

---

[1] Atkinson (1970) also used expression (5.2.5) to examine the relative sensitivity of an inequality measure, but he did not provide a proof.

$$T(x) = V'(x) - V'(x - h) \qquad (5.2.6)$$

Proof. Note that equation (5.2.5) is equivalent to (5.2.3). Substituting $x_i = x$ and $x_j = x - h$ into (5.2.1) yields

$$d\theta = -dx\left[V'(x) - V'(x - h)\right] \qquad (5.2.7)$$

showing that the magnitude of change in inequality depends on $T(x)$. That proves Lemma 5.4.

Lemma 5.4 facilitates an examination of the relative sensitivity of the inequality measures at different income levels. For example, if $T(x)$ is constant for all x, it implies that the transfer effect would be independent of the income levels at which it is made. Further, suppose $T(x)$ is a monotonically decreasing function of x. In that case, the inequality measure gives a higher weight to transfers at the lower end of the income distribution, and weight decreases monotonically as income increases. This condition would satisfy the transfer-sensitivity axiom 5.7. If $T(x)$ is a monotonically increasing function of x, the weight attached to transfers increases with income. The inequality measures satisfying this condition are not regarded as desirable. It can also occur that $T(x)$ increases first and then decreases. This condition implies that the inequality measure attaches more weight to transfers in the middle of the income distribution.

Axiom 5.8 (Subgroup Consistency) *Given that subgroup population shares and subgroup population means remain unchanged, the overall inequality must rise when inequality rises in one group and does not fall in the other groups.*

Axiom 5.8 concerns the relationship between subgroup inequality and overall inequality. In an unpublished note, Frank Cowell (1980) was the first to draw attention to this axiom. He demonstrated that some well-known inequality measures violate this axiom using hypothetical examples. Suppose the population is divided into k mutually exclusive subgroups, then if (a) the mean income in every group is constant, (b) inequality in every group goes up, and (c) the overall inequality falls, these three requirements contradict each other and, therefore, are not subgroup consistent. Cowell identified three inequality measures: the logarithm of variance, the relative mean deviation, and the Gini index, simultaneously satisfying these three requirements. He called them three bad measures of inequality. Shorrocks (1988) introduced subgroup consistency for inequality measures, and Foster and Shorrocks (1991) added subgroup consistency for poverty measures. However, the basic concept of subgroup consistency is similar for both inequality and poverty measures.

Inequality comparison axioms presented in this section provide a framework to evaluate alternative inequality measures proposed in the literature. The subsequent sections in this chapter utilize this framework to assess the properties of various inequality measures.

5.3 Gini Index and Relative Mean Difference

The Gini index is the most widely used to analyze income and wealth distribution of all the inequality measures. If $x_1 \leq x_2 \leq \ldots\ldots\ldots \leq x_n$ is an ordered income distribution among n individuals, the inequality measure proposed by Gini (1912) is defined as

$$G = \frac{\Delta}{2\mu} \tag{5.3.1}$$

where μ is the mean income of all n individuals, and

$$\Delta = \frac{1}{n(n-1)} \sum_{i=1}^{n} \sum_{j=1}^{n} |x_i - x_j| \tag{5.3.2}$$

where Δ is the arithmetic average of the $n(n-1)$ differences taken as absolute values. The minimum value of Δ is zero when every individual in society receives the same income. The maximum value of Δ is equal to 2μ, which would be obtained when one unit receives all the income. Thus, the Gini index lies between 0 (perfect equality) and 1 (perfect inequality).

Subsequently, Gini (1913–14) proposed an inequality measure equal to one minus twice the area under the Lorenz curve. He demonstrated that this new measure corresponds to his earlier measure, defined in terms of relative difference. This correspondence between the two measures does not seem obvious, proving Lemma 5.4.

Lemma 5.4 *As defined in (5.3.1), the Gini index equals one minus twice the area under the Lorenz curve.*

Proof. The Gini index defined in (5.3.1) in the continuous case is written as

$$\begin{aligned}
G &= \frac{1}{2\mu} \int_0^\infty \int_0^\infty |x - y| f(x) f(y)\, dx dy \\
&= \frac{1}{2\mu} \int_0^\infty \left[\int_0^x (x-y) f(y)\, dy + \int_x^\infty (y-x) f(y)\, dy \right] f(x)\, dx \\
&= \frac{1}{\mu} \int_0^\infty [xF(x) - \mu F_1(x)] f(x)\, dx \tag{5.3.3}
\end{aligned}$$

where $F(x)$ is the probability distribution function and $F_1(x)$ is the first-moment distribution function defined in (3.2.2). Integrating the first term in (5.3.3) by parts yields

$$\frac{1}{\mu}\int_0^\infty xF(x)f(x)\,dx = 1 - \int_0^\infty F_1(x)f(x)\,dx, \tag{5.3.4}$$

which on substituting into (5.3.3) yields

$$G = 1 - 2\int_0^\infty F_1(x)f(x)\,dx \tag{5.3.5}$$

The right-hand side of (5.3.5) is one minus twice the area under the Lorenz curve. That completes the proof of Lemma 5.4. This lemma demonstrates that the Gini index is closely related to the Lorenz curve, visually explaining inequality. The popularity of the Gini index stems mainly from its linkage with the Lorenz curve. The Gini index always satisfies Dalton's principle of transfers, as stated in Axiom 5.6, easily demonstrated because of its link with the Lorenz curve. The sensitivity of the Gini index at different income levels is revealed in Lemma 5.5.

Lemma 5.5 *The Gini index attaches the maximum weight to income transfers at the mode of the income distribution.*

Proof. Substituting (5.3.4) into (5.3.5) yields

$$G = \frac{2}{\mu}\int_0^\infty x\left[F(x) - \frac{1}{2}\right]f(x)\,dx, \tag{5.3.6}$$

which yields

$$V(x) = \frac{2}{\mu}x\left[F(x) - \frac{1}{2}\right]. \tag{5.3.7}$$

If the income x of the individual changes to $x + dx$, then because of rank preserving transfers from rich to poor, $F(x)$ will not be affected. The derivative of $V(x)$ with respect to x is, therefore, equal to

$$V'(x) = \frac{2}{\mu}\left[F(x) - \frac{1}{2}\right],$$

which yields

$$T(x) = \frac{2}{\mu}\left[F(x) - F(x - h)\right]. \tag{5.3.8}$$

The sensitivity of the Gini index to transfers depends on $T(x)$. This equation shows that $T(x)$ increases with x and decreases for a typical unimodal distribution.[2] That

---

[2] This is a standard result of unimodel distributions in statistics.

means that $T(x)$ will have a maximum value at the distribution mode. Thus, the Gini index is most sensitive to transfers at the mode of the income distribution, where there is a maximum concentration of individuals. This feature of the Gini index might be attractive to policymakers who want to show the impact of changes in inequality on a maximum number of individuals. Suppose the concern of policymakers is to provide more importance to those who belong at the lower end of the income distribution. In that case, the measure of inequality must satisfy the transfer-sensitive Axiom 5.7. The Gini index violates this axiom.

Policymakers widely understand the Gini index as an aggregate measure of inequality, and it lies between 0 and 1. Its value is 0 when everyone receives equal income, and it takes value 1 when the wealthiest person in society enjoys all the income, and the rest receive no income. The Gini index formula in equation (5.3.1) is somewhat complicated and cannot be explained intuitively to policymakers.

Shorrocks (2005), in an unpublished note, attempted to provide a simple explanation of the Gini index. For example, the Gini index of the United States in 2000 was 0.40, which implies that if $1 is divided between the poor and the rich, the poor get only 10 cents, and the rich get 90 cents. A general formula of shares of incomes of the poor and the rich are $0.5 - G$ and $0.5 + G$, respectively. This formula shows that the larger the Gini index, the higher the income gap between the poor and the rich. The Gini index for Finland, for example, has a value of 0.27, which on using this general formula, translates the division of $1 into 23 cents for the poor and 77 cents for the rich. This simple explanation of the Gini index may be appealing to a layman who is not familiar with the Gini formula.

5.4 Information Measures of Inequality

Theil (1967) proposed two inequality measures based on the notation of entropy in information theory. Entropy is a measure of disorder in thermodynamics. Let x_i be the income of the ith individual in society, where i varies from 1 to n. If μ is the mean income of society, then $y_i = x_i/n\mu$ is the fraction of total income earned by the ith individual. The entropy of income shares is given by

$$H(y) = \sum_{i=1}^{n} y_i \ln\left(\frac{1}{y_i}\right), \qquad (5.4.1)$$

which is the weighted average of the logarithm of the reciprocal of each income share, weights being the respective income shares. The upper limit of $H(y)$ is $\ln(n)$ when all individuals earn equal income, the minimum of $H(y)$ is zero, which is reached when one individual receives all the income. Thus, the inequality measure proposed by Theil in 1967 is

$$I_1 = \ln(n) - H(y) = \sum_{i=1}^{n} y_i \ln(ny_i), \tag{5.4.2}$$

which varies from 0 to $\ln(n)$. The upper limit of this measure approaches infinity as n approaches infinity. Thus, unlike the Gini index, this measure does not lie between 0 and 1.

It may be convenient to express this measure as

$$I_1 = I(y:f) = \sum_{i=1}^{n} y_i \ln\left(\frac{y_i}{f_i}\right) \tag{5.4.3}$$

where f_i is the population share that, in this case, is equal to $1/n$ for all i. One can interpret $I(y:f)$ as the expected information of the indirect message that transforms prior probabilities $f_1, f_2, \ldots \ldots, f_n$ into posterior probabilities $y_1, y_2, \ldots \ldots \ldots, y_n$.

An alternative measure proposed by Theil is

$$I_0 = I(f,p) = \sum_{i=1}^{n} f_i \ln\left(\frac{f_i}{y_i}\right) \tag{5.4.4}$$

which is interpreted as the expected information of the indirect message that transforms prior probabilities $y_1, y_2, \ldots \ldots \ldots, y_n$ into posterior probabilities $f_1, f_2, \ldots \ldots \ldots, f_n$.

When x is a continuous random variable, these measures are written as

$$I_1 = I(y:f) = \frac{1}{\mu} \int_0^{\infty} [x\ln(x)f(x)\,dx - \mu\ln(\mu)]/\mu \tag{5.4.5}$$

$$I_0 = I(f:y) = \int_0^{\infty} [\ln(\mu) - \ln(x)]f(x)\,dx \tag{5.4.6}$$

These measures are relative measures of inequality, satisfying Axiom 5.3, implying that inequality does not change when the same proportion alters each income. Therefore, the inequality measures are independent of the measurement scale.

Theil derived his inequality measures using the notion of entropy in information theory. Entropy is a measure of disorder in thermodynamics, equated to equality in income distribution. That means that inequality is a measure of order in society. Accordingly, the decrease in inequality leads to more disorder in society. Creating disorder cannot be a social objective. The purpose of measuring inequality is to enhance equality of income distribution in society, which leads to higher social welfare, as discussed in Chapter 4. The notion of entropy implies that improving social welfare increases social disorder. These two social objectives contradict each other. Despite this limitation, Theil's inequality measures gained popularity because of their decomposability and subgroup consistency properties. The following section explains the basic idea of decomposability and subgroup consistency.

5.5 Discomposability and Subgroup Consistency

Suppose a population is partitioned into k mutually exclusive subgroups according to specific socio-economic characteristics of individuals (such as age, gender, race, schooling, or occupation). Inequality measures are decomposable if they enable the expression of inequality in the population as the sum of within-group inequality and between-group inequality. The within-group inequality is the weighted sum of the inequality within all the subgroups. On the other hand, the between-group is the inequality that would exist if the incomes of each group were replaced by the group mean.

Decomposition was an exciting innovation among applied economists because it could explain how much inequality is contributed by various subgroups so that policymakers could target specific subgroups to reduce overall inequality. Decomposable inequality measures always satisfy the subgroup consistency stated in Axiom 5.8.

Shorrocks (1980) proved a remarkable theorem that only one class of inequality measures could permit the decomposability of inequality measures. The single-parameter generalized-entropy family gives this class of inequality measures:

$$I_c = \frac{1}{c(c-1)} \int_0^\infty \left[\left(\frac{x}{\mu}\right)^c - 1 \right], c \neq 0, 1. \tag{5.5.1}$$

The square of the coefficient of variation is a member of this class when $c = 2$. The parameter c can be interpreted as a measure of inequality aversion. As c decreases, the measure becomes more sensitive to transfers at the lower end of the distribution. When $c = 2$, the measure attaches the same weight to transfers at all income levels.[3] The higher the value of c, the greater weight given to transfers at the top end of the distribution.

It is easy to establish that as c approaches 0, I_c approaches Theil's inequality measure I_0 defined in (5.4.6). Similarly, as c approaches 1, I_c approaches Theil's inequality measure I_1 defined in (5.4.5). Thus, Theil's two entropy inequality measures are particular cases of Shorrocks (1980) class of inequality measures.

The decomposition equations for the generalized-entropy measures for the k mutually exclusive groups are

$$I_c = \frac{1}{\mu^c} \sum_{j=1}^k a_j \mu_j^c I_c^j + \frac{1}{c(c-1)\mu^c} \sum_{j=1}^k a_j \left[\mu_j^c - \mu^c \right], \quad c \neq 0, 1 \tag{5.5.2}$$

$$I_0 = \sum_{j=1}^k a_j I_0^j + \sum_{j=1}^k a_j [ln(\mu) - ln(\mu_j)] \tag{5.5.3}$$

$$I_1 = \frac{1}{\mu} \sum_{j=1}^k a_j \mu_j I_1^j + \frac{1}{\mu} \sum_{j=1}^k a_j \mu_j [ln(\mu_j) - ln(\mu)]. \tag{5.5.4}$$

[3] Cowell and Kuga (1981) introduced a further axiom of sensitivity which leads to Theil's measure I_1.

a_j and μ_j are the population share and mean of the jth subgroup, respectively. I_c^j is the inequality within the jth subgroup. The first term in these equations is within-group inequality, which is the group inequalities' weighted sum. The second term is between-group inequality, which measures the contribution of inequality due to differences in the group means. The weights are given to different subgroups depending on the chosen inequality measures. Should weights be a criterion in the choice of inequality measure? The literature on decomposition has not addressed this issue. If the population shares are considered as the natural weights, then inequality measure I_0 will be an appropriate choice in the entire class of decomposable inequality measures.

The decomposability of inequality measures ensures that Axiom 5.8 of subgroup consistency is always satisfied, implying an increase in inequality in one subgroup; keeping subgroup means and population shares constant does not decrease inequality.

5.6 Normative Measures of Inequality

Sen (1973), in the preface of his seminal book on economic inequality, stated that the idea of inequality is both simple and very complex. It is simple if defined as the dispersion of income distribution. Many measures of dispersion exist in the literature, which can result in contradictory conclusions about the relative merits of income distributions.[4] In his pioneering paper published in 1970, Atkinson argued that the pure statistical measures of inequality could be misleading in obtaining a complete ranking of distributions without fully specifying the form of the social welfare function. He made a strong case in rejecting such conventional measures by arguing that the social welfare functions implicit in these measures in many cases may not accord with social values.

Dalton (1920) was the first to argue that an inequality measure must be derived directly from a social welfare function. He proposed a measure of inequality defined as the proportional loss of social welfare resulting from income inequality. He assumed a utilitarian social welfare function, defined as the sum of individual utility functions of their respective incomes. Each individual has the same utility function, increasing in income and concave. If the income x is a continuous random variable with density function $f(x)$, the utilitarian social welfare function would be given by

$$W = \int_0^\infty u(x) f(x)\, dx \qquad (5.6.1)$$

[4] Among the most popular measures of dispersion used are the Gini index, coefficient of variation, relative mean deviation, standard deviation of logarithm of income, and Theil's entropy measures. These are viewed as positive measures of inequality because they are not derived from social welfare functions. The social welfare implications of the Gini index have been studied extensively. Sen (1973) derived the Gini index from a social welfare function that captures the relative deprivation suffered by people. A detailed discussion of the Gini index and its generalizations is provided in Sections 5.7 and 5.8.

where $u(x)$ is the individual utility function such that $u'(x) > 0$ and $u''(x) < 0$. Under these conditions, if everyone enjoys the same income equal to μ, then social welfare will be maximum equal to $u(\mu)$, the proportional welfare loss resulting from inequality would be

$$D = \int_0^\infty \frac{u(\mu) - u(x)}{u(\mu)} f(x)\, dx \qquad (5.6.2)$$

which is essentially the inequality measure proposed by Dalton.

Dalton's measure has a limitation that it does not satisfy the basic relative principle of inequality stated in Axiom 5.3, implying that the inequality measure should remain unaffected if each income is altered by the same proportion. The inequality measure should be independent of the mean income or scale of measurement. Further restrictions on the utility function must be considered to satisfy this axiom. If $u(x)$ is a homogenous function, satisfying $u(\lambda x) = \lambda^\alpha u(x)$, D measures the relative inequality. All utility functions do not measure relative inequality. For example, $u(x) = \ln(x)$ is a legitimate utility function because it satisfies the requirement $u'(x) > 0$ and $u''(x) < 0$, but it is not homogenous, so it does not provide a relative measure of inequality.

Particular utility functions may now be considered. First, consider the utility function given by $u(x) = 1 - [\ln(\mu) - \ln(x)]$, which satisfies the restrictions: $u'(x) = \frac{1}{x} > 0$ and $u''(x) = -\frac{1}{x^2} < 0$ when $x>0$. This utility function is legitimate for all positive incomes. Substituting this utility function in (5.6.2) yields Theil's inequality measure I_0 defined in (5.4.6). Thus, Theil's inequality measure I_0 has an implicit social welfare function; this is not considered in the literature, which has maintained that Theil's inequality measures derived from entropy are just the statistical devices devoid of any social welfare interpretation.

Secondly, consider the utility function $u(x) = 1-[\mu \ln(\mu) - x \ln(x)]$, which satisfies the restrictions $u'(x) = 1 + \ln(x) > 0$ and $u''(x) = \frac{1}{x} > 0$ for $x > 0$. Substituting this utility function in (5.6.2) yields Theil's inequality measure I_1 defined in (5.4.5). The social welfare function implicit in this measure is not legitimate because the utility function is convex. Dalton's measure in (5.6.2) is defined only for a concave utility function. Thus, Theil's measure I_1 does not have an implicit social function that is meaningful.

Thirdly, consider the utility function $u(x) = 1 - \frac{1}{c(c-1)}\left[\frac{x^c}{\mu^c} - 1\right]$ for $c \neq 0$ and 1, which satisfies the restriction $u'(x) = \frac{1}{(1-c)}\frac{x^{(c-1)}}{\mu^c} > 0$ if $x > 0$ and $c < 1$; and $u''(x) = -\frac{x^{(c-2)}}{\mu^c} < 0$ if $x > 0$. Substituting this utility function in (5.6.2) yields Shorrocks' (1980) family of generalized-entropy inequality measures defined in (5.5.1). The utility function for this family is increasing and concave if $x > 0$ and $c < 1$. These properties of utility function imply that Shorrocks' generalized-entropy measures have an implicit legitimate social welfare if $x>0$ and $c<1$. This result is also new in the literature.

Summing up, Sen (1997) asserts that Theil's measures are arbitrary and have no intuitive sense. The analysis presented in this section demonstrates that Theil's inequality measure I_0 can be derived from a well-defined social welfare function and, therefore, cannot be considered an arbitrary measure. However, Theil's inequality measure I_1 is arbitrary because it does not have a legitimate implicit social welfare function. This section has also derived a new result that Shorrocks' generalized-entropy measures also have an implicit well-defined social welfare function when c<1.

5.7 Atkinson's Inequality Measures

Atkinson (1970) criticized Dalton's measure on the ground that "it is not invariant with respect to a positive linear transformation of the utility function." Sen (1973) did not consider this criticism seriously since the ordering of Dalton's measure would not be affected by making the measure invariant to a positive linear transformation. Of course, one could agree with Sen if inequality is measured on an ordinal scale. But from a policy point of view, it will be appropriate to measure inequality on a cardinal scale, which is a positive linear transformation of utilities.

Atkinson (1970) proposes a class of inequality measures invariant with respect to any positive linear transformation of individual utilities. He derived measures using the concept of an "equally distributed equivalent level of income." Suppose x^* is the equally distributed equivalent level of income, which is the level received by every individual. In that case, it will result in the same level of social welfare as the present distribution. Like Dalton, Atkinson (1970) also assumed that the social welfare function is utilitarian and every individual has the same utility function [given in (5.5.1)], then x^* is given by

$$u\left(x^*\right) = \int_0^\infty u\left(x\right)f\left(x\right)dx. \tag{5.7.1}$$

It is easy to verify that if we substitute $u(x) = a + bu(x)$, where $b > 0$ into (5.7.1), x^* remains invariant. Thus, Atkinson's measure of social welfare is x^*, invariant to any positive linear transformation of the utility function. The most attractive feature of this measure is that it is a money metric measure of social welfare of actual income distribution and can be measured in income units such as dollars or euros. The mean income μ is a money metric measure of social welfare when everyone receives the same income. The utility function is always assumed to be increasing in income and is concave, which implies that $x^* \leq \mu$, which means that there will be a loss in social welfare when income is unequally distributed. Thus, the inequality measure proposed by Atkinson is given by

$$A = 1 - \frac{x^*}{\mu}. \tag{5.7.2}$$

So the Atkinson measure is interpreted as the proportional loss of social welfare, measured in money metric.

This measure has a considerable intuitive appeal. For example, $A = 0.3$ means that if all individuals had the same income, only 70 % of the current incomes would be required to achieve the same level of welfare.

If Atkinson's measure is scale-independent (i.e., the relative or rightist measure of inequality under Kolm's [1976a, 1976b] terminology), further restrictions on the form of utility function must be considered. It can be easily shown that Atkinson's inequality measure will be scale-independent if and only if the utility function is homothetic. A class of homothetic utility functions is given by

$$u(x) = a + \frac{bx^{(1-\epsilon)}}{(1-\epsilon)}, \qquad\qquad if\ \epsilon \neq 1$$

$$= a + b\ln(x), \qquad\qquad if\ \epsilon = 1 \qquad\qquad (5.7.3)$$

where ϵ is a measure of the degree of inequality aversion or the relative sensitivity of income transfers at different income levels. As ϵ rises, more weight is attached to transfers at the lower end of the income distribution, and less weight is given to transfers at the top. If $\epsilon = 0$, it reflects an inequality-neutral attitude of society, meaning that society has no concern for inequality. Under this scenario, society would mainly be focused on maximizing economic growth without any concern for reducing inequality.

Substituting (5.7.3) into (5.7.1) gives Atkinson's social welfare function:

$$x^* = \left[\int_0^\infty x^{1-\epsilon}f(x)\,dx^{\frac{1}{1-\epsilon}}\right] \qquad\qquad if\ \epsilon \neq 1$$

$$= exp\left[\int_0^\infty \ln(x)f(x)\,dx\right] \qquad if\ \epsilon = 1 \qquad\qquad (5.7.4)$$

x^* is the per capita social welfare measured in monetary units (e.g., dollars).

Both Dalton's and Atkinson's inequality measures rely heavily on value judgments represented by the individual utility function and are normative. Both define inequality measures as the proportional loss of social welfare but in two alternative ways. While Dalton's social welfare is measured in utility units, Atkinson's is measured in monetary units.

Meade (1976), calling the welfare loss "distributional waste," argued that a measure of distribution waste is not really in any fundamental sense a measure of inequality. It is a measure of inefficiency or the loss of utility from a less than optimal distribution of available income. Thus, he rejects these so-called normative measures of inequality. It is difficult to dismiss these measures because the distribution waste occurs because of inequality in income distribution. Hence, they can legitimately measure the degree of inequality. A social welfare function is a function of mean income and inequality, and the efficiency concerns how much total income is available to society. There will be a loss of available income (or social welfare) from a less than optimal production process. In contrast, social welfare loss can occur because everyone does not enjoy the same income, which directly links with inequality in income distribution. Thus, there are no merits in Meade's objection to Atkinson's or Dalton's approaches to measuring inequality.

Atkinson's paper has been the most influential in linking inequality with social welfare functions. His formulation of money metric social welfare is more appealing than Dalton's approach, expressing social welfare in utility units. It has provided a neat social welfare framework for measuring inequality. But this framework is restricted to utilitarian social welfare functions, and the following section extends this framework to general social welfare functions.

5.8 General Social Welfare Framework for Income Inequality

Suppose there are n persons in the society whose incomes are given by a vector

$$\tilde{x} = (x_1, x_2, \ldots \ldots \ldots, x_n).$$

Given this, a general social welfare function can be expressed as a function

$$W = W(\tilde{x}).$$

The following conditions are essential in deriving inequality measures from social welfare.

Condition 1: *Relative homogeneity If $\tilde{y} = \lambda \tilde{x}$ ($\lambda > 0$), $W(\tilde{y}) = \lambda W(\tilde{x})$*

This condition requires that if all incomes are increased (decreased) by the same proportion, social welfare also increases (decreases) by the same ratio. This condition is essential in the derivation of relative measures of inequality.

Condition 2: *Absolute homogeneity If $\tilde{y} = a + \tilde{x}$, $W(\tilde{y}) = a + W(\tilde{x})$*
This condition requires that if all incomes are increased (decreased) by the same absolute amount, social welfare also increases (decreases) by the same absolute amount. This condition is essential in the derivation of absolute measures of inequality.

Condition 3: *Quasi-concavity Minimum $[W(\tilde{x}), W(\tilde{y})] \leq W[\lambda \tilde{x} + (1 - \lambda)\tilde{y}]$*
for any λ in the range $0 < \lambda < 1$ and for any two vectors $\tilde{x}$ and $\tilde{y}$ in the domain of W.

This minimum condition ensures that Dalton's transfer principle stated in Axiom 5.6 is satisfied.

Condition 4: *Social welfare function is invariant to any positive linear transformation if*

$$W(x^* e) = W(\tilde{x}) \qquad (5.8.1)$$

where $e'(1, 1, 1, \ldots \ldots \ldots, 1)$ *and* x^* *is the equally distributed equivalent level of income, which would result in the same level of social welfare as the present distribution if every individual received the same income.*

Suppose solution of x^* from (5.8.1), denoted by x_W^*, is the generalized Atkinson's social welfare. Condition 4 ensures that social welfare is measured in monetary income units such as dollars or euros. Social welfare in income units makes intuitive sense because it measures inequality in the income space. Moreover, social welfare is an abstract concept that policymakers will understand readily if expressed in monetary units.

Using Atkinson's framework, the relative measure of inequality for a general social welfare function in $W(\tilde{x})$ is given by

$$I_W = 1 - \frac{x_W^*}{\mu}, \qquad (5.8.2)$$

which is a relative measure of inequality because of relative homogeneity, Condition 1. This measure is interpreted as the proportionate loss of social welfare due to inequality and can only be derived if the social welfare function is relatively homogeneous of degree one (Condition 1).

The absolute measure of inequality is defined

$$A_W = \mu - x_W^*. \qquad (5.8.3)$$

Kolm (1976a, 1976b) calls this a leftist measure of inequality, which does not show any change in inequality when each income is increased or decreased by the same amount. It is interpreted as the absolute loss of social welfare due to inequality. This measure can also be interpreted as the cost of inequality measured in monetary units. It is essential to emphasize that this measure can only be derived if the social welfare function is absolute homogeneous of degree one (Condition 2). Unfortunately, Atkinson's social welfare function discussed in Section 5.5 is not absolute homogeneous of degree one, so one cannot derive absolute inequality measures.

5.9 Social Welfare Implications of the Gini Index

The welfare implications of the Gini index have been debated extensively by Atkinson (1970), Newbery (1970), Rothschild and Stiglitz (1970, 1973), Kats (1972), Sheshinski

(1972a, 1972b), Dasgupta, Sen, and Starrett (1973), Sen (1973, 1974a, 1974b), and Chipman (1974). A brief review of this debate follows.

Consider income distributions with the same mean income. Lemma 5.4 showed that the Gini index is equal to one minus twice the area under the Lorenz curve. Together with Lemma 4.5, this lemma implies that the Gini index will rank these distributions in the same order as any quasi-concave and symmetric distributions, provided the Lorenz curves of distributions do not intersect. Atkinson (1970) criticized the Gini index by arguing that if the Lorenz curves intersect, one can always find a social welfare function that will rank the distributions in reverse order to the one given by the Gini index. Newbery (1970) strengthened Atkinson's criticism of the Gini index by proving that no additive social welfare function exists that ranks income distributions in the same order as the Gini index. Thus, a strong case is made for rejecting the Gini index as a measure of inequality. Nevertheless, the Gini index is the most widely used measure of inequality. A pertinent question arises: should the empirical studies that have used the Gini index to analyze inequality be abandoned because the Gini social welfare function is not additive separable?

Additive separability may not necessarily be desirable to impose on a social welfare function. The assumption implies that the welfare of individuals crucially depends only on their own consumption and is not impacted by the consumption of others in society; in other words, individuals do not suffer relative deprivation.[5] Sheshinski (1972a) maintained that an additive separable welfare function has no particular significance. He provided an example of a nonadditive welfare function that ranks the distributions similar to the Gini index. The social welfare function implicit in the Gini index is interdependent, whereby the welfare of an individual depends not only on her consumption but also on the consumption of others. If the concept of inequality is based on relative deprivation, as Runciman (1966) defines it, the assumption of additive separability will be too restrictive.

Dasgupta, Sen, and Starrett (1973) and Rothschild and Stiglitz (1973) demonstrated no strictly quasi-concave social welfare function would give the same rankings as the Gini index.[6] Sen (1973, 34) did not, however, consider this criticism of any consequence: "The implied group welfare function may not be strictly quasi-concave, but it is quasi-concave alright, but any transfer from the poor to the rich or vice versa is strictly recorded in the appropriate direction, which is the most crucial requirement of an inequality measure."

So far, only the restrictions on the welfare functions implied by the Gini index have been considered. Chipman (1974) pursued an alternative approach by restricting the kinds of income distributions likely to be observed. He asked if any plausible form of the income distribution would give the ranking of distributions provided by the Gini index in the same order as any social welfare function would offer them. Atkinson (1973), Dasgupta, Sen, and Starrett (1973), and Rothschild and Stiglitz (1973) have

---

[5] See Runciman (1966) on relative deprivation.
[6] Note that the nonadditive social welfare function considered by Sheshinski is quasi-concave but not strictly quasi-concave.

answered this question. Any class of income distributions that give nonintersecting Lorenz curves would permit the ranking of distributions by the Gini index. Chapter 3 demonstrated that any two-parameter distribution functions belong to the noninter-secting Lorenz curves family. Lemma 5.4 showed that the Gini equals one minus twice the area under the Lorenz curve. Together with Lemma 4.5, this lemma implies that the Gini index will rank these distributions in the same order as any quasi-concave and symmetric distributions, provided the Lorenz curves of distributions do not intersect. The two popular income distributions—the Pareto and the lognormal—depend on two parameters and, hence, they belong to nonintersecting Lorenz curves. This leads to the following lemma.

Lemma 5.6 *For both the Pareto and lognormal distributions,*

$$\frac{\partial W}{\partial G} < 0 \tag{5.9.1}$$

where W is the general social welfare function, non-decreasing, symmetric, and quasi-concave.

Chipman (1974) proved inequality (5.9.1) for only the Pareto distribution. His proof is based on the assumption that the social welfare function is utilitarian, and every individual has the same utility function. Lemma 5.6 is more general and follows immediately from Lemmas 5.4 and 4.5.

The criticisms of the Gini index are, for the most part, based on the fact that the welfare function in the Gini index is not additive separable and strictly quasi-concave. As argued, these requirements on the welfare function do not necessarily make the Gini index undesirable as a measure of inequality. Sen (1974a) derived a welfare function satisfying a set of four axioms that would rank distributions the same way as the Gini index. Among the four axioms, the most controversial axiom requires that the difference in the weight given to two incomes depends solely on the number of persons between the two incomes (not on income difference). Therefore, this axiom rules out the cardinality of individual welfares, except that revealed by the number of intermediate positions between any two incomes. However, Sen's (1974a) main aim was to capture the relative deprivation aspects of inequality by making the weight given to an individual's welfare depend on their rank among all individuals. The lower a person is on the welfare scale, the higher the sense of deprivation relative to others in society.[7]

Thus, according to Sen's rank order axiom, the sense of deprivation suffered by an individual with income x depends on the proportion of people who have income

---

[7] The rank-order weighting has been widely used in voting theory (see, for instance, Borda 1781, Black (1958), Fine and Fine (1974), Fishburn (1975), Gardenfors (1973) and Hansson (1973).

higher than x, which led Sen to propose the following social welfare function:

$$W_S = 2 \int_0^\infty x\left[1 - F(x)\right]f(x)\,dx \qquad (5.9.2)$$

where $F(x)$ is the distribution function measuring the proportion of persons who have income higher than x, such that

$$2 \int_0^\infty \left[1 - F(x)\right]f(x)\,dx = 1,$$

which informs that Sen's social welfare function is the weighted average of incomes of all persons in society. The weight given to income x decreases monotonically with x, making the social welfare egalitarian because any transfer of income from the rich to the poor increases welfare, provided the transfer does not change the welfare ranking of individuals.

Using equation (5.3.6), it is easy to show the relationship between the Gini index and Sen's social welfare function W_S as

$$W_S = \mu\left(1 - G\right). \qquad (5.9.3)$$

This result demonstrates that Sen's social welfare function must rank the distributions with the same mean income in precisely the same order as the negative of the Gini index. An interesting result follows from this.

If η_μ and η_G denote as the elasticity of the social welfare function W_S with respect to μ and G, respectively, (5.9.3) yields $\eta_\mu = 1$ and $\eta_G = -\frac{G}{1-G}$, which implies $|\eta_G| < |\eta_\mu|$. Hence, the following Corollary follows:

Corollary 5.1 *Sen's social welfare function is more (less) sensitive to the mean income than income inequality if the initial Gini index is less (greater) than one-half.*

This corollary has an exciting policy implication that if a country's social objective is to maximize its social welfare, it should follow growth-enhancing policies when its initial inequality is less than 0.5, but if its initial inequality is higher than 0.5, then the redistribution policies that reduce inequality would be more appropriate.

The social welfare function implicit in the Gini index is interdependent, implying that the individual welfare is dependent on the welfare (income) of others; it makes little sense to measure inequality in a subgroup of the population without considering the incomes of individuals elsewhere. The assumption that the satisfaction an individual derives is independent of the consumption of others is restrictive because people compare themselves with others and feel deprived when they see others having higher consumption. The essential requirement of this assumption is that the social welfare function must be additive separable, which is the minimum requirement for any decomposable measure. Sen (1973) has argued that even if the additive-separable framework is accepted, the social welfare function implied by decomposable measures is not the one that is overflowing with intuitive sense. This criticism does not always hold, as shown in Section 5.6. Yes, Sen is right about Theil's inequality measure I_1, which does not imply a legitimate social welfare function. This section demonstrated that Theil's inequality measure I_0 and Shorrocks' (1980) class of general-entropy measures, which are decomposable, have social welfare interpretation.

5.10   Is the Gini Index Decomposable and Subgroup Consistent?

As noted, the Gini index came under severe criticism because it is not decomposable and subgroup consistent. This section shows that this criticism is unjustified. The social welfare implicit in the Gini index is interdependent, so decomposability needs to be defined differently. A new decomposition is developed in this section.

Section 3.10 presented the relative deprivation curve. The idea of this curve is that individuals with income x compare their income with all other individuals in society. They select other individuals one by one at random and make all possible comparisons. They suffer from deprivation upon discovering that their income is lower. However, they do not feel deprived when they find their income is higher. Sen (1973) proposed measuring the degree of deprivation they suffer depending on how much lower their income is. He also suggested measuring the deprivation suffered by the whole society by the average of all such deprivations in all possible pairwise comparisons—Sen's idea of quantifying deprivation generated enormous attention, which led to many conceptual and measurement issues. Among the crucial contributions made were Yitzhaki (1979, 1982), Hey and Lambert (1980), and many others.[8] Kakwani (1984d) developed the idea of the relative deprivation curve, which is invariant to proportional changes in all incomes.

The relative deprivation suffered by an individual with income x is given by

$$d(x) = \left[1 - F_1(x)\right] - \frac{x}{\mu}\left[1 - F(x)\right] \qquad (5.10.1)$$

where μ is the mean of the population; $F(x)$ is the probability distribution function; and $F_1(x)$, the first-moment probability distribution function, is interpreted as the proportion of income enjoyed by individuals with income less than or equal to x.

---

[8] For many other extensions of the measures of deprivation, see Berrebi and Silber (1985), Chakravarty and Chakraborty (1984), Paul (1991), Chakravarty and Mukherjee (1999), Donaldson and Weymark (1980) and Chakravarty and Chattopadhyay (1995). Chakravarty (2009) has provided an excellent survey on this topic so it is not necessary to review here the entire literature. This literature, however, does not add much to the main thrust of the decomposability methodology developed here.

Integrating both sides of (5.10.1) shows the Gini index is the average deprivation suffered by society:[9]

$$G = \int_0^\infty d(x)f(x)\,dx.$$

(5.10.2)

This idea is now extended to derive the decomposability of the Gini index not discussed in the literature.

Suppose a population is divided into k mutually exclusive groups and a_j is the population share of the jth group, then $\sum_{j=1}^k a_j = 1$ must hold. Further, if $f_j(x)$ is the density function of the distribution in the jth group, then the average deprivation suffered by the population in the jth group will be given by

$$D_j = \int_0^\infty d(x)f_j(x)\,dx.$$

(5.10.3)

The average deprivation suffered by any group can be compared with the average deprivation suffered by society, measured by the Gini index. This comparison informs which social group suffers more (or less) deprivation than society. Note that D_j is not the Gini index of the jth group because, in its calculations, individuals in the jth group make comparisons with all the groups including their group, whereas the Gini index is the average deprivation when the individuals make comparisons with only the jth group, which implies $D_j > G_j$, where G_j being the Gini index of the jth group.

It is easy to show from the properties' density functions that

$$f(x) = \sum_{j=1}^k a_j f_j(x),$$

(5.10.4)

which on substituting (5.10.2) yields

$$G = \sum_{j=1}^k a_j D_j,$$

(5.10.5)

which demonstrates that the relative deprivation suffered by the whole society is the weighted average of the deprivation suffered by each social group, with weights equal to population shares of the social groups. This decomposition explains how much each group's contribution to total inequality is. Given $D_j > G_j$, it follows from (5.10.5):

$$G > \sum_{j=1}^k a_j G_j.$$

(5.10.6)

That formally demonstrates that the Gini index violates the subgroup consistency (Axiom 5.8), which states that given subgroup population shares and subgroup population means remain unchanged, the overall inequality must rise when inequality rises

---

[9] Yitzhaki proposed this result in 1979, which was followed by Hey and Lambert (1980) who provided an alternative motivation of this result. Berrebi and Silber (1985) showed that many of the commonly used inequality indices can also provide measures of relative deprivation.

in one group and does not fall in the rest of the groups. This requirement may not hold because of inequality in (5.10.6). Based on equation (5.10.5), the following new axiom of subgroup relative deprivation consistency is proposed:

Axiom 5.9 (*Subgroup relative deprivation consistency*) *Given that subgroup popu-lation shares and subgroup population means remain unchanged, the overall in-equality must not decrease when relative deprivation in any one group increases but does not change in the other groups.*

The Gini index will always satisfy this axiom.

This section also presents a dynamic version of the Gini decomposition proposed by Kakwani and Son (2016). From (5.10.5), the change in the Gini index can be explained by two factors: (i) change in population shares and (ii) change in average deprivation. Defining G_t as the Gini index in period t, a_{jt} as the population share of the jth group in period t, and D_{jt} average deprivation suffered by the jth group in period t, then we obtain the following dynamic decomposition as

$$\Delta G_t = \sum_{j=1}^{k} \left(\frac{D_{jt} + D_{j(t-1)}}{2} \right) \Delta a_{jt} + \sum_{j=1}^{k} \left(\frac{a_{jt} + a_{j(t-1)}}{2} \right) \Delta D_{jt}, \qquad (5.10.7)$$

which shows that two factors explain the change in the Gini index. The first factor is the changes in population shares, similar to Kuznets' (1955) idea of structural trans-formation. The second factor is the change in average deprivations of different social groups. This decomposition explains to what extent social groups' changes are taking place.[10]

The literature has pointed out that the Gini index's main limitation is that it can-not be decomposed as the sum of between-group and within-group inequalities. That would be true under the assumption that the individuals within each group do not compare their income with individuals in other groups. Since the Gini social welfare function is interdependent, it would be odd to assume that the individuals within a group do not compare their incomes with individuals in other groups. The average deprivations D_j is derived when all possible comparisons are made among all social groups in the population. That is a valid assumption given the Gini social welfare function is interdependent.

It will now be demonstrated that the Gini index can be decomposed as the sum of between-group relative deprivation (BGRD) and within-group relative deprivation (WGRD). The BGRD is the relative deprivation generated when all individual in-comes in each group are replaced with the average income of that group, implying that all persons within groups have the same income. The following results will be

---

[10] See Kakwani and Son (2016) for application of this decomposition to the contributions of social groups in explaining changes in inequality.

used to derive it.

$$F(x) = \sum_{j=1}^{k} a_j F_j(x) \tag{5.10.8}$$

$$F_1(x) = \frac{1}{\mu}\sum_{j=1}^{k} a_j \mu_j F_{1j}(x) \tag{5.10.9}$$

where μ_j is the mean income of the jth group; and $F_j(x)$ and $F_{1j}(x)$ are the probability distribution and the first-moment distribution functions in the jth group, respectively. Substituting (5.10.8) and (5.10.9) into (5.10.1) yields

$$d(x) = 1 - \frac{1}{\mu}\sum_{j=1}^{k} a_j \mu_j F_{1j}(x) - \frac{x}{\mu}\left[1 - \sum_{j=1}^{k} a_j F_j(x)\right] \tag{5.10.10}$$

The inequality within each group would be zero if $F_{1j}(x) = F_j(x)$ for all j, which leads to

$$\hat{d}(x) = 1 - \frac{1}{\mu}\sum_{j=1}^{k} a_j \mu_j F_j(x) - \frac{x}{\mu}\left[1 - \sum_{j=1}^{k} a_j F_j(x)\right], \tag{5.10.11}$$

which is the relative deprivation suffered by an individual with income x when inequality within each group is zero (i.e., the mean income of that group replaces income in each group). Thus, the BGRD is obtained as

$$BGRD = \int_0^{\infty} \hat{d}(x) f(x) \, dx, \tag{5.10.12}$$

which from (5.10.10) and (5.10.11) yields

$$d(x) - \hat{d}(x) = \frac{1}{\mu}\sum_{j=1}^{k} a_j \mu_j \left[F_j(x) - F_{1j}(x)\right]. \tag{5.10.13}$$

In this equation, $\left[F_j(x) - F_{1j}(x)\right]$ represents the deviation of the Lorenz curve from the egalitarian line within each group, measuring the inequality within each group. Further, substituting $\mu_j = \mu$ for all j in (5.10.13) yields

$$d(x) - \hat{d}(x) = \sum_{j=1}^{k} a_j \left[F_j(x) - F_{1j}(x) \right], \qquad (5.10.14)$$

which is the relative deprivation suffered by an individual with income x caused by inequality within each group under the counterfactual that all groups have the same mean income. The WGRD is defined as the relative deprivation suffered by society caused by relative deprivation within each group when all the groups have the same mean income. Thus, the WGRD is obtained as

$$WGRD = \int_{0}^{\infty} \left[d(x) - \hat{d}(x) \right] f(x) \, dx = \sum_{j=1}^{k} a_j \int_{0}^{\infty} \left[F_j(x) - F_{1j}(x) \right] f(x) \, dx.$$

$$(5.10.15)$$

Combining (5.10.2) with (5.10.12) and (5.10.16) leads to a new Gini decomposition:

$$G = BGRD + WGRD. \qquad (5.10.16)$$

This decomposition explains the relative deprivation suffered by society in terms of between-group and within-group components, but the decomposition can be easily extended to absolute deprivation. The absolute deprivation suffered by society is μG, and, hence, obtaining the absolute Gini decomposition by multiplying both sides of (5.10.16) by μ. Thus, the absolute deprivation for society will be the sum of the between-group absolute deprivation (BGAD) and the within-group absolute deprivation (WGAD), measured in money metric. The absolute BGAD and WGAD are interpreted as the cost to society because of between- and within-group deprivation among the social groups.

5.11 Generalized Gini Index

As noted in Section 5.10, the Gini social welfare function is interdependent, implying that the welfare of an individual depends on only her income and the incomes of others in society. This welfare function captures the relative deprivation aspects of inequality by making the weight given to an individual's welfare depend on her rank among all individuals. According to Sen's (1974a) rank order axiom, the sense of deprivation suffered by an individual with income x depends on the proportion of people with income higher than x, leading Sen to propose the Gini social welfare function.

This section discusses a general class of social welfare functions that capture the relative deprivation suffered by society. These functions lead to a family of inequality measures that give different weights to transfers at different income levels in the distribution. A general class of social welfare functions is provided by

$$W_v = \int_0^\infty xv\left(F(x)\right)f(x)\,dx \qquad\qquad (5.11.1)$$

where $f(x)$ is the density function and $F(x)$ is the distribution function, which measures the proportion of persons with income less than x. $v\left(F(x)\right)$ is the weight attached to the income level x such that $v'\left(F(x)\right) < 0$, implying that the weight must decrease monotonically with $F(x)$ such that higher weight is given to poorer persons than richer ones. The total weight adds to 1:

$$\int_0^\infty v\left(F(x)\right)f(x)\,dx = 1.$$

This social welfare function captures the idea of relative deprivation by assigning a weight to income x depending on the ranking of all individuals in society. The lower a person is on a welfare scale, the higher is the person's sense of deprivation with respect to others in society. This social welfare class will be called rank order social welfare functions. The most attractive feature of this class of social welfare functions is that it is both relatively and absolutely homogeneous of degree one, implying that both relative and absolute inequality measures can be derived.

Kakwani (1980b) proposed a generalization of the Gini index that makes it possible to give higher weights to the income of the poor.[11] His generalized Gini social welfare function is a particular member of W_v obtained when

$$v\left(F(x)\right) = (k+1)\left[1 - F(x)\right]^k,$$

which leads to the general social welfare function implicit in the generalized Gini index as

$$W_k = (k+1)\int_0^\infty x\left[1 - F(x)\right]^k f(x)\,dx = \mu\left(1 - G_k\right) \qquad (5.11.2)$$

where μ is the mean income and G_k is the generalized Gini index. The parameter k is similar to the inequality aversion parameter introduced by Atkinson (1970). When $k=0$, $W_k = \mu$, in which case the income of all individuals gets the same weight, reflecting an inequality-neutral attitude of society, meaning that it does not concern inequality at all and focuses solely on enhancing economic growth.

When $k = 1$, G_k equals the Gini index G, in which case the deprivation suffered by an individual with income x is two times the proportion of individuals with income higher than x. When $k=2$, the deprivation suffered by an individual with income x is three times the square of the proportion of individuals with income higher than x. Thus, as k increases, the deprivation suffered by individuals with lower incomes increases.

[11] Yitzhaki (1983) has provided many properties of Kakwani's generalization of the Gini index.

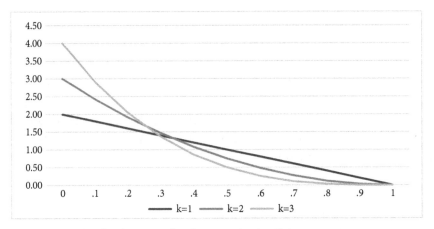

Fig. 5.1 Weights for the generalized Gini index in China, 1988–2013

Note: Data for Figure 5.1 comes from the weight function: weight(k) = (1+k)[1−F(x)]k
F(x) =0.0, 0.1, 0.2, 0.3, 0.4, 0.5, 0.6, 0.7, 0.8, 0.9, 1.0 is the x-axis, and weight (k) is the y-axis

In Figure 5.1, the x-axis is the cumulative proportion of the population. The diagram shows that as k increases, the generalized Gini index gives higher weight to the lower end of the income distribution. The higher value of k would be desirable if society desires greater concern for the weaker sections of society.

G_k is a family of relative inequality measures, implying that inequality does not change if everyone's income changes by the same proportion. Following Kolm (1976a, 1976b), the family of absolute measures of inequality is obtained as μG_k, implying that inequality remains unchanged when everyone's income changes by an absolute amount.

Substituting $v\left(F\left(x\right)\right) = -\ln\left(F\left(x\right)\right)$ in (5.13.1) yields the Bonferroni (1930) social welfare function as

$$W_B = -\int_0^\infty x \ln\left(F\left(x\right)\right)f\left(x\right)dx = \mu\left(1 - B\right) \qquad (5.11.3)$$

where B is the relative Bonferroni measure of inequality, thus, proving that the social welfare function implicit in the Bonferroni inequality B is a particular member of the general rank order social welfare functions (5.11.1). Like the Gini index, it also captures the relative deprivation aspect of inequality. It also lends to the absolute Bonferroni inequality measure equal to μB.

The Gini and Bonferroni social functions have all the desirable properties of a social welfare function, increasing individual welfare, quasi-concave, and decreasing monotonically as individual welfare increases. A pertinent question is which index of inequality should be used in practice. The Gini index is most widely used, while hardly any study uses the Bonferroni index. It is easy to see that the Gini social welfare function's weights decrease monotonically at a constant rate. On the other hand, weights in the Bonferroni social welfare function fall monotonically at an increasing rate. In other words, Bonferroni weights decline more steeply than the Gini weights.

Since the total weight for both functions adds up to unity, the Bonferroni social welfare function gives higher weight to the individuals at the lower end of the distribution than the Gini social welfare function. Based on this result, one can conclude that the Bonferroni social welfare function is more egalitarian (pro-poor) than the Gini social welfare function.

5.12 Trends in Inequality in China

It is well-known that China has achieved unprecedented economic growth rates during the last three decades. Economists have been concerned whether the Chinese economic growth has been accompanied by rising inequality. This section presents the trends in income inequality in China. How much is the income inequality in China? How rapidly has inequality been increasing? Are there signs of slowing trends in inequality? Analyzing inequality using urban-rural decomposition is exciting due to the increasing concerns about China's urban-rural divide. This section attempts to answer these questions utilizing five rounds of the Chinese Household Income Project surveys, covering 1988–2013. Per capita household income derived from the surveys has been adjusted for spatial prices across rural and urban areas and provinces. Furthermore, the incomes of all households have been adjusted to take account of inflation over time. Thus, the per capita household incomes are measured in the 2013 Beijing prices and are comparable across the country and over time.

China had been expanding its output at an unprecedented rate. The population ultimately consumes the output produced in an economy. In theory, individuals must get entitlement to consumption depending on how much they have contributed to the production. But, that may not be true. Several factors can impact people's entitlement. It is not essential to identify the factors determining people's entitlement. It suffices to say that a composite measure of people's entitlement is their income, which they can exchange for goods and services. It is the consumption of goods and services that offer people material welfare. Hence, the chapter uses real per capita income to measure the average standard of living. This section attempts to answer the question: Has the rapid economic growth in China contributed to the rising average standard of living? The changes in per capita income provide real increases or decreases in the average standard of living.

Table 5.1 shows that the average standard of living in China in 1988 was 2,680 yuan per person per year, which increased to 17,017 yuan in 2013. Furthermore, the trend growth rate shows that the average standard of living rose at an annual rate of 627 yuan per person, which is a highly significant rise. Thus, the unprecedented economic growth in China has indeed contributed to enormous prosperity in China.

Table 5.1 also presents the generalized Gini index estimates for three alternative values of inequality aversion parameter k. The larger the value of k, the higher the weight given to the poorer individuals. The empirical estimates use three values of k: 1, 2, and 3. When $k = 1$, inequality is measured by the Gini index. The empirical

Table 5.1 Trends in generalized Gini in China, 1988–2013

Year	1988	1995	2002	2007	2013	Trend growth
Per capita real income	2,680	4,295	5,478	11,056	17,017	627
Relative generalized Gini (percent)						
$k=1$	33.77	35.95	38.47	41.03	41.51	0.32
$k=2$	46.28	48.69	51.63	54.56	55.94	0.4
$k=3$	53.33	55.69	58.64	61.6	63.77	0.43
Bonferroni index	46.76	48.87	50.96	53.67	56.28	0.39
Absolute generalized Gini (yuan per person per year)						
$k=1$	905	1544	2107	4536	7065	270
$k=2$	1240	2091	2828	6033	9520	362
$k=3$	1429	2392	3212	6811	10,852	412
Bonferroni index	1253	2099	2791	5934	9578	364

Source: Authors' estimates.

estimates also include the Bonferroni inequality measure, which, as shown, is more egalitarian than the Gini index. The four relative measures of inequality presented in the table show that inequality in China rose monotonically over the 1988–2013 period. For instance, the trend growth rate indicates that the Gini index increased at an annual rate of 0.32%. An important conclusion emerging from the table is that the trend increase in inequality is even higher when the inequality measure gives higher weight to the poorer segment of the income distribution. Thus, the extremely poor in China have benefited even less from economic growth.

The absolute inequality measures indicate the loss of social welfare due to inequality, and they measure the social cost of inequality in money terms. According to the absolute Gini index, per capita loss of income was 905 yuan per annum in 1988, which increased to 7,065 yuan in 2013, increasing the trend at 270 yuan per person per year in 1988–2013. The trend increase is higher at 412 yuan when $k=3$. The Bonferroni index gives a higher social cost of inequality than the Gini index.

The empirical analysis presented in this section provides overwhelming evidence that inequality in China has been rising throughout the 25 years. There has also been an increasing concern in China that the gap between urban and rural areas has increased, contributing to increasing inequality. The rising trend growth in inequality is explained using the urban-rural decomposition developed in Section 5.10.

Table 5.2 presents empirical estimates of the decomposition of the Gini index between and within urban–rural areas. The trend growth in incomes shows that the average living standard in China, measured by the price-adjusted per capita income, had increased at the rate of 627 yuan per person per year in the 1988–2013 period, an increase in rural areas being only 365 yuan compared with 791 yuan in urban areas. Thus, the urban-rural gap had significantly widened in China, resulting in increased

Table 5.2 Urban–rural relative deprivation decomposition in China, 1988–2013

	1988	1995	2002	2007	2013	Trend growth
	Per capita mean income adjusted for prices					
Rural	2,242	3,479	4,027	6,814	10,701	365
Urban	4,478	6,275	7,987	16,078	22,347	791
Total	2,680	4,295	5,478	11,056	17,017	627
Gini index	33.77	35.95	38.47	41.03	41.51	0.32
	Population shares					
Rural	80.39	70.82	63.37	54.21	45.77	−1.42
Urban	19.61	29.18	36.63	45.79	54.23	1.42
	Average relative deprivation					
Rural	38.97	42.72	47.37	54.07	54.96	0.67
Urban	12.44	19.52	23.08	25.59	30.16	0.7
	Contribution to total inequality (percent)					
Rural	92.78	84.15	78.02	71.43	60.59	−1.31
Urban	7.22	15.84	21.98	28.57	39.41	1.31
BGRD and WGRD						
BGRD	13.15	13.45	16.78	20.8	16.99	0.17
WGRD	20.62	22.5	21.69	20.23	24.53	0.15

Source: Authors' estimates based on 1988, 1995, 2002, 2007, and 2013 CHIPs.

BGRD at an annual rate of 0.17% during 1988–2013 (Figure 5.1). On the other hand, the WGRD rose at a yearly rate of 0.15 percentage points. As a result, the Gini index in China grew at a yearly rate of 0.32 percentage points, which is the sum of growth rates in BGRD and WGRD. These observations conclude that growing inequality in China has been due to a rise in BGRD and WGRD, but BGRD is more pronounced.

Furthermore, the rural areas reduced relative deprivation at an annual rate of 1.31%, while the urban areas increased by the same rate. Thus, the increasing disparity between the rural and urban areas has been a significant factor in rising inequality in China. These observations suggest that the government policy in China should focus on reducing the between-group urban-rural deprivation, but the within-group urban-rural deprivations should also receive attention.

5.13 Polarization

The current political environment in the United States can readily explain the concept of polarization. Since the election of President Donald Trump, the political system in the United States has become highly polarized. The ideological gaps between the two major political parties, Republicans and Democrats, have widened so much that the Congress and the Senate have almost become unfunctional. The voters belonging to the two parties are almost equally divided, and they cluster around their parties and have entirely lost the sense of right and wrong within their parties. This party-line solidarity is the basic idea of polarization.

Human beings are pretty diverse. They differ concerning their socio-economic and demographic characteristics such as age, gender, education level, occupation, religion, and ethnicity. Given these differences, a society is classified into various social groups, which leads to polarization. As the US political system demonstrates, the high degree of polarization has severe consequences for the well-being of the people and even the survival of a functioning democracy. It is essential to reduce polarization, but the literature has not provided much help to formulate appropriate policies to reduce polarization. No policy framework could give any guidelines on the optimal strategies in developing such systems. The development of such structures requires monitoring the degree of polarization across society over time. The measurement of the degree of polarization is essential in developing a policy framework for polarization.

The measurement of polarization has recently attracted much attention in economics. In the 1970s and 1980s, academic research focused on measures of inequality and poverty. In the 1990s, the focus shifted to measurements of polarization. The research on this issue began because of concerns among some economists about the shrinking of the middle class. Foster and Wolfson (1992) wrote an outstanding paper that links polarization and the shrinking size of the middle class. This paper gave rise to the concept of bi-polarization. Esteban and Ray (1994) were the first to develop a general notion of polarization for any number of social groups. These two notions of polarizations are distinct, so both will be discussed separately.

5.13.1 Size of the Middle Class and Bi-Polarization

The phenomenon of the "disappearing middle class" has concerned many economists. The emerging consensus among them was that an increase in the size of the middle class increases economic activity, leading to a rise in per capita income. Easterly (2001) suggested that the rise of the middle-class share contributes to higher economic growth. There was also a belief that higher middle-class shares result in better health and education outcomes. Birdsall (2007a, 2007b) even defined inclusive growth as growth that builds the middle class. According to her, there is a linkage between a weak middle class and weak state institutions and unsustainable growth. Berkowitz and Jackson (2005) even suggested that a solid middle class is conducive to lower inequality. Many studies have indicated that a sizable middle class contributes to overall economic development, including Thurow (1984), Foster and Wolfson (1992), Easterly (2001), Birdsall (2007a, 2007b), and Pressman (2007). These studies, however, do not provide conclusive findings.

How should the middle class be measured? However, there is no agreement on how the middle class should be defined. Thurow (1984) first identified the middle class as those households whose income ranges from 75% to 125% of the median household income. Subsequently, Blackburn and Bloom (1985) increased the range from 60% to 225%. Davis and Huston (1992) suggested 50% and 150% of the median income. Fuchs (1969) proposed a relative definition of poverty, according to which poor households are those whose per capita income is less than 50% of the household median income. So, Davis and Huston's lower middle-class range coincided with the Fuchs' (1969) proposal for identifying the poor. More recently, Birdsall (2007a, 2007b) proposed measuring the middle class by the absolute per capita income between $10 in 2005 PPP and below the 90th percentile of the income distribution. There are still more proposals; the overall message is that economists cannot define the middle class, although they believe it plays an essential role in economic development. It is, therefore, necessary to know whether the size and share of the middle class are increasing or decreasing during economic growth.

Foster and Wolfson (1992) linked bi-polarization and size and middle-class share. The link can be explained by considering a society divided into three groups: the poor, the middle class, and the rich. A larger spread from the median implies moving away from the intermediate position to the tails of the income distribution. The rich become more affluent, and the poor become poorer. Hence, the gap between the poor and rich widens, leading to a smaller and poorer middle class. Thus, a polarized society has a smaller middle class and sizable poor and rich classes, with a large gap. This is basically the idea of bi-polarization as articulated by Foster and Wolfson (2009).

The literature distinguishes between alienation and polarization. A person is alienated if her income spreads from the middle; the larger the spread, the higher the alienation. The idea of alienation can be readily explained by relating it to the deprivation suffered by an individual. Assume that a person suffers deprivation if her income deviates from the median; the larger the deviation, the higher the deprivation. Suppose m is the median income, and $d(x)$ is the deprivation suffered by an individual with income x; the following simple model of capturing alienation is proposed:

$$
\begin{aligned}
d(x) &= (m - x) \text{ if } x < m \\
&= (x - m) \text{ if } x > m.
\end{aligned}
\tag{5.13.1}
$$

It measures the degree of alienation by the average deprivation suffered by society:

$$
A = \int_0^m (m - x) f(x)\, dx + \int_m^\infty (x - m) f(x)\, dx
\tag{5.13.2}
$$

where $f(x)$ is the probability density function. Denoting m_1 and m_2 the mean income of the population having income below and above the median income, respectively, then A is derived as

$$A = \frac{(m_2 - m_1)}{2}. \qquad (5.13.3)$$

The larger is A, the higher is the alienation in society. A is an absolute measure of alienation because it does not change if everyone's income changes by the same absolute amount. It measures the cost to society because of alienation in monetary units. If everyone has the same income, A will be zero, so there is no alienation in society. A person with zero income suffers the most alienation, equal to m. Thus, the proposed relative measure of alienation is given by

$$R = \frac{m_2 - m_1}{2m}, \qquad (5.13.4)$$

which does not change if everyone's income changes by the same proportion.

The second requirement of bi-polarization is when incomes below the median or above the median become closer. This situation is called a "bunching of the two groups" because the two groups have become more homogeneous (Nissanov, Poggi, and Silber 2011). In such a case, the individuals identify themselves as belonging to one of the two groups. This situation is assumed to increase polarization.

The social welfare function implicit in alienation gives equal weights to the incomes below and above the median, which is why the alienation index is entirely insensitive to any income transfer on either side of the median. However, such transfers can be sensitive to transfers at all income levels by giving different weights to income gaps within the two groups. How should then weights be determined?

The social welfare functions implicit in inequality measures give the highest weight to the worst-off individuals in society and the least weight to the most affluent individuals, which means the weight function $v(x)$ should decrease monotonically as income x increases. In the measurement of polarization, however, society is most concerned with the welfare of the middle-income groups; the weight $v(x)$ should be maximum at the median when $x=m$, which tapers off to zero at the tails of the distribution. Kakwani and Son (2016) proposed the following simple weighting scheme:

$$v(x) = 4F(x) \qquad \qquad if\ x < m$$
$$v(x) = 4[1 - F(x)] \qquad if\ x > m \qquad (5.13.5)$$

such that $\int_0^\infty v(x)f(x)\,dx = 1$.

There are two non-overlapping groups: one having income less than the median and the other higher than the median, each group having the same proportion of individuals. Then the per capita mean income of the whole population is given by

$$\mu = \frac{(m_1 + m_2)}{2}. \qquad (5.13.6)$$

Given the two non-overlapping groups, the Gini index of the population can be decomposed as the sum of between- and within-group components (Kakwani 1980a):[12]

$$G = G_B + G_W \qquad (5.13.7)$$

where

$$G_B = \frac{(m_2 - m_1)}{4\mu} \qquad (5.13.8)$$

and

$$G_W = \frac{(m_1 G_1 + m_2 G_2)}{4\mu}. \qquad (5.13.9)$$

G_1 and G_2 are the Gini indices of groups 1 and 2, respectively and G_B is the between-group Gini index and G_W is the within-group Gini index.

Using (5.13.1) and (5.13.4), the average deprivation suffered by society is given by

$$P_A = 4 \int_0^m (m - x) F(x) f(x)\, dx + 4 \int_m^\infty (x - m)\left[1 - F(x)\right] f(x)\, dx$$

which simplifies to

$$P_A = 2\mu (1 - G) - 2m_1$$

which on utilizing (5.13.7) and (5.13.8) in conjunction with (5.13.3) simplifies to

$$P_A = A - 2\mu G_w. \qquad (5.13.10)$$

The proposed measure of absolute polarization is the average deprivation suffered by society in monetary units. Note that as the absolute alienation A increases, the absolute polarization also increases by the same magnitude. Furthermore, μG_w is the absolute measure of within-group Gini, which informs to what extent the two groups bunch together. In other words, the extent to which overall income differences between the two groups decrease. Hence, it is an absolute measure of identification. As absolute identification decreases, the polarization increases. Thus, P_A is a composite measure of absolute alienation and identification, an increasing function of absolute alienation, and a decreasing function of absolute identification.

---

[12] If the groups are overlapping, then this decomposition is not valid.

The relative measure of polarization is obtained by dividing both sides of (5.13.10) by m

$$P_R = R - 2\mu G_W/m \qquad (5.13.11)$$

where R is the relative measure of alienation defined in (5.13.4). Utilizing (5.13.7) into (5.5.10) yields

$$P_R = 2\mu \left(G_B - G_W\right)/m, \qquad (5.13.12)$$

which is similar but not the same as the measure of polarization proposed by Foster and Wolfson (2009).

The notions of inequality and polarization seem related but are distinct concepts. Their deprivation functions have different weighting schemes. Inequality measures give maximum importance to the worst-off individuals in society. In contrast, polarization measures give the utmost importance to people with medium income, and weights taper off to zero at the tails of the income distribution. The differences in weighting can result in different rankings of the income distribution.

The consensus does not exist in the literature on defining the middle class. The various definitions of the middle class proposed in the literature are ad hoc. However, there is consensus among economists that the size and share of the middle class are essential indicators of development. Therefore, it is crucial to ask whether or not the middle class is shrinking. Kakwani and Son (2016) empirically attempted to answer this question. They used Brazilian data for 1992–2012 and found a robust significant relationship between the size and share of the middle class and alienation. They concluded that a decrease (increase) in alienation leads to an increase (decrease) in the size and share of the middle class. Their empirical finding suggested that there is no need to arbitrarily specify the middle-class range to determine whether or not the middle class is increasing or decreasing in size and share. The empirical estimate of alienation determines whether the society faces increasing or decreasing the size and share of the middle class.

5.13.2 Multi-Group Polarization

Polarization deals with conflicts in society, and it became an essential topic in economics in the mid-1990s. Polarization arises when the population is clustered around a few social groups formed by religion, ethnicity, regions, linguistic, economic differences, political beliefs, etc. Conflict in society arises when social groups become more clustered, and the gaps between them widen. The two concepts that are intrinsic to polarization are "identification" and "alienation." Esteban and Ray (1994) were the first to conceptualize the index of polarization that simultaneously considers these two concepts. They developed an index of polarization that captures social conflict with more

than two social groups. Their work gave rise to many papers providing many variations and interpretations of the measures of polarization, including Zhang and Kanbur
(2001), Reynal-Querol (2002), Duclos, Esteban and Ray (2004), Laso de la Vega and
Urrutia (2006), Deutsch and Silber (2007), Estbal, Gradin, and Ray (2007), Permanyer
(2008), and Gigliano and Mosler (2009). It is beyond the scope of this chapter to provide a review of this literature. This section utilizes the Gini decomposition, developed
in the previous section, to measure the degree of multi-group polarization.

A composite measure of polarization considers both the measures of identification
and alienation. Income is the main attribute used in defining identification and alienation. It is assumed that as the incomes of individuals belonging to a social group
become closer, their feeling of identification increases. In contrast, as gaps in income
between social groups widen, alienation increases. The literature on polarization in
economics has only focused on measuring polarization in income. However, the polarization measurement does not have to be restricted to income space. Polarization
can occur in many other dimensions of well-being. For instance, polarization in delivering health and education services can also create social tension in society. Thus,
the idea of polarization in income space can easily be extended to various well-being
spaces.

Zhang and Kanbur (2001) have provided a simple measure of multi-group polarization. They based their measurements on decomposable inequality measures. Their
idea is simple: high between-group inequality increases the distance between social
groups, increasing alienation. In contrast, smaller within-group inequality implies
higher homogeneity within the groups, which should increase identification. Thus, polarization would increase the between-group inequality and decrease the within-group
inequality. Therefore, they proposed the following measure of polarization:

$$P_{ZK} = \frac{BGRI}{WGRI} \qquad (5.13.13)$$

where $BGRI$ and $WFRI$ refer, respectively, to the between-group and the within-group
relative inequality. P_{ZK} is derived from Theil's (1967) decomposition of inequality
measures. In the case of a perfect polarization, $BGRI$ must be maximum, and $WGRI$
must be minimum. The minimum of $WGRI = 0$, implying discontinuity of the ZK
measure. Therefore, it would be more appropriate to measure polarization by the difference between the between-group and within-group relative inequality measures.
Theil's decomposable inequality measures readily define these measures. Section 5.10
developed the Gini decomposition, expressing the inequality in populations as the
sum of $BGRD$ and $WGRD$. Thus, a new measure of multi-group polarization based on
the Gini relative deprivation decomposition is proposed:

$$P_{KS} = (BGRD - WGRD). \qquad (5.13.14)$$

In perfect polarization, every group is homogeneous, implying $WGRD=0$, which from
(5.13.7) gives $BGRD=G$. Then $P_{KS} = G$, and in the case of no polarization, $BDRD=0$,

Table 5.3 Size and share of the middle class, and alienation and polarization in China, 1988–2013

Year	Middle class		Absolute		Relative	
	Size (Percent)	Share (Percent)	Alienation	Polarization	Alienation	Polarization
1988	61.3	25.7	1241	672	0.55	0.30
1995	57.3	23.5	2112	1137	0.60	0.32
2002	53.5	21.1	2886	1558	0.67	0.36
2007	49.8	18.9	6206	3339	0.74	0.40
2013	48.5	19.0	9681	5233	0.72	0.39
Trend	−0.5	−0.3	369.5	199.6	0.70	0.38

Source: Authors' estimates.

and $WGRD=G$, $P_{KS} = -G$. Thus, the proposed multi-group polarization index P_{KS} lies between $-G$ and G. The central idea of this index is that the $BGRD$ increases polarization, and the $WGRD$ has a decreasing relationship with polarization.

5.14 Size and Share of the Middle Class in China

As noted in Figure 5.1, the Gini index increased in China from 1988–2013. Many development economists would be interested in knowing whether the shrinking of the middle class is accompanied by rising inequality. This section attempts to answer this question utilizing five rounds of Chinese Household Income Project surveys.

The median income is used as the reference point in classifying the middle class. The middle class is defined as those persons whose per capita income adjusted for prices is above 50% and below 150% of the median. This definition is arbitrary, but the measures of alienation and polarization supplement it. Defining the middle class would involve two components: (i) the size of the middle class and (ii) the income share of the middle class. Table 5.3 and Figure 5.2 present the empirical estimates of the size and the share of the middle class covering 1988–2013.

The empirical results show that the middle-class size declined monotonically in China from 1988 to 2013, but the middle-class income share has registered a slight increase from 2007 to 2013. Both components show a declining trend in the middle class. The overall conclusion is that the middle class in China had been shrinking, and this conclusion is based on an arbitrary definition of the middle class. Still, the empirical estimates of alienation and polarization presented in Table 5.3, Figures 5.3 and 5.4 support the phenomenon of the shrinking middle class in China.

Many economists have argued that a weak middle class has a bearing on economic growth. Could the shrinking middle class be the reason for China's recent economic growth slowing down? It is not feasible to provide a definitive answer to this question, but the most one can say is that it is a conjecture which requires further evidence.

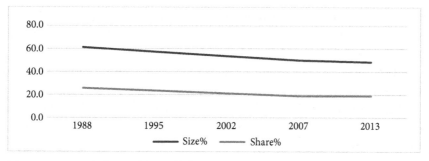

Fig. 5.2 Size and share of the middle class in China, 1988–2013
Note: Data for Figures 5.2–5.4 are given in Table 5.3.

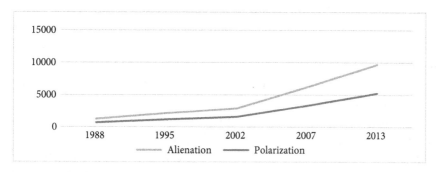

Fig. 5.3 Absolute alienation and polarization in China, 1988–2013

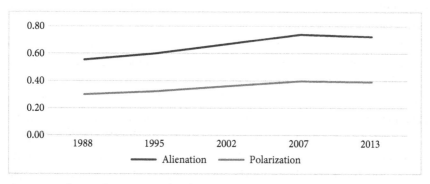

Fig. 5.4 Relative alienation and polarization in China, 1988–2013

5.15 Concluding Remarks

This chapter has dealt with the issue of measuring inequality of income distribution. Since Atkinson's publication of his seminal paper in 1970, the research on inequality measurement has expanded considerably. This chapter has attempted to cover most of the research undertaken in the last fifty years. A brief review of alternative inequality measures has suggested that there could be no single "best" measure. The choice of a measure should depend on the particular aspect of inequality in which one is interested. Some measures are more suited to reflect specific characteristics of distribution than others. This chapter has provided an extensive discussion of evaluating inequality measures.

In the 1970s, the axiomatic approach to assessing inequality measures became fashionable. This chapter has provided the most comprehensive set of axioms. These axioms have ethical implications that became the basis of evaluating alternative inequality measures. The chapter has also proved many lemmas, providing a practical method of assessing inequality.

Atkinson's paper, published in 1970, was groundbreaking, and it emphasized deriving inequality measures from some social welfare functions. Economists increasingly recognized that inequality measures should not be viewed as statistical devices measuring relative dispersions in income distribution. Since they have policy relevance, their measurement must incorporate society's preferences. Thus, inequality research focused on finding social welfare functions implicit in the conventional inequality measures.

The Gini index is by far the most widely used inequality measure. Several well-known authors debated the welfare implications of this index, and Amartya Sen's contribution had been the most influential. He developed the Gini social welfare function, relating the Gini index with the relative deprivation suffered by society. This chapter has described the properties of the Gini social welfare function, and it has developed a generalized Gini social welfare function. It derives a family of inequality measures that give different weights to transfers at different income levels in the distribution. The Gini index is a particular member of this family of inequality measures.

China has achieved unprecedented economic growth rates during the last three decades. Using the family of generalized Gini index, this chapter has analyzed the trends in income inequality in China.

The empirical analysis presented provides overwhelming evidence of rising inequality in China over the 25 years studied. There was also an increasing concern in China that the gap between urban and rural areas increased. The chapter has developed a new Gini decomposition to explain how the urban-rural disparity has contributed to rising trends in inequality. The empirical results indicated that the increasing gap between the rural and urban areas had been a significant factor in rising inequality in China. Thus, the government policy in China should focus on reducing the between-group urban-rural inequality, but within-group urban-rural inequalities should also receive attention.

In the 1990s, the measurement of polarization attracted much attention from researchers. The research on this issue began because of concerns among some economists about the shrinking of the middle class. The chapter has provided a linkage between polarization and the shrinking size of the middle class. Defining the middle class involves two components: (i) the size of the middle class and (ii) the income share of the middle class. The chapter has explored whether the rising inequality in China accompanies a shrinking middle class.

The empirical evidence has suggested that the middle-class size had been declining monotonically in China between 1988 and 2013. Still, the income share of the middle class has registered a slight increase in this period, and both components show a declining trend in the middle class. The overall conclusion is that the middle class in China had been shrinking. This conclusion is at odds with the belief of many economists that a robust middle class is necessary to achieve sustained economic growth.

6

Specifying Poverty Lines

6.1 Introduction

The measurement of poverty involves two distinct problems, as Sen (1976) pointed out. First is the identification of the poor. The poor are those who lack resources to meet their basic minimum needs. Defining basic needs sounds simple, but their determination is not that easy. The "poverty line" specification is a practical method to identify basic human needs. In his study on poverty in 1901, Rowntree defined families in primary poverty if their total earnings were insufficient to obtain the "minimum necessities of merely physical efficiency." First, he estimated the minimum money costs for food, satisfying the average nutritional need for families of different sizes. Then, he added the rent paid and specific minimum amounts for clothing, fuel, and sundries to arrive at a poverty line of a family of a given size. The poverty line is the total cost of maintaining the minimum necessities of merely physical efficiency. A family is classified as poor if its total income is less than its poverty line from all sources.

Once the poverty line is determined, the second problem is constructing an index to measure the intensity of poverty suffered by those below the poverty line. This issue is concerned with the aggregation of individuals' poverty over the population utilizing the poverty line.

Rowntree's approach to measuring poverty may be called the "income approach." It identifies the poor based on monetary income or consumption. Poverty under this approach measures the degree of the lowness of income or consumption in society; poverty occurs because some sections of society cannot satisfy their minimum basic needs.

Although income deprivation may give rise to several other denials, people may still suffer acute lack in many aspects of life, even if they possess adequate command over commodities. Thus, the lowness of well-being can be deemed more critical than the lowness of income. In this context, Sen (1999) argues that poverty should be viewed as depriving necessary capabilities rather than merely a lowness of income. This approach to poverty has recently attracted much attention, leading to significant literature called "multidimensional poverty."

The income approach to identifying and measuring poverty is the most common in analyzing poverty. It determines the minimum income levels sufficient to meet people's basic food and non-food needs. These income levels are the poverty thresholds.

Economic Inequality and Poverty. Nanak Kakwani and Hyun Son, Oxford University Press.
© Nanak Kakwani and Hyun Son (2022). DOI: 10.1093/oso/9780198852841.003.0006

This chapter focuses on constructing poverty thresholds, while Chapter 7 discusses the aggregate measures of poverty utilizing the poverty lines. Finally, Chapter 8 is devoted to measuring multidimensional poverty, which has recently come into existence.

This chapter presents a new model for constructing poverty lines, developed by Kakwani (2011). The model uses consumer theory to create both food and non-food poverty lines. Based on consumer theory, the model defines the minimum standard of living by the minimum utility level u^* allowing the families or households to satisfy their calorie requirements and essential non-food needs such as education, shelter, and health. A family whose actual enjoyment of utility is less than u^* is identified as poor. A poverty line is a metric money value of u^*.

Although the construction of poverty lines incurs value judgments, this model helps make ad hoc assumptions more justifiable. The methodology developed in the chapter is applied to construct poverty thresholds to data obtained from Pakistan. The poverty thresholds obtained from the model are country-specific and therefore cannot be used to make international comparisons of poverty. This chapter also provides the construction of global poverty lines used to produce global poverty counts.

6.2 Absolute versus Relative Poverty Lines

There are two main approaches to specifying poverty lines. The first approach is the "absolute approach," based on Rowntree's minimum subsistence standard of living. Persons are identified as poor if they cannot enjoy this minimum standard of living. The alternative approach is the "relative approach," which defines the poverty line in relation to the average standard of living of a particular society at a specific time (Atkinson, 1974). This approach is based on "relative deprivation," which denotes the deprivation suffered by the worse-off persons in society.[1]

Rich industrialized countries prefer to use the relative approach. For example, Fuchs (1969) defined the poverty line in the United States as equal to one-half of the median family income. Drewnowski (1977) suggested that the poverty line should be the mean income of society. Under this definition, the poor gain when income becomes more equally distributed, and the non-poor are those who lose. In Australia, the Commission of Inquiry into Poverty (Henderson 1975) suggested that a household consisting of the head, dependent wife, and two children would be in poverty if its weekly income fell short of 56.6% of seasonally adjusted average weekly earnings of wage and salary earners for Australia. The poverty line under this approach changes with the average earnings of the wage and salary earners.[2]

Is the relative approach appropriate to measure poverty? The absolute approach is vital if society wants to ensure that nobody lives below society's predetermined minimum living standards. This predetermined minimum standard of living is fixed over

[1] The term "relative deprivation" was coined by Stouffer (1949) and subsequently developed by Merton (1957) and Runciman (1966).
[2] It must be pointed out that all the rich industrial countries do not follow a relative approach to measuring poverty. The first official poverty line for the United States, constructed by Orshansky (1965) was an absolute poverty line based on the cost of the United States Department of Agriculture's low-cost food plan.

time and space. In the relative approach, society's minimum living standards align with society's average standard of living.

The major criticism of the relative approach is that it may reduce poverty when people's income may be falling all around, resulting in a fall in the standard of living of the poor and the non-poor. A reduction (or increase) in poverty will show up only if there is a change in the relative income distribution. A poverty measure based on a relative approach is, in fact, a measure of inequality. It means that poverty is viewed as an issue of inequality. If that is the view of poverty, it is unnecessary to specify poverty lines. Instead, one should look at various measures of inequality discussed in Chapter 5. Poverty is distinct from inequality. Sen (1983) has put this view as follows:

> A sharp fall in general prosperity, causing widespread starvation and hardship, must be seen by an acceptable criterion of poverty as an intensification of poverty. But the stated view of poverty "as an issue of inequality" can easily miss this if the relative distribution is unchanged. There is no change in the differences between the bottom 20 or 10 percent and the rest of the society.

Under the relative approach, poverty is entirely insensitive to economic growth if income inequality does not worsen or improve. Thus, the only way to reduce poverty will be to reduce inequality. Therefore, the impressive economic growth enjoyed by many East Asian countries will play absolutely no role in reducing poverty. Similarly, negative growth rates in the early 1990s in former Soviet republics would have shown no increase in poverty, even if the standards of living of the poor and the non-poor fell sharply in these countries. Such scenarios may be unacceptable.

The OECD countries set their poverty line at half of the median income. However, there is no technical justification for this. Moreover, this poverty line will not always correspond to the socially accepted minimum standard of living. If, for instance, society's objective is to ensure that everyone should meet their nutrition needs and basic non-food requirements, this poverty line is entirely inadequate.

The relative approach also raises questions when measuring poverty within different regions in a country. In that case, the most prosperous areas should have a higher poverty line than the more impoverished areas because of their higher average living standards. Thus, the more prosperous regions may have a higher incidence of poverty than the more disadvantaged areas, leading to higher government resources flowing to more affluent areas and fewer resources to the more impoverished areas. This situation is undesirable.

6.2.1 Absolute Poverty Line Is Relative in the Long Run

Rejection of relative views of poverty must not be confused with being indifferent to society's contemporary standard of living. The poverty line should, of course, take into account current standards of living and should only be defined in relation to the living standards of a particular society at a specific time. The poverty threshold must change gradually as the standard of society adapts itself to new conditions. The relative approach implies that the poverty threshold should vary monthly or quarterly as data become available. The standard of living is more stable than indicated by monthly or quarterly changes in economic situations.

It should be emphasized that an absolute poverty line cannot remain absolute forever. It should change in line with the long-run changes in society's average standard of living. Thus, the absolute poverty line becomes a relative poverty line in the long run. As society's average standard of living changes, people's consumption patterns also change as they adapt to the new living standards. Thus, the absolute poverty line should be revised in the long run to consider the changes in people's living standards and consumption patterns.

6.2.2 Absolute Poverty Line Is Relative across Countries

As pointed out, the poverty line specifies the society's minimum standard of living to which everybody should be entitled. Every society has its views on what constitutes its minimum standard of living. So, the poverty line is a concept which is very much country-specific. For instance, poverty in the United States cannot be and should not be compared with, say, poverty in India. Even if it is absolute, the poverty line should reflect the country's standard of living. Ravallion (1998) has examined the cross-country relationship between poverty lines and per capita real GDP. He found an almost one-to-one relationship between the poverty lines and per capita GDP. Thus, even if they are absolute within countries, the poverty lines are generally relative across countries.

6.3 A New Model of Specifying Absolute Poverty Thresholds

This section discusses the new model of absolute poverty lines developed by Kakwani (2011).

The calorie requirements of individuals vary with their age, sex, body weight, and activity levels. So the food basket will not be the same for all individuals. Similarly, if individuals live in different areas, such as rural and urban, their basic non-food requirements will differ. That means that the minimum utility function must take account of their differences.

The proposed model is based on individual utility functions reflecting their different calorie requirements and non-food needs as:

$$u = \left[\frac{q_f}{r}, \frac{q_n}{n} \right] \qquad (6.3.1)$$

where q_f and q_n are the vectors of food and non-food items of consumption.

The minimum standard of living is fixed at $u=u^*$, then (6.3.1) will provide the food and non-food baskets for individuals with given calorie requirement r and basic non-food requirement n. For a predetermined minimum utility u^* the food and non-food poverty baskets will depend on individuals' calorie and basic non-food needs. Hence, the food and non-food poverty lines will differ for different individuals.

Let p_f and p_n be the price vectors of food and non-food baskets; respectively, the conventional utility theory maximizes the utility function in (6.3.1) subject to the budget constraint

$$p_f q_f + p_n q_n \leq x, \tag{6.3.2}$$

where x is the total expenditure or income available to the consumer. This yields the demand functions

$$q_f = rg_f(x, rp_f, np_n) \tag{6.3.3}$$

and

$$q_n = ng_n(x, rp_r, np_n) \tag{6.3.4}$$

respectively. These equations are the Marshallian demand functions (Marshall 1930). Substituting (6.3.3) and (6.3.4) into (6.3.2) yields the cost function[3]

$$x = e(u, rp_r, np_n), \tag{6.3.5}$$

which is the minimum cost of buying the individual utility u at given food and non-food prices, and individual's caloric needs r and non-food basic needs n.

Substituting (6.3.5) into (6.3.3) and (6.3.4) yields the Hicksian food and non-food demand equations (Hicks 1957) as:

$$q_f = rg_f(u, rp_f, np_n) \tag{6.3.6}$$

and

$$q_n = ng_n(u, rp_f, np_n) \tag{6.3.7}$$

respectively.

---

[3] This cost function is also called the expenditure function in the literature.

The minimum standard of living, measured by u^*, provides the food and non-food poverty lines. Substituting $u=u^*$ into (6.3.6) and (6.3.7) yields the food and non-food poverty lines as

$$F = p_f q_f = r p_f g_f (u^*, r p_f, n p_n) \tag{6.3.8}$$

and

$$NF = p_n q_n = n p_n g_n (u^*, r p_f, n p_n). \tag{6.3.9}$$

Equations (6.3.8) and (6.3.9) give the food and non-food poverty lines corresponding to the consumers' minimum utility u^* enjoyed. These lines will differ for individuals depending on their calorie requirements and non-food needs. The sum of the food and non-food poverty lines yields the total poverty lines, consistent with consumers' minimum utility function u^* enjoyed. If the minimum utility u^* is known, the food and non-food poverty lines are determined from (6.3.8) and (6.3.9), respectively. The critical question is: How does one choose u^*? The following method is proposed.

The food poverty lines should satisfy the requirement that calorie intake equals every individual's calorie requirement (or need). Suppose c is the vector that converts food quantity vector q_f into calories. And, hence, $c q_f$ will be the number of calories obtained by consuming the food basket q_f, which should be equal to calorie requirement r. Then using (6.3.8) yields the restriction:

$$c g_f (u^*, r p_f, n p_n) = 1 \tag{6.3.10}$$

which should hold for all exogenously determined values of r, p_f, n and p_n. That means that the demand function $g_f (u^*, r p_f, n p_n)$ should not contain $r p_f$ and $n p_n$ as its arguments and, hence, depend only on u^*. The food poverty line in (6.3.8) will then be given by

$$F = p_f q_f = r p_f g_f (u^*) \tag{6.3.11}$$

Suppose the calorie cost denoted by c_cost is the expenditure on food per calorie, then the food poverty line will be equal to calorie requirement, and calorie cost, which from (6.3.11) immediately gives

$$c\_cost = p_f g_f (u^*). \tag{6.3.12}$$

This shows that calorie cost depends on food prices and u^*. The real calorie cost is the nominal calorie cost adjusted for food prices. That means that the real calorie cost, adjusted for food prices, is given by

$$c\_cost^* = g_f(u^*). \tag{6.3.13}$$

Note that $g_f(u^*)$ is a monotonically increasing function of u^*. This implies from (6.3.13) that the real calorie cost is a monotonically increasing function of u^*, which measures individuals' minimum living standards. Thus, this proves the following theorem:

Theorem 6.1 *If any two persons have the same real calorie cost at the point when they satisfy the calorie requirements, they will enjoy the same minimum standard of living.*

This theorem implies that one can determine the minimum standard of living measured by the minimum utility u^* by the real calorie cost. If, for instance, two persons meet their calorie requirements, the person who incurs a higher real calorie cost enjoys a higher standard of living. The more affluent individuals may not consume more calories, but they consume food rich in protein, which has a higher calorie cost. The more impoverished individuals consume more carbohydrates, which have a lower calorie cost. Theorem 6.1 emphasizes that it is not the number of calories that determines living standards, and the calorie cost is the critical factor that determines standard of living.

It is not feasible to directly estimate the minimum standard of living given by the minimum utility u^*. However, the calorie cost can be calculated from the data from household surveys. Hence, the theorem provides a practical method of comparing the minimum living standards of individuals with different circumstances. The following section discusses utilizing the theorem in estimating the food and non-food poverty lines.

6.4 Food Poverty Line

The first step in constructing a minimum consumption basket is to specify the nutritional requirements of an individual or a family. Determining the dietary needs of individuals or families is a difficult task. To maintain the required physical efficiency, an individual requires several nutrients such as calories, protein, fat, and carbohydrates in proper combination and at appropriate times (Gopalan 1992). The Food and Agriculture Organization (FAO) has been concerned with determining the nutritional norms of individuals of different age and sex groups. The concept of absolute poverty should be closely related to malnutrition in the population.

The measurement of malnutrition is indeed problematic. Still, as Sen (1981) argues, "malnutrition can provide a basis for standard poverty without poverty being identified as the extent of malnutrition; the level of income at which an average person will be able to meet his or her nutritional requirements has a claim to be considered as an appropriate poverty line when it is explicitly recognized that nutritional requirement varies interpersonally around the average."

The caloric needs of individuals are the starting point to construct food baskets for poverty measurements. The calorie norms are generally available for each country. If some countries do not have such norms, using the FAO norms will be feasible. These norms differ for different persons because of differences in age and sex. Household expenditure surveys provide information on the age and sex of each individual within a household. Given the caloric norms and information on the age and sex of each individual, one can calculate the per capita caloric requirement of each household.

The per capita food poverty line can be obtained for each household if we multiply the household's per capita calorie requirement by the calorie cost. The food poverty lines are consistent if all households at the food poverty line enjoy the same minimum standard of living. This is an essential requirement of the poverty line. It should be emphasized that all households do not have to consume the same food basket to maintain the consistency of food poverty lines, and they only need to have the same minimum standard of living. Theorem 6.1 ensures that households enjoy the same minimum standard of living if they consume food baskets with the same calorie cost. Thus, the calorie cost adjusted for price differences provides a practical method of ensuring the consistency of food poverty lines.

A critical question remains of how one should determine the calorie cost that reflects the consumption pattern of the population regarded as poor in a given country. In other words, one must choose a reference group in a country considered poor. The determination of the reference group should be related to the overall standard of living prevalent in a country. This requirement is essential because poverty cannot be the same for developed and developing countries. The idea of poverty in the United States, for instance, is different from that of, say, India. The poor in the United States can appear pretty affluent when their standard of living is compared to the standard of living in India.

Every society has its notion of poverty. So, one cannot avoid value judgment in determining the reference group that society regards as poor. The choice of reference group should also be determined based on governments' commitment to allocating resources to poverty reduction programs.

The calorie cost can be calculated for different population quintiles based on per capita household consumption. This chapter makes a judgment that the people belonging to the bottom quintile are relatively more impoverished than society. Thus, the people belonging to the bottom quintile are chosen as a reference group. Admittedly, this choice is arbitrary. When the government in a country specifies a poverty line, it is committing to allocate resources to poverty reduction programs. The government could choose the bottom decile as a reference group if it could not spare resources to uplift the bottom quintile people. In this chapter, the average calorie cost of the bottom quintile is used to determine the minimum standard of living in a country.

Having determined the reference group's calorie cost at the national level, one needs to adjust for regional cost of living differences. Thus, the regional cost of living index estimate for food consumption items will be required. The regional cost of living indices can be estimated if the average prices of different food items consumed by the population are known. The appropriate food basket will be the reference group's food basket to calculate the regional or spatial price indices. These indices will allow the estimation of separate calorie costs for each region. Multiplying the regional caloric costs by the household's per capita calorie requirement will immediately give us the per capita food poverty line for each household belonging to different regions.

6.5 Non-Food Poverty Line

Suppose F is the per capita food poverty line that meets the caloric needs of a household. Substituting F into the food expenditure function (derived from the consumer theory), one can solve the utility level u^*, society's minimum standard of living. Thus, the food poverty line is the minimum expenditure on food that gives the consumer u^* level of utility at the given food price vector p_f. At this utility level, the family will buy nutritionally adequate food baskets. Using u^* into the total expenditure function, one can obtain the overall poverty line, z, consistent with the utility level u^*. The non-food poverty line will be equal to $z-F$. This procedure can be described using a simple diagram.

In Figure 6.1, the horizontal axis represents the utility level, and the vertical axis represents expenditures. The figure depicts the food and the total expenditure curves, increasing with the utility level. C is the point that corresponds to the food poverty line on the food expenditure curve. At this point, the family will enjoy the minimum utility u^*. Corresponding to point C, point D on the total expenditure curve corresponds to the total poverty line z, consistent with the utility level u^*.

In the diagram, BC is the food poverty line, and BD is the total poverty line, which yields the non-food poverty line given by CD. The non-food poverty line obtained will be consistent with the minimum utility u^*. Thus, the non-food poverty line is determined when the food expenditure equals the food poverty line. Thus, both the food and non-food poverty lines are determined endogenously, consistent with the society's minimum living standard.

Ravallion (1998) suggested estimating the non-food poverty line using the idea that if a person's total income is just enough to reach the food threshold, anything a person spends on non-food items will reflect the basic non-food needs. According to this idea, the non-food poverty line is the household's non-food expenditure at which the household's total spending is equal to the food poverty line. At this point, the household's income is sufficient to buy only the nutritionally adequate food basket, so any expenditure a household incurs on non-food will be essential.

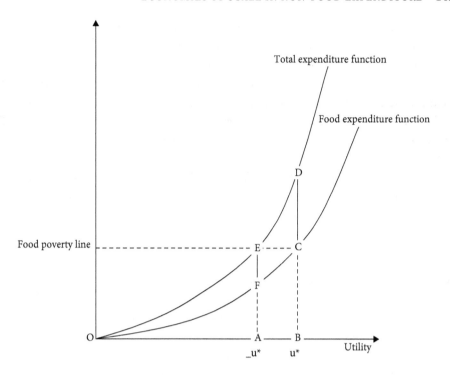

Fig. 6.1 Determination of non-food poverty line

In the figure, at point E, the total expenditure equals the food poverty line. At this point, AE is the total poverty line, which will always be less than the BD. The total poverty line corresponds to the utility level $\_u^*$, smaller than the utility level u^*. Thus, Ravallion's proposed poverty line will not meet society's minimum living standard. This limitation is severe, so his poverty line is not recommended for specifying the poverty line. The following section provides a practical method of computing the food and non-food poverty lines using Pakistan's national household expenditure survey.

The non-food poverty line consists of several components: clothing and footwear, housing, water, electricity and gas, furnishing and household equipment, health, transport, communication, and education. The following section shows how to calculate these individual components of the non-food poverty line using a national household expenditure survey.

6.6 Economies of Scale in Non-food Expenditure

Households have different needs and cannot have the same non-food expenditures. In food expenditures, an assumption is made that the household needs are proportional to per capita calorie requirements. The per capita calorie requirements depend on the age and sex of household members. In non-food, one does not have any logical basis for allocating the non-food expenditure to each household according to age and sex. However, there is ample literature on households enjoying economies of scale because of their size. A person living alone will incur more per person expenditure than two persons living together because they share many household goods. In a household, there are two kinds of items of consumption. One is personal items such as toothbrushes, and the second is public goods that members of the household share without affecting their welfare. These items may include a television, which household members can watch together, or a jointly-used refrigerator.

Kakwani (2011) has proposed the following adjustment to take account of economies of scale. Suppose there are k non-food consumption components, then the average per capita non-food poverty line $(NFPL)$ is the sum of the k components:

$$(NFPL) = \sum_{j=1}^{k} (NFPL)_j \qquad (6.6.1)$$

where $(NFPL)_j$ is the average per capita jth non-food component, where j varies from 1 to k. The different non-food components have different degrees of economies of scale depending on their degree of sharing. Suppose θ_j is the economies of scale parameter for the jth component of the non-food poverty line, which takes value 1 if the jth component is a purely private good and takes value 0 if the jth component is a purely public good. Suppose n_i is the size of the ith household, then the consumption of the jth component by the ith household will be given by

$$(NFPL)_{ij} = c(NFPL)_j n_i^{(\theta_j - 1)} \qquad (6.6.2)$$

where c is the constant of proportionality, if θ_j is equal to 1, every household will be allocated the same per capita expenditure $(NFPL)_j$, implying no economies of scale for the jth component. If θ_j is equal to 0, the ith household will be allocated the per capita expenditure of $(NFPL)_j/n_i$. The parameter c is determined so that the mean of $(NFPL)_{ij}$ across all households is equal to $(NFPL)_j$, ensuring that the economies of scale do not change the mean national poverty line for the non-food component. The per capita non-food poverty line for the ith household will then be given by

$$(NFPL)_i = \sum_{j=1}^{k} (NFPL)_{ij} \qquad (6.6.3)$$

This methodology is implementable if the economies of scale parameters θ_j are known. However, the estimation of θ_j is challenging. In the literature, there exist no credible methods. Lanjouw and Ravallion (1994) estimated the economies of scale using Engel's (1957) model. They assumed that the budget share devoted to food correctly indicates welfare between households of different sizes and compositions. The main objection against this approach, as Kakwani (2011) points out, is the implicit assumption that all commodities provide the same degree of economies of scale. Since there are both private and public goods, it is not correct to assume that all goods offer the same economies of scale. Therefore, it is not feasible to estimate the economies scale

Table 6.1 Economies of scale parameter

Food	0.95
Clothing	0.9
Transport	Share of workers
Personal care	0.8
Recreation	Share of children
Education	Share of children
Housing	0.0
Fuel	0.0
Rent	0.0
Medical	1.0

Source: Kakwani (2011).

parameter from the consumption patterns of the households. The only viable option is to determine the values of the economies of scale parameter using judgment about the characteristics of the commodities included in determining the poverty line. This approach is followed here.

Food is generally a private good, but some households can economize on it by making bulk purchases. Therefore, savings due to economies of scale are not expected to be considerable. Thus, the economies of scale parameter is assumed to be 0.95, implying a saving of only 5% due to bulk buying.

While clothing is generally a private good attributed to household members, some sharing of clothing does go on within the households. So θ_j for clothing may be equal to 0.9, implying a saving of 10%. Housing (including utilities, furnishing, and household equipment) is a public good; it is reasonable to assume θ_j for this good to be equal to 0. Health services are a purely private good (because there cannot be sharing of health services); it is reasonable to assume the economies of scale parameter for health expenditure equals 1. Households incur expenses on education only where children are present, so the assumption is made that spending on education is proportional to the number of children in the household (divided by household size). Working adults incur expenditure on transport and communication, so the spending on transportation is proportional to the number of working adults divided by household size.

Table 6.1 presents the values of the economies of scale parameters suggested by Kakwani (2011), which are considered reasonable. However, one can always do some simulations to test the robustness of the poverty counts.

6.7 Updating the Poverty Line

The poverty lines need to be updated to maintain the same minimum standard of living implied by the poverty lines over time. Several things may change over time. For instance, household size and composition may change, which has important implications for caloric requirements. The changes in household size also affect the distribution of non-food poverty lines across households because of economies of scale that occur within households. Thus, the following procedure is proposed to address this issue.

First, the method must ensure that the real calorie cost remains the same over time. To achieve this, it is essential to know the regional consumer price indices for food, generally available in most countries. Since the nominal calorie cost in each region in the base year is known from household surveys, the nominal caloric cost in each region in the terminal year is estimated using regional consumer price indices for food.

Each household's per capita caloric requirement is estimated from the household survey in the terminal year. Multiplying the per capita caloric requirement in the latest survey by the nominal caloric cost for each region will readily give each household's per capita food poverty line in the terminal year.

To maintain consistency, the procedure must also ensure that the real average expenditures on various non-food components do not change over time. That requires the consumer price indices for each of the k non-food components. Generally, consumer price indices are available in countries and can estimate each component's average non-food poverty line in the terminal period. Given these estimates, the next step is to estimate the non-food poverty lines for each sample household. That requires economies of scale adjusting of each household's non-food component poverty line using the economies of scale parameters in Table 6.1. Each sample household then yields the non-food poverty line for various components. The total non-food poverty line for each sample household is estimated using (6.6.3).

6.8 Development of Poverty Lines for Pakistan: A Case Study

This section presents a case study for Pakistan, illustrating the construction of poverty lines. It utilizes the Pakistan Integrated Household Survey (PIHS). The 2001–2 survey is used as the base year to perform the main calculations of poverty lines, but the terminal year 2004–5 survey illustrates the updating of the poverty lines over time.

6.8.1 Calorie Requirements

First, the food poverty lines require the caloric norms of individuals. Since the caloric norms vary from country to country depending on race, climatic conditions, and so on, it is appropriate to adopt norms specific to the country. Therefore, the caloric norms applicable to Pakistan are used to construct the food poverty line. Table 6.2 presents these norms.

Table 6.2 illustrates that the calorie requirements vary with age and sex. Pakistan currently uses a single calorie requirement of 2,350 calories per equivalent adult per day for every household member. Since the calorie requirements vary with age and

Table 6.2 Caloric requirements per person per day in Pakistan

Age groups	Males	Females
<1	1,010	1,010
01–04	1,304	1,304
05–09	1,768	1,768
10–14	2,816	2,464
15–19	3,087	2,322
20–39	2,760	2,080
40–49	2,640	1,976
50–59	2,460	1,872
60+	2,146	1,632
Average per capita caloric requirement		
2001–2	2,154.3	
2004–5	2,175.9	

Source: Kakwani (2011).

sex, it will be desirable to calculate the actual calorie requirements by age and sex, as shown in Table 6.2. As the PIHS provides information on age and sex for each household member, it was possible to calculate each household's per capita caloric requirement using the surveys. Given this information for each household, the average per capita (per day) calorie requirement for Pakistan was calculated employing a weighted average method. The weights used were proportional to the population and are readily available from the household surveys.

The empirical calculations showed that the Pakistani population in 2001–2 required an average of 2,154 calories per person per day. This average increased to 2,176 in 2004–5. This increase is because the population structure in Pakistan is changing, and the proportion of children in the population is declining, which is a worldwide phenomenon.

6.8.2 Calorie Cost

Given the calorie requirements for each household, the next step is to convert the required calories into a food poverty line, which is the expenditure on food needed to meet the exogenously determined calorie requirements. Thus, each household's per capita food poverty line equals per capita household calorie requirements multiplied by the per calorie cost.

The PIHS 2001–2 provided information on quantities of different food items consumed by households. These food quantities can be converted into calories, employing food calorie conversion factors for typical Pakistani food.

Given the quantities of food consumed by each sample household, it was possible to compute the actual calorie intake of each sample household by multiplying the

Table 6.3 Average calorie cost by
quintile in Pakistan (Rupees per 1,000
calories)

Quintiles	Calorie Cost
Quintile 1	5.72
Quintile 2	6.41
Quintile 3	6.92
Quintile 4	7.65
Quintile 5	9.84
Total	7.56

Source: Kakwani (2011).

quantities by the calorie conversion factors. Dividing the calorie intake of each household by its size gave us each household's per capita calorie intake.

Given the per capita calorie intake and the per capita food expenditure incurred, the calorie cost for each sample household is obtained by dividing the food expenditure by the calorie intake. The calorie cost varies with a household's standard of living; the more affluent the household, the higher the calorie cost. To see how the calorie cost varies with the per capita final consumption, Pakistan's population was divided into five quintiles by ranking them by their per capita consumption. Then, the calorie cost was calculated for each quintile. Table 6.3 presents the calorie cost for each quintile.

It is seen from the table that the households belonging to the first quintile spend Rs 5.72 on food to consume 1,000 calories. As expected, the calorie cost increases monotonically from the first quintile to the fifth quintile. The more affluent households have greater calorie costs than the poorer households because they tend to consume richer food, which is more expensive. This result is consistent with Theorem 6.1.

The calorie cost for determining the food poverty line must correspond to some reference group. How should the reference group be selected? Indeed, the reference group cannot be the most affluent, those with the most expensive taste. If the most affluent reference group is chosen, the poverty line will be so high that most of the population would be considered poor. When the government adopts a poverty line, it agrees on a minimum standard of living to which everyone should be entitled. If the poverty line is too high, the government will not fulfill its commitment to maintaining society's minimum living standard.

On the other hand, the poverty line should not be so low that almost everyone is non-poor. In such a situation, the government may not be motivated enough to raise the standard of living of those unable to meet the absolute basic needs. These absolute basic needs are not entirely absolute, and they are relative to society's overall standard of living.

The reference group should contain the population that is representative of the poor. For example, around 30% of the population in Pakistan is perceived as poor.

Therefore, it is reasonable to set the calorie cost of the poorest 30% of Pakistan's population. Table 6.3 shows that the calorie costs of quintiles 1 and 2 are Rs 5.72 and Rs 6.41 per 1,000 calories, respectively. Therefore, the calorie cost of Rs 6.07 per 1,000 calories approximately corresponds to the poorest 30% of the population, which seems to be a typical calorie cost for the poor in Pakistan. The food poverty line is calculated using this calorie cost.

The calorie costs presented in Table 6.3 are calculated based on the consumption patterns of Pakistan's population. Thus, the food poverty lines developed in this study, based on the actual calorie costs derived from household surveys, account for the consumption patterns prevalent in Pakistan.

6.8.3 Spatial Price Indices

The calorie cost depends on food prices, and the higher the food prices, the higher will be the calorie cost. Since Pakistan is a vast country, the food prices will not be the same across regions. Therefore, the calorie cost will vary across regions because of differences in the relative costs of food.

Spatial price indices measure the relative living costs in different regions and communities. These indices are essential for poverty measurement because they allow one to consider the regional cost of living differences. The spatial price indices for food were estimated for the eight regions given in Table 6.4, utilizing unit prices obtained from the PIHS 2001–2.[4]

Table 6.4 presents the spatial price index for food in the survey year 2001–2. The index value is set at 1 at the national level for Pakistan. The index values for other regions provide the living costs relative to the national cost of living. The food cost of

Table 6.4 Spatial price indices for food and caloric cost in Pakistan, 2001–2

	Spatial price	Caloric cost	Food inflation (2004–5)	Calorie cost (2004–5)
Urban areas	1.07	6.50	24.12	8.06
Punjab	1.02	6.21	24.79	7.75
Sind	1.15	6.99	23.20	8.61
Frontier	1.05	6.39	18.97	7.60
Baluchistan	1.13	6.84	26.52	8.66
Rural area	0.97	5.90	24.19	7.33
Punjab	0.93	5.64	26.73	7.15
Sind	0.99	6.02	22.23	7.36
Frontier	1.05	6.38	16.93	7.46
Baluchistan	1.13	6.84	27.67	8.73
Pakistan	1.00	6.07	24.32	7.54

Source: Kakwani (2011).

[4] The detailed methodology is described in the Appendix.

living in urban areas is 7% higher than the national average. In contrast, the food cost of living in rural areas is 3% lower than the national average. Baluchistan is the most expensive region for food, where the food cost is 13% higher than the national average in urban and rural areas.

The calorie cost at the national level is set at Rs 6.07 per 1,000 calories. The calorie cost for each region is calculated using the regional spatial price indices presented in the first column of Table 6.4. The second column in Table 6.4 presents the caloric costs for different regions. These costs are used to calculate the food poverty lines in different regions in the survey year 2001–2.

6.8.4 Inflation Rates between the Survey Periods

The caloric costs in the second survey period, 2004–5, change according to the food inflation rates between the two survey periods 2001–2 and 2004–5. The Tornqvist price index is utilized to calculate the food inflation rates separately for each region.[5] The food inflation rates are presented in the third column of Table 6.4, showing that the food prices in Pakistan increased by 24.3% between the two survey periods. The inflation rates are different in various regions. For example, the food inflation rate is highest in Baluchistan.

Applying the food inflation rates on caloric costs in 2001–2 yielded the caloric costs for each region in the terminal survey period 2004–5, as presented in the fourth column of Table 6.4. For example, the caloric cost in Pakistan increased from Rs 6.07 in 2001–2 to Rs 7.54 in 2004–5 because of increased food prices.

6.8.5 Food Poverty Lines

The food poverty line equals the calorie requirements multiplied by calorie costs. The food poverty lines will differ depending on household size, composition, and region. Table 6.5 presents the average per capita food poverty lines in the different regions. These are the weighted averages with weights proportional to the population; the household surveys provide its information. The food poverty line for Pakistan is the weighted average of regional poverty lines, with weight proportional to the regions' population.

The differences in average food poverty lines across regions reflect two factors: (a) the regional cost of living differences and (b) regional differences in household demographics. Over time, the differences in food poverty lines reflect the inflation rates in each region and changes in household demographics.

---

[5] The detailed methodology is described in the Appendix.

Table 6.5 Average per capita food poverty line in Pakistan

	2001–2	2004–5	Percent change
Urban areas	389	487	25.2
Punjab	373	466	25.1
Sindh	416	526	26.3
Frontier	376	447	19.0
Balochistan	399	521	30.4
Rural area	341	429	25.5
Punjab	328	419	28.0
Sindh	345	430	24.5
Frontier	364	430	18.1
Balochistan	401	519	29.4
Pakistan	355	447	25.9

Source: Kakwani (2011).

6.8.6 Non-food Poverty Lines

Once the food poverty line is determined, one can estimate the non-food poverty line using the consumer theory outlined in Sections 6.5 and 6.6. This method avoids making many demanding normative judgments in the literature on constructing the non-food poverty line. Instead, it utilizes the population's consumption patterns in household budget surveys. The method involves calculating the non-food poverty line when the per capita food expenditure equals the per capita food poverty line. Food welfare is defined as the per capita food expenditure divided by the per capita food poverty line multiplied by 100. The food welfare was constructed because the food poverty line is different for different households, and it takes 100 when per capita food expenditure equals the per capita food poverty line. Therefore, the per capita non-food expenditure at this point will be the average per capita non-food poverty line. At this point, it was also possible to estimate the various components of the non-food poverty line. These components include clothing and footwear, transport, personal care, recreation, education, fuel and light, house rent, and medical. The average non-food poverty line and its components are presented in Table 6.6.

The first column in Table 6.6 gives the average per capita non-food poverty lines for various non-food components for the survey year 2001–2. The third column in the table provides the inflation rates for different non-food items obtained from the consumer price indices. Applying these indices on the first column yielded the average per capita non-food poverty lines for various components for the survey year 2004–5.

Table 6.6 reveals that housing rent is the major non-food component of household expenditure after food. The house rent varies substantially across the regions, and the rent is much higher in urban areas than that in rural areas. The rent component of the total poverty line in the different regions was determined so that households on the

Table 6.6 Average per capita non-food poverty lines in Pakistan

	2001–2	2004–5	Inflation rate
Clothing	55.26	61.44	11.2
Transport	24.13	28.94	19.9
Personal care	29.70	34.02	14.5
Recreation	1.04	1.06	2.2
Education	26.33	30.08	14.2
Fuel & light	63.30	75.56	19.4
Medical	34.01	36.44	7.1
House rent	85.32	101.10	18.5
Non-food	319.08	368.63	15.5

Source: Kakwani (2011).

Table 6.7 The poverty line for house rent in Pakistan

	2001–2	2004–5
Urban areas	167.7	198.7
Punjab	173.6	205.8
Sindh	174.5	206.8
Frontier	87.0	103.1
Balochistan	168.7	199.9
Rural area	51.7	61.3
Punjab	53.3	63.2
Sindh	41.8	49.5
Frontier	44.1	52.3
Baluchistan	102.0	120.9
Pakistan	85.3	101.1

poverty line enjoy the same level of welfare. Table 6.7 informs how much poor households are expected to spend on housing in the different regions in 2001–2. From the consumer price index for the housing rent, it is noted that the rents increased by about 18.5% between the survey periods. Applying this inflation rate in column 1 in Table 6.7 yielded the per capita rent at the poverty line in 2004–5, presented in column 2 of Table 6.7.

Having estimated the minimum required non-food component for each household, the total non-food poverty line was calculated by adding eight non-food components. Thus, the per capita overall poverty line is the sum of the food and non-food poverty lines, which differs for each household.

Figure 6.2 shows that the per capita poverty line declines monotonically with household size, reflecting the different needs in food consumption of various household members and the economies of scale within the large household.

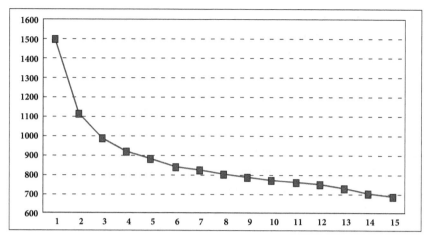

Fig. 6.2 Per capita poverty line by household size

6.8.7 Incidence of Poverty in Pakistan

The poverty line is essential in identifying the poor. A person is poor if their income falls below the poverty line. This chapter has covered a range of issues in the specification of the poverty line. Once the poverty line is determined, the second issue is constructing an index to measure the degree of poverty suffered by those below the poverty line. Chapter 7 will provide a critical evaluation of alternative indices of poverty. This section presents the percentage of poor individuals in Pakistan based on the poverty lines developed in the chapter.

Table 6.8 reveals that the number of poor has declined by 10% between 2001–2 and 2004–5. The rural areas have achieved a much more substantial reduction in the

Table 6.8 Percentage of poor in Pakistan

	2001–2	2004–5	Change
Urban areas	30.5	23.0	−7.5
Punjab	34.2	26.0	−8.2
Sindh	25.2	18.5	−6.7
Frontier	27.6	20.5	−7.1
Balochistan	29.6	26.0	−3.5
Rural area	37.8	26.9	−10.9
Punjab	37.3	27.8	−9.5
Sindh	42.1	23.1	−19.0
Frontier	32.4	26.3	−6.1
Balochistan	41.5	34.6	−7.0
Pakistan	35.7	25.7	−10.0

Source: Kakwani (2011).

percentage of poor. The poverty lines developed in this chapter can be applied to calculate more refined measures of poverty that would provide greater insight into the
intensity of poverty in Pakistan.

6.9 International Poverty Line

The World Bank has championed the production of global poverty counts. How many
people are suffering from extreme poverty in the world? This issue is vital to understanding the causes of world poverty and what one can do to eliminate global poverty
or reduce its intensity.

International development communities widely used the poverty line of $1.25 per
person per day in 2005 purchasing power parity (PPP) to gauge poverty reduction
efforts. The poverty rates based on this line became a key indicator to monitor the Millennium Development Goals (MDGs). The United Nations' more recent Sustainable
Development Goals have also adopted these global poverty rates as a critical indicator to assess economic development in the post-MDG era. The poverty line of $1.25
would continue to be a benchmark for calculating global poverty rates.

In 2014, the World Bank released its estimates of the 2011 PPP currency conversions
to compare the size and price levels in countries worldwide. The PPP estimates play a
crucial role in producing global poverty counts. The new PPP estimates cover many
countries, with much-improved methodology and more detailed coverage of price
data. Hence, the international development community must adopt the latest currency
conversions to calculate global poverty rates. The 2011 PPP estimates have sparked
debates about calculating global poverty thresholds based on the new conversion rates.

Since the poverty line of $1.25 in 2005 PPP has been widely adopted as a benchmark
for calculating global poverty rates, the change in PPPs should not sharply shift global
poverty counts. However, the World Bank's calculations have shown otherwise. With
the modification of the 1993 PPP to the 2005 PPP, the World Bank estimated that the
number of poor in the world increased by about 500 million. Given the same absolute
poverty line and distributions, such a change in PPP conversions should not substantially increase the number of poor in the world. Kakwani and Son (2016a, 2016b)
argued that a substantial increase in poverty counts of about 500 million could only
happen when the real poverty line has increased significantly. They raised a pertinent
question: what poverty line in 2011 PPP is equivalent to the current poverty line of
$1.25 in 2005 PPP? The equivalence requirement should ensure that the new poverty
line in 2011 PPP should preserve the real purchasing power of the earlier poverty
line of $1.25 in 2005 PPP. They proposed the following methodology of equivalence
poverty lines to calculate a single international poverty line in this context.

Suppose the poverty line in 2005 at 2005 PPP was $1.25 per person per day, then
how should the equivalent poverty line in 2011 PPP be calculated? These calculations
require the following definitions:

- PPP (2005): Purchasing power parity in 2005
- PPP (2011): Purchasing power parity in 2011
- PL_{LOCAL} (2005): Poverty line in local currency in 2005
- PL_{LOCAL} (2011): Poverty line in local currency in 2011
- CPI (2005): Consumer price index in 2005
- CPI (2011): Consumer price index in 2011
- PL_{US} (2005, 2005 PPP): Poverty line in US dollars in 2005 PPP
- PL_{US} (2011, 2011 PPP): Poverty line in US dollars in 2011 PPP

The following relations will always hold:

$$PL_{LOCAL}(2005) = PL_{US}(2005,\ 2005\ PPP) \times PPP(2005) \qquad (6.9.1)$$

$$PL_{LOCAL}(2011) = PL_{US}(2011,\ 2011\ PPP) \times PPP(2011) \qquad (6.9.2)$$

Adjusting the poverty lines in local currency for inflation in the country gives:

$$PL_{LOCAL}(2011) = PL_{LOCAL}(2005) \times CPI(2011) mathord/ CPI(2005) \qquad (6.9.3)$$

Substituting (6.9.1) and (6.9.2) into (6.9.3) gives:

$$PL_{US}(2011,\ 2011\ PPP) = PL_{US}(2005,\ 2005\ PPP) \times \left[\frac{PPP(2005)}{PPP(2011)}\right] \times \left[\frac{CPI(2011)}{CPI(2005)}\right]$$

This equation gives the two poverty lines: PL_{US} (2005, 2005 PPP) and PL_{US} (2011, 2011 PPP), which are equivalent because they imply the same real poverty lines in local currency in 2005 and 2011. If PL_{US} (2005, 2005 PPP) is set equal to \$1.25, then the equivalent poverty line in 2011 in 2011 PPP will be given by

$$PL(2011) = 1.25 \times \left[\frac{PPP(2005)}{PPP(2011)}\right] \times \left[\frac{CPI(2011)}{CPI(2005)}\right]. \qquad (6.9.4)$$

PL(2011) is the international poverty line in 2011, which provided the same poverty rates as \$1.25 per person a day in 2005. From (6.9.4), it is noted that PL(2011) is not unique for all countries and varies with inflation rates between 2005 and 2011 and PPP rates in 2005 and 2011. A country with a high inflation rate will have a higher poverty line in 2011. Similarly, if the PPP exchange rate for the country appreciates in 2011, relative to that in 2005, the poverty line will also be higher. Therefore, no single equivalent poverty line exists in the 2011 PPP.

PPP(2011) is the PPP exchange rate in 2011, which the International Comparison Program has recently estimated. If PPP(2011) were not available, then one could still calculate the exchange rates using the 2005 PPP as

$$EX(2011,\ 2005\ PPP) = PPP(2005) \times \left[\frac{CPI(2011)\ CPI_R(2005)}{CPI(2005)\ CPI_R(2011)} \right] \qquad (6.9.5)$$

where $CPI_R(2005)$ and $CPI_R(2011)$ are the consumer price index for the reference country (US) in 2005 and 2011, respectively. The relative inflation rates determine the exchange rate in 2011 in a country compared to that of the United States. Equating this exchange rate to PPP(2011), equations (6.9.4) and (6.9.5) yield

$$PL(2011) = 1.25 \times \left[\frac{CPI_R(2011)}{CPI_R(2005)} \right], \qquad (6.9.6)$$

which shows that the poverty line in 2011 equivalent to the poverty line of $1.25 depends on the inflation rate in the United States: the larger the inflation rate, the larger the poverty line in 2011. Therefore, it has been suggested that the equivalent poverty line should be calculated based on the rate of inflation in the United States. Still, this method is problematic because it estimates poverty counts only under the highly restricted assumption that the 2011 PPP conversion rates are equal to the 2005 PPP rates when adjusted for the relative inflation rates of comparator countries to the United States.

Kakwani and Son (2016a) developed the idea of equivalence poverty lines published in the *Journal of Economic Inequality*. The World Bank based its new official poverty line on the same concept of equivalent poverty lines given in this paper. It applied this idea to the same fifteen countries to construct the $1.25 poverty line in 2005 PPP. The World Bank used the simple average of the equivalent poverty lines for these fifteen countries. In contrast, it is shown here that—strictly speaking—there is no equivalent single poverty line calculated from the new 2011 PPP equivalent to $1.25 in 2005 PPP. Every country will have its own 2011 PPP poverty line equivalent to the $1.25 line in 2005 PPP. Kakwani and Son (2016) recommended using the weighted average of equivalent poverty lines for as many countries as possible, with weights proportional to their population if a single poverty line is required. Given data availability on inflation rates, they calculated the weighted average of equivalent poverty lines of 101 countries worldwide. This method arrived at the poverty line of $1.93 in 2011 PPP, while the World Bank's official poverty line is $1.90.

Although the two poverty lines are close, Kakwani and Son (2016) demonstrated that the poverty line of $1.93 performed better than the World Bank's official poverty line of $1.90 to preserve the real purchasing power of the $1.25 in 2005 PPP.

The poverty rates and the number of poor for 126 countries using the three poverty lines: (i) $1.25 at 2005 PPP, (ii) $1.90 at 2011 PPP, and (iii) $1.93 at 2011 PPP are presented in Table 6.9. The calculations were performed using PovcalNet (World Bank's interactive program online). The poverty rates and the number of poor are presented for six regions. The global estimates are the weighted regional-poverty rates with weights proportional to each region's population.

Table 6.9 Percentage and number of poor by region in Pakistan

All countries	Population (million)	Percentage of poor (Percent)			Number of poor (million)		
		$1.25 (2005 PPP)	$1.90 (2011 PPP)	$1.93 (2011 PPP)	$1.25 (2005 PPP)	$1.90 (2011 PPP)	$1.93 (2011 PPP)
East Asia and Pacific	1,896.37	7.93	8.54	8.97	150.30	161.96	170.16
Europe and Central Asia	447.98	0.49	0.49	0.53	2.21	2.21	2.37
Latin America and Caribbean	585.22	4.63	5.90	6.03	27.12	34.52	35.28
Middle East and North Africa	125.18	1.06	0.85	0.91	1.33	1.07	1.14
South Asia	1,599.28	24.49	22.20	23.24	391.69	355.10	371.74
Sub-Saharan Africa	847.84	46.85	44.35	45.14	397.20	376.02	382.74
Total	5,501.87	17.63	16.92	17.51	969.85	930.88	963.43

Source: Kakwani and Son (2016).
Note: PPP = purchasing power parity.

Many interesting findings emerge from comparing poverty estimates at the country level. One striking result involves the comparison of poverty incidence in India and China. Based on the poverty line of $1.25 in 2005 PPP, 24.67% of India's population lived in poverty in 2011 (with the number of poor equal to 301 million), while in China, only 6.26% were poor in the same year (with the number of poor equal to 84.14 million). When the calculations are performed using the $1.93 poverty line in 2011 PPP, India's poverty decreased to 23.63% (with the number of poor equal to about 288.56 million), while the poor in China increased to 8.27% (with the number of poor equal to 111.16 million). Although the gap in poverty incidence between India and China has narrowed, India has a long way to go to catch up with China's progress. The change in PPP has appeared to favor India and disfavor China.

Based on the poverty line of $1.93 in 2011 PPP, the total number of poor in South Asia and Sub-Saharan Africa is 754.48 million, while the total number of poor in the world based on the same poverty line is 963.43 million. About 79% of the world poor are concentrated in the two regions, and the incidence of extreme poverty outside these two regions is almost negligible.

Shifting from $1.25 in 2005 PPP to $1.93 in 2011, PPP reduced the global poor by 6.42 million. The decline occurred mainly in South Asia (19.95 million) and Sub-Saharan Africa (14.46 million). The substantial reduction in the number of poor in these two poorest regions has been offset by an increase in the number of poor in more affluent areas, resulting in the poor's net reduction by 6.42 million. South Asia and Sub-Saharan Africa achieved a considerable reduction in poverty because prices in these two regions fell relative to their richer counterparts.

6.10 Concluding Remarks

In his influential paper published in 1976, Sen pointed out that poverty measurement involves two distinct issues: (i) identifying the poor in the population and (ii) constructing an index of poverty, measuring the degree of poverty suffered by a society. The literature on poverty measurement has primarily focused on the second issue. Identifying the poor depends critically on the poverty line, and poverty indices cannot precisely reflect poverty in a society without an accurate poverty line estimate. Surprisingly, the literature has almost ignored the specification of poverty lines, which requires rigorous research.

This chapter has attempted to fill this gap by presenting a new model for constructing poverty lines, using consumer theory to generate food and non-food poverty lines. A poverty line is a metric money value of u^*. It defines the minimum standard of living by the utility level u^*, allowing the families or households to satisfy their calorie requirements and essential non-food needs such as education, shelter, and health. A family whose actual utility u is less than u^* is defined as poor.

The utility u^* is unobservable; it cannot be estimated from real-world data. This chapter has proved an important theorem that indirectly enables us to estimate u^* from household surveys. The theorem shows a monotonic relationship between utility u^* and the calorie cost adjusted for prices. In conjunction with food prices, the household surveys provide estimates of real calorie costs for every household.

The primary message of the theorem is that if, for instance, there are two persons, both of whom meet their calorie requirements, the person who incurs higher real calorie costs enjoys a higher standard of living. The more affluent individuals may not consume more calories, but they consume food rich in protein, which is more expensive, resulting in higher calorie costs. The more impoverished individuals consume more carbohydrates, which have a lower calorie cost. The theorem proved in the chapter informs that it is not the number of calories that determines people's living standards, but rather the calorie cost, which provides a practical method of comparing individuals' minimum standard of living with different circumstances.

Having estimated the minimum living standard that meets people's caloric requirements, the chapter has provided a novel method of estimating the non-food poverty line, consistent with the minimum living standards determined corresponding to the food poverty line. Thus, the chapter has demonstrated that the food and non-food poverty lines are linked to minimum living standards. This linkage is essential in determining food and non-food poverty lines.

The chapter shows that household surveys using standard consumer theory can estimate the non-food poverty line's components (housing and water). This avoids the ad hoc methods used in the poverty line literature to determine non-food poverty lines.

This chapter has presented a detailed case study utilizing the Pakistan Integrated Household Survey to demonstrate how the complex issues of constructing poverty lines can be addressed. The topics include comparing the cost of living in different regions, updating poverty lines over time, economies of scale that larger households enjoy, and so on.

The study has presented the percentage of the poor in Pakistan based on the poverty lines constructed. The number of poor has declined by 10% between 2001-2 and 2004-5, and the rural areas have achieved a much more substantial reduction in the percentage of poor. Poverty in Pakistan may be revisited, utilizing more refined measures of poverty that would provide greater insight into the intensity of poverty.

The poverty lines constructed for Pakistan are country-specific and cannot be applied to make international poverty comparisons. The international development community has widely used the World Bank's poverty line of $1.25 per person per day in 2005 PPP to gauge poverty reduction efforts. The World Bank's release of 2011 PPP estimates in 2014 sparked debates about calculating global poverty thresholds based on the new conversion rates. This chapter has addressed the pertinent question—what poverty line in 2011 PPP is equivalent to the current poverty line of $1.25 in 2005 PPP?—and developed a methodology of equivalence poverty lines to calculate a single international poverty line in this context.

The chapter demonstrates that this method is superior, arriving at the poverty line of $1.93 in 2011 PPP to the World Bank's official poverty line of $1.90. The chapter applied the poverty line of \$1.93 in 2011 PPP to make international comparisons. The total number of poor in South Asia and Sub-Saharan Africa was 754.48 million, while the total number of poor in the world was 963.43 million. Thus, about 79% of the world's poor concentrated in the two regions. The incidence of extreme poverty outside these two regions was almost negligible.

Appendix A

Regional Cost of Living Indices for Food

Pakistan has four provinces, each of which has rural and urban areas, so there is a total of eight regions.

The spatial price indices needed were for the eight regions. The PHIS 2001–02 informed that people consume about 80 food items in all eight regions. The budget shares were constructed for 80 items for each region. The PHIS also provided the unit prices of different food items for each household. The median prices of 80 food items were computed from households for each region.

Suppose a_j is the population share of the jth region (j varies from 1 to 8) and w_{ij} is the budget share of the ith food item in the jth region, then the national basket (or budget share) was calculated for each food item as

$$\bar{w}_i = \sum_{j=1}^{8} a_j w_{ij}. \tag{a.1}$$

Similarly, if p_{ij} is the median price of the ith food item in the jth region, then one can construct a national price for the ith food item as

$$log(\bar{p}_i) = \sum_{j=1}^{8} a_j log(p_{ij}) \tag{a.2}$$

where $\bar{p}_i$ is the national price of the ith food item.

The regional price indices are constructed relative to the national prices. Two alternative approaches were followed, namely, Laspeyres and Paasche. These approaches are described in Deaton and Zaidi (2002). In the Laspeyres approach, the fixed national basket is used to calculate price relatives of each region:

$$log(P_j^L) = \sum_{i=1}^{n} \bar{w}_i log(p_{ij}/\bar{p}_i) \tag{a.3}$$

The Paasche approach uses the basket of each region to calculate the regional price relatives:

$$log(P_j^P) = \sum_{i=1}^{n} w_{ij} log(p_{ij}/\bar{p}_i) \tag{a.4}$$

The calculations for Pakistan showed that both approaches gave almost identical results to use any of the two approaches.

Regional Inflation Rate between Two Time Periods

The poverty line over time is updated using a price index that captures changes in prices over time. The prices do not change uniformly in all regions, so the inflation rates separately for each region are required. Each region has a different food basket, and baskets also vary between the two periods. This study uses the Tornquist (1936) price index to calculate the inflation rates at the regional and national levels.

Suppose w_{ijt} is the budget share of the ith food item in the jth region in year t, then the inflation rate from year $t-1$ to year t is given by

$$I_{jt} = \sum_{i=1}^{n} \left(\frac{w_{ijt-1} + w_{ijt}}{2} \right) [log(p_{ijt}) - log(p_{ijt-1})] \tag{a.5}$$

and the inflation rate between the two periods at the national level is provided by

$$\bar{I}_t = \sum_{i=1}^{n} \left(\frac{\bar{w}_{it-1} + \bar{w}_{it}}{2} \right) [log(\bar{p}_{it}) - log(\bar{p}_{it-1})] \tag{a.6}$$

where $\bar{w}_{it}$ is the national budget share of the ith food item in year t, and $\bar{p}_{it}$ is the national price in year t.

7

Poverty Measures

7.1 Introduction

Chapter 6 discussed issues relating to the specification of the poverty line, which is the level of income just sufficient to buy the minimum necessities of life. The poor are those who cannot meet their minimum needs of life. The poverty line is a practical method of quantifying the essential goods and services people require in monetary units to maintain a minimum standard of living that society requires everyone to enjoy. A person is poor if their income falls below that line.

Once the poverty line is determined, the next problem is constructing an aggregate measure of poverty to measure the intensity of poverty suffered by those below the poverty line.

Most of the literature on poverty focused on the percentage of poor in society. This measure is popularly known as the head-count ratio. Empirical studies have been extensively using this ratio. However, a paper published by Sen (1976) became the most influential on poverty measurement. According to Sen, the poor suffer a different degree of deprivation that an aggregate poverty measure must capture. He developed a poverty measure that incorporated three aspects of poverty: (i) the percentage of poor, (ii) the aggregate income gap, and (iii) the inequality among the poor. His poverty measure was a composite measure, combining these three distinct aspects of poverty. He proposed an axiomatic approach to deriving his poverty measure.[1]

Chapter 5 discussed the relationship between inequality and social welfare functions. Every inequality has an implicit social welfare function, and the literature has not explored the relationship between social welfare functions and poverty measures. This chapter shows that, as with inequality measures, every poverty measure also has an implicit social welfare function. This contribution is significant because it helps evaluate poverty measures using society's ethical values. This chapter develops poverty social welfare functions that give positive weights to the poor (or those who have income less than or equal to the poverty line) and zero weight to the non-poor (who have income above the poverty line). Like inequality measures, poverty measures can be derived from poverty social welfare functions.

Chapter 5 provided an extensive discussion of absolute measures of inequality proposed by Kolm (1976a, 1976b). Absolute or leftist inequality measures do not show

---

[1] An excellent discussion of aggregate poverty measures, see Foster (1984).

Economic Inequality and Poverty. Nanak Kakwani and Hyun Son, Oxford University Press.
© Nanak Kakwani and Hyun Son (2022). DOI: 10.1093/oso/9780198852841.003.0007

any change in inequality when each income is increased or decreased by the same amount. Like inequality measures, it is proposed to derive absolute poverty measures that imply that poverty does not change when the poverty line and incomes increase or decrease by the same absolute amount. All poverty measures proposed in the literature are relative measures, showing that poverty does not change when the poverty line and incomes increase or decrease by the same proportion. This chapter develops absolute poverty measures of poverty, which are new in the literature. They inform the total social cost of poverty (TSCP) in monetary units. The chapter presents the TSCP for China for the period 1988–2018. The TSCP provides policy insights into how much the Chinese government needs to incur social costs to alleviate or reduce poverty.

The publication of Sen's paper set a benchmark for poverty measures, and it led to the development of many variants of his poverty measure, including Hamada and Takyama (1977), Takayama (1979), Thon (1979), and Shorrocks (1995). Kakwani (1980a, 1980b) developed a generalization of Sen's poverty measure that satisfies the three additional sensitivity axioms that became desirable for poverty measures to satisfy. This chapter provides the intuitive justification of these axioms, and it also provides a critical evaluation of some variants of Sen's poverty measure.

Sen's poverty measure and variants are based on interdependent social welfare functions. Since the groundbreaking paper by Foster, Greer, and Thorbecke (1984), the interdependent social welfare function, capturing the poor's relative deprivation, came under much criticism. The focus shifted to utilitarian social welfare functions, which assume that social welfare is the sum of the individual utility functions of their respective incomes. Each individual has the same utility function, which is increasing and concave. Thus, the utilitarian framework is highly restrictive. Although these are restricted assumptions, the poverty measures are additively decomposable and subgroup consistent. This chapter has gone deeper into the issue of decomposability and subgroup consistency of poverty measures. It has made a new contribution that Sen's poverty measure and its variants can also be decomposable and are subgroup consistent. The application to China illustrates these properties using Sen's poverty measures.

7.2 Head-Count Ratio: A Popular Measure of Poverty

Suppose income x of a person is a random variable with probability density function $f(x)$, and if z is the poverty line, then the proportion of persons in society with income less than the poverty line is given by

$$H = \int_0^z f(x)\, dx \qquad (7.2.1)$$

Measure H is called the head-count ratio. Empirical studies extensively use this ratio. This measure also plays a prominent role in public debates on poverty. Sen (1976) has called it a crude measure of poverty despite its popularity. Its main drawback is that it does not distinguish between the two extreme situations; all the poor have zero income or non-zero income but are below the poverty line. The poor suffer different degrees of deprivation, but the measure is entirely insensitive to such differences.

Sen (1976) proposed the following two axioms which a poverty measure must satisfy.

Axiom 7.1 (Monotonicity) *Given other things, a reduction in a person's income below the poverty line must increase poverty.*

Axiom 7.2 (Transfer) *Given other things, a pure transfer of income from a person below the poverty line to anyone richer must increase poverty.*

The head-count ratio is insensitive to any decrease in income below the poverty line and income transfers among the poor. Thus, the head-count ratio violates both axioms.

7.3 Poverty Gap Ratio

Persons are identified as poor if their income is less than the poverty line. The problem is how poor the poor are. Suppose the deviation of a poor person from the poverty line is proportional to the degree of misery suffered by her. In that case, the average of these deviations may be considered a desirable measure of aggregate poverty. Assuming that the non-poor do not suffer any deprivation due to lack of income, then the average deprivation suffered by all poor will be given by

$$g_A = \frac{1}{H} \int_0^z (z - x) f(x) \, dx, \qquad (7.3.1)$$

which can also be written as

$$g_A = (z - \mu_z) \qquad (7.3.2)$$

where μ_z is the mean income of the poor. g_A is the aggregate income gap measured in monetary units. It tells how much is society's total income shortfall from the poverty line. This indicator is helpful for policymakers in assessing how much it will cost to eliminate poverty. This measure may be called an absolute income gap.

The relative income gap ratio is given by

$$g_R = \frac{(z - \mu_z)}{z},$$ (7.3.3)

which measures the aggregate income shortfall from the poverty line as the proportion of the poverty line. This index, used by the United States Social Security
Administration, is called the "income gap ratio."

Sen (1976) has argued that the head-count ratio is insensitive to the extent of the
income shortfall per person, and the income gap ratio is insensitive to the proportion
of the poor. But, the product of H and g_R provides adequate information in the particular case in which all the poor have precisely the same income. Thus, Sen proposed
the following normalization axiom.

Axiom 7.3 (Relative normalization) *If all the poor have the same income, then the
poverty gap ratio given by*

$$P_R = \int_0^z \frac{(z - x)}{z} f(x)\, dx = H g_R$$ (7.3.4)

is a suitable poverty measure.

The following implications of the poverty gap ratio are drawn:

1. If the income of every poor person is raised to the poverty line, the poverty
   measure becomes zero, implying that poverty is eliminated.
2. When all the poor have zero income, the poverty measure equals the head-count
   ratio, the proportion of the poor population. The head-count ratio is an extreme
   measure of poverty, and it may be considered a suitable poverty measure if all
   the poor have zero income.
3. When everyone in the population is poor and has zero income, the poverty measure equals 1. This is the worst situation of extreme poverty that any society can
   ever suffer.
4. Any reduction in income of the poor increases the poverty measure. Thus, the
   measure satisfies the monotonicity Axiom 7.2.

Similar to the normalized poverty gap ratio, the following normalized absolute poverty
gap is proposed.

Axiom 7.4 (absolute normalization) *If all the poor have the same income, then the
absolute poverty gap is given by*

$$P_A = \int_0^z (z - x) f(x)\, dx = H(z - \mu_z)$$ (7.3.5)

The following are implications of the absolute poverty gap:

1. If the income of every poor person is raised to the poverty line, the poverty measure becomes zero, implying that poverty is eliminated.
2. When all the poor have zero income, the absolute poverty gap is Hz.
3. When everyone in the population is poor and has zero income, the absolute poverty gap equals the poverty line z.
4. Any reduction in income of the poor increases the poverty measure. Thus, the measure satisfies the monotonicity of Axiom 7.2.

Pattanaik and Sengupta (1995) argued that normalization axioms are a strong requirement unnecessary for poverty measurement. Accordingly, they proposed two substantially weaker versions of normalization axioms. These two axioms are stated as follows:

Axiom 7.5 (relative weaker normalization I) *When every poor person has zero income, the relative poverty measure equals the head-count ratio.*

Axiom 7.6 (relative weaker normalization II) *When every person has zero income, the relative poverty measure equals 1.*

Axiom 7.5 implies that the head-count ratio will be a suitable measure of poverty if every poor person has zero income. This is a situation of extreme poverty. Axiom 7.6 implies the maximum poverty of 1, when everyone has zero income. This situation is extraordinary and unlikely to be true in any economy. However, every poverty measure must satisfy this axiom. If any poverty measure violates this axiom, it cannot be considered meaningful.

The following weaker axioms of absolute poverty measures are proposed:

Axiom 7.7 (absolute weaker normalization I) *When every poor person has zero income, the absolute poverty measures equals zH.*

Axiom 7.8 (absolute weaker normalization II) *When everyone in society has zero income, the absolute poverty measure equals z.*

Both poverty measures P_R and P_A satisfy the monotonicity axiom but violate the transfer axioms. The transfer axiom is related to the relative deprivation suffered by the poor. Sen's (1976) focus was on how a poverty measure should capture relative deprivation among the poor. The violation of the transfer axiom led Sen to develop an axiomatic framework to measure poverty. His paper led to many contributions in the literature on poverty measurement. His axiomatic framework became central to the poverty measures that followed Sen's pioneering work. P_R satisfies Axioms 7.5 and 7.6, while P_A satisfies Axioms 7.7 and 7.8.

7.4 A Social Welfare Framework of Poverty Measures

Chapter 5 provided an extensive discussion of the relationship between inequality and social welfare functions. Every inequality has an implicit social welfare function. However, no literature gives the relationship between social welfare functions and poverty measures. Poverty measures are essential tools for designing poverty alleviation policies. In evaluating such policies, normative judgments cannot be avoided, and social welfare functions explicitly specify judgments by assigning weights to different individuals. It is, therefore, critical that poverty measures must be derived from social welfare functions. This section explores the relationships between social welfare functions and poverty measures.

The poverty line specifies the society's minimum standard of living. Individuals suffer deprivation, resulting in welfare loss when their income is less than the poverty line. The welfare of an individual with income x is given by

$$
\begin{aligned}
w(x) \quad &= x - g(z,x) \quad && \text{if } x < z \\
&= x && \text{if } x \geq z
\end{aligned}
\tag{7.4.1}
$$

where z is the poverty line, and

$$
\begin{aligned}
g(z,x) &> 0 \quad \text{if } x < z \\
&= 0 \quad \text{if } x \geq z
\end{aligned}
\tag{7.4.2}
$$

is the deprivation function characterizing the deprivation suffered by the poor. The non-poor do not suffer any deprivation. This model yields the average welfare of society as

$$
W(P) = \mu - \int_0^z g(z,x) f(x)\, dx
\tag{7.4.3}
$$

where μ is the mean income of society. The second term on the right-hand side of (7.4.3) is the average deprivation suffered by society due to poverty. $W(P)$ is the proposed poverty social welfare function. Since μ is measured in monetary units, $W(P)$ is defined only when the average deprivation in (7.4.3) is measured in monetary units.

The function $g(z, x)$ is the monetary value of an individual's deprivation when their income is below the poverty line. This function depends on society's value judgments. $W(P)$ is the general class of social welfare functions implicit in any poverty measure. Chapter 5 discussed that every inequality measure has an implicit social welfare function. This framework implies that, similar to inequality measures, every poverty measure also has an implicit social welfare function. All poverty measures proposed in the literature can be derived from this general social welfare framework.

The existence of poverty must incur social costs to society, which may be called the social cost of poverty (SCP). The policymakers readily understand such costs if they are presented in monetary units. The (SCP) is the average loss of social welfare a society suffers due to poverty. It is given by

$$(SCP) = \int_0^z g(z,x)f(x)\,dx, \qquad (7.4.4)$$

which must be measured in monetary units. The (SCP) is the absolute cost of poverty. The relative social cost of poverty RSCP may be defined as the (SCP) as the proportion of the mean income:

$$(RSCP) = \frac{1}{\mu}\int_0^z g(z,x)f(x)\,dx. \qquad (7.4.5)$$

Suppose a society judges that the deprivation suffered by a person whose income is less than the poverty line is given by $g(z,x) = (z-x)$, which on substituting in (7.4.3) gives

$$W(P_R) = \mu - zP_R, \qquad (7.4.6)$$

which is the poverty social welfare function for the poverty gap ratio defined in (7.3.4). The second term on the right-hand side of (7.4.6) is the (SCP) for the poverty gap ratio. It is also equal to society's economic cost incurred in eliminating poverty. The (RSCP) for the poverty gap ratio is given by zP_R/μ.

If all poor persons in society have zero income, it is easy to see that $P_R = H$, in which case social welfare loss will be zH. This result yields the poverty social welfare for the head-count ratio as

$$W(H) = \mu - zH. \qquad (7.4.7)$$

It is easy to see that $W(H) < W(P_R)$. Following a similar logic, the poverty social welfare function for P_A will be given by

$$W(P_A) = \mu - P_A. \qquad (7.4.8)$$

When every poor person has zero income, $P_A = zH$, implying that $W(P_A) = W(H)$ as given in (7.4.7).

7.5 Sen's Relative Poverty Measure

Inequality and poverty measures differ because of the weights given to individual incomes. Inequality measures are derived by giving positive weights to all individuals' incomes. Poverty measures focus on the poor, giving positive weights to the poor (who have income less than or equal to the poverty line) and zero to the non-poor (who have income above the poverty line). For example, in the derivation of the poverty gap ratio in (7.3.4), every poor person received an equal weight of 1, and the non-poor received the 0 weight. This poverty measure violated the transfer axiom because of equal weights given to the poor.

Sen (1976) derived his poverty measure using an axiomatic approach which became a new mantra for the derivation of poverty measures. His axioms also became a target for much critical evaluation.[2] It is not essential to discuss Sen's complete axiomatic derivation of his poverty measure because it does not add value to the empirical applications of the measure.[3] It suffices to confer the weighting he proposed. He proposed to give different weights to every poor person's income to make the poverty measure sensitive of income transfers among the poor. Suppose $v(z,x)$ is the weight given to a poor person with income x, Sen proposed the following weighting:

$$v(z,x) = \frac{2[H-F(x)]}{H} \ if \ x < z$$
$$= 0 \ \ if \ x \geq z$$

(7.5.1)

$F(x)$ is the probability distribution function. The total weight in the domain of x is given by

$$\int_0^\infty v(z,x)f(x)\,dx = 2\int_0^z \frac{[H-F(x)]}{H}f(x)\,dx = H$$

(7.5.2)

The poorest person receives the maximum weight of 2, which decreases monotonically as income increases and becomes 0 at the poverty line.

Thus, Sen's poverty measure is given by

$$S_R = 2\int_0^z \left[\frac{z-x}{z}\right]\left[\frac{H-F(x)}{H}\right]f(x)\,dx = P_R + \frac{H\mu_z G_z}{z}$$

(7.5.3)

where μ_z and G_z are the mean income and the Gini index of the poor, respectively, and, S_R is a relative poverty measure, implying that if the poverty line and everyone's income are increased or decreased by the same proportion, poverty does not change, When all the poor have income equal to μ_z, S_R equals the poverty gap ratio P_R as defined in (7.3.4), hence satisfying Sen's normalization axiom 7.3. Society does not suffer any poverty when everyone has income equal to or higher than z. In that case, Sen's poverty measure equals zero. When every poor person has zero income, $S_R = H$, and when everyone in society has zero income, $S_R = 1$. Sen's poverty measure satisfies Axioms 7.4 and 7.5.

[2] See for instance, Thon (1983), Foster, Greer, and Thorbecke (1984), and Shorrocks (1995).
[3] Pattanaik and Sengupta (1995) derived the Sen measure using a version of Sen's rank order axiom, and a weaker form of his normalization axiom.

Sen's weighting depends on the income ranking among the poor, implying that his measure's implicit social welfare function is interdependent. It means that each person's utility depends not only on their income but also on the incomes of other persons in society. People compare their income with others and feel relatively deprived when poorer than others. A basic intuition behind the rank ordering is that the lower a person is on a welfare scale, the higher this person's sense of deprivation.

Sen assumed that the poor compare their incomes only among the poor. So, the poor are not concerned about the non-poor in society. This is an assertion and has no justification. In the following section, this assumption is relaxed.

Sen's poverty measure has an implicit social welfare function derived using the poverty social welfare framework proposed in Section 7.4. Suppose the deprivation function $g(z,x)$ is assumed as

$$g(z,x) = v(z,x)[z-x] \tag{7.5.4}$$

where the weight $v(z,x)$ for a given poverty line, z, is a monotonically decreasing function of income x. This function implies that a poor person with the highest income shortfall from the poverty line receives the maximum weight. The weight takes value 0 when the income equals or exceeds the poverty line. Following Sen's proposed weighting defined in (7.5.1) and substituting (7.5.6) into (7.4.3) yields the poverty social welfare function for Sen's poverty measure:

$$W(S_R) = \mu - zS_R \tag{7.5.5}$$

The second term on the right-hand side of this equation is the social welfare loss due to poverty in society, measuring the (SCP) for the Sen poverty measure. The social welfare function $W(S_R)$ is homogeneous of degree 1 in incomes and poverty line. Therefore, it implies that if the poverty line and all incomes increase or decrease by the same proportion, the poverty social welfare function also increases or decreases by the same proportion.

When everyone in society has income equal to or higher than z, $S_R = 0$ and thus, $W(S_R) = \mu$, which is the maximum social welfare. When every poor person has zero income, then equation (7.5.5) gives $S_R = H$, in which case $W(S_R) = \mu - zH$, implying the maximum social welfare loss equal to Hz.

7.6 Sen's Absolute Measure of Poverty

Alternatively, Kolm (1976a, 1976b) proposed the absolute or leftist measures of inequality, which do not show any change in inequality when each income is increased or decreased by the same amount. One can have absolute poverty measures like inequality measures, implying that poverty does not change when the poverty line and all incomes increase or decrease by the absolute amount. Such measures inform how much is the monetary cost of eliminating poverty. These measures make more practical sense and may readily be understood by policymakers.

Sen (1976) did not propose an absolute measure of poverty, but it is easy to derive an absolute measure of poverty using his framework as

$$S_A = 2 \int_0^z (z - x) \left[\frac{H - F(x)}{H} \right] f(x) \, dx = H \left[z - \mu_z (1 - G_z) \right] \tag{7.6.1}$$

This measure remains invariant when the poverty line and all incomes increase or decrease by the same absolute amount. The poverty social welfare function implicit in this measure is given by

$$W(S_A) = \mu - S_A \tag{7.6.2}$$

It is interesting to note that Sen's absolute poverty measure is the average per person social welfare loss. This social welfare function is an absolutely homogeneous function of degree one in poverty line and incomes. If the poverty line and all incomes are increased or decreased by the same absolute amount, the social welfare also increases or reduces by the same absolute amount.

7.7 Variants of Sen's Poverty Measures

7.7.1 A New Variant of Sen's Poverty Measure

Sen's social welfare function assumes that the poor compare their incomes only with other poor people. So, the poor are not concerned about the non-poor in society. As pointed out, this is an assertion and has no empirical basis. This section now re-laxes this restriction and assumes that the poor can compare their incomes with all the persons in society. Following Sen (1976), it is postulated that the relative depri-vation suffered by a person with income x is captured by the weight proportional to the number of richer persons than x in society (not just the poor). This weighting is given by

$$v_1(z, x) = \frac{2[1 - F(x)]}{2 - H} \quad \text{if } x < z \atop = 0 \qquad\qquad \text{if } x \geq z \tag{7.7.1}$$

so that

$$\int_0^\infty v_1(z, x) f(x) \, dx = 2 \int_0^z \frac{[1 - F(x)]}{2 - H} f(x) \, dx = H \tag{7.7.2}$$

All the non-poor get zero weight in this weighting, and all the poor get a positive weight. The poorest person receives the maximum $2/(2-H)$ weight, decreasing monotonically as x increases. Note that $\lim_{x \to z} v_1(z,x) = 2(1-H)/(2-H)$ and the weight is zero when $x=z$, meaning the weight function is not continuous. This discontinuity makes no difference to the derivation of a poverty measure.

Using the weighting function in (7.7.1) yields a new variant of Sen's relative poverty measure as

$$S_{R1} = \int_0^z \frac{z-x}{z} v_1(z,x) f(x)\, dx = \frac{2}{2-H} \int_0^z \frac{z-x}{z} [1-F(x)] f(x)\, dx$$

$$= P_R + \frac{H^2 \mu_z G_z}{z(2-H)} \tag{7.7.3}$$

Note that S_{R1} is a relative poverty measure, meaning that if the poverty line and all incomes increase or decrease by the same proportion, the incidence of poverty does not change. When all the poor have equal income μ_z, S_{R1} is equal to the relative poverty gap ratio P_R in (7.3.4). Therefore, it satisfies Sen's normalization Axiom 7.3. When every poor person has zero income, S_{R1} equals H, the head-count ratio. When everyone in society has zero income, which is a scenario of extreme poverty, $S_{R1} = 1$. Therefore, this proposed new variant of Sen's poverty measure satisfies the normalization Axiom 7.3 and weaker normalization Axioms 7.5 and 7.6. Concluding that the proposed new variant satisfies all Sen's poverty measure properties, it uses a more realistic assumption that the poor compare their income with the poor and non-poor. This proposed poverty measure can substitute Sen's poverty measure.

The poverty social welfare function implicit in this new variant is derived by substituting

$$g(z,x) = v_1(z,x)[z-x] \tag{7.7.4}$$

into (7.4.3), yielding

$$W(S_{R1}) = \mu - z \int_0^z \frac{z-x}{z} v_1(z,x) f(x)\, dx = \mu - z S_{R1} \tag{7.7.5}$$

This social welfare function is homogeneous of degree 1 in the poverty line and income.

7.7.2 Thon–Shorrocks Measures

In the case of the discrete income distribution, Thon (1979) proposed the following weighting:

$$v_2(z,x) = \frac{2}{n(n+1)}(n+1-i) \quad \text{if } x < z$$
$$= 0 \qquad\qquad\qquad\quad \text{if } x \geq z \tag{7.7.6}$$

which in the case of the continuous income distribution is equivalent to the weighting given by

$$v_2(z, x) = 2[1 - F(x)] \quad if \, x < z$$
$$= 0 \qquad\qquad\qquad if \, x \geq z \tag{7.7.7}$$

so that

$$\int_0^\infty v_2(z, x) f(x) \, dx = 2 \int_0^z [1 - F(x)] f(x) \, dx = H(2 - H) \tag{7.7.8}$$

which implies that the total weight over the whole income distribution of the poor does not add up to H. This weighting function leads to Thon's poverty measure:

$$S_{R2} = \int_0^z \frac{z - x}{z} v_2(z, x) f(x) \, dx = 2 \int_0^z \frac{z - x}{z} [1 - F(x)] f(x) \, dx$$
$$= (2 - H) P_R + \frac{H^2 \mu_z G_z}{z} \tag{7.7.9}$$

When all the poor have equal income, that is, $G_z = 0$, S_{R2} equals $(2 - H) P_R$. That concludes that Thon's poverty measure violates the normalization Axiom 7.3. When every poor person has zero income, S_{R2} equals $(2 - H)H$, implying that S_{R2} violates Axiom 7.5. However, it satisfies Axiom 7.6, which is that when everyone in society has zero income, poverty must equal 1.

Shorrocks (1995) proposed the following weighting for discrete income distribution:[4]

$$v(z, x) = \frac{1}{n^2}(2n + 1 - 2i) \quad if \, x < z$$
$$= 0 \qquad\qquad\qquad\qquad if \, x \geq z \tag{7.7.10}$$

In the case of continuous income distributions, it is equivalent to weighting given in (7.7.5). Thus, Shorrock's poverty measure is identical to Thon's measure for continuous income distributions.

Thon and Shorrock proposed identical poverty measures in continuous income distributions, though they published their research independently. However, these measures violate the normalization axiom. When every poor person has zero income, they lead to poverty measure $H(2 - H)$. Hence, they also violate Axiom 7.5, which is a fundamental poverty axiom.

---

[4] Chakravarty (1997) showed that Shorrock's modification of Sen's measure can be derived by applying the Gini social evaluation on the censored income distribution.

7.7.3 Takayama's Measure of Poverty

Takayama (1979) and Hamada and Takayama (1977) introduced the notion of a "censored distribution." Suppose income x is a random variable with density function $f(x)$, then the censored income distribution x^* is defined as

$$
\begin{aligned}
x^* &= x \quad if\ x < z \\
&= z \quad if\ x \geq z,
\end{aligned}
\tag{7.7.11}
$$

which yields the mean income of the censored income distribution as

$$
\mu^* = \int_0^z x f(x)\, dx + \int_z^\infty z f(x)\, dx = H\mu_z + z(1-H)
\tag{7.7.12}
$$

The Gini social welfare function for the censored income distribution, obtained from (7.6.11), is given by

$$
W(S_3) = 2\int_0^z x\left[1 - F(x)\right]f(x)\, dx + 2\int_z^\infty z\left[1 - F(x)\right]f(x)\, dx,
\tag{7.7.13}
$$

which is referred to as Takayama's social welfare function. It simplifies to

$$
W(S_3) = (2 - H)\, H\mu_z - H^2\mu_z G_z + z(1 - H)^2,
\tag{7.7.14}
$$

which is related to the Gini index of censored distribution denoted by G^* as

$$
W(S_3) = \mu^*\left(1 - G^*\right),
\tag{7.7.15}
$$

which yields

$$
S_{R3} = G^* = \frac{(1 - H)\, zP_R + H^2\mu_z G_z}{z - zP_R}
\tag{7.7.16}
$$

Takayama (1979) proposed the Gini index of the censored income distribution as a measure of poverty, which is given by S_{R3} in (7.7.16). When all the poor have equal income, then $S_{R3} = \frac{(1-H)zP_R}{(z-zP_R)}$, which is not equal to P_R, proving that the Takayama poverty measure violates Sen's normalization axiom. When all persons falling below the poverty line have income equal to z, the Takayama measure correctly shows zero poverty.

Similarly, when the poor have zero income, the Takayama measure equals the headcount ratio, satisfying Axiom 7.5. When everyone in society has zero income, which is the extreme poverty suffered by society, the measure satisfies Axiom 7.6.

Kakwani (1981b) has demonstrated that Takayama's poverty measure violates Sen's monotonicity Axiom 7.1 when the poverty line strictly exceeds the median income of the income distribution. This result is undesirable.

7.8 Troublesome Axiom of Income Transfers

Sen (1976) developed his poverty measure using an axiomatic framework. He proposed two fundamental axioms: monotonicity and transfers among the poor. These axioms stated as Axioms 7.1 and 7.2 in Section 7.2 have been scrutinized in the literature on poverty measurement. Thon (1979, 1983) championed the attack on the transfer axiom, pointing out that "the axiom has been from the very beginning plagued with difficulty." He demonstrated that Sen's poverty measure violates the axiom.

Sen (1976) proposed the transfer axiom to make the poverty measure sensitive to the inequality among the poor. He viewed that the greater the inequality among the poor, the higher the poor's relative deprivation. Thus, he proposed the transfer axiom to capture the impact of inequality among the poor on poverty. He did not realize that his proposed transfer axiom was too demanding and could be violated when the poor cross the poverty line.

In response to Thon's criticisms, Sen (1981) introduced the following weaker transfer axiom:

Axiom 7.9 (Weak Transfer) *Given other things, a pure transfer of income from a person below the poverty line to anyone richer must increase the poverty measure if no poor cross the poverty line.*

This revised axiom rules out the possibility that the transfer makes any poor person crossing the poverty line and becoming non-poor due to a transfer of income. Both the head-count and poverty gap ratios violate even this weak transfer axiom.

Thon (1979) and Shorrocks (1995) developed two alternative poverty measures; the main motive was to satisfy Sen's original transfer axiom. The previous section demonstrated that their measures are identical for continuous income distributions. Effectively, they proposed only one poverty measure but published it independently in two separate papers. Their papers satisfy Sen's original transfer axiom, but their measures encounter more severe problems explained below.

An aggregate poverty measure is a function of three variables:

1. Head-count ratio (H)
2. Mean income of the poor (μ_z)
3. Inequality of income among the poor (G_z).

If no poor cross the poverty line due to a regressive transfer, the regressive transfer does not change the head-count ratio and mean income, but the Gini index among the poor increases, then Sen's poverty measure will always show an increase in poverty, hence satisfying Sen's weaker transfer Axiom 7.5.

When some poor cross the poverty line due to regressive transfers among them, all these three variables may reduce, from which one cannot infer whether poverty increases or decreases. It will illuminate to explain the violation of Axiom 7.5 by different poverty measures using Thon's (1983) hypothetical example. This example assumes three persons with incomes 1, 2, and 3, and the poverty line is 2.1, which gives 0.67% poor. Suppose the transfer of income takes place from the poorest person to the second poorest person so that the three persons' incomes after transfer are 0.8, 2.2, and 3. The head-count ratio now declines to 0.33. Table 7.1 shows that due to regressive income transfer, both Sen's and the proposed new variant of poverty reduce poverty, while Thon–Shorrocks' and Takayama's poverty measures increase poverty. Thus, both the poverty measures S_R and S_{R1} violate while S_{R2} and S_{R3} satisfy Sen's transfer axiom.

The primary motivation for Thon's and Shorrock's measures is that any poverty measure must satisfy the transfer axiom, even when the poor person crosses the poverty line. But is it a compelling argument for adopting their poverty measure? To answer this question, it would be relevant to mention two "population monotonicity" properties proposed by Kundu and Smith (1982). The two properties are: (a) given other things when a non-poor person is added to the population, poverty should decrease, and (b) when a poor person is added to the population, poverty should not fall. They proved that any poverty measure satisfying (a) and (b) must violate the transfer axiom. Sen (1981) argued that the population monotonicity requires the poverty line, while the transfer axiom takes no note of the poverty line. This result suggests that the transfer Axioms 7.2 may be too demanding because the weaker transfer Axiom 7.9 does consider the poverty line. Thus, according to Sen, the weaker transfer axiom is more relevant. His poverty measure always satisfies the weaker transfer axiom, and it also does not conflict with the population monotonicity properties.

Sen's (1976) characterization of relative deprivation assumes that the poor compare their economic situation only with the poor in society, and this assumption is restrictive. Could this be the reason that his measure violates the unrestricted transfer Axioms 7.2? This restriction is relaxed in deriving the proposed variant S_{R1}, whereby the poor compare their economic situation with all persons in society, both the rich and the poor. Still, this new variant violates the stronger transfer Axioms 7.2, as shown in Table 7.1.

The formulation of the Thon–Shorrocks measures also assumes that the poor compare with all persons in society, similar to the proposed variant, but they satisfy the stronger transfer Axioms 7.2, allowing some poor to cross the poverty line. Their poverty measure suffers from three severe limitations.

The poverty measures are defined as the weighted average of income shortfall of the poor such that the total weight over the distribution of the poor adds up to H. In the derivation of the proposed variant S_{R1}, the total weight does add up to H. In contrast, in the Thon–Shorrocks poverty measure derivation, the total weight adds up to $H(2 - H)$. That means their measure violates the fundamental Axiom 7.5. Consequently, their measure also violates Sen's normalization Axiom 7.3.

Table 7.1 Effect of transfer on poverty

Variable	Before transfer	After transfer	Change
z	2.1	2.1	0
H	0.67	0.33	−0.33
μ_z	1.50	0.80	−0.70
G_z	0.17	0.00	−0.17
S_R	0.27	0.21	−0.06
S_{R1}	0.23	0.21	−0.02
S_{R2}	0.31	0.34	0.04
S_{R3}	0.14	0.17	0.03

Poverty measures are crucial in formulating policies to reduce or alleviate poverty, so they must have meaningful social welfare implications. However, the most severe criticism of the Thon–Shorrocks measure is that they do not have a meaningful implicit poverty social welfare function. Their social welfare function is given by

$$W\left(S_{R2}\right) = \mu - z \int_0^z \frac{z-x}{z} v_2\left(z,x\right) f\left(x\right) dx \qquad (7.8.1)$$

where the second term in this equation must measure the average deprivation suffered by society due to poverty. This term is not a weighted average but is a weighted sum. As such, $W\left(S_{R2}\right)$ is not considered as a legitimate social welfare function.

Both Sen's poverty measure and the proposed new variant S_{R1} satisfy the weak transfer axiom, have a meaningful social welfare function, and satisfy Axioms 7.1, 7.3, 7.5, and 7.6.

7.9 Monotonicity and Transfer-Sensitivity Axioms

Kakwani (1980b) proposed three sensitivity axioms, which attracted much attention in poverty measurement (Foster, Greer, and Thorbecke 1984). He introduced these axioms as an extension of Sen's monotonicity and transfer Axioms 7.1 and 7.2.

Axiom 7.10 (Monotonicity-Sensitivity) *Suppose a poor person with income x suffers a reduction in income by a small amount d, without affecting the ranking of individuals, then the change in poverty denoted by $(\Delta\theta)_x$ must decrease as x increases.*

This axiom implies that the poorer the individual, the larger the increase in poverty due to reduced income. If a poor person's income is reduced, the overall deprivation

increases (monotonicity axiom). According to this axiom, the increase in total deprivation should be higher if the same amount of income is taken away from a still more
destitute individual.

Axiom 7.11 (Transfer-Sensitivity I) *Assume that a small amount d of income is
transferred from a poor person with income x to a richer person y such that* $F(y) =
F(x) + \rho(y) = F(x) + \rho$, *where ρ is the proportion of persons between incomes
x and y, then increase in poverty due to transfer denoted by* $(\Delta\theta)_{x,y}$ *must decrease
as x increases.*

This axiom implies that the poverty measure's sensitivity to income transfers depends
on the transferrer's position in ordering the poor when the number of positions between the transfer recipient is fixed. The poorer the transferrer, the higher the increase
in the poverty measure should be. Sen's measure gives equal weight to income transfers at different income positions; the impact of a small transfer from a person with
income, say, x_i to x_{i+1} is the same for all x. This neutral position may not be desirable if
the poverty measure is based on the concept of relative deprivation. Thus, his measure
violates transfer-sensitivity Axiom 7.7.

Axiom 7.12 (Transfer-Sensitivity II) *If a transfer of income takes place from a poor
person with income x to another poor with income (x + h), then for a given h > 0,
the magnitude of the increase in poverty measure decreases as x increases.*

This axiom gives higher weight to income transfers at the lower end of the distribution than at the higher end. Under this axiom, it is the income difference and not the
number of income positions that are fixed between the transferrer and the transfer
recipient. Sen's measure also violates this axiom.

There is a considerable discussion of this axiom in the literature on income inequality (see Atkinson (1970) and Sen (1973)). Chapter 5 provided in-depth discussion of
this axiom. The same argument applies to poverty measurement. Suppose society is
particularly averse to inequality among the poor. In that case, the poverty measure
must give maximum weight to a transfer from the poorest person, and the weight
should decrease with the income level. Suppose the poverty line is less than the mode
of the income distribution. In that case, Sen's measure implies precisely the opposite weighting system—that is, it gives the least weight to a transfer from the poorest
person, and the weight increases with the level of income. Kakwani (1980a) argues
that such a weighting system is incongruent with existing social values. The following
section derives a class of poverty measures proposed by Kakwani, including all three
possible weighting systems: increasing, decreasing, and constant (or neutral). The
choice of a particular member should then depend on the preference for alternative
weighting schemes.

7.10 A General Class of Poverty Measures

Sen's (1976) measure presented in (7.3.4) violates the three sensitivity Axioms 7.6–7.8. This section offers a generalization of Sen's poverty measure that satisfies these three sensitivity axioms. As argued earlier, the poverty measures must attach positive weights to the poor (who have income less than or equal to the poverty line) and zero weight to the non-poor (who have income above the poverty line) (Sen's focus in Axiom 7.5). Thus, a general class of relative poverty measures is introduced using this weighting:

$$\theta_S = \int_0^z \frac{z-x}{z} v\left[H, F\left(x\right)\right] f\left(x\right) dx, \qquad (7.10.1)$$

such that

$$\int_0^z v\left[H,\ F\left(x\right)\right] f\left(x\right) dx = H \qquad (7.10.2)$$

Note that the weight function $v[H, F(x)]$ depends on individuals' ranking, capturing individuals' relative deprivation. The weight must be maximum for a person with a minimum income in society, which is assumed to be zero, and the weight must become zero when the person has income equal to the poverty line. Since the relative deprivation must decrease as a person's income increases, the weight must decrease monotonically as income increases. Thus, the weight function must have the following requirements:

$$v\left[H, F\left(x\right)\right] > 0 \ \text{if} \ x < z \qquad (7.10.3)$$

$$v\left[H, F\left(x\right)\right] = 0 \ \text{if} \ x \geq z$$

$$v\left[H, F\left(x\right)\right] = v\left[H, 0\right] = v(H) \ \text{if} \ x = 0,$$

$$\frac{\partial[v(H), F\left(x\right)]}{\partial F\left(x\right)} < 0$$

where $v\left(H\right)$ is the maximum weight given to the person with zero income.

Suppose a poor person with income x suffers a reduction in income by a small amount d, without affecting the ranking of individuals, then the change in poverty measure in (7.10.1) will be given by

$$(\Delta\theta_R)_{dx} = dv[H, F(x)]/z, \tag{7.10.4}$$

which implies that poverty will always increase if $d>0$, and $v[H, F(x)] > 0$. Thus, the class of poverty measures will always satisfy Sen's monotonicity axiom. Since the increase in poverty depends on the magnitude of $v[H, F(x)]$, it implies that $\dfrac{\partial[v(H,F(x))]}{\partial F(x)}$ < 0; the magnitude of the increase in poverty will decrease monotonically as x increases. Thus, the poverty measure θ_R will satisfy the monotonicity-sensitivity Axiom 7.10.

Suppose that a small amount d of income is transferred from a poor person with income x to a richer person y, with no change in rankings

$$d\theta_{dR} = \frac{\partial\theta_R}{\partial x}(-d) + \frac{\partial\theta_R}{\partial y}(d),$$

which from (7.10.1) becomes

$$d\theta_{dR} = \frac{d}{z}\left[v(H, F(x)) - v(H, F(y))\right]. \tag{7.10.5}$$

Since $v(H, F(x))> v(H, F(y))$ for $x<y$ if $\dfrac{\partial[v(H,F(x))]}{\partial F(x)} < 0$, the right-hand side of (7.10.5) will always be positive for $d>0$. Thus, the general class of poverty measures (7.11.1) will always satisfy Sen's weak transfer Axiom 7.3.

Suppose $(y) = F(x) + \rho$ and ρ is the proportion of persons between incomes x and y, then increase in poverty measure θ_{dR} due to transfer is given by

$$T_d(x) = \frac{d}{z}\left[v[H, F(x)] - v[H, F(x) + \rho]\right] \tag{7.10.6}$$

Then the transfer-sensitivity Axiom 7.7 will be satisfied if $T_d(x)$ decreases with x.

Under Axiom 7.12, it is the income difference and not the number of fixed income positions between the transferer and the transfer recipient; hence, $F(y)=F(x+d)$. Thus, Axiom 7.12 will be satisfied if

$$T_d^*(x) = \frac{d}{z}[v(H, F(x)) - v(H, F(x + d))] \tag{7.10.7}$$

decreases with x.

7.11 Particular Cases of the General Class of Poverty Measures

The following cases are considered to operationalize the general class of poverty measures (7.11.1).

7.11.1 Kakwani's k Class of Poverty Measures

Kakwani (1980b) proposed a class of poverty measures, motivated by Sen's poverty measure's failure to satisfy transfer-sensitivity axioms. This class of measures is a particular case of the poverty measures in (7.10.1):

$$\theta_k = (k+1) \int_0^z \left(\frac{z-x}{z} \right) \left[\frac{H - F(x)}{H} \right]^k f(x)\, dx \qquad (7.11.1)$$

and weights in these measures satisfy all the requirements in (7.10.3) for $k \geq 0$. Hence, these measures meet Sen's monotonicity Axioms 7.1 for all values of $k \geq 0$. Substituting $k=1$ in θ_k of (7.11.1) leads to Sen's relative poverty measure S_R in equation (7.5.5). If $k = 0$, θ_k reduces to the poverty gap ratio P_R, which is a suitable measure of poverty in the particular case when all poor have the same income. Since the weights in (7.11.1) satisfy restrictions in (7.10.3), the entire k class poverty measures will satisfy the monotonicity-sensitivity Axiom 7.10.

Next, consider the possible values of k for which the transfer-sensitivity axioms are satisfied. For this purpose, we write $T_d(x)$ in (7.10.6) as

$$T_{dk}(x) = \frac{d(k+1)}{z} \left[\left(\frac{H - F(x)}{H} \right)^k - \left(\frac{H - F(x) - \rho}{H} \right)^k \right], \qquad (7.11.2)$$

which on differentiating with respect to $F(x)$ yields

$$\frac{\partial T(x)}{\partial F(x)} = -\frac{dk(k+1)}{zH^k} \left[(H - F(x))^{k-1} - (H - F(x) - \rho)^{k-1} \right] \qquad (7.11.3)$$

Then it can be seen that $\frac{\partial T(x)}{\partial F(x)} < 0$ only for $k>1$, which proves that $T_{dk}(x)$ decreases with $F(x)$ only for $k>1$. Thus, the poverty measures θ_k satisfy the transfer-sensitivity I Axiom 7.11 for $k>1$. Further, note that $\frac{\partial T_k(x)}{\partial F(x)} = 0$ when $k=1$, which demonstrates that Sen's measure violates the transfer-sensitivity axiom.

Next, consider the transfer-sensitivity II Axiom 7.12, which assumes that the income difference between the transferer and the transfer recipient is fixed. For this purpose, write $T^*_{dk}(x)$ obtained from (7.10.7) as

$$T^*_{dk}(x) = \frac{d(k+1)}{z} \left[\left(\frac{H - F(x)}{H} \right)^k - \left(\frac{H - F(x+d)}{H} \right)^k \right], \qquad (7.11.4)$$

which for $k=1$ becomes

$$T^*_{k=1}(x) = \frac{2d}{zH} \left[F(x+d) - F(x) \right], \qquad (7.11.5)$$

which demonstrates that $T^*_{k=1}$ increases with x until it reaches the mode and then decreases as x increases. If the poverty line is less than the mode, which is a likely scenario, it implies that Sen's measure gives the least weight to a transfer from the worse-off poor, and the weight increases with the level of income.

The transfer-sensitivity II will be satisfied if $T^*_{dk}(x)$ in (7.11.4) decreases monotonically as $F(x)$ increases. Even for $k > 1$, the transfer-sensitivity II Axiom 7.12 may not be satisfied. The question arises whether there exists a value (or values) of k for which this axiom is always satisfied. The answer, fortunately, is affirmative, as Kakwani (1980b) has argued. The term in the square bracket of (7.11.4) can be made a decreasing function of k for all $F(x)$ by choosing k sufficiently larger than unity. Thus, both the transfer-sensitivity axioms will be satisfied for a value of k sufficiently larger than one. It can also be shown that the larger the value of k, the higher the weight function's concavity, implying that as k increases, the poverty measure gives greater importance to the more impoverished individuals. It is suggested to choose the value of k greater than 2.

7.11.2 Bonferroni Poverty Measure

Chapter 5 discussed the Bonferroni inequality measure based on a logarithmic weight function. This section proposes a new poverty measure based on a logarithmic weighting called the Bonferroni poverty measure. The poverty literature has not discussed this measure. It is derived from the general class of poverty measures given in (7.10.1) as

$$\theta_B = \int_0^z \frac{z-x}{z} \left[ln\,(H) - ln\,(F\,(x)) \right] f(x)\, dx \qquad (7.11.6)$$

It is easy to show that

$$\int_0^z \left[ln\,(H) - ln\,(F\,(x)) \right] f(x)\, dx = H.$$

When all poor have the same income, θ_B reduces to the poverty gap ratio P_R, and satisfies Sen's normalization Axioms 7.3 and Axioms 7.5 and 7.6. The weight function implicit in this measure satisfies all the requirements given in (7.10.3). Hence, the Bonferroni poverty measure satisfies the monotonicity-sensitive Axiom 7.10.

Next, explore whether the Bonferroni poverty measure satisfies the transfer-sensitivity axioms. So, write $T_d(x)$ in (7.11.6) as

$$T_{dB}(x) = \frac{d}{z} \left[ln\,(F\,(x) + \rho) - ln\,(F\,(x)) \right], \qquad (7.11.7)$$

which on differentiating with respect to $F(x)$ yields

$$\frac{\partial T(x)}{\partial F(x)} = -\frac{d}{z}\left[\frac{\rho}{F(x)(F(x)+\rho)}\right], \qquad (7.11.8)$$

which is negative for all $\rho > 0$.

This demonstrates that the Bonferroni poverty measure satisfies transfer-sensitivity I Axiom 7.11, noting that Sen's measure violates the axiom.

Next, consider transfer-sensitivity Axiom 7.12. For this purpose, write $T^*_{dB}(x)$ obtained from (7.11.7) as

$$T^*_{dB}(x) = \frac{d}{z}\left[ln\left(F(x+d)\right) - ln\left(F(x)\right)\right] \qquad (7.11.9)$$

The Bonferroni poverty measure will satisfy the transfer-sensitivity II Axiom 7.12 if $T^*_B(x)$ decreases monotonically as $F(x)$ increases. The monotonicity of this relationship cannot be established so that the Bonferroni poverty measure can violate Axiom 7.12. The weight function of the Bonferroni measure decreases monotonically with x and is strictly concave. While Sen's measure also decreases monotonically with x but is not strictly concave, it decreases linearly. From this property, it can be concluded that the Bonferroni poverty measure is superior to Sen's because it gives greater importance to the more impoverished individuals.

7.12 Utilitarian Social Welfare Functions

The poverty measures discussed in the previous sections are based on interdependent social welfare functions, whereby the welfare of an individual depends not only on her income but also on the income of others in society. These welfare functions capture the idea of relative deprivation by making weights to rely on the ranking of the poor.

Since the groundbreaking paper by Foster, Greer, and Thorbecke (1984), the interdependent social welfare function, capturing the poor's relative deprivation, came under severe criticism. The focus shifted to utilitarian social welfare functions, which are the sum of the individual utility functions of their respective incomes. Each individual has the same utility function, which is increasing and concave. The utilitarian social welfare framework is highly restrictive but has attracted much attention in the poverty literature.

The poverty measures under the utilitarian framework are defined as the sum of disutilities arising from being poor. Suppose $u(x)$ is the utility function, which is increasing in x, then among the poor individuals, $u(x)<u(z)$ when $x<z$. In the construction of poverty measures, the poor get a positive weight, and the non-poor get

zero weight. Based on this weighting criterion, therefore, a utilitarian social welfare function is defined as

$$W(\tilde{x}) = \int_0^z u(x) f(x) dx \qquad (7.12.1)$$

If persons have income $x \geq z$, they do not suffer any loss of utility due to poverty. If their income is less than the poverty line, $x<z$, they suffer a loss of utility $u(z) - u(x)$. The proportional loss of utility due to poverty suffered by a person with income x is characterized by

$$\begin{aligned} D(z,x) \quad &= \frac{u(z)-u(x)}{u(z)} > 0 \quad if\, x < z \\ &= 0 \qquad\qquad\qquad if\, x \geq z \end{aligned} \qquad (7.12.2)$$

The average proportional utility loss suffered by society is then given by

$$\theta_R = \int_0^z D(z,x) f(x) dx = \frac{\int_0^z [u(z) - u(x)] f(x) dx}{u(z)}, \qquad (7.12.3)$$

which may be referred to as a general class of utilitarian poverty measures. This class of poverty measures reflects the average proportional loss of utility suffered by society due to poverty.

If the utility function is homogeneous, that is, $u(\lambda x) = \lambda^\varepsilon u(x)$ for all δ_ε, then θ_R remains unchanged when the poverty line and income are increased or decreased by the same proportion. This homogeneity condition ensures that θ_R are the relative poverty measures.

Note that the class of utilitarian poverty measures θ_R is new in the literature. Hagenaars (1987) derived it using Dalton's (1920) inequality measure on censored income distribution. He also proved that this measure satisfies both monotonicity and transfer axioms if the utility function increases and is concave. Furthermore, if the utility function is strictly concave, this class of measures will also satisfy transfer-sensitivity axioms presented in the previous section.

If all the poor have the same income equal to the mean income μ_z,

$$\theta_R = H\frac{u(z) - u(\mu_z)}{u(z)},$$

which is equal to the poverty gap ratio P_R defined in (7.3.4) only if $u(x) = \lambda x$ for $\lambda \neq 0$. Thus, in general, θ_R measures will not satisfy Sen's normalization Axiom 7.3. If it is assumed that $u(x)$ approaches 0 as x approaches 0, and all the poor have zero income, θ_R will approach H. Thus, θ_R will satisfy both the weak relative normalization

I and II Axioms 7.5 and 7.6, respectively, if the utility function $u(x)$ approaches 0 as x approaches 0.

7.13 Particular Cases of the General Utilitarian Poverty Measures

It is essential to specify the utility function to operationalize the general class of utilitarian poverty measures (7.12.3). The literature has developed numerous additive separable poverty measures, and Hagenaars (1987) demonstrated that most of them are particular cases of the general utilitarian poverty measures. These measures have found many empirical applications. If the underlying utility function of these measures is increasing and strictly concave, then all the separable additive measures will satisfy monotonicity and transfer axioms. The strict concavity also ensures that these measures satisfy both monotonicity and transfer-sensitivity axioms.

7.13.1 Watts Poverty Index

Watts proposed his poverty index in 1968, much earlier than Sen's (1976) groundbreaking paper on poverty measurement. Although this index was distribution-sensitive, as emphasized by Sen, the poverty literature somehow neglected it. The main reason was that Watts' paper was not published in any mainstream journal. The literature began to realize the usefulness of the index when Zheng (1993) provided an axiomatic characterization of the index.

The index proposed by Watts (1968) is given by

$$\theta_w = \int_0^z \left[ln\left(z \right) - ln\left(x \right) \right] f(x)\, dx \tag{7.13.1}$$

It is easy to verify that the utility function given by

$$u\left(x \right) = 1 + ln\left(x \right) - ln\left(z \right), \tag{7.13.2}$$

on substituting in (7.12.3) yields the Watts poverty measure.

Note that the utility function $u(x)$ in (7.13.2) is increasing with income and is strictly concave. Thus, the Watts measure satisfies both monotonicity and transfer axioms.

Watts poverty measure has recently become popular. However, it has two undesirable features. First, it does not satisfy Sen's normalization of Axiom 7.3. Second, it cannot be defined when any poor person has zero income. Consequently, it violates the weak relative normalization Axioms 7.5 and 7.6.

7.13.2 Foster, Greer, and Thorbecke (FGT) Poverty Measures

Foster, Greer, and Thorbecke (1984) proposed a class of poverty measures that are additively decomposable. These measures are given by

$$\theta_\alpha = \int_0^z \left(\frac{z-x}{z}\right)^\alpha f(x)\, dx \qquad (7.13.3)$$

These poverty measures have become most popular among poverty analysts. They are popularly known as FGT poverty measures. The parameter of these measures is a measure of poverty aversion. A larger α gives greater weight given to the more impoverished poor. When $\alpha = 0$, $\theta_\alpha = H$, the head-count ratio. When $\alpha = 1$, $\theta_\alpha = P_R$, the poverty gap ratio defined in (7.3.4). When $\alpha = 2$, this measure is popularly known as the severity of poverty.

The utility function that leads to the FGT measures is given by

$$u(x) = z^\alpha - (z-x)^\alpha \qquad (7.13.4)$$

It is easy to show that $u(x)$ increases with x when $\alpha > 0$ and is strictly concave when $\alpha > 1$. Thus, both monotonicity and transfer axioms will be satisfied when $\alpha > 1$. When all the poor have the same income μ_z, $\theta_\alpha = \left(\frac{z - \mu_z}{z}\right)^\alpha$, which is equal to the poverty gap ratio P_R only if $\alpha = 1$. Thus, the FGT measures, in general, do not satisfy the normalization Axiom 7.3. However, when all the poor have zero income, $\theta_\alpha = H$. Thus, the FGT measures satisfy the weak normalization Axiom 7.5. When all persons in society have zero income, the FGT measures equal 1, thus satisfying the normalization Axiom 7.6.

7.13.3 Chakravarty Index

Chakravarty (1983b) proposed the following poverty index:

$$\theta_C = \int_0^z \left[\frac{z^e - x^e}{z^e}\right] f(x)\, dx \qquad (7.13.5)$$

The utility function that leads the Chakravarty index is given by

$$u(x) = x^e, \qquad (7.13.6)$$

which is an increasing function of x when $e>0$ and is strictly concave when $e<1$. Thus, the Chakravarty index satisfies both monotonicity and transfer axioms. When all the poor have the same income μ_z, $\theta_C = H\left(\frac{z^e - \mu_z^e}{\mu_z^e}\right)$, which is equal to the poverty gap ratio P_R only if $e = 1$. Thus, the Chakravarty measures generally do not satisfy the normalization Axiom 7.3. However, when all the poor have zero income, $\theta_C = H$. Thus, the Chakravarty measures satisfy the weak normalization Axiom 7.5. If all persons in society have zero income, $\theta_C = 1$, thus satisfying the weak normalization Axiom 7.6.

7.13.4 Atkinson's Index

Atkinson's (1987) index is very similar to the Chakravarty index (except divided by a constant β) and is given by

$$\theta_A = \frac{1}{\beta} \int_0^z \left[\frac{z^\beta - x^\beta}{z^\beta}\right] f(x) \, dx, \tag{7.13.7}$$

which is the same class of poverty measures proposed by Clark, Hemming, and Ulph (1981).

As β approaches zero, θ_A approaches the Watts index given in (7.12.1). The utility function that leads to the Atkinson index is given by

$$u(x) = (\beta - 1) + \frac{x^\beta}{z^\beta}, \tag{7.13.8}$$

which is an increasing function of x if $\beta > 0$ and is strictly concave when $\beta < 1$. Thus, Atkinson's poverty index satisfies both monotonicity and transfer axioms. It is easy to show that Atkinson's measures satisfy the normalization Axiom 7.3 only when $\beta = 1$. Also, they satisfy the weak normalization Axioms 7.5 and 7.6 only when $\beta = 1$.

7.14 Total Social Cost of Poverty (TSCP) for Utilitarian Social Welfare Functions

As pointed out, poverty must incur social costs to society (SCP). Policymakers readily understand such costs if they are presented in monetary units. The general utilitarian poverty measures θ_R in (7.12.3) capture society's average proportional utility loss due to poverty. Utility is an abstract concept, so it will help transform the utility loss into the SCP in monetary units, providing policymakers with a better understanding of the adverse impact of poverty on society.

This section provides a methodology to measure the SCP monetary units for utilitarian poverty measures. These costs are derived using the idea of an "equally distributed equivalent poverty gap," introduced by Clark, Hemming, and Ulph (1981). This section extends their approach to "equally distributed equivalent utility loss due to poverty."

The utilitarian social welfare framework provides the per-person social utility loss (SUL) due to poverty given by

$$(SUL) = \int_0^z [u(z) - u(x)]f(x)\, dx \tag{7.14.1}$$

$u(z) - u(x)$ is the utility loss of the poor person with income x. (SUL) will be zero when the poor's incomes are raised to the poverty line. Suppose $g^* = (z - x^*)$ that the equally distributed utility loss, if shared by all the poor, would yield the same (SUL) as the existing distribution (7.12.1). Hence, g^* is determined by

$$H[u(z) - u(x^*)] = \int_0^z [u(z) - u(x)]f(x)\, dx \tag{7.14.2}$$

Since only the poor suffer utility loss, the (TSCP) will be given by

$$(TSCP) = NH(z - x^*) \tag{7.14.3}$$

where N is the total population. The (TSCP) is measured in monetary units such as millions or billions of dollars. The (TSCP) depends on the utility function that a society chooses.

The utility function in (7.14.2) yields the Watts measure of poverty, which on substituting in (7.14.2) and utilizing (7.14.3) gives

$$(TSCP)_W = NHz\left[1 - e^{-\frac{\theta_W}{H}}\right] \tag{7.14.4}$$

Next, the utility function in (7.13.4) yields FGT poverty measures, which on substituting in (7.14.3) yields

$$(TSCP)_\alpha = NzH^{\frac{(\alpha-1)}{\alpha}}(\theta_\alpha)^{\frac{1}{\alpha}}, \ \alpha \neq 0 \tag{7.14.5}$$

when $\alpha = 1$, $\theta_\alpha = P_R$, the poverty gap ratio, which gives $(SCP) = NzP_R$. When $\alpha = 2$, $(TSCP) = Nz\sqrt{H}\sqrt{\theta_2}$, where θ_2 measures the severity of poverty. Since Sen's class of poverty measures θ_R in (7.9.1) are linear in income, it is easy to show that $(TSCP) = NzS_R$.

The utility function in (7.13.6) yields the Chakravarty index in (7.14.5), which on using in (7.14.2) yields the (TSCP) as

$$(TSCP)_C = NHz[1 - \{1 - \frac{\theta_c}{H}\}^{\frac{1}{e}}]. \tag{7.14.6}$$

If $e=1$, the $(TSCP)_C$ reduces to NzP_R.

Finally, The utility function in (7.13.8) yields Atkinson's (1987) index in (7.13.7), which on substituting in (7.13.2) yields the $(TSCP)$ for the Atkinson index as

$$(TSCP)_A = NH\left[1 - \left\{1 - \frac{\theta_a}{H}\right\}^{\frac{1}{\beta}}\right]. \tag{7.14.7}$$

The $(TSCP)$ derived here depends on the poverty index that society has chosen to formulate its poverty alleviation policies. Section 7.16 will present the empirical estimates of $(TSCP)$ for different poverty measures using the Chinese household survey.

7.15 Decomposable Poverty Indices and Subgroup Consistency

Suppose that the population is divided into m subgroups according to ethnic, socio-economic, and demographic characteristics. It would be of much interest to policy-makers to know how poverty is related to poverty in various subgroups. How much is the contribution of each subgroup to total poverty? This information is helpful in the formulation of national poverty alleviation policies. In this regard, Foster, Greer, and Thorbecke (1984) proposed the idea of additively decomposable poverty measures. According to this idea, total poverty should be a weighted average of poverty levels of subgroups with weights proportional to their population shares. Suppose $f_j(x)$ is the density function of the jth subgroup. The probability density function of the entire population can then be written as

$$f(x) = \sum_{j=1}^{m} a_j f_j(x) \tag{7.15.1}$$

a_j is the proportion of individuals in the jth group such that $\sum_{j}^{m} a_j = 1$, i.e., all subgroups are mutually exclusive.

Assuming that poverty line z is the same for each subgroup,[5] then the class of utilitarian poverty measures for the jth subgroup can be written as

$$\theta_{jR} = \int_{0}^{z} D(z,x) f_j(x)\, dx = \frac{\int_{0}^{z} [u(z) - u(x)] f_j(x)\, dx}{u(z)} \tag{7.15.2}$$

Using (7.15.1) into (7.12.3), and utilizing (7.15.2) yields the poverty decomposition:

$$\theta_R = \sum_{j=1}^{m} a_j \theta_{jR} \tag{7.15.3}$$

---

[5] Note that the nominal poverty line will be different for different regions because of differences in their cost of living. The real poverty line adjusted for costs of living will be the same. The costs of living adjustment is done by spatial price indices constructed for different regions.

The decomposition in (7.15.3) implies that total poverty is a weighted average of the poverty levels of subgroups, with weights proportional to their population shares. The poverty measures that satisfy equation (7.15.3) are called "additively decomposable." It has been demonstrated that the entire class of utilitarian poverty measures is additively decomposable.

The additively decomposable poverty measures enable us to assess the contributions of subgroup poverty to total poverty. As Sen (1992) points out, human beings are diverse in terms of their characteristics, and they differ by age, gender, education, occupation, and ethnicity, among other characteristics. Given these differences, every society consists of social groups that suffer from different degrees of poverty. Identifying such groups is essential and especially useful in formulating poverty alleviation policies. Therefore, it is not surprising that poverty decomposition has become a vital tool for poverty reduction strategies.

The additively decomposable poverty measures have a property that the overall poverty level falls if a subgroup experiences a poverty reduction, while the population shares and poverty in the rest of subgroups remain unchanged. This property led Foster and Shorrocks (1991) to propose the idea of subgroup consistent poverty indices. They viewed subgroup consistency as an essential counterpart to a coherent poverty program. Furthermore, they argued that if a poverty indicator is not subgroup consistent, it faces an undesirable situation. For example, suppose a government has achieved a reduction in poverty in one targeted group; if a poverty measure is not subgroup consistent, it may lead to a situation where poverty in the country has increased when poverty and population shares of other groups have not changed. This is an unintended consequence of a poverty program.

Foster and Shorrocks (1991) have asserted that Sen's measure violates subgroup consistency. They demonstrate this by a hypothetical example. Thus, it will be instructive to discuss their example.

Consider a country with two regions with identical income distributions (1, 9, 9, 9, 20). When the poverty line is set at 10, Sen's index gives a poverty level of 0.36. If the income distribution in region 1 is changed to (5, 9, 9, 9, 20), then region 1's poverty level falls to 0.35. Finally, when the distributions of the two regions are merged, it gives the overall poverty level of 0.365. Thus, Sen's poverty measure shows that poverty in region 1 has declined and has no change in region 2, yet total poverty has increased. Therefore, Sen's measure violates subgroup consistency. Furthermore, it can be shown that the generalized Sen index presented in (7.9.1) also violates the subgroup consistency.

The subgroup consistency property is intuitively appealing, and if it is violated, it has undesirable policy implications. The class of utilitarian poverty measures is additively decomposable and is subgroup consistent. Should Sen's poverty measure and its generalizations be abandoned in favor of utilitarian poverty measures? A vital attribute of Sen's measure is that it captures the sense of "relative deprivation," which Sen considers an essential feature of poverty. Sen (2006) does not think decomposability is necessary or, at most minuscule, a desirable characteristic of indicators to be chosen to reflect poverty. This chapter, however, views decomposability and subgroup consistency as essential attributes of poverty that must be employed in analyzing policies. The poverty literature has wrongly asserted that Sen's poverty measure and its generalizations are not decomposable and violate subgroup consistency.

The following section demonstrates that Sen's entire class of generalized poverty measures are decomposable and subgroup consistent, of which Sen's poverty measure is a particular case.

7.16 Decomposability of Sen's Generalized Poverty Measures

Sen's class of generalized poverty measures given in (7.10.1) is rewritten as

$$\theta_S = \int_0^z \frac{z-x}{z} v\left[H, F\left(x\right)\right] f\left(x\right) dx \tag{7.16.1}$$

where

$$\int_0^z v\left[H, F\left(x\right)\right] f\left(x\right) dx = H.$$

Assuming that poverty line z is the same for each subgroup, and if $f_j\left(x\right)$ is the probability density function of the jth subgroup, then θ_{Sj} for the jth group will be given by

$$\theta_{Sj} = \int_0^z \frac{z-x}{z} v\left[H, F\left(x\right)\right] f_j\left(x\right) dx \tag{7.16.2}$$

Since the social welfare function implicit in Sen's generalizations is interdependent, individuals in the jth subgroup compare their economic situation with individuals in all subgroups in the population.

Substituting (7.15.1) into (7.16.1), and utilizing (7.16.2) yields

$$\theta_S = \sum_0^z a_j \theta_{Sj}, \tag{7.16.3}$$

which demonstrates that the total poverty is a weighted average of the poverty levels of the subgroups, with weights proportional to their population shares. Thus, the entire class of Sen's generalized poverty measures is additively decomposable, implying subgroup consistency. Since Sen's poverty measure is a particular class, it will also be additively decomposable and subgroup consistent.

The utilitarian poverty measures are additively separable and, therefore, one can easily understand their decomposability. The implicit social welfare functions are independent in these measures, so subgroups are also independent. In the generalized Sen measures, the implicit social welfare functions are interdependent, so the subgroups cannot be assumed to be independent. Foster and Shorrocks (1991) measure the subgroup poverty of Sen's poverty measure by considering that the subgroups are independent, which they are not. They define the poverty of the jth group as

$$\theta_{Sj}^* = \int_0^z \frac{z-x}{z} v\left[H_j, F_j(x)\right] f_j(x) \, dx, \qquad (7.16.4)$$

which is not the correct measure of the jth subgroup poverty because the poor are comparing their income only within their group, ignoring the other subgroups in the population. θ_{Sj} in (7.16.2) is the correct measure of the jth subgroup poverty, taking into account the interdependence of social welfare implicit in Sen's poverty measure. This fallacy led Foster and Shorrocks (1991) to conclude that Sen's poverty measure is not subgroup consistent.

The hypothetical example of two subregions provided by Foster and Shorrocks (1991) can be revisited. Their hypothetical example demonstrated that Sen's index showed decreased poverty in region 1, but no change in poverty in region 2, but the total poverty increased. Hence, they concluded that Sen's poverty measure violates the subgroup consistency requirement. Their conclusion is unfounded because they calculated Sen's poverty measure using equation (7.16.4), which assumes that the social welfare function in region 1 is independent of that in region 2. The correct method to estimate Sen's measure for each region would be to use equation (7.16.2), which considers the interdependence of the two regions. Using this correct method, Sen's index for regions 1 and 2 equals 0.345 and 0.385, respectively. This implies that if the distribution in region 1 is changed and there is no change in region 2, poverty will still change in both regions. The decomposition of Sen's measure in (7.16.3) shows that the total poverty has increased because the increase in poverty in region 2 has more than offset the reduction in poverty in region 1. Thus, Sen's poverty measure does not violate subgroup consistency.

7.17 Application to China, 1988–2018

Chapter 5 presented the trends in income inequality in China. This section analyzes the trends in poverty in China. It utilizes the six rounds of Chinese Household Income Project (CHIP) surveys covering 1988–2018. Per capita household income derived from the surveys has been adjusted for spatial prices across urban and rural areas and provinces. Further, the incomes of all households have been adjusted to take account of inflation over time. Thus, the per capita household incomes are measured in the 2013 Beijing prices and are comparable across the country and over time. In China, the official poverty line was 2,736 yuan per person per year in 2013 Beijing prices, used for all years between 1988 and 2018.

Table 7.2 presents the estimates of poverty and the total social cost of poverty (TSCP). The last column in the table shows the trend growth rates for 1988–2018. The population in China increased at an annual growth rate of 0.82%. Compared

Table 7.2 Social cost of poverty in China, 1988–2018

	1988	1995	2002	2007	2013	2018	Trend growth
Poverty estimates (Percent)							
Population (billion)	1.10	1.20	1.27	1.30	1.35	1.37	0.82
Per capita real income	2,732	4,304	5,480	11,074	17,144	20,108	7.08
Percentage of poor	61.82	35.40	26.78	7.77	4.21	3.08	−10.44
Poverty gap ratio	23.45	12.01	8.98	2.07	1.31	1.15	−11.36
Severity of poverty	11.63	5.73	4.28	0.83	0.63	0.65	−11.60
Watts measure	34.04	17.29	12.95	2.77	1.99	2.01	−11.22
Sen's measure	37.01	21.32	16.44	4.03	2.59	2.27	−10.40
Social cost of poverty							
Poverty gap ratio	706.28	393.60	313.07	73.31	48.37	43.03	−10.54
Severity of poverty	807.34	466.55	373.22	90.40	60.14	53.25	−10.20
Watts measure	788.27	448.26	358.07	82.69	58.54	55.36	−10.25
Sen's measure	1,114.57	698.44	573.28	143.22	95.54	85.28	−9.58

with many other countries in the world, the population growth in China has been the slowest. However, China has achieved an impressive growth rate of per capita real income at an annual rate of 7.08%. All poverty measures presented in the table show an outstanding performance in poverty reduction. The incidence of poverty declined on average at an annual rate of almost 11%.

Poverty incurs a social cost, measured in billions of yuan per year. Its value depends on what poverty measure is used. For instance, the poverty gap ratio had a social cost of 706 billion yuan per year in 1988. In contrast, Sen's poverty measure had a much higher cost of 1,114 billion yuan. The social cost had been declining at an average rate of around 10.5%. The lower rate of decline of social cost is attributed to a much slower population growth rate.

The empirical estimates of the SCP presented here provide some policy insight into how much the Chinese government should spend on alleviating or reducing poverty to offset poverty's social cost.

The Chinese government had been much concerned about the extreme gap in urban and rural China's living standards. The poverty decomposition discussed in the previous section will help calculate the contributions of urban and rural areas to the poverty in China. As pointed out, Sen's poverty measures had been subjected to immense criticism because they were not decomposable. Many writers wrongly criticized this because they did not realize that the calculation of subgroup poverty must consider the interdependence of social welfare function implicit in Sen's poverty

Table 7.3 Poverty measures and their shares of urban and rural areas in China, 1988–2018

	1988	1995	2002	2007	2013	2018	Trends growth
Rural China							
Population (billion)	0.88	0.85	0.81	0.70	0.62	0.54	−1.38
Per capita income	2,295	3,489	4,030	6,831	10,807	11,822	5.79
Percent of poor	74.18	47.26	39.19	13.73	8.13	7.11	−8.40
Poverty gap ratio (Percent)	28.66	16.37	13.44	3.65	2.57	2.68	−9.36
Severity of poverty (Percent)	14.30	7.87	6.47	1.47	1.23	1.54	−9.61
Watts measure (Percent)	41.68	23.63	19.48	4.89	3.83	4.74	−9.22
Sen's measure (Percent)	45.39	29.11	24.66	7.14	5.08	5.30	−8.41
Shares (Percent)							
Population	80.02	70.81	63.36	54.19	45.71	39.55	−2.20
Per capita income	67.24	57.40	46.59	33.42	28.81	23.25	−3.49
Percent of poor	96.03	94.53	92.72	95.78	88.19	91.32	−0.16
Poverty gap ratio	97.78	96.48	94.88	95.85	89.63	92.30	−0.20
Severity of poverty	98.39	97.30	95.88	95.50	88.86	93.38	−0.22
Watts measure	97.96	96.74	95.30	95.66	87.97	93.48	−0.21
Sen's measure	98.13	96.69	95.06	95.84	89.63	92.32	−0.21
Urban China							
Population (billion)	0.22	0.35	0.47	0.59	0.73	0.83	4.90
Per capita income	4,479	6,280	7,987	16,092	22,479	25,528	6.24
Percent of poor	12.29	6.63	5.32	0.72	0.92	0.44	−12.22
Poverty gap ratio (Percent)	2.60	1.45	1.25	0.19	0.25	0.15	−11.02
Severity of poverty (Percent)	0.94	0.53	0.48	0.08	0.13	0.07	−9.93
Watts measure (Percent)	3.47	1.93	1.66	0.26	0.44	0.22	−10.55
Sen's measure (Percent)	3.47	2.42	2.22	0.37	0.49	0.29	−9.30
Shares (Percent)							
Population	19.98	29.19	36.64	45.81	54.29	60.45	4.09
Per capita income	32.76	42.60	53.41	66.58	71.19	76.75	3.24
Percent of poor	3.97	5.47	7.28	4.22	11.81	8.68	2.31
Poverty gap ratio	2.22	3.52	5.12	4.15	10.37	7.70	4.43
Severity of poverty	1.61	2.70	4.12	4.50	11.14	6.62	5.75
Watts measure	2.04	3.26	4.70	4.34	12.03	6.52	4.76
Sen's measure	1.87	3.31	4.94	4.16	10.37	7.68	5.18

measure. The estimates of Sen's poverty measure presented in Table 7.2 consider the interdependence of poverty across urban and rural areas. These results show that Sen's measure does provide the poverty contributions of urban and rural areas like all the decomposable poverty measures.

It is striking that the rural population in 1988 was 80.02% of the total population, which declined to only 39.55% in 2018. In contrast, the urban population share increased from 19.98% in 1988 to 60.45% in 2018. It means that China went through a significant structural transformation between 1988 and 2018. There had been a vast migration from the rural to urban areas. According to Kuznets (1955), structural change contributes to more prosperity in a country. An adverse impact of this is the increasing disparity between urban and rural areas. Table 7.3 reveals that this is precisely what is happening in China.

In 1988, the urban population enjoyed 95% higher per capita real income than the rural population. But, in 2018, the per capita income of the urban population became 116% higher. As a result, the per capita real income in rural China increased at a yearly rate of 5.79%, while it increased at 6.24% in urban areas. This result indicates an increasing disparity between the urban and rural populations.

In 1988, 74.18% were poor in rural areas and 6.29% in urban areas, meaning rural poverty was about six times urban poverty. In 2018, 7.11% were poor in rural areas and 0.44% in urban areas, which means that rural poverty was about 16 times higher than urban poverty. Furthermore, it implies that urban-rural poverty disparity has been increasing. That is also indicated by the trend growth rates of the percentage of poor. The percentage of rural poor decreased at an annual rate of 8.4%, while the urban poor declined at 12.22%. Thus, the urban-rural poverty disparity is vast and also increasing. Moreover, these gaps persist even after adjusting for the cost of living differences between urban and rural areas.

Based on Sen's poverty measure, the contribution of rural areas to total poverty was 98.13% in 1988, which declined to 92.32% in 2018. There are two causes of such decline: (i) the trend in the poverty gap and (ii) the trend in population size. Table 7.3 reveals that the urban-rural poverty gap increased while the rural population declined. These trends conclude that the significantly reduced share of the rural population is the leading cause of the declining rural share of total poverty.

7.18 Concluding Remarks

The measurement of poverty involves two distinct issues. First is the identification of the poor. The poor are those who cannot meet the basic needs of life. The poverty line is the income level just sufficient to meet the basic needs of persons belonging to a society. Once the poverty line is determined, the second issue is constructing an aggregate index to measure the intensity of poverty suffered by those who have income below the poverty line. This chapter provided an extensive discussion on the construction of poverty lines. In addition, this chapter has provided the development of poverty measures that reflect the intensity of poverty suffered by society.

The inequality literature has extensively discussed the relationship between inequality and social welfare functions. Every inequality has an implicit social welfare function. The poverty literature does not link poverty measures to social welfare functions. Poverty measures are essential tools for designing poverty alleviation policies. In evaluating such policies, normative judgments cannot be avoided, and social welfare functions explicitly specify judgments by assigning weights to different individuals. This chapter has explored the relationship between poverty measures and social welfare functions, and it has evaluated the poverty measures proposed in the literature based on their social welfare implications.

All poverty measures proposed in the literature are relative measures, showing that poverty does not change when the poverty line and incomes increase or decrease by the same proportion. Therefore, this chapter has developed absolute poverty measures that do not show poverty reduction when the poverty line and incomes rise or drop by the same absolute amount.

Poverty must incur a social cost. The absolute poverty measures provide the total social cost of poverty (TSCP) in monetary units. Social costs incurred by poverty in monetary units are intuitive and can be more readily understood by policymakers. Poverty measures have different social welfare functions, and therefore, the (TSCP) will depend on which poverty measure is used by policymakers. The chapter has presented the (TSCP) for China covering 1988–2018. The results showed that the poverty gap ratio had a social cost of 706 billion yuan per year in 1988, which decreased to 43 billion yuan in 2018. In contrast, Sen's poverty measure had a much higher cost of 1,114.57 billion yuan in 1988, declining to 85 billion yuan in 2018. The magnitudes of (TSCP) are valuable metrics, providing insight into how much governments should spend on alleviating or reducing poverty to offset poverty's social cost.

There are two general social welfare functions: (i) rank order social welfare functions and (ii) additive separable utilitarian social welfare functions. The rank order social welfare functions are interdependent, meaning the welfare of an individual depends not only on her consumption or income but also on the consumption or income of others in society. Thus, these welfare functions capture the relative deprivation individuals suffer. In contrast, the additive utilitarian social welfare functions assert that an individuals' welfare depends only on her consumption or income and is not affected by the consumption of others in society. Thus, these social welfare functions completely ignore the relative deprivation suffered by society. The poverty measures proposed in the literature fall into two categories: (i) measures derived from rank order social welfare functions and (ii) measures based on additive separable utilitarian social welfare functions. Sen's poverty measure and its variants fall into the first category. Foster, Greer, and Thorbecke's (1984) measures and their numerous variants fall into the second category.

Sen's poverty measure and its variants became the focus of severe criticism because they were not additively decomposable and therefore violated the subgroup consistency property. The subgroup consistency property is intuitively appealing. But if it is violated, it has undesirable policy implications. The class of utilitarian poverty measures is additively decomposable and is subgroup consistent. Consequently, the empirical analysts preferred additively decomposable poverty measures to Sen's poverty measures and its variants.

This chapter has revisited this controversy, and it has demonstrated the decomposability and subgroup consistency of Sen's measure using empirical illustrations. Thus, the chapter makes a vital contribution that Sen's poverty measure and its variants are decomposable and subgroup consistent.

8

Multidimensional Poverty

8.1 Introduction

Chapters 6 and 7 focused on income or consumption-based poverty measuring. This approach views poverty only as a lack of income (or consumption). Poverty exists when some persons in society cannot enjoy the minimum subsistence standard of living. Chapter 6 dealt with the specification of the poverty line—that is, the minimum income needed to satisfy minimum basic needs. Chapter 7 focused on developing aggregate poverty measures that would inform the intensity of poverty suffered by society.

People want income because it provides them entitlement to commodities that they consume. The higher the income, the greater the entitlement people have to commodities. The entitlement to commodities, which include services, provides people with the means to lead a better life. Lack of income deprives people of satisfying socially defined basic needs. However, lack of income is not the only kind of deprivation people may suffer. People may suffer deprivation in many aspects of life beyond basic needs (for example, ill-health, lack of education, etc.). A low level of well-being is essential to measure deprivation rather than a low-income level. According to the 2000 World Development Report (WDR), poverty is pronounced deprivation in well-being. As Sen (1985) points out, "ultimately, the focus has to be on what we can or cannot do or cannot be." The entitlement to income is only a means to an end. Thus, well-being must be seen in terms of individual achievements rather than individuals' means to achieve them. This line of reasoning led Sen to develop the idea of functionings and capabilities. Thus, functionings are directly related to the kind of life people lead, whereas capabilities are the opportunities people have to lead lives of their choice. Therefore, the capabilities of a person are an opportunity set of functionings, measuring her freedom to achieve functionings they value.

According to the capability approach, individuals are poor if they do not possess basic capabilities. It may seem obvious that the higher the income people have, the greater their capabilities will be. After all, it is observed that rich countries enjoy more increased well-being than developing countries. But, the relationship between the two is not simple. For instance, consider a country that has succeeded in reducing mortality so much that its per capita GDP falls because of the resulting population increase. Has the country's living standard improved or deteriorated? The answer is not clear. The country's standard of living has fallen in the income space, while the country has

Economic Inequality and Poverty. Nanak Kakwani and Hyun Son, Oxford University Press.
© Nanak Kakwani and Hyun Son (2022). DOI: 10.1093/oso/9780198852841.003.0008

extended the capability of its citizens to live a longer life. Thus, the exclusive focus on income poverty may miss out on the deprivation people may suffer in many other aspects of life.

The United Nations Development Programme (UNDP) in 1990 created the Human Development Index. Then, in 2000 UNDP developed the Millennium Development Goals, which led to a clear shift toward a multidimensional approach to poverty measurement. There is now a widespread consensus that poverty is multifaceted, reflecting deprivation people suffer in many aspects of life. Sen's (1985, 1992, 1999) seminal work on functionings and capabilities has been the most influential in defining poverty in a multidimensional framework. As Thorbecke (2008) points out, Sen's capabilities and functionings framework is the most comprehensive in capturing the concept of multidimensional poverty. This approach provides a holistic definition of poverty, leading to many complex measurement issues in the operational sense.

Although the literature on multidimensional poverty has made considerable progress in identifying the poor and developing multifaceted poverty indices, too many challenges remain to be considered. A principal problem has been that multidimensional poverty measurement requires many arbitrary assumptions that lead to an arbitrary degree of poverty. This chapter briefly reviews unresolved issues and proposes an alternative analysis of multidimensional poverty.

8.2 Unresolved Issues

8.2.1 Basic Capabilities

According to the capability approach, persons are poor if they do not possess the capabilities to achieve basic functionings. What are these basic functionings and the corresponding capabilities? How can they be identified? An answer to this question requires value judgments. It depends on how society prioritizes different capabilities. These priorities may also rely on a country's economic resources.

While there is no universal agreement on these basic capabilities, it may still be possible to agree on some basic capabilities. For example, suppose persons cannot be well-nourished, adequately clothed, and sheltered, not able to avoid preventable morbidity or death. In that case, they can be classified as deprived of basic capabilities. Those capabilities related to health, education, shelter, clothing, nutrition, and clean water can reasonably be considered essential capabilities that provide broad agreement. Thus, the number of basic capabilities determines the dimensions of multidimensional poverty analysis.

Alkire (2008) has made a valuable contribution to choosing dimensions. She listed five practical methods of selecting dimensions. However, the application of these methods is not straightforward. Researchers need to make explicit their reason for making a particular choice. How have they taken account of society's priorities? Should developing countries have a different list or the same list of basic capabilities as developed countries? How many dimensions are sufficient to capture the multidimensional aspects of poverty adequately? There are no clear-cut answers to these questions.

Should there be a one-size-fits-all list of basic core capabilities that could be used to make international comparisons of multidimensional poverty? This issue sparked a sharp exchange between Nussbaum (2003) and Sen (2004), providing no clear answer.

Nussbaum believes that one list should ensure that the capability approach is widely applicable and carries binding force. According to her, if "the approach is too open-ended, then there is a real practical possibility that the wrong freedom will be prioritized and expanded." In response, Sen views that the problem is not listing essential capabilities but insisting on one predetermined canonical list of capabilities chosen by theorists without any general public discussion. This exchange demonstrates there is no agreement on even having a list of capabilities that could be adopted.

8.2.2 Multidimensional Poverty Index (MPI)

The literature on multidimensional poverty assumes that every individual must possess capabilities to achieve some minimum functionings. Suppose n persons have in total m capabilities, called attributes, and $y_{ij} \geq 0$ is the quantity of jth attribute owned by the ith individual, where i varies from 1 to n, and j varies from 1 to m. Suppose each attribute has a threshold z_j, the minimum achievement necessary for maintaining a subsistence living in the jth attribute. A person is defined as poor in the jth attribute if $y_{ij} < z_j$. The person i suffers deprivation in the jth attribute if they bear a shortfall of the jth essential capability. A function can define the magnitude of deprivation experienced by the ith person in the jth attribute: $d_{ij} = d(z_j, y_{ij})$. An MPI is a numerical representation of deprivations and is an aggregate index of multiple deprivations across all individuals in society.

Most of the literature on multidimensional poverty has focused on developing a multifaceted composite index. Sen (1976) pioneered the axiomatic approach to measuring poverty in income space. The literature has extended its unidimensional axiomatic foundation to derive multidimensional poverty indices (Tsui 2002, Bourguignon and Chakravarty 2003, Alkire and Foster 2011). Chakravarty and Silber (2008) developed many functional forms for multidimensional poverty indices, satisfying poverty decomposability and subgroup consistency.[1]

There is now debate on why it is helpful to have a composite MPI. When various dimensions of poverty are collapsed into a single index, some valuable information about the nature of poverty is lost. For policy purposes, the analysis of poverty in

---

[1] The poverty decomposability is thus defined as: "If a population is divided into several mutually exclusive subgroups, then overall poverty is the population weighted average subgroup poverty levels." Foster, Greer, and Thorbecke (1984) were first to introduce this concept. Chapter 7 provided an extensive discussion of poverty decomposability and subgroup consistency.

different dimensions can be indispensable because policymakers want to identify which aspects of poverty have been a capability failure. The composite index can, at best, inform that there has been an overall capability failure. This information does not help formulate policy to reduce or eliminate deprivation in a particular dimension of poverty. There has also been sharp disagreement on whether various dimensions of poverty can be aggregated into a single, multidimensional index in a meaningful way (Lustig 2011).

8.2.3 Poverty Thresholds for Multidimensional Poverty

The measurement of multidimensional poverty requires poverty thresholds for every dimension. But, can poverty thresholds for various dimensions be meaningfully determined? The literature has not dealt with this issue. Chapter 6 showed that the construction of the poverty line, even in income space, is a complex undertaking. The new model of the poverty line developed in that chapter helped justify poverty thresholds for food and non-food poverty lines using the consumer theory. The determination of poverty thresholds for various diverse dimensions is infinitely more complex.

However, no methods exist to construct poverty thresholds for the minimum essential capabilities to identify the poor in different poverty dimensions. For example, it is not apparent how one can place a threshold for life expectancy at birth or infant survival rate. Can one say that a 50% literacy rate is the minimum acceptable rate for society? The fact remains that there is no methodology to determine poverty thresholds in a meaningful way in a multidimensional poverty framework. The papers published on multidimensional poverty have determined thresholds completely ad hoc.

8.2.4 Aggregation across Dimensions

Suppose the thresholds of all attributes are determined and let z_j be the jth attribute's threshold; the deprivation suffered by the ith person in the jth attribute is given by $d_{ij} = d(z_j, y_{ij})$. It is a relative measure of deprivation if it does not change when z_j and y_{ij} change by the same proportion. The ith individual suffers positive deprivation in the jth attribute if $y_{ij} < z_j$ and suffers zero or no deprivation if $y_{ij} \geq z_j$. Given this, the deprivation function will be given by

$$
\begin{aligned}
d_{ij} = d(z_j, y_{ij}) &> 0 \text{ if } y_{ij} < z_j \text{ for all } i \text{ and } j \\
&= 0 \qquad \text{ if } y_{ij} \leq z_j \text{ for all } i \text{ and } j
\end{aligned}
\tag{8.2.1}
$$

This equation yields the aggregate deprivation suffered by society in the jth attribute as

$$
D_j = \frac{1}{n} \sum_{i=1}^{q_j} d(z_j, y_{ij})
\tag{8.2.2}
$$

where q_j is the number of poor in the jth attribute because they suffer a shortfall in capability when $y_{ij} < z_j$. To obtain the MPI, the deprivation in the jth attribute in (8.2.2) needs to be aggregated across m attributes. This aggregation is performed by assigning predetermined weights to each attribute. Thus, the MPI is given by

$$D = \sum_{j=1}^{m} w_j D_j \qquad (8.2.3)$$

w_j is the weight assigned to the deprivation individuals suffer in the jth attribute such that[2]

$$\sum_{j=1}^{m} w_j = 1.$$

Suppose that there are two attributes: the jth attribute denoting longevity and the kth denoting educational attainment. Suppose the deprivation in longevity is increased by 1% if the MPI remains the same. In this case, equation (8.2.3) implies that the deprivation in educational attainment must reduce by w_j/w_k percentage points. This also indicates that one can substitute longevity by educational attainment. It is hard to visualize whether any individual would accept such a substitution. Would they trade, say, one year of life for two years of education? Any such substitution makes little sense at the individual level, but since policymakers have limited resources, they may opt for such a substitution to allocate their budget.

Another serious issue in this field is that there is no meaningful, transparent method of assigning weights to different dimensions of poverty. Researchers tend to rely on their ad hoc judgments in deciding weights across different dimensions.

8.2.5 Capability Deprivation and Income Poverty

Multidimensional poverty describes poverty as the deprivation of essential capabilities. Poverty encompasses many forms of deprivation in different aspects of life, such as ill-health, illiteracy, vulnerability, and social exclusion. Can multidimensional poverty be described only by capability deprivation? Suppose that a millionaire, who has all the economic means to buy anything, has an incurable disease, preventing him from achieving some essential functions. They undoubtedly suffer severe capability deprivation despite having all the best medical facilities at their disposal. Yet, it would be odd to call this millionaire "poor." From a capability perspective, poverty must arise when essential capability failure is caused by inadequate entitlement to resources, whether through markets or public provision or other non-market channels. One may identify a millionaire suffering from deprivation by examining capability deprivation alone. Still, it is odd to call a millionaire poor even if they suffer severe deprivation in some dimensions.

---

[2] Note that the same weight is assigned to each person's deprivation. This may be an heroic assumption because individuals differ with respect to their sufferings in various dimensions.

One needs to make a distinction between poverty and capability deprivation in general. Poverty results from the inadequacy of command over resources needed to generate socially determined essential capabilities, whereas a host of factors may cause capability deprivation. Among them, a lack of income or entitlement to resources may not be the most critical. Thus, a person may suffer capability deprivation but may not always be poor.

Defining poverty from the capability perspective cannot be done independently of income or available resources. The capabilities to function linked to poverty should be derived if people suffer from a lack of resources at their disposal. Income or command over resources cannot be separated from capability, but at the same time, it must be recognized that the link between them is far from simple.

8.3 Global Multidimensional Poverty Index

The UNDP (2020) has taken the primary initiative in developing the global multi-dimensional poverty index. It has computed the global MPI and its components for almost all countries in the globe. The index is now available for 2019. It identifies multiple deprivations at the household level in health, education, and standard of living. All the indicators used to construct the index are derived from the same household survey.

The global MPI uses ten deprivation indicators in three dimensions: health with two indicators, education with two indicators, and living standards with six indicators. Each indicator measures the shortfall in well-being. For instance, a household with no electricity suffers deprivation in living standards. Similarly, a household suffers deprivation in education if any school-age child is not attending school. Table 8.1 describes ten deprivation indicators developed by the UNDP. The UNDP also assigned a deprivation score to each indicator.

Suppose w_j is the deprivation score given to the jth indicator. The total sum of the deprivation score is 1. The maximum score for each dimension is 1/3. For example, the health and education dimensions have two indicators, so each indicator is weighted as 1/6. The standard of living dimension has six indicators, so each is weighted as 1/18.

To identify multidimensionally poor people, the deprivation scores for each indicator are summed to obtain the household deprivation score. A cutoff of 1/3 is used to distinguish between poor and nonpoor households. Households are considered multidimensionally poor if their total deprivation score is 1/3 or higher. Households with a deprivation score of 1/5 but less than 1/3 are considered vulnerable because they are likely to become poor with a slight economic shock. The households with a deprivation score of 1/2 or higher are considered severe multidimensional poor. If a household is identified as poor, all its members are also regarded as poor.

Let p_{ij} be the probability of the ith household being poor in jth indicator, which is given by

Table 8.1 2020 Multidimensional poverty index: dimensions, indicators, deprivation cutoffs, and weights

Dimension	Indicator	Deprivation cutoff	Weight
Health	Nutrition	Any adult under 70 years of age or any child for whom there is nutritional information is undernourished.[1]	1/6
	Child mortality	Any child under the age of 18 years who has died in the family in the five-year period preceding the survey.[2,3]	1/6
Education	Years of schooling	No household member of school entrance age + six[4] years or older has completed six years of schooling.	1/6
	School attendance	Any school-aged child is not attending school up to the age at which he/she would complete class eight.[5]	1/6
Standard of living	Cooking Fuel	The household cooks with dung, wood, charcoal, or coal.	1/18
	Sanitation	The household's sanitation facility is not improved (according to SDG guidelines) or it is improved but shared with other households.[6]	1/18
	Drinking Water	The household does not have access to improved drinking water (according to SDG guidelines) or improved drinking water is at least a 30-minute walk from home, round trip.[7]	1/18
	Electricity	The household has no electricity.[8]	1/18

Continued

Housing	At least one of the three housing materials for roof, walls, and floor are inadequate: the floor is of natural materials and/or the roof and/or walls are of natural or rudimentary materials.[9]	1/18
Assets	The household does not own more than one of these assets: radio, television, telephone, computer, animal cart, bicycle, motorbike, or refrigerator, and does not own a car or truck.[10]	1/18

Source : UNDP (2020)

1. Adults 19 to 70 years of age (229 to 840 months) are considered undernourished if their age-specific BMI values are below minus two standard deviations from the median of the reference population (https://www.who.int/growthref/en/). In the majority of the countries, BMI-for-age covered people aged 15 to 19 years, as anthropometric data was only available for this age group; if other data were available, BMI-for-age was applied for all individuals 5 to 19 years. Children under 5 years (60 months and under) are considered undernourished if their z-score for either height-for-age (stunting) or weight-for-age (underweight) is below minus two standard deviations from the median of the reference population (https://www.who.int/childgrowth/software/en/). Nutritional information is not provided for households without members eligible for measurement, these households are assumed to be not deprived in this indicator.

2. All reported deaths are used if the date of child's death is not known.

3. Child mortality information is typically collected from women of reproductive ages 15–49 years. Households without women of such ages do not provide information about child's deaths and are assumed to be not deprived in this indicator.

4. This country-specific age cutoff was introduced in 2020. Previously, the age cutoff was 10 years which did not recognize the fact that by age 10 children do not normally complete 6 years of schooling.

5. Source for official entrance age to primary school: United Nations Educational, Scientific and Cultural Organization, Institute for Statistics database. Education systems [UIS, http://data.uis.unesco.org/?ReportId=163].

6. A household is considered to have access to improved sanitation if it has some type of flush toilet or latrine, or ventilated improved pit or composting toilet, provided that they are not shared. If the survey report uses other definitions of improved sanitation, we follow the survey report.

7. A household has access to improved drinking water if the water source is any of the following types: piped water, public tap, borehole or pump, protected well, protected spring or rainwater, and it is within 30 minutes' walk (round trip). If the survey report uses other definitions of improved drinking water, we follow the survey report.

8. A few countries do not collect data on electricity because of 100% coverage. In such cases, we identify all households in the country as non-deprived in electricity.

9. A household is considered deprived if the dwelling's floor is made of mud/clay/earth, sand or dung; or if the dwelling has no roof or walls or if either the roof or walls are constructed using natural materials such as cane, palm/trunks, sod/mud, dirt, grass/reeds, thatch, bamboo, sticks or rudimentary materials such as carton, plastic/ polythene sheeting, bamboo with mud/stone with mud, loosely packed stones, uncovered adobe, raw/reused wood, plywood, cardboard, unburned brick or canvas/tent.

10. Television (TV) includes smart TV and black and white TV, telephone includes cell phones, computer includes tablets and laptops, and refrigerator includes freezers.

$$p_{ij} = 1, \quad \text{if the } i\text{th household is poor in the } j\text{th indicator}$$
$$= 0, \quad \text{if the } i\text{th household is nonpoor in the } j\text{th indicator.} \tag{8.3.1}$$

Suppose w_{ij} is the deprivation score of the ith household in the jth indicator, which will be given by

$$w_{ij} = p_{ij} w_j \tag{8.3.2}$$

where w_j is the deprivation score for the jth indicator, which is the same for all households. The total deprivation score for the ith household will be given by

$$w_{i.} = \sum_{j=1}^{10} p_{ij} w_j \tag{8.3.3}$$

Suppose there are n households in the country, the per capita deprivation score for the whole population will be given by

$$\tilde{w} = \frac{\sum_{i=1}^{n} w_{i.}}{n} = \frac{\sum_{i=1}^{n} \sum_{j=1}^{10} p_{ij} w_j}{n} \tag{8.3.4}$$

which is the global MPI.

The product of two components can explain the global MPI: (i) multidimensional headcount ratio and (ii) the average per capita deprivation suffered by the poor. The UNDP derived its index by further assuming that the ith household is multidimensional poor if its deprivation score is greater than 1/3. Thus, the poverty status of the ith household is given by

$$q_i = 1 \quad \text{if } w_{i.} > 1/3$$
$$= 0, \text{otherwise} \tag{8.3.5}$$

which gives the number of multidimensional poor households as

$$q = \sum_{i=1}^{n} q_i \tag{8.3.6}$$

The headcount ratio, H, is the proportion of multidimensional poor households in a country as

$$H = \frac{q}{n}, \tag{8.3.7}$$

n is the total number of households in the country. The headcount ratio does not inform how much is the depth of poverty. To measure the depth of poverty, $w_{i.}$ needs to be calculated for all poor households in the country. The depth of poverty, A, suffered by the average multidimensional poor households q is defined as

$$A = \frac{\sum_{i=1}^{q} w_{i.}}{q} \tag{8.3.8}$$

The numerator in this equation is the total deprivation score of poor households, and A is the society's per capita deprivation score of poor households. The higher the value of A, the greater the depth of poverty. A suitable index of multidimensional poverty will be the product headcount ratio and depth poverty:

$$MPI = HA = \frac{\sum_{i=1}^{q} w_{i.}}{n},$$
(8.3.9)

which is the global multidimensional poverty index. It is the per capita deprivation score of poor households divided by the total number of households. This index is similar to the unidimensional poverty gap ratio proposed by Sen (1976) as given in (7.3.4).

UNDP's MPI arbitrarily assigns weights to each indicator of the three dimensions of poverty. The index has been subjected to criticism because it uses arbitrary weights to determine the deprivation score, providing no rationale for these weights.

8.4 An Alternative Approach to Multidimensional Poverty

This section proposes an alternative approach to measuring the multidimensional poverty index. It develops the deprivation score based on the cost of eliminating poverty in indicators in various poverty dimensions.

Suppose C_{ij} is the cost of eliminating the ith household poverty in the jth indicator, interpreted as the amount of income society needs to give to the ith household to come out of poverty in the jth indicator. The total cost of eliminating the ith household poverty in all indicators is provided by $C_{i.} = \sum_{j=1}^{10} C_{ij}$. Further, suppose that C_j is the cost of eliminating poverty in the jth indicator for all households in the country. Then using the probability p_{ij} defined in (8.3.1) yields

$$C_{ij} = p_{ij} C_j$$
(8.4.1)

which gives the total cost of eliminating poverty of the ith household in all indicators as

$$C_{i.} = \sum_{j=1}^{10} C_{ij} = \sum_{j=1}^{10} p_{ij} C_j$$
(8.4.2)

The total cost of eradicating poverty among all households in all indicators will be given by

$$\tilde{C} = \sum_{i=1}^{n} C_{i.} = \sum_{i=1}^{n} \sum_{j=1}^{10} p_{ij} C_j$$
(8.4.3)

which is the proposed multidimensional poverty index. This index measures the monetary cost of eradicating multidimensional poverty in all dimensions. Since it is measured in monetary units, policymakers will readily understand the degree of multidimensional poverty suffered by society.

The main advantage of this index is that it does not specify the *ad hoc* deprivation weights required by UNDP's MPI. However, it requires estimation of monetary costs of eliminating poverty in different poverty dimensions. It makes an intuitive sense to relate the deprivation weights to the costs of removing the deprivation in different poverty dimensions. The higher the cost, the greater the efforts required to eliminate poverty. The calculation of these costs may be difficult but not impossible.

8.5 Union or Interaction Approaches to Identifying the Poor

UNDP's MPI identifies poor households by the shortfall of deprivation score from a predetermined poverty cutoff point. The cutoff point is arbitrarily set at 33.3 percent or more of the total deprivation score. An alternative approach is to calculate the proportion of poor in each dimension of poverty and then derive the proportion of poor in the population by aggregating across poverty dimensions. Define

$$P_{ij} = 1 \quad if\ y_{ij} < z_j$$
$$= 0, \text{otherwise},$$

$(8.5.1)$

then the proportion of poor in the jth dimension is given by

$$H_j = \frac{1}{n} \sum_{i=1}^{n} P_{ij}$$

$(8.5.2)$

The proportion of multidimensional poor in the population will be given by

$$H = \sum_{j=1}^{m} w_j H_j$$

$(8.5.3)$

where $\sum_{j=1}^{m} w_j = 1$.

This is a simple way of calculating the proportion of multidimensional poor. The weights given to poverty dimensions reflect society's importance to various capabilities. There should be a public debate determining the relative importance of different, essential capabilities in determining these weights.

The researchers have always been uneasy about assigning arbitrary weights to various poverty dimensions. To avoid this arbitrariness, Bourguignon and Chakravarty (2003) proposed to use the union approach to identifying the poor, according to which a person is regarded as poor if they suffer deprivation in at least one dimension of poverty. To explain it, suppose poverty includes two dimensions, A and B. P(A) is the probability of being poor in dimension A, and P(B) is the probability of being poor in dimension B. The probability of the union of A and B is given by

$$P(A \cup B) = P(A) + P(B) - P(A \cap B)$$

$(8.5.4)$

where $P(A \cap B)$ is the probability of being poor simultaneously in dimensions A and B. A nonpoor does not suffer poverty in any dimension, and hence the probability of being nonpoor is given by $1 - P(A \cup B)$.

Alkire and Foster (2011) have rejected the union approach because if the number of dimensions is large, most of the population would often be identified as poor. Consequently, union-based poverty may not help distinguish and target the most extensively deprived.

The other multidimensional identification is the interaction approach, which identifies a person as poor if deprived in all dimensions. Again, if the number of dimensions is large, this approach may show zero multidimensional poverty because it is unlikely that all persons will simultaneously suffer deprivation in all dimensions. Alkire and Foster (2011) also dismiss this approach, arguing that considering persons to be non-poor may suffer considerable multiple deprivations. They proposed a third approach that identifies a person as poor if they suffer deprivation in at least k dimensions, where k varies from 2 to $m-1$. This approach may be called the intermediate between union and interaction approaches as special cases where $k=1$ and $k=m$, respectively.

Alkire and Foster's intermediate approach requires both the within dimension or deprivation cutoff z_j and the across dimensions or poverty cutoff k. It is called the dual cutoff method of identification. The cutoff k is determined arbitrarily, depending on the analyst's judgment. The headcount ratio H is the proportion of the population deprived of at least k dimensions. An additional problem that emerges in a multidimensional setting is that H remains unchanged if a poor person becomes deprived of a new dimension. This violates what Alkire and Foster call "dimensional monotonicity," which states that "if a person becomes newly deprived in an additional dimension, then overall poverty should increase." To satisfy this requirement, Alkire and Foster introduced another indicator B, which is the fraction of possible dimensions m, in which the average poor person is deprived. Thus, Alkire and Foster proposed a composite multidimensional poverty indicator $M_0 = HB$. This index satisfies the dimensional monotonicity since if a person becomes deprived in an additional dimension, then B rises, and so does M_0.

Thus, there are three approaches to identifying the multidimensional poor: union, interaction, and intermediate. These counting methods seem not to require the arbitrarily determined weights assigned to different poverty dimensions, which is incorrect. When choosing the number of dimensions persons are deprived of, it assumes that all attributes or dimensions are equally important to society, implying equal weights for all dimensions. These approaches also make specific value judgments regarding the number of poverty dimensions deprived individuals. There is no meaningful justification for these approaches. The literature has unnecessarily added even more ad hoc assumptions with no added value except making multidimensional poverty highly complex.

8.6 A New Method of Measuring Multidimensional Poverty

There is widespread consensus that poverty is multidimensional. Many research papers have been written on the topic, but many challenging issues remain unresolved.

The literature has primarily focused on developing the multidimensional poverty framework, a straightforward extension of the unidimensional income poverty methods. The research writings have not adequately addressed the new concepts necessary for designing multidimensional poverty. The multifaceted poverty framework developed so far involves many arbitrary judgments that are not intuitively justifiable. This section attempts to resolve some of the challenges of measuring multidimensional poverty.

It is helpful to distinguish between social well-being and social deprivation functions. The social well-being function can be defined in terms of individuals' achievements. Therefore, one can measure social well-being by the social well-being function. However, poverty is the overall deprivation (also referred to as ill-being) that society suffers. Hence, this section proposes measuring multidimensional poverty by the social ill-being functions aggregated across all poverty dimensions. But first, however, the idea of the social ill-being function must be developed for each poverty dimension.

In income poverty, a person suffers deprivation if their income is less than the poverty line. The multidimensional poverty framework follows a similar method to income poverty and requires thresholds for every capability space dimension. In Section 8.2, it was argued that the determination of minimum thresholds for capabilities might not be achievable meaningfully. The method proposed below entirely dispenses with the poverty thresholds in poverty dimensions.

The well-being indicators are generally bounded, lying in a finite range. For instance, the literacy rate is measured by the percentage of the literate population, lying between 0 and 100. Most health indicators have an upper limit. Given this property, one would readily know the maximum possible levels of well-being indicators (Sen1992). The maximum levels provide the ideal achievements that societies can attain, so any deviations of actual achievements from the ideals represent shortfalls in well-being. These shortfalls are the negative indicators of well-being. For instance, the infant survival rate is an indicator of attainment. In contrast, the infant mortality rate is an indicator of a shortfall and can be called an indicator of ill-being.

Similarly, life expectancy at birth is an indicator of achievement, and the deviation of life expectancy at birth from its maximum value would indicate a shortfall in longevity. An aggregate measure of shortfalls suffered by all individuals will measure poverty in longevity. Determining the maximum ideal values of achievements is not as arbitrary as determining the poverty thresholds for minimum achievement levels.

In Section 8.2, it was argued that defining poverty from the capability perspective cannot be independent of income. People may suffer capability deprivation due to a host of factors; poverty concerns the inadequacy of command over resources needed to obtain socially determined necessary capabilities. And hence, multidimensional poverty must be linked with income. This linkage is established using the elasticity of the ill-being function with respect to x.

Suppose $y_j(x)$ is the achievement of the person with income x in the jth attribute (or dimension), and further, suppose a_{1j} and a_{0j} are the society's maximum and minimum achievements in the jth attribute, then a measure of the shortfall suffered in the jth attribute by the person with income x is defined as

$$D_j(x) = \frac{a_{1j} - y_j(x)}{a_{1j} - a_{0j}} \qquad (8.6.1)$$

Note that $D_j(x)$ is the relative measure of ill-being or deprivation in the jth attribute because its value does not change when a_{ij}, a_{0j}, and $y_j(x)$ change by the same proportion. $D_j(x)$ takes value zero if the individual with income x has attained the maximum attainable achievement, and takes value one, if the individual with income x's achievement is the minimum.

The elasticity of the individual ill-being function in the jth dimension with respect to x is defined as

$$\in_j(x) = \frac{x}{D_j(x)} \frac{\partial D_j(x)}{\partial x} \qquad (8.6.2)$$

This elasticity can be both negative and positive. If the elasticity is 0 for all x, all individuals suffer the same ill-being irrespective of their income. In practice, the rich tend to experience less ill-being than the poor. If $\in_j(x) < 0$ for all x, it suggests that as income increases, the ill-being decreases monotonically, implying the poorer an individual, the higher the ill-being. This situation may be referred to as inequity in well-being. $\in_j(x) > 0$ means that the poorer a person, the lower the ill-being they suffer. This situation may be characterized as equity in well-being. The magnitude of elasticity can measure the degree of inequity or equity in ill-being. The idea of inequity (or equity) is utilized to develop multidimensional poverty.

The average ill-being in the jth dimension is defined as

$$\overline{D}_j = \int_0^\infty D_j(x) f(x)\, dx \qquad (8.6.3)$$

where $f(x)$, being the density function of income, measures the average ill-being suffered by society. It is the average ill-being suffered by society in the jth dimension. One can use this to measure poverty in the jth dimension. But, it has one limitation. It does not tell how ill-being is distributed across incomes. Like the social welfare function, the social ill-being function can capture the linkage between ill-being and income. Chapter 5 in equation (5.7.2) presented Sen's (1974a) social welfare function, a generalization of which is the social ill-being $(SIB)_j$ in the jth poverty dimension given by

$$(SIB)_j = 2 \int_0^\infty D_j(x) [1 - F(x)] f(x)\, dx \qquad (8.6.4)$$

where $F(x)$ is the probability distribution function when individuals are arranged in ascending order of their income, satisfying

$$2 \int_0^\infty [1 - F(x)] f(x) \, dx = 1$$

This implies that the social ill-being in (8.6.4) is the weighted average of individual ill-being, with weights proportional to the number of persons in society richer than x. It is an aggregated measure of ill-beings suffered by individuals, reflecting the overall ill-being suffered by society in the jth dimension. Thus, the $(SIB)_j$ is the proposed index of poverty in the jth dimension.

If all persons in society suffer the same degree of ill-being in the jth dimension, $(SIB)_j$ will reduce to the society's average ill-being $\overline{D}_j$. If $D_j(x) = 0$ for all x, the society does not suffer any poverty in the jth dimension because everyone has attained the maximum achievement in the jth dimension. If $D_j(x) = 1$ for all x, $(SIB)_j = 1$, which is the maximum incidence of poverty in the jth dimension, that is, when everyone has the minimum achievement.

Chapter 9 will prove that the elasticity in (8.6.2) has a one-to-one relationship with the concentration index. Suppose $(CI)_j$ is the concentration index of the ill-being $D_j(x)$, which is related to $(SIB)_j$ by the following relationship:

$$(SIB)_j = 2 \int_0^\infty D_j(x) [1 - F(x)] f(x) \, dx = \overline{D}_j [1 - (CI)_j] \tag{8.6.5}$$

$$(CI)_j = \frac{1}{\overline{D}_j} \int_0^\infty D_j(x) [2F(x) - 1] f(x) \, dx$$

Chapter 9 will show that $(CI)_j$ lies between -1 and $+1$. The value of 0 implies that all individuals suffer from the same ill-being irrespective of their income. When $(CI)_j = +1$, only the richest person in society suffers from all the ill-being, and the remaining other persons do not suffer any ill-being. And, if $(CI)_j = -1$, only the poorest person in society suffers from all the ill-being, and the remaining others do not suffer any ill-being. These are the two extreme scenarios.

It will be demonstrated in Chapter 9 that $(CI)_j$ measures the overall elasticity of society's ill-being with respect to income; the higher the absolute magnitude of $(CI)_j$, the larger the absolute magnitude of the overall ill-being elasticity. A measure of inequity in ill-being in the jth dimension is given by $I_j = -(CI)_j$. If $I_j > 0$, it means that the poorer a person, the greater is their ill-being, implying that society suffers inequity in well-being. If $I_j < 0$, it means that the richer a person, the greater their ill-being, indicating that society enjoys equity in well-being. The social objective should be to minimize I_j for all j. Thus, the proposed index of poverty in the jth dimension is given by

$$(SIB)_j = \overline{D}_j \left(1 + I_j\right) \tag{8.6.6}$$

Two factors impact this index: (i) the average ill-being suffered by the population $\overline{D}_j$ and (ii) inequity in ill-being I_j. If the social objective is to reduce poverty in the jth dimension, policymakers must attempt to reduce both $\overline{D}_j$ and I_j. There can be a trade-off between the two, so the function in (8.6.6) provides the magnitude of the trade-off.

Having defined the poverty index in different dimensions, the next step is to determine the MPI, which would require the weights assigned to various dimensions. The literature has resorted to arbitrary weights without providing economic justification. In Section 8.3, it was argued that it makes intuitive sense to relate the deprivation weights to the costs of eliminating the deprivation in different poverty dimensions. But suppose these costs are not readily available. In that case, alternately, society might be most concerned about the inequity in the distribution of ill-being, so it might be appropriate to make weights proportional to the inequity index. The inequity index reflects how the economic resources available to individuals affect the suffering of ill-being in essential capabilities among the poor. This leads to the following MPI.

$$MPI = \sum_{j=1}^{m} \frac{\overline{D}_j I_j}{\sum_{j=1}^{m} I_j} \tag{8.6.7}$$

The total weight assigned to all dimensions adds up to 1. Note that the MPI is the weighted average of ill-being proportional to inequity in ill-being.

The MPI in (8.6.7) also has a limitation. The index gives a higher weight to the poverty dimensions that are more sensitive to economic resources available to indi viduals. This leads to making a distinction between output and outcome indicators. For instance, access to health care is an output, and life expectancy at birth is an outcome. People's economic resources more directly impact output through their income or resources given by the government.

On the other hand, life expectancy at birth is an outcome that is influenced by several health-related individual factors, including access to health care. A critical question arises whether outputs or outcomes measure multidimensional poverty. If the objective is to measure only the overall ill-being suffered by society, it would be appropriate to use outcomes. In contrast, poverty occurs when individuals suffer from ill-being due to their inadequate entitlement to resources. The resources entitle people to have greater access to outputs that enhance people's capabilities. Hence, economic resources directly impact outputs, whereas a host of many other factors, including economic resources, impacts outcomes. The MPI in (8.6.7) will be more meaningful if all dimensions of poverty are outputs. Any aggregation of poverty dimensions will not be meaningful if the various dimensions have a mixture of both outputs and outcomes.

Any public action intended to reduce poverty provides (directly or indirectly) additional entitlements to those who lack them. Public policy generates an output that may or may not result in a desirable outcome, and an excellent public action is the one that leads to more desired outcomes in ill-being. The inequity index developed in this section would be an indispensable tool in formulating public policies to reduce multidimensional poverty.

8.7 Multidimensional Poverty in Brazilian Municipalities: A Case Study

This section presents the calculations of multidimensional poverty in Brazilian municipalities. The study uses data from the 2013 Atlas of Human Development in Brazil, developed by the Brazilian Research Institute for Applied Economics. The Atlas provides human development indicators for more than 5,000 municipalities. In addition, almost 1,000 socio-economic indicators were compiled for each municipality based on census data for 1991, 2000, and 2010. It will suffice to illustrate the calculations of multidimensional poverty only for 2010.[3]

Table 8.2 presents a set of well-being indicators divided into four broad dimensions: health, education, living conditions, and labor market activities. The health dimension has three indicators: life expectancy at birth, infant survival rate, and child survival rate. Life expectancy at birth indicates the numbers of years a newborn would live if patterns of mortality prevailing for all people at the time of delivery were to stay the same throughout her life. It is an index of longevity, influenced by several input variables, such as nutrition, clean water supply, sanitation, and access to medical services. Hence, life expectancy at birth is an indicator of achievement and therefore becomes eligible to be an indicator of well-being.

The household surveys do not provide life expectancy at birth, so none of the studies on multidimensional poverty have included this indicator, even though it is an essential aspect of people's well-being. However, this indicator was available at the municipal level because indirect methods were used to estimate mortality. Information is based on the self-reported number of live births and living children when the census was conducted. From this information, it was possible to get the proportion of deaths. Then, a model was run to apply these death rates to life tables, from which the life expectancy at birth was extracted.

Infant and child survival rates are also important indicators of well-being because society puts a high value on the survival of infants and children. Poor sanitation, unclean drinking water, and poor nutrition are the causes of low survival rates among infants and children. Although infant and child survival rates are the main determinants

---

[3] Kakwani and Son (2016a, chapter 6) have provided a detail discussion of levels and distribution of well-being in Brazil using the same data.

Table 8.2 Calculations of multidimensional poverty index in Brazilian municipalities, 2010

Indicators	Achieved well-being	Maximum value	Average ill-being	Inequity index	Poverty in each dimension
A. Health					
Life expectancy at birth	74.39	85	12.48	0.10	13.76
Infant survival rate	98.35	100	1.65	0.15	1.90
Child survival rate	98.17	100	1.83	0.14	2.09
B. Education					
Adult literacy rate among people aged 15 and above (Percent)	90.04	100	9.96	−0.01	9.91
Expected number of years of schooling for 18-year-olds	9.63	12	19.75	0.01	19.89
People aged 18 and above who completed high school (Percent)	37.24	100	62.76	0.11	69.51
People aged 25 and above who completed higher education (Percent)	10.83	100	89.17	0.04	92.88
Children aged 11–14 attending school (Percent)	96.24	100	3.76	0.05	3.95
Children aged 15–17 attending school (Percent)	83.58	100	16.42	0.07	17.51
Youths aged 18–24 attending school (Percent)	30.62	100	69.38	0.03	71.42
C. Living Conditions					
Population living in households with piped water (Percent)	92.06	100	7.94	0.55	12.29
Population living in households with toilet (Percent)	87.17	100	12.83	0.55	19.86
Population living in households with garbage collection (Percent)	96.17	100	3.83	0.59	6.07
Population living in households with electricity (Percent)	98.58	100	1.42	0.72	2.45
Population living in households with adequate sanitation (Percent)	93.88	100	6.12	0.64	10.01
D. Labor Market Activities					
Employed among aged 18 and above (Percent)	61.45	100	38.55	0.06	41.01
Employed among aged 18 and above with formal contract (Percent)	35.88	100	64.12	0.10	70.67
Employed among aged 18 and above with productive employment (Percent)	47.40	100	52.60	0.14	59.91

of life expectancy at birth, they are included as separate well-being indicators. This is because they are susceptible to poor hygienic conditions and more susceptible to water-borne diseases and malnutrition (Kakwani and Son 2016a, Chapter 6).

The data on education were obtained on seven indicators. Among them, adult literacy can be considered the ultimate achievement of society. If a person is literate, they can access many other capabilities such as reading, writing, communicating with others, and participating in the political process. It is almost impossible for an illiterate person to function in contemporary societies.

Educational attainment is another essential component of well-being. Any additional years of schooling generate positive rates of return, and more school enables individuals to get higher-paying jobs and hence raises their standard of living. The expected number of years of education for 18-year-olds is an indicator of educational attainment. Two additional indicators of educational attainment compiled are: (i) the percentage of people aged 18 years and above who have completed high school, and (ii) the percentage of people aged 25 years and above who have completed higher education. Further, three indicators related to school attendance among children in the school-age group are also included in the analysis.

Well-being is concerned with people's living conditions. For example, a population deprived of clean water, toilet, and adequate sanitation are susceptible to infectious diseases, resulting in poor health and a high mortality rate. This case study has identified four indicators that directly impact people's health: access to pipe water, toilets, adequate sanitation, and garbage disposal. In addition, the study has also added access to electricity, which affects people's necessary capabilities, including education. Thus, five indicators are utilized under the dimension of living conditions.

A large proportion of the population earns its livelihood through labor markets. An income enables people to lead a better life. Those unemployed are likely to have a lower standard of living. Besides material rewards, jobs provide people with work satisfaction. However, not all employees derive the same satisfaction from their jobs. In improving well-being, the quality of employment should also matter. For instance, people in the informal sector work long hours under poor conditions and receive low wages. In Brazil, one-fourth of the workforce is employed in the informal sector. Persons engaged in the informal sector are the ones who do not have a formal employment contract. The proportion of employees with a legal agreement is used as an indicator of well-being.

Similarly, productive employment is also an essential component of well-being. Thus, this case study has included the percentage of the population with productive employment. Productive work ensures that a worker and her dependents have a consumption level above the poverty line. For Brazil, a person with productive employment is defined as earnings at least one minimum wage.

The analysis in this case study does not include many other social and psychological characteristics components of quality of life, such as security, freedom of choice, and human rights, mainly due to the non-availability of the appropriate data. The analysis may be deemed somewhat limited in this context. Nevertheless, while the analysis may appear incomplete, it has still covered a wide range of essential capabilities influencing human well-being, not undertaken by any previous study.

The first column in Table 8.2 provides the average achievement in well-being in Brazil in 2010. For instance, the average life expectancy at birth is 74.39 years, implying that a person born in Brazil in 2010 expects to live just over 74 years. However, poverty is about a shortfall in achieving well-being, called ill-being. The shortfall in the jth attribute is measured by $D_j(x)$, defined in (8.6.1). The shortfall calculation requires the minimum and maximum values of achievement attainable by any society. The minimum value of all shortfalls is set at zero. The maximum value of average life expectancy at birth is set at 85 years. Until now, no country has attained an average life expectancy at birth exceeding 85. Column 2 in Table 8.2 gives the maximum value of achievement in various attributes. The indicators relating to the percentage of the population with given levels of achievement have been given the maximum value of 100. Children in Brazil start their schooling at the age of 6; it is reasonable to set the maximum value of 12 to the expected number of years of education for 18-year-olds.

The average ill-being or shortfall measured by $\overline{D}_j$ is then calculated from columns 2 and 3, presented in column 3. Finally, the inequity index, given in column 4, informs the extent to which income contributes to the particular dimension of ill-being. In the case of Brazil, this index helps answer questions as to whether better-off municipalities are likely to suffer from higher or lower ill-being, and to what extent?

The positive value of the inequity index indicates that the poorer municipalities suffer from greater ill-being than the wealthier ones. As the values of the inequity index are positive for all indicators (except for the adult literacy rate), the better-off municipalities are likely to have lower multidimensional poverty than their worse-off counterparts; the poorer the municipality, the larger would be its poverty.

The poverty in literacy rate is only 9.96%, implying that more than 90% of the adult population in Brazil is literate. Furthermore, the inequity index has a value of −0.01, which signifies that the economic situation of municipalities has no or an insignificant impact on the shortfall in literacy rate.

The value of the inequity index for the life expectancy at birth is 0.10, which implies that inequity in achievement contributes to 10% additional poverty in longevity. Brazilian society suffers from an average shortfall in life expectancy of 12.48%. Since poor municipalities do not have equitable access to health services, ill-being in longevity rises to 13.76%, the proposed measure of aggregate poverty in achieving longevity. Column 5 in Table 8.2 provides the aggregate poverty index in various dimensions.

The aggregate poverty in infant and child survival rates is relatively minor compared to life expectancy at birth. This phenomenon might be widespread worldwide because most countries have developed immunization programs that significantly impact infant and children's survival. Poor sanitation, unclean drinking water, and poor nutrition are the additional causes of low survival rates among infants and children. Economic conditions influence these indicators, explaining the higher inequity in infant and child survival rates.

Under education, the study has presented the incidence of poverty for seven indicators. The magnitude of poverty varies from 3.95% for the children 11 to 14 years attending school to 92.88% for those aged 25 and older who have completed higher education. Given such a wide variation in poverty in different attributes, it is impossible to infer meaningfully the overall poverty in education. It would be more insightful for policymakers to look at poverty in individual education components. Also, the inequity index for various education segments is relatively low, implying that a family's economic circumstances do not play a significant role in providing education to the population in Brazil.

The values of the inequity index show that compared with health and education, living conditions are more directly influenced by income. The more affluent municipalities have lower poverty levels in piped water, electricity, access to a toilet, garbage collection, and adequate sanitation. Also, the overall poverty in living conditions is high. These observations have a clear message that the government of Brazil should pay more considerable attention to improving its necessary infrastructure.

Most economic activities take place through labor markets. Many people earn their livelihood by participating in the labor market, which strongly bears their well-being. The study has presented three indicators of poverty relating to the labor market. It reveals that the overall poverty under labor market activities is higher than all other dimensions of ill-being. It is noted that 70.67% of employees are engaged in the informal sector with no formal contract. These people have lower employment protection, working long hours with lower wages. Almost 60% of employees do not have productive employment, receiving wages below the poverty line. These observations also have a clear message for the government to reform the labor market.

Table 8.2 has a mixture of both output and outcome indicators, and it would be meaningless to aggregate them into a composite index of poverty. From the policy perspective, it is more insightful to analyze poverty in various dimensions instead of constructing a composite index.

8.8 Concluding Remarks

There is now widespread consensus that poverty is multidimensional, reflecting people's deprivation in many aspects of life. It is not enough to measure deprivation in income space. Sen's seminal work on functionings and capabilities led to a clear shift toward a multidimensional poverty measure. There is now a sizable literature focused on developing a multifaceted composite index. For policy purposes, the analysis of poverty in different dimensions can be indispensable because policymakers want to identify which aspects of poverty have a capability failure. A composite index can, at best, inform that there has been an overall capability failure. This information does not help formulate policy to reduce or eliminate deprivation in a particular dimension of poverty.

Sen's capabilities and functionings framework has played a crucial role in developing multidimensional poverty. This approach provides the broadest definition of poverty, leading to many complex measurement issues. Although the literature on multidimensional poverty has made considerable progress in identifying the poor and developing multifaceted poverty indices, many unresolved challenges exist. This chapter has provided a comprehensive discussion of many unresolved issues.

The measurement of multidimensional poverty requires poverty thresholds for every dimension. However, the literature has not dealt with constructing poverty thresholds for the necessary minimum capabilities to identify the poor in different poverty dimensions. For example, it is not apparent how one can place a threshold for life expectancy at birth or infant survival rate. Similarly, can one say that a 50% literacy rate is the minimum acceptable rate to society in literacy rate? Such thresholds are arbitrary, which would lead to arbitrary measures of poverty.

Well-being indicators are different from income. They are generally bounded, lying in a finite range, such as health status, educational attainment, or nutritional intake; therefore, their maximum possible levels are readily known. These maximum levels provide the ideal achievements that societies can attain. Any deviations of actual achievements from the ideals represent shortfalls in well-being. These shortfalls are measures of ill-being, which can be used to measure poverty in different dimensions. For instance, the infant survival rate is an indicator of attainment. In contrast, the infant mortality rate indicates a shortfall and can be called an indicator of ill-being.

Similarly, life expectancy at birth is an indicator of achievement, and the deviation of life expectancy at birth from its maximum value would indicate the shortfall in longevity. Thus, an aggregate measure of shortfalls suffered by all individuals in society will measure poverty in longevity.

Poverty is concerned with the deprivation of basic capabilities. People may suffer capability deprivation due to a host of factors. For instance, if Bill Gates suffers capability deprivation in health, it would be odd to call him poor. He is deprived but not poor. This chapter has argued that poverty occurs when capability deprivation occurs due to the inadequacy of command over resources. Examining capability deprivation alone cannot identify persons as the poor; even they suffer acute deprivation in a dimension. Therefore, income should play a central role in the measurement of poverty. The literature has entirely ignored the role of resources available to individuals. This chapter has provided the multidimensional poverty framework that links capability deprivation with resources. The framework offers aggregate measures of poverty in each dimension.

Furthermore, the framework provides a new index of inequity in ill-being. This index informs whether the poorer persons suffer greater or lesser ill-being than the wealthier persons. The larger the value of this index, the higher the suffering of the poor. Governments have welfare programs to reduce people's deprivation of well-being, and governments transfer resources to those who cannot afford the necessary capabilities through such programs. Hence, income plays a central role in reducing multidimensional poverty. The inequity index developed in the chapter can be a valuable tool in formulating policies to alleviate poverty in its dimensions.

The most contentious issue in measuring multidimensional poverty is the weights assigned to various dimensions. The literature has resorted to arbitrary weights without providing economic justification. This chapter has argued that it makes an intuitive sense to relate the weights to the costs of eliminating the deprivation in different poverty dimensions. But suppose these costs are not readily available. In that case, alternately, society might be most concerned about the inequity in the distribution of ill-being, so it might be appropriate to make weights proportional to the inequity index. However, the MPI so derived also has a limitation. It gives higher weight to the poverty dimensions that are more sensitive to economic resources available to individuals.

The chapter makes a distinction between output and outcome indicators. For instance, access to health care is an output, and life expectancy at birth is an outcome. People's economic resources more directly impact the output through their income or resources, and governments can also provide resources to families through social programs. On the other hand, life expectancy at birth is an outcome that is influenced by several health-related individual factors, including excess to health care or even genes specific to individuals. A critical question arises whether one should measure multidimensional poverty by outputs or outcomes. The literature has not addressed this issue. In the analysis of poverty, it would be more meaningful if all dimensions of poverty are outputs. If dimensions of poverty have a mixture of both outputs and outcomes, any aggregation of poverty dimensions will lead to a meaningless poverty measure.

Individuals have different needs and differ in their ability to convert their income or resources into capabilities to function. Individuals have different circumstances and require different resources to achieve the necessary capabilities. Ideally, any proposed income measure of poverty should be constructed from capabilities. Therefore, income poverty thresholds should reflect the cost of achieving basic capabilities. Chapter 6 developed poverty thresholds to meet people's nutritional needs in income space. This methodology could be extended to calculate the cost of achieving other essential capabilities.

9

Concentration Curves

9.1 Introduction

Relationships among the distributions of various economic variables are the corner-stone of economic analysis. For example, economic theory suggests a relation between total family expenditure and income. Therefore, it is important to know under what conditions a family's total expenditure is more equally distributed than income, especially because expenditure is considered a better indicator of a family's actual economic position than the current income.

This chapter shows how the Lorenz curve technique can help us understand the relationships among economic variables. Mahalanobis (1960) proposed extending and generalizing the Lorenz curve concept to deal with consumer behavior patterns associated with different commodities. He suggested that generalized Lorenz curves be called concentration curves. He used concentration curves as a convenient graphical tool to illustrate consumption patterns for various commodities based on data from the National Sample Survey of India.

Kakwani (1977c) provided a more general and rigorous treatment of concentration curves to study the relations among the distributions of different economic variables. He proved many theorems that led to numerous applications in economics, particularly in public finance, where the effect of taxation and public spending on income distribution is analyzed. Chapter 10 is entirely devoted to the economic applications of theorems proved in this chapter.

This chapter has developed a new method of estimating aggregate elasticity for the whole population using the concentration index. Empirical estimates of concentration indices can readily be obtained from household surveys, providing the estimates of aggregate elasticity. Chapter 10 provides numerous applications of the aggregate elasticity estimated from concentration indices.

9.2 Derivation of Concentration Curves

Suppose income X is a random variable with probability density function $f(X)$ and distribution function $F(X)$. Hence, we define $F(x)$ as the proportion of persons having an income less than or equal to x. Let $g(X)$ be a continuous function of X so that its first

Economic Inequality and Poverty. Nanak Kakwani and Hyun Son, Oxford University Press.
© Nanak Kakwani and Hyun Son (2022). DOI: 10.1093/oso/9780198852841.003.0009

derivative exists, and the following condition holds, $g(X) \geq 0$ *for all* $X \geq 0$. If $E[g(x)]$ exists, one can define

$$F_1[g(x)] = \frac{1}{E[g(X)]} \int_0^x g(X)f(X)\,dX \qquad (9.2.1)$$

where

$$E[g(X)] = \int_0^\infty g(X)f(X)\,dX$$

so that

$$\lim_{x \to 0} F_1[g(x)] = 0 \qquad (9.2.2)$$

and

$$\lim_{x \to \infty} F_1[g(x)] = 1. \qquad (9.2.3)$$

The relationship between $F_1[g(x)]$ and $F(x)$ will be called the $g(x)$ function's concentration curve. The curve is obtained by inverting the functions $F_1[g(x)]$ and $F(x)$ and eliminating x if the functions are invertible. Alternatively, one plots the curve by generating the $F_1[g(x)]\,F(x)$ values by giving some arbitrary values to x. Like the Lorenz curve, this curve is represented in a unit square. The ordinate and abscissa of the curve are $F_1[g(x)]$ and $F(x)$, respectively. Equations (9.2.2) and (9.2.3) imply that the curve passes through (0, 0) and (1, 1). $F_1(g(x)) = F(x)$ is called the egalitarian line, on which $g(x)$ has the same value for all x.

If $F(X)$ is continuous, the derivative of $F_1[g(x)]$ with respect to x exists and is given by

$$\frac{dF_1[g(x)]}{dx} = \frac{g(x)f(x)}{E[g(X)]} \geq 0, \qquad (9.2.4)$$

which implies that $F_1[g(x)]$ is a monotonically nondecreasing function of x.

Using $\frac{d}{dX}F(X) = f(X)$ and (9.2.4), the slope of the concentration curve can be defined as

$$\frac{dF_1[g(x)]}{dF(x)} = \frac{g(x)}{E[g(x)]}, \qquad (9.2.5)$$

which is nonnegative if $g(x) \geq 0$. Assuming $g(x) > 0$ for all $x > 0$, then equation (9.2.5) implies that the concentration curve is monotonically increasing function of x.

The second derivative of the concentration curve is

$$\frac{d^2 F_1 [g(x)]}{dF^2 (x)} = \frac{g'(x)}{E[g(X)]} \cdot \frac{1}{f(x)},$$

(9.2.6)

which may be positive or negative depending on the sign of $g'(x)$. If $g'(x) >$ 0 *for all* $x > 0$, the concentration curve is convex to the F-axis, implying $F_1 [g(x)] <$ $F(x)$ *for all* x. In this case, the concentration curve falls below the egalitarian line. If $g'(x) < 0$, the concentration curve is concave to the F-axis and $F_1 [g(x)] > F(x)$ for all x. Under this scenario, the concentration curve lies above the egalitarian line. If, however, $g'(x) = 0$ *for all* x, the concentration curve coincides with the egalitarian line.

The Lorenz curve defined in (3.2.2) is the relationship between $F_1 (x)$ and $F(x)$, where $F_1 (x)$ is the proportion of total income enjoyed by persons with income less than or equal to x. It follows that the Lorenz curve of income x is a particular case of the concentration curve for the function $g(x)$ when $g(x) = x$. The relationship between $F_1 [g(x)]$ and $F_1 (x)$ will be called the relative concentration curve of $g(x)$ with respect to x. Similarly, let $g^*(x)$ be another continuous function of x, the graph of $F_1 [g(x)]$ versus $F_1 [g^*(x)]$ will be called the relative concentration curve of $g(x)$ with respect to $g^*(x)$.

9.3 The Concentration Curve for Well-Known Income Distributions

9.3.1 The Pareto Distribution

The Pareto distribution has a probability distribution function given by

$$F(x) = 1 - \left(\frac{x}{x_0}\right)^{-\alpha} \quad when\ x \geq x_0$$

(9.3.1)

where x_0 is the scale factor, and α is the Pareto parameter.[1] The density function of the Pareto is given by

$$f(x) = \alpha x_0^{\alpha} x^{-1-\alpha} \quad when\ x \geq x_0$$
$$= 0 \qquad\qquad when\ x < x_0.$$

If it is assumed that

$$g(x) = Ax^{\eta},$$

(9.3.2)

---

[1] Note that is found to be approximately 1.5. See Pareto (1897).

which on substituting in (9.2.1) gives

$$F_1\left[g\left(x\right)\right] = \frac{1}{E\left[g\left(x\right)\right]} \int_0^x A\alpha x_0^\alpha X^{\eta-\alpha-1} dX. \tag{9.3.3}$$

This equation is evaluated as

$$F_1\left[g\left(x\right)\right] = \frac{A\alpha x_0^\eta}{E\left[g\left(X\right)\right]\left(\alpha - \eta\right)}\left[1 - \left(\frac{x_0}{x}\right)^{\alpha-\eta}\right], \tag{9.3.4}$$

which should approach unity as x approaches infinity. Note that this limit exists only if $\alpha > \eta$, which, if satisfied, yields

$$E\left[g\left(x\right)\right] = \frac{A\alpha x_0^\eta}{\alpha - \eta}. \tag{9.3.5}$$

Now, eliminating x from (9.3.1) and (9.3.4) and using (9.3.5) yields

$$1 - F_1\left[g\left(x\right)\right] = \left[1 - F\left(x\right)\right]^{(\alpha-\eta)/\alpha}, \tag{9.3.6}$$

which is the equation of the concentration curve for the function $g(x)$ defined in (9.3.2). When $\eta = 1$, equation (9.3.6) reduces to the Lorenz curve for the Pareto distribution, derived in (3.3.4) in Chapter 3. Note that the concentration curve in (9.3.6) is defined if and only if $\eta < \alpha$.

9.3.2 The Lognormal Distribution

The probability distribution function of the lognormal distribution defined in (3.3.10), Chapter 3 is given by

$$F\left(x\right) = \Lambda\left(x/\mu, \sigma^2\right)$$

where

$$\Lambda\left(x/\mu, \sigma^2\right) = \int_0^x \frac{1}{X\sigma\sqrt{2\pi}} \exp\{-\frac{1}{2\sigma^2}(\log X - \mu)^2\} dX \, for \, x > 0. \tag{9.3.7}$$

Given this, the following equation is derived from (9.2.1), using (9.3.2)

$$F_1\left[g\left(x\right)\right] = \frac{1}{E\left[g\left(x\right)\right]} \int_0^x A X^\eta d\Lambda\left(x \mid \mu, \sigma^2\right),$$

which on using Theorem 2.6 in Aitchison and Brown (1957, 12), simplifies to

$$F_1\left[g\left(x\right)\right] = \Lambda\left(x \mid \mu + \eta\sigma^2, \sigma^2\right). \tag{9.3.8}$$

It is helpful to define

$$x = \varphi\left(t\right)$$

where $t = \frac{1}{\sqrt{2\pi}} \int_0^x \exp\left(-X^2/2\right) dX$ is the standard normal distribution function. Then if $F\left(x\right) = \Lambda\left(x/\mu, \sigma^2\right)$, it follows that

$$\frac{\log x - \mu}{\sigma} = \phi\left[F\left(x\right)\right] \tag{9.3.9}$$

and

$$\frac{\log x - \mu - \eta\sigma^2}{\sigma} = \phi\left[F_1\left\{g\left(x\right)\right\}\right] \tag{9.3.10}$$

respectively. Eliminating $\log(x)$ from (9.3.9) and (9.3.10) yields the equation of the concentration curve as[2]

$$\phi\left[F_1\left\{g\left(x\right)\right\}\right] = \phi\left[F\left(x\right)\right] - \eta\sigma, \tag{9.3.11}$$

which depends on the two parameters, η and σ. Substituting $\eta = 1$ into (9.3.11) gives the equation of the Lorenz curve for the lognormal distribution as given in (3.3.15), Chapter 3.

9.4 Relationships between Elasticity and Concentration Curves

Elasticity has numerous economic applications. This section reveals the linkage between the elasticity of a function and concentration curves, and this linkage opens the door to many economic applications.

Let $\eta_g\left(x\right)$ be the elasticity of $g\left(x\right)$ with respect to x given by

$$\eta_g\left(x\right) = \frac{g'\left(x\right)x}{g\left(x\right)} \tag{9.4.1}$$

---

[2] This result was derived by Iyenger (1960).

where $g'(x)$ is the first derivative of $g(x)$. Similarly, denote $\eta_{g^*}(x)$ as the elasticity of $g^*(x)$ with respect to x. The relationship between the elasticity of the two functions is stated in the following theorem, which has a wide range of economic applications.

Theorem 9.1 *The concentration curve for the function $g(x)$ will lie above (below) the concentration curve for the function $g^*(x)$ if and only if $\eta_g(x)$ is less (greater) than $\eta_{g^*}(x)$ for all $x \geq 0$.*

Proof. Utilizing (9.2.5), the slope of the relative concentration curve of $g(x)$ with respect to that of $g^*(x)$ is

$$\frac{dF_1[g(x)]}{dF_1[g^*(x)]} = \frac{E[g^*(X)]\ g(x)}{E[g(X)]\ g^*(x)} > 0, \qquad (9.4.2)$$

which implies that the relative concentration curve of $g(x)$ with respect to $g^*(x)$ is monotonically increasing. Because the curve must pass through $(0, 0)$ and $(1, 1)$, a sufficient condition for $F_1[g(x)]$ to be greater (less) than $F_1[g^*(x)]$ is that the curve be convex (concave) from above. To establish the curvature, the second derivative of $F_1[g(x)]$ with respect to $F_1[g^*(x)]$ is obtained as

$$\frac{d^2F_1[g(x)]}{dF_1^2[g^*(x)]} = \frac{(E[g^*(X)])^2}{E[g(X)]} \frac{g(x)}{g^{*2}(x)} \frac{[\eta_g - \eta_{g^*}]}{xf(x)}. \qquad (9.4.3)$$

This derivation uses equations (9.2.6) and (9.4.1). The sign of the second derivative is given by $\eta_g(x) - \eta_{g^*}(x)$. Thus, the second derivative is positive (negative) if $\eta_g(x)$ is greater (less) than $\eta_{g^*}(x)$ for all x. The concentration curve for $g(x)$ lies, therefore, above (below) the concentration curve for $g^*(x)$ if $\eta_g(x)$ is less (greater) than $\eta_{g^*}(x)$ for all $x \geq 0$. This proves sufficient condition. The necessary condition follows immediately from equation (9.4.3), which completes the proof of the theorem.

If $g^*(x)$ is constant for all $x \geq 0$, then elasticity $\eta_{g^*}(x) = 0$ and $F_1[g^*(x)] = F(x)$, which is the equation of the egalitarian line. This leads to the following corollary.

Corollary 9.1 *The concentration curve for the function $g(x)$ will be above (below) the egalitarian line if and only if $\eta_g(x)$ is less (greater) than zero for all $x \geq 0$.*[3]

Substituting $g^*(x) = x$ such that $\eta_{g^*}(x) = 1$, the concentration curve for $g^*(x)$ becomes the Lorenz curve for x. It follows from Corollary 9.1 that the Lorenz curve for

---

[3] Roy, Chakravarty, and Laha (1959) have provided the proof of this corollary.

x lies below the egalitarian line and that, therefore, the curve is concave from above. Hence, Corollary 9.2 follows from Theorem 9.1.

Corollary 9.2 *The concentration curve for the function $g(x)$ lies above (below) the Lorenz curve for the distribution of x if and only if $\eta_g(x)$ is less (greater) than unity for all $x \geq 0$.*

Suppose the function $g(x)$ has unit elasticity for all $x \geq 0$; the second derivative of the relative concentration curve of $g(x)$ with respect to x will be zero—implying that the relative concentration curve slope will be zero for all values of x. Because the curve must pass through $(0, 0)$ and $(1, 1)$, the relative concentration curve of $g(x)$ with respect to x coincides with the egalitarian line. Thus, $F_1[g(x)] = F_1(x)$ for all $x \geq 0$. Similarly, if $F_1[g(x)] = F_1(x)$, the slope of the relative concentration curve will be constant, which from (9.4.3) implies that $g(x)/x$ is constant for all x. This gives $\eta_g(x) = 1$ for all x and proves the following corollary.

Corollary 9.3 *The concentration curve for $g(x)$ coincides with the Lorenz curve for x if and only if $\eta_g(x)$ is unity for all $x \geq 0$.*

Note that the concentration curve $g(x)$ is not the same as the Lorenz curve for $g(x)$. The following conditions are derived so that both are identical.

Let $Y = g(X)$ be a random variable with the probability density function $f^*(Y)$ and the distribution function $F^*(Y)$; if the mean of Y exists, the first-moment distribution function of Y is given by

$$F_1^*(y) = \frac{1}{E(Y)} \int_0^y Yf^*(Y)\, dY. \tag{9.4.4}$$

Then, $[F^*(y), F_1^*(y)]$ is a point on the Lorenz curve for $g(x)$. The two curves will be identical if

$$F^*[g(x)] = F(x)\, F_1^*[g(x)] = F_1[g(x)] \tag{9.4.5}$$

for all values of x. The following theorem provides the conditions under which the two curves are identical.

Theorem 9.2 *If the function $g(x)$ has a continuous derivative $g'(x)$ strictly positive for all $x \geq 0$, the concentration curve for $g(x)$ coincides with the Lorenz curve for the distribution of $g(x)$.*

Proof. The condition $g'(x) > 0$ for all x implies that $g(x)$ is strictly monotonic. Further, if $g(x)$ has a continuous non-vanishing derivative in the region $x \geq 0$, the probability density function of Y is given by[4]

---

[4] See Wilks (1944, 55).

$$F^* (Y) = f[h(Y)] \mid h'(Y) \tag{9.4.6}$$

where $X = h(Y)$ is the solution of $Y = g(X)$.

Now, consider the graph of $F(x)$ against $F^*[g(x)]$, which has the slope

$$\frac{dF^*[g(x)]}{dF(x)} = \frac{F^*(y)}{f(x)h'(y)}$$

that, on using (9.4.6), becomes unity if $h'(y) > 0$. Furthermore, $g'(x) > 0$ necessarily implies that $h'(y) > 0$. Because the curve of $F(x)$ versus $F^*[g(x)]$ passes through $(0, 0)$ and $(1, 1)$ and has the slope of unity for all x; it must coincide with the line through $(0, 0)$ and $(1, 1)$. Hence, $F^*[g(x)] = F(x)$.

Likewise, we can prove that the graph of $F_1[g(x)]$ against $F_1^*[g(x)]$ has the slope of unity for all $x \geq 0$. Because the curve passes through $(0, 0)$ and $(1, 1)$, it must coincide with the straight line joining $(0, 0)$ and $(1, 1)$—implying that $F_1^*[g(x)] = F_1[g(x)]$. This proves Theorem 9.2.

The following corollaries follow immediately from Theorems 9.1 and 9.2.

Corollary 9.4 *If the functions $g(x)$ and $g^*(x)$ have continuous derivatives strictly greater than zero for all x, $g(x)$ is Lorenz superior (inferior) to $g^*(x)$ if $\eta_g(x)$ is less (greater) than $\eta_{g^*}(x)$ for all $x \geq 0$.*

Corollary 9.5 *If the function $g(x)$ has a continuous derivative $g'(x) > 0$ for all x, $g(x)$ is Lorenz superior (inferior) to x if $\eta_g(x)$ is less (greater) than unity for all $x \geq 0$.*

Theorem 9.3 *If $g(x) = \sum_{i=1}^{k} g_i(x)$ so that $E[g(x)] = \sum_{i=1}^{k} E[g_i(x)]$ where E is the expected value operator,*

$$E[g(x)] F_1[g(x)] = \sum_{i=1}^{k} E[g_i(x)] F_1[g_i(x)]. \tag{9.4.7}$$

Proof. Substituting $g(x) = \sum_{i=1}^{k} g_i(x)$ into (9.2.1) and interchanging the summation and integral signs gives[5]

$$F_1[g(x)] = \frac{1}{E[g(x)]} \sum_{i=1}^{k} \int_0^x g_i(X) f(x)\, dx \tag{9.4.8}$$

Note that $F_1[g_i(x)]$ can be expressed as

$$F_1[g_i(x)] = \frac{1}{E[g_i(x)]} \int_0^x g_i(X) f(X)\, dX,$$

[5] The interchange of summation and integral signs is permissible if k is finite.

which, substituting into (9.4.8), provides the result stated in the theorem.

Let $g(x) = a + bx$ such that $E[g(x)] = a + b\mu$ where $E(x) = \mu$. Given this, $g(x)$ is the sum of two functions, a and bx. Thus, Theorem 9.3 yields

$$F_1[a + bx] = \frac{1}{a + b\mu}[aF(x) + b\mu F_1(x)].$$

(9.4.9)

This holds because the constant function's concentration curve coincides with the egalitarian line. Equation (9.4.9) can also be written as

$$F_1[a + bx] - F_1(x) = \frac{a}{a + b\mu}[F(x) - F_1(x)].$$

(9.4.10)

Because $F(x) \geq F_1(x)$ for all x, it implies that the concentration curve for a linear function $(a + bx)$ lies above (below) the Lorenz curve for x if a is greater (less) than zero. Further, if $b > 0$, the function $g(x) = a + bx$ is a monotonic increasing function of x and has a continuous first derivative $g'(x)$ strictly greater than zero. In that case, the concentration curve for $(a + bx)$ coincides with the Lorenz curve of function $(a + bx)$. This leads to the following corollary.

Corollary 9.6 *If $b > 0$, the linear function $(a + bx)$ is Lorenz superior (inferior) to x if a is greater (less) than zero.*

In Corollary 9.6, if $a < 0$, the linear function $(a + bx)$ will be negative for $x \leq -a/b$. Consider the case in which the function $(a + bx)$ is forced to be equal to zero. Under this assumption, the mean value of the function is

$$E[a + bx] = \int_{-a/b}^{\infty}(a + bx)f(x)\, dx$$
$$= a + b\mu - aF\left(\frac{-a}{b}\right) - b\mu\left(\frac{-a}{b}\right)$$

(9.4.11)

and the first-moment distribution function becomes

$$F_1[a + bx] = \frac{1}{E[a+bx]}\int_{-a/b}^{x}(a + bx)f(x)\, dx$$
$$= \frac{a}{\mu^*}\left[F(x) - F\left(\frac{-a}{b}\right)\right] + \frac{b\mu}{\mu^*}\left[F_1(x) - F_1\left(\frac{-a}{b}\right)\right]$$

(9.4.12)

for $x \geq -a/b$ where $\mu^* = E(a + bx)$. Note that $F_1(a + bx) = 0$ for $x < -a/b$.

Utilizing (9.4.11), equation (9.4.12) can be expressed as

$$F_1(a + bx) - F_1(x) = \frac{a}{\mu^*}[F(x) - F_1(x)] - \frac{1 - F_1(x)}{\mu^*}[a + b\mu - \mu^*].$$

(9.4.13)

The right-hand side of (9.4.13) can be negative or positive, depending on the value of x. Thus, the Lorenz curves for x and $(a + bx)$ may intersect. Hence, it is impossible to conclude that $(a+bx)$ will be more (less) equally distributed than x.

9.5 Concentration Index of a Function

This section introduces the concentration index for a function $g(x)$ and proves some of its theorems.

The concentration index for a function $g(x)$ is defined as one minus twice the area under the $g(x)$ concentration curve. It is given by

$$C_g = 1 - 2\int_0^\infty F_1\left[g(x)\right] dF(x). \tag{9.5.1}$$

It is easy to verify that

$$E\left[F(x)\right] = \int_0^\infty F(x)f(x)\,dx = 1/2 \tag{9.5.2}$$

which shows that the probability distribution function $F(x)$ always has a mean equal to ½. Utilizing (9.5.2) into (9.5.1) and $dF(x) = f(x)\,dx$, the concentration index of $g(x)$ can be written as

$$C_g = 2\int_0^\infty \left[F(x) - F_1\left(g(x)\right)\right]f(x)\,dx. \tag{9.5.3}$$

It will be helpful to express the concentration index differently. Integration (9.5.3) by parts yields

$$C_g = \frac{2}{\mu_g}\int_0^\infty g(x)F(x)f(x)\,dx - 1 \tag{9.5.4}$$

where $\mu_g = E\left[g(x)\right] = \int_0^\infty g(x)f(x)\,dx$ is the mean of g(x). Further, combining (9.5.2) and (9.5.4) gives

$$C_g = 2\int_0^\infty \left[\frac{\mu_g - g(x)}{\mu_g}\right]\left[1 - F(x)\right]f(x)\,dx \tag{9.5.5}$$

Note that substituting $g(x)=x$ in (9.5.5) immediately gives $C_g = G$, where G is the Gini index of income x. Thus, the $g(x)$ concentration index is the Gini index of x when $g(x)=x$.

It is important to emphasize that $g(x)$'s concentration index will not be the same as the Gini index of $g(x)$. But, the condition under which both will be identical is derived below.

The covariance of functions $g(x)$ and $F(x)$ is given by

$$cov\left[g\left(x\right), F\left(x\right)\right] = \int_0^\infty \left[g\left(x\right) - \mu_g\right]\left[F\left(x\right) - \frac{1}{2}\right]f(x)\,dx \qquad (9.5.6)$$

which on using (9.5.5), gives

$$C_g = \frac{2}{\mu_g}cov\left[g\left(x\right), F\left(x\right)\right]. \qquad (9.5.7)$$

The Gini index of the variable $y=g(x)$ is

$$G_g = 1 - 2\int_0^\infty F_1^*\left(y\right)F^*\left(x\right)dx \qquad (9.5.8)$$

where $F_1^*\left(y\right)$, defined in (9.4.4), is the first-moment distribution function of y and $F^*\left(x\right)$ is the probability distribution function of y. Integrating (9.5.8) by parts and following similar steps as in the derivation of (9.5.5) gives

$$G_g = 2\int_0^\infty \left[\frac{\mu_g - g\left(x\right)}{\mu_g}\right]\left[1 - F^*\left(y\right)\right]F^*\left(y\right)dy \qquad (9.5.9)$$

where $F^*\left(y\right) = F^*\left(g\left(x\right)\right)$ is the probability distribution function of y. From (9.5.9), it is not difficult to show that

$$G_g = \frac{2}{\mu_g}cov[g\left(x\right), F^*\left(g\left(x\right)\right)], \qquad (9.5.10)$$

which on combining with (9.5.7) yields the relationship between C_g and G_g as

$$C_g = \frac{cov\left[g\left(x\right), F\left(x\right)\right]}{cov\left[g\left(x\right), F^*\left(g\left(x\right)\right)\right]}G_g. \qquad (9.5.11)$$

If the total number of persons is fixed, the variance of $F(x)$ will be identical to the variance of $F^*(g(x))$.[6] That gives

$$C_g = \frac{R\left[g\left(x\right), F\left(x\right)\right]}{R\left[g\left(x\right), F^*\left(g\left(x\right)\right)\right]}G_g, \qquad (9.5.12)$$

where $R(a, b)$ stands for the rank correlation coefficient between a and b, noting that the probability distribution $F(x)$ is the cumulative proportion of persons when arranged in ascending order of their income x. Similarly, $F^*(g(x))$ is the cumulative

---

[6] In fact, all the moments of $F(x)$ and $F^*(g(x))$ will be identical.

proportion of persons when the same persons are arranged in ascending order of their $g(x)$ values. Therefore, their difference will be ranking between x and $g(x)$. Thus, if $F(x)$ and $F^*(g(x))$ are replaced by the rankings of x and $g(x)$, the rank correlation coefficients in (9.5.12) will remain the same. That leads to the following theorem.

Theorem 9.4 *The concentration index of $g(x)$ is related to the Gini index of $g(x)$ as*

$$C_g = \frac{R[g(x),\, r(x)]}{R[g(x),\, r(g(x))]} G_g,$$ (9.5.13)

where $r(x)$ stands for a rank of x, and $r(g(x))$ for the rank of $g(x)$.

From this theorem it follows that if $r(x)=r(g(x))$, $C_g = G_g$. If $g'(x) > 0$ for all x, and $g(x)$ will have the same raking, in which case the concentration index of $g(x)$ will be equal to the Gini index of $g(x)$. If $g'(x) < 0$ for all x and $g(x)$ will have the opposite ranking, and hence $R[g(x),\, r(x)] = -R[g(x),\, r(g(x))]$, $C_g = -G_g$. If there is no monotonic relationship between x and $g(x)$, $R[g(x),\, r(x)] \le R[g(x),\, r(g(x))]$, which from (7.9.13) implies that C_g lies between $-G_g$ and $+G_g$. This leads to Theorem 9.5.

Theorem 9.5

$$-G_g \le C_g \le G_g$$

where C_g and G_g are the concentration and Gini indices, respectively, of any function $g(x)$.

Theorem 9.3, in conjunction with the definition of the concentration index of $g(x)$ in (9.5.1), leads to Theorem 9.6

Theorem 9.6
If

$$g(x) = \sum_{j=1}^{k} g_j(x)$$ (9.5.14)

so that

$$\mu_g = \sum_{j=1}^{k} \mu_{gj}$$ (9.5.15)

where μ_g is the mean of $g(x)$ and μ_{gj} is the mean of $g_j(x)$, then

$$\mu_g C_g = \sum_{j=1}^{k} \mu_{gj} C_{gj}$$ (9.5.16)

where C_g and C_{gj} are concentration indices of functions $g(x)$ and $g_j(x)$, respectively.

Proof. Utilizing (9.5.5), the concentration index of $g_j(x)$ is given by

$$\mu_{gj}C_{gj} = 2\int_0^\infty \mu_{gj} - g_j(x)[1 - F(x)]f(x)\,dx,$$

which on summing both sides from j to k and utilizing (9.5.14) and (9.5.15) yields (9.5.16). This proves Theorem 9.6.

Note that Theorem 9.6 does not require that functions $g(x)$ and $g_j(x)$ be monotonic. If, however, $g'(x) > 0$ for all x, that is, $g(x)$ is a monotonically increasing function of x, $r(x)=r(g(x))$, then it follows from Theorem 9.4 that $C_g = G_g$. Furthermore, if $g_j(x)$ is any function (not necessarily monotonic), it follows from Theorem 9.5 that $C_{gj} \leq G_{gj}$, where G_{gj} is the Gini index of $g_j(x)$. Substituting these results into (9.5.15) leads to the following corollary.

Corollary 9.7

$$\mu_g G_g \leq \sum_{j=1}^{k} \mu_{gj} G_{gj}$$

where G_g and G_{gj} are the Gini indices for $g(x)$ and $g_j(x)$, respectively.

Suppose $g(x)$ is a linear function $g(x)=a+bx$ so that $\mu_g = a + b\mu$, where μ is the mean of x. If $b > 0$, $g'(x)>0$, which from Theorem 9.4 implies that the concentration index of $(a+bx)$ is the same as its Gini index. Further, if the Gini index of a constant is zero, and the Gini index of bx is the same as the Gini index of x, then it follows from Theorem 9.6 that

$$(a + b\mu)\,G^* = b\mu G$$

where G is the Gini index of x, and G^* is the Gini index of the linear function $(a+bx)$. This leads to the following corollary.

Corollary 9.8 For the linear function $(a+bx)$, if $b>0$

$$G^* = \frac{b\mu G}{(a + b\mu)} \qquad\qquad (9.5.17)$$

In this Corollary, if $a=0$, $G^* = G$, which implies that income inequality remains unchanged if all incomes are multiplied by the same constant. Furthermore, G^* is less (greater) than G if a is greater (less) than zero.

The simple result in (9.5.16) has many practical applications discussed in subsequent chapters.

9.6 Relative Concentration Curve and Index

As noted, the graph of $F_1[g(x)]$ versus $F_1[g^*(x)]$ is called the relative concentration curve of $g(x)$ with respect to $g^*(x)$. Substituting $g^*(x)=x$, the relationship between $F_1[g(x)]$ and $F_1(x)$ will be called the relative concentration curve of $g(x)$ with respect to x. This curve is also represented in the unit square, with $F_1(x)$ as x-axis, and $F_1[g(x)]$ as ordinate. From (9.4.2), it follows that the slope of the relative concentration curve of $g(x)$ with respect to x is positive, implying that the curve increases monotonically as $F_1(x)$ increases from 0 to 1.

The curve $F_1[g(x)] = F_1(x)$ is the equation of the diagonal of the unit square, on which $g(x)$ and x increase at the same rate; for instance, if x increases by 1%, then $g(x)$ also increases by 1%. It means that the function $g(x)$ has an elasticity equal to one at all diagonal points. The diagonal is the line of unit elasticity. From (9.4.3), it is noted that the second derivative of the relative concentration curve is positive (negative) if the elasticity of $g(x)$ with respect to x is greater (less) than one. This proves the following theorem.

Theorem 9.7 $F_1(x) \geq F_1[g(x)]$ *for all x implies* $\eta_g(x) \geq 1$ *for all x. Similarly,* $F_1(x) \leq F_1[g(x)]$ *for all x implies* $\eta_g(x) \leq 1$ *for all x.*

This theorem implies that the relative concentration curve of $g(x)$ with respect to x lies above (below) the line of unit elasticity if the elasticity $\eta_g(x)$ is smaller (larger) than one. The elasticity will be equal to one at all points when the curve coincides with the line of unit elasticity.

The relative concentration index is defined as one minus twice the area under the relative concentration curve. Similar to the concentration index in (9.5.1), the relative concentration index of $g(x)$ with respect to x will be given by

$$C_{g,x} = 1 - 2\int_0^\infty F_1[g(x)]\, d[F_1(x)]. \tag{9.6.1}$$

It is easy to verify that

$$2\int_0^\infty F_1(x)\, dF_1(x) = 1, \tag{9.6.2}$$

which on using in (9.6.1) gives

$$C_{g,x} = 2\int_0^\infty [F_1(x) - F_1(g(x))]\, dF_1(x). \tag{9.6.3}$$

Since $dF_1(x) = \frac{x}{\mu} f(x)\, dx$, this equation is given by

$$C_{gx} = 2 \int_0^\infty \left[F_1(x) - F_1\{g(x)\} \right] f^*(x)\, dx \qquad (9.6.4)$$

where $f^*(x) = \frac{x}{\pi} f(x)$ such that $\int_0^\infty f^*(x) = 1$. Hence, $f^*(x)$ is a legitimate density function.

From Theorem 9.7, if $\left[F_1(x) - F_1\{g(x)\} \right] \geq 0$, it implies that $\eta_g(x) \geq 1$ for all x, and similarly if $\left[F_1(x) - F_1\{g(x)\} \right] \leq 0$, it implies that $\eta_g(x) \leq 1$ for all x. In conjunction with (9.6.4), this result leads to Theorem 9.8.

Theorem 9.8

(i) $\eta_g(x) > 1$ *for all x implies* $C_{gx} > 0$.
(ii) $\eta_g(x) < 1$ *for all x implies* $C_{gx} < 0$
(iii) $\eta_g(x) = 1$ *for all x implies* $C_{gx} = 0$

9.7 Generalization of Social Welfare Functions

Chapter 5 discussed Sen's (1973) social welfare function:

$$S = 2 \int_0^\infty x\left[1 - F(x) \right] f(x)\, dx \qquad (9.7.1)$$

where $F(x)$ is the distribution function measuring the proportion of persons who have income higher than x, such that

$$2 \int_0^\infty \left[1 - F(x) \right] f(x)\, dx = 1.$$

Sen's social welfare function is the weighted average of income of all persons in society. The weight given to income x decreases monotonically with x, making the social welfare egalitarian because any transfer of income from the rich to the poor increases social welfare, provided the transfer does not change the welfare ranking of individuals.

It will help generalize Sen's social welfare function for any function $g(x)$ for many economic applications. Thus, the following generalization for a function $g(x)$ is proposed:

$$S_g = 2 \int_0^\infty g(x) \left[1 - F(x) \right] f(x) \, dx. \qquad (9.7.2)$$

Then from the concentration index defined in (9.5.4), it is easy to show that

$$S_g = \mu_g \left(1 - C_g \right) \qquad (9.7.3)$$

where $\mu_g = \int_0^\infty g(x) f(x) \, dx$ is the average well-being of society and C_g is the concentration index of $g(x)$.

It will be instructive to illustrate the economic application of the generalized social welfare function in (9.7.3). Suppose $g(x)$ is the well-being enjoyed by a person with income x. Noting from (9.5.1) if the concentration curve for $g(x)$ coincides with the egalitarian line, that is, if $F[g(x)] = F(x)$, then the concentration index C_g equals 0, which implies that everyone in society enjoys the same well-being. If $F[g(x)]=1$ for all x, then from (9.5.1), $C_g = -1$, which implies that the poorest person in society enjoys all the well-being. If $F[g(x)]=0$ for all x, then from (9.5.1), $C_g = +1$, which implies that the wealthiest person in society enjoys all the well-being. Thus, C_g lies between -1 to $+1$. The concentration index measures the inequity in well-being. The positive (negative) value indicates that the rich (poor) enjoy higher well-being. The magnitude of the concentration index measures the degree of disparity of well-being across incomes. Well-being is a multidimensional concept, and one can use the concentration index to determine which dimension of well-being is equitable or inequitable and to what degree. This concept is beneficial in assessing how individuals' income matters for well-being.[7]

9.8 Aggregate Elasticity

The previous section denoted $g(x)$ as the well-being of an individual with income x. This function does not have to be the well-being function, and it can signify the expenditure on a commodity incurred by an individual with income x. It can also represent access to essential services by a person with income x. The elasticity of this function has many economic applications that will be explored in the following chapter. This elasticity, defined at a particular point, is called point elasticity. But, the aggregate elasticity for the whole population is required for many applications. This section discusses a method of estimating aggregate elasticity using the idea of the concentration index.

The point elasticity of $g(x)$ with respect to x, denoted by $\eta_g(x)$, was defined in (9.4.1). There can be many methods of estimating aggregate elasticity from the point elasticity. There has been extensive literature on estimating Engel elasticity from econometric models, including Allen and Bowley (1935), Prais and Houthakker (1955), Cramer (1964), Mahalanobis (1960), and Iyenger (1960).

---

[7] See Chapter 8 for a detailed discussion of well-being.

This literature defines the aggregate elasticity at $x = \mu$, the mean income, or expenditure. A better way of estimating the aggregate elasticity will be by the average point elasticity across the whole income distribution. Thus, the aggregate elasticity is defined as

$$\bar{\eta}_g = \int_0^\infty \eta_g(x) f(x)\, dx. \tag{9.8.1}$$

This aggregation method utilizes the point elasticity at all income levels and should be preferable to the single point.

Using Corollary 9.1, the following two inequalities follow:

(i) If $F(x) - F_1\left[(g(x))\right] \geq 0$ for all x implies $\eta_g(x) \geq 0$ for all x

(ii) If $F(x) - F_1(g) \leq 0$ for all x implies $\eta_g(x) \leq 0$ for all x.

Integrating equation (i) over the whole range of x, we obtain

$$2\int_0^\infty \{F(x) - F_1[g(x)]\}\, f(x)\, dx \geq 0 \text{ implies } \int_0^\infty \eta_g(x) f(x)\, dx \geq 0. \tag{9.8.2}$$

It is easy to show that the left-hand side of this inequality is equal to C_g, which is the concentration index of $g(x)$. The right-hand side of this inequality from (9.8.2) is equal to the aggregate elasticity $\bar{\eta}_g$. And, that proves that $C_g \geq 0$ implies $\bar{\eta}_g \geq 0$. Similarly, equation (ii) proves that $C_g \leq 0$ implies $\bar{\eta}_g \leq 0$. Thus, there is a close relationship between $g(x)$ concentration index and $g(x)$ aggregate elasticity.

This leads to Theorem 9.9.

Theorem 9.9

(i) $C_g > 0$ *implies* $\bar{\eta}_g > 0$

(ii) $C_g < 0$ *implies* $\bar{\eta}_g < 0$

(iii) $C_g = 0$ *implies* $\bar{\eta}_g = 0$

Using Corollary 9.2, the following two inequalities are also obtained:

(i) If $F_1(x) - F_1[g(x)] \leq 0$ for all x implies $\eta_g(x) \leq 1$ for all x

(ii) If $F_1(x) - F_1[g(x)] \geq 0$ for all x implies $\eta_g(x) \geq 1$ for all x $\qquad$ (9.8.3)

Integrating the equation in (i) over the whole range of x yields

$$2\int_0^\infty \{F_1(x) - F_1[g(x)]\}\, f(x)\, dx \leq 0 \text{ implies } \int_0^\infty \eta_g(x) f(x)\, dx \leq 1. \tag{9.8.4}$$

It is easy to show that the left-hand side of this inequality is equal to $C_g \leq G$, where G is the Gini index of x. The right-hand side of this inequality is equal to $\bar{\eta}_g \leq 1$. Hence, that proves that $C_g \leq G$ implies $\tilde{\eta}_g \leq 1$. Similarly, inequality (ii) follows that $C_g \geq G$ implies $\tilde{\eta}_g \geq 1$. This leads to Theorem 9.10.

Theorem 9.10

>   (i) $C_g < G$ *implies* $\tilde{\eta}_g < 1$
> (ii) $C_g > G$ *implies* $\tilde{\eta}_g > 1$
> (iii) $C_g = G$ *implies* $\tilde{\eta}_g = 1$

The following implications follow immediately from Theorems 9.9 and 9.10:

>   (i) If $\frac{C_g}{G} < 0 \rightarrow \tilde{\eta}_g < 0$
> (ii) If $\frac{C_g}{G} = 0 \rightarrow \tilde{\eta}_g = 0$
> (iii) If $\frac{C_g}{G} > 0 \rightarrow \tilde{\eta}_g > 0$
> (iv) If $\frac{C_g}{G} < 1 \rightarrow \tilde{\eta}_g < 1$
>   (v) If $\frac{C_g}{G} = 1 \rightarrow \tilde{\eta}_g = 1$
> (vi) If $\frac{C_g}{G} > 1 \rightarrow \tilde{\eta}_g > 1$

These inequalities demonstrate that there is a close relationship between $\frac{C_g}{G}$ and $\tilde{\eta}_g$. Thus, it is proposed to measure the aggregate elasticity of $g(x)$ with respect to x by the ratio of the concentration index of $g(x)$ to the Gini index of income x:

$$\tilde{\eta}_g = \frac{C_g}{G}. \tag{9.8.5}$$

This ratio informs whether the function $g(x)$ is inelastic (elastic) if $0 < \tilde{\eta}_g < 1$ ($\tilde{\eta}_g > 1$) based on the ratio of concentration index of $g(x)$ and the Gini index of income x, which can be calculated from household surveys.

An alternative method of defining the aggregate elasticity is given by

$$\tilde{\eta}_g = \int_0^\infty \eta_g(x) f^*(x) \, dx \tag{9.8.6}$$

where $f^*(x) = \frac{x}{\mu}f(x)$ such that $\int_0^\infty f^*(x) = 1$ is an alternative density function. How does the aggregate elasticity $\tilde{\eta}_g$ differ from $\tilde{\eta}_g$? The answer depends on the weights given to different individuals. $\tilde{\eta}_g$ gives equal weight to all individuals irrespective of their income, whereas $\tilde{\eta}_g$ gives weight proportional to the income shares of individuals, meaning that the richer the individual, the greater the elasticity weight.

Integrating both sides of (9.8.3) using the density function $f^*(x)$ yields from (9.8.4) that $C_{gx} < 0$ implies $\tilde{\eta}_g < 1$, and $C_{gx} > 0$ implies $\tilde{\eta}_g > 1$, and $C_{gx} = 0$ implies $\tilde{\eta}_g = 1$. This proves Theorem 9.11.

Theorem 9.11

(i) $C_{gx} < 0$ **implies** $\tilde{\eta}_g < 1$

(ii) $C_{gx} > 0$ **implies** $\tilde{\eta}_g > 1$

(iii) $C_{gx} = 0$ **implies** $\tilde{\eta}_g = 1$

Theorem 9.11 shows a close relationship between the relative concentration index of $g(x)$ and the $g(x)$ aggregate elasticity in (9.8.6). Thus, the relative concentration index C_{gx} can also be used as an indicator of aggregate elasticity $\tilde{\eta}_g$.

Chapter 10 will provide several applications of aggregate elasticity in economic analysis.

9.9 Concluding Remarks

This chapter has provided a detailed discussion of concentration curves and related theorems. Relationships among the distributions of various economic variables are the cornerstone of economic analysis. This chapter has revealed how the concentration curves can help understand the relationships among economic variables. These theorems have numerous economic applications, and Chapter 10 is entirely devoted to many practical economic applications.

Economists use social welfare functions to evaluate the allocation of resources to understand whether people are becoming better off. Social welfare is defined in income space. This chapter has generalized social welfare to define it for any function $g(x)$, representing an economic variable. As an illustration, suppose $g(x)$ denotes the well-being of a person with income x; the chapter has proposed a social well-being function as a function of average well-being and the concentration index of well-being. The concentration index of well-being measures the inequity in well-being, the positive (negative) value of which indicates that the rich (poor) enjoy higher (lower) well-being than the poor. Chapter 10 provides applications of the concentration index of a function to evaluate equity in many economic phenomena.

Economists use the idea of elasticity to understand the relationships among economic variables. This elasticity, defined at a particular point, is called point elasticity. But, for many applications, the aggregate elasticity for the whole population is needed. This chapter has developed the concept of aggregate elasticity using the concentration indices. This chapter has discussed the method of estimating the aggregate elasticity utilizing the idea of the concentration index. Chapter 10 will explore numerous economic applications of aggregate elasticity. Chapters 11–13 will apply the notion of aggregate elasticity to analyze equity in taxations, deriving several tax progressivity measures.

10

Applications of Concentration Curves to Economic Analysis

10.1 Introduction

In many areas of economics, the relationships among economic variables play a crucial role in understanding economic phenomena. It is essential to know how various economic variables are related, but many economic phenomena require analyzing the relationships among individuals' or families' distribution of economic variables. Chapter 9 showed how the concentration curves could quantify the relationship between the distribution of one economic variable and the distribution of another economic variable.

Chapter 9 proved many theorems and corollaries relating to the concentration curves. This chapter provides numerous economic applications of those theorems and corollaries, which provided the conditions under which the variable $y = g(x)$ is more or less equally distributed than the variable x. Some of the applications are discussed in this chapter; others are considered in detail in subsequent chapters. The purpose of these applications is to illustrate the power of techniques presented to analyze economic phenomena. There might be many more applications not covered in this volume. The readers of this chapter will discover new applications, leading to enhanced economic policies.

10.2 The Engel Curve

The Engle curve is the relationship between expenditure on a commodity and the total expenditure (also used as a proxy for income). Suppose $g(x)$ represents the equation of the Engel function of a commodity. In that case, the elasticity of the function $g(x)$ with respect to total expenditure (or income) x, denoted by $\eta_g(x)$, indicates whether the commodity is inferior, necessary, or luxury. If its elasticity is negative, the commodity is inferior, implying that the expenditure on an inferior commodity decreases as income increases. The positive elasticity means that the consumption of the commodity increases as income increases. The commodity is necessary (luxury) if its elasticity is less (higher) than unity.

Economic Inequality and Poverty. Nanak Kakwani and Hyun Son, Oxford University Press.
© Nanak Kakwani and Hyun Son (2022). DOI: 10.1093/oso/9780198852841.003.0010

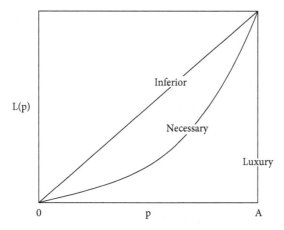

Fig. 10.1 Concentration curve for commodities

From Corollaries 9.1 and 9.2, it follows that if the concentration curve of a commodity lies above the egalitarian line, then elasticity $\eta_g(x) < 0$ for all x, it means that it is an inferior commodity; if the concentration curve lies between the Lorenz curve for x and the egalitarian line, then $0 < \eta_g(x) < 1$ for all x, it is a necessary commodity; and if the concentration curve lies below the Lorenz curve, then $\eta_g(x) > 1$ for all x, the commodity is luxury.

The concentration curve indicates whether the commodity is an inferior, necessity, or luxury. Figure 10.1 is the Lorenz curve of income. In the same figure, the concentration curves of various commodities are depicted by plotting $F(x)$ and $F_1[g(x)]$ for different values of x. The cumulative proportion of expenditure on a commodity, when individuals are arranged in ascending order of their income, is denoted by $F_1[g(x)]$. The position of the concentration curve in Figure 10.1 indicates whether the commodity is inferior, necessary, or luxury.

The aggregate Engel elasticity for the entire income range is needed for many economic applications. The aggregate elasticity can be calculated directly from estimated coefficients if the Engel function is specified in a linear double-logarithm. If the Engel function is not linear double-logarithm, the aggregate elasticity is determined at the mean expenditure or income. This is a point elasticity that does not capture the distribution of variables among individuals or households. The aggregate elasticity developed in Chapter 9 is more suitable for distributional variables.

Equation (9.8.1) in Chapter 9 proposed a definition of the aggregate elasticity of $g(x)$ as

$$\bar{\eta}_g = \int_0^{\infty} \eta_g(x) f(x)\, dx, \qquad (10.2.1)$$

which is the average elasticity at all points. Equation (9.8.5) proposed to measure the aggregate elasticity using the idea of concentration indices:

$$\bar{\eta}_g = \frac{C_g}{G} \qquad (10.2.2)$$

where C_g is the concentration index of $g(x)$, and G is the Gini index of x. From this elasticity, it can be concluded that the commodity is inferior if $\frac{C_g}{G} < 0$, necessary if $0 < \frac{C_g}{G} < 1$, and luxury if $\frac{C_g}{G} > 1$. Thus, $\frac{C_g}{G}$ is the proposed aggregate elasticity index.

Suppose an expenditure system consists of k commodities, let $g_j(x)$ be the per capita expenditure on the jth commodity by a household with per capita income x, then the following identity always holds:

$$x = \sum_{j=1}^{k} g_j(x). \qquad (10.2.3)$$

Applying Theorem 9.6 on this equation yields

$$G = \frac{1}{\mu} \sum_{j=1}^{k} \mu_j C_j, \qquad (10.2.4)$$

where μ_j is the per capita expenditure on the jth commodity and μ is the mean of the total expenditure so that $\mu = \sum_{j=1}^{k} \mu_j$, C_j is the concentration index of the expenditure on the jth commodity, and G is the Gini index of the total expenditure. From (10.2.2), the aggregate elasticity index of the jth commodity from (10.2.4) yields

$$\frac{1}{\mu} \sum_{j=1}^{k} \mu_j \bar{\eta}_j = 1, \qquad (10.2.5)$$

which proves that the weighted average of the aggregate elasticity indices of all commodities equals 1, the weights being proportional to the shares of expenditures on commodities. Thus, the proposed elasticity index satisfies the adding up criterion, which says the weighted average of elasticities of all commodities must always equal one. This criterion is essential for estimating Engel elasticities for any expenditure system. The elasticities calculated from individually specified Engel curves seldom satisfy this criterion.

Table 10.1 illustrates the aggregate Engel elasticities using the Indonesian National Social and Economic Survey data for October 1969–April 1970. The estimates of the elasticity index indicate that cereal and cassava are most inelastic, with an index value of 0.56. In contrast, meat, egg, and milk products are highly elastic, with an index value of 1.8. Also, total food is inelastic, with an index value equal to 0.94. Among the non-food commodities, durables and semi-durables are highly elastic, whereas housing (shelter) expenditure is inelastic.

The methodology discussed in this section has a practical application in indirect taxation; if the indirect tax is levied on a necessary (luxury) commodity, the poor pay proportionally more (less) tax than the non-poor. An equitable indirect tax system will be achieved when policymakers can either exempt or impose a low tax rate on inelastic goods and services and charge higher rates on elastic goods and services.

Table 10.1 Aggregate elasticity of commodities, urban and rural Indonesia, 1969–70

Commodities	Concentration index	Elasticity index
Cereal and cassava	0.196	0.56
Sea food	0.430	1.24
Meat	0.623	1.80
Eggs and milk	0.625	1.80
Vegetables	0.295	0.85
Fruit and peas	0.479	1.38
Other food	0.386	1.11
Total food	0.326	0.94
Tobacco and alcohol	0.402	1.16
Housing	0.324	0.93
Miscellaneous goods	0.544	1.57
Clothing	0.392	1.13
Durables and semidurables	0.598	1.72
Other expenditure	0.397	1.14
Total expenditure	0.347	1.00

10.3 Consumption and Saving Functions

In the Keynesian case, consumption is related to income, either linearly or curvilinearly. First, assume that the relationship is linear:

$$c = \alpha + \beta x \tag{10.3.1}$$

where β is the marginal propensity to consume, x is the disposable income, and c is the consumption expenditure of an individual. Because α and β are greater than zero, Corollary 9.8 in Chapter 9 implies that personal consumption expenditure is Lorenz superior to personal income. Therefore, personal consumption expenditure will be more equally distributed than personal disposable income.

The saving function corresponding to (10.3.1) is

$$s = -\alpha + (1 - \beta)x. \tag{10.3.2}$$

Corollary 9.8 implies that personal savings will be more unequally distributed than personal disposable income, provided the marginal propensity to consume is less than unity. Note that the marginal propensity to consume cannot exceed unity in this model; otherwise, society's average savings will be negative.

The disposable income $x = y - T(x)$, where y is the gross income and $T(y)$ is the tax function; the consumption function in (10.3.1) then becomes

$$c = \alpha + \beta\left[y - T(y)\right]$$

which, on differentiating with respect to y, yields

$$\frac{dc}{dy} = \beta\left[1 - T'(y)\right].$$

Note that $T'(y)$ is the marginal tax rate at income level y. When $T'(y) < 1$, which, from Theorem 9.2 in Chapter 9, shows that the concentration curve for the personal consumption expenditure coincides with its Lorenz curve if the marginal tax rate is less than unity for all y. The elasticity of c with respect to y will be

$$\eta_{cy} = \frac{\beta\left[1 - T'(y)\right]y}{\alpha + \beta\left[y - T'(y)\right]},$$

which will be less than or equal to unity provided that

$$\beta T(y)\left[1 - \eta_T(y)\right] \leq \alpha \tag{10.3.3}$$

where $\eta_T(y)$ is the elasticity of $T(y)$ with respect to y. It is well known that if $\eta_T(y) > 1$ for all y, the tax function is progressive; if $\eta_t(y) = 1$ for all y, the tax function is proportional; otherwise, it is regressive.[1] If it is assumed that $T(y) \geq 0$ for all y, excluding the possibility of negative income tax, the inequality in (10.3.3) will hold when the $T(y)$ function is progressive or proportional throughout the income range. From Corollary 9.2, it thus follows that personal consumption expenditure will be more equally distributed than pre-tax income for both proportional and progressive tax systems. If the tax system is regressive, it is not possible to make any *a priori* statement regarding the distribution of consumption expenditure.

The elasticity of personal savings with respect to gross income is

$$\eta_{sy} = \frac{(1 - \beta)\left[1 - T'(y)y\right]}{-\alpha + (1 - \beta)\left[y - T(y)\right]},$$

which will be higher than or equal to unity provided that

$$(1 - \beta)T(y)\left[1 - \eta_t(y)\right] + \alpha \geq 0. \tag{10.3.4}$$

Suppose $\beta < 1$ and $\eta_t(y) \leq 1$, equation (10.3.4) will hold. Therefore, Corollary 9.2 follows that if the marginal propensity to consume is less than unity, savings will be more unequally distributed than pre-tax income for both regressive and proportional tax systems. However, if taxes are progressive, no statements regarding the distribution of savings can be made.

---

[1] A more detailed discussion of tax progressivity is provided in Chapter 11.

The macroeconomic literature informs that the interest rate has a direct impact on savings, so the rate of interest has been included in the savings function as an additional variable:

$$s = -\alpha + (1 - \beta)x + \lambda r \qquad (10.3.5)$$

where r is the rate of interest, and $\lambda \geq 0$ is the corresponding parameter. The elasticity of savings with respect to disposable income x will then be

$$\eta_s(x) = \frac{(1-\beta)x}{-\alpha + (1-\beta)x + \lambda r}. \qquad (10.3.6)$$

This equation indicates that as r increases, $\eta_s(x)$ decreases. Thus it follows from Theorem 9.1, Chapter 9 that the concentration curve for savings will shift upward as r increases. If the marginal propensity to consume is less than unity, s will be an increasing function of x, and the concentration curve for savings will coincide with its Lorenz curve. Therefore, one can conclude that the higher the interest rate, the more equal the distribution of savings—a conclusion based on the assumption that an increase in the interest rate does not alter the distribution of disposable income.

The linear consumption function may be too restrictive. So, curvilinear consumption and savings functions are considered. Suppose the average propensity to consume decreases as income increases. In that case, the income elasticity of consumption will be less than unity, and the income elasticity of savings will be higher than unity. It immediately follows from Corollary 9.2 that the concentration of personal consumption expenditure (personal savings) will be above (below) the Lorenz curve for disposable income. Because personal consumption and savings are both increasing functions of disposable income, their concentration curves will coincide with their respective Lorenz curves. That concludes that if the average propensity to consume decreases as income rises, disposable income inequality will be greater for curvilinear consumption and savings functions than personal consumption but less than that of personal savings.

10.4 The Stiglitz Model of Distribution of Income and Wealth among Individuals

Stiglitz (1969) considered a simple accumulation model with a linear savings function, a constant reproduction rate, homogeneous labor, and equal division of wealth among one's heirs. He proved that the distribution of wealth and income would tend to a state of complete equalization if the balanced growth is stable in such a model. He further demonstrated that his necessary conclusions are unaltered under alternative savings assumptions. His proof of these propositions depends on comparing wealth growth rates between an arbitrary pair of rich and poor income groups.

Tsuji (1972) proved some of these propositions using the variance and the Gini coefficient as inequality measures. This section demonstrates below that the theorems on concentration curves presented in Chapter 9 can provide an unambiguous conclusion for any inequality measure to prove all the Stiglitz propositions in terms of Lorenz's preference.

Stiglitz's basic model is described as follows. Consider a society divided into a number of groups arranged in ascending order of wealth. Labor is homogeneous; hence, all workers receive the same wage. Also, all the members of any one group possess the same wealth. Under these assumptions, the per capita income of group i is given by

$$y_i = w + rc_i \tag{10.4.1}$$

where c_i is the capital per person in the ith group, w is the wage rate, and r is the interest rate. Let s_i be the per capita savings of the ith group and a linear function of per capita income. It then follows that

$$s_i = my_i + b \tag{10.4.2}$$

where m is the marginal propensity to save, and b is the per capita savings at zero income and can be negative or positive.

Suppose that the population of each group is increasing at the same constant rate n, and there is no intermarriage among the groups. These assumptions ensure that the relative proportion of the population of each group, f_i, remains constant. The per capita wealth accumulation for group i is then given by

$$\frac{1}{c_{it}}\frac{dc_{it}}{dt} = \frac{s_{it}}{c_{it}} - n \tag{10.4.3}$$

where the suffix t stands for time. Substituting (10.4.1) and (10.4.2) into (10.4.3) yields

$$\frac{dc_{it}}{dt} = (b + mw) + (mr - n)\,c_{it},$$

which is a first-order differential equation. Its solution is

$$c_{it} = \frac{(b + mw)}{(n - mr)}\left[1 - e^{-(n-mr)t}\right] + e^{-(n-mr)t}c_i \tag{10.4.4}$$

where c_i now represents the wealth of the ith group at $t = 0$.

Consider how the distribution of wealth changes with time. The coefficient of C_i in (10.4.4) is always greater than zero, and thus, from Theorem 9.2, the concentration curve c_{it} coincides with its Lorenz curve. It immediately follows from Corollary 9.8

that the distribution of c_{it} will be Lorenz superior (inferior) to the distribution of c_i if a given by

$$a = \frac{(b + mw)}{(n - mr)} \left[1 - e^{-(n-mr)t} \right] \qquad (10.4.5)$$

is greater (less) than zero.

Now consider the conditions of equilibrium under which a is negative or positive. For this purpose, a concave production function exhibiting constant returns to scale must be assumed. If y is the output per worker and k is the aggregate capital-labor ratio, it follows that

$$y = f(k) \text{ where } f'(k) > 0 \text{ and } f''(k) < 0.$$

If each factor of production is paid with its marginal product, the wage rate w and interest rate r are given by

$$r = f'(k), w = f(k) - kf'(k). \qquad (10.4.6)$$

If k_i denotes the capital in the ith group divided by the total production, then $k_i = f_i c_i$ yields

$$k = \sum_i k_i = \sum_i f_i c_i \qquad (10.4.7)$$

The differential equation of the aggregate capital accumulation is, therefore,

$$a = \frac{(b + mw)}{(n - mr)} \left[1 - e^{-(n-mr)t} \right] \qquad (10.4.8)$$

where the relative proportion of population f_i in each group remains constant.

If the economy is in balanced growth, $dk/dt = 0$, from (10.4.8) it follows

$$m(w + rk) = nk - b \qquad (10.4.9)$$

Substituting $y = \sum_i f_i y_i$ into (10.4.1) and (10.4.7), this equation becomes

$$mf(k) = nk - b, \qquad (10.4.10)$$

the solution of which yields the aggregate capital-labor ratio, leading to balanced growth. If $b > 0$, there is a unique solution. By contrast, if $b < 0$, there will be two balanced growth paths.[2] The balanced growth path is stable (unstable) if

---

[2] See Stiglitz (1969).

$\partial (dk/dt) /\partial k$ at $dk/dt = 0$ is less (greater) than zero. Differentiating (10.4.8) partially with respect to k gives

$$\frac{\partial}{\partial k}\left(\frac{dk}{dt}\right) = -(n - mr), \tag{10.4.11}$$

which implies that the balanced growth path will be stable (unstable) if $(n - mr)$ is greater (less) than zero.

From (10.4.10), note that the intersection of the line $(nk-b)$ and curve $mf(k)$ yields the solution for the balanced growth path. If there is only one balanced growth path, the slope of the line $(nk-b)$ at this point must be greater than the slope of curve $mf(k)$. The slope of curve $mf(k)$ is $mf'(k)$, which from (10.4.6) is equal to mr. This gives $n > mr$, which from (10.4.11), leads to the result that if there is only one balanced growth path, it is globally stable. In contrast, if there are two balanced growth paths, one can show that the lower growth path will be locally unstable and the upper locally stable.

If the economy is in balanced growth, the equation (10.4.9) will hold. Substituting this equation into (10.4.5), a becomes

$$a = k\left[1 - e^{-(n-mr)t}\right], \tag{10.4.12}$$

which is positive (negative) if $(n - mr)$ is greater (less) than zero. Therefore, the distribution of c_{it} will be Lorenz superior (inferior) to c_i if $(n - mr)$ is greater (less) than zero. This leads to the conclusion that *the distribution of wealth must eventually become more (less) egalitarian if the economy is at a stable (unstable) balanced growth path.*

Now consider the movement of the distribution of income over time. Substituting (10.4.1) into (10.4.4) yields the income of the ith group at time t as

$$y_{it} = \left[w + \frac{r(b + mw)}{(n - mr)}\right]\left[1 - e^{-(n-mr)t}\right] + e^{-(n-mr)t}y_i \tag{10.4.13}$$

where y_i now represents the wealth of the ith group at $t = 0$. If the economy is in a balanced growth path, using (10.4.9), this equation becomes

$$y_{it} = (w + kr)\left[1 - e^{-(n-mr)t}\right] + e^{-(n-mr)t}y_i. \tag{10.4.14}$$

Utilizing Corollary 9.8 in Chapter 9, the distribution of y_{it} will be Lorenz superior (inferior) to the distribution of y_i if $(n - mr)$ is greater (less) than zero. Therefore, income distribution will eventually become more (less) egalitarian if the economy is stable (unstable) balanced growth path.

10.5 Employment-Growth Elasticity

Every economy produces thousands of goods and services every day. Gross domestic product (GDP) is a gross measure of total output produced in an economy. The activities in the economy occur through the participation of people in the labor market or their entrepreneurial activities. A large proportion of people earn their livelihood through employment—the growth in output results from employment growth. Every working-age person aspires to have a decent job. Public policy debate often revolves around promoting full and productive employment. The employment elasticity of economic growth is a valuable tool economists use to explore the relationship between employment, productivity, and economic growth.

Suppose Y is the total output, and E is employment, then employment elasticity of growth is defined as

$$\eta_e = \frac{YdE}{EdY} = \frac{dln\,(E)}{dln\,(Y)}, \qquad (10.5.1)$$

which is interpreted as follows: If Y increases by 1%, the employment increases by η_e%. A high elasticity indicates that growth in output leads to increased job creation. Policymakers often want to know to what extent economic growth creates employment in the economy, i.e., how much is the employment intensity of economic growth? This elasticity is highly relevant in policy debates promoting employment and economic growth productivity.

Productivity at the macro level is defined as the total output produced by one unit of employment. Then the growth in productivity will be given by

$$dln\,(P) = dln\left[\frac{Y}{E}\right] = dln\,(Y) - dln\,(E), \qquad (10.5.2)$$

which immediately yields the elasticity of productivity with respect to Y as

$$\eta_P = 1 - \eta_e, \qquad (10.5.3)$$

which provides the relationship between the growth in employment and productivity, when output grows by 1%. If $\eta_e < 1$, then $\eta_P > 0$, implying that if employment grows at lower than 1%, there will be positive productivity growth; the higher the employment intensity, the lower the productivity growth. Productivity growth is negative when the employment elasticity exceeds one.

Labor productivity is the primary determinant of wages earned by workers. If the government follows the policy of expanding employment for the same output growth, the economy will suffer lower productivity growth, which results in lower wages. Thus, that may result in a phenomenon of working poor, which is widely prevalent in developing countries. There is a trade-off between employment growth and productivity growth, provided the economic growth rate is fixed. But, by increasing economic growth, one can improve both employment and productivity. Hence, the key to avoiding the phenomenon of working poor is to enhance economic growth. Suppose, hypothetically, the employment elasticity is 0.4; then, the productivity elasticity will be 0.6. If the economic growth rate increases to 5%, then employment will increase by 2%, and the income per worker will increase by 3%.

10.5.1 The ILO Method of Estimating Employment Elasticity

What is the optimum level of employment elasticity? How does the elasticity vary across different sectors of the economy or socio-economic and demographic groups? The literature does not provide guidance on these issues. However, there is a sizable literature on estimating employment–economic growth elasticity, including the International Labour Organization (ILO 1995), Boltho and Glyn (1995), and Padalino and Vivarelli (1997). The elasticity estimation uses a cross-country employment and GDP data panel. The ILO has pioneered many studies on the econometric estimation of elasticity, and it has primarily used the following log-linear regression model:

$$ln\left(E\right) = \alpha + \beta_1 ln\left(Y\right) + \beta_2 \left[ln\left(Y\right) D\right] + \beta_3 D + u. \qquad (10.5.4)$$

Y is GDP, D is the country dummy, and u is the random error term. The dummy variable D interacts with ln (GDP) for generating the point elasticity. The model is estimated using the pooled cross-section and time series. The estimated elasticity of employment with respect to GDP in a country from (10.5.4) is given as $b_1 + b_2$, where b_1 and b_2 are the least-square estimates of β_1 and β_2, respectively.

The cross-country regression models are the only tools used in estimating these elasticities. The ILO has estimated employment elasticity for 160 economies using the most extensive cross-country comparable employment data set. The model uses the aggregate data for each country on GDP and employment derived from different sources. The employment data are obtained from labor force surveys conducted in each country, while the GDP data are from national accounts. Not all countries follow the same methodology to conduct the labor force surveys, so there is a wide variation in compiling employment data for different countries. One of the essential requirements of cross-country regression models is that all data across countries are comparable, which is unlikely to hold. It is natural to be skeptical about the ILO's employment data comparability across 160 countries.

The statistical inferences drawn from cross-country regression models suffer from many well-known conceptual problems. In such models, the countries represent individual observations that are independent of each other, and this essential requirement is unlikely to hold. Even the ILO, which has pioneered the estimation of elasticities, has noted several shortcomings of cross-country models. It points out that the model it uses suffers from omitted variable bias, as no other variable that may influence either employment performance or overall economic performance is controlled for. Given these limitations, this section proposes a new approach to analyzing employment–productivity performance. In this approach, the employment–productivity relationship is explored at the household level.

10.5.2 A New Method of Analyzing the Employment–Productivity Relationship

A new method of analyzing the employment–productivity relationship is proposed. Many household surveys provide data on employment and income at the household level. These surveys quantify the contributions of labor market indicators and non-labor income to the per capita household income.

The following indicators are constructed from household surveys:

1. Per capita income x: the gross income of a household divided by the number of household members.
2. Per capita labor income $l(x)$: the total wage and salary income of a household, including all work-related in-kind benefits of the household with income x, divided by the number of household members.
3. Per capita employment $e(x)$: the total number of employed persons in the household with income x divided by household members.
4. Per capita hours of work in the labor market, $h(x)$: the total number of hours worked by all household members of the household with income x divided by the number of household members.

The following identity follows from these indicators

$$x = e(x) \cdot \frac{h(x)}{e(x)} \cdot \frac{l(x)}{h(x)} \cdot \frac{x}{l(x)}. \tag{10.5.5}$$

This equation shows that per capita household income is determined by four factors:

(i) Per capita household employment: The higher per capita employment, the higher per capita household income.

(ii) Hours of work per employed person: Persons are considered employed if they work at least one hour a week. The employed persons work different hours, so the per capita household income depends on how many hours the employed person works.

(iii) Productivity: It is the per capita labor income divided by per capita hours of work by household members. It is a measure of wage rate per hour of work.

(iv) The ratio of total income to labor income: This measures the non-labor income to the household income.

Taking logarithm and differences both sides of (10.5.5) gives

$$dln(x) = dln(e(x)) + [dln(h(x)) - dln(e(x))] + [dln(l(x)) - dln(h(x))]$$
$$+ [dln(x) - dln(l(x))],$$

which on dividing both sides by $dln(x)$ yields

$$1 = \eta(e(x)) + [\eta(h(x)) - \eta(e(x))] + [\eta(l(x)) - \eta(h(x))] + [1 - \eta(l(x))]$$
$$(10.5.6)$$

where $\eta(e(x)) = \frac{dln(e(x))}{dln(x)}$ is the economic growth elasticity of employment. In the same way, one can define growth elasticities of $h(x)$ and $l(x)$. Integrating both sides of (10.5.6) over the entire range of x yields the aggregate growth elasticity of employment as

$$\bar{\eta}_e = \int_0^\infty \eta(e(x))f(x)\,dx, \qquad (10.5.7)$$

which from (9.8.1) in Chapter 9 is given by

$$\bar{\eta}_e = \frac{C_e}{G} \qquad (10.5.8)$$

where C_e is the concentration index of employment function $e(x)$, and G is the Gini index of per capita income x. Then using (10.5.8) into (10.5.6) yields

$$1 = \frac{C_e}{G} + \left[\frac{C_h}{G} - \frac{C_e}{G}\right] + \left[\frac{C_l}{G} - \frac{C_h}{G}\right] + \left[1 - \frac{C_l}{G}\right] \qquad (10.5.9)$$

where C_h and C_l are the concentration indices of the functions $h(x)$ and $l(h)$, respectively. This equation is an identity relating to the growth elasticities of employment, hours of work per employed person, productivity, and the non-labor income. These elasticities inform how each of these factors is contributing to the growth in per capita income.

Multiplying both sides of (10.5.9) by G results in

$$G = C_e + [C_h - C_e] + [C_l - C_h] + [G - C_l], \qquad (10.5.10)$$

which explains the inequality by four factors: (i) employment, (ii) hours of work per employed person, (iii) productivity, and (vi) non-labor income. This equation provides the contributions of the four factors to explain the inequality of per capita household income. The following section applies this methodology to Brazil.

10.6 Application of Employment-Growth Elasticity to Brazil

This section analyzes the employment–productivity relationships for Brazil. The empirical analysis presented is based on Brazil's National household survey called PNAD for 2011. PNAD contains extensive information on labor market questions that facilitated the construction of relevant indicators on employment, productivity, and hours of work. Per capita household income is used as individuals' welfare, and growth in per capita income is used to measure economic growth. Per capita employment for each household provides the measure of employment level. The PNAD also had information on the regional sectors: metropolitan, urban non-metropolitan areas, and rural areas. The employment–productivity relationships patterns are likely to vary across these three areas. This application analyzes these three regional sectors, plus Brazil as a whole. Table 10.2 shows the labor market indicators.

In metropolitan areas, per capita income is 905 reais per month, 2.6 times the per capita income in rural areas. Per capita income in urban non-metropolitan areas is in between at 6.93 reais per month. These differences in standards of living are mainly due to the earnings in the labor market. For instance, in the metropolitan regions, all three indicators—employment, hours of work, and productivity—are higher, contributing to higher earnings in the labor market. Productivity is the leading cause of the vast difference in the standard of living in the three regions. In the metropolitan area, the hourly wage income, measuring hourly productivity, is 105.2 reais, whereas it is as low as 43.0 reais in a rural area.

Table 10.3 presents the aggregate growth elasticity of the labor market indicators. These elasticities are calculated by dividing the concentration index of an indicator divided by the Gini index of per capita income. For instance, for Brazil, the growth elasticity of per capita employment in Brazil is 0.23. As per capita income increases by 1%, growth in per capita employment is 0.23%. The growth elasticity of per capita work hours is 0.43, implying as per capita income increases, growth in per capita hours of work is 0.43% to per capita aggregate income growth. The growth elasticity of labor income is elastic at 1.02, which means that the rise in labor income contributes to a more than 1% increase in per capita income.

Table 10.2 Labor market indicators in Brazil, 2011

Indicators	Metropolitan areas	Urban non-metropolitan areas	Rural areas	Brazil
Per capita income	905.4	693.7	361.1	711.2
Gini index of per capita income	0.57	0.52	0.51	0.55
Per capita labor income	715.40	538.20	240.6	550.10
Per capita employment	0.48	0.47	0.51	0.48
Per capita hours	6.80	6.30	5.60	6.38
Share of labor income	0.79	0.78	0.67	0.77
Hours/employed	14.17	13.4	10.98	13.29
Productivity	105.2	85.4	43.00	86.20

Table 10.3 Elasticity estimates in Brazil, 2011

Indicators	Metropolitan areas	Urban non-metropolitan areas	Rural areas	Brazil
Per capita employment	0.23	0.28	0.2	0.23
Per capita hours of work	0.38	0.47	0.5	0.43
Per capita labor income	0.99	1.02	1.05	1.02

Suppose an objective of policymakers is to achieve an overall increase in per capita household income. Then it is essential to know what factors can contribute to such growth. The identity in (10.5.9) can provide an answer. The growth elasticity of four factors—per capita employment, work hours per employed person, productivity, and per capita non-labor income—must be calculated. Table 10.4 presents these elasticities.

If policymakers promote the expansion of employment in the economy, this policy for Brazil will contribute only 0.23% to the increase in income of 1%. Another strategy could be to increase hours of work by promoting, for instance, full-time employment. This policy will contribute to an additional increase in income by 0.20%. However, a more critical strategy will be to create more productive jobs, which adds almost 0.59% to the household income, according to the decomposition presented in Table 10.4. For the metropolitan region, the productivity increase can contribute as much as 0.62% to the household income. The non-labor income makes an insignificant contribution to enhancing household income. The labor market policies play a key role in advancing households' standard of living.

Next, the causes of inequality in per capita income are explored in Brazil. The identity in (10.5.10) helps to calculate the contributions of the labor indicators to this inequality. Table 10.5 shows the empirical estimates. In Brazil, the Gini index of per capita income is 0.55, of which employment contributes 0.13, hours of work per employed 0.11, and productivity 0.33. Thus, productivity makes the most significant contribution to inequality. This pattern is evident in all three regions. Public policy always revolves around increasing productive employment, which contributes to a

Table 10.4 Elasticity decomposition in Brazil, 2011

Indicators	Metropolitan areas	Urban non-metropolitan areas	Rural areas	Brazil
Per capita employment	0.23	0.28	0.20	0.23
Hours/employed	0.15	0.19	0.30	0.20
Productivity	0.62	0.56	0.54	0.59
Per capita non-labor income	0.01	−0.02	−0.05	−0.02
Total	1.00	1.00	1.00	1.00

Table 10.5 Inequality explained by labor market indicators in Brazil, 2011

Indicators	Metropolitan areas	Urban non-metropolitan areas	Rural areas	Brazil
Gini index (per capita income)	0.570	0.520	0.510	0.550
Contributions by				
Per capita employment	0.131	0.145	0.101	0.127
Hours/employed	0.083	0.098	0.155	0.107
Productivity	0.352	0.289	0.277	0.327
Per capita non-labor income	0.004	−0.012	−0.023	−0.012

higher standard of living. But such a policy leads to higher inequality. Even expanding jobs and hours of work contribute positively to inequality. The labor market activities have an overall impact on increasing inequality. The non-labor income seems to lower the inequality, but its effect is insignificant.

A conclusion emerging from the evidence presented is that the labor market policies in Brazil are not of much help in reducing inequality. A possible strategy may be to increase the labor productivity of those at the lower end of the income distribution. To achieve this requires the expansion of education among the poor or those with unskilled jobs.

10.7 Income Inequality by Factor Components

Households derive income from many sources, such as wages and salaries, business income, dividends from shares, property income, and government transfers. The income derived from various sources is called factor incomes. The factor incomes reveal the income structure of the economy, which can explain income inequality and poverty in an economy. This section analyzes the contribution of each factor's income to the inequality of total per capita household income. A dynamic decomposition is proposed to explain the contributions of factor income to the trends in inequality over time.

Suppose there are k factor incomes, and $g_j(x)$ is the jth factor income of the household with income x, we can write

$$x = \sum_{j=1}^{k} g_j(x) \tag{10.7.1}$$

so that

$$\mu = \sum_{j=1}^{k} \mu_j, \tag{10.7.2}$$

which gives $s_j = \frac{\mu_j}{\mu}$ equal to the income share of the jth factor income. If households are arranged in ascending order of their income, applying Theorem 9.6 (Chapter 9) to (10.7.1) yields

$$G = \sum_{j=1}^{k} s_j C_j \qquad (10.7.3)$$

where G is the Gini index of household income x and C_j is the concentration index of the jth factor income $g_j(x)$. In (10.7.3), $s_j C_j$ is the contribution of the jth factor income to the inequality of household income. Dividing both sides of (10.7.3) by G gives the proportional contribution of each factor income as

$$\frac{1}{G} \sum_{j=1}^{k} s_j C_j = 1 \qquad (10.7.4)$$

where $100 \times s_j C_j / G$ is the percentage contribution of the jth factor income to the inequality of total household income. This equation tells how the structure of income explains income inequality, measured by the Gini index.

The concentration index of a factor income measures how evenly or unevenly a factor income is distributed over the total household income. The concentration index's negative value implies that the factor income goes more to the poorer households and contributes to reducing income inequality. The positive value of the concentration index increases inequality. Suppose the concentration index exceeds the Gini index of income. In that case, the income from that factor income is highly unevenly distributed in favor of the wealthier households and contributes to much higher inequality.

Table 10.6 presents the empirical results of the inequality decomposition presented in this section using data obtained from the Family Budget Surveys for Ukraine. The methodology is illustrated for three years: 1989–92. Ukraine faced an unprecedented economic crisis during the late 1980s and early 1990s. Per capita family income declined by 23.56% during the 1991–92 period. This led to a drastic reduction in the average standard of living of the Ukrainian people. Wage and salary income declined by a massive 31.44%. This is revealed in Table 10.6, which shows that the income share of wage and salary income fell from 56.9% in 1989 to 46.4% in 1992.

Furthermore, the income from smallholding farms increased from 9.9% in 1989 to 19.6% in 1992. Most of the smallholding income comes from the output of small household plots. The massive increase in the share of smallholding is understandable because people lost their jobs due to the recession, so they diverted their efforts to smallholdings to maintain their livelihood.

The substantial changes in the structure of income happened in a short duration of only three years, and these changes led to a decline in the Gini index from 26.4 to 23.4%. In 1989, the contribution of wage and salary to inequality was 70.4%, which fell substantially to only 62.1% in 1992. Thus, the decline in labor market activities alone contributed to a decrease in inequality by 8.3%. The concentration index of wage and salary was 32.8% in 1989, considerably higher than the Gini index of income. This observation implies that the income from wages and salaries is highly unequalizing, contributing to increased inequality, which means that if labor income

Table 10.6 Income inequality by factor incomes in Ukraine

Factor incomes	Income shares (Percent)	Concentration index (Percent)	Contribution (Percent)
	1989		
Wage and salary	56.9	32.8	70.4
Collective farm income	10.4	28.5	11.2
Government cash benefits	12.8	−0.07	0
Smallholding income	9.9	23.8	8.9
Other sources	10	25.4	9.6
Total income	100	26.5	100
	1992		
Wage and salary	46.4	31.3	62.1
Collective farm income	13.5	12.4	7.2
Government cash benefits	10.3	14.2	6.3
Smallholding income	19.6	19.8	16.6
Other sources	10.2	18	7.9
Total income	100	23.4	100

share decreases, it will reduce inequality. A sharp drop in the share of wage and salary income is the dominant factor contributing to the reduction in inequality in 1992. But at the same time, the concentration index of wage and salary decreased slightly from 32.8 to 31.3, which would have reduced inequality. But, this impact would not have been significant.

The government transfers' concentration index was −0.07, implying that this income component was distributed more or less proportional to the household income with no focus on the poor.[3] Although the overall aim of government transfers should be to reduce inequality, the magnitude of reduction is small. In 1992, the concentration index of government transfers increased to 14.2, implying that a higher proportion of government transfers went to wealthier households. During a recession, governments should target their scarce resources to the poor, but in Ukraine, precisely the opposite happened.

Two factors determine changes in inequality (i) income shares and (ii) the concentration index of each factor income. The separate effects of each factor on inequality changes must be analyzed. Kakwani (1996) developed the methodology of disentangling the impact of each factor on in equality changes. Dynamic decomposition of inequality changes can explain the inequality changes. The following section presents this methodology.

[3] The absence of targeting of government transfers is a common finding for socialists countries (Milanvic 1992).

10.8 A Dynamic Decomposition of Inequality

Suppose that over a period, the income shares of the jth factor changed from s_j to s_j^*, which accompanied changes in their concentration indices from C_j to C_j^* for all j from 1 to k. These changes would change the inequality of total income from G to G^*, which from (10.7.3) is given by

$$G^* - G = \sum_{j=1}^{k} \left(s_j^* C_j^* - s_j C_j \right) \tag{10.8.1}$$

which implies that $\left(s_j^* C_j^* - s_j C_j \right)$ is the contribution of the jth factor income to the change in the inequality of total income. This contribution can be further decomposed into two components; one due to a change in the share, and second, due to a change in the concentration index of the jth factor income:

$$\left(s_j^* C_j^* - s_j C_j \right) = \frac{1}{2} \left(C_j + C_j^* \right) \left(s_j^* - s_j \right) + \frac{1}{2} \left(s_j + s_j^* \right) \left(C_j^* - C_j \right) \tag{10.8.2}$$

The first term on the right-hand side of this equation measures the impact of a change in the share of the jth factor income, and the second term measures the effect of the change in the concentration index of the jth factor income.

Substituting (10.8.2) into (10.8.1) gives

$$G^* - G = \frac{1}{2} \sum_{j=1}^{k} \left(C_j + C_j^* \right) \left(s_j^* - s_j \right) + \frac{1}{2} \sum_{j=1}^{k} \left(s_j + s_j^* \right) \left(C_j^* - C_j \right). \tag{10.8.3}$$

This equation explains the change in income inequality by two factors: changes in income shares and changes in concentration indices. The changes in concentration indices inform how the changes in distributions of factor incomes impact the change in inequality. Table 10.7 explains the factors contributing to the change in inequality in Ukraine between 1989 and 1992.

The Gini index of total income declined by 3.14%. The primary cause of this reduction was the wage and salary income, contributing to a decrease of 4.14%. The decrease in the share of wage and salary income caused a reduction in total inequality by 3.37%. The remaining decline of 0.77% was caused by the redistribution of wages and salaries favoring poor households.

Changes in collective farm income led to a reduction of 1.29% in total inequality. Of this, a decrease of 1.92% was due to redistributing this factor favoring the poor. The increase in the share of the factor contributed to a rise in total income inequality of 0.63%. That the redistribution of collective farm income favors poorer households is an interesting observation, particularly when the country is faced with a severe economic downturn. The shrinking labor market led poor people to work on farms, making this income component pro-poor.

Government cash transfers aim to help the poor cope with recessions. Surprisingly, the government transfers increased inequality by 1.65% because they benefited the

Table 10.7 Explaining changes in inequality by factor incomes in Ukraine, 1989–92

Factor incomes	Changes in factor income shares	Changes in concentration index	Contributions by factor income
Wage and salary	−3.37	−0.77	−4.14
Collective farm income	0.63	−1.92	−1.29
Government cash transfers	−0.18	1.65	1.47
Smallholding income	2.11	−0.59	1.52
Other sources	0.04	−0.75	−0.7
Total income	−0.75	−2.39	−3.14

non-poor families proportionally more than the low-income families. These results strongly suggest that the social sector policies did not target the poor; they instead supported the rich.

10.9 Inequity in Opportunity

Roemer (1998) developed the conceptual framework of measuring inequity in opportunity. The basic idea of his framework is that inequality can be partitioned into two components: (i) inequality caused by individuals' circumstances and (ii) inequality caused by individuals' efforts. The idea is that inequalities caused by circumstances are unjust, and those caused by efforts are just. Suppose I is the inequality of income, which is partitioned as the sum of two components:

$$I = I(C) + I(E) \tag{10.9.1}$$

where $I(C)$ is the inequality attributed to individuals' circumstances, and $I(E)$ is the inequality caused due to individuals' efforts. $I(C)$ is the inequality for which individuals cannot be held responsible and is, therefore, unjust or illegitimate. $I(E)$, created due to individuals' efforts, would yield greater prosperity for all, is just, and should be promoted by society. In this framework, I is called the inequality of outcome, and $I(C)$ is the inequality of opportunity.

The World Bank devoted its 2006 World Development Report to analyzing inequality in opportunity worldwide. It adopted Roamer's idea of defining inequality of opportunity. According to the report, public policies need not necessarily eliminate or reduce all inequality of outcomes. Societies may only be concerned about the inequality generated by individuals' circumstances, and it is appropriate for nations to have inequality created by people's efforts.

Kanbur and Wagstaff (2014) raised concerns about this approach. Their concern was whether it could develop a consensus on the sets of circumstance and effort variables. They raised many conceptual issues concerning the partitioning of inequality (10.9.1), arguing that this partitioning is not meaningful in practical applications.

Kakwani and Son (2016, Chapter 7) built upon more severe problems implementing the World Bank's methodology.

Opportunities are created for people to enhance their well-being. Economic growth can directly create opportunities through market operations. More importantly, it generates tax revenues that governments use to create opportunities in education, health, nutrition, and living conditions, such as providing clean water, electricity, and sanitation. A fair society offers equal opportunities for all. Incredibly, the World Bank measured inequality in opportunity without specifying essential opportunities that every person should access. How equitably people can avail themselves of these opportunities should be a principal goal for every society. This section develops a measure of inequity in opportunity.

Suppose x is the household's per capita income, which measures the economic resources available to all household members. Further, let $o(x)$ be the opportunity available to a household with income x, then the opportunity elasticity of the household with per capita income x is given by

$$\eta_o(x) = \frac{d\ln\left[o\left(x\right)\right]}{d\ln\left(x\right)}, \tag{10.9.2}$$

which is a point elasticity at income level x. Utilizing (10.2.1), an aggregate opportunity elasticity is provided by

$$\bar{\eta}_o = \int_0^\infty \eta_o\left(x\right) f(x)\, dx \tag{10.9.3}$$

where $f(x)$ is the probability density function of x. Now using the idea of aggregate elasticity developed in equation (9.8.1) in Chapter 9, yields

$$\bar{\eta}_o = \frac{C_o}{G} \tag{10.9.4}$$

where C_o is the opportunity function $o(x)$ concentration index, and G is the Gini index of x. The interpretation of the aggregate elasticity of opportunity in (10.9.4) is as follows.

$\bar{\eta}_o < 0$ (when $C_o < 0$) implies that as x increases, the opportunity available to that household decreases, meaning that the poorer a household, the higher its opportunity will be. This situation is called an equitable opportunity. If $\bar{\eta}_o = 0$ (when $C_o = 0$), it implies that all individuals in society enjoy equal opportunity. $0 < \bar{\eta}_o < 1$ (when $0 < C_o < G$) means that opportunities are inequitable because the rich enjoy more opportunities than the poor. In this scenario, the opportunity increases with income but at a lower rate than income increases. If $0 < C_o < G$ (when $C_o > G$), the opportunity for the rich increases more rapidly than income. This scenario is highly inequitable. $\bar{\eta}_o$ is the proposed inequity index of opportunity; the larger its value, the more inequitable the opportunity.

10.10 Opportunities in Education and Health in Indonesia

This section analyzes inequity in opportunities in education and health in Indonesia. The data from the National Socioeconomic Survey are utilized. These are the large-scale, multi-purpose, socio-economic surveys initiated in 1963–64 and fielded every year or two. This application illustrates the methodology developed in the previous section; it suffices to analyze only 2014. Table 10.8 shows the empirical results.

Education begins for children at an early age. All children of school age must attend school, irrespective of their families' economic circumstances. If some children from low-income families cannot participate in school, there is inequity in the education system. In 2014, Indonesia had 24.6 million children in the primary school age group between 6 and 11 years, of which 99.61% of children attended school. This means that only 0.39% of the children were deprived of their opportunity to attend school. This tiny fraction of children who did not participate in school is insignificant. This absence from school could be due to unavoidable reasons due to sickness or disability. The inequity index is −0.21, implying that poor children have greater access to this opportunity than the rich. The index value is small and not significant. Thus, it can be concluded that all children in the primary school age group have equal opportunity to attend school.

Among the children in the secondary school age group, from 12 to 17 years, 88.17% attended school in 2014, meaning that 11.83% did not participate in school. The inequity index is −0.06, which is too small to be significant. Hence, it is concluded that all

Table 10.8 Inequity in opportunity in education and health in Indonesia, 2014

	Average opportunity (Percent)	Inequity Index
Percentage of children attending school		
Primary school-age group (6–11 years)	99.61	−0.21
Secondary school-age group (12–17 years)	88.17	−0.06
Tertiary school-age group (18–24 years)	22.57	0.82
Percentage of childbirth attended by health personnel		
Doctors	18.7	0.59
Midwife	65.1	−0.30
Others	16.2	−0.89
Percentage of children vaccinated		
BCG	93.4	0.025
DPT	90.7	0.025
Polio	90.7	0.025
Measles	78.5	0.025
Hepatitis	87.5	0.05
Utilization of healthcare		
Government hospitals	2.88	0.54
Private hospitals	1.77	1.13
Community health centers	0.45	−0.42

children in the secondary school age group also have equal opportunity to participate in school.

The children in the age group 18–24 fall in the tertiary age group when they go to university. Of these children, only 22.57% are pursuing higher education. The inequity index for this group is 0.82, signifying a high level of inequity. Thus, in acquiring higher education in Indonesia, family income does matter significantly; only wealthy families can send their children to pursue higher education.

Inadequate healthcare access can cause poor health outcomes such as life expectancy at birth, infant mortality rate, or maternal mortality rate. This section examines the opportunities in access to healthcare in Indonesia. Childbirth is a critical period for the health of mothers and infants, and many complications may arise if qualified health personnel are not available at the time of childbirth. In Indonesia, only 18.7% of babies were delivered by qualified doctors. Midwives and other unqualified health personnel attended the remaining 81.1% of the total number of childbirths. The inequity index for childbirth attended by doctors is 0.59, which is high, indicating that a large proportion of women are deprived of this basic health service, critical for both the mother's and the child's health. The main reason for this deprivation is lack of income.

Access to immunization is critical for the health of infants and children, and children who are not immunized can suffer severe health issues or even death. For instance, 90.7% of children in Indonesia received a polio vaccination in 2014, which means that 9.3% of children were unprotected from polio vaccination. The inequity index for polio is 0.025, showing almost insignificant inequity in accessing protection from polio. Hence, one can conclude that children from poor and non-poor families have a more or less equal probability of polio vaccination. The measles vaccination coverage is only 78.5%, which is relatively low and needs to be expanded.

Providing vaccination to all children is one of the least expensive health interventions governments can support. The values of the inequity index are low in Indonesia for all kinds of vaccinations, meaning the government has done well in immunizing children from both poor and non-poor families. Family circumstances play a minor role in protecting children from serious diseases.

Indonesia provides both private and public access to healthcare. Private healthcare is generally of high quality but may not be affordable to a large percentage of people belonging to low-income families. Public healthcare might be cheaper, but the quality of service is unknown. Community health centers also provide healthcare to people, particularly in rural areas. Healthcare utilization is measured by people's average number of visits during the last six months of the survey year. The Indonesian population, on average, made 2.88 visits to public hospitals and 1.77 visits to private hospitals in 2014.

The inequity index for private hospitals is 1.13, meaning that utilizing private hospitals is elastic with respect to income. Patients from low-income families have little probability of accessing private hospitals. The inequity index for access to public hospitals is 0.54, which, although inelastic, is still highly inequitable. Hence, the poor enjoy less opportunity than the non-poor, even in the utilization of government hospitals. Since the government primarily funds the government hospitals, it would be reasonable to expect people to access their services, irrespective of their economic circumstances. However, in Indonesia, wealthier individuals have greater access than poorer individuals. This could be because the government hospitals employ the user principle that the patients pay for the services.

People with low incomes are the primary users of community health services, as evidenced by the inequity index of −0.42. Community health centers are not as well equipped as hospitals to deal with serious illnesses, and the poor have less opportunity for treatment when they face life-threatening conditions.

The empirical evidence presented here shows that Indonesia's healthcare system is not equitable overall. The economic circumstances of individuals do matter in accessing healthcare. While Indonesia has recently performed well in enhancing its economic growth, inequities in healthcare provision remain.

10.11 Concluding Remarks

Chapter 9 proved many theorems and corollaries relating to the concentration curves. This chapter has provided numerous economic applications of the theorems and corollaries presented therein. The primary purpose of this chapter has been to illustrate the usefulness of techniques developed in Chapter 9 in analyzing economic phenomena. Chapter 11 will discuss the applications relating to equity in taxation. There may be many more applications not covered in this chapter. This chapter has provided a framework for quantifying the distributional relations among economic variables. The readers of this chapter will indeed discover new applications that could enhance economic policies.

In his 1957 study of family budgets, Ernest Engel made empirical observations on family expenditures on various commodities and their income. He concluded that the proportion of expenditure on food decreases as a family's standard of living rises. This observation is now universally valid and known as Engel's law.

Engel's empirical investigations suggested that the expenditure on a given commodity varies with income in accordance with an underlying mathematical relationship. Such a relationship became known as the Engel curve. Many empirical studies have been undertaken to estimate the Engel elasticity that revealed the consumption patterns of various socio-economic groups. This Engel elasticity revealed the consumption patterns of different socio-economic groups. The elasticity also has a practical application in indirect taxation; if the indirect tax is levied on a necessary (luxury) commodity, the poor pay proportionally more (less) tax than the non-poor.

The estimation of Engel elasticity requires the specification of the Engel function. The econometric studies investigated both the linear and nonlinear forms of Engel curves. This chapter has provided a novel method of estimating Engle elasticity using the idea of aggregate elasticity based on the concentration index developed in Chapter 9.

In Keynesian economics, the consumption income is the crucial relation, and this relation can be either linearly or curvilinearly. This chapter has drawn some conclusions based on a linear consumption function. The findings emerging from this model are interesting when taxation and interest rates are considered in the consumption function. The following conclusions emerged:

- Personal consumption expenditure will be more equally distributed than pre-tax income for both proportional and progressive tax systems. If the tax system is regressive, it is not possible to make any *a priori* statement regarding the distribution of consumption expenditure.
- If the marginal propensity to consume is less than unity, savings will be more unequally distributed than pre-tax income for regressive and proportional tax systems. However, if taxes are progressive, no statements regarding the distribution of savings can be made.
- The higher the interest rate, the more equal the distribution of savings.
- Suppose the average propensity to consume decreases as income rises. In that case, disposable income inequality will be higher than personal consumption but less than personal savings for curvilinear consumption and savings functions.

Using a simple accumulation model with a linear savings function, a constant reproduction rate, homogeneous labor, and equal division of wealth among one's heirs, Stiglitz (1969) proved that the distribution of wealth and income would tend to a state of complete equalization if the balanced growth is stable in such a model. He established his proposition by comparing wealth growth rates between an arbitrary pair of rich and poor income groups. This chapter has proved that the Stiglitz propositions are unambiguously valid for any inequality based on Lorenz dominance.

The employment elasticity of economic growth is a valuable tool economists use to explore the relationship between employment, productivity, and economic growth. There is a sizable literature on estimating employment-growth elasticity using a cross-country employment and GDP data panel. In this regard, the ILO has pioneered many studies on the econometric estimation of elasticity. This chapter has pointed out many limitations of these studies and has proposed a new method of analyzing the employment–productivity relationships using aggregate elasticity.

The empirical application to Brazil suggested that the policies of employment expansion in the economy and increasing work hours by promoting full employment contribute 43% to the total per capita household income. However, a more effective strategy will increase labor productivity, creating more productive jobs, adding almost 0.59% to the per capita household income. The productivity increase contributed as much as 62% to the household income for the metropolitan region. The non-labor income made an insignificant contribution to enhancing household income. The labor market policies played a crucial role in advancing Brazil's living standards.

This chapter has also developed a methodology to quantify the contributions of labor market indicators and non-labor income to the inequality in per capita household income. The empirical application to Brazil indicated that expanding jobs and hours of work contributed positively to inequality. But, productivity increase made the most significant contribution to inequality. The public debate generally revolves around increasing productive employment. The productive employment contributed significantly to a higher standard of living, but such a policy led to higher inequality. The non-labor income seemed to lower the inequality, but its effect was insignificant.

Households derive income from many sources, such as wages and salary, business income, dividends from shares, property income, and government transfers. These income sources are called factor incomes that reveal the income structure in the economy. This chapter has analyzed the contribution of each factor's income to the inequality of total per capita household income. The chapter further extended this idea to a dynamic decomposition to explain the trends in inequality over time.

The chapter illustrated the application of inequality decomposition to the Family Budget Surveys for Ukraine. During the late 1980s and early 1990s, Ukraine faced an economic crisis, which was unprecedented. Per capita family income declined by 23.56% during the 1991–92 period. This led to a drastic reduction in the average standard of living of the Ukrainian people. Wage and Salary income declined by a massive 31.44%.

The substantial changes in the structure of income happened in a short duration of only three years. These changes led to a decline in the Gini index from 26.4 to 23.4%. The contribution of wage and salary to inequality fell from 70.4% in 1989 to 62.1% in 1992. Thus, the decline in labor market activities alone contributed to a decrease in inequality by 8.3%. The concentration index of wage and salary was 32.8% in 1989, considerably higher than the Gini index of income. This observation implied that the income from wage and salary is highly unequalizing, contributing to increased inequality. A sharp drop in the share of wage and salary income was the dominant factor contributing to the reduction in inequality in 1992.

Government cash transfers aim to help the poor cope with the recession. Surprisingly, the government transfers increased inequality by 1.65% points. They benefited the non-poor families proportionally more than the low-income families. These results strongly suggested that the social sector policies did not target the poor; they instead supported the rich.

The World Bank devoted the 2006 World Development Report to analyzing inequality in opportunity. It viewed inequality in opportunity as the inequality caused by the individuals' circumstances. This chapter took a different view, defining inequity in opportunity as the inequity in access to essential education, health, clean water, electricity, etc. It derived the inequity index of opportunity using the aggregate elasticity developed in Chapter 9; the larger its value, the more inequitable the opportunity.

This chapter analyzed inequity in opportunities in education and health in Indonesia utilizing the National Socioeconomic Survey data. The chapter concluded that children in the primary and secondary school-age groups enjoyed equal opportunity to attend school in Indonesia. In acquiring higher education in Indonesia, the chapter concluded that family income does matter significantly; only wealthy families can send their children to pursue higher education.

Inadequate healthcare access can cause poor health outcomes such as life expectancy at birth, infant mortality rate, or maternal mortality rate. This chapter has examined the opportunities in access to healthcare in Indonesia. The healthcare included (i) childbirth attended by qualified health personnel, (ii) children immunization, and (iii) access to private and public health facilities. The empirical evidence presented here showed that overall, Indonesia's healthcare system is not equitable. The economic circumstances of individuals do matter in accessing healthcare. While Indonesia has recently performed well in enhancing its economic growth, inequities in healthcare provision remain.

11

Tax Progressivity and Redistribution Effect of Taxes

11.1 Introduction

The tax literature emphasizes two fundamental principles: Efficiency and equity. If a tax system distorts agents' behavior, it leads to a social welfare loss. Such distortions occur when agents minimize their tax, creating many distortions such as discouraging work or distorting prices. Efficiency is concerned with reducing the loss of social welfare caused by distortions. On the other hand, equity focuses on how the citizens share the tax burden, and it focuses on distributive justice, meaning that taxes should be fair.

What are the criteria for determining the fairness of taxes? In the taxation literature, horizontal equity (HE) and vertical equity (VE) are the two fundamental commands of social justice. The HE requires equal treatment of equals, and the VE requires unequal treatment of unequals. These concepts have been widely applied to assess equity in taxation. The two commands are not precise enough to measure them quantitatively. There may be few or no equals in the real world, making it practically difficult to measure HE. Similarly, it is difficult to know to what degree the unequal be treated unequally in the real world, making it difficult to measure VE.

Kakwani and Lambert (1998) introduced a set of three equity axioms, which can measure the HE and VE using real-world data. These axioms may be called the equity principles of taxation. This chapter discusses these axioms and shows how they facilitate measuring the tax's progressivity and redistribution effect. The four hypothetical tax systems presented in the chapter for the same income distribution clarify the three equity axioms in practical situations.

The measurement of tax progressivity requires a precise definition of tax progressivity. Pigou (1928) was the first to define tax progressivity in his book *A Study in Public Finance*. Following this work, an influential paper by Musgrave and Thin (1948) proposed four alternative definitions of tax progressivity, which are briefly discussed in this chapter. Based on these definitions, they suggested four alternative measures of progressivity belonging to the same family. They relate to progression at a given point on the income scale. They did not measure the actual incidence of progressivity of taxes, direct and indirect, or public expenditures. This chapter primarily measures overall tax progressivity that depends on the distribution of taxes paid, the benefits received, and pre-tax income distribution.

Economic Inequality and Poverty. Nanak Kakwani and Hyun Son, Oxford University Press.
© Nanak Kakwani and Hyun Son (2022). DOI: 10.1093/oso/9780198852841.003.0011

It is essential to distinguish concepts of tax progressivity and the redistribution effect of taxation. Tax progressivity deals with an equity principle of taxation, suggesting that wealthier persons must pay more or even higher rates. On the other hand, the redistributive effect of taxation is an outcome of the equity principle. It measures the impact of taxes on income inequality; the progressive tax reduces inequality, while the regressive tax increases it, and the proportional tax does not affect inequality. While the two concepts are related, they are distinct. This chapter shows that the violation of the three equity axioms negatively influences the redistribution effect of taxation. It also develops HE and VE measures and shows that redistributive tax impact is the sum of HE and VE. This decomposition shows that the violation of HE reduces the redistribution impact of taxes, while VE increases the redistributive effect of the tax.

This chapter distinguishes between relative and absolute measures of tax progressivity. Relative measures of progressivity remain unchanged if everyone's tax is increased or decreased by the same proportion. Similarly, absolute measures of progressivity remain unchanged when everyone's tax is increased or decreased by the same absolute amount. The chapter derives tax progressivity measures using the equity axioms of taxation.

Among several relative measures of tax progressivity proposed in the literature, the Kakwani index, proposed by Kakwani in 1977, is extensively used to analyze equity in taxation and government expenditures. The index is also applied to analyzing equity in access to health, education, and essential services. This chapter develops the absolute Kakwani measure of tax progressivity, indicating the extent to which a tax system deviates from a situation where everyone pays the same amount of tax.

Governments collect revenue from various taxes, such as personal income tax, company tax, estate gift duties, and indirect taxes. In designing a tax system, it helps determine the progressivity of various kinds of taxes and how much they contribute to the total tax system's progressivity. This chapter proposes a tax progressivity decomposition to answer this question.

The HE requires no systematic discrimination against any social group in tax payment. Different social groups must pay taxes based on one tax code, and if various social groups face different tax codes, then the tax system is discriminatory. Kakwani and Lambert (1999) proved that systematic discrimination against any social groups necessarily results in social welfare loss. The loss of social welfare in monetary units provides a valuable measure of horizontal inequity. This chapter revisits this study and offers helpful insights.

Many governments in developed countries are offering relief packages to their population in response to the COVID-19 pandemic. The relief packages aim to provide cash payments to people to maintain their minimum needs. Governments may exclude some specific groups from these transfers because of resource constraints. For instance, temporary residents, overseas students, and undocumented migrants may be excluded from the pandemic relief. This section provides a model to calculate the social welfare loss caused by excluding a social group from government relief initiatives.

11.2 Equity Axioms

HE and VE are the two fundamental commands of social justice in the taxation literature. The HE means that the equal must be treated equally, and the VE means that the unequal must be treated unequally. The two commands are not precise enough to measure them quantitatively, and there may be few or no equals in the real world. Similarly, it is difficult to know to what degree the unequal are treated unequally in the real world.

Kakwani and Lambert (1998) introduced a set of three equity axioms that can measure HE and VE using real-world data. These axioms may be called the equity principles of taxation. This section discusses these axioms and shows how they measure tax progressivity and tax redistribution.

Suppose $x_1, x_2, \ldots \ldots \ldots, x_n$ are the pre-tax incomes of n individuals who are paying $t_1, t_2, \ldots \ldots \ldots, t_n$ tax amounts. The following three axioms are introduced.

Axiom 11.1 $x_i \geq x_j \rightarrow t_i \geq t_j$ for all i and j.

This axiom implies that the richer a person, the more tax she should pay because a richer person has more ability to pay tax than a poorer person. It means that the tax paid by individuals should increase monotonically with income. Fei (1981) calls this requirement minimal progressivity (see also Moyes 1988).

Axiom 11.2 $x_i \geq x_j$ and $t_i \geq t_j \rightarrow t_i/x_i \geq t_j/x_j$ for all i and j.

According to this axiom, richer persons pay more tax and must pay taxes at higher rates. This principle is most widely used in defining tax progressivity (see Pigou 1928, Blum and Kalven 1953, Blum 1979, and Bos and Felderer 1989). Note that this axiom is more demanding than Axiom 11.1. The violation of Axiom 11.1 automatically entails the violation of Axiom 11.2. If Axiom 11.2 holds, then Axiom 11.1 will always be satisfied.

Axiom 11.3 $x_i \geq x_j$ and $t_i \geq t_j$ and $t_i/x_i \geq t_j/x_j \rightarrow x_i - t_i \geq x_j - t_j$ for all i and j.

If Axioms 11.1 and 11.2 are satisfied, then Axiom 11.3 implies that the post-tax income must increase monotonically as pre-tax income increases. This axiom ensures that tax must not make the richer person poorer and the poorer person richer. This can happen when the richer persons pay so much tax that they become poorer. In other words, the tax should not change the rankings of persons in the pre- and post-income distributions.

The three Axioms 11.1–11.3 are independent of each other and are shown by four hypothetical tax systems for the same income distribution for three taxpayers in Table 11.1.

Table 11.1 Independence of axioms

Income	100	150	200	
Tax system 1	20	60	100	Axiom 11.1 satisfied
Tax rate	0.2	0.4	0.5	Axiom 11.2 satisfied
Post-tax income	80	90	100	Axiom 11.3 satisfied
Tax system 2	20	60	50	Axiom 11.1 violated
Tax rate	0.2	0.4	0.25	Axiom 11.2 violated
Post-tax income	80	90	150	Axiom 11.3 satisfied
Tax system 3	20	60	70	Axiom 11.1 satisfied
Tax rate	0.2	0.4	0.35	Axiom 11.2 violated
Post-tax income	80	90	130	Axiom 11.3 satisfied

Tax system 1 is equitable: it satisfies all Axioms 11.1–11.3. Tax system 2 violates Axiom 11.1 and 11.2 but satisfies Axiom 11.3. Tax system 3 satisfies Axiom 11.1 and 11.3 but violates Axiom 11.2. Tax system 4 satisfies Axiom 11.1 and 11.2 but violates Axiom 11.3.

11.3 Linkage between Tax Elasticity and Equity Axioms

This section shows the linkage between the three equity axioms and tax elasticity.

Suppose $T(x)$ is the tax paid by an individual with pre-tax income x, tax elasticity is given by

$$\eta_T(x) = \frac{dln(T(x))}{dln(x)}. \tag{11.3.1}$$

When $\eta_T(x) = 0$ for all x, everyone pays the same amount of tax, irrespective of pre-tax income. If $\eta_T(x) > 0$ for all x, it implies that the richer a person, the higher the tax she pays. Thus, Axiom 11.1 will be satisfied if $\eta_T(x) \geq 0$ for all x.

The average tax rate is defined as the share of tax paid by a person with pre-tax income x, given by $e(x) = \frac{T(x)}{x}$, which on differentiating with respect to x gives

$$\frac{de(x)}{dx} = \frac{e(x)}{x}[\eta_T(x) - 1]. \tag{11.3.2}$$

If $\eta_T(x) = 1$ for all x, it implies that everyone pays the tax at the same rate irrespective of their pre-tax income. Such a tax system is called proportional. If $\eta_T(x) > 1$ for all x, it means that the richer a person, the higher the tax rate she pays. Such a tax system is called progressive. Thus, Axiom 11.2 will be satisfied if $\eta_T(x) \geq 1$ for all x.

Suppose $y(x) = x - T(x)$ is the post-tax income, the elasticity of which with respect to the pre-tax income is given by

$$\eta_y(x) = \frac{d\ln\left[x - T(x)\right]}{d\ln(x)} = \frac{1 - m(x)}{1 - e(x)} \tag{11.3.3}$$

where $m(x) = \frac{dT(x)}{dx}$ is the marginal tax rate. $\eta_y(x) = 0$ for all x implies that every person has the same post-tax income, meaning that the tax has equalized the post-tax income for every person. Such a tax system will be most equitable. If $\eta_y(x) > 0$ the post-tax income increases monotonically as the pre-tax income increases. Axiom 11.3 will be satisfied if $\eta_y(x) \geq 0$ for all x, which is equivalent to using (11.3.3) $\eta_T(x) \leq \frac{1}{e(x)}$.

This leads to the following lemma:

Lemma 11.1 *A tax system T(x) satisfies all three equity Axioms 11.1–11.3 if* $1 \leq \eta_T(x) \leq \frac{1}{e(x)}$ *for all x, where $\eta_T(x)$ is the tax elasticity, and e(x) is the average tax rate at the pre-tax income x.*

Further, from (11.3.3), Axiom 11.3 will always be satisfied if $m(x) \leq 1$ for all x. If, for some x, $m(x)$ exceeds 1, then Axiom 11.3 will be violated. An implication is that some taxpayers pay more than one dollar of tax when they earn an additional income of one dollar. Such a situation will lead to a disincentive to earn extra income. It changes the ranking between the pre- and post-tax income distributions. Axiom 11.3 rules out the possibility that the marginal tax rate should exceed 100% (Lambert and Yitzhaki 1995). In other words, a tax should never make the richer person poorer and the poorer person richer.

11.4 Four Alternative Definitions of Tax Progressivity

Musgrave and Thin (1948) proposed four alternative definitions of tax progressivity, briefly discussed in this section.

1. **Average rate progressivity**: A tax structure is defined to be progressive, proportional, and regressive when the average tax rate increases ($\frac{de(x)}{dx} > 0$), remains constant ($\frac{de(x)}{dx} = 0$), and decreases ($\frac{de(x)}{dx} < 0$), respectively, as pre-tax income rises with income x. Pigou (1928, 1932) suggested this definition of progressivity, but subsequently, Musgrave and Thin (1948) considered it. Equation (11.3.2) implies that this definition is equivalent to saying that the tax structure is progressive if $\eta_T(x) > 1$, proportional if $\eta_T(x) = 1$, and regressive $\eta_T(x) < 1$ for all x. This demonstrates that if a tax structure is progressive or proportional, it satisfies Axiom 11.2. If the tax structure is regressive for some x, Axiom 11.2 is violated.

2. **Liability progressivity**: A tax structure is defined as progressive if the tax elasticity $\eta_T(x) > 1$, proportional if $\eta_T(x) = 1$, and regressive $\eta_T(x) < 1$ for all x.

That concludes that if a tax structure is progressive or proportional, it satisfies Axiom 11.2. The axiom is violated if the tax structure is regressive for some x.

3. **Residual progressivity**: A tax structure is said to be progressive, proportional, and regressive if the post-tax income elasticity is less than one $[\eta_y(x) < 1]$, equal to one $[\eta_y(x) = 1]$, and greater than one $[\eta_y(x) > 0]$, for all x, respectively.

Equation (11.3.3) also shows that $\eta_y(x) = \frac{1-\eta_T(x)e(x)}{1-e(x)}$, which implies that if $\eta_T(x) > 1$, $\eta_y(x) < 1$, if $\eta_T(x) = 1$, $\eta_y(x) = 1$, and if $\eta_T(x) < 1$, $\eta_y(x) > 1$. These inequalities demonstrate that the residual progressivity is compatible with Axiom 11.2, implying that a tax system is progressive or proportional based on the residual progressivity. Furthermore, $\eta_y(x) \leq 1$ may yield $\eta_y(x) \leq 0$ in some cases, implying that a tax structure can satisfy Axiom 11.2 but violate Axiom 11.3. Similarly, $\eta_y(x) > 1$ yields $\eta_y(x) > 0$, suggesting that a tax structure violates Axiom 11.2 but satisfies Axiom 11.3.

4. **Marginal rate progressivity**: A tax structure is said to be progressive, proportional, and regressive if the marginal tax rate increases $[\frac{dm(x)}{dx} > 0]$, remains constant $[\frac{dm(x)}{dx} = 0]$, and decreases $[\frac{dm(x)}{dx} < 0]$, respectively, as x increases. The increasing marginal tax rate is stronger than the increasing average tax rate, and the former necessarily implies the latter, but not *vice versa*. The marginal tax rate does not, in general, rise continuously but steps up by income brackets. But if there is an overall increasing trend in the marginal tax rate, one can say that the tax structure is progressive.

The average rate, liability, and residual progressivity definitions are compatible with Axiom 11.2. The marginal rate progressivity will be compatible with Axiom 11.2 if there is an increasing (or decreasing) trend in the marginal tax rate. The four alternative measures of progressivity proposed by Musgrave belong to the same family. They relate to progression at a given point on the income scale. They do not provide a single index of overall tax progressivity. For many practical applications, the overall tax progressivity measure is needed. This chapter is primarily concerned with measuring overall tax progressivity. The chapter also distinguishes between the tax progressivity and the redistribution effect of taxation. Some of the tax literature does not differentiate the two concepts. It is argued here that the two concepts are distinct but closely related.

11.5 Relative and Absolute Measures of Tax Progressivity

The literature on taxation distinguishes between relative and absolute measures of tax progressivity (Urban 2014, 2019). Relative measures of progressivity remain unchanged if everyone's tax is increased or decreased by the same proportion. Similarly, absolute measures of progressivity remain unchanged when everyone's tax is increased or decreased by the same absolute amount.

Among several relative measures of tax progressivity proposed in the literature, the Kakwani index, proposed by Kakwani in 1977, is extensively used to analyze equity in taxation and government expenditures. The index is also applied to analyzing equity in access to health, education, and essential services. In particular, the index has become a popular tool for analyzing equity in public finance and delivering healthcare. His measure indicates the extent to which a given tax system deviates from proportionality when everyone pays the tax at the same rate.

A tax system is relatively progressive (regressive) when the tax rate rises (falls) with income, satisfying Axiom 11.2.

In contrast, an absolute measure of progressivity indicates the extent to which a tax system deviates from a situation where everyone pays the same amount of tax. A tax system is progressive (regressive) when richer people pay more taxes than their poorer counterparts, satisfying Axiom 11.1.[1] This chapter discusses both the relative and absolute measures of progressivity.

The following section provides a derivation of this index using aggregate tax elasticity developed in Chapter 9.

11.6 The Kakwani Index of Tax Progressivity and Its Variants

Suppose $T(x)$ is the tax paid by an individual with pre-tax income x. If $F_1[T(x)]$ denotes the proportion of taxes paid by an individual with income less than equal to x, and $F(x)$ is the proportion of individuals with income less than or equal to x, the relationship between $F(x)$ and $F_1[T(x)]$ is called the concentration curve of taxes.

Corollary 9.2 in Chapter 9 states the following two inequalities:

(i) If $F_1(x) - F_1[T(x)] \leq 0$ for all x implies $\eta_T(x) \leq 1$ for all x

(ii) If $F_1(x) - F_1[T(x)] \geq 0$ for all x implies $\eta_T(x) \geq 1$ for all x

where $\eta_T(x)$ is the tax elasticity at the income level x. If $\eta_T(x) \geq 1$ for all x, then the equity Axiom 11.2 is satisfied; thus, the tax system $T(x)$ will be progressive. The vertical distance between the curves $F_1(x)$ and $F_1[T(x)]$ depends on the tax elasticity. If this elasticity is unity at all income levels, the two curves coincide. The inequality (ii) shows that the larger the distance between the two curves, the higher deviation of the tax elasticity from unity at all income levels. A single measure of tax progressivity measures the overall deviation of the tax elasticity from unity.

In Chapter 9, in Theorem 9.11, the idea of aggregate elasticity of a function $g(x)$ with respect to x was developed. Utilizing this theorem, the aggregate elasticity of the tax function $T(x)$ with respect to x is obtained as

[1] This is the minimal concept of tax progressivity introduced by Fei (1981). Moyes (1988) demonstrated that a progressive tax under this concept reduces absolute inequality.

$$\overline{\eta}_T = \frac{C_T}{G} \qquad\qquad (11.6.1)$$

where C_T is the concentration index of tax and G the Gini index of pre-tax income. The tax system is progressive (regressive) if $\overline{\eta}_T$ is higher (lower) than one. The tax system will be proportional if $\overline{\eta}_T$ equals one. Thus, aggregate elasticity $\overline{\eta}_T$ provides a suitable measure of overall tax progressivity.

It is evident that $\overline{\eta}_T$ has a one-to-one relationship with $(C_T - G)$, and hence an appropriate measure of tax progressivity will be given by

$$K = (C_T - G), \qquad\qquad (11.6.2)$$

which is the well-known Kakwani index. The positive value of K implies a progressive tax system, and the negative value indicates a regressive tax system. The tax system will be proportional when K equals zero.

The Kakwani index is a relative measure of tax progressivity because it remains unchanged if the tax liability of everyone is increasing or decreasing by the same proportion. It always satisfies Axiom 11.2.

The absolute measure of tax progressivity remains unchanged if the tax liability of everyone is increased or decreased by the same absolute amount of tax. A tax system is progressive (regressive) when richer persons pay more taxes than poorer ones, satisfying Axiom 11.1. The absolute measure of tax progressivity indicates the overall deviation of the aggregate tax elasticity from zero. Thus, a tax system will be absolutely progressive (regressive) if the tax elasticity $\overline{\eta}_T$ is greater (smaller) than zero. Everyone has the same tax liability if $\overline{\eta}_T$ equals zero. Thus, from (11.6.1), an absolute measure of tax progressivity will be given by

$$K_A = C_T, \qquad\qquad (11.6.3)$$

which is the proposed index of overall absolute tax progressivity. This index will be referred to as the absolute Kakwani index of tax progressivity.

Khetan and Poddar (1976) proposed a relative measure of progressivity that has a similarity with the Kakwani index, given by

$$KP = \frac{1 - G}{1 - C_T}. \qquad\qquad (11.6.4)$$

By this measure, a tax is judged as progressive if $KP>1$, proportional if $KP=1$, and regressive if $KP <1$. It is not difficult to show that the Khetan–Poddar index has a one-to-one relationship with the Kakwani index. This index also satisfies Axiom 11.2 and therefore is a suitable measure of tax progressivity. The following section shows that the Kakwani index has a convenient decomposability property that the Khetan–Poddar index does not possess.

11.7 A Tax Progressivity Decomposition

Governments collect revenues from various taxes, such as personal income tax, company tax, estate gift duties, and indirect taxes. In designing a tax system, it helps to determine the progressivity of various kinds of taxes and how much they contribute to the total tax system's progressivity. This section discusses a tax progressivity decomposition to aid this process.

Suppose the total tax $T(x)$ is the sum of the k individual taxes $T_1(x), T_2(x),$ ... ..., $T_k(x)$:

$$T(x) = \sum_{j=1}^{k} T_j(x). \qquad (11.7.1)$$

Suppose $\overline{T}$ is the average tax revenue collected by the government and μ is the mean income, then $e = \dfrac{\overline{T}}{\mu}$ is the average tax rate of society. Similarly, if the average tax rate of the jth individual tax is defined as $e_j = \dfrac{\overline{T_j}}{\mu}$, then (11.7.1) yields

$$e = \sum_{j=1}^{k} e_j. \qquad (11.7.2)$$

Utilizing Theorem 9.3 in Chapter 9 gives

$$C_T = \sum_{j=1}^{k} \frac{e_j}{e} C_{Tj} \qquad (11.7.3)$$

where C_{Tj} is the concentration index of the jth tax, and C is the concentration index of all taxes together.

From (11.6.2), it follows

$$K = \sum_{j=1}^{k} \frac{e_j}{e} K_j \qquad (11.7.4)$$

where K is the Kakwani index of all taxes and K_j the Kakwani index of the jth type tax. This equation shows that the relative progressivity of all combined taxes is equal to the weighted average of the progressivity of each tax, with weights proportional to their tax shares. $100\frac{e_j}{e}K_j$ is the percentage contribution of the jth tax to total tax progressivity. This equation helps to analyze the contributions of each kind of tax to total tax progressivity.

Utilizing (11.6.3) on (11.7.3) provides an absolute tax progressivity decomposition:

$$K_A = \sum_{j=1}^{k} \frac{e_j}{e} K_{Aj} \qquad (11.7.5)$$

where K_{Aj} is the Kakwani index of absolute tax progressivity. This equation shows that the absolute progressivity of all taxes together is equal to the weighted average of the

Table 11.2 Progressivity of taxes and their contributions in Australia, 1967

Tax	Percent share taxes	Absolute progressivity	Relative progressivity	Contributions to absolute progressivity	Contributions to relative progressivity
Personal income tax	37	0.45	0.14	47.54	127.43
Company tax	13.5	0.43	0.12	16.5	39.7
Estate gift tax	1	0.98	0.67	2.8	16.44
Indirect taxes	30.8	0.21	−0.1	18.44	−75.14
State motor taxes	3.2	0.21	−0.1	1.93	−7.86
Sate probate duties	2.1	0.94	0.63	5.5	31.68
Other state taxes	7.2	0.23	−0.08	4.7	−13.97
Local government taxes	5.3	0.17	−0.14	2.59	−18.28
Total tax	100	0.35	0.04	100	100

progressivity of each tax, with weights proportional to their shares of tax. $100\frac{e_j}{e}K_{Aj}$ is the percentage contribution of the jth tax to total tax progressivity. The relative and absolute progressivity measures can give very different contributions of each type of tax to the total progressivity.

Table 11.2 presents the estimates of tax progressivity of different types of taxes in Australia. The table has five columns, the first showing the percentage share of different kinds of taxes. The second and third columns present absolute and relative indices of tax progressivity, respectively. The fourth and fifth columns show each type of tax's percentage contributions to the total absolute and relative progressivity, respectively.

The Australian tax system is dominated by personal income taxes contributing 37% to the total revenue, followed by indirect taxes, contributing 30.8% to the total revenue. The company tax is the third dominant tax adding 13.5% to the total tax revenue.

It is striking that the values of absolute progressivity in column 3 are positive for all types of taxes. It means that all kinds of taxes are absolutely progressive, implying that wealthier persons pay higher taxes than the poor, satisfying the equity Axiom 11.1. The relative progressivity index values in column 4 are negative for indirect taxes, state motor taxes, other state taxes, and local taxes, signifying that these taxes are regressive. These are the indirect taxes, where the poor pay proportionally more taxes than the rich, which make negative contributions to the total relative progressivity.

Table 11.3 presents a progressivity comparison of federal and state taxes in three developed countries: Australia, Canada, and the United States. Federal and state taxes are progressive for all three countries based on the absolute concept of progressivity. It means that the wealthier people are paying more taxes than the more impoverished people. The relative progressivity index shows that the federal taxes are progressive in Australia and the United States, while the state taxes are regressive. However, in Canada, the state taxes are proportional.

The absolute and relative concepts of progressivity provide different implications of tax progressivity. Economists have been arguing for many years that indirect taxes are regressive, and this is why they have preferred to rely on personal income taxes, which

Table 11.3 International comparisons of tax progressivity

Tax	Percent share taxes	Absolute progressivity	Relative progressivity	Contributions to absolute progressivity	Contributions to relative progressivity
			Australia 1967		
Federal taxes	82.1	0.36	0.05	85.06	109.03
State taxes	17.9	0.29	−0.02	14.94	−9.03
Total taxes	100	0.35	0.04	100	100
			Canada 1970		
Federal taxes	49.8	0.41	0.04	52.36	91.68
State taxes	50.2	0.37	0.00	47.64	8.32
Total taxes	100	0.39	0.02	100	100
			United States 1970		
Federal taxes	63.24	0.46	0.06	69.95	238.82
State taxes	36.76	0.34	−0.06	30.05	−138.82
Total taxes	100	0.42	0.02	100	100

are usually deemed progressive. The analysis presented here shows that the regressive taxes based on the relative measure can become progressive when using the absolute measure of tax progressivity. Hence, a crucial question arises as to what progressivity concept policymakers should rely on to formulate tax policies.

The idea of an absolute measure of tax progressivity stems from the pioneering paper by Kolm (1976a, 1976b), who proposed the absolute measures of inequality, which do not change when each income is increased or decreased by the same amount. Until the publication of Kolm's paper, the discussion on inequality focused on the relative measures of inequality, which remain unchanged when every income is increased or decreased by the same proportion. Kolm called the relative measures "rightist measures" and the absolute measures "leftist measures." This classification suggests that absolute measures are more egalitarian than relative measures. However, absolute measures of progressivity are derived from a weaker Axiom 11.1, implying that the rich should pay more tax than the poor.

On the other hand, relative measures are based on the stronger Axiom 11.2, meaning that the rich should pay tax at a higher tax rate. Hence, one can say that the relative concept of tax progressivity is more egalitarian than the absolute concept. It is appropriate to point out that the absolute concept will be more egalitarian than the relative concept in social welfare programs that provide transfers to the poor.

The two concepts of progressivity have different value judgments. It is impossible to provide a definitive answer to which concept policymakers should adopt to assess a tax system. A compromise will be to present the analysis to policymakers based on both ideas.

11.8 The Suits Tax Progressivity Measure

Suits (1977) proposed a measure of tax progressivity based on a relative concentration curve concept. A detailed discussion of relative concentration curves is given in Chapter 9. Suppose $T(x)$ is the tax function, then the relative concentration of $T(x)$ with respect to x is the relationship between $F_1[T(x)]$ and $F_1(x)$, where $F_1(x)$ and $F_1[T(x)]$ are the proportion of income received and tax paid by the individuals with pre-tax income less than or equal to x, respectively. The concentration and relative concentration curves have different interpretations, and the concentration curve informs the tax shares of individuals with income less than or equal to x. In contrast, the relative concentration curve is the relationship between individuals' tax share and income share. It indicates the poorest individuals' tax share with respect to their income share.

It will help explain the two curves by a simple hypothetical example. Suppose 10% of individuals have pre-tax income less than $1,000, whose income share is, say, 6%. The Lorenz curve informs that 10% of individuals with less than $1,000 have a 6% income share. Suppose these 10% of individuals pay a 4% share of tax. In that case, the concentration curve informs that the 10% of individuals with pre-tax income less than $1,000 contribute 4% to the total tax revenue. Thus, the concentration curve is the relationship between the proportion of individuals with income less than $1,000 and their tax share. The relative concentration curve shows that the poorest individuals with 6% of income share contribute the tax share of 4%. It is the relationship between the income share and the tax share.

Theorem 9.7 in Chapter 9 showed that $F_1(x)$ is greater (smaller) than $F_1[T(x)]$ for all x implies the tax elasticity $\eta_T(x)$ is greater (less) than one for all x. The elasticity $\eta_T(x)$ equals one for all x when the two curves $F_1(x)$ and $F_1[T(x)]$ coincide at all points. That means that when the two curves coincide, the tax system will be proportional assuming everyone pays tax at the same rate. The deviation of $F_1(x)$ from $F_1[T(x)]$ at all points measures the deviation of the tax system from proportionality. Following this idea, Suits (1977) defined his measure of tax progressivity as

$$S = 2 \int_0^\infty (F_1(x) - F_1[T(x)]) dF_1(x). \qquad (11.8.1)$$

It will help to write $dF_1(x) = (1 + G) f_1(x) dx$, where G is the Gini index income x. It is thus easy to show that $\int_0^\infty f_1(x) dx = 1$. As such, $f_1(x)$ will be a legitimate density function. Then, S is given by

$$S = 2(1 + G) \int_0^\infty (F_1(x) - F_1[T(x)]) f_1(x) dx. \qquad (11.8.2)$$

Chapter 9 defined the relative concentration index of the tax function $T(x)$ with respect to x as

$$C_{Tx} = 2 \int_0^\infty [F_1(x) - F_1(T(x))] f_1(x) \, dx. \tag{11.8.3}$$

Theorem 9.8 in Chapter 9 showed that the aggregate elasticity of $T(x)$ denoted by $\tilde{\eta}_T$ will be higher (lower) than one, if C_{Tx} is higher (lower) than zero. Thus, C_{Tx} measures the deviation of aggregate tax elasticity from unity. The tax system $T(x)$ will be progressive (regressive) if C_{Tx} is greater (less) than zero and proportional when $C_{Tx} = 0$. Thus, C_{Tx} is the appropriate measure of tax progressivity.

Suits' measure S in (11.8.2) is not the same as the relative concentration index C_{Tx}. To obtain the correct measure of tax progressivity, S has to be normalized by $(1+G)$:

$$C_{Tx} = \frac{S}{(1 + G)}. \tag{11.8.4}$$

Although Suits' measure is widely used in analyzing tax progressivity, this error has not been spotted in over 43 years.

Formby, Seaks, and Smith (1981) compared the Kakwani and Suits measures using the United States income tax data for 1962–76. They revealed that the two measures display different magnitudes of change in progressivity. More importantly, in three out of fourteen years, the two measures moved in opposite directions. One possible explanation for such divergence may be that they did not normalize the Suits measure. If the Gini index of pre-tax income changes continuously over time, the two measures are not comparable, although both are derived from the tax elasticity. Table 2 of their paper revealed that the magnitude of the Suits measure was consistently higher than the magnitude of the Kakwani measure. If the Suits measure is normalized by $(1+G)$, the magnitudes of the two measures will be closer to each other.

11.9 Horizontal and Vertical Equity

As pointed out, the principles of horizontal equity (HE) and vertical equity (VE) are the two fundamental commands of social justice. The HE requires that two persons with identical incomes and needs pay the same tax; in other words, equal treatment of equals. Various individual circumstances can violate this principle. For instance, people earning income from businesses pay taxes lower than those earning income from wages and salaries. These inequities in taxation may alter the ranking of individuals in pre- and post-tax income distribution. The VE relates to unequal treatment of the unequal, that is, wealthier persons must pay taxes at a higher rate. The quantification of the two principles raises many complex issues. However, Kakwani (1984b) proposed a methodology to quantify the two principles. This section provides a more detailed discussion of this methodology.

Suppose $T(x)$ is the tax paid by a person with income x, then the post-tax income of the person is given by

$$y(x) = x - T(x). \tag{11.9.1}$$

If the persons are ranked by their pre-tax income, then applying Theorem 9.3 in Chapter 9 on (11.9.1) yields

$$\mu_y F_1\left[y(x)\right] = \mu F_1\left(x\right) - \overline{T} F_1\left[T(x)\right] \tag{11.9.2}$$

where $F_1\left[y(x)\right]$ is the concentration curve of $y(x)$, $F_1\left(x\right)$ is the Lorenz curve of pre-tax income, and $F_1\left[T(x)\right]$ is the concentration curve of taxes. μ_y is the mean of the post-tax income given by

$$\mu_y = \mu - \overline{T} \tag{11.9.3}$$

μ being the mean pre-tax income and $\overline{T}$ the average tax paid by society.

Rearranging equation (11.9.2) yields

$$F_1\left[y(x)\right] = F_1\left(x\right) + \frac{e}{(1-e)}\left\{F_1\left(x\right) - F_1\left[T(x)\right]\right\} \tag{11.9.4}$$

where $e = \dfrac{\overline{T}}{\mu}$ is the average tax rate of the entire society.

$F_1\left[y(x)\right]$ is the share of post-tax income received by persons with a pre-tax income less than or equal to x when they are ranked in ascending order of their pre-tax income. Let $F_1^*\left[y(x)\right]$ be the proportion of the post-tax income received by persons with the pre-tax income less than or equal to x when they are ranked by their post-tax income. The Lorenz curve of the post-tax income will be the same as the concentration curve $F_1\left[y(x)\right]$ only if the ranking of persons is unaltered between the pre- and post-tax incomes. Chapter 9 showed that if the *ranking* changes, then $F_1^*\left[y(x)\right] < F_1\left[y(x)\right]$ *for all x*, and hence the two curves will be different.

The redistribution effect of a tax, defined by the criterion of Lorenz dominance, is measured by the deviation of the Lorenz curve of the post-tax income from that of pre-tax income. Thus, the redistribution effect of the tax will be given by

$$R(x) = F_1^*\left[y(x)\right] - F_1\left(x\right) \tag{11.9.5}$$

so the tax system reduces (increases) inequality if $R(x)$ is positive (negative) for all x.

Combining (11.9.4) and (11.9.5), we obtain

$$R(x) = F_1^* [y(x)] - F_1(x) = F_1^* [y(x)] - F_1[y(x)] + \frac{e}{(1-e)} \{F_1(x) - F_1[T(x)]\},$$

which can be written as

$$R(x) = H(x) + V(x) \tag{11.9.6}$$

where

$$H(x) = F_1^* [y(x)] - F_1[y(x)] \tag{11.9.7}$$

and

$$V(x) = F_1[y(x)] - F_1(x) = \frac{e}{(1-e)} \{F_1(x) - F_1[T(x)]\}. \tag{11.9.8}$$

$H(x)=0$ for all x if there is no change in ranking between pre- and post-tax income distributions. If there is a change in ranking, then $H(x)<0$, indicating the change in ranking reduces the tax system's redistributive effect.

Suppose the rankings of individuals between the pre- and post-tax income distributions change. In that case, the tax system does not treat some individuals equally, and there is a HE violation. Therefore, Feldstein (1976) and Rosen (1978) proposed measuring the horizontal inequity by the rank correlation coefficient between individuals' utilities' pre- and post-tax orderings. In this context, Atkinson (1980) proved that the change in ranking increases the Gini index of the post-tax income. This result implies that the change in ranking impacts the redistribution of taxes. It is evident from (11.9.7) that $H(x)$ directly affects the redistribution of taxes and can indicate horizontal inequity.

The principle of VE requires that people with different economic circumstances pay different amounts of tax. This principle is rather ambiguous and its measurement requires a more precise definition of VE. A clear description of VE will be that wealthier persons pay higher taxes (Axiom 11.1) or pay taxes at a higher rate (Axiom 11.2). Hence, the idea of VE is closely related to tax progressivity. But, the two concepts differ, and how they differ is explained below.

Musgrave and Thin (1948) proposed a measure of progressivity obtained from the difference between the inequality indexes of the post-tax and pre-tax income distributions. Their measure of progressivity indicates the extent to which a given tax system leads to a reduction in income inequality. The progressive tax is associated with decreased income inequality, whereas a regressive tax is related to increased income inequality. Musgrave and Thin (1948) measured the redistributive effect of taxation and not tax progressivity. Tax progressivity deals with an equity principle of taxation, suggesting that wealthier persons must pay more or even higher rates. The redistributive effect of taxation is, on the other hand, an outcome of the equity principle. It would be natural to relate the principles of HE and VE to the outcome of equity principles of taxation, which is the redistributive effect of the tax.

The appropriate index of tax progressivity is obtained by comparing the Lorenz curve of the pre-tax income and the concentration of taxes. It informs to what extent taxes are distributed across income. The distribution of taxes alone does not affect the outcome because one also needs to know the size of individuals' taxes. In (11.9.8), $V(x)$ depends on the average tax rate and tax progressivity. The average tax rate measures the size of the tax, and progressivity measures the distribution of taxes. Together, these two factors provide how individuals with different incomes pay taxes differently. Thus, $V(x)$, which directly impacts the redistribution of taxes, provides a measure of VE.

Section 11.4 discussed four alternative measures of tax progressivity proposed by Musgrave and Thin (1948). Among them, the residual measure is the only one that has linkage with the redistributive effect of tax, and this linkage must be explored.

According to the residual measure, a tax structure is said to be progressive, proportional, and regressive if the post-tax income elasticity is less than one $[\eta_y(x) < 1$ for all $x]$, equal to one $[\eta_y(x) = 1$ for all $x]$, and greater than one $[\eta_y(x) > 1$ for all $x]$, for all x, respectively. Applying Corollary 9.2 on (11.9.8), it can be shown that there is a one-to-one relationship between the residual measure of tax progressivity and VE, meaning that for all x, $V(x)>0$ if $\eta_y(x) < 1$, $V(x)=0$ if $\eta_y(x) = 1$, and $V(x)<0$ if $\eta_y(x) > 1$. But, Jakobsson (1976) demonstrated that residual progressivity is the only logical measure directly linked with the tax system's redistributive effect judged by the Lorenz domination. He proved a one-to-one relationship between the residual measure of tax progressivity and the redistribution effect of taxation. Since $R(x)=H(x)+V(x)$, Jakobsson's result can be valid only if for a particular case when $H(x)=0$ for all x, that is, when the tax system does not change the rankings of individuals.

Integrating both sides of (11.9.6) over the entire range of x, we obtain

$$R = \frac{G - G^*}{G} = \frac{(C_y - G^*)}{G} + \frac{e\,K}{(1 - e)\,G} \tag{11.9.9}$$

where G and G^* are the Gini indices of the pre- and post-tax income, respectively, C_y is the concentration index of the post-tax income, and K is the Kakwani index given in (11.6.2). R is an index of the tax redistribution, measured by the percentage change in the Gini index of the pre- and post-tax income. It is given by

$$R = H + V \tag{11.9.10}$$

where

$$H = \frac{C_y - G^*}{G} \tag{11.9.11}$$

and

$$V = \frac{e\,K}{(1-e)\,G} \tag{11.9.12}$$

are the indices measuring the HE and VE, respectively.[2]

Theorem 9.5 in Chapter 9 showed that $C_y < G^*$, which implies $H \leq 0$. Note that $H=0$ when the ranking remains the same between the pre- and post-tax incomes, and if the ranking changes, then $H<0$. Thus, the violation of HE in the Feldstein sense will have the effect of reducing the redistributive impact of taxation. Further, note that V is greater (less) than zero if the tax system is progressive (regressive) and equal to zero when the tax system is proportional. It follows that a progressive tax system reduces inequality, and a regressive tax system increases inequality. The proportional tax system has no impact on inequality.

11.10 A Hypothetical Example

This section draws some conclusions from a hypothetical example of four tax systems developed by Kakwani (1984c), described in Table 11.4. From this table, the summary measures are calculated and presented in Table 11.5. The conclusions that follow are:

Tax system 1 is progressive and results in a 10% decrease in income inequality. It does not violate the principle of HE, and as a result, the index of VE is equal to the index of the redistributive effect of the tax.

Tax system 2 is more progressive than tax system 1 and has a higher average tax rate. As a result, the index of VE increases substantially from 10% to 110.24%, but at the same time, horizontal inequity is introduced, which has the

Table 11.4 A hypothetical example of four tax systems

Pre-tax income	Tax liability	Post-tax income
	Tax system 1	
100	20	80
500	180	320
	Tax system 2	
100	20	80
500	430	70
	Tax system 3	
100	10	90
500	440	60
	Tax system 4	
100	11	89
500	484	16

[2] Plotnick (1981) also suggested a similar index of HE, but did not relate it to the redistributive effect of taxes.

Table 11.5 Summary table of four tax systems

	Tax system 1	Tax system 2	Tax system 3	Tax system 4
Average tax rate	0.33	0.75	0.75	0.83
Pre-tax Gini index	0.67	0.67	0.67	0.67
Progressivity	0.13	0.25	0.39	0.29
Horizontal equity	0.00	−20.25	−60.04	−208.62
Vertical equity	10.00	110.24	130.04	204.35
Redistributive effect	10.00	89.99	70.00	−4.27

effect of increased inequality by 20.25%. This example shows that there can be a possible clash between HE and VE, and increasing VE may lead to horizontal inequity.

Tax system 3 is even more progressive than tax system 2 while keeping the same average tax rate. The index of VE increased further from 110.24% to 130.04%, which could have increased the index of tax redistribution; but its effect was offset by substantial increases in horizontal inequity, resulting in a decline in income redistribution from 89.9% to 70%. Interestingly, although the two tax systems give precisely the same ranking of individuals, the magnitude of horizontal inequity is substantially higher for tax system 3. This result indicates that horizontal inequity is sensitive to changes in tax progressivity.

Tax systems 3 and 4 have the same progressivity but differ concerning the average tax rate. It is noted that increasing the average tax rate while keeping the same progressivity increases VE substantially from 130.04% to 204.35%. An even greater increase in horizontal inequity accompanies the increase in VE. As a result, the redistribution effect decreases from 70% to −4.27%. Thus, a change in the average tax rate can vastly alter VE and HE, even if the progressivity of taxation has remained constant.

This hypothetical example reveals that taxation's progressivity and redistribution effect are related but distinct concepts. Three factors affect the relative redistribution effect: taxation progressivity, the change in ranking due to taxation, and the average tax rate.

Musgrave and Thin (1948) measured progressivity by the extent to which a given tax system reduces income inequality, which is essentially a measure of the redistributive effect of taxation. Tax progressivity deals with an equity principle of taxation, suggesting that wealthier persons must pay more or even higher rates. Axioms 11.1 and 11.2 form the basis of equity principles of taxation. Thus, the two principles of taxation are crucial in deriving measures of progressivity.

11.11 Violation of Equity Axioms

The three axioms presented in Section 11.2 formed the basis for measuring tax progressivity and redistribution effect. Kakwani and Lambert (1998) showed that the violation of the axioms exerts negative influences on the redistributive impact of tax. These negative influences on the redistributive effect of tax provide the means to characterize the type of inequity present in a tax system and assess its significance. It would be helpful to explain it intuitively.

Axiom 11.1 says that tax should increase monotonically with people's ability to pay. Thus, $T(x)$ and x should have the same ranking. If the ranking is not the same, then the axiom is violated. Suppose G_T and C_T are the Gini and concentration indices of $T(x)$, respectively, then from Theorem 9.5 in Chapter 9, it follows that $T(x)$ and x will have the same ranking if $G_T = C_T$. If $G_T > C_T$, the ranking of $T(x)$ and x will not be the same. Thus, the positive value of $G_T - C_T$ measures the degree of violation of Axiom 11.1.

Axiom 11.3 requires that the post-tax income $y(x)$ have the same ranking as x. The axiom will be violated if the ranking between $y(x)$ and x is not the same. If G_y and C_y are the Gini and concentration indices of $y(x)$, respectively, then $y(x)$ and x will have the same ranking if $G_y = C_y$. And the ranking will be different if $G_y > C_y$. Thus, the magnitude of $G_y - C_y$ measures the degree of violation of Axiom 11.3.

Axiom 11.2 is more complicated. If Axiom 11.1 is violated, then Axiom 11.2 is also violated. Axiom 11.1 is weaker than Axiom 11.2, so if Axiom 11.1 is satisfied, Axiom 11.2 may be either satisfied or violated. Suppose $e(x)$ is the average tax rate, then if $e(x)$ and x have the same ranking, Axiom 11.2 will be satisfied only if $T(x)$ and x have the same ranking. Suppose G_e and C_e are the Gini and concentration indices of $e(x)$, respectively, then if $G_e - C_e = 0$, Axiom 11.2 is satisfied provided $G_T - C_T = 0$. And, if $G_e - C_e > 0$, Axiom 11.2 violated. Thus, $G_e - C_e$ measures the difference in rankings between $e(x)$ and x, which also includes the cases of $G_T - C_T > 0$. Thus, $(G_e - C_e) - (G_T - C_T) > 0$ measures the net effect of the violation of Axiom 11.2, while $G_T - C_T > 0$ measures the violation of Axiom 11.1.

It will be helpful to introduce the following variables:

$$S_1 = \frac{e}{(1-e)G}(G_T - C_T) \tag{11.11.1}$$

$$S_2 = \frac{e}{(1-e)G}[(G_e - C_e) - (G_T - C_T)] \tag{11.11.2}$$

$$S_3 = \frac{(G^* - C_y)}{G} \tag{11.11.3}$$

where $G^* = G_y$ is the Gini index of the post-tax income.

From (11.9.9), the redistributive effect of taxation can be written as

$$R = \frac{e}{(1-e)G}[K + (G_e - C_e)] - S_1 - S_2 - S_3 \tag{11.11.4}$$

where S_1, S_2, and S_3 measure the redistributive effects of taxation when Axioms 11.1, 11.2, and 11.3 are violated, respectively. Their magnitudes inform the quantitative departures of equity in taxation. Their negative contributions signify that violation of equity increases inequality of post-tax income. The first term on the right-hand side of (11.11.4) measures the potential equity in a tax system, a value of the redistributive effect that might be achieved if an appropriately designed tax system could eliminate all inequities. There is, of course, no uniquely well-defined way to abolish axiom violation. Thus, the equation (11.11.4) is the decomposition of the redistributive effect of taxation into a potential equity component and three inequity components, each contributing to an increase in inequality due to tax.

11.12 An International Comparison of Inequities in Taxation

The violation by an income tax system of each of the three equity axioms would negatively influence the redistribution effect of the tax. These negative influences provide a means to characterize the inequities present in an income tax system and assess their significance.

   This section offers an international comparison of inequity in taxation in nine developed countries. The income distribution data for these countries were obtained from the Luxembourg Income Study (LIS) database for 2013. Gross household income is the total monetary and non-monetary current income. Disposable income is the gross income net of taxes and social security contributions. Thus taxes include both income tax and social security payments.

   The household income and taxes (including social security payments) are equalized by dividing them by the square root of the number of household members. This equalizing procedure accounts for different needs of household members and economies of scale that occur in larger households. The redistribution effect of the tax is measured by the percentage change in the pre- and post-tax Gini index.

   Table 11.6 reveals that the Australian income tax system reduces inequality in living standards by 12.16%. The inequity due to violation of Axiom 11.1 reduces the overall redistribution effect by 1.31%. The violation of this axiom implies that some more affluent taxpayers pay lower income tax than some poorer taxpayers.

   The inequity due to breach of equity Axiom 11.2 increases the post-tax income inequality by 2.64%. That implies that some richer individuals pay income tax lower than poorer individuals. The inequity due to violation of Axiom 11.3 reduces the overall redistribution effect by 0.34%. This principle relates to HE, implying that the tax system changes the rankings of individuals between the pre- and post-tax income distributions. The rank change happens because the tax system makes some poorer individuals more affluent than average poor individuals. It also means that the tax system does not treat taxpayers equally with the same economic circumstances.

Table 11.6 Inequities in taxation: an international comparison

Countries	Redistributive effect of the income tax system (Percent)	Inequity due to violation of axioms (Percent)			Total tax Inequity (Percent)	Potential redistribution effect (Percent)
		Axiom 1	Axiom 2	Axiom 3		
Russia	−1.73	1.74	3.35	0.23	5.32	−7.05
South Korea	−2.50	2.36	10.82	0.32	13.50	−16.00
UK	−10.72	2.69	4.58	0.91	8.19	−18.90
Israel	−11.28	1.38	5.75	0.45	7.58	−18.85
Germany	−13.18	2.10	5.15	1.45	8.70	−21.89
Finland	−10.83	1.36	3.43	0.59	5.39	−16.22
Canada	−8.49	1.40	7.40	0.46	9.26	−17.75
Australia	−12.16	1.31	2.64	0.46	4.40	−16.56
United States	−9.67	1.10	2.83	0.34	4.27	−13.95

The total inequity in the Australian tax system reduces the redistribution effect of tax by 4.40%. The results suggest that the Australian tax system could have reduced income inequality by 16.56% (instead of 12.16%) because of inequities in the tax system. Thus, removing inequities could improve taxation's redistribution effect without increasing marginal tax rates on higher-income groups.

Table 11.6 reveals that the violation of the three axioms in the United States tax system contributes to the total inequity of 4.27%, the lowest among the nine developed countries. The total inequity is the highest in South Korea at 13.50%, followed by Canada at 9.26%.

The violation of Axiom 11.2 has the most severe impact on the redistributive effect in all nine countries. That is a striking finding, suggesting substantial regressivity in the income tax systems of all nations. The inequity is much smaller if the tax system requires that wealthier taxpayers pay more tax, but inequity increases significantly when the system requires them to pay tax at higher rates. Thus, progressive income taxes induce the taxpayers to indulge in tax avoidance or even tax evasion schemes.

11.13 Income Tax Discrimination

Equity in taxation requires that there should not be any systematic discrimination against any social group in tax payment. Different social groups must not face different tax schedules. Still, in many countries, tax systems discriminate against some groups of taxpayers. For instance, income tax may discriminate against workers because of the tax breaks business people enjoy. In some countries, government treats rural people more leniently in tax payments, particularly farmers. Intuitively, any discrimination must result in a loss of social welfare. Kakwani and Lambert (1999) provided a framework to measure welfare loss caused when a tax system discriminates against some social group. They focused only on income tax, but their framework can be extended to other kinds of taxes. They proved that tax discrimination against any group results in social welfare loss. Their methodology computed welfare loss in money metric, meaning that the loss is in monetary units. This section revisits their study, providing further insight into the issue.

Suppose that the population is divided into k mutually exclusive social groups. Further, suppose that the jth group has the population share a_j and the density function of the pre-tax income x is $f_j(x)$ with mean $\mu_j = \int_0^\infty x f_j(x)\,dx$.

If the tax function $T(x)$ is applied uniformly to the whole population and if any persons have the same income x, they pay the same tax irrespective of which social group they belong. Such a tax system is said to be nondiscriminatory. Suppose different tax functions $T_j(x)$ for $j=1$ to k are applied to each group, then differences in $T_j(x)$ constitute tax discrimination, meaning that individuals belonging to different social groups pay a different amount of tax for the same income. Let e_j be the average tax rate paid by the jth group, which is given by

$$e_j = \frac{1}{\mu_j} \int_0^\infty T_j(x) f_j(x)\,dx = \frac{\overline{T}_j}{\mu_j} \qquad (11.13.1)$$

where $\overline{T}_j$ is the average tax paid by the jth social group.

The overall probability density function $f(x)$ for x is defined as

$$f(x) = \sum_{j=1}^{k} a_j f_j(x) \qquad (11.13.2)$$

Given this, $\mu = \int_0^\infty x f(x)\,dx$ and $\overline{T} = \int_0^\infty T(x) f(x)\,dx$ are the mean income and mean tax paid by the whole population, which from (11.12.1) and (11.12.2) are also given by $\mu = \sum_{j=1}^{k} a_j \mu_j$ and $\overline{T} = \sum_{j=1}^{k} a_j \overline{T}_j$, respectively. These results provide the overall tax rate of the entire population as $e = \frac{\overline{T}}{\mu}$, which from (11.12.1) is given by

$$e = \frac{\sum_{j=1}^{k} a_j \mu_j e_j}{\mu} \qquad (11.13.3)$$

If $e_j = e$ for all j, then there will not be any tax discrimination.

The tax function $T(x)$ for the entire population must relate to the individual group tax functions $T_j(x)$ where $j=1$ to k, at every income level x. Thus, using (11.12.2), $T(x)$ is determined by the weighted average of tax functions $T_j(x)$ at every income level x:

$$T(x) = \frac{1}{f(x)} \sum_{j=1}^{k} a_j f_j(x) T_j(x) = \sum_{j=1}^{k} \lambda_j(x) T_j(x) \qquad (11.13.4)$$

where $\lambda_j(x) = \frac{1}{f(x)} \sum_{j=1}^{k} a_j f_j(x)$ so that $\sum_{j=1}^{k} \lambda_j(x) = 1$.

Substitute $T_j(x) = T(x)$ for all j in this equation gives (11.12.2). Integrating (11.12.4) and dividing by μ both sides yields (11.12.3). The deviation of $T(x)$ in (11.12.4) from $T_j(x)$ for $j=1$ to k measures the tax discrimination. Note that e_j is the average tax rate of the jth group when the tax function $T_j(x)$ is imposed on the group. Suppose another group l, which with a tax function $T_l(x)$ has an average tax rate of e_l, there are two reasons that e_l can exceed e_j: one is that group l is wealthier than group j, in which case with progressive tax code, e_l will exceed e_j; and another is tax discrimination against group l relative to group j. The tax discrimination can be measured if one can separate the two effects. For this, the following procedure can be adopted.

An appropriate method will apply the same tax function $T(x)$ to each social group. Therefore, $\bar{T}_j^* = \int_0^\infty T(x) f_j(x)\, dx$ is the average tax paid by the jth group when there is no discrimination. As such, $e_j^* = \dfrac{\bar{T}_j^*}{\mu_j}$ will be the average tax rate of the jth group when there is no tax discrimination. It is, thus, easy to verify that

$$e = \frac{\sum_{j=1}^{k} a_j \mu_j e_j^*}{\mu},\qquad (11.13.5)$$

which has a similarity with (11.13.3). The effect of discrimination against the jth group can then be measured by $d_j = e_j - e_j^*$. If $d_j = 0$, there is no discrimination against the jth group. But, if d_j is greater (less) than zero, the tax system discriminates against (favoring) the jth group.

It will now be shown that tax discrimination against any social group reduces welfare. Atkinson's general class of social welfare functions is utilized for this purpose (see Chapter 5 for details). Every individual is assumed to have the same utility function:

$$u(x^*) = \int_0^\infty u(x) f(x)\, dx \qquad (11.13.6)$$

where $u(x)$ is increasing in x and is concave. x^* is the equally distributed equivalent level of the pre-tax income, interpreted as the level if received by every individual, it will result in the same level of social welfare as the present distribution. x^* is the dollar value of the pre-tax social welfare. Substituting (11.12.2) into (11.12.6) yields

$$u(x^*) = \sum_{j=1}^{k} a_j \int_0^\infty u(x) f_j(x)\, dx = \sum_{j=1}^{k} a_j u(x_j^*) \qquad (11.13.7)$$

where x_j^* is the dollar value of the pre-tax social welfare of the jth group.

Similarly, the dollar value of the post-tax social welfare, when the same tax function $T(x)$ is applied to all social groups, is given by

$$u\left(y^{*}\right) = \int_{0}^{\infty} u\left(x - T\left(x\right)\right) f\left(x\right) dx. \tag{11.13.8}$$

y^{*} is the dollar value of post-tax social welfare when there is no tax discrimination against any social group. Substituting (11.12.2) into (11.12.8) yields

$$u\left(y^{*}\right) = \sum_{j=1}^{k} a_{j} \int_{0}^{\infty} u\left(x - T\left(x\right)\right) f_{j}\left(x\right) dx = \sum_{j=1}^{k} a_{j} u\left(y_{j}^{*}\right), \tag{11.13.9}$$

which relates the dollar value of the post-tax social welfare of each social group to the dollar value of social welfare of all taxpayers when there is no discrimination.

Suppose each social group faces different tax functions, when there is discrimination, then the post-tax social welfare of the jth group will be given by

$$u\left(\tilde{y}_{j}^{*}\right) = \int_{0}^{\infty} u\left(x - T_{j}\left(x\right)\right) f_{j}\left(x\right) dx, \tag{11.13.10}$$

which on utilizing (11.13.2) yields

$$u\left(\tilde{y}^{*}\right) = \sum_{j=1}^{k} a_{j} \int_{0}^{\infty} u\left(x - T_{j}\left(x\right)\right) f_{j}\left(x\right) dx = \sum_{j=1}^{k} a_{j} u\left(\tilde{y}_{j}^{*}\right) \tag{11.13.11}$$

where $\tilde{y}^{*}$ and $\tilde{y}_{j}^{*}$ are the dollar values of the whole population's social welfare and the jth group when different tax functions are applied to each social group, respectively.

The central proposition of Kakwani and Lambert (1999) is that tax discrimination is welfare-reducing. Theorem 11.1 formally presents their proposition.

Theorem 11.1 $\tilde{y}^{*}$ *and* y^{*} *are the money values of social welfare of the post-tax income with and without tax discrimination, respectively. Given this, if* $T\left(x\right) = T_{j}\left(x\right)$ *for all* $j=1$ *to* k, *then* $\tilde{y}^{*} = y^{*}$; *otherwise,* $\tilde{y}^{*} < y^{*}$.

Proof: By equation (11.12.4) and using $\sum_{j=1}^{k} \lambda_{j} = 1, x - T\left(x\right) = \sum_{j=1}^{k} \lambda_{j}\left(x - T_{j}\left(x\right)\right)$, which on using in (11.12.7) gives

$$u\left(y^{*}\right) = \int_{0}^{\infty} u\left(\sum_{j=1}^{k} \lambda_{j}\left(x - T_{j}\left(x\right)\right)\right) f\left(x\right) dx. \tag{11.13.12}$$

By equation (11.12.10) and using $\lambda_{j} = \frac{1}{f(x)} \sum_{j=1}^{k} a_{j} f_{j}\left(x\right)$ gives

$$u\left(\tilde{y}^{*}\right) = \int_{0}^{\infty} \sum_{j=1}^{k} \lambda_{j} u\left(\left(x - T_{j}\left(x\right)\right)\right) f\left(x\right) dx. \tag{11.13.13}$$

From Jensen's inequality, we have

$$u\left[\sum_{j=1}^{k} \lambda_j \left(x - T_j\left(x\right)\right)\right] \geq \sum_{k}^{k} \lambda_j u \left(x - T_j\left(x\right)\right), \qquad (11.13.14)$$

which from (11.12.12) and (11.12.13) immediately yields $u\left(y^*\right) \geq u\left(\tilde{y}^*\right)$, which proves that $y^* \geq \tilde{y}^*$. If there is no discrimination in the tax treatment of different social groups, then $y^* = \tilde{y}^*$, which completes the proof of Theorem 11.1.

The empirical estimation of discrimination requires specifying the utility function. In the application to Australian income tax in the next section, Atkinson's class of homothetic utility functions is utilized:

$$u\left(x\right) = \frac{x^{1-\epsilon}}{1-\epsilon}, \quad \epsilon \neq 1$$
$$= \ln\left(x\right), \quad \epsilon = 1 \qquad (11.13.15)$$

where $\epsilon > 0$ captures inequality aversion (see Chapter 5).

11.14 Is There Discrimination in Australian Income Tax?

The Australian tax system levies tax on individuals' taxable income, a net of deductions for the out-of-pocket cost of earning their income. Although wage and salary earners are allowed certain deductions, they have little scope to inflate their deductions. At the same time, many business and self-employed earners have more significant opportunities to inflate their deductions. Somehow, many wealthy individuals manage to get income-related tax breaks that flatten the degree of progression in the tax system. The Australian tax code does not indicate de facto tax discrimination between wage and salary earners and the rest of the taxpayers (such as entrepreneurs, pensioners, and the wealthy living on unearned income). Based on the previous section's methodology, Kakwani and Lambert (1999) provided an empirical exploration of tax discrimination in Australia in 1984. They utilized data from the Australian Household Expenditure survey in 1984. This section summarizes their findings, shown in Table 11.7.

The wage and salary earners pay an average tax rate of 19.4%, while others have a tax rate of only 13%. The wage and salary earners could be expected to pay tax at a higher tax rate because they generally have higher incomes. They may also be discriminated against because they cannot inflate their deductions. The same tax function $T(x)$ is applied to both wage and salary earners and others to separate discrimination from progressive tax structure. The empirical results showed that if the tax discrimination had been eliminated, the average tax rate of wage and salary earners would be reduced to 18.55%. In comparison, that of other taxpayers would be increased to 14.96%. The

Table 11.7 Change in social welfare when tax discrimination is eliminated in Australia, 1984

	Wage/salary earners	All others	All taxpayers
Average tax rate (%)	19.4	13	17.46
Change in social welfare			
$\in = 1$	2.98	−2.51	0.05
$\in = 1.5$	3.46	−2.03	0.06
$\in = 2$	3.95	−1.4	0.05

net effect of tax discrimination on wage and salary earners would boost the average tax rate by 0.85%, while the average tax rate would decrease by 1.96% on other taxpayers.

Table 11.7 shows that wage and salary earners would benefit from removing discrimination: their after-tax welfare would increase by $2.98, $3.46, and $3.95 per person when the values of inequality aversion parameter $\in$ are 1, 1.5, and 2, respectively. Other taxpayers would lose from removing discrimination: their post-tax welfare would reduce by $2.51, $2.03, and $1.40, when values $\in$ are 1, 1.5, and 2, respectively. Due to discrimination, the overall social welfare loss is very small: for $\in = 2$, it is only five cents per person.

The welfare loss due to wage and salary earners' discrimination increases monotonically with the inequality aversion parameter $\in$, suggesting that welfare gain for other taxpayers reduces. This observation suggests that the unequal tax treatment of the two groups affects the poor more than the rich.

The conclusion emerging from this illustration is that the wage and salary earners suffer tax discrimination, but the magnitude of their welfare loss is not significant.

11.15 Relief Package in Response to COVID-19 Pandemic

In response to the Coronavirus pandemic, many governments in developed countries offer relief packages to their population. Their main concern has been that economic fallout can drastically curtail economic activities leading to high unemployment and falling incomes. The relief packages aim to provide cash payments to people to meet their minimum needs. Also, they can generate demand for goods and services so that businesses can survive during the pandemic. Governments may exclude specific groups from these transfers because of resource constraints, such as temporary residents, overseas students, and undocumented migrants. A government may also decide to exclude rural households because they are unlikely to be impacted by the pandemic. The exclusion of any social group from the relief package is an example of discrimination and must result in social welfare loss. This section extends the idea of tax discrimination discussed in the previous section to calculate the social welfare loss caused by excluding a social group from the government relief initiatives.

Suppose the government makes a cash transfer of $b(x)$ to an individual with pre-transfer income x. If there is no discrimination, then the transfer function $b(x)$ will apply to every social group. If the government applies different transfer functions to various groups, that means that the government is not treating all social groups equally, and, therefore, there is discrimination. Under this scenario, suppose $b_j(x)$ is the transfer function applied to the jth social group, then similar to (11.12.4), the following transfer function follows

$$b(x) = \sum_{j=1}^{k} \lambda_j(x) b_j(x) \tag{11.15.1}$$

where $\lambda_j(x) = \frac{a_j f_j(x)}{f(x)}$ so that $\sum_{j=1}^{k} \lambda_j(x) = 1$.

Theorem 11.2 follows from this.

Theorem 11.2 *Suppose $\tilde{z}^*$ and z^* are the post-transfer money metric social welfare with and without discrimination, then discrimination against any social group leads to social welfare loss of $z^* - \tilde{z}^* > 0$. The social welfare loss will be zero if there is no discrimination against any social group.*

Proof: If there is no discrimination, then using (11.14.1), the post-transfer income of a person with pre-transfer income x is given by

$$x + b(x) = \sum_{j=1}^{k} \lambda_j(x)(x + b_j(x)). \tag{11.15.2}$$

This equation gives the dollar value of the post-transfer social welfare z^*, under no discrimination as given by

$$u(z^*) = \int_0^{\infty} u(x + b(x)) f(x)\, dx = \int_0^{\infty} u\left(\sum_{j=1}^{k} \lambda_j(x + b_j(x))\right) f(x)\, dx. \tag{11.15.3}$$

If there is discrimination, then the dollar value of social welfare is given by

$$u(\tilde{z}^*) = \int_0^{\infty} \sum_{j=1}^{k} a_j u(x + b_j(x)) f_j(x)\, dx = \int_0^{\infty} \sum_{j=1}^{k} \lambda_j(x) u(x + b_j(x)) f(x)\, dx. \tag{11.15.4}$$

From Jensen's inequality under the requirement that the utility function $u(x)$ is concave gives

$$u\left[\sum_{j=1}^{k} \lambda_j(x)(x + b_j(x))\right] \geq \sum_{j=1}^{k} \lambda_j(x) u(x + b_j(x)), \tag{11.15.5}$$

which on comparing (11.15.3) and (11.15.4) yields $z^* \geq \tilde{z}^*$, which implies $z^* \geq \tilde{z}^*$. Thus, discrimination against any social group will result in social welfare loss.

The relief packages are short-term initiatives and are not targeted at the poor. Governments aim to make transfers as quickly as possible, bypassing any targeting and providing transfers of the same amount to everyone in the population. If there is no discrimination, everyone gets the same transfer amount equal to b. Suppose there are k social groups; social group 1 is the core group, the only group receiving transfers, and the remaining $(k-1)$ groups do not receive any transfer. If everyone in group 1 gets the same amount of transfer equal to b_1, and if the total cost of transfers to the government is the same under the two scenarios of with and without discrimination, then from (11.15.1), it is easy to show that $b_1 = \dfrac{b}{a_1}$, where a_1 is the population share of group 1. It is appropriate to calculate the welfare effect of discrimination by keeping the same transfer cost to the government.

Suppose x^* is the money metric social welfare of the population before the relief transfers, and if there is no discrimination, everyone receiving the same relief transfer of amount b, then the post-transfer social welfare of the whole population will be given by $y^* = x^* + b$.

Under the scenario of no discrimination, when everyone receives the same amount of transfer b, social welfare of the post-transfer income is given by

$$u(z^*) = \int_0^\infty u(x+b)f(x)\,dx = \sum_{j=1}^k u(x_j^* + b).\qquad(11.15.6)$$

x_j^* is the pre-transfer money metric social welfare of the jth group.

When everyone belonging to the first social group receives the same amount of transfer, $b_1 = \dfrac{b}{a_1}$, and the remaining $(k-1)$ social groups receive no transfers, the social welfare under this scenario is given by

$$u(\tilde{z}^*) = a_1 \int_0^\infty u(x+b_1)f_1(x)\,dx + \sum_{j\neq 1}^k \int_0^\infty u(x)f_j(x)\,dx.\qquad(11.15.7)$$

From Theorem 11.2, it immediately follows that $z^* - \tilde{z}^* > 0$ will be the loss of social welfare.

11.16 An Illustration of Welfare Loss Due to Discrimination Using Brazilian Data

This section illustrates the calculations of welfare loss due to discrimination using Brazilian data. These data are from the National Household Survey 2012. The survey is conducted in Brazil every year and is popularly known as PNAD. The COVID-19 pandemic has recently spread severely in Brazil, ranked third globally in infection and death rates. The economy is in free fall due to the lockdown. Still, Brazil did not have any significant relief package initiated by the government.

The methodology of welfare loss due to discrimination is illustrated assuming that everyone in the country would receive a transfer of 200 reals per person under no discrimination. Suppose hypothetically, the government believes that the urban residents felt most severely the economic impact of COVID-19. So, it is assumed that only the urban residents received the cash handouts of the amount 200/0.85 = 235 reais. Table 11.8 presents empirical results.

Table 11.8 shows that based on the risk aversion parameter of $\epsilon = 2$, rural residents had the pre-transfer welfare of 141 reais per person. In contrast, the urban residents enjoyed a much higher welfare level of 473 reais per person, implying that the urban residents had 335% higher welfare than the rural residents. The relief package under no discrimination with the same aversion parameter increased rural and urban residents' welfare to 431 and 634 reais, respectively. Under the scenario of no discrimination, the welfare gap between the rural and urban residents reduced significantly to only 147%. But if the government discriminated against the rural residents and provided transfers to only urban residents, the welfare of the rural residents remained at 141 reais. In contrast, that of urban residents increased to 681 reais. The welfare gap between the two rose to 483%. Thus, discrimination led to the welfare loss of 290 reais per person for the rural residents, whereas the urban residents gained only 47 reais per person. The country suffered an overall welfare loss of 159 reais per person due to discrimination. This illustration demonstrates that discrimination can cause significant welfare loss to society. However, it must be understood that this illustration is hypothetical and has no bearing on the Brazilian government's

Table 11.8 Impact of discrimination on welfare loss due to discrimination in Brazil, 2012

	Rural	Urban	Total
Social welfare without the stimulus package			
$\epsilon = 0$	377	823	754
$\epsilon = 1$	241	525	459
$\epsilon = 1.5$	189	496	358
$\epsilon = 2$	141	473	268
Social welfare with no discrimination			
$\epsilon = 0$	577	1023	954
$\epsilon = 1$	485	768	716
$\epsilon = 1.5$	455	693	645
$\epsilon = 2$	431	634	591
Social welfare with discrimination			
$\epsilon = 0$	377	1023	926
$\epsilon = 1$	241	811	676
$\epsilon = 1.5$	189	737	561
$\epsilon = 2$	141	681	432
Loss of social welfare due to discrimination			
$\epsilon = 0$	200	0	28
$\epsilon = 1$	244	−42	40
$\epsilon = 1.5$	266	−45	84
$\epsilon = 2$	290	−47	159

relief package if any. The purpose has only been to track discriminatory welfare effects between socio-economic groups.

11.17 Concluding Remarks

Efficiency and equity are the fundamental principles of taxation. This chapter has been concerned with equity in tax, focusing on how the tax burden is distributed among people. The measures of tax progressivity and the redistributive effect of taxation are used to assess the fairness of taxes. This chapter has utilized three equity axioms, also called equity principles, to derive the tax progressivity and redistributive effect.

The violation of any equity axioms exerts negative influences on the redistributive impact of tax. These negative influences on the redistributive effect of tax provide the means to characterize the type of inequity present in a tax system and assess its significance. The chapter has analyzed the degree of inequities in the Australian tax system.

The Australian household survey showed that the Gini indices of pre- and post-tax incomes were 31.13% and 28.73%, respectively. The index gave the overall redistributive effect of taxes equal to 7.71%, which is the percentage reduction in inequality in living standards in Australia contributed by the income tax. Thus, the Australian tax system is progressive, but still has inequities. The inequity due to the violation of Axiom 11.3 reduced the overall redistributive effect by 2.13%. This inequity is attributed to excess tax progressivity, resulting in changes in the rankings of individuals. It is a measure of horizontal inequity, contributing to post-tax income inequality.

The inequities due to violation of Axioms 11.1 and 11.2 contributed to further reductions in income redistribution by 6.26% and 28.14%, respectively. The violation of Axiom 11.2 had the most severe impact on the redistributive effect of the tax system. It meant that some taxpayers were not paying taxes proportional to their income, contributing to a substantial regressivity in the tax system. The total inequity in the Australian tax system reduced the redistributive effect by 36.71%. In the absence of these significant inequities, the Australian tax system could have reduced income inequality by 44.42% instead of only 7.71%. Thus, the conclusion emerging from this analysis is that removing inequities could improve the redistributive effect of taxation without increasing the marginal tax rates on higher-income groups.

Governments collect revenue from various taxes, such as personal income tax, company tax, estate gift duties, and indirect taxes. In designing a tax system, it helps to determine the progressivity of various kinds of taxes and how much they contribute to the total tax system's progressivity. This chapter has discussed a tax progressivity decomposition to aid this process.

Economists have been arguing for many years that indirect taxes are regressive. This is why they have preferred to rely on personal income tax in tax reforms, as these are usually deemed progressive. The analysis presented in this chapter shows that the regressive taxes based on the relative measure can become progressive when using the absolute measure of tax progressivity. Hence, a crucial question arises as to what progressivity concept policymakers should establish to analyze equity in taxation. The two concepts of progressivity have different value judgments, and it is impossible to provide a definitive answer as to which concept should be adopted to assess a tax system. A compromise will be to present the analysis to policymakers based on both ideas.

Inequity in taxation can arise when systematic discrimination exists against a social group in tax payment. Tax discrimination happens when different social groups face different tax schedules. For instance, income tax may discriminate against wage and salary earners compared to self-employed earners, who can overestimate their deductible business expenses. This chapter demonstrates that tax discrimination against any social group results in necessary social welfare loss. The dollar loss of social welfare quantifies the magnitude of discrimination.

The Australian tax system showed that wage and salary earners pay an average tax rate of 19.4%, while the non-wage earners have a tax rate of only 13%. The wage and salary earners may pay a higher tax rate because they have higher incomes, and they may also be paying a higher tax rate because they are unable to inflate their business expenses. This chapter has provided a method of separating the effect of discrimination from the progressive tax structure. The empirical result showed that if the tax discrimination were eliminated, the average tax rate of wage and salary earners would be reduced to 18.55%. In comparison, that of the non-wage earners increased to 14.96%. The net effect of tax discrimination on wage and salary earners would boost the average tax rate by 0.85%, while the average tax rate would decrease by 1.96% on other taxpayers.

The tax system shows that wage and salary earners would benefit from removing discrimination: their after-tax welfare would increase by $2.98, $3.46, and $3.95 per person when the values of inequality aversion parameter $\in$ are 1, 1.5, and 2, respectively. Non-wage earners would lose from removing discrimination: their post-tax welfare would reduce by $2.51, $2.03, and $1.4, when values $\in$ are 1, 1.5, and 2, respectively. The overall loss of social welfare due to discrimination is very small: for $\in = 2$, it is only five cents per person. It is also found that the welfare loss due to discrimination against wage and salary earner increases monotonically with the inequality aversion parameter $\in$, suggesting that unequal tax treatment affects the poor more than the rich.

The chapter has extended the idea of tax discrimination to designing the government relief packages in response to the COVID-19 pandemic. Governments may exclude specific groups from these transfers because of resource constraints, such as temporary residents, overseas students, and undocumented migrants. The exclusion of any social group from the relief package is an example of discrimination and must result in welfare loss. Using Brazilian data, the chapter has illustrated the calculation of social welfare loss caused due to the exclusion of some social groups from the relief package. This illustration demonstrates that discrimination can cause significant welfare loss to society.

12

Normative Measures of Tax Progressivity

12.1 Introduction

Chapter 5 showed that the relationship between inequality indices and social welfare functions is well established (Atkinson 1970, Sen 1974a). Although understanding the links between tax progressivity and social welfare functions has important policy implications, the tax literature has not explored it. In a recent paper, Kakwani and Son (2021) have developed a social welfare function framework that links the measurement of tax progressivity with social welfare function. They created a general social welfare framework to obtain tax progressivity measures. This chapter elaborates on this framework and derives several measures of tax progressivity that have practical social welfare interpretations. Thus, the framework enables the evaluation of alternative progressivity measures using society's distributive judgments.

The Kakwani index, discussed in the previous chapter, is extensively used to analyze equity in taxation and government expenditures and equity in access to health, education, and essential services. In particular, the index has become a popular tool for analyzing equity in public finance and delivering healthcare.[1] This chapter derives the Kakwani index of tax progressivity from Sen's social welfare function, which captures the idea of relative deprivation suffered by society. Thus, the chapter demonstrates that the Kakwani index has a normative interpretation, enhancing its usefulness in policy applications.

Kakwani (1980a, 1980b) proposed a generalization of the Gini social welfare function that makes it possible to assign higher weights to income transfers at the lower end of the income distribution.[2] This chapter derives a class of progressivity measures from the generalized Gini social welfare functions. The Kakwani index is a particular case of generalized progressivity measures. This general class of progressivity measures depends on a parameter k similar to Atkinson's (1970) inequality aversion parameter. The higher the inequality aversion parameter, the higher the weight given to the more impoverished persons.

The chapter utilizes the general social welfare function framework presented to derive new progressivity measures from Atkinson's class of social welfare functions. The

---

[1] For a discussion of the upper bound of the Kakwani index, see Mantovani, Pellegrino, and Vernizzi (2018). Gerber, Klemm, Liu, and Mylonas (2019) have examined the relationship between tax progressivity and economic growth based on the Kakwani index.

[2] Yitzhaki (1983) published the same generalization of the Gini index.

Economic Inequality and Poverty. Nanak Kakwani and Hyun Son, Oxford University Press.
© Nanak Kakwani and Hyun Son (2022). DOI: 10.1093/oso/9780198852841.003.0012

chapter also identifies the social welfare implications of Suits' index of tax progressivity. It demonstrates that the Suits index used widely in analyzing tax policies, as such, does not lend itself to a social welfare interpretation. Chapter 11 proposed a modification of the Suits index, and this chapter shows that only the modified Suits index has a social welfare interpretation. Finally, the chapter derives a new measure of tax progressivity using the Bonferroni social welfare function (Bonferroni, 1930).

The publication of two seminal papers by Kolm (1976a, 1976b) introduced two alternative concepts of relative and absolute inequality to the literature. Urban (2019) conceived a range of intermediate inequality concepts, which he referred to as "intermediate" because they reflect a combination of the relative and absolute transformations (Bossert and Pfingsten, 1990; Ebert, 2004; Bosmans, Decancq, and Decoster, 2014). Measures of tax progressivity can have both relative and absolute notions.[3] The social welfare functions framework proposed in the chapter can provide both relative and absolute tax progressivity measures from any social welfare function.[4] This chapter has also derived a new index of absolute tax progressivity using a social welfare function offered by Pollak (1971), popularly known as the Kolm–Pollak social welfare function.

The available empirical evidence suggests that taxes can change the rankings between the pre- and post-tax incomes. This chapter proves that the ranking will always result in social welfare loss. It proposes to measure horizontal inequity by the loss of social welfare caused by the change in ranking.

Finally, this chapter makes international comparisons of tax progressivity and redistributive effects of taxation. The comparisons are based on the income distribution data for 32 countries obtained from the Luxembourg Income Study (LIS) database. These data sets are the largest available from about 50 countries in Europe, North America, Latin America, Africa, Asia, and Australasia, spanning five decades.[5]

12.2 Relative and Absolute Measures of Tax Progressivity

The social welfare framework proposed in this chapter requires the usual restriction on a social welfare function—that is, it should be increasing, concave, or quasi-concave in incomes. An additional requirement is that the social welfare framework should be homogeneous of degree one, implying that if all incomes are increased (decreased) by

---

[3] Many papers have been written on the impact of taxation on income inequality, exploring the conditions under which a tax reduces inequality for alternative concepts of inequality. See Pfingsten (1987, 1988), Moyes (1988), Ebert and Moyes (2000), Ebert (2010), and Urban (2014, 2019).

[4] The distinction can be made between local and global measures of tax progressivity; local measures relate to progression at a given point in the income scale, whereas the global measures are single indices of overall tax progressivity. The focus of this paper is on global measures of tax progressivity. Pfingsten (1987) and Ebert (2010) formulated both relative and absolute indices of local tax progressivity. Urban (2019) dealt with the generalization of both relative and absolute measures of tax progressivity.

[5] Of the 50 countries, we have selected 32 countries based on the availability of comparable tax data around 2013. The list of these 32 countries is provided in the supplementary Excel file, available in Kakwani and Son (2021).

the same proportion, social welfare should also increase (decrease) by the same proportion. Atkinson's (1970) social welfare function derived from a class of homothetic utility functions is homogeneous of degree one and has become a basis for many empirical studies. The homogeneity requirement is essential to obtain relative inequality measures from social welfare functions. These measures are mean independent, implying that the value of inequality remains unchanged if the same proportion alters each income. Such social welfare functions are referred to as relative homogeneous functions of degree one.

Chapter 5 discussed Kolm's (1976a, 1976b) absolute or leftist measures of inequality which do not show any change in inequality when each income is increased or decreased by the same amount. The social welfare functions yielding such inequality measures must satisfy the requirement that if all incomes are increased (decreased) by the same amount, the social welfare function must also increase (decrease) by the same amount. Such social welfare functions are referred to as absolute homogeneous functions of degree one, and Atkinson's class of social welfare function does not satisfy this requirement.

This chapter distinguishes between relative and absolute tax progressivity measures (Urban, 2019). Relative measures of progressivity remain unchanged if everyone's tax is increased or decreased by the same proportion. Similarly, absolute measures of progressivity remain unchanged when everyone's tax is increased or decreased by the same absolute amount.

As discussed in Chapter 11, the relative measures of tax progressivity indicate the extent to which a given tax system deviates from proportionality when everyone pays tax at the same rate. A tax system is said to be progressive (regressive) when the tax rate rises (falls) with income (see Axiom 11.2 in Chapter 11). An absolute measure of progressivity indicates the extent to which a tax system deviates from a situation where everyone pays the same amount of tax. A tax system is an absolute progressive (regressive) when wealthier persons pay more tax than the more impoverished persons (see Axiom 11.1 in chapter 11).[6] This chapter provides welfare interpretations of both the relative and absolute measures of progressivity.

The relative tax progressivity measures can only be derived from social welfare functions relatively homogeneous of degree one. In contrast, absolute tax progressivity measures can only be derived from absolute homogeneous social welfare functions of degree one.

12.3 Additive Separable and Rank Order Social Welfare Functions

Suppose n persons in society have pre-tax incomes given by a vector

$$\tilde{x} = (x_1, x_2, ..., x_n).$$

---

[6] This is the minimal concept of tax progressivity introduced by Fei (1981). Moyes (1988) demonstrated that a progressive tax under this concept reduces absolute inequality.

Given this, a general social welfare function can be written as

$$W_x = W(\tilde{x}).$$

This welfare function qualifies as relatively homogeneous of degree one if $W(\lambda\tilde{x}) = \lambda W(\tilde{x})$, implying that if all incomes are increased (decreased) by the same proportion, social welfare should also increase (decrease) by the same proportion. The social welfare function will be called as absolute homogeneous of degree one if $W(\tilde{x} + a) = W_x + a$, implying that if all incomes are increased (decreased) by the same amount, the social welfare function must also increase (decrease) by the same amount.

Let $T(x)$ be the tax paid by an individual with income x. The post-tax or disposable income of the individual will then be $y(x) = x - T(x)$. The vector

$$\tilde{y} = (y_1, y_2, \ldots\ldots\ldots, y_n)$$

provides the social welfare of the post-tax income of n individuals as

$$W_y = W(\tilde{y}).$$

The difference in social welfare between the pre- and post-tax income distributions given by $(W_y - W_x)$ is the contribution of the tax system to social welfare. This chapter considers two kinds of general social welfare functions to derive tax progressivity measures. One is the class of additive separable social welfare functions, defined as

$$u(W_x) = \int_0^\infty u(x)f(x)\,dx \qquad (12.3.1)$$

where pre-tax income x is assumed to be a random variable with density function $f(x)$ and $u(x)$ is the utility function, which is increasing in x and is concave. As discussed in Chapter 5, W_x is Atkinson's (1970) social welfare function based on the idea of the equally distributed equivalent (EDE) level of income. The EDE income W_x is the income that, if each individual gets it, provides the same level of social welfare as the present distribution. If the utility function $u(x)$ is homothetic, then the social welfare function W_x is relatively homogeneous of degree one. A homothetic utility function has constant elasticity of marginal utility $u'(x)$ with respect to x, given by $u''(x)x/u'$. Atkinson (1970) identified an entire class of homothetic utility functions given by

$$u(x) = A + B\frac{x^{(1-\epsilon)}}{(1-\epsilon)} \quad if\ \epsilon \neq 1$$

$$= A + Bln(x) \quad if\ \epsilon = 1 \qquad (12.3.2)$$

where ϵ is the inequality aversion parameter, which equals minus times the elasticity of marginal utility with respect to income (for a detailed discussion of this utility function, see equation (5.5.5) in Chapter 5).

If the utility function satisfies the conditions either $u(x+a)=u(x)+u(a)$ or $u(x+a)=u(x)\,u(a)$, then W_x in (12.3.1) is absolutely homogenous of degree one, meaning that if everyone's income changes by the same absolute amount, then social welfare also changes by the same amount.

The class of additively separable social welfare functions in (12.3.1) has the property that each person's welfare depends only on their income or consumption and not on the income or consumption of others in society. Such welfare functions do not capture the relative deprivation suffered by society.

Chapter 5 discussed the Gini social welfare function developed by Sen (1974a). He defined it as the weighted average of income levels with weights depending on individuals' rankings. A general form of this function can be written as[7]

$$W(\tilde{x}) = \int_0^\infty xv\left(F\left(x\right)\right)f\left(x\right)dx \qquad (12.3.3)$$

where $f(x)$ is the density function of x, and $F(x)$ is the distribution function that measures the proportion of persons with income less than x. $v\left(F\left(x\right)\right)$ is the weight attached to the income level x such that $v'\left(F\left(x\right)\right) < 0$, implying that weights must decrease monotonically with $F(x)$, meaning that the more impoverished persons get higher weights, and the total weight adds up to 1:

$$\int_0^\infty v\left(F\left(x\right)\right)f\left(x\right)dx = 1. \qquad (12.3.4)$$

The social welfare functions in (12.3.3) depend on rankings of the individuals, and therefore, are referred to as the rank order social welfare functions. These functions are interdependent and nonadditive separable since they depend on the ranks of all individuals in society, which, as Sen (1974a) argued, captures the relative deprivation suffered by society.

The most attractive feature of the rank order social welfare functions is that they are both relatively and absolutely homogeneous of degree one. Hence, they provide both relative and absolute measures of tax progressivity.

12.4 Horizontal Inequity and Rank Change

Chapter 11 defined horizontal inequity in taxation when persons with the same pre-tax income are not treated equally. This definition is the classical definition of horizontal inequity. Alternatively, horizontal inequity occurs when a tax system alters the rankings of the pre- and post-tax income distributions. This definition was promoted by Feldstein (1976) and Rosen (1978). Following this idea, they proposed measuring

---

[7] This social welfare function was proposed by Yaari (1988).

horizontal inequity by the rank correlation between individuals' pre- and post-tax incomes. How are these two definitions compatible with each other? The distinction between the two is as follows:

A change in ranking occurs when a richer person becomes poorer, and a poorer person becomes richer. That can only happen when persons with the same pre-tax income are not treated equally, implying horizontal equity violation. But, when there is a violation of horizontal equity, rank changes may or may not happen.[8] Suppose income distributions are anonymous concerning the identity of individuals; in that case, if any two persons interchange their positions, the ranking by incomes does not change, and hence, the tax system has not changed the income distributions. But, the classical definition implies a clear violation of horizontal equity.

The taxation literature has explored the consequence of rank change. Atkinson (1980) showed that the re-ranking of individuals based on post-tax income increases the Gini index of the post-tax income distribution. Plotnick (1981) and Kakwani (1984c) have suggested a measure of horizontal inequity based on the increase in the Gini index, which happens when the tax system changes the ranking of individuals. A detailed discussion of this was provided in Chapter 11.

This section demonstrates that the change in ranking between the pre- and post-tax incomes will result in social welfare loss for both the classes of additive separable and rank order social welfare functions.

12.4.1 Additive Social Welfare Functions

Atkinson's class of additive social welfare functions for the pre-tax income x presented in (12.3.1) provides the social welfare function of the post-tax income $y(x) = x - T(x)$ as

$$u\left(W_y\right) = \int_0^\infty u\left[y\left(x\right)\right]f^*\left(y\right)dy \qquad (12.4.1)$$

where $f^*\left(y\right)$ is the density function of the post-tax income. It will be helpful to introduce the idea of the pseudo-social welfare function of $y(x)$ as

$$u\left(\widehat{W}_y\right) = \int_0^\infty u\left[y\left(x\right)\right]f(x)\,dx, \qquad (12.4.2)$$

which uses the density function of pre-tax income x. If $y'(x) = \left[1 - T'(x)\right] > 0$ for all x, it means that the marginal tax rate $T'(x) < 1$ for all x. This requirement implies that $y(x)$ increases monotonically with x. This monotonic relationship between

---

[8] For a detailed discussion of the two notions of horizontal inequity, see Duclos, Jalbert, and Araar (2003).

x and $y(x)$ gives the density function of $y(x)$ as

$$f^*(y) = \frac{f(x)}{[1 - T'(x)]},$$

(12.4.3)

which immediately implies that $f^*(y) \, dx = f(x) \, dx$. Thus, equations (12.4.1) and (12.4.2) yield $W_y = \hat{W}_y$, proving that $y(x)$'s social welfare will be the same as the pseudo-social welfare of $y(x)$ when the tax system does not change the ranking.

The monotonicity will not hold if $T'(x) > 1$ *for some x*, implying taxpayers pay a tax of more than one dollar for every additional dollar they earn. This situation also means that $y(x)$ does not increase monotonically with x, implying that the ranking between pre- and post-tax incomes would change. Hence, the relationship in (12.4.3) will not hold.

Partitioning income of all individuals into a finite number of k intervals such that $y(x)$ is strictly monotone and differentiable on each partition. In that case, $f^*(y)$ is given by

$$f^*(y) = \sum_{j=1}^{k} \frac{f(x_j)}{1 - T'(x_j)}.$$

(12.4.4)

If $T'(x_j) < 1$ *for all j*, then $f^*(y) \, dy = f(x) \, dx$. Suppose for some j, $T'(x_j) > 1$, then $1 - T'(x_j) < 0$, which from (12.4.3) would imply $f^*(y) \, dy < f(x) \, dx$. Therefore, from (12.4.1) and (12.4.2) will yield $(W_y) < u(\hat{W}_y)$, which on using $u'(x) > 0$ *for all x*, leads to $W_y < \hat{W}_y$. That leads to Theorem 12.1.

Theorem 12.1 *For a general class of Atkinson's class of social welfare functions, if there is a change in ranking between the pre- and post-tax incomes, then there will always be loss of social welfare given by $H = W_y - \hat{W}_y < 0$, and if there is no change in ranking, H=0.*

12.4.2 Rank Order Social Welfare Functions

A general form of rank order social welfare function presented in (12.3.3) yields the social welfare of $y(x) = x - T(x)$ as

$$W_y = \int_0^\infty y(x) \, v \, (F^*(y)) f^*(y) \, dy,$$

(12.4.5)

which on using (12.3.4) gives

$$W_y = Covariance \, [y(x), \, v(F^*(y))].$$

(12.4.6)

The pseudo-social welfare function of $y(x)$ using the weights of the pre-tax income is

$$\widehat{W}_y = \int_0^\infty y(x) \, v\,(F(x)) f(x) \, dx, \qquad (12.4.7)$$

which on using (12.3.4) gives

$$\widehat{W}_y = Covariance\,[y(x),\, v\,(F(x))]. \qquad (12.4.8)$$

Given a fixed number of persons in the population, the variance of $F(x)$ and $F^*(y)$ will be the same. (12.4.7) and (12.4.8) will, thus, yield

$$\frac{\widehat{W}_y}{W_y} = \frac{R[y(x),(F(x))]}{R[y(x),v(f^*(y))]}. \qquad (12.4.9)$$

$R(a,\, b)$ stands for the coefficient of rank correlation between a and b. Note that $F(x)$ is the cumulative proportion of individuals when arranged in ascending order of their pre-tax income, while $F^*(y)$ is the cumulative proportion of individuals when arranged by their post-tax income. The difference between $F(x)$ and $F^*(y)$ will, therefore, be due to the difference in rankings between x and y. Thus, if $F(x)$ and $F^*(y)$ are replaced by rankings of x and y, the correlation coefficients in (12.4.9) will not change. Since $v\,(F(x))$ and $v\,(F^*(y))$ are monotonically decreasing functions of $F(x)$ and $f^*(y)$, respectively, equation (12.4.9) becomes

$$\frac{\widehat{W}_y}{W_y} = \frac{R[y(x),r(-x)]}{R[y(x),r(-y)]}. \qquad (12.4.10)$$

If $y'(x) > 0$, x and y will have the same rank; thus from (12.4.10), $W_y = \widehat{W}_y$, But if $y'(x) < 0$ for some x, then x and y will have a different rank, in which case $W_y < \widehat{W}_y$. That leads to the following theorem.

Theorem 12.2. *For a general class of rank order social welfare functions in (12.3.3), if there is a change in ranking between the pre- and post-tax incomes, there will always be a loss of social welfare given by $H = W(\tilde{y}) - \widehat{W}(\tilde{y}) < 0$. If there is no change in ranking, H=0.*

Theorems 12.1 and 12.2 show that the rank change due to taxation will always result in social welfare loss for the two general classes of social welfare functions. Since the change in ranking implies horizontal inequity, the magnitude of loss in social welfare can provide a measure of horizontal inequity.[9] The difference in social welfare

---

[9] Kakwani and Lambert (1998) developed a methodology to measure classical horizontal inequity in terms of welfare loss due to tax discrimination among social groups. They based their measurement on Atkinson's (1970) social welfare function, which is not a rank order social welfare function.

functions defines the absolute measure of horizontal inequity:

$$H_A = W_y - \widehat{W}_y < 0, \tag{12.4.11}$$

which is interpreted as the monetary cost of horizontal inequity when the tax system discriminates against some taxpayers.

Similarly, the relative measure of horizontal inequity is given by

$$H_R = \frac{W_y - \widehat{W}_y}{\overline{T}} < 0 \tag{12.4.12}$$

where $\overline{T}$ is the average tax collected by the government. H_R is the loss of social welfare caused by horizontal inequity when the government collects an average of one dollar tax.[10] Hypothetically, suppose the loss of social welfare is $0.05 for every dollar collected by the government, the relative measure of horizontal inequity will be 5%. That is the proportional social cost society bears when the tax system discriminates against some taxpayers.

12.5 Social Welfare Framework for Measuring Tax Progressivity

A tax system is said to be proportional if every person pays taxes at the same tax rate $e = \frac{\overline{T}}{\overline{x}}$, where $\overline{x}$ is the average pre-tax income and $\overline{T}$ is the average tax collected by the government. Under the proportional tax system, the relative homogeneity requirement implies that the post-tax social welfare is given by $\widetilde{W}_y = (1 - e) W_x$, which leads to the following decomposition.

$$
\begin{aligned}
(W_y - W_x) &= H_A + (\widetilde{W}_y - W_x) + (\widehat{W}_y - \widetilde{W}_y) \\
&= H_A - eW_x + (\widehat{W}_y - (1 - e) W_x). \tag{12.5.1}
\end{aligned}
$$

The left-hand side of this equation is the welfare impact of taxation. It implies that the welfare impacts of the tax system have three components. The first component is social welfare loss due to horizontal inequity caused by rank change. The second is a social welfare loss when there is no change in income distribution due to taxes when the tax system is proportional. The third component would be the difference between the pseudo-social welfare of the post-tax income and the social welfare under the counterfactual if the tax system were to be proportional. This term can be either positive or negative as it measures the gain (loss) of social welfare when the tax system is progressive (regressive). There would be no gain or loss of welfare if the taxes were proportional.

---

[10] There are many other contributions on horizontal inequity, for which see Jenkins (1988), Jenkins and Lambert (1999), Kaplow (1989), and Lambert and Ramos (1997).

The progressivity indices proposed in the literature do not tell policymakers the extent of gains or losses in social welfare a tax system contributes. The framework presented here derives the progressivity indices with direct social welfare implications for tax systems. Dividing (12.5.1) by the average tax collected from society gives

$$\frac{W_y - W_x}{\overline{T}} = H_R - \frac{W_x}{\overline{x}} + \frac{\widehat{W}_y - (1 - e) W_x}{\overline{T}}. \tag{12.5.2}$$

On the left-hand side of this equation, the term is the tax system's welfare contribution when the government collects an average of one dollar of tax from society. This term is the sum of three contributions, as shown in the equation. The first contribution is the relative horizontal inequity, the social welfare loss due to a change in ranking between pre- and post-tax incomes. The second term on the right-hand side of the equation (12.5.2) is the loss of social welfare if there are no changes in income distribution because of taxation; that is when the tax system is proportional. The third contribution is the gain (loss) of social welfare contributed by a progressive (regressive) tax system when the government collects an average tax of one dollar per person from society. A general measure of relative tax progressivity is proposed as

$$\theta_R = \frac{\widehat{W}_y - (1 - e) W_x}{\overline{T}}, \tag{12.5.3}$$

which is the relative measure of progressivity as it remains unchanged if the tax paid by everyone in a society increases or decreases by the same proportion. This measure is the monetary gain (loss) of social welfare per dollar of tax collected by the government when the tax system is progressive (regressive). If the tax system is proportional, then θ_R will be equal to zero. This general class of relative tax progressivity will always satisfy tax equity Axiom 11.2 in Chapter 11. Equation (12.5.3) enables the derivation of a progressivity measure from any specific social welfare function. Hence, every relative tax progressivity has an implicit social welfare function.

A tax system is absolutely progressive if the wealthier persons pay more tax than the poorer persons. Thus, an absolute tax progressivity measure indicates the extent of the overall deviation of a tax system from a situation when everyone pays the same absolute amount of tax. If everyone pays the same tax equal to $\overline{T}$, the after-tax social welfare will be given by

$$\widetilde{w}_y = W\left(\widetilde{x} - \overline{T}\right) = W\left(\widetilde{x}\right) - \overline{T}, \tag{12.5.4}$$

which must always hold if the social welfare function is absolutely homogeneous of degree one.

So a general measure of absolute progressivity is the deviation of $\widehat{W}_y$ from $\widecheck{W}_y$

$$\theta_A = \widehat{W}_y - W_x + \overline{T}, \tag{12.5.5}$$

which will be positive (negative) if tax is absolutely progressive (regressive) and 0 if everyone pays the same tax. Similar to inequality measures, these progressivity measures remain unchanged when everyone's tax increases or decreases by the same amount. This general class of absolute tax progressivity measures will always satisfy tax equity Axiom 11.1 in Chapter 11.

The loss of social welfare due to taxation is related to the absolute measure of progressivity by

$$W_y - W_x = H_A - \overline{T} + \theta_A \tag{12.5.6}$$

where H_A is the absolute measure of horizontal inequity. This equation demonstrates that the absolutely progressive (regressive) tax system increases (decreases) social welfare. If everyone pays the same amount of tax, that is, $\theta_A = 0$, the ranking of individuals does not change; social welfare loss would be equal to society's average tax. The larger the government's tax, the higher would be the welfare loss. Sections 12.7 to 12.9 derive the progressivity measures from particular social welfare functions.

12.6 Redistributive Effect of Taxation

Musgrave and Thin (1948) pioneered the measurement of tax progressivity. They proposed to measure tax progressivity by the difference between the inequality of the post-tax and pre-tax income distributions. Their measure of progressivity indicates the extent to which a given tax system reduces income inequality. A progressive tax is associated with decreased income inequality, whereas a regressive tax is related to increased income inequality. Jakobsson (1976) justified Musgrave and Thin's (1948) measure of tax progressivity.

Chapter 11 distinguished between tax progressivity and redistribution of taxes. Tax progressivity deals with an equity principle of taxation, suggesting that wealthier persons must pay more taxes or even at a higher rate. The chapter presented three tax equity Axioms 11.1–11.3 and demonstrated that violations of these principles negatively influence the redistribution effect of taxation. These principles deal with fairness in taxation, which impacts tax redistribution. The redistributive effect of taxation is an outcome of the equity principle. While the two concepts are related, they are distinct. It will help explain the relationship between the two relative and absolute tax redistribution in more general terms.

12.6.1 Relative Measure of Tax Redistribution

Given that the social welfare function is relatively homogeneous of degree one, one can derive the relative measure of inequality of the pre-tax income distribution as[11]

$$W_x = \bar{x}(1 - I_x) \tag{12.6.1}$$

where $\bar{x}$ is the average of pre-tax income, and I_x is the inequality of pre-tax income (Atkinson, 1970). Similarly, the post-tax social welfare is related to post-tax income inequality as

$$W_y = (1 - e)\bar{x}(1 - I_y) \tag{12.6.2}$$

where I_y is the inequality of post-tax income distribution. Similarly, the pseudo-social welfare function for post-tax income distribution, when the ranking is by the pre-tax income, gives a pseudo-post-tax inequality measure $\hat{I}_y$ and is defined by[12]

$$\hat{W}_y = (1 - e)\bar{x}(1 - \hat{I}_y). \tag{12.6.3}$$

Theorem 12.1 proved $\hat{W}_y > W_y$, which implies $\hat{I}_y < I_y$.

Substituting (12.6.1) and (12.6.3) into (12.5.3) yields the relative measure of tax progressivity as

$$\theta_R = \frac{(1 - e)}{e}\left[I_x - \hat{I}_y\right] \tag{12.6.4}$$

The relative measure of income redistribution is the change in relative inequality due to taxation, which is the difference between inequality of the post-tax and pre-tax income, which on using in (12.6.4) yields:

$$\varphi_R = I_y - I_x = (I_y - \hat{I}_y) - \frac{\theta_R e}{(1 - e)}. \tag{12.6.5}$$

φ_R is a relative measure of income redistribution due to taxation. The first term on the right-hand side of the equation (12.6.5) is positive, implying that the change in ranking between pre- and post-tax incomes always contributes to increases in inequality. The second term on the right-hand side of equation (12.6.5) demonstrates that the tax system reduces (raises) the relative inequality if the relative measure of tax progressivity θ_R is positive (negative). This result proves that the relative progressive tax system reduces relative inequality while the regressive tax system increases it. When tax is proportional—that is, $\theta_R = 0$—the ranking of individuals will not change, and taxation will have no impact on inequality.

---

[11] A relative measure of inequality is defined as the proportionate loss of social welfare due to inequality.
[12] Note that $\hat{I}_y$ is the concentration index of post-tax income discussed in Chapter 11.

The result in (12.6.5) is the generalization of redistribution of taxes similar to the one derived, as presented in Chapter 11 for the Kakwani index of progressivity. The first term in this equation measures horizontal inequity, and the second term is vertical equity. The horizontal inequity increases inequality, whereas the vertical equity decreases it. The net effect of the two is called the redistributive effect of taxes.

12.6.2 Absolute Measure of Tax Redistribution

If the social welfare function is absolutely homogeneous of degree one, one can then calculate the absolute measures of inequality of the pre- and post- tax income distributions—with the difference between them providing an absolute measure of income redistribution as[13]

$$\varphi_A = (1 - e)\bar{x}I_y - \bar{x}I_x = \bar{y}(I_y - \widehat{I}_y) - \theta_A \tag{12.6.6}$$

where $\bar{y}$ is the mean of the post-tax income. The first term on the right-hand side of equation (12.6.6) shows that the change in ranking between the pre- and post-tax incomes always increases the absolute inequality, while the second term indicates that the tax system reduces (increases) the absolute inequality if the absolute measure of progressivity θ_A is positive (negative). This result proves that an absolutely progressive tax system (when the richer persons pay higher taxes than the poorer persons) reduces absolute inequality. In contrast, the absolutely regressive tax system (when the poorer persons pay higher taxes than the richer) raises absolute inequality. When everyone pays the same amount of tax, absolute inequality due to taxation does not change.

This section, therefore, concludes that the progressivity and the redistribution effect of taxation are related but distinct concepts. Three factors affect the relative redistribution effect: taxation progress, the change in ranking due to taxation, and the average tax rate. The absolute redistribution is affected by the change in ranking and absolute progressivity.

12.7 A General Class of the Gini Social Welfare Functions

Chapter 5, Section 5.13 discussed a generalization of the Gini index that makes it possible to assign higher weights to the income of the poor. The general social welfare function implicit in the generalized Gini index is

$$W_x(k) = (k + 1)\int_0^\infty x[1 - F(x)]^k f(x)\, dx = \bar{x}(1 - G_x(k)) \tag{12.7.1}$$

---

[13] An absolute measure progressivity is defined as the absolute loss of social welfare due to inequality.

where $G_x(k)$ is the generalized Gini index of the pre-tax income distribution. The parameter k is similar to the inequality aversion parameter introduced by Atkinson (1973). When $k = 0$, $W_x(k) = \bar{x}$, the mean income of the pre-tax distribution. In such a case, the income of everyone receives the same weight, which reflects an inequality-neutral attitude—that is, society does not care about inequality at all and focuses solely on enhancing economic growth. When $k = 1$, $W_x(k)$ equals the Gini social welfare function. The larger the value of k, the higher the relative weight given to the lower end of the income distribution. A higher value of k, therefore, would be appropriate if society desires to give greater importance to transfers of income to its weaker sections.

The generalized Gini social welfare for the post-tax income distribution is given by

$$W_y(k) = (k+1) \int_0^\infty y[1 - F^*(y)]^k f^*(y)\, dy = \bar{y}(1 - G_y(k)) \qquad (12.7.2)$$

where $y = x - T(x)$ and $G_y(k)$ is the generalized Gini index of the post-tax income distribution.

The pseudo-social welfare function of the post-tax income is derived using weights of the pre-tax income. Hence, the pseudo-social welfare for the generalized Gini social welfare function is given by

$$\widehat{W}_y(k) = (1+k) \int_0^\infty [x - T(x)][1 - F(x)]^k f(x)\, dx = \bar{y}(1 - C_y(k)) \qquad (12.7.3)$$

where $C_y(k)$ is the generalized concentration index of the post-tax income distribution. As demonstrated in Theorem 12.1, $\widehat{W}_y(k) > W_y(k)$ when there is a change in ranking. Hence, using (12.7.2) and (12.7.3) yields the absolute measure of horizontal inequity in taxation by the index

$$H_A(k) = \bar{y}[C_y(k) - G_y(k)]. \qquad (12.7.4)$$

The relative measure of horizontal inequity as defined in (12.4.12) is obtained as

$$H_R(k) = \frac{(1-e)}{e}[C_y(k) - G_y(k)] < 0. \qquad (12.7.5)$$

Similarly, the pseudo-social welfare function of tax is given by

$$W_T(k) = (k+1) \int_0^\infty T(x)[1 - F(x)]^k f(x)\, dx = \bar{T}(1 - C_T(k)) \qquad (12.7.6)$$

where $C_T(k)$ is the generalized concentration index of tax. It is easy to verify from (12.7.1), (12.7.3), and (12.7.6) that

$$\widehat{W}_y(k) = W_x(k) - W_T(k), \qquad (12.7.7)$$

which on substituting into (12.5.3) and utilizing (12.7.1) and (12.7.6) gives a relative measure of tax progressivity

$$\theta_R(k) = K(k) = C_T(k) - G_x(k), \tag{12.7.8}$$

which is referred to as the generalized Kakwani index of tax progressivity. When $k = 1$, $\theta_R(k) = K$, given by $C_T - G_x$, being the Kakwani index of progressivity. When k is greater than 1, a higher weight is given to transfers among those with less income than the mode. Combining (12.7.1), (12.7.2), and (12.7.3) and (12.7. 5) with (12.7. 8) yields

$$\frac{W_y(k) - W_x(k)}{\bar{T}} = H_R(k) - (1 - G_x(k)) + K(k) \tag{12.7.9}$$

where $H_R(k)$ is the measure of relative horizontal inequity for the generalized Gini social welfare function.

The left-hand side of equation (12.7.9) is the change in social welfare when society pays an average of one dollar of tax. The right-hand side of equation (12.7.9) shows that the total welfare impact of taxation is the sum of three contributions: (i) the loss of welfare when there is a change in ranking, (ii) the loss of welfare when the tax system is proportional, and (iii) the gain (loss) of welfare when the tax system is progressive (regressive).

The taxation system is progressive when the generalized Kakwani index $K(k)$ is positive, which means that the progressive tax contributes to a gain in social welfare. Conversely, if $K(k)$ is negative, the tax system is regressive and contributes to a welfare loss. Hence, one can now ascribe a social welfare interpretation to the generalized Kakwani index. The value of $K(k)$ measures the magnitude of the gain (loss) of social welfare if the tax system is progressive (regressive) when society pays an average of one dollar in tax. Even if taxes are proportional, society suffers a loss of social welfare equal to $(1 - G_k)$. Since Kakwani developed his index by measuring the deviation of a tax system from proportionality, the index had seemingly no social welfare implication. The section has shown that the Kakwani index has a valid social welfare interpretation.

The relative redistributive effect for the generalized social welfare functions, derived from (12.6.5), is given by

$$\varphi_R(k) = [G_y(k) - C_y(k)] - \frac{e\,K(k)}{(1-e)}, \tag{12.7.10}$$

which leads to the Kakwani (1984c) decomposition when $k = 1$. The first term in (12.7.10) measures horizontal inequity, and the second term measures vertical equity. The first term is always positive when there is horizontal inequity, implying that horizontal inequity always increases income inequality. There is no change in inequality when there is no horizontal inequity. The second term is negative (positive) when tax is progressive (regressive).

Aronson, Johnson, and Lambert (1994) and Duclos, Jalbert, and Araar (2003) proposed another version of this decomposition in their models of horizontal inequity:

$$-\varphi_R(k) = [G_x(k) - G_y(k)] = \frac{e}{(1-e)}K(k) - [G_y(k) - C_y(k)]. \qquad (12.7.11)$$

Note that (12.7.10) and (12.7.11) are identical but have different interpretations. The first term on the right-hand side of (12.7.11) is the "vertical effect," which represents the "potential" redistributive effect that would be achieved in the absence of horizontal inequity. The term $G_y(k) - C_y(k) \geq 0$ is the re-ranking effect, representing the reduction of the redistributive impact due to horizontal inequity.

Similarly, one can derive the absolute measure of tax progressivity by substituting (12.7.6) into (12.5.5) as

$$\theta_A(k) = C_T(k) \qquad (12.7.12)$$

where $C_T(k)$ is the generalized concentration index of tax. A tax system is absolutely progressive when the rich pay more tax than the poor, in which case $C_T(k) > 0$. When $k = 1$, $C_T(k)$ equals the concentration index of tax C_T. The change in social welfare due to tax will thus be

$$w_y(k) - W_x(k) = H_k - \overline{T} + C_T(k). \qquad (12.7.13)$$

If everyone pays the same amount of tax, there will be no change in ranking. Hence, society suffers a loss of social welfare equal to society's average tax.

The absolute measure of the redistribution effect of taxes will be given by

$$\varphi_A(k) = (1-e)\overline{x}\,G_y(k) - \overline{x}\,G_x(k) = -H_k - C_T(k), \qquad (12.7.14)$$

which shows that if taxes are absolute progressive, absolute inequality declines because of taxation. If $C_T(k) = 0$, everyone pays the same tax, and the ranking of individuals will not change. Hence, absolute inequality does not change.

12.8 A Class of Atkinson and Kolm Social Welfare Functions

Atkinson's (1970) general class of social welfare functions given in (12.3.1) are additive separable. As discussed in Section 12.3, he derived it based on the EDE income level. He assumed that the social welfare function is utilitarian, and every individual has the same utility function that is increasing and is concave in income. He further assumed that the utility function implicit in his social welfare function is homothetic as defined in (12.3.2), which on substituting into (12.3.1) gives his social welfare function for the pre-tax income distribution as

$$W_x(\epsilon) = \left[\int_0^\infty x^{1-\epsilon} f(x)\, dx\right]^{\frac{1}{(1-\epsilon)}} \quad \text{if } \epsilon \neq 1$$

$$= \exp\left[\int_0^\infty \ln(x) f(x)\, dx\right] \text{if } \epsilon = 1 \qquad (12.8.1)$$

This class of Atkinson's social welfare functions is relatively homogeneous of degree one, and hence they can provide the class of relative tax progressivity measures. ϵ measures the degree of inequality aversion—that is, the relative sensitivity to income transfers at different income levels.

The social welfare function for the post-tax income distribution from (12.8.1) is obtained as

$$W_y(\epsilon) = \left[\int_0^\infty (x - T(x))^{(1-\epsilon)} f^*(y)\, dy\right]^{\frac{1}{(1-\epsilon)}} \quad \text{if } \epsilon \neq 1$$

$$= \exp\left[\int_0^\infty \ln(x - T(x)) f^*(y)\, dy\right] \quad \text{if } \epsilon = 1 \qquad (12.8.2)$$

The pseudo-social welfare function for the post-tax income distribution obtained by using the pre-tax weights is given by

$$\widehat{W}_y(\epsilon) = \left[\int_0^\infty (x - T(x))^{(1-\epsilon)} f(x)\, dx\right]^{\frac{1}{(1-\epsilon)}} \quad \text{if } \epsilon \neq 1$$

$$= \exp\left[\int_0^\infty \ln(x - T(x)) f(x)\, dx\right] \quad \text{if } \epsilon = 1. \qquad (12.8.3)$$

Under the proportional tax system, everyone pays tax at the same rate. Since the social welfare function is homogeneous of degree one, the social welfare function of the post-tax distribution, when the tax system is proportional, is $(1 - e) W_x(\epsilon)$, where e is the average tax rate of society. Substituting (12.8.1) and (12.8.3) into (12.5.3) yields a class of progressivity measures based on Atkinson's social welfare functions as

$$\theta_\epsilon = \frac{\widehat{W}_y(\epsilon) - (1 - e) W_x(\epsilon)}{T}. \qquad (12.8.4)$$

This equation defines a measure of tax progressivity for any given value of the inequality aversion parameter ϵ. The inequality aversion parameter in the context of tax progressivity measures the relative sensitivity of tax rates at different income levels. As ϵ rises, a higher weight is assigned to tax rates at the lower end of the income distribution and a lower weight to tax rates at the top end of the distribution. If $\in = 0$, all individuals pay the same tax rate, and the tax system is thus proportional. These are relative measures of tax progressivity. Since Atkinson's social welfare functions are not absolutely homogeneous of degree one, they do not lend themselves to absolute tax progressivity measures.

Can a utilitarian social welfare function give an absolute measure of tax progressivity? The answer is yes. Its derivation is as follows:

Kolm (1976a, 1976b) proposed a class of absolute measures of inequality given by

$$I_{KOM} = \frac{1}{\beta} ln \left[\int_0^\infty exp\{\beta (\bar{x} - x)\} f(x) \, dx \right],$$ (12.8.5)

where $\beta > 0$ is the parameter and $\bar{x}$ is the mean income. An absolute measure of inequality is related to social welfare as

$$I_K = \bar{x} - W_{KOM}$$ (12.8.6)

where W_{KOM} is the class of absolute social welfare functions underlying the Kolm inequality measures. It is easy to verify that W_{KOM} is given by

$$-exp\left(-\beta W_{KOM}\right) = \int_0^\infty -exp\left(-\beta x\right) f(x) dx.$$ (12.8.7)

The utility function implicit in these social welfare functions is given by

$$u(x) = -exp\left(-\beta x\right),$$ (12.8.8)

which on substituting in (12.3.1) gives the Kolm social welfare function (12.8.7). Thus, these results demonstrate that the Kolm social welfare function belongs to the general social welfare function class (12.3.1). The utility function $u(x)$ in (12.8.8) is increasing in x and is concave. The utility function also satisfies $u(x + a) = u(a) u(x)$, which from (12.3.1) implies that the social welfare function in (12.8.7) is absolutely homogeneous of degree one; if everyone's income is increased (decreased) by the same amount, the social welfare function also increases (decreases) by the same amount.

It is appropriate to note that Pollak (1971) proposed precisely the same social welfare function as derived in (12.8.8), but in the context of multiple commodity utility functions. This social welfare function is popularly known as the Kolm–Pollak social welfare function (See Blackorby, Bossert, and Donaldson 1999; Ebert 1988; Gajdos 2001; Mas-Colell, Whinston, and Green 1995).

Utilizing (12.5.5) in conjunction with (12.8.7) yields the class of absolute progressivity measures underlying the social welfare function in (12.8.7) as

$$\theta_{KP} = -\frac{1}{\beta} \ln \left[\int_0^\infty exp\left(-\beta x\right) \cdot exp\left(\beta T\left(x\right)\right) f\left(x\right) dx \right]$$

$$+ \frac{1}{\beta} \ln \left[\int_0^\infty exp\left(-\beta x\right) f\left(x\right) dx \right] + \bar{T}, \tag{12.8.9}$$

which is a new measure of absolute tax progressivity underlying the Kolm–Pollak social welfare function. Substituting $T(x) = a$ for all x in (12.8.9), $\theta_{KP} = 0$; if everyone pays the same tax, the progressivity index equals zero.

12.9 Welfare Interpretation of Suits' Measure of Tax Progressivity

Suppose $C(p)$ is the proportion of taxes paid by the bottom p proportion of individuals, and $L(p)$ is the proportion of their income. The graph of $C(p)$ and $L(p)$ is called the relative concentration curve of taxes with respect to income (Chapter 8 and Kakwani, 1977, 1980a). Suits (1977) proposed a measure of progressivity that is equal to 1 minus twice the area under the relative concentration curve:

$$S = 1 - 2 \int_0^1 C(p) dL(p) \tag{12.9.1}$$

When $C(p) = L(p)$ for all p, all individuals pay the same share of taxes, equal to their share of incomes, implying that the tax system is proportional and thus, $S = 0$. When $C(p) = 0$ for all p (when the wealthiest person in society pays all the taxes), $S = 1$; this scenario shows extreme progressivity. When $C(p) = 1$ for all p (the poorest person in society pays all the taxes), $S = -1$. Hence, S lies between -1 and $+1$.

The social welfare function that provides the Suits measure of progressivity is somewhat unclear. To determine this, it will be necessary to evaluate the integral in (12.9.1) as

$$S = 1 - \frac{2}{\bar{T}} \int_0^\infty T(x) \left[1 - F_1(x)\right] f(x) dx \tag{12.9.2}$$

where $F_1(x)$ is the cumulative proportion of incomes of individuals with income less than or equal to x.

Kakwani (1980a) introduced the following social welfare function, which for the pre-tax income is given by

$$W_x^S = \frac{2}{(1 + G_x)} \int_0^\infty x \left[1 - F_1(x)\right] f(x) dx \tag{12.9.3}$$

where G_x is the Gini index of the pre-tax income distribution. This social welfare function is the weighted average of income levels. The weight given to an individual with income x is $\frac{2}{(1+G_x)}[1 - F_1(x)]$, which adds up to 1 for the whole population. When integrating (12.9.3) by parts, W_x^S simplifies to $\frac{\bar{x}}{(1+G_x)}$. Like Sen's social welfare function, this function captures the relative deprivation suffered by a society. The extent of deprivation experienced by an individual with income x is proportional to the total income of individuals in a society who are richer than the person with income x. In Sen's social welfare function, the deprivation is proportional to the number of individuals richer than the person with income x. This social welfare function has different normative judgments from Sen's. Although Kakwani (1980a) proposed it, it will be appropriate to refer to it as the Suits social welfare function for convenience. The post-tax social welfare of this function would be

$$W_y^S = \frac{2}{(1 + G_y)} \int_0^\infty y\left[1 - F_1^*(y)\right] f^*(y)\, dy \tag{12.9.4}$$

where G_y is the Gini index of the post-tax income distribution. The pseudo-social welfare of the post-tax income distribution uses the pre-tax weights and is given by

$$\widehat{W}_y^S = \frac{2}{(1 + G)} \int_0^\infty [x - T(x)]\left[1 - F_1(x)\right] f(x)\, dx. \tag{12.9.5}$$

Thus, the relative measure of horizontal inequity for the Suits social welfare function would be

$$H_S = \frac{W_y^S - \widehat{W}_y^S}{\bar{T}} < 0 \tag{12.9.6}$$

Using (12.9.3) and (12.9.4) in conjunction with (12.9.5) and (12.9.6) yields the following decomposition:

$$\frac{W_y^S - W_x^S}{\bar{T}} = H_S - \frac{1}{(1 + G_x)} + \frac{S}{(1 + G_x)} \tag{12.9.7}$$

where S is the Suits index of tax progressivity. This decomposition shows that the total welfare impact of taxation when the government collects an average of one dollar of tax from society has three components: (i) the loss of welfare when there is a change in ranking, (ii) the loss of welfare when the tax system is proportional, and (iii) the gain (loss) of welfare when the tax system is progressive (regressive). A taxation system is progressive when the Suits index (S) is positive—that is, tax contributes to a gain in welfare. Conversely, if S is negative, taxation is regressive and contributes to a welfare loss.

The gain (loss) of social welfare is $\frac{S}{(1+G_x)}$ when the tax system is progressive (regressive), and society pays an average of one dollar tax. Like other progressivity measures, one can ascribe social welfare interpretation to the Suits index provided it is normalized by $(1 + G_x)$. Hence, a modified Suits measure of progressivity is proposed by $\frac{S}{(1+G_x)}$, which has a social welfare interpretation. This proposed modification is the first in the literature. Furthermore, the social welfare function implicit in Suits is not absolutely homogeneous of degree one, so it does not give the absolute measure of progressivity.

12.10 A New Progressivity Index Based on the Bonferroni Social Welfare Function

In 1930, Carlo Emilio Bonferroni proposed a curve similar to the Lorenz curve based on the cumulative means of the income distribution. This curve is given by

$$B(p) = \frac{L(p)}{p}.$$

Based on this curve, Son (2011) derived a social welfare function given by

$$W_x^B = -\int_0^\infty x \ln(F(x)) f(x)\, dx = \bar{x}(1 - B_x) \qquad (12.10.1)$$

where $F(x)$ is the probability distribution function; this social welfare function is the weighted average of income levels. The weight given to an individual with income x is $-\ln(F(x))$, which decreases monotonically with income, and the total weight adds up to 1 for the entire population. B_x is the Bonferroni inequality measure of the pre-tax income distribution.

The social welfare function of the post-tax income $y = x - T(x)$ is given by

$$W_y^B = -\int_0^\infty (x - T(x)) \ln(f^*(y)) f^*(y)\, dx = \bar{x}(1 - e)(1 - B_y) \qquad (12.10.2)$$

where B_y is the Bonferroni inequality measure for the post-tax income. The Bonferroni pseudo-social welfare function of the post-tax income distribution is given by

$$\widehat{W}_y^B = -\int_0^\infty (x - T(x)) \ln(F(x)) f(x)\, dx = \bar{x}(1 - e)(1 - C_y^B) \qquad (12.10.3)$$

where C_y^B is the concentration index of the post-tax income for the Bonferroni social welfare function.

Similarly, the Bonferroni pseudo-social welfare function for taxes is given by

$$W_T{}^B = -\int_0^\infty T(x) \ln\left(F(x)\right) f(x)\, dx = \overline{T}\left(1 - C_T^B\right) \tag{12.10.4}$$

where C_T^B is the Bonferroni concentration index of the taxes. Horizontal inequity, measured by the loss of social welfare caused by the change in rankings, is given by

$$H_B = W_y^B - \widehat{W}_y^B < 0 \tag{12.10.5}$$

From (12.10.1), (12. 10.3), and (12. 10.4), it is easy to verify that

$$\widehat{W}_y^B = W_x^B - W_T^B, \tag{12.10.6}$$

which upon substituting in (12.5.3) and using (12.10.1) and (12.10.4) yields a new tax progressivity index based on the Bonferroni social welfare function as

$$\theta_B = C_T^B - B_x \tag{12.10.7}$$

which we will be referred to as the Bonferroni tax progressivity index. The tax system is progressive (regressive) when θ_B is positive (negative) and proportional when $\theta_B = 0$.

Substituting (12.10.6) into (12.5.2) and using (12.10.1), (12.10.2), (12.10.5), (12.10.6), and (12.10.7) gives the decomposition:

$$\frac{W_y^B - W_x^B}{\overline{T}} = \frac{H_B}{\overline{T}} - \left(1 - B_x\right) + \theta_B, \tag{12.10.8}$$

which shows that the total welfare impact of taxation, when society pays an average of one dollar tax, is the sum of three components: (i) the loss of social welfare when there is a change in ranking between the pre- and post-tax incomes, (ii) the loss of social welfare when the tax system is proportional, and (iii) the gain (loss) of social welfare when the tax system is progressive (regressive). The progressivity index θ_B is interpreted as the welfare contribution of tax progressivity when society pays an average of one dollar tax. Therefore, the progressive tax system contributes to a gain in social welfare, while the regressive tax system contributes to a social welfare loss.

The Bonferroni social welfare function is absolutely homogeneous of degree one; one can obtain the absolute measure of tax progressivity as

$$\theta_A = C_B, \tag{12.10.9}$$

which upon substituting in (12.5.6) yields the change in social welfare as

$$y_B^* - x_B^* = H_B - \overline{T} + C_B. \tag{12.10.10}$$

When $C_B = 0$, everyone pays the same amount of tax, and there is no change in ranking. The resulting loss of social welfare is thus equal to the average tax paid by society.

12.11 International Comparison of Tax Progressivity

This section presents an international comparison of tax progressivity using the measures discussed in this chapter. It uses the income distribution data for 32 countries obtained from the Luxembourg Income Study database, providing the most comprehensive income data for around 50 countries in Europe, North America, Latin America, Africa, Asia, and Australasia, spanning five decades. This comparison has selected 32 countries based on (i) the availability of comparable tax data (observed only for industrialized countries) that allows for the comparisons of tax progressivity across countries, and (ii) the availability of household surveys conducted around 2013.

The gross household income is defined as total monetary and non-monetary current income; gross disposable income is the household gross income net of taxes and social security contributions. Household incomes and taxes (including social security payments) were equalized by dividing them by the square root of the number of household members. This equalizing procedure accounts for different needs of household members and economies of scale that occur in larger households. The local currency's income and taxes were converted to the 2011 purchasing power parity (PPP) international dollars, legitimizing international comparisons.

Linear regression and correlation techniques are the tools to measure relationships between variables. The relationships involving social welfare functions and tax progressivity are often nonlinear. Thus, the correlation coefficients that measure a deviation from linearity may invariably show that the variables are not significantly or only weakly related. Given the nonlinear nature of variables, some analysts have estimated linear regressions after applying a nonlinear transformation to the original data. Since the exact forms of nonlinear relationships are unknown, incorrect conclusions on the significance of relationships may emerge. Rank correlation methods are more robust (Iman and Conover, 1978). Therefore, this chapter uses the Spearman correlation coefficient to test a significant relationship between variables, and it uses the following t statistics to test the significance of relationships.

$$t = \frac{r\sqrt{n-2}}{\sqrt{1-r^2}} \tag{12.11.1}$$

where r is the Spearman rank correlation, which is distributed approximately as Student's t distribution with $(n-2)$ degrees of freedom. Pitman (1937) proposed this test procedure, which performs better than the normal approximation (Iman and Conover, 1978).

This chapter does not attempt to establish a causal relationship between the variables, which would require a highly complex general equilibrium model. Its aim is limited to determining whether significant monotonic relationships exist between the variables. It carried out the rank correlation analysis using the household surveys of 32 countries. The level of statistical significance is set at 1%. If the rank correlation coefficients among the variables are significant, one can conclude that their relationships would exist with a high degree of confidence.

12.11.1 Relative Measures of Tax Progressivity

Table 12.1 presents the relative tax progressivity measures for the nine wealthiest countries of the 32 selected for this study. In the generalized Gini social welfare function, when $k = 0$, the social welfare function collapses to the mean income of society; that is, everyone has the same income and pays the same tax rate, in which case taxes will be proportional. In this scenario, for every dollar of the government's average tax collection, society loses one dollar per person of social welfare.

When $k = 1$, the progressivity index derived from the generalized Gini social welfare function is the Kakwani index based on Sen's social welfare function. Taking Australia as an example, the value of the index is 0.22, implying that the Australian tax system is progressive and contributes to a social welfare gain of 22 cents. If the tax system were proportional, there would be a social welfare loss equal to 59 cents. Thus, the net loss of social welfare contributed by the Australian tax system is 37 cents. The Australian tax system also incurs a welfare loss of 0.01 cents due to horizontal inequity. Therefore, the Australian tax system contributes to the total social welfare loss of 38 cents. The Australian government mobilizes revenues of one dollar from the tax to invest in the provision of public goods and public services such as education, health, and welfare programs. For the Australian government to break even, it has to generate a social rate of return of 38% from its investments.

The social welfare lost due to taxation in other countries is much larger. For instance, the social welfare loss for South Korea is 59 cents, which implies the Korean government has to generate a social rate of return of 59% when it invests its tax dollars in public investments. The main reason for this high social welfare loss is that the Korean tax system is relatively less progressive.

Almost all governments worldwide mobilize a significant proportion of their tax revenues from indirect taxation, which is always regressive. Hence, the loss of social welfare from taxation would be much higher. Suppose the tax is mildly regressive with the value of progressivity index $K = -0.10$. Under this scenario, Korea's total social welfare loss would be 78 cents for every tax dollar collected. Hence, the government needs to generate a social rate of 78% from its public programs to break even. Society suffers a net loss in social welfare due to taxation if the Korean government fails to create high returns.

Furthermore, since the government incurs the administrative costs of tax collection, it will need to create a much higher social rate of return to break even. Optimal social welfare, therefore, requires three factors: (i) a tax system to be progressive; (ii) minimum administrative costs in collecting taxes; and (iii) efficient investments of tax revenues to maximize the social rates of return.

The progressivity index must increase when a tax is transferred from a richer individual to a poorer one, provided the transfer does not change the ranking. This requirement is satisfied by all the measures of tax progressivity discussed in the chapter. However, an additional element is that the progressivity index must be more sensitive to such transfers if they take place among relatively poorer individuals. In the generalized Gini social welfare function, k is the parameter of inequality aversion. As k increases, the progressivity index becomes more sensitive to tax transfers among poorer individuals. If a society's objective is to have a tax system that is more sensitive to tax transfers among those relatively poorer persons, it should choose the progressivity index with a higher value of k. Table 12.1 shows that as k rises from 1 to 3, the social welfare losses fall for all nine countries, implying that the social rate of return from their public investments needed for governments to break even also decreases. This observation has a similarity with the "leaky bucket experiment." As k rise, society tolerates more waste and inefficiency.

Atkinson's social welfare functions also consider the different degrees of the aversion parameter, making it possible to assign higher weights to the transfers at the lower end of the income distribution. As expected, their conclusions are similar to those from the generalized Gini social welfare functions.

This chapter has also computed tax progressivity measures using the Bonferroni and Suits social welfare functions. Table 12.1 reveals that the Bonferroni social welfare function for the Australian tax system results in a welfare loss of 25 cents, while the Suits social welfare function yields a much higher welfare loss of 42 cents. The welfare gain due to the progressivity of taxation is also much higher for the Bonferroni social welfare function at 25 cents compared with 18 cents when the Suits social welfare function is used. Although social welfare functions result in different magnitudes of tax progressivity measures and welfare losses, the overall conclusions emerging from these empirical results are not much different.

12.11.2 Absolute Measures of Tax Progressivity

Table 12.2 presents the absolute measures of tax progressivity and welfare losses due to taxation based on 2011 PPP international dollars. Taking Canada as an example, tax progressivity derived from the Gini social welfare function contributes to an increase in social welfare equivalent to $7,737 per person, resulting in a social welfare gain due to the progressive tax structure. The tax structure also generates horizontal inequity, resulting in a social welfare loss of $110 per person. The Canadian tax system incurs a net social welfare loss of $6,900 per person. The Canadian government mobilizes tax

Table 12.1 Relative progressivity and social welfare contributions of taxation when the average tax collected is $1

Countries	Russia	Korea	UK	Israel	Germany	Finland	Canada	Australia	United States
Generalized Gini social welfare k=1									
Horizontal inequity	-0.01	-0.01	-0.03	-0.03	-0.02	-0.01	-0.01	-0.01	-0.01
Proportional tax	-0.62	-0.67	-0.61	-0.6	-0.62	-0.65	-0.61	-0.59	-0.56
Progressivity	0.08	0.09	0.17	0.2	0.15	0.12	0.15	0.22	0.18
Total welfare loss	-0.55	-0.59	-0.47	-0.43	-0.48	-0.53	-0.48	-0.38	-0.39
Generalized Gini social welfare k=2									
Horizontal inequity	-0.01	-0.01	-0.04	-0.04	-0.02	-0.01	-0.01	-0.01	-0.01
Proportional tax	-0.49	-0.53	-0.48	-0.46	-0.48	-0.52	-0.48	-0.46	-0.42
Progressivity	0.11	0.1	0.21	0.19	0.18	0.15	0.18	0.24	0.19
Total welfare loss	-0.39	-0.44	-0.31	-0.31	-0.32	-0.38	-0.31	-0.22	-0.24
Generalized Gini social welfare k=3									
Horizontal inequity	-0.01	-0.01	-0.05	-0.05	-0.02	-0.01	-0.01	-0.01	-0.01
Proportional tax	-0.42	-0.45	-0.41	-0.38	-0.41	-0.44	-0.4	-0.38	-0.35
Progressivity	0.12	0.09	0.22	0.17	0.19	0.16	0.19	0.24	0.18
Total welfare loss	-0.31	-0.36	-0.24	-0.27	-0.24	-0.29	-0.22	-0.15	-0.17

Continued

Table 12.1 Continued

Countries	Russia	Korea	UK	Israel	Germany	Finland	Canada	Australia	United States
Bonferroni social welfare function									
Horizontal inequity	-0.01	-0.01	-0.07	-0.12	-0.02	-0.01	-0.01	-0.01	-0.01
Proportional tax	-0.49	-0.52	-0.48	-0.46	-0.49	-0.52	-0.48	-0.46	-0.43
Progressivity	0.1	0.08	0.18	0.14	0.16	0.14	0.16	0.22	0.17
Total welfare loss	-0.41	-0.46	-0.37	-0.44	-0.35	-0.39	-0.33	-0.25	-0.27
Suits social welfare function									
Horizontal inequity	-0.02	-0.03	-0.03	-0.06	-0.06	-0.06	-0.06	-0.1	-0.08
Proportional tax	-0.68	-0.69	-0.66	-0.6	-0.61	-0.63	-0.59	-0.5	-0.54
Progressivity	0.05	0.08	0.13	0.18	0.12	0.1	0.12	0.18	0.15
Total welfare loss	-0.65	-0.64	-0.56	-0.48	-0.55	-0.58	-0.54	-0.42	-0.46
Atkinson's social welfare function: inequality aversion parameter=0.5									
Proportional tax	-0.88	-0.9	-0.88	-0.87	-0.88	-0.9	-0.88	-0.86	-0.84
Progressivity	0.04	0.12	0.1	0.16	0.08	0.06	0.09	0.14	0.12
Total welfare loss	-0.84	-0.78	-0.77	-0.71	-0.8	-0.83	-0.79	-0.72	-0.72

Atkinson's social welfare function: inequality aversion parameter=1.0

Proportional tax	-0.77	-0.79	-0.77	-0.75	-0.77	-0.8	-0.75	-0.74	-0.7
Progressivity	0.09	0.15	0.17	0.22	0.15	0.12	0.16	0.23	0.2
Total welfare loss	-0.69	-0.64	-0.6	-0.52	-0.62	-0.68	-0.59	-0.51	-0.5

Atkinson's social welfare function: inequality aversion parameter=1.5

Proportional tax	-0.68	-0.68	-0.65	-0.62	-0.68	-0.71	-0.59	-0.53	-0.49
Progressivity	0.16	0.26	0.25	0.26	0.16	0.1	0.23	0.21	0.21
Total welfare loss	-0.51	-0.42	-0.4	-0.36	-0.52	-0.6	-0.36	-0.32	-0.27

Note: Results for 32 countries are available in the supplementary Excel file.
Source: Authors' calculations.

revenues worth $14,527 per person. The government needs to produce social welfare of an amount equivalent to more than $6,900 per person to break even. Otherwise, the Canadian society would suffer a net social welfare loss, in which case the government should not be imposing a tax on the population. If administrative cost is also considered, the government will need to generate even higher social welfare from its investment of tax revenue.

12.11.3 Rank Correlation Analysis

This chapter has presented eight alternative social welfare functions that generate eight alternative tax progressivity measures. All progressivity measures satisfy the fundamental axiom of equity in taxation. The absolute measures satisfy the fundamental axiom: the rich should pay more tax than the poor. Similarly, the relative measures satisfy a stronger axiom: the rich should pay tax at a higher rate. Empirical calculations of the tax progressivity show different magnitudes of the change in progressivity. Accordingly, this section attempts to answer whether the various measures derived from different social welfare functions result in significantly different rankings of countries.

Formby, Seaks, and Smith (1981) presented an empirical study using the United States income tax system for 1962–76 and concluded that the Kakwani and Suits measures of progressivity displayed opposite rankings in 3 of 14 years. If this conclusion is generally correct, it is essential to know which social welfare functions one should use to analyze progressivity in taxation. This issue is addressed using the rank correlation method.

Table 12.3 presents the empirical results on the Spearman rank correlation that indicates changes in the rankings of 32 countries by various progressivity measures. As shown in the table, the estimates of the rank correlation are all positive and statistically significant at the 1% level of significance. From these results, one can conclude a significant monotonic relationship among the measures of progressivity derived from different social welfare functions. This conclusion implies that various social welfare functions do not significantly change a country's ranking. These observations are inconsistent with Formby, Seaks, and Smith's conclusion that the measures of progressivity are fundamentally different and can move in the opposite direction. One possible explanation for such divergence is that, as pointed out earlier, Suits' measure does not have a social welfare interpretation unless it is normalized by $(1 + G_x)$. Unfortunately, Formby, Seaks, and Smith (1981) did not perform this normalization.

Various measures of redistribution of taxation also depend on social welfare functions. The empirical results in Table 12.3 also reveal a significant monotonic relationship among multiple measurements of the redistribution effects of taxation. Therefore, the rankings of countries by the progressivity and redistribution effects of tax do not change significantly. As noted, for a given degree of progressivity, the average tax rate contributes to a reduction in post-tax income inequality—that is, it increases the redistribution of taxation. The rank correlation analysis is consistent with this theory.

Table 12.2 Absolute progressivity and social welfare contributions of taxation

Countries	Russia	Korea	UK	Israel	Germany	Finland	Canada	Australia	United States
Generalized Gini social welfare k=1									
Horizontal inequity	−35	−40	−284	−286	−249	−96	−110	−118	−98
Proportional tax	−3796	−4382	9241	9789	−16,494	−15,076	−14,527	−14,770	−16,050
Progressivity	1746	1856	5191	5880	8808	7145	7737	9267	9898
Total welfare loss	−2084	−2566	4335	4194	−7935	−8027	−6900	−5620	−6250
Generalized Gini social welfare k=2									
Horizontal inequity	−42	−46	−368	−404	−324	−108	−127	−128	−111
Proportional tax	−3796	−4382	9241	9789	−16,494	−15,076	−14,527	−14,770	−16,050
Progressivity	2346	2498	6744	7198	11,549	9524	10,221	11,601	12,337
Total welfare loss	−1492	−1930	2865	2994	−5269	−5660	−4433	−3296	−3824
Generalized Gini social welfare k=3									
Horizontal inequity	−44	−47	−431	−501	−355	−112	−131	−121	−111
Proportional tax	−3796	−4382	9241	9789	−16,494	−15,076	−14,527	−14,770	−16,050
Progressivity	2661	2842	7461	7674	12,876	10,767	11,473	12,707	13,450
Total welfare loss	−1179	−1587	2211	2616	−3973	−4421	−3185	−2184	−2711

Continued

Table 12.2 *Continued*

Countries	Russia	Korea	UK	Israel	Germany	Finland	Canada	Australia	United States
Bonferroni social welfare function									
Horizontal inequity	-38	-51	-651	1174	-370	-100	-112	-106	-95
Proportional tax	-3796	-4382	9241	9789	-16,494	-15,076	-14,527	-14,770	-16,050
Progressivity	2291	2438	6436	6630	11,077	9289	9861	11,157	11,880
Total welfare loss	-1543	-1995	3456	4333	-5788	-5886	-4778	-3719	-4265
Suits social welfare function									
Horizontal inequity	-84	-130	-294	-557	-908	-850	-921	-1522	-1280
Proportional tax	-3796	-4382	9241	9789	-16,494	-15,076	-14,527	-14,770	-16,050
Progressivity	1421	1710	4363	5677	8343	7123	7593	10,023	9877
Total welfare loss	-2458	-2802	5172	4668	-9059	-8803	-7856	-6268	-7453
Atkinson's social welfare function: inequality aversion parameter=0.5									
Proportional tax	-3796	-4382	9241	9789	-16,494	-15,076	-14,527	-14,770	-16,050
Progressivity	615	949	2096	2858	3314	2488	3038	4118	4547
Total welfare loss	-3181	-3433	7146	6931	-13,180	-12,588	-11,489	-10,652	-11,504

Atkinson's social welfare function: inequality aversion parameter=1.0

Proportional tax	−3796	−4382	9241	9789	−16,494	−15,076	−14,527	−14,770	−16,050
Progressivity	1194	1583	3697	4666	6204	4787	5942	7299	8011
Total welfare loss	−2601	−2799	5544	5122	−10,290	−10,289	−8585	−7471	−8039

Atkinson's social welfare function: inequality aversion parameter=1.5

Proportional tax	−3796	−4382	9241	9789	−16,494	−15,076	−14,527	−14,770	−16,050
Progressivity	1847	2542	5529	6274	7903	5967	9258	10,103	11,650
Total welfare loss	−1949	−1840	3712	3515	−8591	−9109	−5269	−4667	−4400

Table 12.3 Spearman rank correlation for 32 countries

	Income	Tax Rate	Generalized Gini			Bonferroni	Suits	Atkinson with aversion		
			k=1	k=2	k=3			0.5	1.0	1.5
Income	1.00									
Tax rate	0.68*	1.00								
Progressivity measures										
Generalized Gini k=1	-0.32	-0.24	1							
Generalized Gini k=2	-0.31	-0.27	0.96*	1						
Generalized Gini k=3	-0.25	-0.25	0.88*	0.97*	1					
Bonferroni	-0.32	-0.24	0.94*	0.97*	0.96*	1				
Suits	-0.27	-0.24	0.98*	0.91*	0.81*	0.90*	1			
Atkinson aversion=0.5	-0.41	-0.44	0.79	0.69*	0.58*	0.67*	0.83*	1		
Atkinson aversion=1	-0.39	-0.38	0.90*	0.83*	0.75*	0.81*	0.91*	0.94*	1	
Atkinson aversion=1.5	-0.38	-0.47	0.68*	0.66*	0.61*	0.62*	0.67*	0.72*	0.81*	1
Redistribution of tax										
Generalized Gini k=1	-0.52*	0.72*	1							
Generalized Gini k=2	-0.50*	0.72*	0.98*	1						
Generalized Gini k=3	-0.47*	0.70*	0.95*	0.99*	1					
Bonferroni	-0.36	0.62*	0.89*	0.94*	0.96*	1				
Suits	-0.56*	0.70*	0.98*	0.95*	0.92*	0.84*	1			
Atkinson aversion=0.5	-0.58*	0.71*	0.91*	0.86*	0.82*	0.68*	0.92*	1		
Atkinson aversion=1	-0.57*	0.71*	0.95*	0.94*	0.92*	0.80*	0.95*	0.95*	1	
Atkinson aversion=1.5	-0.39	-0.43	0.64*	0.64*	0.62*	0.53*	0.62*	0.73*	0.70*	1

Note: * indicates statistical significance at 1%.
Source: Authors' calculations.

The rank correlations presented in Table 12.3 also reveal that a tax rate has no significant relationship among various measures of progressivity. As expected, there is a significant relationship between the tax rate and the redistribution of taxation.

12.12 Concluding Remarks

The concept of tax progressivity is the most relevant to analyzing equity in taxation and government expenditures. It has also found applications to examine access to health, education, and essential services. The Kakwani index has become a popular tool for analyzing equity in public finance and delivering healthcare. Measures of tax progressivity inform the design of public policies and programs. The public debates on taxation revolve around tax progressivity and the redistribution effects of taxation and government social programs. It is, therefore, essential to assess the extent to which tax systems lead to social welfare gains or losses.

However, the literature on taxation has yet to explore the social welfare implications of the measures of progressivity. This chapter has undertaken a pioneering effort to develop a social welfare function framework for deriving tax progressivity measures and exploring their social welfare implications. This social welfare framework has helped derive progressivity measures from eight alternative social welfare functions. Every tax progressivity measure has an implicit social welfare function that determines the society's normative values.

This chapter has developed a generalized Kakwani index depending on a parameter k, similar to Atkinson's inequality aversion parameter that assigns a higher weight to the more impoverished populations in the income distribution.

This chapter also proposed an essential modification of the Suits measure of progressivity. While this measure is widely used to analyze equity in taxation, it needs to be appropriately normalized to assign a social welfare interpretation. This chapter also has developed a new progressivity measure based on the Bonferroni social welfare function.

The chapter has compared tax progressivity in household surveys from 32 developed countries, selected based on comparable tax data, and conducted in 2013. The relative measures of progressivity are interpreted as the welfare gains (losses) of social welfare when taxes are progressive (regressive) and when society pays an average of one dollar tax. Taking Australia as an example, the value of the Kakwani index of tax progressivity for the Australian tax system is at $0.22. Since the gain is positive, the Australian tax system is progressive. For every dollar in tax the Australian government mobilizes, the tax system contributes to a social welfare gain of 22 cents. If the Australian tax system were proportional, there would be a loss of social welfare equal to 59 cents, resulting in a net loss of 37 cents. The empirical application found that the Australian tax system also incurs a welfare loss of 0.01 cents due to horizontal inequity; hence, the tax system's contribution to the total social welfare loss was 38 cents. These results imply that the Australian government needs to generate a rate of return of 38% from its public investments funded by the revenue collected from taxes. This interpretation of tax systems is new in the literature and must help policymakers design an equitable tax system. The required investment returns will be even higher if the administrative costs are also considered.

The chapter concluded that optimizing social welfare requires three factors: (i) a progressive tax system, (ii) minimum administrative costs for collecting taxes, and (iii) efficient investments of tax revenues to maximize the social rates of return.

Although different social welfare functions result in varying magnitudes of tax progressivity measures and welfare losses, the overall conclusions are by and large similar, and the overall results are pretty robust, whichever social welfare function we use.

Considering various distortions that lead to lower efficiency in the tax system, the optimum taxation literature has attempted to determine how progressive a tax system should be. Covering both the issues of efficiency and equity deals with determining the optimal tax structure associated with maximizing social welfare. This chapter has shown that the welfare loss of taxation can be substantial and may worsen if the tax system is inefficient. The efficiency in taxation is beyond the scope of this chapter. However, the chapter has emphasized the importance of efficient and equitable investments of government tax revenues so that society does not suffer too much from welfare loss of taxation. Thus, maximizing social returns from government investments should be an essential component of any debate on tax policy.

13

Negative Income Tax Plans

13.1 Introduction

Negative income tax and guaranteed annual income are the two commonly suggested fiscal measures to transfer income from the rich to the poor to reduce income inequality and poverty. Negative income tax proposals aim to extend income tax rates beyond zero to negative levels. Families having an income below a break-even level obtain an allowance from the government. A break-even income level is when a family neither pays an income tax nor receives a government cash allowance.

Guaranteed income schemes, also referred to as social dividend taxation, pay cash subsidies to every family, depending on the family composition; in turn, each family pays a proportional income tax, excluding cash benefits.

Friedman (1962) proposed the first formula for negative income tax. His plan determined the break-even income level by the total value of exemptions and deductions allowed under existing tax laws to a family of a given size. Lampman (1964, 1971) and Green (1966) proposed an almost identical plan but differed slightly from the Friedman plan. All three determine the break-even level of income based on the poverty standard for a family of a given size. Besides, these plans have the same marginal tax rate, although the Friedman plan provides more benefits to larger families than the Lampman and Green plans.

Among several guaranteed income plans, the Smith (1965) plan is the only one that provides for the differing needs of children and adults within a family. In contrast, the Tobin (1965) plan gave every family member the same allowance: the Rolph (1967) plan was similar to the Tobin plan, and it applied a lower tax rate on family income other than the allowance.

This chapter develops a general framework that incorporates all the negative income tax plans discussed above. This framework is defined with three parameters: marginal tax rate, the lump-sum subsidy given to each family, and tax credit per family member. This chapter evaluates the negative income plans using the two equity principles of taxation: progressivity and redistributive effects.

Chapter 12 discussed the two concepts of tax progressivity—absolute and relative. This chapter derives both absolute and relative measures of progressivity from the general framework of negative income plans. It evaluates the various negative income plans by the elasticities of progressivity measures with respect to the three parameters of negative income tax plans.

Economic Inequality and Poverty. Nanak Kakwani and Hyun Son, Oxford University Press.
© Nanak Kakwani and Hyun Son (2022). DOI: 10.1093/oso/9780198852841.003.0013

Chapter 11 discussed the redistributive effect of taxation. This chapter explores the redistributive impact of negative tax plans, measuring how they reduce income inequality. If they increase inequality, such plans should be deemed anti-poor. The chapter also distinguishes the relative and absolute measures of redistributive effects. It demonstrates that the negative tax plans may increase income inequality under certain conditions.

13.2 A General Framework of Income Tax Plans

Suppose x is the family's income, assuming a random probability distribution with density function $f(x)$. The proposed general framework of negative tax plans, denoted by $T(x)$, extends the income tax rates beyond zero to negative levels. Families having an income below a break-even level obtain an allowance from the government. The break-even income is the level at which a family neither pays an income tax nor receives a cash allowance from the government. If a family of size $n \geq 1$ has an income less than the break-even income $R(n)$, the family receives a cash allowance from the government; if the family income is higher than $R(n)$, it pays a tax.

Assuming that the marginal tax rate β is the same for both positive and negative income tax, the net tax paid by the family with income x is given by

$$
\begin{aligned}
T(x) &= -\beta\left[R(n) - x\right] \quad && if\, x \leq R(n)\\
&= \beta\left[x - R(n)\right] \quad && if\, x \geq R(n),
\end{aligned}
\tag{13.2.1}
$$

which is also given by

$$
T(x) = \beta x - \beta R(n).
\tag{13.2.2}
$$

The simplest break-even level of income is the linear function:

$$
R(n) = a + bn
\tag{13.2.3}
$$

where $a>0$ is the cash allowance allowed for the family, and $b>0$ is the deduction for each family member.

The elasticity of the break-even level with respect to n is given by

$$
\eta_R = \frac{n}{R}\frac{\partial R(n)}{\partial n} = \frac{bn}{a + bn} < 1
$$

This shows that as the family size increases by 1%, the break-even income increases by less than 1%, implying that the plan considers the economy of scale that larger households enjoy. If there were no economies of scale, the elasticity would equal 1.

Substituting (13.2.3) into (13.2.2) yields

$$T(x) = \beta x - a\beta - b\beta n = \beta x - a^* - b^* n \tag{13.2.4}$$

where $a^* = \beta a > 0$ is the lump-sum subsidy given to every family and $b^* = \beta b > 0$ is the size of credit per family member. Every family receives a total cash transfer $a^* + b^* n$, irrespective of its income. This amount is the negative income tax, but every family becomes subject to a β tax rate. βx is the positive tax paid by the family with income x.

If μ is the mean family income before taxes and transfers and μ_n is the mean family size, the average net tax collected by the government is given by

$$\overline{T} = \beta\mu - a^* - b^* \mu_n, \tag{13.2.5}$$

which is nonnegative if $\mu > \frac{a^* + b^* \mu_n}{\beta}$. However, if $\mu < \frac{a^* + b^* \mu_n}{\beta}$, the government will not collect any tax revenue. The average tax rate is given by

$$e = \frac{\overline{T}}{\mu} = \frac{\beta\mu - a^* - b^* \mu_n}{\mu}, \tag{13.2.6}$$

which will always be less than one if the marginal tax rate $\beta < 1$. Further, $\beta > e$ will always hold. Thus, the marginal tax rate must satisfy $e < \beta < 1$. Also, it is easy to show from (13.2.6) that the average tax rate e increases as β increases and decreases as a^* and b^* increase.

The disposable income or net income of the family with pre-tax income $x \geq 0$ is given by

$$y(x) = (1 - \beta)x + a^* + b^* n, \tag{13.2.7}$$

which will always be positive if the marginal tax rate is less than unity.

This general framework does not consider the differing needs of children and adults within families. One method of doing so is to specify the break-even level of a family as

$$R(n) = a + b_1 n_1 + b_2 n_2 \tag{13.2.8}$$

where $n = n_1 + n_2$, n_1 and n_2 are the number of children (say, under 15) and adults (over 15) in the family, respectively. Accordingly, (13.2.2) becomes

$$T(x) = \beta x - a\beta - \beta b_1 n_1 - \beta b_2 n_2 = \beta x - a^* - b_1^* n_1 - b_2^* n_2 \tag{13.2.9}$$

where $a^* = a\beta > 0$ is the lump-sum subsidy given to every family, $b_1^* = \beta b_1 > 0$ is the credit per child, and $b_2^* = \beta b_2 > 0$ is the credit per adult in the family. Every family receives a total cash transfer $a^* + b_1^* n_1 + b_2^* n_2$, irrespective of its income. This amount is the negative income tax, but every family becomes subject to a β tax rate other than the allowance. βx is the tax paid by the family with income x.

Equation (13.2.9) yields the average tax per family collected by the government as

$$\bar{T} = \beta\mu - a^* - b_1^*\mu_{n_1} - b_2^*\mu_{n_2} \qquad (13.2.10)$$

where μ_{n_1} is the mean number of children, and μ_{n_2} is the mean number of adults in families. The government collects on average the positive amount of tax per family if $\mu > \frac{a^* + b_1^*\mu_{n_1} + b_2^*\mu_{n_2}}{\beta}$. The disposable income of the family with pre-tax income x will be

$$y(x) = (1 - \beta)x + a^* + b_1^*n_1 + b_2^*n_2, \qquad (13.2.11)$$

which also will always be positive if $0 < \beta < 1$.

The average tax rate under this plan is given by

$$\tilde{e} = \frac{\bar{T}}{\mu} = \frac{\beta\mu - a^* - b_1^*\mu_{n_1} - b_2^*\mu_{n_2}}{\mu}, \qquad (13.2.12)$$

which will always be less than one if the marginal tax rate $\beta < 1$. Further, $\beta > e$ will always hold. Thus, the marginal tax rate must satisfy $e < \beta < 1$. Also, it is easy to show from (13.2.12) that the average tax rate $\tilde{e}$ increases as β increases and decreases as a^*, b_1^* and b_2^* increase.

13.3 Alternative Negative Income Tax Plans

This section summarizes the well-known alternative negative income tax plans proposed in the literature.

13.3.1 The Friedman Plan

This plan determines the family's break-even level by the total value of exemptions and deductions for each family member. According to the 1964 tax laws in the United States, each family member has a $600 exemption and a $100 deduction, and the head of the family is allowed a deduction of $300. Each member is entitled to $700, but the family head receives an additional ($300 − $100) = $200. The plan applies a tax rate of 50% for both positive and negative income tax. Thus, under this plan $\beta = 0.5$, $a = 200, and $b = 700. The lump-sum cash subsidy given to each family is the tax credit per member of the family $b^* = 0.5 \times 700 = 350. Data from the United States Bureau of the Census for 1965 shows the average family size equal to 3.17. Thus, on average, the US families under this plan would receive a cash transfer of $100 + 3.17 \times 350 = $1,209$. The mean pre-tax income of the United States in 1965 was $6,603. Thus, on average, families would pay the tax of $3,301, so the net government revenue would be 3301− 1209 = $2,092. The plan generates the average tax revenue for the government equal to 2092/6603=31.7%.

13.3.2 The Lampman–Green Plan

This plan applies a rate of 50% on how the family's poverty standard differs from the actual income. The poverty level is $1,500 for the family head plus $500 for each dependant. So, the poverty threshold equals $1,500 + 500 (n - 1)$ for the family size n. Thus, under this plan $\beta = 0.5$, $a = \$1,000$, and $b = \$500$. The lump-sum cash subsidy to each family is $a^* = 0.5 \times \$1,000 = \$500$, and the tax credit per family member is $b^* = 0.5 \times 500 = \$250$. Using the US Census data, the families under this plan would receive, on average, the cash subsidy of $500 + 3.17 \times 250 = \$1,292$, and pay the average tax of $3,301, so the net government revenue would be $3,301-$1,292=$2,009$. The plan generates the average tax rate for the government equal to 30.4%.

13.3.3 The Tobin Plan

This plan pays a basic allowance of $500 to every family member, which is subject to tax at a rate of 33.33% on income other than the allowance. Tobin also merges the negative tax with the present positive tax system, but this scenario will not be explored. Thus under this plan, $\beta = 0.333$, $a = 0$, and $b\beta = 500$, which means that the lump-sum cash subsidy to each family is $a^* = 0$, and the tax credit per member of the family is $b^* = \$500$. Using the US Census data, the US families under this plan would receive, on average, the total cash subsidy of $0 + 3.17 \times 500 = \$1,585$. The families would, on average, pay a tax equal to $0.333 \times 6603 = \$2,199$. The government's average net tax revenue would be $2199-1585=$614$. The plan generates the average tax rate for the government equal to 9.3%.

13.3.4 The Rolph Plan

This plan is similar to Tobin's plan, except that a tax rate of 30% instead of 33.33% is applied. Under this plan, $\beta = 0.3$ and $b^* = 500$. The average cash subsidy to families is $1,585, which would pay an average tax equal to $0.3 \times 6603 = \$1,981$. The government's average net tax revenue would be $1981-1585=$396$. The plan generates the average tax rate for the government equal to 6%.

13.3.5 The Smith Plan

This plan is the only one that provides for the differing needs of children and adults within a family. The plan pays $1,000 a year for each adult and $200 a year for each child. Each family is then subject to a tax rate of 40%. Thus, under this plan, $\beta = 0.40$, $a^* = 0$, $b_1^* = \$200$, and $b_2^* = \$1,000$. Using the US Census data, the average number of children is 1.16, and the average number of adults is 2.01, so the average family size is 3.17. The families under this plan would receive, on average, the cash subsidy of $0 + 1.16 \times 200 + 2.01 \times 1,000 = \$2,242$. The families pay an average tax of $0.4 \times 6,603 = \$2,641$. The average net tax revenue to the government would be $399. The plan generates the average tax rate for the government equal to 6.1%.

13.4 Progressivity of Negative Income Tax Plans

Applying Theorem 9.6 in Chapter 9 on (13.2.4) gives the concentration index of tax as

$$C_T = \left(\beta\mu G - b^*\mu_n C_n\right)/\overline{T} \tag{13.4.1}$$

where G is the Gini index of family income, and $\overline{T}$ is the average tax collected by the government, defined in (13.2.5). Note that the derivation of (13.4.1) utilized the following facts: the concentration index of a constant is zero; the Gini index of βx is β times the Gini index of x; and the concentration index of $b^* n$ is equal to b^* times the concentration index of n, denoted by C_n.

Chapter 12 distinguished between absolute and relative measures of tax progressivity. An absolute measure of progressivity indicates the extent to which a tax system deviates from a situation where everyone pays the same amount of tax. A tax system is absolutely progressive (regressive) when wealthier persons pay more (less) tax than the more impoverished persons (see Axiom 11.1 in Chapter 11). The concentration index of tax measures absolute tax progressivity. Thus, the absolute measure of tax progressivity obtained from (13.4.1) is given by

$$\theta_A = C_T = \frac{\left(\beta\mu G - b^*\mu_n C_n\right)}{\overline{T}} > 0 \ if \ C_n < 0. \tag{13.4.2}$$

This equation implies that if the family size decreases as family income increases (meaning the numbers of family members are more concentrated among the lower-income families), the negative income tax plans will always be absolutely progressive. But, if the family size increases with the family income, when $C_n > 0$, from (13.4.2), one cannot infer whether negative income tax plans are absolutely progressive or regressive. Under this scenario, one cannot know whether the poor will pay more taxes relative to the rich. This situation is at odds with the essential purpose of negative income tax plans to support the poor. In practice, this situation might be unlikely because wealthier families tend to be smaller in size.

Differentiating partially θ_A with respect to $\beta, a,^*$ and b^* results in the following elasticities

$$\eta_\beta^A = \frac{\partial\theta_A\beta}{\partial\beta\theta_A} = \frac{\mu\beta\left(G - \theta_A\right)}{\overline{T}\theta_A} < 0 \ if \ C_n < 0 \tag{13.4.3}$$

$$\eta_{a^*}^A = \frac{\partial\theta_A a^*}{\partial a^*\theta_A} = \frac{a^*}{\overline{T}} > 0 \tag{13.4.4}$$

$$\eta_{b^*}^A = \frac{\partial \theta_A b^*}{\partial b^* \theta_A} = \frac{\mu_n \left(\theta_A - C_n\right) b^*}{T\theta_A} > 0 \; if \, C_n < 0 \qquad (13.4.5)$$

If $C_n < 0$, equation (13.4.3) shows that the absolute tax progressivity of the negative income tax plans continuously decreases as the marginal tax rate increases. Equations (13.4.4) and (13.4.5) show that the lump-sum cash subsidy a^* and the size of credit per family member b^* increase absolute progressivity. The elasticities in these equations will inform how sensitive absolute tax progressivity is with respect to changes in β, a^*, and b^*. If the social objective is to increase tax progressivity, it is essential to minimize the marginal tax rate and maximize the lump-sum cash subsidy and credit per family member.

Next, consider the Smith plan, which distinguishes the differing needs of children and adults within a family. The tax function for this plan is given in (13.2.9). Applying Theorem 9.6 in Chapter 9 on (13.2.9) yields the absolute tax progressivity index as

$$\tilde{\theta}_A = C_T = \frac{\beta \mu G - b_1^* \mu_{n_1} C_{n_1} - b_2^* \mu_{n_2} C_{n_2}}{\overline{T}} \qquad (13.4.6)$$

where C_{n_1} and C_{n_2} are the concentration indices of children and adults within the families, and $\overline{T}$ is given in (13.2.10). From (13.4.6), note that $\tilde{\theta}_A > 0$ if $C_{n_1} < 0$ and $C_{n_2} < 0$, implying that the tax function in (13.2.9) will always be absolutely progressive if the number of adults and children in the families decreases with the family income. If these requirements are not met, one cannot infer whether the rich will pay more tax than the poor.

Differentiating both sides of $\tilde{\theta}_A$ in (13.4.6) with respect to β, a^*, b_1^*, b_2^* yields the tax progressivity elasticities:

$$\tilde{\eta}_{\beta}^A = \frac{\partial \tilde{\theta}_A \beta}{\partial \beta \tilde{\theta}_A} = \frac{\mu \beta \left(G - \tilde{\theta}_A\right)}{\overline{T}\tilde{\theta}_A} < 0 \; if \, C_{n_1} < 0 \, and \, C_{n_1} < 0 \qquad (13.4.7)$$

$$\tilde{\eta}_{a^*}^A = \frac{\partial \tilde{\theta}_A a^*}{\partial a^* \tilde{\theta}_A} = \frac{a^*}{\overline{T}} > 0 \qquad (13.4.8)$$

$$\tilde{\eta}_{b_1^*}^A = \frac{\partial \tilde{\theta}_A b_1^*}{\partial b_1^* \tilde{\theta}_A} = \frac{\mu_{n_1} \left(\tilde{\theta}_A - C_{n_1}\right) b_1^*}{\overline{T}\tilde{\theta}_A} < 0 \; if \, C_{n_1} < 0 \, and \, C_{n_2} < 0 \qquad (13.4.9)$$

$$\tilde{\eta}_{b_2^*}^A = \frac{\partial \tilde{\theta}_A b_2^*}{\partial b_2^* \tilde{\theta}_A} = \frac{\mu_{n_2} \left(\tilde{\theta}_A - C_{n_2}\right) b_2^*}{\overline{T}\tilde{\theta}_A} < 0 \; if \, C_{n_1} < 0 \, and \, C_{n_2} < 0. \qquad (13.4.10)$$

The elasticities will help evaluate the alternative Smith negative income tax plans.

As discussed in Chapter 11, the relative measures of tax progressivity indicate the extent to which a given tax system deviates from proportionality when everyone pays tax at the same rate. The Kakwani index is a relative measure of tax progressivity, which from (13.4.2) is obtained as

$$\theta_R = \theta_A - G = \frac{a^* G + b^* \mu_n (G - C_n)}{\overline{T}} > 0 \, if \, G > C_n \qquad (13.4.11)$$

From equation (9.7.3) in Chapter 9, it follows that the aggregate elasticity of family size n with respect to x will be less than one if $G > C_n$. Under this scenario, negative tax plans will always be relatively progressive; the wealthier families pay taxes at a higher rate. If $G < C_n$, the aggregate elasticity of family with respect to x will be greater than one; it is impossible to make a priori judgment whether the negative income tax plans will always be relatively progressive. In practice, the family size elasticity is unlikely to exceed one because the proportional increase in family size is generally less than the proportional increase in income.

From (13.4.11), note that if $\theta_R > 0$, $\theta_A > G$, implying that if a negative income tax plan is relatively progressive, it will also be absolute progressive. But vice-versa is not valid—that is, if a negative income tax plan is an absolute progressive, it may not be necessarily relatively progressive. Relative progressivity is a stronger requirement than absolute progressivity.

Elasticities of θ_R with respect to β, a^* and b^* are derived as

$$\eta_\beta^R = \frac{\partial \theta_R \beta}{\partial \beta \theta_R} = -\frac{\mu \beta}{\overline{T}} < 0 \qquad (13.4.12)$$

$$\eta_{a^*}^R = \frac{\partial \theta_R a^*}{\partial a^* \theta_R} = \frac{a^* (\theta_R + G)}{\overline{T} \theta_R} > 0 \, if \, G > C_n$$

$$\eta_{b^*}^R = \frac{\partial \theta_R b^*}{\partial b^* \theta_R} = \frac{\mu_n ((\theta_R + G - C_n) b^*}{\overline{T} \theta_R} > 0 \, if \, G > C_n.$$

The relative measure of progressivity of the Smith negative income tax plan will be given by

$$\tilde{\theta}_R = \tilde{\theta}_A - G = \frac{a^* G + b_1^* \mu_{n_1} (G - _{n_1}) + b_2^* \mu_{n_2} (G - C_{n_2})}{\overline{T}} > 0$$

$$if \, G - C_{n_1} > 0 \, and \, G - C_{n_2} > 0 \qquad (13.4.13)$$

$\tilde{\theta}_A$ is the absolute measure of progressivity given in (13.4.6). This equation implies that the Smith plan will always be relatively progressive if the overall elasticities of children and adults within a family with respect to the family income are less than unity. It is unlikely that these elasticities will be greater than one because the number of children and adults does not, in reality, increase at the same proportion as family income.

Differentiating both sides of $\tilde{\theta}_R$ in (13.4.13) with respect to $\beta, a^*, b_1^*,$ and b_2^* yields the tax progressivity elasticities:

$$\tilde{\eta}_\beta^R = \frac{\partial \tilde{\theta}_R \beta}{\partial \beta \tilde{\theta}_R} = -\frac{\mu \beta}{\overline{T}} < 0$$

$$\tilde{\eta}_{a^*}^R = \frac{\partial \tilde{\theta}_R a^*}{\partial a^* \tilde{\theta}_R} = \frac{a^* \left(\theta_R + G\right)}{\overline{T}\theta_R} > 0 \, if \, G - C_{n_1} > 0 \, and \, G - C_{n_1} > 0$$

$$\tilde{\eta}_{b_1^*}^R = \frac{\partial \tilde{\theta}_R b_1^*}{\partial b_1^* \tilde{\theta}_R} = \frac{\left[\mu_{n_1} \left(G - C_{n_1}\right) + \tilde{\theta}_R \mu_{n_1}\right] b_1^*}{\overline{T}\theta_R} > 0 \, if \, G - C_{n_1} > 0 \, and \, G - C_{n_1} > 0$$

$$\tilde{\eta}_{b_2^*}^R = \frac{\partial \tilde{\theta}_R b_2^*}{\partial b_2^* \tilde{\theta}_R} = \frac{\left[\mu_{n_1} \left(G - C_{n_1}\right) + \tilde{\theta}_R \mu_{n_1}\right] b_1^*}{\overline{T}\theta_R} > 0 \, if \, G - C_{n_1} > 0 \, and \, G - C_{n_1} > 0.$$

These elasticities enable evaluating the sensitivity of negative income tax plans to their relative progressivity. They can be crucial in designing negative tax plans to maximize their progressivity.

13.5 Redistributive Impacts of Negative Income Tax

The previous section analyzed the impact of negative income tax plans on tax progressivity. This section explores their redistributive effects, meaning how much they reduce income inequality. If they increase inequality, such plans should be deemed anti-poor. This section also distinguishes the relative and absolute measures of redistributive effects.

13.5.1 Relative Measures of Redistributive Effect

Suppose G_y is the Gini index of the disposable income $y(x)$ defined in (13.2.7), and G is the Gini index of the pre-tax income x, then the relative measure of redistributive effect of negative income tax plans is given by

$$\tau_R = \frac{G_y - G}{G}. \tag{13.5.1}$$

If τ_R is less (greater) than zero, the negative income tax plans reduce (increase) income inequality. Equation (11.9.7) in Chapter 11 presented the following decomposition:

$$\tau_R = \frac{G_y - G}{G} = \left(\frac{G_y - C_y}{G}\right) - \frac{e\theta_R}{(1-e)\,G} \tag{13.5.2}$$

where e is the average tax rate defined in (13.2.6), and C_y is the concentration index of the disposable income $y(x)$. θ_R is the relative measure of tax progressivity defined in (13.4.11). The first term on the right-hand side of (13.5.2) measures the impact of change in ranking between the pre-tax and post-tax incomes, which equals zero if there is no change in ranking due to the negative income tax plans. And, if $H = \left(\frac{G_y - C_y}{G}\right) > 0$, it implies that the change in ranking increases income inequality. In Chapter 11, H was interpreted as a measure of horizontal inequity.

It is clear from (13.5.2) that given other things constant, the progressive negative income plans reduced the after-tax inequality. Also, the larger the value of e, the smaller the after-tax income inequality. As θ_R and e increase, the after-tax income inequality decreases. Chapter 11 interpreted $V = -\frac{e\theta_R}{(1-e)G}$ as a measure of vertical equity in taxation.

The concentration curve for the disposable income $y(x)$ as defined in (13.2.7) coincides with the Lorenz curve for $y(x)$ if the ranking of families according to their disposable income is identical to their ranking according to their pre-tax income. If there is no change in ranking, the first term on the right-hand side of (13.5.1) will be zero. There will be no change in ranking if $\frac{\partial y(x)}{dx} > 0$ for all x. This condition is satisfied if

$$\frac{\partial n}{\partial x} > -\frac{1-\beta}{b^*} \text{ for all } x. \tag{13.5.3}$$

In practice, it is not known if $\partial n/\partial x$ is positive or negative at all income levels. If it is positive for all x, then the condition in (13.5.3) will always be satisfied, implying $H=0$, in which case only the vertical equity will determine the redistributive effect of the negative income tax. It is noted from (13.4.11) that θ_R is always positive if $C_n < G$. From Theorem 9.9 in Chapter 9, note that $\frac{\partial n}{\partial x} > 0$ for all x implies that $C_n > 0$, but the converse of which may not hold, meaning that $C_n > 0$ does not imply $\frac{\partial n}{\partial x} > 0$ for all x. Hence, there may be a change in ranking between the post- and pre-tax incomes so that H would be positive, meaning that the first term on the right-hand side of (13.5.2) would be positive. Therefore, it is not possible to infer that the relatively progressive negative income tax plan will always show a reduction in income inequality.

Next, consider the Smith plan, the relative redistributive effect of which will be given by

$$\tilde{\tau}_R = \frac{\tilde{G}_y - G}{G} = \left(\frac{\tilde{G}_y - \tilde{C}_y}{G}\right) - \frac{\tilde{e}\tilde{\theta}_R}{(1-\tilde{e})G}. \qquad (13.5.4)$$

$\tilde{G}_y$ and $\tilde{C}_y$ are the Gini and concentration indices of the disposable income $y(x)$ of the Smith plan defined in (13.2.11), respectively. $\tilde{e}$ is the average tax rate of the Smith plan given in (13.2.12) and $\tilde{\theta}_R$ is the relative measure of tax progressivity of the Smith plan defined in (13.4.12). Under the Smith plan, the disposable income $y(x)$ defined in (13.2.11) will have the same ranking as x if $\frac{\partial y(x)}{dx} > 0$ if for all x, which will always be satisfied if $\frac{\partial n_1}{\partial x} > 0$ and $\frac{\partial n_2}{\partial x} > 0$ for all x. Hence under these conditions, there will be no change in ranking between $y(x)$ and x. So, the first term on the right-hand side of (13.5.3), measuring the horizontal inequity of the Smith plan given by $\tilde{H}$, will be zero, and therefore, the redistributive effect of the Smith plan will be determined by the vertical equity $\tilde{V} = -\frac{\tilde{e}\tilde{\theta}_R}{(1-\tilde{e})G}$. It is also noted from (13.4.12) that $\tilde{\theta}_R$ will always be positive if $C_{n_1} < G$ and $C_{n_2} < G$. From Theorem 9.9 in Chapter 9, it follows that $\frac{\partial n_1}{\partial x} > 0$ and $\frac{\partial n_2}{\partial x} > 0$ for all x always imply $C_{n_1} > 0$ and $C_{n_2} > 0$, respectively, but the converse of which may not hold, meaning that $C_{n_1} > 0$ and $C_{n_2} > 0$ do not necessarily imply $\frac{\partial n_1}{\partial x} > 0$ and $\frac{\partial n_2}{\partial x} > 0$ for all x. Hence, the first term on the right-hand side of (13.5.3) given by $\tilde{H}$ could be positive. Therefore, it is not possible to infer that the relatively progressive Smith plan will always show a reduction in income inequality.

This section concludes that negative income plans may not always reduce income inequality even though they are relatively progressive. If the negative income tax plans increase income inequality, the introduction of such plans should be deemed questionable.

13.5.2 Absolute Measure of Redistributive Effect

The absolute measure of redistributive effect is the change in absolute inequality between pre- and post-income inequality:

$$\tau_A = \mu_y G_y - \mu G \qquad (13.5.5)$$

where μ is the mean income of the pre-tax income and $\mu_y = \mu(1-e)$ is the mean income of the post-tax income. Note that τ_A does not change when everyone's pre-tax income increases or decreases by the same amount. If τ_A is less (greater) than zero, the negative income tax plans reduce (increase) absolute income inequality.

Substituting $k = 1$ in equation (12.7.14), Chapter 12 yields the absolute redistributive effect of negative income tax plans as

$$\tau_A = \mu_y \left(G_y - C_y \right) - \theta_A \tag{13.5.6}$$

where θ_A is the absolute measure of tax progressivity defined in (13.4.2). This equation shows that if a negative income tax plan is absolute progressive, it reduces the post-tax income inequality, provided there is no change in ranking. $H_A = \mu_y \left(G_y - C_y \right)$ is an absolute measure of horizontal inequity, which is zero when there is no change in ranking due to a negative income tax plan. If there is a change in ranking, $H_A > 0$, it implies that the horizontal inequity increases the post-tax income inequality. The vertical equity is given by $V = -\theta_A$, which is negative when the progressivity index $\theta_A > 0$. The absolute progressive negative income tax contributes to a reduction in absolute inequality. If there is a change in ranking, the first term on the right-hand side of (13.5.6) is positive, and the second term is negative. Hence, absolute inequality can increase even when a negative income tax system is absolute progressive.

No change in ranking requires $\frac{\partial n}{\partial x} > 0$ for all x, which implies $C_n > 0$. From (13.4.2), it noted that $\theta_A > 0$ will always hold if $C_n < 0$. The two conditions $C_n > 0$ and $C_n < 0$ cannot hold simultaneously, so one cannot infer if the negative income tax plans will always reduce the post-tax absolute income inequality. The same conclusion will emerge for the Smith negative income tax plan.

13.6 A Numerical Illustration Using US data

Based on 1964 income data from Current Population Reports of the US Bureau of the Census Department of Commerce, Series P-60, No. 47, this section evaluates the five negative income tax plans discussed above. Income includes money wages or salary, net income from non-farm self-employment, net income from farm self-employment, social security, interest (on savings or bonds), dividends and income from estates or trusts, rent, unemployment compensation, and other sources, such as private or government pensions.

The data were available in groups consisting of 17 income classes. Each income class's midpoint was used to approximate each income class's mean income below $15,000. A $19,000 was used as the mean income for the group $15,000 to $24,000 interval. For the income interval $25,000 and over, the Pareto curve was fitted to estimate the mean income. The average family size and the average number of children and adults in each income class were extracted from the first five current population reports. The Gini index of income and concentration indices of the average family size and number of children and adults were estimated by fitting the new coordinate curve equation discussed in Chapter 3. Table 13.1 gives these estimates.

The concentration indices were calculated by arranging all families in the increasing order of their income. The family size has a concentration index of 0.115, which is

Table 13.1 Distribution of income and family composition: United States, 1965

Mean income: $ per year	6,603
Mean household size	3.17
Mean number of children	1.16
Mean number of adults	2.01
Gini of pre-tax income	0.407
Concentration index of household size	0.115
Concentration index of number of children	0.14
Concentration index of number of adults	0.10

Table 13.2 Alternative negative income tax plans

Negative income tax plans	Marginal tax rate	Lump-sum cash subsidy	Tax credit per family member
Friedman	0.5	100	350
Lampman–Green	0.5	500	250
Tobin	0.33	0	500
Rolph	0.3	0	500
Smith	0.4	0	
Children			200
Adults			1,000

positive, implying the family size increases as the family income increases. Also, the concentration index is much lower than the Gini index of income, 0.407. This means that family members are more evenly distributed across income ranges than the family income. Similarly, the adults' concentration index is 0.10, smaller than the children's, 0.14. This implies that adults within families are more evenly distributed across income ranges than children.

Table 13.2 presents a summary of the alternative negative income tax plans. The plans differ in three parameters: average tax rate, lump-sum cash subsidy, and tax credit. Smith's plan distinguishes between children and adults in the family, and it specifies the tax credit for each child equal to $200 and each adult equal to $1,000. All five plans assume that the tax rate is the same for positive and negative income tax plans.

The first two plans have the same marginal tax rates, but Friedman's plan provides more benefits to the larger families than the Lampman–Green plan. The Tobin, Rolph, and Smith plans do not offer any lump-sum cash subsidy, so family benefits are proportional to family size or composition. They do not take account of economies of scale that occur in larger families.

Table 13.3 shows that all negative income tax plans have positive and negative income taxes. The average positive income tax paid by families is proportional to the tax rate applied to the family income; the higher the tax rate, the higher the average positive income tax. The average negative income tax depends on two factors: lump-sum cash subsidy given to each family and tax credit, which depends on family size.

Table 13.3 Average positive, negative, and net average government revenue

Negative income plans	Average positive income tax	Average negative income tax	Net average government tax revenue	Average tax rate
Friedman	3302	1210	2092	0.32
Lampman–Green	3302	1293	2009	0.30
Tobin	2179	1585	594	0.09
Rolph	1981	1585	396	0.06
Smith	2641	2242	399	0.06

All five plans generate positive net revenue for the government to finance expenditures other than transfers to families. Thus, the effect of these alternative plans is not purely redistributive.

The average negative income tax is highest for the Smith plan, and Tobin's and Rolph's plans have the same average negative income tax but differ in the average positive income tax. The last column in the table shows that the average tax rate, defined as the average net government revenue as the proportion of average total household income, differs considerably under different plans. The Friedman and Lampman–Green plans provide substantial tax revenue to the government but smaller transfers to families. At the same time, the remaining three plans offer significantly larger transfers to families but generate smaller revenue for the government.

Table 13.4 presents the different plans' absolute and relative tax progressivity measures. The plans differ considerably in their degree of progressivity, and Friedman's plan is the least progressive, whereas Smith's plan is the most progressive. The relative progressivity measure for Rolph's and Smith's plans exceeds one, which indicates that a larger proportion of lower-income families are paying negative taxes, meaning that they are receiving cash transfers and not paying taxes. Chapter 12 discussed the welfare implications of tax progressivity, which showed that the greater the progressivity index's value, the greater the social welfare gain. Tables 13.3 and 13.4 show that higher social welfare gain leads to lower net tax revenue for the government. The Friedman and Lampman–Green plans generate minor social welfare gains compared with the remaining three plans but generate higher net tax revenue for the government. Thus, the empirical results suggest that there can be a trade-off between social welfare gains and government revenue.

How do the different negative income tax plans redistribute income? In other words, how do they impact post-tax income inequality? As discussed, the redistributive effect depends on the sum of horizontal inequity, which increases income inequality when there is a change in ranking, and vertical equity decreases income inequality when tax is progressive. The vertical equity further depends on tax progressivity and the average tax rate, and the vertical equity for an absolute redistributive effect does not depend on the average tax rate.

Table 13.4 Tax progressivity and redistributive effects of alternative negative income tax plans

	Progressivity		Vertical equity	
	Absolute	Relative	Absolute	Relative
Friedman	0.62	0.22	−0.62	−0.10
Lampman–Green	0.65	0.25	−0.65	−0.11
Tobin	1.40	0.99	−1.40	−0.10
Rolph	1.89	1.48	−1.89	−0.09
Smith	2.11	1.70	−2.11	−0.11

The US data used in this application are available only in group form. Therefore, it was not possible to calculate the horizontal inequity from these data because the grouped data could not capture the effect of rank change. The individual unit record data could only capture the rank change to measure horizontal inequity. Many empirical studies have shown that the impact of horizontal inequity on inequality is relatively insignificant. Hence, the redistributive effect could be approximated by vertical equity. The last two columns of Table 13.4 present vertical equity estimates for absolute and relative redistributive effect concepts.

The absolute concept of vertical equity measures how much a negative income tax plan impacts absolute inequality. At the same time, the relative concept of vertical equity measures the impact on relative inequality. The two concepts lead to different conclusions about the equity of negative income tax plans. According to the absolute concept, the Friedman plan is the least redistributive, and the Smith plan has the most impact on the redistributive effect. The relative notion of vertical equity shows that all negative income tax plans do not differ significantly from their redistributive effects. The reason is that the plans differ substantially from their average tax rates. The Friedman plan generates an average tax rate of 32%, while the Smith plan has only 6%. The larger is the average tax rate, the higher is the relative vertical equity. While it does not impact vertical equity's absolute measure, the average rate significantly impacts the relative measure of vertical equity.

Which of the two notions of redistributive effect should be used in evaluating tax policies? It is not simple to answer this question. Both absolute and relative inequality concepts have attractive features, but most of the literature focuses on the relative notion of inequality. A compromised solution is that policymakers should be presented with both concepts.

The various negative income tax plans generate vastly different tax rates for the government. Comparing the tax progressivity of these plans would be more meaningful if they yielded the same tax rate. It would then be possible to know how much the progressivity of different plans would be if they produced the same average tax rate (or the same average revenue for the government). It would be simple to assume that all plans maintain the same lump-sum cash subsidy given to each family and tax credit, depending on family size, but vary the marginal tax rates so that all plans would yield

Table 13.5 Tax progressivity when alternative negative income tax plans have the same tax rate

	Tax rate of 10%		Tax rate of 20%		Tax rate of 30%	
Progressivity	Absolute	Relative	Absolute	Relative	Absolute	Relative
Friedman	1.09	0.68	0.75	0.34	0.64	0.23
Lampman–Green	1.14	0.74	0.77	0.37	0.65	0.25
Tobin	1.32	0.92	0.87	0.46	0.71	0.31
Rolph	1.32	0.92	0.87	0.46	0.71	0.31
Smith	1.44	1.03	0.92	0.51	0.75	0.34

Table 13.6 Redistributive effect of negative income tax plans with different average tax rates

	Tax rate of 10%		Tax rate of 20%		Tax rate of 30%	
	Absolute	Relative	Absolute	Relative	Absolute	Relative
Friedman	−1.09	−0.08	−0.75	−0.09	−0.64	−0.10
Lampman–Green	−1.14	−0.08	−0.77	−0.09	−0.65	−0.11
Tobin	−1.32	−0.10	−0.87	−0.11	−0.71	−0.13
Rolph	−1.32	−0.10	−0.87	−0.11	−0.71	−0.13
Smith	−1.44	−0.11	−0.92	−0.13	−0.75	−0.15

the same average tax rates. The marginal tax rates for each negative income tax plan were determined to generate the same average tax rates. The simulations were performed using 10%, 15%, and 20% tax rates. Table 13.5 gives the empirical estimates of tax progressivity of plans for three alternative average tax rates.

The empirical results show that the progressivity decreases as the average tax rate increases from 10% to 30% for each negative income tax plan. There is a monotonically declining relationship between progressivity and the average tax rate. Further, although all plans yield the same average tax rate, they differ considerably in their progressivity. Smith's plan gives the highest value of progressivity, and the Friedman plan the lowest value. These results show that if governments want to increase their revenue, society achieves lower progressivity. Thus, in designing negative tax plans, the trade-off between government revenue and progressivity must be considered.

Table 13.6 shows how vertical equity changes as the average tax rate increases. The net effect of the two factors, as indicated in Table 13.6, is that the vertical equity rises with the rising average tax rate. This result is at odds with the declining progressivity when the average tax rate increases, and this can be explained. The rise in the average tax rate dominates the fall in tax progressivity, resulting in a net decrease in relative inequality. However, the vertical equity based on the absolute concept is unchanged as the average tax rate changes.

This empirical application has evaluated the five well-known negative income tax plans using the two tax principles: tax progressivity and redistributive effect of taxes. The two alternative concepts of tax progressivity, absolute and relative, can lead to different conclusions.

13.7 Concluding Remarks

The idea of negative income tax plans and guaranteed income schemes evolved in the 1960s. They instantly became a popular policy. They had dual purposes: first, they generate revenue for governments to perform their regular operations, and second, they provide the minimum guaranteed income to low-income families. The objective of negative income tax proposals was to extend the income tax rates beyond zero to negative levels. The cash transfers to families were viewed as a negative income tax. Families having an income below a break-even level received transfers, and those above the threshold paid tax.

The negative tax plans determine the break-even income by the size or composition of the family. This chapter has developed a general framework incorporating all the well-known negative income tax plans proposed in the literature. Using this framework, the chapter has developed methods of comparing the progressivity and redistribution effects of alternative negative income plans.

The chapter derived absolute and relative tax progressivity measures from the general framework of negative income tax plans. Absolute progressivity implies that wealthier persons pay higher taxes. In contrast, relative progressivity means that the wealthier persons pay taxes at a higher rate. Relative progressivity is a stronger requirement than absolute progressivity.

The evaluation of alternative negative income tax plans combines family income and family size and composition. A family's needs crucially depend on their composition; therefore, it is more realistic to consider family income and family composition in the design of negative income plans. This realism makes the evaluation of plans considerably complex.

The first complexity that arises is that it is unknown whether the wealthier families have larger or smaller family sizes. Also, the relationship between family composition and family income is not known. Given these problems, the evaluation of negative income tax plans becomes complex. This chapter, however, has derived the conditions under which the negative income plans are always progressive. It demonstrates that negative income tax plans will always be progressive if the family size decreases as family income increases (meaning the family members are more concentrated among the lower-income families). But, if the family size increases with the family income, it is impossible to infer whether negative income tax plans are absolutely progressive or regressive. Under this scenario, it is impossible to figure out whether the poor will pay more taxes than the rich. This situation is at odds with the essential purpose of negative income tax plans to support the poor. However, this situation might be unlikely in practice because wealthier families tend to be smaller in size.

This chapter has also provided an empirical assessment of alternative negative income tax plans using the 1964 income data from Current Population Reports of the US Bureau of the Census. The empirical results showed that Friedman's plan is the least progressive, whereas Smith's plan is the most progressive. The relative progressivity measure for Rolph's and Smith's plans exceeds one, which indicated that a larger proportion of lower-income families are paying negative taxes, meaning that they are receiving cash transfers and not paying tax.

As argued in Chapter 12, progressivity measures have welfare interpretations; the greater the progressivity measures, the higher the social welfare gains. The empirical results showed that the Friedman and Lampman–Green plans generate minor social welfare gains compared with the remaining three plans from Tobin, Rolph, and Smith but generate higher net tax revenue for the government. Thus, it is concluded that there could be a trade-off between social welfare gains and government revenue.

This chapter also explored how the different negative income tax plans redistribute income, that is, how they impact post-tax income inequality. If they increase inequality, such plans should be deemed anti-poor and not recommended. The chapter showed analytically that negative tax plans might increase income inequality under certain conditions. A striking result emerging from this analysis is that absolute and relative inequality concepts can give conflicting conclusions about their impact on post-tax income inequality.

Which of the two notions of redistributive effect should be used in evaluating tax policies? It is not simple to answer this question. Both absolute and relative inequality concepts have attractive features, but most of the literature focuses on the relative notion of inequality. A compromise will be to analyze tax-transfer policies using both concepts.

In the 1960s and 1970s, the negative income tax plans attracted enormous attention from policymakers and academic economists. Many experiments were conducted to simulate the disincentive effects of the plans. Economists showed deep interest in the plans. However, no country in the world has ever adopted any such plan. These plans have attractive features that consider the incomes of households and their needs based on their household composition. They can play an essential role in simultaneously reducing poverty and inequality. This chapter has provided a rigorous evaluation of the alternative negative income tax plans. It is hoped that the analysis presented in the chapter will revive interest in these plans.

14

Targeting Tools to Evaluate Social Programs

14.1 Introduction

Governments need revenue to perform their everyday operations. They collect revenues from several sources. Among them, taxation provides the largest share of their total revenue. Since the introduction of progressive income tax, many government taxation policies have included income redistribution as a major goal. With the recent emergence of welfare states, social programs, particularly in developed countries, have been accepted as social norms. A growing number of developing countries invest in various social programs to improve the welfare of their people, particularly the poor and vulnerable.

These programs have become an essential pillar of economic development policies. The number of targeted programs has increased many folds in developing countries. For example, Coady, Grosh, and Hoddinott (2004) have listed 85 programs in 36 developing countries. The World Bank report, "The State of Social Safety Nets 2015," states that as many as 1.9 billion people are beneficiaries of safety net programs (Kakwani and Son 2016). These programs intend to provide income to the poor or those who face a potential risk of falling into poverty.

Given the popularity of these programs, it has become essential to evaluate them rigorously so that policymakers know the extent to which they meet their intended objectives. The primary goals of these programs are to reduce poverty and improve people's welfare. Targeting is a method to improve program efficiency to achieve the program objectives of maximizing poverty reduction with minimum cost. This chapter discusses evaluation methodologies of social programs to know whether they reach their intended purpose.

There are two distinct issues in designing targeted programs: First is identifying the deserving beneficiaries who are the neediest, and second is deciding how much transfers should be given to them to meet their minimum basic needs. Thus, targeting efficiency is judged by two targeting methods: (i) beneficiary incidence and (ii) benefit incidence. This chapter discusses both types of targeting methods to assess the effectiveness of government social programs.

When anyone invests in any project, their concern is how much the rate of return from investment would be. Using a similar idea, when the government invests in a social program, it should be concerned with the program's social rate of return (SRR). It should judge the efficacy of a social program based on how much it generates social welfare in relation to its operational cost. The chapter introduces the SRR, defined as

Economic Inequality and Poverty. Nanak Kakwani and Hyun Son, Oxford University Press.
© Nanak Kakwani and Hyun Son (2022). DOI: 10.1093/oso/9780198852841.003.0014

social welfare as a percentage of the program's cost.[1] A low or negative SRR signifies that the program does not achieve its intended objective of reducing poverty with minimum cost. Targeting indicators proposed in the literature do not consider the cost of programs. It is essential to judge a program's efficiency based on how much the government invests in it and how much social welfare the program generates.

China's Minimum Living Standard Guarantee program (Dibao) is the world's most extensive social safety net program. The government first introduced the program in urban areas in the 1990s but extended it to rural areas in early 2000s. The rural Dibao became more popular than the urban Dibao, covering 42.72 million individual beneficiaries. Kakwani, Li, Wang, and Zhu (2019) evaluated the program. This chapter describes several methods for assessing government programs' effectiveness and applying them to China's rural Dibao program.

14.2 Targeting Indicators

Targeting the poor is not a problem if people's economic situation is known. The primary challenge in designing social programs is that accurate information about people's economic situation is often unknown. In the absence of such information, targeting methods are used to obtain the maximum benefits for the needy and most vulnerable members of society. Targeting is a means of reaching the poor. Targeting indicators evaluate the existing programs so that policymakers know whether they meet the intended objectives of maximizing poverty reduction with minimum cost. This chapter provides a thorough review of several targeting tools proposed in the literature.

In his influential paper, Ravallion (2009) concluded that the standard targeting indicators are uninformative, or even deceptive, about the impact of poverty programs and cost-effectiveness in reducing poverty. He arrived at this conclusion without exploring the welfare implications of the targeting indicators. This chapter shows that all targeting indicators presented in the literature have a meaningful social welfare interpretation. Using the Chi-square distribution, it also develops a new targeting indicator derived from a contingency table.

14.3 Poverty Status and Selection of Beneficiaries

Perfect targeting must ensure that all beneficiaries are poor and non-beneficiaries are non-poor. If all persons' exact economic situation is unknown, it is impossible to achieve perfect targeting. This chapter attempts to derive a targeting method that selects beneficiaries whose economic situation correlates positively with their poverty status. The higher is this correlation, the better will be the targeting.

---

[1] The idea of SRR has been developed by Kakwani and Son (2016).

Suppose N is the total population of individuals; among them N_p are the poor, then the head-count ratio of poverty is given by

$$H = \frac{N_p}{N}$$

Assume that N_b are the total number of program beneficiaries, then the probability of selecting a beneficiary in the population is given by

$$B = \frac{N_b}{N}$$

Ideally, all program beneficiaries must be poor, and it is impossible to achieve this without complete information about people's financial situation.

Suppose among N_b beneficiaries N_{bp} are poor, and the remaining $N_b - N_{bp}$ are non-poor. The probability of selecting a beneficiary among the poor is given by

$$B_p = \frac{N_{bp}}{N_p}$$

Similarly, the probability of selecting a beneficiary among the non-poor is given by

$$B_n = \frac{(N_b - N_{bp})}{(N - N_p)}.$$

Suppose there is no association between the actual poor and the selection of a benefi-ciary. In that case, the probability of choosing a beneficiary among the poor must be equal to the probability of selecting a beneficiary among the non-poor. In other words, the poor are as likely to be chosen as the non-poor, in which case $B_p = B_n$. This situ-ation may have no information about the poor, so everyone has the same probability of being selected in the program.

A program may be called pro poor if the probability of selecting a beneficiary among the poor is higher than that among the non-poor—that is, when

$$B_p - B_n > 0.$$

In a pro-poor program, the poor are more likely to be selected as beneficiaries than the non-poor. Therefore, the degree of pro-poorness may be measured by how much higher the probability of choosing a poor person is than the probability of selecting a non-poor person in the program, which is as measured by the pro-poor index

$$\gamma = B_p - B_n. \tag{14.3.1}$$

In the case of perfect targeting, only the poor are selected as beneficiaries, and all non-poor are entirely left out, which can happen only if $B_p = 1$ and $B_n = 0$, which gives the maximum pro-poor index γ equal to 1. The maximum value of γ cannot be attained unless the proportion of beneficiaries in the program is precisely equal to the proportion of poor—that is, $B=H$. If $B<H$, then some poor will always be left out of the program, and some non-poor will be included in the program—that is, $B_p < 1$ and $B_n > 0$. Similarly, if $B>H$, then all the poor can be included in the program, but all the non-poor cannot be excluded—that is, $B_p = 1$ and $B_n > 0$. Thus, the maximum value of γ cannot be attained unless $B=H$.

A program is said to mismatch if $B \neq H$. In almost all targeted programs, B is never equal to H. An important implication is that even if perfect information about households' poverty status (which household is poor and non-poor) is available, the program's pro-poorness is diminished due to mismatch.

There are two kinds of mismatch. The most common mismatch is when $B<H$. The cost of any targeted program depends on the proportion of beneficiaries included in the program; the larger the B, the higher its cost will be. Most governments in developing countries have budget constraints, so there is always a tendency to design programs with B as small as possible. In such a situation, it is impossible to evaluate the targeting efficiency by the pro-poor index given in (14.3.1). When there is a mismatch, which often is the case, one can assess a program by measuring the association between poverty status and the selection of beneficiaries. A measure of this association is derived from a 2×2 contingency table as

$$\phi = (B_p - B_n) \sqrt{\frac{H(1-H)}{B(1-B)}}. \tag{14.3.2}$$

When $\phi = 0$, it implies no association between poverty and the selection of beneficiaries. In other words, the poor are just as likely to be selected in the program as the non-poor. When there is no mismatch, $B=H$, ϕ is equal to the pro-poor index γ given in (14.3.1).

A standard 2×2 contingency table shows that $N\psi^2$ follows a χ^2 distribution with 1 degree of freedom. This result allows the testing of the null hypothesis of no association between poverty status and the selection of beneficiaries. This test is applicable in the situation of both mismatch and no mismatch.

The larger the value of ϕ, the higher is the association between poverty status and the selection of beneficiaries. As shown above, this statistic is also related to the program's degree of pro-poorness; the larger ϕ, the higher the program's pro-poorness. One can test the statistical significance of ϕ using household surveys; if it is statistically insignificant, the program is not explicitly targeted at the poor. Such a result implies that the program will have no significant impact on poverty reduction. Thus, the test statistic for ϕ provides a practical method of assessing the efficacy of a program.

14.4 Beneficiary Incidence

Beneficiary incidence is concerned with the selection of beneficiaries of the program. The programs may target a variety of individuals or families. For instance, the old-age pension targets the elderly who are 65 years and older. An unemployment benefits program provides cash transfers to individuals who have become unemployed. Brazil's well-known program of conditional cash transfers gives cash transfers to families with children. Under this program, the beneficiary families must fulfill certain conditions—that their children regularly attend a school or have a full immunization course, for example. Many programs target disabled children in the family. Although such programs are designed to provide direct benefits—cash or in-kind—to specific individuals within a beneficiary family, all families indirectly benefit from them. Thus, there are both direct and indirect beneficiaries. If a family is enrolled in the program, all its members are assumed to be the beneficiaries. This assumption is commonly used to evaluate programs.

Many social programs are unconditional programs designed to provide a safety net for chronically poor and vulnerable families. If a family is identified as poor, with income less than the poverty line, all its members are assumed to be poor and counted as the program beneficiaries.

Exclusion error and leakage are the most common indicators to evaluate targeting efficiency. The exclusion error is the percentage of the poor who are excluded from the program and is given by

$$E = 1 - B_p \qquad (14.4.1)$$

The exclusion error informs the percentage of eligible persons excluded from the program. It measures the program's horizontal inequity, implying that all individuals in the same economic circumstances are not treated equally.

Leakage of a program is defined as the number of non-poor as the percentage of all program beneficiaries (or percentage of not eligible beneficiaries of the program),

$$L = \frac{B - HB_p}{B}. \qquad (14.4.2)$$

This measures the resources going to unintended beneficiaries of the program.

Exclusion error and leakage are related as

$$L = 1 - \frac{H}{B}(1 - E). \qquad (14.4.3)$$

If the probability of selecting a beneficiary is equal to the head-count ratio of poverty ($B = H$), then leakage L is equal to exclusion error E. If $B < H$, $L<E$, and similarly, if $B > H$, then $L>E$. The difference between leakage and exclusion error indicates the degree of mismatch in the program.

Both exclusion error and leakage are undesirable, but they cannot simultaneously be reduced. If the number of beneficiaries increases by expanding the program, the exclusion error can be reduced, but the leakage increases. A reduction in one error may cause the other to rise. There is no simple formula to evaluate how well-targeted a program is, and there might be a trade-off between the two errors; therefore, one needs a normative judgment in assessing the program.

14.5 Benefit Incidence

Targeting efficiency should be judged on two accounts: (i) the distribution of the beneficiaries among the poor and the non-poor, and (ii) the distribution of the program's benefits among the poor and non-poor beneficiaries. After selecting beneficiaries, the next issue is how the program distributes total transfers among the poor and the non-poor. The proportion of beneficiaries in the population is B, and suppose β is the average transfers given to each beneficiary, then the average benefits per person in the population will be given by $\bar{b} = \beta B$. Similarly, if β_p and β_n are the average transfers given to each beneficiary among the poor and the non-poor, respectively, then $\bar{b}_p = \beta_p B_p$ and $\bar{b}_n = \beta_n B_n$ are the average benefits per person among the poor and the non-poor, respectively. The average per-person benefit in the population must be equal to the weighted average of the per-person benefits going to the poor and the non-poor, with weights proportional to proportions of poor and non-poor:

$$\bar{b} = H\bar{b}_p + (1 - H)\,\bar{b}_n,$$

which we can write as

$$\beta B = H\beta_p B_p + (1 - H)\,\beta_n B_n.$$

Leakage of benefits (or resources) is an essential targeting indicator, defined as the proportion of total transfers going to the non-poor:

$$l = \frac{\beta B - H\beta_p B_p}{\beta B} \tag{14.5.1}$$

Recall that L is the proportion of the total number of beneficiaries selected from the non-poor. The relationships between l and L is shown by

$$l = L + \frac{H B_p}{\beta B}\,(\beta - \beta_p), \tag{14.5.2}$$

which implies that if $l > (<)L$, then $\beta > (<)\beta_p$. If the leakage of benefits is higher (lower) than the leakage of beneficiaries, the transfer per beneficiary will be higher among the non-poor (poor). If the poor and non-poor beneficiaries receive the same benefits, the leakage of benefits will be the same as the beneficiaries' leakage. The difference in leakage between benefits and beneficiaries indicates the degree of inequity in beneficiaries' benefits among the poor and the non-poor, respectively.

14.6 Universal Basic Income (UBI)

A UBI scheme is a form of social security in which all individuals in society receive government transfers. The World Bank is now promoting this idea on its blog "Basic Income: Can we transfer our way out of poverty?". Finland is currently testing this idea, which ultimately gets rid of targeting the poor for all social transfers. The poor and the rich are all equal beneficiaries of social programs.

Since the UBI scheme includes all the poor, the exclusion error is always zero, but there will be high leakage. The probability of being a beneficiary is the same for the poor and the non-poor, then $B_p = B_n = B = 1$, which on substituting in (14.4.2) gives the leakage $L=(1-H)$. For instance, in China, the official estimate of the poor is about 10%. If the UBI scheme is introduced in China, about 90% of beneficiaries will be non-poor. Similarly, since all beneficiaries receive the same transfer amount, the leakage of benefits or resources will also be about 90%. Thus, the UBI scheme eliminates exclusion errors, introducing massive leakage to the non-poor. This scheme does not target the poor and is a scenario of no targeting. The UBI can be used as a benchmark to evaluate a program such as the Dibao.

The comparison of the Dibao with the UBI must be made by keeping the operational cost of the two same. Suppose $\bar{b}$ is the per person transfer cost of the Dibao, the transfer received by a person with income x for the UBI will be given by

$$b\left(x\right) = \bar{b} \text{ for all } x. \tag{14.6.1}$$

The UBI is used as a benchmark to evaluate the Dibao. Social programs aim to achieve the maximum reduction in poverty with a given program cost. Poverty reduction is used as a criterion to assess the Dibao relative to the UBI while controlling for the total program cost.

14.7 Perfect Targeting

If everyone's income in the population is precisely known, it is easy to correctly identify every poor person, providing income shortfall of everyone's income from the poverty line z. The perfect targeting is achieved if the program benefit of a person with income x is given by

$$\begin{aligned} b\left(x\right) &= k\left(z - x\right) \text{ if } x < z \\ b\left(x\right) &= 0 \qquad\qquad \text{ if } x \geq z \end{aligned} \tag{14.7.1}$$

This perfect targeting ensures that the program transfers go only to the poor, and the transfer amount is proportional to every poor person's income shortfall. The non-poor receive zero transfer. Under this scenario, there will be no exclusion error or leakage in either beneficiaries or benefits.

Per capita cost of such a program (excluding administrative cost) will be given by

$$\bar{b}_k = k\left(zH - \mu_p H\right) \qquad (14.7.2)$$

where μ_p is the mean income of the poor. To assess the performance of the Dibao against perfect targeting as a benchmark, the per capita transfer of the two must be the same. Hence, k is determined so that $\bar{b}_k = \bar{b}$, which gives

$$k = \frac{\bar{b}}{H\left(z - \mu_p\right)} \qquad (14.7.3)$$

The program's impact on poverty under perfect targeting can now be calculated using the transfer scheme (14.7.1) with k given in (14.7.3).

14.8 The Social Rate of Return (SRR)

In practice, investors make decisions based on how much their investments generate returns, and they assess how suitable an investment is by its rate of return. A similar approach may be adopted when governments make investments in social programs.

Cost is an essential component of any social program, and programs ought to be judged based on how much social welfare they generate on their operational costs. Kakwani and Son (2016) proposed evaluating programs using the SRR. The calculation of SRR uses a social welfare function that specifies normative judgments by assigning weights to different individuals.

The SRR is defined as the social welfare generated by a program as a percentage of the program's cost. The SRR requires social welfare to be measured in the money metric. As measured in a country's currency, it is essential to know how the social program generates social welfare compared to its cost estimated in the same currency. Social welfare generated by the program should outweigh the program's operational cost. This requirement must be considered essential in designing any social welfare program.

Suppose there are n persons in a society whose incomes are given by a vector:

$$\tilde{x} = \left(x_1, x_2, \ldots \ldots \ldots, x_n\right).$$

We define a general social welfare function as

$$W = W(\tilde{x}).$$

The minimum requirements of a social welfare function are: (i) it should be non-decreasing in its arguments, and (ii) it should be quasi-concave.[2]

A social welfare program provides cash transfers to its beneficiaries, but not everyone receives the same amount. A vector can represent the distribution of the program's benefits:

$$\tilde{b} = (b_1, b_2, \dots\dots\dots, b_n)$$

In this vector, if $b_i > 0$, then the ith individual is a beneficiary; otherwise, the individual is a non-beneficiary. To calculate the SRR, it is essential to specify a social welfare function.

Suppose $W(\tilde{x})$ is the social welfare without the program, then the usual procedure of estimating the contribution of the program to social welfare is to measure the change in social welfare given by

$$\Delta W = W(\tilde{x} + \tilde{b}) - W(\tilde{x}),$$

which is the post-transfer minus pre-transfer social welfare function. However, this procedure assumes that the program does not impact other sources of income. When a program is introduced, some people may change their behaviors. For instance, beneficiaries may have a reduced incentive to work or cease to receive private transfers that they were receiving in the program's absence. So the program may change the pre-transfer distribution of income.

Suppose that with the introduction of the program, initial income distribution $\tilde{x}$ changes to $\tilde{x}^*$ defined by

$$\tilde{x}^* = (x_1^*, x_2^*, \dots\dots\dots, x_n^*)$$

then $(\tilde{x}^* + \tilde{b})$ is the observed distribution of income after the program is implemented and $\tilde{x}$ is the counterfactual distribution of income—the distribution of income if the program had not existed. The net impact of the program on social welfare will be given by

$$\Delta W^* = W(\tilde{x}^* + \tilde{b}) - W(\tilde{x}), \tag{14.8.1}$$

which can be decomposed into two components: (i) direct impact of transfers on social welfare and (ii) indirect impact due to change of individuals' behavior. The two components can be separated using Shapley (1953) decomposition:

[2] A social welfare function is quasi-concave if $min[W(x), W(y)] \leq W(\rho x + (1 - \rho)y)$ for any ρ with $0 < \rho < 1$ and for any two vectors x and y in the domain of W.

$$\Delta W^* = \frac{\left[W\left(\tilde{x}^* + \tilde{b}\right) - W(\tilde{x}^*) + W\left(\tilde{x} + \tilde{b}\right) - W(\tilde{x})\right]}{2}$$

$$+\frac{\left[W\left(\tilde{x}^* + \tilde{b}\right) - W\left(\tilde{x} + \tilde{b}\right) + W(\tilde{x}^*) - W(\tilde{x})\right]}{2} \qquad (14.8.2)$$

The first term on the right-hand side of this equation measures the direct impact of transfers on social welfare, while the second term is the indirect impact of behavior change.

Some simplifying assumptions must be made to measure the program's impact on social welfare. It is helpful to define a social welfare function that is decomposable by components:

$$W\left(\tilde{x} + \tilde{y}\right) = W(\tilde{x}) + W(\tilde{y})$$

for any vectors $\tilde{x}$ and $\tilde{y}$. Applying this definition on (14.8.2) gives

$$\Delta W^* = \left[W\left(\tilde{b}\right)\right] + \left[W(\tilde{x}^*) - W(\tilde{x})\right] \qquad (14.8.3)$$

The first term on the right-hand side of this equation is the direct impact, estimated if the vector of program benefits (obtained from benefit analysis) and social welfare function are known. The second term on the right-hand side of (14.8.3) is the indirect impact, the estimation of which requires the income distribution vector $\tilde{x}$, not observed from the household surveys. The counterfactual distribution of income would be if the program were not implemented. The post-transfer income distribution given by $\left(\tilde{x}^* + \tilde{b}\right)$ is known from the household surveys that provide income information from various sources, including transfers from the program. Since the vector $\tilde{x}$ is not observed from the household surveys, the indirect impact of the program cannot be readily estimated from household surveys.

However, the program's direct impact on social welfare given by $W\left(\tilde{b}\right)$ is readily estimable from the household surveys. This effect will always be positive because social welfare will increase when transfers are made to families. The indirect impact—which may be referred to as the behavioral impact—can be negative or positive. For instance, if the program leads to disincentives to work, some people may become worse off with the program, given that the loss of employment income is offset by the transfer they receive from the program.

It is not easy to measure the indirect effects of using household surveys, and there are hardly any impact evaluation studies that have captured the indirect impacts.

According to the World Bank's report "The State of Social Safety Nets 2015," as many as 86 impact evaluation studies focusing on social safety nets have been conducted between 2010 and 2015. These studies confirm safety net programs' positive, significant

impact on school attendance, health, nutrition, and food security. Program evaluations in Brazil, Chile, Honduras, Mexico, Nicaragua, and the Philippines show that
the disincentive to labor market participation has been insignificant. The World Bank
report does not mention any study conducted to measure the indirect impact of programs on income distribution. Impact evaluations are generally carried out after the
program has been implemented for a few years. Hence, it becomes almost impossible
to measure the income distribution before implementing the program or counterfactual income distribution (Kakwani and Son 2016). Thus, it becomes essential to
assume that the indirect impact on social welfare is insignificant; the estimation of
SRRs is based on social welfare functions derived from the programs' direct impact.

The calculation of the SRR requires the total program cost. There are two types of
costs associated with running a program. One is the amount of money transferred to
households, denoted by T, and the other is the administrative cost of the program,
denoted by A. The total cost of the program is given by $C = T + A$.

Kakwani and Son (2016a) point out that administrative costs vary from one program to another, and similar programs are implemented in different countries. They
also depend on how well the targeting method is applied. Programs are primarily
means-tested, requiring detailed information on households' economic situation, and
collecting such information is associated with costs. As such, the more information is
collected, the less likely it is to leak resources to unintended beneficiaries.

The delivery of transfers to beneficiaries also incurs costs. Electronic transfers
have become a standard method of delivering transfers directly to households, reducing administrative costs. Suppose the administrative cost is $\in$ % of the total
transfers provided to the beneficiary households, then the total program cost will be
$C = (1+ \in) T$.

The program generates social welfare, which must be measured in monetary units.
Such social welfare is called money metric social welfare. The SRR is calculated using
the program's money metric social welfare as a percentage of the program cost. If W
$\left(\tilde{b}\right)$, defined in (14.8.3), is the money metric social welfare contributed by the program,
then the SRR is defined as

$$(SRR) = \frac{W\left(\tilde{b}\right)}{(1+ \in) T} - 1. \qquad (14.8.4)$$

Hypothetically, suppose the program's total cost is $100 million, including both the
transfer and administrative costs, and the increase in social welfare is $160 million.
The SRR is 60%, meaning that the social investment of $1 generates social welfare of
$1.60.

A negative SRR can occur for two reasons: one, the program gives more benefits to
the rich than the poor—that is, the program has high leakage. Another reason is that
the program's administrative cost is so high that it removes the targeted beneficiaries'
benefits.

It must emphasize that the administrative cost's assumption being a fixed proportion of total transfers may be too simplistic. The relationship between administrative costs and transfers is not linear. When a program starts, it must develop a social infrastructure that requires sizable fixed costs, but the variable costs become more important over time. When several local governments run the program, it cannot be assumed that all will have the same efficiency levels. Hence, the administrative cost calculation is highly complex, requiring all its complexities to calculate it accurately.

This chapter calculates the SRR under the three alternative transfer schemes:

- Actual transfers under the program
- Transfers under the UBI (no targeting)
- Transfers under perfect targeting.

Comparing these three SRR provides a new evaluation method for social programs.

14.9 Operationalizing Social Rate of Return

To make the idea of the SRR operational, one must specify a social welfare function that meets the following conditions: (i) non-decreasing in its arguments, (ii) quasi-concave, (iii) measurable in money metric terms, and (iv) decomposable by components. This chapter considers two general social welfare functions satisfying these conditions: the generalized Rawlsian and Sen's (1976) Gini social welfare functions. This section discusses how to make the SRR operational using these two social welfare functions.

14.9.1 Generalized Rawl's Social Welfare Function

This social welfare function is attributed to Rawls (1971), who proposed the idea of "maximin rule," according to which the social objective is to maximize the welfare of the worst-off individual in society. It is formally defined for a population of n persons as

$$W = min\left[u_1, u_2, \ldots \ldots \ldots \ldots \ldots, u_n\right]$$

where u_i is the welfare of the ith person. Without loss of generality, it can be assumed that income measures an individual's welfare. Kakwani and Son (2016) proposed a generalized maximin criterion, under which society maximizes the average income of the bottom $100 \times H\%$ of the population, H being the proportion of the poor. When $H=1$, social welfare becomes the average income of the society, whereby average inequality aversion is equal to zero. When H takes the value of $1/n$, society maximizes the welfare of the worst-off person, which corresponds to Rawl's maximin social welfare function. These are the two extreme values of H; however, H can take any value between $1/n$ to 1.

Suppose x is the individual's income under the counterfactual that the program had not been introduced, which can be assumed to be a random variable with density function $f(x)$. With the introduction of the program, people can change their behavior. As pointed out, it is not easy to measure the effect of people's change in behavior on their income. For practical purposes, it can be assumed that the impact of people's change in behavior is insignificant. Under this assumption, the post-transfer income of an individual with pre-transfer income x is given by

$$y(x) = x + b(x). \tag{14.8.5}$$

Assuming that x is a random variable with the probability density function $f(x)$, then the poverty line z_H is given by

$$H = \int_0^{z_H} f(x)dx$$

which yields the generalized Rawl's social welfare function as

$$W(x) = \frac{\int_0^{z_H} xf(x)\,dx}{\int_0^{z_H} f(x)\,dx} \tag{14.8.6}$$

which shows that the generalized Rawl's social welfare function is a weighted average of individual incomes. It is a money metric social welfare function decomposable by components.

Substituting (14.8.5) into (14.8.6) yields

$$W(y) = W(x) + W(b)$$

where

$$W(b) = \frac{\int_0^{z_H} b(x)f(x)\,dx}{\int_0^{z_H} f(y)\,dx}$$

is the contribution of the program to the total social welfare, noting that $W(b) = \bar{b}_p$ is the average transfer received by the poor. The average transfer per person going to the whole population is given by $\bar{b} = \int_0^\infty b(x) f(x)\,dx$. If the administrative cost is $\in$ % of the total amount of transfers delivered to the beneficiary households, then the average cost of the program to the society is given by $(1+ \in)\bar{b}$. Given the average contribution of the program to social welfare is $\bar{b}_p$, then the (SRR) is given by

$$SRR = \frac{\overline{b_p}}{(1+\epsilon)\,\overline{b}} - 1 \tag{14.8.7}$$

Hypothetically, suppose the program's average transfer cost is \$50 per person, and the administrative cost is 10% of the transfers delivered to beneficiary households. In this case, the average cost of the program to society is \$55. If the poor receive an average transfer of \$100, which is the average social welfare per person generated by the program, then \$1 spent on the program will yield \$100/\$55=\$1.82 of social welfare, and thus, the SRR is 82%.

Suppose β_p is the average transfer per person going to the poor beneficiaries, and β is the average transfer per person to all beneficiaries in the population, then $\overline{b}_p = \beta_p B_p$ and $\overline{b} = \beta B$, which on substituting in (14.8.7) yields

$$(SRR) = \frac{\beta_p B_p}{(1+\epsilon)\,\beta B} - 1. \tag{14.8.8}$$

Suppose all beneficiaries, whether poor or non-poor, receive equal transfer per person, then $\beta = \beta_p$ then the SRR in (14.8.8) will be given by

$$(SRR)_e = \frac{B_p}{(1+\epsilon)\,B} - 1. \tag{14.8.9}$$

From (14.8.8) and (14.8.9), the relationship between the two SRRs can be expressed as

$$(SRR) = (SRR)_e + \frac{B_p\,(\beta_p - \beta)}{(1+\epsilon)\,\beta B} \tag{14.8.10}$$

which shows that the (SRR) will be higher (lower) than $(SRR)_e$ when the poor (non-poor) beneficiaries receive on average higher (lower) benefits per capita than the non-poor. A program is pro-poor (anti-poor) if the poor receive more (less) per capita benefits than the non-poor. The pro-poorness of a program is given by the statistic ϕ:

$$\phi = (SRR) - (SRR)_e \tag{14.8.11}$$

The program is pro-poor (anti-poor) if ϕ is greater (less) than zero.

The leakage of benefits defined in (14.5.1) is the essential targeting indicator. It is related to the (SRR) in (14.8.8) through the following:

$$(SRR) = \frac{(1-l)}{H(1+\epsilon)} - 1, \tag{14.8.12}$$

which shows that for a fixed administrative cost, the (SRR) is a monotonically decreasing function of leakage; the larger (smaller) the leakage, the smaller (larger) the

(*SRR*). Thus, this section has demonstrated that the leakage has a direct social welfare interpretation.

The leakage is not independent of the administrative cost, and there is even a trade-off between the two. Reducing the leakage requires more resources spent on identifying beneficiaries. To this end, policymakers would be interested in knowing whether they should channel more resources toward administering the program to reduce leakage. Policymakers should aim to achieve higher SRRs and, by implication, improve a program's targeting performance.

The trade-off between the leakage and the administrative cost can be assessed from the total differentiation of (14.8.12) as

$$d\left(SRR\right) = -\frac{dl}{H\left(1+ \in\right)} - \frac{\left(1 - l\right)d\in}{H(1+ \in)^2},$$

which yields the trade-off between the two as

$$\frac{d\in}{dl} = -\frac{\left(1+ \in\right)}{\left(1 + l\right)}.$$

This equation informs how much the policymakers should increase the administrative cost to reduce the leakage while keeping the (SRR) unchanged. For example, suppose $l = 0.50$, implying that 50% of the program benefits go to the non-poor, and the administrative cost is 10% of the benefits delivered to beneficiary households. The trade-off between the leakage and the administrative cost is −2.2, which means that by reducing the leakage by 1%, the administrative cost would increase by 2.2%. Policymakers should devote more (less) resources to improving targeting efficiency if the reduction of leakage by 1% increases the administrative cost by less (more) than 2.2%, in which case the (SRR) will increase (decrease). This analysis helps policymakers decide whether to divert resources to administrative costs to reduce leakage.

14.9.2 Sen's Social Welfare Function

The generalized Rawl's social welfare function focuses on the poorest H% of the population. It gives positive but equal weight to all individuals' incomes belonging to the bottom H% of the people and zero weight to all those belonging to the top $(1-H)$%. Hence, the evaluation of programs can exclude a large proportion of the population. Suppose, hypothetically, the poverty line is set at $1,000 per month, then all those having a monthly income of more than $1,000 are excluded from such an evaluation. Thus, if a poor person earns even one extra dollar, society has no concern for such a person, even if his poverty situation remains almost unchanged.

Although safety net programs are intended to help the poor and the vulnerable population, they can also reduce inequality. Any social program designed to target only the poor can create disincentives to work because one additional dollar earned can completely disqualify a person from benefiting from the program. As an alternative, one must consider a social welfare function that gives the highest weight to the poorest person, and the weight declines monotonically as the income increases. Sen's social welfare, discussed in Chapter 5, has this property.

Suppose x is the pre-transfer income of an individual, assumed to be a random variable with density function $f(x)$, then Sen's social welfare function is given by

$$W_S = 2 \int_0^\infty x [1 - F(x)] f(x) \, dx \qquad (14.8.13)$$

where $F(x)$ is the distribution function measuring the proportion of persons who have income higher than x, such that

$$2 \int_0^\infty [1 - F(x)] f(x) \, dx = 1.$$

Equation (14.8.3) yielded $W(\tilde{b})$ as the social welfare contributed by the program, which for Sen's social welfare function is given by

$$W_s(\tilde{b}) = 2 \int_0^\infty b(x) [1 - F(x)] f(x) \, dx \qquad (14.8.14)$$

where $b(x)$ is the transfer received by an individual with income x. Equation (9.7.3) in Chapter 9 yields

$$W_s(\tilde{b}) = \bar{b}(1 - C_b) \qquad (14.8.15)$$

where $\bar{b}$ is the average program transfers delivered to the population or also the average transfer cost of the program, and C_b is the concentration index of the program benefits.

The concentration index can be either negative or positive. A negative value means that transfers from the program decrease as income increases; the poorer the person is, the greater the benefits are. Similarly, the concentration index's positive value implies that the richer the person is, the greater the benefits are. Thus, a program is pro-poor (anti-poor) if the concentration index is negative (positive). The targeting efficiency of a program can be measured by

$$\rho = (1 - C_b), \qquad (14.8.16)$$

which implies that the program is pro-poor (anti-poor) if ρ is greater (less) than 1; the larger the value of ρ, the greater the targeting efficiency of the program. When

ρ = 1, everyone receives the same cash transfer, corresponding to the UBI scheme.

If the administrative cost is $\in$ % of the total amount of transfers delivered to households, then the average cost of the program to the society is given by $(1+ \in)\,\bar{b}$. The SRR is then obtained by comparing the program's social welfare with the total program cost measured in the money metric. Thus, the SRR for Sen's social welfare function is given by

$$(SRR)_S = \frac{(1 - C_b)}{(1+ \in)} - 1 = \frac{\rho}{(1+ \in)} - 1 \qquad (14.8\ 17)$$

This demonstrates that the targeting indicator ρ has a direct linkage with the SRR derived from Sen's social welfare function. Suppose that the concentration index is -0.40, which gives the targeting indicator ρ = 1.40. The administrative cost is 10% of the transfers delivered to beneficiary households, then the SRR calculated from (14.8.17) is 27.3%. This means that a dollar spent on the program will generate social welfare worth \$1.27. Under the UBI scheme, ρ =1, and if the administrative cost of the program is negligible, it yields the SRR equal to zero. This scenario will be our benchmark in assessing any program.

14.9.3 The Social Welfare Functions Implicit in Foster, Greer, and Thorbecke's (FGT) Poverty Measures

Since the primary objective of welfare programs is to reduce poverty, it will be appropriate to use social welfare functions that incorporate normative judgments implicit in poverty measures. FGT poverty measures are most widely used to measure poverty. Kakwani and Son (2016a, chapter 3) have developed social welfare functions corresponding to the entire class of FGT poverty measures:

$$W_\alpha = \mu - Hz\left(\frac{\theta_\alpha}{H}\right)^{\frac{1}{\alpha}}, \qquad (14.9.1)$$

where θ_α is the FGT class of poverty measures, which is the head-count ratio (H) if α = 0, the poverty gap ratio if α = 1, and the severity of poverty ratio if α = 2, and z is the poverty line. The social welfare measured in the money metric is yuan per year. The second term on the right-hand side of (14.9.1) is the loss of social welfare caused by poverty. It depends on which poverty measure is used.

Note that W_α is not decomposable by components, so a program's contribution will differ in pre- and post-transfer programs' social welfare. The change in social welfare due to the program is given by:

$$\Delta W_{\alpha} = \Delta\mu - z\,\Delta H\left(\frac{\theta_{\alpha}}{H}\right)^{\frac{1}{\alpha}} \tag{14.9.2}$$

which is the social benefit of the program. The SRR is calculated by comparing the program's social benefit with its total cost. The total program cost is $(1+\in)\,T$, therefore, the SRR for the FGT social welfare functions will be given by

$$(SSR)_{\alpha} = \frac{\Delta W_{\alpha}}{(1+\in)\,T} - 1 \tag{14.9.3}$$

For instance, a hypothetical program generates total welfare equal to 30 billion yuan per year, and the total transfers going to beneficiaries are 19 billion yuan per year. Suppose 5% of the transfers are the program's administrative cost. The total program cost will be 19.95 billion yuan, which gives the SRR equal to 50%, implying a social investment of 1 yuan generates social welfare of 1.50 yuan.

14.10 China's Dibao Program

China's Dibao program is the minimum living standard guarantee program designed to provide cash support to those whose income falls short of a certain poverty threshold. It was launched in the 1990s by China's more developed urban regions to assist urban workers during economic reform and structural change. The program was extended to rural areas in 2007. This chapter provides the most rigorous evaluation of rural Dibao. Golan et al. (2017) provided a detailed description of the rural Dibao.

Both the central and local governments fund the program. The central government allocates funds to provinces based on the estimated number of people in poverty and the extent of their poverty. Provincial governments then give the funds to its subdominant until it gets into the hands of those in need.

The local areas administer the program, and they select the beneficiary households from a list of registered households called Hukou. In principle, a household is eligible to apply for the Dibao assistance as long as its income is lower than the threshold level determined by the officials in the local area without satisfying any other conditions. The beneficiary household receives the cash transfer; usually, the difference between the income threshold level and the household's income, to close the gap between them. Since actual household incomes are not known to officials, there is a possibility of a high degree of inequity in distributing cash transfers.

Implementation remains decentralized. The local authorities determine eligibility thresholds, beneficiary selection, and transfer payment amounts. The local governments' income threshold level usually depends on local areas' economic conditions, such as the consumption level, capacity, and funding for the local areas. Due to the fiscal interactions among regions, local governments tend to reduce the minimum living standard guarantee in their jurisdiction if there is a decrease in the minimum living standard in their neighbors. Thus, regions race to the bottom regarding these welfare spending expenditures.

The income threshold level varies across regions and is different between urban and rural areas, and it is higher in urban areas than in rural areas. Regions with better economic conditions tend to have a higher income threshold than those with worse economic conditions. Poor counties tend to have lower Dibao thresholds and transfer amounts than affluent counties. Thus, there exists no uniform criterion for identifying the poor. The transfers are given to beneficiaries also vary across counties.

The management of the Dibao is highly decentralized, based on a de facto quota system. In practice, authorities estimate the number of poor in a region and then distribute the fund accordingly. For a given amount of funds, county-level officials decide the Dibao line and distribute certain funds to their subsidiaries in the villages, where local cadre or villagers determine who should get the money. A more affluent village may get more quota than it needs, and another region may get much less, which can only barely cover the extremely poor.

Dibao households were often not means-tested at the village level but democratically decided by villagers based on their perception. For instance, in some places, the recipients are selected by counting off incomes ranked from highest to lowest and choosing from the poorest, while in other areas, villagers decide it through voting.

This chapter reports some field studies and interviews with many local officials and villagers. It found that villagers often gather to discuss and decide who should get the transfers. It is usually easy to identify a couple of extremely poor households who should get the money, but it is not easy to settle those who should get the rest. If there are more equally poor households than the number of households the Dibao can support, some households may rotate yearly to get the Dibao subsidies.

Villagers often decide on a pool of households and give them Dibao based on rotation. When this happens, the household survey would only pick those who get the Dibao in that year and have no information about the others who might benefit later. Thus, the targeting shown in the data may not be accurate.

14.11 Evaluation Methodology

The rural Dibao's evaluation is based on the fifth round of the Chinese Household Income Project (CHIP) covering rural households in 2013. These surveys were carried out by the China Institute of Income Distribution, supported by the Beijing Normal University.

The rural survey sample contains more than 10,000 households in 12 provinces and two province-level municipalities, representing China, across eastern, middle, and western regions: Beijing, Liaoning, Jiangsu, Shandong, Guangdong, Shanxi, Anhui, Henan, Hubei, Hunan, Gansu, Sichuan, Chongqing, and Yunnan. The sample is a subset of the National Bureau of Statistics (NBS) annual rural household survey (approximately 65,000 rural households).

The CHIP surveys are the best publicly available data source on Chinese household income and expenditures. These data remain the only source of household-level information on income and other individual and household characteristics representing China as a whole (Gustafsson, Li, and Sicular, 2008).

The primary objective of social assistance programs is to reduce poverty. Therefore, it is essential to identify the poor who genuinely need help from the government. Identifying the poor requires a money metric individual-level household welfare. In most countries, the per capita income is used to measure household welfare. Household welfare should include all income components that contribute to household welfare. The households also make transfers to other households and pay taxes, which do not contribute to their welfare, so these expenditures must be deducted from their gross income. So the household welfare is determined by their disposable income, which is the net income available to households for consumption.

Many developing countries use per capita expenditure as a measure of household welfare. It is not easy to accurately measure income in these countries due to a significant informal sector. However, from the welfare point of view, consumption is regarded as a better basis for determining who is poor who is not. There is much more significant income fluctuation in any given month or year than in actual household consumption. Households tend to smooth their consumption across periods by saving or dissaving as needed. So household consumption during the survey period provides a better measure of their permanent standard of living than their current income.

The CHIP survey provided both income and consumption. Since there are pros and cons of using income or consumption as household welfare measures, this chapter uses both as a basis for evaluating the Dibao program. Since the cost of living varies across provinces, the household income was deflated by the spatial price indices for different provinces of China (numeracies equals national average consumption basket). Thus, the two alternative household welfare measures are the real per capita disposable income and per capita household consumption.

To measure poverty among individuals, one needs to know the welfare of individuals. To derive the welfare of individuals, it is essential to assume that all households enjoy the same living standard. If a household is identified as poor, then all individuals belonging to this household are also poor. This assumption is commonly used in poverty measurement because the intra-household distribution of household resources is unknown from household surveys. The poverty estimates presented here relate to poverty among individuals (not households).

An evaluation should be carried out against some poverty line. As pointed out, the Dibao is a highly decentralized program in which each local authority determines eligibility thresholds and transfer payments. Each county has its poverty line for identifying the poor. Should then the Dibao be evaluated separately for each county? A problem with this approach is that counties do not have clear criteria and do not use any explicit poverty line to identify the beneficiaries. They make their decisions on an ad hoc basis. Since Dibao is a national program, this paper evaluates it using a national benchmark. An appropriate benchmark is federal poverty for rural areas.

This chapter has used the rural official poverty line of 2,736 yuan per person per year for 2013, about 28% of the average per capita real income. The 2011 PPP exchange rate for the Chinese yuan per dollar was 3.545 in 2013, which gave the per person per day official poverty line equal to $2.11 in 2011 PPP. The World Bank has recommended the poverty line of $1.90 in 2011 PPP for the extremely poor. Thus, the Chinese official poverty line is about 11% higher than the World Bank's poverty line, a reasonable poverty line for the extremely poor. Given the Chinese economic development level, it is unnecessary to use the World Bank's extreme poverty line.

14.12 Evaluation of the Dibao, 2013

Table 14.1 presents the estimates of various targeting indicators discussed in this chapter. As pointed out, this evaluation is based on two alternative welfare measures: (i) per capita real disposable income and (ii) per capita real household consumption. The estimates of targeting indicators are presented separately for the two welfare measures. The total rural population of rural China, from the CHIP survey, is 620.22 million. According to the *2014 Statistical Yearbook* published by the National Bureau of Statistics, the total rural population in 2013 was 630 million, close to 620.22 million used in this evaluation.

Per capita real disposable income in 2013 prices is estimated equal to 9,850 yuan per year, whereas per capita real household consumption is calculated equal to 7,731 yuan. The per capita household consumption is about 78% of the per capita household disposable income. The two welfare measures also have different inequality as measured by the Gini index. The Gini index of per capita consumption is estimated equal to 36.44%, much lower than that of the per capita disposable income calculated equal to 40.73%. Commonly, the inequality of consumption welfare is lower than that of income welfare.

The chapter uses the same poverty line for the two welfare measures, resulting in different poverty estimates. The percentage of poor based on per capita disposable income is 10.12%, while per capita consumption is 9.40%. Consumption poverty is lower than income poverty because consumption has lower inequality than income. In most situations, the poverty gap and severity of poverty have lower values than the percentage of poor because they consider both the poor and how poor they are. The empirical estimates in the table provide somewhat unusual estimates of the poverty gap and severity of poverty, whose values based on per capita income are 4.85% and 13.33%, respectively. The main reason for these unusual estimates is that about 70 sample households in the CHIP had high negative incomes. Although negative income is typical in many household surveys, such high negative incomes are somewhat unusual. The calculations presented here are based on all the negative incomes observed in the study. The survey does not know whether households with such high negative incomes were genuinely poor or were not poor but had temporary

Table 14.1 Targeting indicators of China's rural Dibao program, 2013

Targeting Indicators	Per capita real disposable income	Per capita real consumption
Total rural population (millions)	620.22	620.22
Gini index	40.73	36.44
Poverty indicators		
Official poverty line (yuan per year)	2736	2,736
Percent of poor	10.12	9.4
Poverty gap ratio (%)	4.85	1.98
Severity of poverty (%)	13.33	0.63
Number of poor (millions)	62.79	58.29
Number of non-poor (millions)	557.43	561.93
Welfare indicators		
Per capita household welfare (yuan per year)	9850	7,731
Per capita household welfare of poor (yuan per year)	1425	2,160
Per capita household welfare of non-poor (yuan per year)	10,799	8,309
Per capita welfare of Dibao beneficiaries (yuan per year)	6080	5,382
Beneficiary incidence		
Percent of beneficiaries	6.89	6.89
Number of beneficiaries (millions)	42.72	42.72
Number of poor included in the Dibao (millions)	7.61	7.66
Number of poor excluded from the Dibao (millions)	55.18	50.63
Exclusion error (Percent of poor excluded)	87.89	86.86
Number of non-poor included in the Dibao (millions)	35.11	35.06
Percent of beneficiaries among poor	12.11	13.14
Percent of beneficiaries among non-poor	6.3	6.24
Percent of all beneficiaries from non-poor	82.2	82.07
Benefit incidence		
Average transfer in the population (yuan per year)	31.96	31.96
Average transfer among the poor (yuan per year)	42.2	50.63
Average transfer among the non-poor (yuan per year)	30.81	30.02
Total transfers to beneficiaries (billions)	19.8	19.8
Total transfers to poor beneficiaries (billions)	2.6	3
Total transfers to non-poor beneficiaries (billions)	17.2	16.9
Proportion of total transfers to non-poor (%)	86.63	85.11
Average transfer per beneficiary (yuan per year)	464	464
Average transfer per beneficiary among poor (yuan per year)	348	385
Average transfer per beneficiary among non-poor (yuan per year)	489	481

Source: Kakwani, N., S. Li, X. Wang, M. Zhu (2019).

setbacks. The main advantage of using consumption welfare is that it cannot have negative values. The poverty gap and severity of poverty on consumption-based welfare are 1.98% and 0.63%, respectively, which seem reasonable when comparing them with estimates obtained from many other countries.

The number of poor in rural China is 62.79 million based on per capita disposable income and 58.29 million based on per capita consumption.

As discussed in Section 14.2, exclusion error and leakage are commonly used indicators to evaluate targeting efficiency. The exclusion error is the percentage of poor excluded from the program. Meanwhile, leakage is the percentage of all beneficiaries who are not poor (or not eligible for the program). Therefore, leakage measures the resources going to unintended beneficiaries of the program.

Of 62.79 million poor, only 7.61 million were the program beneficiaries, which means that 55.18 million poor were not included in the program. Thus, the Dibao excludes 87.89% poor from receiving any benefit, a very high degree of exclusion error. The exclusion error based on per capita consumption is 86.6%, slightly lower but still very high compared to many international social assistance programs. Thus, the program generates a high degree of horizontal inequity, meaning that all the poor are not treated equally.

Of the total 42.72 million beneficiaries, 35.11 million are non-poor, which gives the leakage of beneficiaries in the program an equal 82.2%. Leakage is also very high at 82.07% when the per capita consumption is used as a welfare measure. High leakage of this magnitude amounts to substantial resources going to unintended beneficiaries of the program.

Both exclusion error and leakage are incredibly high in comparison with international standards. It seems that in selecting beneficiaries, the program did not use the poverty status of individuals. Section 14.2 developed a test statistic φ, which measures the association between poverty status and the selection of beneficiaries. When $\phi = 0$, it implies that there is no association between poverty and the selection of beneficiaries. In other words, the poor are as likely to be selected in the program as the non-poor. It was shown that $N\phi^2$ is distributed as a χ^2 distribution with 1 degree of freedom. This result allows testing the null hypothesis of no association between poverty status and the selection of beneficiaries.

The metric ϕ for the Dibao is calculated to be 0.07 on the income-based welfare measure and 0.08 on consumption-based welfare, both of which are not statistically significant at the 5% level of significance. Thus, the hypothesis of no association cannot be rejected whatever welfare measure is used. A considerable conclusion emerging from this analysis is that the program did not use individuals' poverty status in selecting individuals. The program chose beneficiaries by factors other than their poverty status.

The benefit incidence is concerned with how the program distributes total transfers among the poor and the non-poor. The average transfer from the Dibao to the whole population is 31.96 yuan per person per year. Multiplying this by the total rural population of 620.22 million gives the program's total transfer cost equal to

19.8 billion yuan per year. Also, there may be some administrative costs of running the program. Although the exact amount of administrative cost of the Dibao is not known, its funding came from both the central government and local governments. Official Statistics for China's rural Dibao program reported that the total transfers going to the Dibao from all levels of government were about 87 billion yuan in 2013 (Golan, Sicular, and Umapathi 2017). Given the actual transfers going to beneficiaries is 19.8 billion yuan, the non-transfer (or administrative) cost of the program is about 67.2 billion yuan, which is a tremendous cost of running a program. It means that 3.4 yuan is eaten away in administrative costs for every yuan transferred to beneficiaries.

The average transfers to each beneficiary are obtained by dividing the total transfers to the population by the number of beneficiaries, which gives the average transfers per beneficiary equal to 464.02 yuan per year. The poor and non-poor have different beneficiaries and will have different transfers per beneficiary. The average amount of transfers to poor beneficiaries was 348.43 yuan per year. Non-poor beneficiaries received the transfer of 489.06 yuan per year, which shows a significant inequity in the program benefits to the poor and non-poor. Thus, the Dibao suffers from serious inequity in distributing benefits to the poor and non-poor. On average, poor beneficiaries get much less than the non-poor beneficiaries who were not supposed to get in the first place.

The leakage is the percentage of total benefits going to the non-poor. This indicator measures the allocation of resources in monetary terms that will benefit unintended beneficiaries. The number of non-poor beneficiaries in the Dibao is equal to 35.11 million. Each non-poor beneficiary receives 489.06 yuan, which gives the total resources leaked to the non-poor equal 17.37 billion yuan. The total transfer cost of the program is 19.8 billion yuan. Thus, 86.63% of total funds leaked out to the non-poor. This represents the leakage rate of resources, and this leakage is even higher than the leakage of beneficiaries, which was calculated to be 82.2%. The leakage is 85.11% when welfare measured is per capita consumption, which is also high by any international standard.

In summary, this section has shown that the Dibao, the most extensive rural safety net program globally, performs poorly based on all targeting indicators.

14.13 Impact of the Dibao on Poverty Reduction

The primary objective of the Dibao is to reduce poverty. How much does the program contribute to poverty alleviation? An answer to this question requires the calculation of poverty with and without program transfers going to beneficiaries. Table 14.2 presents the actual magnitude of poverty reduction separately for the two alternative welfare measures: per capita disposable income and per capita consumption. The program reduces the poor by 0.42% when welfare measured is per capita real disposable

Table 14.2 Contribution of the Dibao to poverty reduction

Poverty measure	Per capita real disposable income	Per capita real consumption
Percent of poor	−0.42	−0.63
Poverty gap ratio (Percent)	−0.22	−0.27
Severity of poverty (Percent)	−0.2	−0.16

Source: Kakwani, Li, Wang, and Zhu (2019).

Table 14.3 Poverty reduction under the UBI program

Poverty measure	Per capita real disposable income	Per capita real consumption
Percent of poor	−0.3	−0.5
Poverty gap ratio (Percent)	−0.16	−0.21
Severity of poverty (Percent)	−0.14	−0.12

Source: Kakwani, Li, and Zhu (2019).

income. The reduction in the percentage of the poor is even higher at 0.63% when welfare measured is per capita consumption. The poverty gap ratio and severity of poverty also show a reduction in poverty but of lesser magnitude. These results indicate that the Dibao does contribute to poverty reduction. Still, one cannot infer how effectively the program reduces poverty without comparing it with benchmarks. Table 14.3 presents the magnitude of poverty reduction under the UBI, keeping the same transfer cost.

Comparing the magnitude of poverty reduction in Table 14.2 and 14.3 shows that the Dibao has a greater poverty reduction than the UBI with the same transfer costs. The magnitudes of poverty reduction under the two scenarios are not that different, and they may be insignificant.

Any program under no targeting has the least administrative cost. As noted earlier, according to official statistics for China's rural Dibao program, the total transfers going to the Dibao from all levels of government was approximately 87 billion yuan in 2013. The actual transfers going to beneficiary households are estimated as equal to approximately 19.8 billion yuan (Table 14.1), which gives the program a non-transfer cost of approximately 67.2 billion yuan, which is the tremendous cost of running a program. A policy question is whether it is worth pouring so much money into the Dibao to achieve such a slight additional reduction in poverty. Would it not be better to replace the Dibao with the UBI program, with almost negligible administrative cost. The main advantage of a UBI program is that it has zero exclusion error, and hence it does not suffer from horizontal inequity. Leakage will be about 90%, but the Dibao also has a high leakage rate of about 86%. Thus, the Dibao does not have much advantage over the UBI scheme.

14.14 Social Rate of Return for the Dibao

The social rate of return (SRR) is the social welfare generated by a program as a percentage of its cost. This section uses the social welfare function given in (14.9.2), which captures the deprivation suffered by the population due to poverty.

Table 14.4 presents social welfare in monetary values for four alternative scenarios: (i) the current situation when the Dibao is operational, (ii) if the Dibao did not exist, (iii) if the Dibao had perfect targeting, and (iv) if the Dibao had no targeting, with everyone receiving the same transfer. In calculating social welfare under the first, third, and fourth scenarios, the total transfers to beneficiaries are kept equal to 19.8 billion yuan.

Per capita disposable income is 9,850 yuan per year, which, when multiplied by the rural population of 620.22 million, gives the total disposable income of the rural population as 6,109 billion yuan, including the total transfers of 19.8 billion yuan to beneficiaries of the program. The existence of poverty incurs a loss of social welfare, which depends on the poverty measure used. The loss of social welfare for the poverty gap ratio, as calculated from (14.9.2), is equal to 82 billion yuan. When subtracted from the total disposable income, social welfare equals 6,027 billion yuan, the rural population's social welfare when Dibao is operational.

The total rural population's counterfactual income, if Dibao had not existed, would be equal to the total disposable income minus the total program transfers of 19.8 billion yuan. If the program were not operational, then poverty would have been higher, leading to higher social welfare loss due to poverty. This loss equals 86 billion yuan, which, when subtracted from the disposable income available to the population without a program, gives social welfare equal to 6,003 billion yuan. The calculation of social welfare under the perfect targeting and UBI follows the same procedure.

Each scenario generates a different value of social welfare. A scenario that creates the highest social welfare level will contribute most to the poverty reduction with a

Table 14.4 Social welfare under various scenarios (billion yuan per year)

Poverty measure	Per capita real disposable income	Per capita real consumption
Dibao operational		
Poverty gap ratio	6,027	4,761
Severity of poverty	5,912	4,754
With no Dibao		
Poverty gap ratio	6,003	4,737
Severity of poverty	5,887	4,727
Perfect Targeting		
Poverty gap ratio	6,043	4,777
Severity of poverty	5,955	4770
No Targeting		
Poverty gap ratio	6,024	4,758
Severity of poverty	5,908	4,749

Source: Kakwani, Li, Wang, and Zhu (2019).

Table 14.5 Contribution to social welfare for three alternative scenarios (billion yuan per year)

Poverty measure	Per capita real disposable income	Per capita real consumption
Existing Dibao		
Poverty gap ratio	24	24
Severity of poverty	25	26
Perfect Targeting		
Poverty gap ratio	40	40
Severity of poverty	68	42
No Targeting		
Poverty gap ratio	21	21
Severity of poverty	21	21

Source: Kakwani, Li, Wang, and Zhu (2019).

given program cost. The difference in social welfare with the program and without the program contributes to that program. For instance, the Dibao generates social welfare equal to 6,027 billion yuan. In contrast, social welfare without a program is 6,003 yuan, implying that the Dibao contributes to social welfare equal to 24 billion yuan per year.

Table 14.5 presents the contributions to social welfare for three alternative scenarios. As expected, perfect targeting generates much greater social welfare than the other two. Although the Dibao creates more social welfare than the UBI, their difference is slight, which may not be significant. A critical policy question is: should a UBI replace the currently run Dibao? The answer depends on the costs of running the two programs.

The SRR takes into account the operational costs of running a program. The UBI does not explicitly target the poor. It makes equal transfers to all individuals, so the administrative cost share of total transfers will be almost negligible. It does not require identifying the poor. It is reasonable to assume that the administrative cost of sending transfers to all citizens will not be more than 5% of the total transfers. The total transfers going to beneficiaries are Y19.8 billion yuan, and with 5% administrative cost, the entire program cost will be 20.8 billion yuan. So the SRR will be 0.01% ((21/20.8)−1), which is almost zero. Thus, the UBI scheme generates an insignificant SRR.

As pointed out earlier, the total transfers going to the Dibao from all levels of government was approximately 87 billion yuan in 2013, as reported by official statistics for China's rural Dibao program. Assuming that 87 billion yuan is the correct cost of running the Dibao, which is justified because it is an official figure, social rates of returns for the Dibao are profoundly negative at around −70%, as shown in Table 14.6. Any program with such high negative rates of return cannot sustain itself in the long run. There is an urgent need to reform the targeting methodology used for the Dibao. If the local governments had followed a UBI scheme, which does not require targeting the poor, the rural Dibao could have avoided such high negative rates of return.

It is impossible to report the estimates of SRR under the scenario of perfect targeting because the administrative cost of perfect targeting is unknown. It is also doubtful

Table 14.6 Social rates of return for the Dibao (Percent)

Poverty Measure	Per capita real disposable income	Per capita real consumption
Poverty gap ratio	−72.99	−71.89
Severity of poverty	−70.81	−69.87

Source: Kakwani, Li, Wang, and Zhu (2019).

whether it is possible to achieve perfect targeting. Even developed countries do not have perfect targeting in their social programs. Undoubtedly, developed countries have evolved more efficient targeting than developing countries; still, they have some degree of leakage. To aspire to perfect targeting is an unachievable goal, which is not recommended for the Dibao, but targeting could be improved substantially.

14.15 Concluding Remarks

This chapter has presented several new methods for evaluating the targeting efficiency and the SRR for social programs applied to assess the Chinese rural Dibao using CHIP 2013 data. All indicators showed poor targeting efficiency of the Dibao, yielding a significantly negative SRR.

This chapter has identified the following causes of such a high degree of inefficiency in the program:

1) The selection of an individual in the Dibao program is almost random, not determined by the individual's poverty status.
2) It excluded almost 87% of the poor while including about 82% of the non-poor.
3) There is considerable inequity in the program benefits to the poor and non-poor, where the poor beneficiaries get much less than those non-poor beneficiaries.
4) The percentage of total resources leaked to the non-poor is even higher than the leakage to beneficiaries.
5) It yielded a high negative SRR for both the poverty gap ratio and the severity of poverty.

The evaluation of the Dibao is carried out using two alternative household welfare measures:

(i) real per capita disposable income, and
(ii) real per capita household consumption.

Both welfare measures tell the same story that the Dibao does not achieve its primary objective of reducing poverty with minimum cost. The cost of running the Dibao is extraordinarily high, with an insignificant impact on poverty reduction. The Chinese government aims to eliminate poverty by 2030, so to achieve this goal, Dibao needs to be urgently reformed by improving its targeting efficiency and reducing its administrative cost.

This chapter's central message is that rural Dibao requires an efficient mechanism and methodology to identify the poor and determine the subsidy needed. The management of the Dibao is highly decentralized, and local governments do not follow any precise targeting system. The evaluation does not recommend that Dibao be completely centralized, and local authorities should run the program because they are more familiar with the local conditions.

What they may lack is the technical capacity to implement targeting methodology. Some central authorities must develop a consistent targeting framework that local governments could use. However, local governments should carry out the implementation of such a framework. The central authority could provide training from time to time on targeting methods to the local administration officials and communities involved in the operation of the Dibao. It could also develop a monitoring system to ensure that the program runs smoothly at the local level.

Given the limitations of accurately obtaining data on people's income or consumption, many developing countries use the proxy means test as a targeting framework. The basic idea of a proxy means test is identifying beneficiaries by easily identifiable variables that predict a household in poverty. A nationally representative household survey makes it possible to design such a proxy means test.

The first step in designing a proxy means testing is identifying a set of variables highly correlated with the poverty status of households. These selected variables must be accessible to measure but at the same time should be able to predict with reasonable accuracy. To accomplish this objective, a proxy means test develops a formula to calculate a correlation coefficient between any proxy variable and households' poverty status. This correlation coefficient helps in identifying the proxy variables.

The basic idea of a proxy means test is to provide a decision rule to identify which households should or should not be included in the program. One can arrive at such a decision rule by setting easily identifiable proxy variables at the household level. Local authorities can collect information on proxy variables from households using a small questionnaire.

Such a system would be an objective way of selecting program beneficiaries and should significantly improve targeting and reduce the cost of running the program. That should help China achieve its goal of eradicating extreme poverty by 2030.

15

Social Price Indices and Inequality

15.1 Introduction

There is a vast literature on the economic theory of price indices. This theory provides a precise meaning to price indices used to make comparisons in the welfare of individuals when they face continuously changing consumer prices. Many economists have contributed to the development of the theoretical foundation of consumer price indices, the most important being those of Hicks (1946), Pollak (1980, 1981, 1983, 1998), Diewert (1976, 1983, 1990a, 1990b 1993, 1998), Samuelson and Swamey (1979), and Konüs (1924).

Most of the literature on the price index theory focuses on comparing the welfare of a single consumer in different price situations. The Laspeyres price index is most widely used to measure the cost of living over time, and most countries in the world have adopted it as an essential price metric. The index measures the cost of living for an average consumer. However, the price index, defined for an average consumer, is insensitive to the impact of relative price changes on income inequality. It does not inform how the relative price changes affect the poor and non-poor.

Muellbauer (1974a) showed that the United Kingdom's price changes since 1974 had an increasing inequality bias. He used the Atkinson (1970) inequality index in conjunction with the linear expenditure system to define a real index of expenditure inequality.

This chapter's main objective is to measure the impact of changes in relative prices on inequality. The effects of price changes on income inequality can only be measured if the price index uses a social welfare function defined for many individuals in society. Such an index is called a social cost of living index, and it takes into account specific value judgments of the society.

Pollak (1981) developed a social cost of living index defined as the ratio of the total expenditure required to enable each individual to attain their reference indifference curve at comparison prices to that needed at reference prices. He called this index a Scitovsky–Laspeyres group cost of living index. Prais (1959) refers to this index as a plutocratic price index. This chapter demonstrates that this index has an implicit social welfare function, which assumes that society is inequality neutral in its attitude. It means that the index is entirely insensitive to changes in income inequality caused by price changes.

Economic Inequality and Poverty. Nanak Kakwani and Hyun Son, Oxford University Press.
© Nanak Kakwani and Hyun Son (2022). DOI: 10.1093/oso/9780198852841.003.0015

This chapter develops the social expenditure function, which defines the true social price indices. This expenditure function is more general than the one suggested by Pollak (1981). His function assumes the neutral inequality aversion, but the framework presented in this chapter considers all possible values of the inequality aversion parameter.

Following Son and Kakwani (2006), this chapter provides a detailed derivation of social price indices based on two alternative classes of social welfare functions. The first social welfare function class is utilitarian, which purports that every individual has the same utility function. A class of social price indices is derived using a homothetic utility function proposed by Atkinson (1970). The chapter shows that Diewert's (1993) multiplicative democratic cost of living index is a particular case of this class.

The second class of social cost of living indices is derived based on a class of Kakwani's social welfare functions proposed by Kakwani (1980b), which considers the interdependence of individual utilities.[1] These cost of living indices capture the idea of relative deprivation suffered by individuals with different income levels.

This chapter also derives the explicit relationship between social price indices and aggregate inequality measures. This relationship shows that in a society with high inequality, the usual computing method of the inflation rate (based on a single consumer) is likely to give highly biased results.

The methodology developed in the chapter is applied to estimate social price indices for Thailand. This study covers the period from 1986 to 1995, and it utilizes Thailand's Socio-economic Survey (SES) data for 1990. The market prices of various goods and services were obtained from the Department of Business Economics, Ministry of Commerce, Bangkok, Thailand.

The chapter also presents the social price indices for South Korea. Comparing the impact of relative prices on inequality between Thailand and South Korea is interesting because South Korea has maintained a more egalitarian income distribution than Thailand.

15.2 Individual Price Indices

This section explains the economic theory of price indices for a single consumer.

Suppose q is a $n \times 1$ quantity vector, which contains everything relevant to a representative consumer. Suppose $u(q)$ is the utility level consumers enjoy if they consume vector q. The conventional treatment of consumer behavior maximizes the utility function $u(q)$ subject to the constraint $p'q = x$, where p is a column vector of n market prices and x is income.[2] This maximization problem yields a system of n Marshallian demand equations $q = q(x, p)$.

---

[1] Individual utility depends not only on her consumption but also on the consumption of others in the society. Sen's (1974a) social welfare function is a particular member of this class.

[2] The literature on consumer theory assumes that the income of consumers equals their total expenditure, meaning that the consumers do not save. Following this tradition, this chapter uses income and total expenditure interchangeably.

The maximum attainable utility consumers enjoy is obtained by substituting demand equations $q = q(x, p)$ into the utility function $u(q)$ to get

$$u = u[q(x,p)] = \Psi(x,p) \tag{15.2.1}$$

which is called the indirect utility function. Solving (15.2.1) for x gives the expenditure function[3]

$$x = e(u,p), \tag{15.2.2}$$

which is interpreted as the minimum expenditure required to enjoy utility level u at the price vector p.

If the utility function $u(q)$ is continuous, increasing, and concave in q, then the expenditure function in (15.2.2) has the following properties, according to Diamond and McFadden (1974):

(i) $e(u, p)$ is strictly increasing in u for every p.
(ii) $e(u, p)$ is continuous jointly in prices and u.
(iii) $e(u, p)$ is (positively) linearly homogeneous in p for every u—that is, $e(u, \lambda p) = \lambda e(u, p)$ for $\lambda > 0$.
(iv) $e(u, p)$ is concave in p for every u.
(v) $\frac{\partial e(u,p)}{\partial p_i} = q_i$.

This expenditure function is the basis for measuring the price indices.

Suppose the price vector p changes to p^*, and then a true consumer price index measures the relative cost of buying a given level of utility at the new prices p^* compared to that at the old prices p. Diewert (1983) defined the Laspeyres–Konüs index as

$$LK(x) = \frac{e(u, p^*)}{e(u, p)} \tag{15.2.3}$$

where u is the base period utility level a consumer enjoys with income (or total expenditure) x.

$LK(x)$ is the true cost of living index of a consumer with income x. It can only be calculated if the expenditure function is known. It is difficult to estimate the expenditure function without knowing the utility function. A practical solution is to assume that the price elasticities of substitution are zero. Using Property (v) above, proved by Diamond and McFadden (1974), and applying Taylor's expansion, yields

---

[3] This function is also known as cost function in the literature but is also called expenditure function. This chapter will refer to it as expenditure function.

$$e(u, p^*) = e(u, p) + \sum_i^n \frac{(p_i^* - p_i)}{p_i} v_i(x) \qquad (15.2.4)$$

where $v_i(x) = p_i q_i(x)$, $q_i(x)$ is the consumption of the ith commodity by an individual with income x. The terms of the higher order of smallness in (15.2.4) have been ignored because of the assumption of zero substitution elasticities. Utilizing (15.2.4) into (15.2.3), $LK(x)$ index becomes

$$L(x) = \sum_{i=1}^n \frac{p_i^*}{p_i} w_i(x) \qquad (15.2.5)$$

where $w_i(x) = \frac{v_i(x)}{x}$ is the budget share of the ith commodity in the consumption of the individual with income x. $L(x)$ is the well-known Laspeyres price index of an individual with income x.

15.3 Social Price Indices

Since societies have many consumers, the single-person cost of living indices is of limited value to measure the impact of prices on inequality. This section reviews the three well-known social cost of living indices.

15.3.1 The Democratic Price Index

The democratic price index (DPI) proposed by Prais (1959) is defined as the average of the price indices of each individual in society.

Since there are many individuals in society, their income distribution can be described by the probability distribution $f(x)$. The DPI is given by

$$DPI = \int_0^\infty LK(x) f(x)\, dx = \int_0^\infty \frac{e(u, p^*)}{e(u, p)} f(x)\, dx \qquad (15.3.1)$$

To make the index (15.3.1) operational, it is necessary to assume that substitution elasticity is zero. Thus utilizing (15.2.4) into (15.3.1) gives

$$LDPI = \sum_{i=1}^n \frac{p_i^*}{p_i} \tilde{w}_i \qquad (15.3.2)$$

where

$$\tilde{w}_i = \int_0^\infty w_i(x) f(x)\, dx, \qquad (15.3.3)$$

where $\tilde{w}_i$ is the average of the individual budget shares of the society, and the LDPI is the Laspeyres democratic price index (Diewert 1983).

The LDPI has an interesting interpretation, which is highlighted below: $\overline{w}_i$ defined by

$$\overline{w}_i = \frac{\int_0^\infty v_i(x) f(x) dx}{\int_0^\infty x f(x) dx} \tag{15.3.4}$$

is the ratio of average expenditure of the society on the ith commodity divided by the average total expenditure. $\overline{w}_i$ is the ith commodity budget share of an average consumer in society. $\overline{w}_i$ will generally be different from $\widetilde{w}_i$. If the ith commodity is a necessary good such as food, $\widetilde{w}_i$ will be higher (lower) than $\widetilde{w}_i$ for the poor (non-poor). However, if the ith commodity is a luxury good, $\widetilde{w}_i$ will be lower (higher) than $\overline{w}_i$ for the poor (non-poor).

It will be informative to write equation (15.3.2) as

$$LDPI = \sum_{i=1}^n \frac{p_i^*}{p_i} \overline{w}_i - \sum_{i=1}^n \frac{p_i^*}{p_i} (\overline{w}_i - \widetilde{w}_i) \tag{15.3.5}$$

The first term in (15.3.5), given by $LPI = \sum_{i=1}^n \frac{p_i^*}{p_i} \overline{w}_i$ is the Laspeyres price index for an average consumer in the society (because $\overline{w}_i$ are the budget shares of a consumer who has an average income μ). This index is most commonly used to measure the price index, and almost all countries in the world use this index to measure the inflation rate over time.

The second term in (15.3.5) will be positive (negative) if the prices of necessary (luxury) goods increase at a faster rate than the prices of luxury (necessary) goods. Thus, the second term in (15.3.5) indicates whether the price changes hurt the poor more than the rich. Therefore, the price changes will be pro-poor (anti-poor) if the second term in (15.3.5) given by (LDPI–LPI) is negative (positive). This implies that the LDPI is sensitive to inequality changes due to relative price changes. Thus, the most commonly used Laspeyres price index L will underestimate (overestimate) the inflation rate if the prices of necessary (luxury) goods increase at faster rates than the prices of luxury (necessary) goods.

15.3.2 Multiplicative Democratic Price Index

Diewert (1993) proposed a multiplicative democratic price index (MDPI) given by

$$ln(MDPI) = \int_0^\infty [ln\{e(u, p^*)\} - ln\{e(u, p)\}] f(x) dx \tag{15.3.6}$$

The MDPI is the geometric mean of the price indices of each individual in society.

Again assuming that the price substitution elasticities are zero, Taylor's expansion yields

$$ln\left[e\left(u,p^*\right)\right] = ln\left[e\left(u,p\right)\right] + \sum_{i=1}^{n}\left[ln\left(p_i^*\right) - ln(p_i)\right]w_i\left(x\right) \qquad (15.3.7)$$

The terms of the higher order of smallness have been ignored (because of the assumption of zero substitution elasticities). Substituting (15.3.7) into (15.3.6) gives

$$ln(LMDPI) = \sum_{i=1}^{n}\left[ln(p_i^*) - ln(p_i)\right]\tilde{w}_i \qquad (15.3.8)$$

where $\tilde{w}_i$ is defined in (15.3.3). LMDPI may be called the Laspeyres multiplicative democratic price index. Similar to the LMDPI index in (15.3.8), the Laspeyres multiplicative price index (LMPI) for an average consumer in the society is proposed as

$$ln(LMPI) = \sum_{i=1}^{n}\left[ln(p_i^*) - ln(p_i)\right]\overline{w}_i \qquad (15.3.9)$$

$\overline{w}$ is defined in (15.3.4). This index is similar to Tornqvist's (1936) price index, but it differs in one respect. It only uses the average budget share for the base year, whereas Tornqvist's index uses the average budget shares of both base year and terminal years. Since the LMPI is defined for a single average consumer, it is entirely insensitive to society's inequality changes.

From (15.3.8) and (15.3.9), we can write

$$ln(LMDPI) = ln(LMPI) - \sum_{i=1}^{n}\left[ln(p_i^*) - ln(p_i)\right]\left(\overline{w}_i - \tilde{w}_i\right) \qquad (15.3.10)$$

The second term in (15.3.10) will be positive (negative) if the prices of necessary (luxury) goods increase at a faster rate than the prices of luxury (necessary) goods. Thus, this term indicates whether the price changes hurt the poor more than the rich. Therefore, the changes in prices will be pro-poor (anti-poor) if $[ln\left(LMDPI\right) - ln\left(LMPI\right)]$ is negative (positive). This implies that the LMDPI is sensitive to inequality changes due to relative price changes. Hence, it can capture the effect of change in relative prices on income inequality.

15.3.3 The Plutocratic Price Index

Pollak (1981) proposed a cost of living index, defined as the ratio of total expenditure required to enable each individual to attain her reference indifference curve at comparison prices, to that needed at reference prices. He calls this index the Scitovsky–Laspeyres index (SL). Prais (1959) refers to this index as a plutocratic price index. This index may be written as

$$SL = \frac{\int_0^\infty e(u, p^*) f(x)\, dx}{\int_0^\infty e(u, p) f(x)\, dx} = \frac{\mu(p^*)}{\mu(p)} \qquad (15.3.11)$$

where $\mu(p)$ is the mean income of the population at the base year price vector p, and $\mu(p^*)$ was the mean income of the population when the price vector p had changed to p^*. But the utility had remained the same. SL can also be written as

$$SL = \frac{1}{\mu(p)} \int_0^\infty \frac{e(u, p^*)}{e(u, p)} x f(x)\, dx = \frac{1}{\mu(p)} \int_0^\infty LK(x)\, x f(x)\, dx \qquad (15.3.12)$$

where $LK(x) = \frac{e(u, p^*)}{e(u, p)}$ is the individual Laspeyres–Konüs price index for an individual with income x, defined in (15.2.3).

SL in (15.3.12) is the weighted average of individual price indices, where weights are proportional to individuals' income. The rich, therefore, are given greater weight than the poor in the measurement of inflation. A rich man's price index motivated Prais (1959) to name it a plutocratic price index. This index will be insensitive to relative inequality changes since the weights are proportional to the individual's aggregate income share. The changes in prices will affect every individual proportionally to their income. Thus, the index does not inform whether the price changes hurt the poor proportionally than the rich.

15.4 Social Expenditure Function

The group cost of living indices discussed in the previous section were obtained by aggregating the individuals' price indices. The aggregation procedures were defined on an ad hoc basis. Any group price index construction should be based on a social welfare function. This section describes the true social cost of living indices in terms of the social expenditure function.

Suppose there are n persons in a society, and each person has its utility, u_i, i varies from 1 to n, then the vector utilities is given by

$$\tilde{u} = (u_1, u_2, \ldots \ldots \ldots u_n)$$

The social expenditure function $e(\tilde{u}, p)$ is the minimum money income given to every person in society. Each of them enjoys $\tilde{u}$ levels of utilities at a given price vector p. Formally, one can describe it as

$$f[e(\tilde{u}, p)] = f[e(u_1, p),\, e(u_2, p),\, \ldots \ldots \ldots e(u_n, p)]$$

The social expenditure function $e\left(\tilde{u}, p\right)$ is the money metric social expenditure function, measured in monetary units (for instance, in dollars). It has the following properties, according to Son and Kakwani (2006):

(i) $e\left(\tilde{u}, p\right)$ is an increasing function of $\tilde{u}$ for all p.[4]
(ii) $e\left(\tilde{u}, p\right)$ is increasing and concave in p for every $\tilde{u}$.[5]
(iii) $e\left(\tilde{u}, p\right)$ is (positively) linearly homogeneous in p for every $\tilde{u}$—that is, $e\left(\tilde{u}, \lambda p\right) = \lambda e\left(\tilde{u}, p\right)$.

If the price vector p changes to p*, every person should receive the minimum income $e\left(\tilde{u}, p^*\right)$ so that everyone in society enjoys the same utility level as before the price change; therefore, the true social price index can be defined as (TSPI) (Son and Kakwani 2006):

$$TSPI = \frac{e(\tilde{u}, p)}{e(\tilde{u}, p)} \tag{15.4.1}$$

From Property (iii) above, if all prices increase by the same proportion—that is, $p^* = \lambda p$—TSPI must be equal to λ. This is an essential requirement of a price index, which is satisfied by TSPI.

Again, assuming that price elasticities of substitution are zero, then from Taylor's expansion, we obtain

$$e\left(\tilde{u}, p^*\right) = e\left(\tilde{u}, p\right) + \sum_{i=1}^{n} \left(p_i^* - p_i\right) \frac{\partial e\left(\tilde{u}, p\right)}{\partial p_i} \tag{15.4.2}$$

where terms of higher-order of smallness have been ignored. Substituting (15.4.2) into (15.4.1), TSPI can be approximated by

$$LSPI = \sum_{i=1}^{n} \frac{p_i^*}{p_i} \tilde{\eta}_i \tag{15.4.3}$$

where

$$\tilde{\eta}_i = \frac{p_i}{e\left(\tilde{u}, p\right)} \frac{\partial e\left(\tilde{u}, p\right)}{\partial p_i}. \tag{15.4.4}$$

LSPI in (15.4.3) is the Laspeyres social price index. $\tilde{\eta}_i$ is the elasticity of $e\left(\tilde{u}, p\right)$ with respect to p_i, which is called the social price elasticity. The interpretation of this elasticity is that if the price of the ith commodity increases by 1%, the minimum income given to everyone in society must increase by $\tilde{\eta}_i$% so that everyone in society enjoys

---

[4] It means that $e(\tilde{u}, \mathbf{p})$ increases as any u_i increases for all $\mathbf{p}$.
[5] It means that $e(\tilde{u}, \mathbf{p})$ increases as any p_i increases for all $\tilde{u}$.

the same levels of utility as before price changes. If all prices rise by 1%, intuitively, everyone should be compensated by 1% so that they all enjoy the same level of utility as before the price increases. Therefore, the sum of elasticity of all commodities must add up to one:

$$\sum_{i=1}^{n} \tilde{\eta}_i = 1. \tag{15.4.5}$$

If all prices increase by the same proportion, equation (15.4.5) ensures that LSPI will increase by the same proportion, which is the minimum requirement of a price index.

This section has presented a general framework of social price indices. It is essential to specify a social expenditure function to make these indices operational. The following section derives the social price indices for alternative social welfare functions.

15.5 Class of Atkinson's Social Expenditure Functions

Suppose $x = e(u, p)$ is the expenditure (or income) of a consumer who faces the base year price vector p. Following Atkinson (1970), the social expenditure function is utilitarian, and every individual has the same utility function $g[e(u, p)]$, where $g(x)$ is increasing in x and concave, then the social expenditure function is given by

$$W = \int_0^\infty g[e(u, p)]f(x)dx \tag{15.5.1}$$

Atkinson (1970) required that the social expenditure function be invariant to any positive linear transformation of the utility function. He utilized the concept of "the equally distributed equivalent level of income" to derive such a social expenditure function. Suppose $e(\tilde{u}, p)$ is the equally distributed equivalent level of income, which would result in the same level of social expenditure as the present distribution if received by every individual. Then Atkinson's social expenditure function $e(\tilde{u}, p)$ is given by

$$g[e(\tilde{u}, p)] = \int_0^\infty g[e(u, p)]f(x)\,dx \tag{15.5.2}$$

As shown above, this equation's social expenditure function will satisfy properties (i) to (ii) given above. The third property (iii) of social expenditure function is that it is positively linearly homogeneous in p for every $\tilde{u}$, and will be satisfied if it is assumed that $g(x)$ is a homothetic function of x. A class of homothetic functions is given by (Atkinson 1970):

$$g(x) = A + \frac{Bx^{1-\epsilon}}{1-\epsilon}, \quad \epsilon \neq 1$$

$$= A + B\log_e(x), \quad \epsilon = 1 \tag{15.5.3}$$

where $\in > 0$ is a measure of relative risk-aversion, constant for all x for this function. Substituting (15.5.3) into (15.5.2) yields the social expenditure function

$$e_\in (\tilde{u}, p) = \left[\int_0^\infty \{e(u,p)\}^{1-\varepsilon} f(x)\, dx \right]^{\frac{1}{1-\varepsilon}}, \quad if\ \varepsilon \neq 1$$

$$= exp \left[\int_0^\infty \log\{e(u,p)\} f(x)\, dx \right], \qquad if\ \varepsilon = 1 \qquad (15.5.4)$$

where exp stands for the exponential function and the parameter ε measures relative sensitivity to income transfers at various income or expenditure levels. As ε rises, more and more weight is attached to income transfers at the lower end of the distribution and less weight to transfers at the top. If $\in = 0$, $e(\tilde{u}, p) = \mu(p)$, the society's mean income in the base year prices. This situation reflects society's inequality-neutral attitude, where society does not care about inequality.

As ε approaches infinity, $e(\tilde{u}, p)$ in (15.5.4) approaches the utility function of the poorest person in society.

Substituting (15.5.4) into (15.4.1) yields the true social price index (TSPI) for the class of Atkinson social welfare functions as

$$ITSPI (\in) = \frac{[\int_0^\infty \{e(u,p^*)\}^{(1-\in)} f(x)\, dx]^{\frac{1}{(1-\in)}}}{\int_0^\infty \{e(u,p)\}^{(1-\in)} f(x)\, dx]^{\frac{1}{(1-\in)}}}, \quad \in \neq 1$$

$$= \frac{exp[\int_0^\infty ln\{e(u,p^*)\} f(x)\, dx}{exp[\int_0^\infty ln\{e(u,p)\} f(x)\, dx}, \quad \in = 1$$

$$= \frac{e(u_p, p^*)}{e(u_p, p)}, \quad \in \rightarrow \infty \qquad (15.5.5)$$

where exp stands for the exponential function.

The different members of this class can now be discussed. Substituting $\varepsilon = 0$ in (15.5.5) gives Pollak's (1981) Scitovsky–Laspeyres group price index (SL) as given in (15.3.11). Thus, Pollak's SL price index is based on a social welfare function that is not strictly concave or quasi-concave. Therefore, this index cannot measure the impact of price changes on income inequality.

When $\varepsilon = 1$, from the social welfare in (15.5.4) yields $TSPI (\varepsilon)$, which is identical to Diewert's (1993) multiplicative democratic price index (MDPI), as defined in (15.3.6). Therefore, the social welfare function implied by Diewert's index is strictly concave, and, therefore, this index will be sensitive to changes in real inequality in society. When $\in \rightarrow \infty$ equation (15.5.5) yields the $TSPI$ for the poorest person in society.

The elasticity of $e\left(\tilde{u},\boldsymbol{p}\right)$ with respect to p_i given in (15.5.4) is given by

$$\tilde{\eta}_i\left(\varepsilon\right) = \frac{\int_0^\infty w_i\left(x\right)x^{(1-\epsilon)}f\left(x\right)dx}{\int_0^\infty x^{(1-\epsilon)}f\left(x\right)dx}, \qquad \epsilon \neq 1$$

$$= \int_0^\infty w_i\left(x\right)f\left(x\right)dx, \qquad \epsilon = 1$$

$$= w_{ip}, \qquad\qquad\qquad \epsilon \to \infty \qquad (15.5.6)$$

where $w_i\left(x\right)$ is the ith budget share of the consumer with income x, and w_{ip} is the ith budget share of the poorest person in society. Assuming that the substitution elasticities are zero, using the elasticities in (15.5.6) into (15.4.3) yields the approximations to the TSPI for the members of Atkinson's social welfare function.

The Laspeyres price indices for different values of ϵ can now be derived. When $\epsilon = 0, \tilde{\eta}_i\left(\varepsilon\right) = \overline{w}_i$ defined in (15.3.4) is the average budget share of society. Substituting this elasticity into (15.4.3) yields an average consumer's Laspeyres Price Index (LPI).

When $\epsilon = 1, \tilde{\eta}_i\left(\varepsilon\right) = \tilde{w}_i$, defined in (15.3.3), is the average of the individual budget shares of the society. Substituting this elasticity into (15.4.3) gives the Laspeyres Democratic price index (LDPI). As ϵ approaches ∞, the elasticity in (15.5.6) approaches the budget share of the poorest person in society; substituting in (15.4.3) gives the Laspeyres price index of the poorest person in society.

15.6 Class of Interdependent Social Expenditure Functions

The previous section derived social price indices from the Atkinson social welfare functions. These functions assume that an individual's utility depends only on their income or consumption. This section derives a social price index class that considers the interdependence of individual utilities. Such social welfare functions capture the idea of relative deprivation suffered by individuals with different income levels; the lower a person is on the welfare scale, the greater is her sense of deprivation with respect to others in the society.

Chapter 5 discussed Sen's (1974a) social welfare function, which considers the proportion of wealthier persons and captures the relative deprivation suffered by a person. Kakwani (1980b) proposed a generalization of Sen's social welfare function, allowing one to judge society's degree of aversion to inequality. Chapter 5 discussed this general class of social welfare function of which Sen's social welfare function is a particular case. The social expenditure function for this general class of social welfare function may be written as

$$e_k\left(\tilde{u},p\right) = (k+1)\int_0^\infty x\left(1 - F\left(x\right)\right)^k f\left(x\right)dx = \mu\left(p\right)\left(1 - G_k\left(p\right)\right) \qquad (15.6.1)$$

$F(x)$ is the distribution function; the proportion of people with income less than or equal to x. $\mu(p)$ is the mean income and G_k is the generalized Gini index. The parameter k is similar to the inequality aversion parameter discussed in the previous section.

When $k = 0$, $e_k(\tilde{u},p) = \mu(p)$, in which case the income of all individuals is given the same weight, reflecting an inequality-neutral attitude of society, which does not care about inequality at all and focuses solely on enhancing economic growth.

When $k=1$, G_k equals the Gini index G, in which the deprivation suffered by an individual with income x is two times the proportion of individuals with income higher than x. When $k=2$, the deprivation suffered by an individual with income x is three times the square of the proportion of individuals with income higher than x. Thus, as k increases, the deprivation suffered by individuals with lower incomes increases.

The elasticity of $e_k(\tilde{u},p)$ with respect to ith price p_i is obtained as

$$\tilde{\eta}_i(k) = \frac{\int_0^\infty w_i(x) x [1 - F(x)]^k f(x)\, dx}{\int_0^\infty x [1 - F(x)]^k f(x)\, dx} \tag{15.6.2}$$

which on substituting in (15.4.3) gives the k-class Laspeyres class of social price indices

$$LSPI(k) = \sum_{i=1}^n \frac{p_i^*}{p_i} \tilde{\eta}_i(k) \tag{15.6.3}$$

The k is the inequality aversion parameter. Substituting $k=0$ in (15.6.2) yields $\tilde{\eta}_i(k) = \overline{w}_i$, and therefore, $LSPI(k)$ in (15.6.3) leads to the widely used Laspeyres price index (LPI) for an average consumer. When $k=1$, $LSPI(k)$ leads to

$$LSPI(1) = \sum_{i=1}^n \frac{p_i^*}{p_i} \overline{w}_i - \frac{1}{(1-G)} \sum_{i=1}^n \frac{p_i^*}{p_i} \overline{w}_i E_i \tag{15.6.4}$$

where $E_i = C_i - G$, C_i is the concentration index of the ith commodity, which is defined by

$$2 \int_0^\infty v_i(x)\, [1 - F(x)] f(x)\, dx = \overline{v}_i (1 - C_i) \tag{15.6.5}$$

$v_i(x) = p_i q_i(x)$ is the expenditure of a person on an ith commodity with income x, and $\overline{v}_i$ is the average expenditure on the ith commodity.

$E_i = C_i - G$ is the aggregate elasticity of the ith commodity developed in Chapter 9. The ith commodity is luxury (necessity) if E_i is greater (less) than zero. If the prices of necessities (luxuries) increase at faster rates than those of luxuries (necessities), the second term in (15.6.4) will be positive (negative). Thus, the second term's sign in this equation indicates whether or not the price changes have a relatively larger (smaller) adverse impact on the poor.

15.7 Impact of Price Change on Inequality

As noted in the previous sections, the social price indices provide a means of assessing whether or not price changes hurt the poor or the non-poor (or how price changes affect aggregate inequality). This section derives the explicit relationship between social price indices and growth in aggregate inequality.

For any general money metric social welfare function, inequality in society at the base year price vector, according to Atkinson (1970), is defined as:

$$A(p) = 1 - \frac{e(\tilde{u}, p)}{\mu(p)} \tag{15.7.1}$$

where

$$\mu(p) = \int_0^\infty e(u, p)f(x)dx \tag{15.7.2}$$

is the mean income of the society in the base period and $e(\tilde{u}, p)$ is the money metric measure of Atkinson's social welfare function defined in (15.5.4).

Suppose the price vector p changes to p^* in the next period, then $e(\tilde{u}, p^*)$ is the social expenditure per person so that the society enjoys the same level of social welfare $\tilde{u}$ (as in the base period). Because of the price changes, the consumers' real income will change. Every person in society will need to be compensated by an amount $[e(\tilde{u}, p^*) - e(\tilde{u}, p)]$ to maintain social welfare before the price changes. This implies that the society's real standard of living after the price change will be given by

$$e(\tilde{u}^*, p^*) = e(\tilde{u}, p) - [e(\tilde{u}, p^*) - e(\tilde{u}, p)] = 2e(\tilde{u}, p) - e(\tilde{u}, p^*) \tag{15.7.3}$$

where $\tilde{u}^*$ is society's utility vector after the price changes.

Similarly, the real standard of living of an individual with income $x = e(u, p)$ after the price changes will be given by

$$e(u^*, p^*) = 2e(u, p) - e(u, p^*), \tag{15.7.4}$$

which on substituting in (15.7.2) gives the average real income of the society after the price change as

$$\mu(p^*) = 2\mu(p) - \mu(p^*) \tag{15.7.5}$$

where

$$\mu(p^*) = \int_0^\infty e(u, p^*)f(x)\,dx.$$

Combining (15.7.3) and (15.7.5) with (15.7.1) yields the real inequality in the society after the price change as

$$A\left(p^*\right) = 1 - \frac{e\left(\tilde{u}^*, p^*\right)}{\mu\left(p^*\right)} = 1 - \frac{2e\left(\tilde{u}, p\right) - e\left(\tilde{u}, p^*\right)}{2\mu\left(p\right) - \mu\left(p^*\right)} \qquad (15.7.6)$$

Using (14.7.1) and (15.7.6) into (15.4.1) yields the true social price index (TSPI) as

$$TSPI = \frac{\mu(p^*)}{\mu(p)} + \frac{\mu^*(p^*)[(A(p^*) - A(p)]}{\mu(p)[1 - A(p)]} \qquad (15.7.7)$$

$\frac{[(A(p^*) - A(p)]}{[(1 - A(p))]}$ is the percentage change in inequality caused due to price change. The first term on the right-hand side of (15.7.7) is the Scitovsky–Laspeyres social price index, which Pollak introduced (1981). This measure is neutral to any growth in inequality. The second term on the right-hand side of (15.7.7) measures the distributional impact of price change. This term is positive if changes in prices increase the aggregate inequality and will be negative if price changes reduce inequality in society.

It is interesting to note from (15.7.7) that the initial inequality level affects the social price index. This suggests that the usual approach to computing inflation rate based on a single average consumer method will give biased results in a society with high inequality. Most countries measure their inflation rates using the Laspeyres price index that ignores inequality, which results in an inaccurate inflation rate.

15.8 Social Price Indices: A Case Study of Thailand

This section presents the empirical estimates of social price indices for Thailand. These indices were computed for 1986–1995, and Thailand's Socio-economic Survey (SES) data was used for 1990. The market prices of various goods and services from 1986 to 1995 were obtained from the Department of Business Economics, Ministry of Commerce, Bangkok, Thailand.

The National Statistical Office (NSO) of Thailand conducts SES regularly. The surveys cover all private non-institutional households residing permanently in municipal areas, sanitary districts, and villages. However, they exclude that part of the population living in transient hotels, rooming houses, boarding schools, military barracks, temples, hospitals, prisons, and other institutions (see Report of the 1990 Household Socio-economic Survey, NSO, Thailand).

The NSO Thailand provided unit record data for this study, giving expenditures on various goods and services for 13,186 households. These surveys provided a detailed disaggregation of goods and sources; matching these data with market prices was not a problem.

The surveys provided weights for each sample household to expand estimates for the defined populations. The calculations of weights are explained as follows. Suppose N is the number of households in the people and n is the sample of households selected in the survey, then the weight attached to every household will be N/n. This weight is not correct because it is based on the assumption that every household in the population has the same probability of being selected. The weight given to each household must be determined by the probability of selection within a stratum adjusted to account for non-responding households. These weights depend on the sample design adopted by the survey. These weights are called the household weights, the sum of which must add up to the total number of households in Thailand.

The population weights were determined by multiplying the population household weights by the household size. The sum of all population weights must add to the total number of persons in Thailand.

Table 15.1 presents the social price indices based on Atkinson's class of social welfare functions. These indices are used to calculate the annual inflation rates. The social price indices and underlying inflation rates were calculated for different inequality aversion parameter values.

As pointed out, when the inequality aversion parameter is zero, the society is inequality neutral or indifferent to inequality. The higher the inequality aversion parameter, the greater the importance society attaches to inequality. The empirical estimates are presented for five alternative inequality aversion parameters: 0, 0.5, 1, 1.5, and 2.

The annual inflation rate for the zero value of inequality aversion is 3.8% for 1987–88. When the inequality aversion parameter increases to 2, the inflation rate becomes 5.2%. The increase in the inequality aversion parameter from 0 to 2 increases the annual inflation rate by 1.4%. This increase in the inflation rate signifies an increase in inequality. This concludes that changes in consumer prices during the 1987–88 period affected the poor more than the rich. Consequently, the real inequality in society increased due to price changes.

Table 15.1 Social price indices and inflation rates in Thailand based on Atkinson's social welfare function

Years	Social price indices Inequality aversion parameter equal to					Inflation rate Inequality aversion parameter equal to				
	0	0.5	1	1.5	2	0	0.5	1	1.5	2
1986	100	100	100	100	100	–	–	–	–	–
1987	102.4	102.5	102.5	102.6	102.6	2.4	2.5	2.5	2.6	2.6
1988	106.3	106.8	107.2	107.6	107.9	3.8	4.2	4.5	4.9	5.2
1989	110.7	111.5	112.1	112.6	113.0	4.2	4.4	4.6	4.7	4.7
1990	116.4	117.2	117.7	118.2	118.5	5.1	5.1	5.0	5.0	4.9
1991	122.8	123.5	124.1	124.5	124.9	5.5	5.4	5.4	5.4	5.3
1992	127.4	128.3	128.9	129.4	129.7	3.8	3.9	3.9	3.9	3.9
1993	131.9	132.3	132.6	132.7	132.9	3.5	3.2	2.8	2.6	2.4
1994	137.4	138.1	138.4	138.6	138.7	4.2	4.4	4.4	4.4	4.4
1995	144.3	145.3	145.8	146.1	146.2	5.0	5.2	5.3	5.4	5.4

Source: Son and Kakwani (2006).

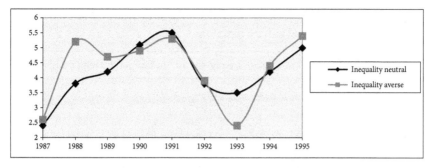

Fig. 15.1 Inflation rates in Thailand

The entire period from 1986 to 1995 shows that the overall price index has increased by 44.3% when the inequality aversion parameter equals zero. Still, when it takes a value equal to 2, the prices have increased by 46.2%. That means that the changes in prices in the 1986–1995 period favored the rich more than the poor because they contributed to an additional annual inflation rate of 1.9%. And hence, the increases in prices led to a rise in real income inequality in Thailand.

Figure 15.1 depicts Thailand's inflation rates between 1986 and 1995 based on the two values of inequality aversion parameter: (i) when the inequality aversion parameter is 0, and (ii) when it is equal to 2. The gap in the two inflation rates indicates the impact of price changes on inequality. If the inflation rate for $\in = 2$ is higher than that for $\in = 0$, it means that the changes in prices have led to an increase in real inequality; otherwise, it has reduced real inequality. Figure 15.1 depicts the increasing or decreasing trends in inequality due to changes in relative prices. It shows that price-induced inequality increased between 1986 and 1989, followed by a decreasing trend between 1989 and 1991. But, the overall picture emerging is that changes in prices hurt the poor more than the rich,

Table 15.2 presents social price indices and their underlying inflation rates calculated using Kakwani's class of social welfare functions. In these functions, k is the inequality aversion parameter, and the four alternative values of k used were 0, 1, 2, and 3.

When the inequality aversion parameter k is zero, the society is inequality neutral, meaning indifferent to inequality. The higher the inequality aversion parameter, the greater the importance society attaches to inequality

Table 15.2 shows that the adverse effects of price changes on inequality are significant. When $k=0$, the price index is 44.3%, but when k increases to 3, the price index increases to 48.4% between 1986 and 1995. This means that an inflation rate of 4.1% is attributed to the inequality increasing bias of price changes.

Next, it is helpful to know the impact of price changes on inequality. Inequality can be measured in many ways, depending on the assumed social welfare function. For the Kakwani class of interdependent social welfare functions, inequality measure will vary with the inequality aversion parameter k; the larger the inequality aversion

Table 15.2 Social price indices and inflation rates in Thailand based on Kakwani's class of social welfare functions

	Social price indices with k equal to				Inflation rates with k equal to			
	0	**1**	**2**	**3**	**0**	**1**	**2**	**3**
1986	100	100	100	100	–	–	–	–
1987	102.4	102.6	102.6	102.6	2.4	2.6	2.6	2.6
1988	106.3	107.3	107.9	108.2	3.8	4.6	5.1	5.4
1989	110.7	112.3	113.1	113.5	4.2	4.7	4.8	4.9
1990	116.4	118.0	118.7	119.1	5.1	5.1	5.0	4.9
1991	122.8	124.5	125.3	125.8	5.5	5.5	5.6	5.6
1992	127.4	129.5	130.4	130.9	3.8	4.0	4.1	4.1
1993	131.9	133.0	133.5	133.8	3.5	2.8	2.4	2.2
1994	137.4	139.2	139.7	140.1	4.2	4.6	4.7	4.7
1995	144.3	147.0	147.8	148.4	5.0	5.6	5.8	5.9

Source: Son and Kakwani (2006).

parameter, the greater is the weight attached to poor individuals in the society. When $k=1$, the inequality measure is the well-known Gini index.

Table 15.3 presents the values of inequality measures for different values of k. The values in 1990 are the actual values of inequality measures calculated from the 1990 SES data. The values in other years measure the impact of real price changes on inequality.

Table 15.3 shows that the annual increases in prices have generally increased inequality every year except in 1989–90 and 1992–93. The last row in the table indicates

Table 15.3 Impact of prices on inequality in Thailand based on the Kakwani social welfare functions

Year	Inequality measures with k equals			Annual change in inequality with k equals		
	1	**2**	**3**	**1**	**2**	**3**
1986	49.8	49.8	49.8	–	–	–
1987	49.9	49.9	49.9	0.2	0.3	0.3
1988	50.4	50.7	50.9	1	1.5	1.8
1989	50.7	51.1	51.4	0.6	0.9	1
1990	49.8	49.8	49.8	−1.8	−2.5	−3
1991	50.9	51.5	51.8	2.3	3.3	3.9
1992	51.2	51.9	52.3	0.6	0.8	1
1993	50.6	51	51.2	−1.2	−1.7	−2
1994	51.2	51.7	52	1.1	1.3	1.4
1995	52.2	53	53.5	2	2.6	2.9
1986–1995	–	–	–	4.8	6.4	7.3

Source: Son and Kakwani (2006).

the impact of price changes on inequality for the entire period from 1986 to 1995. A conclusion emerging from it is that price changes have generally contributed to increased inequality. For instance, the inequality measure for $k=1$ is the Gini index, which has increased by 4.8% due to changes in relative prices between 1986 and 1995. Thus, the increases in relative prices have led to a higher degree of relative deprivation in society. Interestingly, when $k=3$, the percentage increase in inequality is 7.3%, meaning that the magnitude of inequality increases significantly if the higher weight to the poor increases. This result concludes that the ultra-poor have suffered the most due to changes in relative prices.

15.9 A Comparison with South Korea

This section presents the social price indices for South Korea. Comparing Thailand and South Korea is interesting because the latter has maintained a significantly more equal income distribution than the former.

South Korea conducts the Family Income and Expenditure surveys every year, so it is possible to compute yearly social price indices and their underlying inflation rates from 1990 to 1999.

Tables 15.4 presents the social price indices and their underlying inflation rates in South Korea based on Atkinson's social welfare functions. The social budget shares were computed using the 1990 Family Income and Expenditure Survey.

The results show that the inflation rates in South Korea had generally been much higher than in Thailand. The inflation rate became more than 8% in the 1997–98

Table 15.4 Social price indices and inflation rates in South Korea based on Atkinson's social welfare function

Year	Social price indices 1990–99				Annual inflation rates			
	Inequality aversion parameter equal to				Inequality aversion parameter equal to			
	0	1	2	3	0	1	2	3
1990	100.0	100.0	100.0	100.0	–	–	–	–
1991	108.7	108.9	109.1	109.2	8.7	8.9	9.1	9.2
1992	114.9	115.1	115.3	115.5	5.7	5.7	5.7	5.7
1993	120.1	120.2	120.4	120.5	4.5	4.5	4.4	4.4
1994	128.0	128.3	128.6	128.8	6.6	6.7	6.8	6.9
1995	133.2	133.5	133.7	133.9	4.1	4.0	4.0	4.0
1996	140.0	140.2	140.4	140.6	5.1	5.1	5.0	5.0
1997	146.3	146.5	146.7	147.0	4.5	4.5	4.5	4.5
1998	158.1	158.5	159.0	159.6	8.1	8.2	8.3	8.5
1999	159.8	160.3	160.9	161.6	1.1	1.2	1.2	1.3

Source: Son and Kakwani (2006).

period when the most severe economic crisis struck the country. The South Korean won depreciated substantially, which fueled inflation. However, the inflation rate dropped to just over 1% in the subsequent period, mainly due to a drastic contraction of the aggregate GDP. It is interesting to note that increasing the value of the inequality aversion parameter did not change the annual inflation rates much, as happened in Thailand.

Figure 15.2 depicts the two curves of inflation rates for the inequality parameter 0 and 2. The two curves almost coincide in the entire period. It means that relative price changes on inequality had a minimal impact—almost insignificant. A similar conclusion is reached for Kakwani's social welfare functions in Table 15.6.

The impact of relative price changes on inequality depends on the population's variation in consumption patterns across income groups. South Korea is a relatively

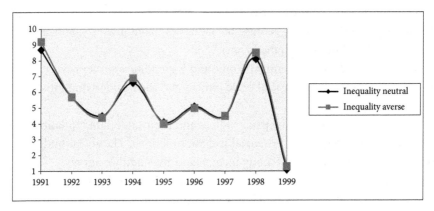

Fig. 15.2 Inflation rates in South Korea based on Atkinson's welfare function

Table 15.5 Social price indices and inflation rates in South Korea based on Kakwani's social welfare function

	Social price indices				Annual inflation rates			
	Inequality aversion parameter k equal to				Inequality aversion parameter k equal to			
Year	0	1	2	3	0	1	2	3
1990	100.0	100.0	100.0	100.0	–	–	–	–
1991	108.7	109.0	109.1	109.2	8.7	9.0	9.1	9.2
1992	114.9	115.2	115.3	115.4	5.7	5.7	5.7	5.7
1993	120.1	120.3	120.4	120.5	4.5	4.4	4.4	4.4
1994	128.0	128.4	128.6	128.8	6.6	6.8	6.8	6.9
1995	133.2	133.6	133.8	133.9	4.1	4.0	4.0	4.0
1996	140.0	140.3	140.5	140.6	5.1	5.0	5.0	5.0
1997	146.3	146.6	146.8	146.9	4.5	4.5	4.5	4.5
1998	158.1	158.7	159.1	159.4	8.1	8.3	8.4	8.5
1999	159.8	160.6	161.1	161.4	1.1	1.2	1.2	1.3

Source: Son and Kakwani (2006).

Table 15.6 Impact of price changes on inequality in South Korea based on Kakwani's social welfare function

Year	Inequality measures for *k* equal to			% Annual change in inequality for *k* equal to		
	1	2	3	1	2	3
1990	29.9	39.4	44.7	–	–	–
1991	30.1	39.7	44.9	0.7	0.6	0.6
1992	30.1	39.7	45	0.2	0.2	0.2
1993	30	39.7	44.9	−0.3	−0.2	−0.2
1994	30.3	39.9	45.2	0.8	0.7	0.7
1995	30.2	39.9	45.2	−0.2	−0.1	−0.1
1996	30.2	39.9	45.2	−0.1	0	0
1997	30.3	40	45.3	0.3	0.4	0.4
1998	30.9	40.9	46.4	2	2.2	2.2
1999	31.2	41.3	46.8	1.1	1.1	1
1990–99	–	–	–	4.6	4.8	4.8

Source: Son and Kakwani (2006).

homogeneous country with relatively low inequality; it is conjectured that the changes in relative prices on inequality would be relatively small. The comparison between Thailand and South Korea supports this conjecture. A significant conclusion emerging from this analysis is that relative price changes on inequality are more critical in highly unequal countries than in low inequality countries with homogeneous populations.

15.10 Concluding Remarks

This chapter has discussed new methodologies for the computation of social price indices. These indices indicate whether or not the price changes have a favorable (or unfavorable) impact on the welfare of the poor; in other words, whether the price changes have decreased (increases) in inequality. Applying this methodology to the Thai and South Korean data shows that the price changes have affected the poor more than the rich in both countries. But, the impact of prices on inequality had been more pronounced in Thailand.

Compared with South Korea, Thailand has experienced much higher inequality, increasing more or less monotonically (Kakwani 1997). The government of Thailand has been deeply concerned with the increasing trend in inequality. Formulating inequality-reducing policies requires knowledge of the causes of the increase in inequality. This chapter has provided a valuable link between price changes and income inequality. The chapter has recommended that Thailand's Department of Business Economics produces social price indices that capture the impact of prices on inequality. The usual Laspeyres price index that it currently uses is insensitive to any change in inequality.

In South Korea, the usual Laspeyres method of computing price indices seems to provide reasonable inflation rates.

This chapter has developed true social price indices using the economic theory of expenditure functions. But such indices cannot be computed from household surveys unless individuals' utility functions are known. These indices can be made empirically operational if it is assumed that the substitution elasticities are zero, and this assumption exaggerates the welfare losses associated with increases in prices. From the theoretical point of view, it is correct to say that the estimates presented in the chapter are biased; it is assumed that there is no consumer substitution taking place in response to changes in relative prices. But many empirical studies have indicated that the bias is small enough that it can probably be ignored.

The empirical results in the chapter assume that all households face the same prices of various commodities. This may be an unrealistic assumption because regional price differences exist in both Thailand and South Korea. Fortunately, the information on regional prices is generally available in many countries, so extending the methodologies presented in the chapter will be worthwhile to account for regional differences in prices.

16

Poverty Price Indices

16.1 Introduction

People have different economic circumstances and consumption patterns, so the impact of prices on living standards also differs from one person to another. Kenneth Arrow (1958) noted that people with lower incomes are likely to have consumption patterns that differ from those with higher incomes. Consumption patterns reveal, on average, those with lower incomes spend more of their income on necessities than on luxuries. Thus, if the prices of necessities increase faster than those of luxuries, the poor will be more adversely affected than the non-poor. Hence, prices can have a significant effect on poverty. Still, there is hardly a study dealing with measuring prices' effect on poverty. However, Son and Kakwani (2008) were the first to develop a methodology to capture the impact of consumer prices on poverty. This chapter elaborates on their methodology, providing policy insights.

This chapter provides a systematic measurement of the impact of prices on poverty. Several indices can measure poverty; the most common among them is the class of Foster, Greer, and Thorbecke (FGT) (1984) poverty measures. The chapter measures the effect of prices on poverty measured by the entire class of FGT poverty measures. The price effect is captured by employing the price elasticity of poverty. The chapter demonstrates that this elasticity can be decomposed into the sum of two components. The first component is the income effect, and the second component is the distribution effect. The distribution effect determines whether price changes are pro-poor or anti-poor.

However, this chapter's main contribution is a new price index for the poor (PIP). The weights used in the new index are derived from the price elasticity of poverty. Thus, there will be a monotonic relationship between the PIP and the poverty changes; the higher the index, the greater the increase in poverty.

Most countries in the world calculate inflation rates using the Laspeyres price index, and this index cannot capture the impact of inflation on poverty. The chapter demonstrates that the difference between the PIP and the Laspeyres price index informs whether inflation is pro-poor or anti-poor; whether inflation contributes to an increase or decrease in poverty.

This chapter presents a case study of Brazil's price indices and their underlying inflation rates over 1999–2006. The study uses the 2002–3 Brazilian National Household Survey (PNAD) as the base year survey, covering 48,470 households throughout the

Economic Inequality and Poverty. Nanak Kakwani and Hyun Son, Oxford University Press.
© Nanak Kakwani and Hyun Son (2022). DOI: 10.1093/oso/9780198852841.003.0016

entire country. The empirical results show that Brazil's inflation has increased poverty during the 1999–2006 period.

16.2 Price Elasticity of Individual Money Metric Utility

Suppose $\mathbf{p}$ is a $n \times 1$ price vector in the base year, changing to $\mathbf{p}^*$ in the terminal period. Following that, how much will the price changes affect an individual's real income (or expenditure)?[1] This question is answered using the expenditure function discussed in Chapter 15. An expenditure function is a function of consumer utility level u and market prices consumers face. The vector of market prices $\mathbf{p}$, given by $x = e(u, \mathbf{p})$, is the minimum expenditure a consumer requires to enjoy u level of utility when the price vector is $\mathbf{p}$.[2] The expenditure function can also be called the money metric utility function.

Hicks (1946) developed two methods of calculating the welfare change due to price changes: compensation variation (CV) and equivalent variation (EV). The CV is the individual's compensation to maintain the same utility level before the price change.[3]

Using the CV, the real income of the individual with income x will change by

$$\Delta x = -[e(u, \mathbf{p}^*) - e(u, \mathbf{p})],   \tag{16.2.1}$$

which on using Taylor expansion and assuming that the substitution elasticities are zero, yields

$$dx = - \sum_{i=1}^{n} (p_i^* - p_i) q_i(x) = \sum_{i=1}^{n} dp_i q_i(x),   \tag{16.2.2}$$

which is derived using the property of expenditure function $q_i(x) = \frac{\partial e(u,p)}{\partial p_i}$, where $q_i(x)$ is the demand for the ith commodity by the individual with income x. It is easy to show from (16.2.2) that the elasticity of the individual money metric utility with respect to the ith price is given by

$$\frac{\partial x}{\partial p_i} \frac{p_i}{x} = - \frac{p_i q_i(x)}{x} = -w_i(x)   \tag{16.2.3}$$

where $w_i(x)$ is the budget share of the ith commodity at income level x. This equation shows that if the price of the ith commodity increases by 1%, the real income (money metric individual utility) x will decline by $w_i(x)$ percent. This result would be helpful when deriving the poverty elasticity with respect to prices.

---

[1] In this chapter, expenditure and income are interchangeably used as a welfare measure.
[2] This function is also referred to as the cost function in the literature. See Deaton and Muellbauer (1980).
[3] The EV is the extra income required to reach the terminal year utility at the base year prices. It is given by $\Delta x = -[e(u^*, \mathbf{p}^*) - e(u^*, \mathbf{p})]$. Most price indices use the base year as a reference, so it will be more appropriate to use the CV as a measure of welfare change due to price changes.

16.3 Price Elasticity of Poverty

This section derives the price elasticity of various poverty measures. Taxes on goods and services are generally regressive, meaning that the poor pay proportionally more taxes than the rich. If the government is to rely on such taxes, the degree of regressivity must be minimized. That raises the question of how to determine the tax rates for various goods and services to reduce the poor's tax burden. Poverty elasticity with respect to prices measures the impact of change in prices on a poverty measure.

Suppose a government wants to determine tax rates on various commodities in consumption taxes. The taxes on commodities will have direct and indirect impacts on commodity prices. The government can determine these tax rates to have a minimum effect on poverty. The poverty elasticity with respect to prices provides a valuable tool to determine tax rates.

Suppose individuals consume n goods and services and t_1, t_2, ..., t_n are the tax rates imposed on them. In practice, the consumers may not fully pay these taxes; the producers may bear some of the tax burdens. If h_i is the proportion of indirect tax on the ith commodity that is passed on to consumers, the observed market price of the ith commodity after tax will be given by

$$p_i = \bar{p}_i + h_i t_i, \tag{16.3.1}$$

where $\bar{p}_i$ is the price of the ith commodity in the absence of the indirect tax. Note that if $h_i=1$, consumers bear the burden of all the tax. In other words, the tax burden on the ith commodity is passed on to consumers. If, however $h_i = 0$, the producers bear all the tax burden on the ith commodity. In practice, h_i will lie between 0 and 1. The magnitude of h_i depends on the demand and supply elasticity of the ith commodity. If the ith commodity is necessary, the producers are more likely to pass on the tax to consumers. But, for luxury goods, the producers are less likely to pass on the tax to consumers.

The percentage increase in the price of the ith commodity due to indirect tax is given by

$$\frac{(p_i - \bar{p}_i)}{\bar{p}_i} = \frac{h_i t_i}{\bar{p}_i}.$$

Chapter 7 discussed several poverty measures; any one of those measures can measure the effect of price change on poverty. Suppose poverty is measured by the index θ and $\eta_{\theta i}$ is the poverty elasticity of θ with respect to the price of the ith commodity. The impact of the ith commodity indirect tax on poverty is measured by $\eta_{\theta i} \left(\frac{h_i t_i}{\bar{p}_i} \right)$. Suppose a priori, the values of h_i (as estimated from the demand and supply elasticities) are known, then the poverty elasticity can help determine the impact of tax rates of various commodities on aggregate poverty. The quantitative magnitudes of these effects can help policymakers determine the tax rates on different commodities.

The derivations of poverty elasticity for alternative poverty measures are presented as follows.

16.3.1 Head-Count Ratio

First, the elasticity of the percentage of the poor, called the head-count ratio, is derived with respect to the ith price. Suppose z is the poverty line and $f(x)$ is the probability density function of x, then the head-count ratio is written as

$$H = \int_0^z f(x)dx = F(z). \tag{16.3.2}$$

$F(z)$ is the probability distribution function at the income level equal to the poverty line z.

Suppose $u(z)$ is the utility enjoyed by a person with income z at the base price vector $\mathbf{p}$, then the expenditure function at the poverty line is given by

$$z = e(u(z), \mathbf{p}) \tag{16.3.3}$$

which on differentiating with respect to p_i gives

$$\frac{p_i}{z}\frac{\partial z}{\partial p_i} = \frac{p_i q_i(z)}{z} = w_i(z) \tag{16.3.4}$$

where $w_i(z)$ is the budget share of the ith commodity at the poverty line. Differentiating (16.3.2) with respect to p_i, yields the elasticity of the head-count ratio H with respect to p_i as

$$\eta_{Hi} = \frac{\partial H}{\partial p_i}\frac{p_i}{H} = \frac{zf(z)w_i(z)}{H} \tag{16.3.5}$$

The interpretation of this elasticity is that if the price of the ith commodity increases by 1%, the head-count ratio H will increase by η_{Hi} percent. If all prices rise by 1%, then H will increase by η_H percent, where η_H is given by

$$\eta_H = \sum_{i=1}^m \eta_{Hi} = \frac{zf(z)}{H}. \tag{16.3.6}$$

16.3.2 A Class of Additive Separative Poverty Measures

A class of additive separable poverty measures is given by

$$\theta = \int_0^z P(z,x)f(x)dx \tag{16.3.7}$$

where $P(z,x)$ can be interpreted as the deprivation, an individual suffers from income x because of poverty. The individual suffers positive deprivation if her income is less than the poverty line z; otherwise, the deprivation is zero. The poverty measure θ is the average deprivation suffered by society due to poverty.

Foster, Greer, and Thorbecke's (1984) (FGT) class of poverty measures, discussed in (7.12.3) of Chapter 7, can be obtained on substituting $P(z,x) = \left(\frac{z-x}{z}\right)^{\alpha}$ in (16.3.7):

$$\theta_{\alpha} = \int_0^z \left(\frac{z-x}{z}\right)^{\alpha} f(x)dx \tag{16.3.8}$$

where α is the parameter of inequality aversion. When $\alpha = 0$, $\theta_0 = H$, the head-count measure. As discussed in Chapter 7, $\alpha = 1$, this measure yields the poverty gap ratio when each poor individual's weight is the income shortfall from the poverty line. It simplifies to $\theta_1 = \frac{H(z-\mu_z)}{z}$, where μ_z is the mean income of the poor. For $\alpha = 2$, the weight given to each poor person is proportional to the square of the income shortfall of the poor from the poverty line. This measure is called the severity of poverty measure.

The price elasticity of poverty for the entire class of these poverty measures can be derived as follows.

Differentiating (16.3.7) with respect to p_i and using (16.2.3) yields

$$\eta_{\theta i} = \frac{\partial \theta}{\partial p_i} \frac{p_i}{\theta} = -\frac{1}{\theta} \int_0^z \frac{\partial P}{\partial x} x w_i(x) f(x)dx \tag{16.3.9}$$

This elasticity has a similar interpretation as the elasticity of the head-count ratio: if the price of the ith commodity increases by 1%, the poverty measured by θ will increase by $\eta_{\theta i}$ percent. If all prices rise by 1%, then θ will increase by η_{θ} percent, where η_{θ} is given by

$$\eta_{\theta} = \sum_{i=1}^n \eta_{\theta i} = -\frac{1}{\theta} \int_0^z \frac{\partial P}{\partial x} x f(x)dx, \tag{16.3.10}$$

which is the total poverty elasticity, and where n is the total number of commodities. Substituting $P(z,x) = \left(\frac{z-x}{z}\right)^{\alpha}$ into (16.3.9), the poverty elasticity of the FGT class of poverty measures with respect to the ith price is given by

$$\eta_{\alpha i} = \frac{\partial \theta_{\alpha}}{\partial p_i} \frac{p_i}{\theta_{\alpha}} = \frac{\alpha}{z\theta_{\alpha}} \left[\int_0^z \left(\frac{z-x}{z} \right)^{\alpha-1} x w_i(x) f(x) dx \right] \tag{16.3.11}$$

for $\alpha \neq 0$. Summing over all commodities, this equation gives the total elasticity of the FGT measures as

$$\eta_{\alpha} = \sum_{i=1}^n \eta_{\alpha i} = \frac{\alpha}{z\theta_{\alpha}} \int_0^z \left(\frac{z-x}{z} \right)^{\alpha-1} x f(x) dx. \tag{16.3.12}$$

Substituting $\alpha = 1$ into (16.3.11) yields the poverty elasticity of the poverty gap ratio as

$$\eta_{1i} = \frac{\partial \theta_1}{\partial p_i} \frac{p_i}{\theta_1} = \frac{\mu_z \overline{w}_{iz}}{(z - \mu_z)} \tag{16.3.13}$$

where $\overline{w}_{iz}$ is the average budget share of the ith commodity of the poor, those with income less than z, satisfying $\sum_{i=1}^1 \overline{w}_{iz} = 1$. The total elasticity of the poverty gap will be given by

$$\eta_1 = \frac{\mu_z}{(z - \mu_z)}, \tag{16.3.14}$$

which measures the impact on the poverty gap ratio when all prices increase by 1%.

16.4 Measuring the Impact of Prices on Poverty

Since $x = e(u, p)$, the poverty measure in (16.3.7) can be written as

$$\theta(p) = \int_0^z P\left(z, e(u, p) \right) f(x) dx, \tag{16.4.1}$$

which shows that $\theta(p)$ is a function of price vector p. Suppose the price vector p changes to p^*, while individuals' utility u remains the same, the poverty measure $\theta(p)$ will change to $\theta(p^*)$, given by

$$\theta(p^*) = \int_0^z P\left(z, e(u, p^*) \right) f(x) dx. \tag{16.4.2}$$

Accordingly, the proportional change in poverty θ due to the change in prices will be given by $\frac{\theta(p^*) - \theta(p)}{\theta(p)}$, which on applying Taylor expansion can be approximated as

$$\frac{\theta(p^*) - \theta(p)}{\theta(p)} = \sum_{i=1}^n \left(\frac{p_i^* - p_i}{p_i} \right) \eta_{\theta i} \tag{16.4.3}$$

where $\eta_{\theta i}$ is the elasticity of θ with respect to the ith commodity price as defined in (16.3.9). The term on the right-hand side of (16.4.3) measures the impact of the change in prices on poverty.

When the ith price p_i increases, it has two impacts on poverty: (i) income effect and (ii) distribution impact. An increase in any price reduces the real income of consumers, which increases poverty. The income effect measures the impact on poverty due to the decline in real income. The distribution effect depends on whether the ith commodity is consumed proportionally more or less by the poor. If the ith commodity is consumed proportionally more (less) by the poor, then an increase in that commodity's price will increase (reduce) poverty.

It is easy to show that if the price of the ith commodity increases by 1%, the real income of an average consumer will decline by $\overline{w}_i$, which is the average budget share of the ith commodity given by

$$\overline{w}_i = \frac{\int_0^\infty x w_i(x) f(x)\,dx}{\int_0^\infty x f(x)\,dx}. \tag{16.4.4}$$

Thus, the income effect is measured by $\overline{w}_i \eta_\theta$, where η_θ is the total poverty elasticity when all prices increase by 1%.

Policymakers need to know whether changes in prices are pro-poor or anti-poor. To answer this question, the decomposition of the poverty elasticity $\eta_{\theta i}$ with respect to the ith price is derived as the sum of two components:

$$\eta_{\theta i} = \overline{w}_i \eta_\theta + \left(\eta_{\theta i} - \overline{w}_i \eta_\theta\right) \tag{16.4.5}$$

The first term on the right-hand side of this equation is the ith price change's income effect, which is always positive. The second term on the right-hand side of (16.4.5) is the ith price change's distribution effect, which is negative or positive. The distribution effect indicates whether increasing the ith price redistributes income favoring the poor or the non-poor. If the income is redistributed in favor of the poor (non-poor), it will reduce (increase) poverty. Hence, if the distribution effect in (16.4.5) is negative (positive), the increase in the ith price reduces (increases) poverty. This leads to a pro-poor price index as[4]

$$\phi_i = \frac{\eta_{\theta i}}{\overline{w}_i \eta_\theta}. \tag{16.4.6}$$

If ϕ_i is less than 1, an increase in the ith price hurts the poor proportionally less than the non-poor; that is, the price increase in the ith commodity is pro-poor. Similarly, if ϕ_i is greater than 1, then the ith price increase is anti-poor. Thus, ϕ_i can be used to analyze how changes in the prices of various commodities would affect poverty.

---

[4] Son (2006) has used this index to analyze the pro-poorness of government fiscal policy in Thailand.

To measure the impact of prices on poverty, substitute (16.4.5) into (16.4.3). This leads to the total effect of the changes in prices on poverty:

$$\sum_{i=1}^{n} \left(\frac{p_i^* - p_i}{p_i} \right) \eta_{\theta i} = \sum_{i=1}^{n} \left(\frac{p_i^* - p_i}{p_i} \right) \overline{w}_i \eta_\theta + \sum_{i=1}^{n} \left(\frac{p_i^* - p_i}{p_i} \right) \overline{w}_i \eta_\theta \left(\phi_i - 1 \right). \quad (16.4.7)$$

The first term on the right-hand side of (16.4.7) measures the income effect, and the increase in poverty was caused by a reduction in real income when all prices had increased at the same rate. The second term on the right-hand side of (16.4.7) is the distribution effect of relative price changes on poverty. Thus, the overall effect of relative price changes is pro-poor (or anti-poor) if the second term on the right-hand side of (16.4.7) is negative (or positive).

16.5 Price Index for the Poor

This section derives a price index for the poor (PIP). Equation (16.4.3) estimates the proportional change in the poverty measure θ when the price vector p changes to p^*. Suppose there is a counterfactual situation whereby all prices change by λ percent, $p_i^* = \lambda p_i$, which on substituting in (16.4.3) yields the proportional change in poverty equal to $\lambda \eta_\theta$. Then λ will be the PIP if it gives the same proportional change in a poverty measure θ as the given change in the price vector from p to p^*.[5] Thus, equation (16.4.3) yields λ as:

$$\lambda = \sum_{i=1}^{n} \frac{p_i^*}{p_i} \left(\frac{\eta_{\theta i}}{\eta_\theta} \right), \quad (16.5.1)$$

which is the PIP for the poverty measure θ. Weights implied by this index are the poverty weights implicit in poverty measures. Various poverty measures indicate different PIPs. The PIP is computed separately for three poverty measures: the head-count ratio, the poverty gap ratio, and the severity of poverty ratio.

The widely used Laspeyres price index is given by

$$L = \sum_{i=1}^{m} \frac{p_i^*}{p_i} \overline{w}_i \quad (16.5.2)$$

where $\overline{w}_i$ is the average budget share of the ith commodity. Utilizing (16.4.6) into (16.5.2) yields

$$\lambda = L + \sum_{i=1}^{m} \frac{p_i^*}{p_i} \overline{w}_i \left(\phi_i - 1 \right) \quad (16.5.3)$$

---

[5] Note that an idea similar to Atkinson's (1970) equally distributed equivalent income level is applied. If all prices increase at the same rate of λ, then λ is determined so that it gives the same proportional change in poverty as the actual change in the price vector from p to p^*.

This chapter provides the main contribution that a relative price change is pro-poor (or anti-poor) if λ is less (or greater) than L.

16.6 A Case Study for Brazil

This section presents a case study of Brazil's price indices and their underlying inflation rates.[6] The study uses the 2002–3 Brazilian Family Expenditure Survey, covering 48,470 households throughout the entire country. The survey provided detailed incomes and consumption expenditures for each household. The poverty weights were calculated using the unit Brazilian record data to calculate the poverty weights.

The monthly price data were obtained from the Institute of Geography and Statistics. These data were collected for 12 metropolitan regions from August 1999 to July 2006. The 12 regions include:

1. Belem, Para
2. Fortaleza, Ceara
3. Recife, Pernambuco
4. Salvador, Bahia
5. Belo Horizonte
6. Rio de Janeiro
7. Sao Paulo
8. Curitiba, Parana
9. The Rio Grande do Sul
10. Goiania, Goias
11. Brasilia, Federal District
12. Non-metropolitan region

These data provided detailed prices for 472 household consumption items, including 219 food items and 253 non-food items. This case study aggregates all the food and non-food items of consumption into 51 commodity groups, precisely matched with the Brazilian Family Expenditure Survey. The national prices for the 51 commodity groups were calculated as the weighted average of the prices for the same 51 commodity groups available from the 12 regions, with weights proportional to each region's population.

The price elasticity of poverty was calculated for the three poverty measures—the head-count ratio, the poverty gap ratio, and the severity of poverty. These elasticities were calculated for 51 commodity groups, but Table 16.1 presents the aggregated elasticity estimates for only eight broad consumption categories. The table also shows the estimates of the pro-poor price index defined in (16.4.6). The empirical results show that the price elasticity of food for the head-count ratio is 0.42, suggesting that

[6] The empirical analysis presented here draws extensively from Son and Kakwani (2008).

Table 16.1 Price elasticity of poverty and pro-poor price index

Items of consumption	Head-count ratio		Poverty gap ratio		Severity of poverty	
	Price elasticity	Pro-poor price index	Price elasticity	Pro-poor price index	Price elasticity	Pro-poor price index
Food	0.42	1.62	0.56	1.77	0.65	1.81
Non-food	1.02	0.86	1.21	0.83	1.36	0.82
Housing	0.63	1.11	0.77	1.11	0.89	1.12
Clothing	0.11	1.24	0.14	1.28	0.16	1.26
Transport	0.11	0.46	0.11	0.36	0.11	0.32
Health	0.09	0.68	0.10	0.61	0.10	0.56
Entertainment	0.05	0.76	0.06	0.70	0.06	0.69
Education and communication	0.03	0.33	0.03	0.30	0.04	0.30
Total	1.44	1.00	1.77	1.00	2.01	1.00

Source: Son and Kakwani (2008).

if food prices increase by 1%, the head-count ratio will increase by 0.42%. Similarly, if non-food prices increase by 1%, the head-count poverty measure will increase by 1.02%. If all prices increase by 1%, the rise in the head-count ratio will be 1.44%.

The results also reveal that the price elasticity increases with a higher-order poverty index, such as poverty severity. This implies that the ultra-poor are more adversely affected by price increases than the poor.

The pro-poor price index informs how each consumption item's prices would affect income distribution among the poor and the non-poor. If the pro-poor index for a commodity group is greater (less) than one, the increase in the price of that commodity group will hurt the poor more (less) than the non-poor. The pro-poor price index for food, clothing, and housing is greater than unity for all three poverty measures, and that implies that increasing the prices of these items will adversely affect the poor more than the non-poor. The remaining four non-food items index—transport, health, entertainment, and education and communication—is less than 1. This result suggests that the price increases of these items will hurt the poor relatively less than the non-poor. This information could help formulate indirect tax policies.

Furthermore, in many countries, the government provides services to the general population for which it charges the users. In formulating such price policies, it is crucial to know how prices impact poverty, and the pro-poor price index can also help develop the government's price policies.

The pro-poor price index facilitates an *ex-ante* analysis of price effects on poverty. It is also interesting to determine how *ex-post* changes in prices have impacted poverty. Table 16.2 presents the *ex-post* percentage changes in poverty due to the changes in prices. These estimates capture the pure price effects when other factors remain constant.

Table 16.2 Percentage change in poverty due to changes in prices explained by income and distribution effects

Period	Total change	Income effect	Distribution effect
	Percent change in head-count ratio		
1999–2000 to 2000–2001	9.75	9.87	−0.12
2000–2001 to 2001–2	14.81	11.74	3.07
2001–2 to 2002–3	23.54	19.15	4.38
2002–3 to 2003–4	13.56	12.22	1.35
2003–4 to 2004–5	7.57	9.80	−2.23
2004–5 to 2005–6	4.77	6.88	−2.11
1999–2000 to 2005–6	91.93	86.20	5.73
	Percent change in poverty gap ratio		
1999–2000 to 2000–2001	12.11	12.16	−0.05
2000–2001 to 2001–2	18.97	14.45	4.52
2001–2 to 2002–3	30.20	23.58	6.62
2002–3 to 2003–4	16.63	15.04	1.59
2003–4 to 2004–5	8.59	12.07	−3.47
2004–5 to 2005–6	5.18	8.47	−3.29
1999–2000 to 2005–6	113.48	106.13	7.35
	Percent change in severity of poverty		
1999–2000 to 2000–2001	13.82	13.78	0.04
2000–2001 to 2001–2	22.09	16.38	5.71
2001–2 to 2002–3	34.89	26.73	8.16
2002–3 to 2003–4	18.90	17.05	1.86
2003–4 to 2004–5	9.37	13.67	−4.31
2004–5 to 2005–6	5.57	9.60	−4.03
1999–2000 to 2005–6	129.41	120.28	9.13

Source: Son and Kakwani (2008).

The empirical results show that the head-count ratio has increased by 91.93% due to price changes from 1999 to 2006. The percentage increases in the poverty gap ratio and the severity of poverty are much higher, at 113.48% and 129.40%, respectively.

The percentage change in poverty due to price changes can be decomposed into two effects, income and distribution. The income effect measures the change in poverty when all prices increase uniformly, whereas the distribution effect captures the change in poverty because of changes in relative prices. The distribution effect reveals how changes in relative prices affect the poor relatively more than the non-poor. The distribution effect implied by the head-count ratio is 5.73 in the 1999–2006 period, suggesting that changes in relative prices have contributed to a rise in the head-count ratio by 5.73% between 1999 and 2006. In comparison, the effect of price changes on the poverty gap ratio and the severity of poverty is far greater, at 7.35 and 9.13, respectively. The overall changes in relative prices have not been pro-poor in Brazil during 1999–2006.

The empirical results for each period reveal a negative distribution effect for 2003–4 to 2004–5 and 2004–5 to 2005–6. Hence, for two to three years, the changes in prices became pro-poor. According to Kakwani, Neri, and Son's (2006) study, Brazil's income inequality declined for the two years before 2006. The results suggest that the real income inequality in Brazil also fell even more than nominal income.

The most widely used Laspeyres price index uses the average budget shares of commodities as weights. These weights do not capture the consumption patterns of the poor. The PIP takes into account the consumption patterns of the poor. It uses the price elasticity of poverty, which depends on what poverty measure is used. Thus, every poverty measure will have a different PIP.

This section has computed PIPs for three poverty measures: the head-count ratio, the poverty gap ratio, and the severity of poverty. Table 16.3 presents the weights implicit in these poverty measures for the eight broad expenditure groups. It is noted that the weights implied by the Laspeyres price index differ vastly from the one indicated by the three price indices for the poor. However, it is interesting to note that the PIPs for the three poverty measures have very similar weights for the seven commodity groups. This implies that the findings are pretty robust irrespective of poverty measures.

Table 16.4 presents the inflation rates computed based on the Laspeyres and PIP indices. The results show that the PIP inflation rates are higher than the Laspeyres inflation rate for 1999–2000 to 2003–4. However, in the two periods 2003–4 to 2004–5 and 2004–5 to 2005–6, the Laspeyres inflation rates are higher than the PIP inflation rates. Figure 16.1 depicts that overall, relative prices have adversely impacted

Table 16.3 Weights implied by poverty indices

Items of consumption	Laspeyres Index	Price Index for the Poor		
		Head-count ratio	Poverty gap ratio	Severity of poverty
Food	17.95	29.06	31.70	32.43
Non-food	82.05	70.94	68.30	67.57
Housing	39.32	43.74	43.64	44.09
Clothing	6.39	7.91	8.16	8.09
Transport	16.97	7.84	6.18	5.43
Health	8.91	6.10	5.40	5.03
Entertainment	4.49	3.40	3.14	3.11
Education and communication	5.98	1.95	1.78	1.81
Total	100.00	100.00	100.00	100.00

Source: Son and Kakwani (2008).

Table 16.4 Inflation rates based on Laspeyres and PIP indices

Period	Laspeyres Index	The Price Index for the Poor		
		Head-count ratio	Poverty gap ratio	Severity of poverty
1999–2000 to 2000–2001	6.86	6.77	6.83	6.88
2000–2001 to 2001–2	8.15	10.28	10.70	10.99
2001–2 to 2002–3	13.30	16.34	17.04	17.36
2002–3 to 2003–4	8.48	9.42	9.38	9.41
2003–4 to 2004–5	6.81	5.26	4.85	4.66
2004–5 to 2005–6	4.78	3.31	2.92	2.77
1999–2000 to 2005–6	59.86	63.84	64.01	64.40

Source: Son and Kakwani (2008)

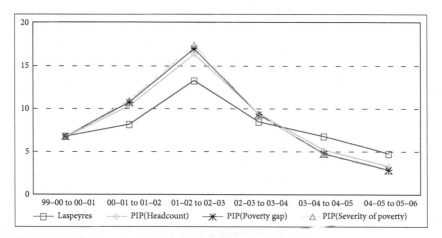

Fig. 16.1 Inflation rates based on Laspeyres and PIP indices

the poor during the entire period. Still, relative prices changed in favor of the poor in the last two sub-periods.

This case study also computed Laspeyres and PIP indices separately for food and non-food items of consumption. The results showed that Laspeyres and PIP indices give very similar inflation rates for food, but the differences are pretty vast for non-food items. These differences can be explained by differences in the consumption patterns of the poor and the non-poor in the food and non-food groups. The consumption patterns of the poor and the non-poor are similar in food items, so vast differences in food inflation rates between the Laspeyres and PIP indices are not observed. However, in non-food items, there are significant differences in the consumption patterns of the poor and the non-poor, which results in substantial differences in price indices.

16.7 Concluding Remarks

Prices play an essential role in people's lives. People have different economic circumstances and consumption patterns, so the impact of prices on people's lives will differ from one person to another. If the prices of necessities increase faster than those of luxuries, the poor will suffer more adversely than the non-poor. If society's concern is to protect the poor, knowing how prices affect them is essential. The main objective of this chapter has been to measure the impact of price changes on poverty. The chapter has achieved this objective by developing a new consumer demand theory methodology.

Developing countries collect a significant amount of revenue from indirect taxes. How should governments determine tax rates on various goods and services? These rates have both direct and indirect impacts on the prices of goods and services. The government can determine these tax rates to have a minimum effect on poverty. The poverty elasticity with respect to prices and the pro-poor index developed in the chapter provide valuable tools to determine tax rates.

Government policies have both direct and indirect impacts on the prices of various commodities. For instance, governments provide health, education, utilities, and transportation services. Many governments tend to recover the cost by charging private users a price for various services. How should the government then determine the charges on multiple services? A social objective should be that such services are available to everyone irrespective of their economic circumstances. Alternatively, the poor should be able to afford the utilization of such services. It is crucial to know how prices of basic services impact the poor in formulating such price policies. This chapter has developed a pro-poor price index, which helps us understand how the price of each consumption item would affect income distribution. This index can help formulate government price policies with the minimum adverse impact on the poor.

Economists have paid enormous attention to controlling inflation. Central banks perform this task by managing interest rates when the inflation rate falls outside a narrow band. Most countries measure inflation rates using the Laspeyres price index, which uses the average budget shares as the weights. This index does not inform how the prices affect the poor and the most vulnerable population. National macroeconomic policies primarily focus on the aggregate inflation rate of an average consumer. Government policies must pay attention to how inflation impacts various population groups, particularly the poor. Based on the Brazilian experience, this chapter has shown that the impact of inflation on the living conditions of the poor can be significantly higher than that of the average population. The primary focus on aggregate inflation in macroeconomic policies must change.

This chapter has developed a price index for the poor (PIP), systematically capturing the poor's consumption patterns through poverty price elasticity. While this index can be computed for any poverty measure, this chapter has focused on three poverty measures: the head-count ratio, the poverty gap ratio, and the severity of poverty. All three poverty measures show that Brazil's price changes during the 1999–2006 period have favored the non-poor proportionally more than the poor.

National statistical offices (NSOs) regularly report inflation rates using the Laspeyres price index. This chapter recommends that the NSOs regularly publish the PIP indices and their regular Laspeyres price index. The difference between the PIP and Laspeyres price index informs the degree to which inflation contributes to poverty, and this information will help formulate poverty alleviation strategies.

17

Economic Growth and Poverty

17.1 Introduction

Growth performance differs among countries, and some countries have experienced a higher growth rate than others. Likewise, cross-country experience in poverty reduction also varies between countries. Many cross-country studies have shown that economic growth leads to a significant decrease in poverty. The cross-country evidence also indicates a considerable variation in poverty reduction for the same growth rate. Given such wide variations across countries, it is essential to understand the linkage between economic growth and poverty. This chapter will illuminate the empirical inter-relationship between economic growth and poverty reduction.

Suppose a society seeks to eliminate or reduce poverty as rapidly as possible. In that case, the core question development economists often ask is whether economic growth is sufficient to achieve this social objective or whether public policies should directly target the poor. A Harvard economist Dani Rodrik (2000) points out that "the recent debate on these questions has generated more heat than light because it has become embroiled in a wider, political debate in globalization, and the role of World Bank/IMF conditionality." This chapter suggests that policies on poverty reduction must be based on empirical evidence.

The answer to these questions requires calculating the trade-offs between growth and inequality. The trade-offs could be better understood using the idea of growth and inequality elasticities of poverty. Economists have attempted to calculate these elasticities using cross-country regression models. This chapter critically reviews these models. The review's objective will be to understand whether the literature answers the core question. Unfortunately, the literature on this issue has offered conflicting answers, making an informed policy difficult. This chapter attempts to explain why the cross-country regression models cause conflicting answers.

Before answering these questions, it is essential to clarify how economic growth should be measured. The chapter has identified three alternative definitions of economic growth: (i) growth rate of GDP, (ii) per capita GDP growth rate, and (iii) per capita income or consumption. The poverty and inequality literature uses these definitions interchangeably. Still, the chapter shows that their magnitudes differ across countries and regions in the world. Thus, their impact on the rate of poverty reduction will also be different. Economists have not formed any consensus on which definition is the best for measuring the effect of economic growth on poverty and inequality.

Economic Inequality and Poverty. Nanak Kakwani and Hyun Son, Oxford University Press.
© Nanak Kakwani and Hyun Son (2022). DOI: 10.1093/oso/9780198852841.003.0017

That is perhaps why various studies arrive at conflicting conclusions about the impact of economic growth on poverty.

This chapter develops a discrete-time decomposition that explains poverty's growth as the sum of the growth and inequality components. It quantifies the contributions of economic growth and change in inequality to growth in poverty. Thus, this decomposition can help governments to develop a mix of policies that achieve rapid poverty reduction.

This chapter has followed the non-parametric approach to estimating growth and inequality elasticities of poverty for individual countries using household surveys. It has derived the growth and inequality elasticity for several poverty measures that estimate them from the individual country's household surveys. It has developed the inequality–growth trade-off index (IGTI), which provides an empirical estimate of the trade-off between the impact of economic growth and inequality change on poverty. This index will be of value to policymakers in assessing how much they should focus on growth and how much they should focus on inequality reduction through poverty alleviation interventions.

Finally, the chapter provides a case study exploring the linkage between economic growth and poverty reduction. It utilizes five rounds of the Chinese Household Income Project surveys covering 1988–2018.

17.2 Three Alternative Measures of Economic Growth

Every economy produces thousands of goods and services every day or even every hour. The output so produced is ultimately consumed by the people. Every person gets entitlement to consumption mainly depending on their contribution to production. There may be many other factors that determine people's entitlements. Many people can also get entitlements through public and private transfers. Income is a composite measure of entitlement, which people exchange for goods and services.

Gross domestic product (GDP) is the most widely used indicator for assessing a country's economic performance. It is the money value of all goods and services produced in the economy.

Suppose the total output produced in an economy consists of k goods and services[1] expressed as the output vector:

$$\tilde{O} \approx (O_1, O_2, \dots \dots \dots, O_k) \qquad (17.2.1)$$

In market economies, people exchange the goods and services produced in the economy at market prices determined by demand and supply. Suppose all market prices are denoted by a vector expressed as:

$$\tilde{p} \approx (p_1, p_2, \dots \dots \dots, p_k)$$

---

[1] Only finished goods are included in GDP. Intermediate goods are not included.

The nominal GDP is the market value of all goods and services, expressed as:

$$GDP = \sum_{j=1}^{k} p_j o_k$$

Comparing GDP over time requires controlling the prices that change over time to measure real output changes. When market prices change, the nominal GDP also changes, even if there is no real output change. Chapters 15 and 16 discussed various price indices to calculate production's real value.

Economic growth is the change in the price-adjusted market value of goods and services produced in the economy over time. All countries calculate economic growth rates regularly from their national accounts, and they report growth rates annually, but some countries also report them quarterly. These growth rates are essential for economic policies in almost all countries.

Some countries also report economic growth by the rate of increase in per capita real GDP. Kakwani and Son (2018) point out that the idea behind this is that since the whole population shares the total output produced in the economy, it would be intuitive to calculate the growth rate of the entire production available for consumption per person in the economy. The per capita GDP growth rate may be more relevant for social welfare and poverty reduction. It can be written as

$$\Delta ln \left(\frac{Y}{N} \right) = \Delta ln(Y) - \Delta ln(N)$$

where ln stands for logarithm, N is the total population, and Y is the real GDP. This equation implies that if the growth rate of real GDP is 5% and the population's growth rate is 2%, then the per capita real GDP growth rate will only be 3%. Thus, the growth rate of 2% is lost due to population growth.

Does the per capita GDP growth rate imply that the living standards in countries with a higher population growth rate will be lower than those with a lower population growth rate? The answer is yes if population growth is unrelated to economic growth. Simultaneously, the higher population growth provides a more productive labor force to the economy, contributing to higher economic growth. The two growth rates are related, but the strength of the relationship can vary across countries. There may not always be a trade-off between population growth and standard of living.

How should economic growth be measured? Should it by growth rates of total GDP or per capita GDP? Kakwani and Son (2018) have attempted to answer this question. They argue that different processes determine GDP and population growths. Total GDP growth is about the accumulation of physical capital, the stock of technology or knowledge, innovations, and how production factors are used and managed. Stern (1991), Barro (1989), Lucas (1988), and Romer (1994) have argued that investment in human capital leads to an increase in the efficiency of labor, which in turn results in output growth. Many economists agree that globalization (openness to trade), liberalization (fewer regulations), sound macroeconomic policies, and the rule of law contribute to economic growth. On the other hand, population growth is determined by a swathe of factors including culture and religion. GDP growth is a short-term phenomenon, while population growth is a long-term phenomenon determined by past events over an extended period.[2]

The GDP growth rate, which measures the expansion of economic activities or recovery, is the most widely reported and debated indicator among economists and international development agencies. The World Bank and the International Monetary Fund regularly provide updates of growth rates of world GDP, and they seldom discuss per capita GDP growth rates.

Ultimately, the population consumes the output produced in an economy via their income, which they can exchange for goods and services produced in the economy. The most significant proportion of individuals' income comes directly from productive economic activities through labor market participation or entrepreneurial activities. However, many people also derive income from non-labor sources such as interest payments, rent on the property, dividends, bonds, and transfer payments. Thus, people derive income from wages and salary receipts, other labor income, proprietors and rental income, dividends, interest income, and transfer payments. Different individuals have different entitlements because they have various sources of income. Suppose these different sources generate an income vector:

$$\tilde{y} \approx (y_1, y_2, \dots \dots \dots, y_N) \tag{17.2.2}$$

where N is the number of individuals in a country and y_i is the income of the ith individual. The income vector measures the country's capability to enjoy the consumption of goods and services produced by the economy—the standard of living measures the actual consumption of goods and services by individuals. Individuals have the discretion to determine how much they consume out of their income. Generally, individuals tend to smooth their consumption over time by borrowing or dissaving when they have lower income and saving when they have excess income. Friedman (1957) introduced the concept of permanent income against transitory income. He argued that consumption reflects people's permanent income and is a better measure of living standards.

The vector of consumption expenditures emerges from the vector of entitlement:

$$\tilde{c} \approx (c_1, c_2, \dots \dots \dots, c_N) \tag{17.2.3}$$

which may be used to measure society's standard of living.

Poverty is estimated either from a vector of income or consumption expenditures. The data for these vectors come from nationally representative, randomly selected

---

[2] For instance, China's population growth is low because it introduced a one-child policy some time ago.

household surveys that collect household income and household consumption data. Developing countries often use per capita consumption as a basis for poverty measurement. However, developed countries use per capita income to measure poverty because they have a smaller informal sector, which is relatively cheaper to collect. The vectors $\tilde{y}$ and $\tilde{c}$ are the outcomes of the growth process, while vector $\tilde{O}$ in (17.2.1) is the outputs produced in the economy that give rise to these outcomes. How close the transformation of outputs is to outcomes determines the effectiveness of economic growth in reducing poverty.

Average consumption expenditure is defined by $\tilde{c} = C/N$, where C, the real total household consumption, is commonly used to measure society's average standard of living. The poverty literature often uses the growth rate of $\tilde{c}$ as a measure of economic growth; however, as noted above, most economists define economic growth as a growth rate of real GDP. The following decomposition gives the link between the two growth rates, according to Kakwani and Son (2018):

$$\Delta ln(\tilde{c}) = \Delta ln(Y) - \Delta ln(N) + \left(\Delta ln(C) - \Delta ln(Y) \right) \qquad (17.2.4)$$

which explains the growth rate of real per capita consumption by three factors: (i) growth rate of GDP, (ii) growth rate of population, and (iii) the difference between household consumption growth and GDP growth. This equation shows no one-to-one relationship between the average standard of living and GDP growth rates. Economic growth, as measured conventionally, is not sufficient to achieve a higher average standard of living. Population growth reduces growth in the average standard of living. The third term on the right-hand side of (17.2.4) indicates the extent to which economic growth contributes to growth in total household consumption. Society's ultimate objective is to provide consumption to individuals through households. The expansion of output is a means of achieving this aim. If the total household consumption grows at the same rate as GDP, then the average standard of living will be the same as the per capita GDP growth rate.

The poverty and inequality literature uses interchangeably three alternative definitions of economic growth. These are growth rates of (i) average per capita consumption (or income), (ii) real GDP, and (iii) per capita GDP. The literature on growth does not provide consensus among economists on which definition is the best for measuring the impact of economic growth on poverty and inequality. It will be safe to assume that the three concepts of economic growth are interrelated but are different. The GDP growth measures the rate at which the productive capacity of an economy is expanding or contracting. The growth in per capita GDP, on the other hand, measures the rate at which the total output available to each person in the economy is increasing or decreasing. The per capita consumption is the actual average standard of living enjoyed by the population in the country. Their magnitudes differ across countries and regions in the world.

All developing countries fall into six broad regions using the World Bank definition. Table 17.1 presents the three alternative growth rates for five regions. The sixth region,

Table 17.1 Annual economic growth rates, 2002–13

Regions	Per capita consumption	GDP	Per capita GDP
East Asia and Pacific	7.01	8.42	7.68
Europe and Central Asia	5.3	4.25	4
Latin America and the Caribbean	3.41	3.79	2.5
South Asia	2.63	6.86	5.37
Sub-Saharan Africa	2.71	5.79	3.08
All developing countries	4.6	6.26	4.98

Source: Kakwani and Son (2018), who based their calculations on Povcal Net and other World Bank data tables.

"the Middle East and North Africa," is excluded because no reliable data could be used to calculate these growth rates.

Table 17.1 reveals that all five regions had significantly positive growth rates between 2002 and 2013, whichever way the economic growth is measured. East Asia and the Pacific region had the most rapid economic growth. South Asia had an economic growth rate of 6.86 per annum in real GDP, but the per capita consumption had the lowest growth rate of only 2.63%.

Economic growth measured by the three alternative growth rates varied widely across the five regions; the economic literature still uses them interchangeably. Variation across countries might be even wider. Adams' (2004) study on international comparisons of growth rates indicated that the growth rate in per capita consumption and per capita GDP move in opposite directions about one-third of the time. The positive (negative) growth rate in per capita GDP accompanied the negative (positive) growth in per capita household expenditure in 47 of 126 growth spells. Therefore, the positive growth in per capita GDP does not necessarily guarantee an improvement in average living standard.

The differences in growth rates of the three alternative definitions are distinct, and their impact on poverty reduction will also be different. That is probably the main reason why many studies arrive at conflicting conclusions about the effects of economic growth on poverty.

17.3 Growth Elasticity of Poverty: Cross-Country Regressions

If Y is the real GDP and θ is a poverty measure, the growth elasticity of poverty with respect to real GDP is given by

$$\eta = \frac{\Delta ln\,(\theta)}{\Delta ln\,(Y)} \qquad (17.3.1)$$

This elasticity answers the key policy question: to what extent does economic growth reduce poverty? Suppose real GDP grows by 1%, the incidence of poverty changes by η percent. In other words, how high a rate of economic growth is required to re-duce or eliminate poverty? The elasticity is generally negative because GDP growth should increase society's overall standard of living by providing additional goods and services in the economy. However, there are some exceptional circumstances under which positive economic growth increases poverty.

There is now a sizable literature on estimating the growth–poverty elasticity from cross-country regressions models (Adams 2004, Ravallion and Chen 1997, Ravallion 2001, Squire 1993, Foster and Székely 2008). These studies utilize the mean income growth rate (or consumption) to measure economic growth. This approach may be called a parametric approach because it requires specifying the regression model. Adams (2004) has suggested the following expanded version of the model proposed by Ravalion and Chen (1997),

$$ln(\theta_{it}) = \alpha_i + \beta ln(\mu_{it}) + \rho ln(G_{it}) + \delta t + \varepsilon_{it} \qquad (17.3.2)$$

where θ_{it} is the measure of poverty in the country i at time t, α_i is a fixed-effect reflecting time differences between countries, β is the growth elasticity of poverty with respect to mean expenditure (income) μ_{it}, ρ is the elasticity of poverty with respect to the Gini index G_{it}, δ is a trend rate of growth over time t, and ε_{it} is the error term in the poverty measure.

This model assumes the growth elasticity of poverty β to be the same in every coun-try. It means that the same growth rate in mean income has the same effect on reducing poverty in all countries. This assumption is unlikely to hold. Countries have different growth patterns and, therefore, with the same level of economic growth, they should have different effects on poverty.

The poverty elasticity with respect to the Gini index denoted by ρ is also assumed to be the same for all countries. Again, this assumption is questionable. The change in poverty depends on how the distribution of expenditure (income) changes over time and across countries. The distribution can change in many ways, each impacting poverty differently. The Gini index is unlikely to capture changes in distribution. Thus, the poverty elasticity with respect to the Gini index may not necessarily pick up the actual change in distribution.

Ravallion (1995) abandoned the idea of estimating the poverty elasticity with re-spect to the Gini index and focused only on estimating the total elasticity with respect to the per capita mean expenditure (income). He estimated the following difference equation model, which eliminates the country fixed-effect term:

$$\Delta ln(\theta_{it}) = \delta + \beta \Delta ln(\mu_{it}) + \Delta \varepsilon_{it} \qquad (17.3.3)$$

In another paper, Ravallion (1997) demonstrated that the higher the initial inequal-ity at any positive growth, the lower the rate at which poverty falls. He provided an interesting link between economic growth, poverty, and inequality. Surprisingly, he ignored the effect of inequality in his model when estimating the growth–poverty elasticity. Thus, his model suffers from the omitted variable bias.

Suppose that there are n countries and the ith country has T_i observations so that the cross-country estimation of this equation is carried out using the total number of $\sum_{i=1}^{n} T_i$ spells. The growth elasticity of poverty can vary across the spells. Kakwani and Son (2018) derived the following expression of the estimator of elasticity disaggregated by spells:

$$\hat{\beta} = \frac{\sum_{i=1}^{n} \sum_{t=1}^{T_i} \Delta ln(\theta_{it})}{\sum_{i=1}^{n} \sum_{t=1}^{T_i} \Delta ln(\mu_{it})} = \frac{\sum_{i=1}^{n} \sum_{t=1}^{T_i} \eta_{it}\gamma_{it}}{\sum_{i=1}^{n} \sum_{t=1}^{T_i} \gamma_{it}} \qquad (17.3.4)$$

where $\hat{\beta}$ is the least-square estimate of β from (17.3.3), $\eta_{it} = \frac{\Delta ln(\theta_{it})}{\Delta ln(\mu_{it})}$ is the growth elasticity of poverty with respect to the per capita expenditure, and $\gamma_{it} = \Delta ln(\mu_{it})$ is the growth rate of the per capita expenditure in the ith country and at year t. Equation (17.3.4) shows that the poverty estimate $\hat{\beta}$ is the weighted average of the growth elasticity in the country i at time t with weights proportional to the growth rates of mean per capita expenditure (income) in the country i at time t. This result implies that the cross-country regression estimates the weighted average of growth elasticity of poverty in each spell with weights proportional to their growth rates of mean expenditure. This estimate gives a higher weight to the countries with higher growth rates, which leads to higher magnitudes of growth elasticity of poverty from the cross-country regression model. It is questionable why this weighting is socially desirable.

The cross-country regression models can only estimate the average poverty elasticity for a selected country set. These estimates will be sensitive to what countries are included in the sample. Moreover, these average elasticities are of little policy relevance in individual countries.

17.4 Linkage between Poverty, Economic Growth, and Income Inequality: A Non-Parametric Approach

Kakwani (1993) developed a non-parametric approach to measure the linkage between poverty, economic growth, and income inequality. This approach applies to individual countries and is of greater relevance for country-specific policies. This section explores the approach thoroughly, discussing the decomposition of poverty change into two components: change in per capita income (consumption) and the change in inequality. The change in per capita income (consumption) is used to measure economic growth.

Ravallion and Huppi (1991) also attempted to measure the impact of per capita income and the Gini index on poverty separately. They employed the cross-country regression models that suffer from serious biases, as argued in the previous section.

The conclusions emerging from these models are so broad that they are not policy-relevant in individual countries. This section has followed Kakwani's non-parametric approach to analyze the inter-relationship between poverty, economic growth, and income inequality.

The degree of poverty depends on three factors: the poverty line, the average income, and the relative income distribution, which the Lorenz curve can measure. A general poverty measure θ can formally be expressed by the relationship

$$\theta = \theta(z, \mu, L(p)) \qquad (17.4.1)$$

where z is the poverty line, which is fixed and determined exogenously. μ is the average income, and $L(p)$ is the Lorenz curve. Any shift in the Lorenz curve implies a change in income inequality. Suppose the k parameters $m_1, m_2, ...\ ...,\ m_k$ characterize the Lorenz curve, then any shift in the Lorenz curve occurs due to changes in these parameters. The decomposition can express the growth in poverty:

$$\frac{d\theta}{\theta} = \eta_\theta \frac{d\mu}{\mu} + \sum_{i=1}^{k} \in_{mi} \frac{dm_i}{m_i} \qquad (17.4.2)$$

where $\eta_\theta = \frac{\partial\theta\mu}{\partial\mu\theta}$ is the growth elasticity of poverty, and $\in_{mi} = \frac{\partial\theta m_i}{\partial m_i\theta}$ is the poverty elasticity with respect to the Lorenz curve parameter m_i.

Equation (17.4.2) decomposes the growth in poverty into two components: (i) the impact of economic growth when the distribution of income does not change, and (ii) the effect of income redistribution when the mean income remains unchanged. The first term on the right-hand side of (17.4.2) may be called pure growth, and the second term is the inequality effect.

If economic growth is positive (negative), the first component in (17.4.2) will always be negative (positive). However, if a redistribution of income accompanies economic growth favoring the poor (non-poor), the second component will be negative (positive). It means the growth process is pro-poor if income redistribution reduces poverty. If the second component is positive, the growth process is accompanied by increased inequality, contributing to greater poverty.

The decomposition (17.4.2) is crucial to understanding the linkage between poverty, economic growth, and income inequality, and household surveys quantify it. It is a valuable decomposition for answering the policy question: should governments follow growth first and foremost policies or follow policies to reduce inequality directly benefiting the poor? Most debate on this issue has depended on using cross-country models that have produced conflicting results. This chapter analyzes the linkage between poverty, economic growth, and income inequality based on the poverty decomposition (17.4.2). However, the estimation of the decomposition requires calculating growth and inequality elasticities. The following section systematically provides derivations of the elasticities for alternative poverty measures.

17.5 Growth Elasticity of Poverty Measures

17.5.1 Head-Count Ratio

The head-count ratio is the percentage of poor persons in the population. Assuming that x is a continuous random variable with density function $f(x)$, and if z is the poverty line, then the head-count ratio $H=F(z)$ is given by

$$H = \int_0^z f(x)dx \tag{17.5.1}$$

The growth elasticity of H is derived so that the Lorenz curve does not shift. Equation (3.2.8) in Chapter 3 derived the following property of the Lorenz curve:

$$L'(H) = \frac{z}{\mu} \tag{17.5.2}$$

Assuming that the Lorenz curve does not shift as μ changes, then differentiating this equation with respect to μ yields

$$\frac{\partial H}{\partial \mu} = -\frac{z}{\mu^2 L''(p)} \tag{17.5.3}$$

where $L''(p)$ is the second derivative of $L(p)$ with respect to p, which from (3.2.8) is given by

$$L'(p) = \frac{1}{zf(z)} \tag{17.5.4}$$

Substituting (17.5.4) into (17.5.3) gives the elasticity of H with respect to μ as

$$\eta_H = -\frac{zf(z)}{H} < 0, \tag{17.5.5}$$

which is the growth elasticity of the head-count ratio based on the assumption that the relative income distribution measured by the Lorenz curve does not change. This elasticity is interpreted as the percentage of poor who cross the poverty line due to 1% growth in the mean income when the Lorenz curve does not shift.

17.5.2 A Class of Utilitarian Poverty Measures

Chapter 7 discussed a class of utilitarian poverty measures. They measure the average proportional loss of utility suffered by society due to poverty. Suppose $u(z)$ is the utility enjoyed by a person with income equal to the poverty line z, and $u(x)$ is the utility enjoyed by a person with income x, a person is poor if $x<z$, in which cases the person with income x suffers the proportional loss of utility given by the function:

$$\varphi(z,x) = \frac{u(z) - u(x)}{u(z)} \qquad (17.5.6)$$

where the utility function $u(x)$ satisfies $u'(x) > 0$ and $u''(x) < 0$. The person with income x does not suffer any utility loss if $x > z$. The average loss of utility suffered by society is given by

$$\theta = \int_0^z \left[\frac{u(z) - u(x)}{u(z)} \right] f(x)dx = \int_0^z \varphi(z,x)\, f(x)dx, \qquad (17.5.7)$$

which is referred to as a class of utilitarian poverty measures. A relative poverty measure must satisfy the requirement that poverty does not change if the poverty line z and everyone's income increases or decreases by the same proportion. This requirement is met by poverty measures in (17.5.7) if the utility function is homogeneous—that is, $u(\lambda x) = \lambda^\varepsilon$ for all ε, which implies that $\varphi(z,x)$ in (17.5.6) is a homogeneous function of degree zero, in z and x, meaning that it does not change when z and x increase by the same proportion. From the mathematical property of homogeneous functions, $\varphi(z,x)$ must satisfy the following relationship:

$$z\frac{\partial\varphi(z,x)}{\partial z} + x\frac{\partial\varphi(z,x)}{\partial x} = 0,$$

which gives

$$zu(x)\,u'(z) = xu(z)\,u'(x) \qquad (17.5.8)$$

Differentiating both sides of (17.5.7) and using (17.5.8) yields

$$\frac{d\theta}{\theta} = -\frac{\int_0^z xu'(x)\,g(x)f(x)\,dx}{\theta u(z)}. \qquad (17.5.9)$$

where $g(x) = \frac{dx}{x}$ is the growth rate of income x. A property of the Lorenz curve in (3.2.8) in Chapter 3 is $x = \mu L'(p)$. This implies that the relative income distribution does not change when all income increases or decreases by the same proportion, which means that the Lorenz curve does not shift. Using this assumption yields $g(x) = \frac{d\mu}{\mu}$, which on substituting into (17.5.9) gives the growth elasticity of poverty measure θ:

$$\eta_\theta = \frac{\mu\partial\theta}{\theta\partial\mu} = -\frac{\int_0^z xu'(x)f(x)\,dx}{\theta u(z)} \qquad (17.5.10)$$

This is the growth elasticity of the utilitarian poverty measures and will always be negative. It implies that positive growth in mean income will always decrease poverty if the Lorenz curve does not shift. The particular cases of this general class can now be considered.

17.5.3 Foster, Greer, and Thorbecke (FGT) Class of Poverty Measures

Substituting

$$u(x) = z^\alpha - (z - x)^\alpha \qquad (17.5.11)$$

into (17.5.7) yields the class of FGT poverty measures

$$\theta_\alpha = \int_0^z \left(\frac{z - x}{z}\right)^\alpha f(x)\, dx \qquad (17.5.12)$$

where α is the parameter of inequality aversion. Using (17.5.11) into (17.5.10) gives the growth elasticity of the FGT poverty measures as

$$\eta_\alpha = -\frac{\alpha[\theta_{\alpha-1} - \theta_\alpha]}{\theta_\alpha} \text{ for } \alpha \neq 0 \qquad (17.5.13)$$

Note that $\eta_\alpha < 0$ will always hold. Thus, as the mean increases, poverty always declines when the relative distribution does not change.

When $\alpha = 1$, θ_α is equal to the poverty gap ratio, its growth elasticity, obtained from (17.5.13), is given by

$$\eta_1 = -\frac{\mu_p}{z - \mu_p} < 0 \qquad (17.5.14)$$

where μ_p is the mean income of the poor.

17.5.4 Watts' Poverty Measure

Watts (1968) proposed a poverty measure

$$W = \int_0^z [ln(z) - ln(x)] f(x) dx. \qquad (17.5.15)$$

The utility function implicit in the Watts measure is given by

$$u(x) = 1 + ln(x) - ln(z), \qquad (17.5.16)$$

which on substituting in (17.5.10) yields the growth elasticity of Watts' measure given by

$$\eta_W = -\frac{H}{W} < 0 \qquad (17.5.17)$$

17.5.5 Chakravarty's Indices

Chakravarty (1983b) proposed the following poverty class of indices:

$$\theta_{CH} = \int_0^z \left(\frac{z^e - x^e}{z^e} \right) f(x)dx. \tag{17.5.18}$$

The utility function that leads to the Chakravarty index is given by

$$u(x) = x^e, \tag{17.5.19}$$

which is an increasing function of x when $e>0$ and is strictly concave when $e<1$. Thus, the Chakravarty index satisfies both monotonicity and transfer axioms.

Using (17.5.19) into (17.5.10) yields the growth elasticity of the Chakravarty index:

$$\eta_{CH} = -\frac{e}{\theta_C z^e} \int_0^z x^e f(x)dx \tag{17.5.20}$$

17.5.6 Atkinson's Class of Poverty Measures

Atkinson's (1987) class of poverty measures are very similar to that of the Chakravarty class of poverty measures (except divided by a constant β) and is given by

$$\theta_A = \frac{1}{\beta} \int_0^z \left[\frac{z^\beta - x^\beta}{z^\beta} \right] f(x)\,dx \tag{17.5.21}$$

As β approaches zero, θ_A approaches the Watts index given in (7.5.15). The utility function that leads to the Atkinson index is given by

$$u(x) = (\beta - 1) + \frac{x^\beta}{z^\beta}, \tag{17.5.22}$$

which is an increasing function of x if $\beta > 0$ and is strictly concave when $\beta < 1$. Thus Atkinson's poverty index satisfies both monotonicity and transfer axioms.

Substituting (17.5.22) into (17.5.11) yields the growth elasticity of Atkinson's class of poverty measures as

$$\eta_A = -\frac{1}{\theta_A z^\beta} \int_0^z x^\beta f(x)dx \tag{17.5.23}$$

Note that Atkinson's poverty measure is the same as the one proposed by Clark, Hemming, and Ulph (1981).

This section has derived the growth elasticity of poverty. The following section will derive the inequality elasticity of poverty.

17.6 Inequality Elasticity of Poverty

Economic growth increases the mean income of the population. But at the same time, growth can accompany an increase in inequality. If economic growth does not change—that is, the mean income remains unchanged—an increase in inequality must intuitively increase poverty. Whether poverty will increase or decrease depends on the net effect of growth and inequality components.

The measurement of the change in inequality on poverty is complex because inequality in distribution can change in infinite ways. Kakwani (1993) assumed that the entire Lorenz curve shifts upward or downward to solve this problem. If it shifts upward, inequality decreases, and if it shifts downward, inequality increases.

Suppose the entire Lorenz curve $L(p)$ shifts by λ percent according to the following formula:

$$L^*(p) = L(p) - \lambda[p - L(p)],\qquad (17.6.1)$$

which implies that when $\lambda > 0$ ($\lambda < 0$), the Lorenz curve shifts downward (upward), increasing (decreasing) inequality. The Gini index is equal to one minus twice the area under the Lorenz curve, which from (17.6.1) follows that the shifting of the Lorenz curve is equivalent to the change in the Gini index by λ percent. If $\lambda = 0.01$ (-0.01), it means that the Gini index has increased (decreased) by 1%.

Suppose, as a result of the shift in the Lorenz curve, with no change in the mean income, the head-count ratio H changes to $H(\lambda)$. Using (17.5.2), it yields

$$L^{*'}[H(\lambda)] = \frac{z}{\mu}.\qquad (17.6.2)$$

Now differentiating both sides of (17.6.1) with respect to p at $H[(\lambda)]$ gives

$$L^{*'}(H(\lambda)) = L'(H(\lambda)) - \lambda[1 - L'(H(\lambda))].\qquad (17.6.3)$$

From the Lorenz curve, H is the proportion of individuals with income less than or equal to z such that $L'(H) = \frac{z}{\mu}$. Substituting $H(\lambda)$ for H in this equation, then supposing poverty line z changes to a new level $z(\lambda)$, gives

$$L'[H(\lambda)] = \frac{z(\lambda)}{\mu}.\qquad (17.6.4)$$

Substituting (17.6.2) and (17.6.4) into (17.6.3) yields

$$z(\lambda) = \frac{z + \lambda\mu}{(1+\lambda)} = z + \frac{(\mu - z)}{(1+\lambda)}.\qquad (17.6.5)$$

Thus, the shift in the Lorenz curve defined by (17.6.1) is equivalent to the change in the poverty line from z to $z(\lambda)$. This equation implies that as the Lorenz curve shifts downward (upward), the poverty line increases (decreases) if the mean income is greater (smaller) than the poverty line. Keeping other things constant, the increase (decrease) in the poverty line must increase (decrease) poverty. Intuitively, if the mean income and the poverty line remain unchanged, the incidence of poverty must increase (decrease) as the Lorenz curve shifts downward (upward). This intuitive result only holds when the poverty line is less than the mean income. The result is significant because many countries have a poverty line that exceeds the mean income. In such situations, the linkage between inequality and poverty breaks down. Therefore, a perverse result can be obtained if a government succeeds in reducing income inequality, but at the same time, such a policy increases poverty incidence. Thus, the poverty line must always be less than the mean income in measuring poverty.

The inequality elasticity of the head-count index of poverty is derived as follows. As the poverty line changes due to a shift in the Lorenz curve by λ percent, suppose the head-count ratio changes from $H=F(z)$ to $H(\lambda) = F(z(\lambda))$, where $F(x)$ is the probability distribution function. The elasticity of the head-count ratio with respect to the Gini index is given by

$$\varepsilon_H = \lim_{\lambda \to 0} \frac{H^*-H}{H\lambda} = \frac{(\mu - z)f(z)}{H} = -\frac{(\mu - z)}{z}\eta_H \qquad (17.6.6)$$

where $f(z)$ is the probability density function at $x=z$, and η_H is the growth elasticity of head-count ratio derived in (7.5.5). This equation shows that when the Gini index increases by 1% due to the downward shift in the Lorenz curve, the head-count ratio increases if the poverty line is less than the mean income.

The inequality elasticity of the utilitarian poverty measures defined in (17.5.7), when the Lorenz curve shifts by λ percent, changes the poverty line z to $z(\lambda)$. Thus, the utilitarian poverty measures after the Lorenz curve has shifted is given by

$$\theta[z(\lambda)] = \int_0^{z(\lambda)} \frac{u[z(\lambda)] - u(x)}{u[z(\lambda)]} f(x)dx \qquad (17.6.7)$$

The inequality elasticity of utilitarian poverty measures will be given by

$$\varepsilon_\theta = \lim_{\lambda \to 0} \frac{\theta[z(\lambda)] - \theta}{\lambda\theta}. \qquad (17.6.8)$$

To evaluate this limit, differentiate both sides of (17.6.7) with respect to λ, yielding

$$\frac{\partial\theta[z(\lambda)]}{\partial\lambda} = \int_0^{z(\lambda)} \frac{u(x)u'(z)}{u^2(z)} \frac{\partial z(\lambda)}{\partial\lambda} f(x)dx. \qquad (17.6.9)$$

Similarly, differentiating both sides of (17.6.5) with respect to λ yields

$$\frac{\partial z(\lambda)}{\partial\lambda} = \frac{(\mu - z)}{(1 + \lambda)}, \qquad (17.6.10)$$

which on substituting in (17.6.9) provides

$$\frac{\partial \theta[z(\lambda)]}{\partial \lambda} = \int_0^{z(\lambda)} \frac{u(x)u'(z)(\mu - z)}{u^2(z)\,(1 + \lambda)} f(x)dx. \tag{17.6.11}$$

The limit of which when λ approaches 0 gives

$$\lim_{\lambda \to 0} \frac{\partial \theta[z(\lambda)]}{\partial \lambda} = \int_0^z \frac{u(x)u'(z)(\mu - z)}{u^2(z)} f(x)dx,$$

which on substituting into (17.6.8) gives

$$\varepsilon_\theta = \frac{(\mu - z)}{z\theta} \int_0^z u(x) \frac{zu'(z)}{u^2(z)} f(x). \tag{17.6.12}$$

The relative poverty measures must satisfy the utility function restriction derived in (17.5.7), which on substituting in (17.6.12) yields

$$\varepsilon_\theta = -\frac{(\mu - z)}{z\theta u(z)} \int_0^z xu'(x)\, f(x)dx = -\frac{(\mu - z)}{z}\eta_\theta > 0 \; if\, \mu > z \tag{17.6.13}$$

where η_θ is the growth elasticity of utilitarian poverty measures derived in (17.5.11). This equation shows that an increase (decrease) in inequality will increase (decrease) poverty for the entire class of utilitarian poverty measures when the poverty line is less than the mean income. This result is fundamental in the measurement of poverty. In all poverty measurements, the poverty line must not exceed the mean income; otherwise, one obtains a perverse result in which the increase in inequality reduces poverty.

17.7 Trade-off between Economic Growth and Income Inequality

Economic growth increases the mean income, which reduces poverty. If economic growth also increases inequality, then poverty increases. Since economic growth and change in inequality impact poverty, a relevant question must be asked: What is the trade-off between the two? Putting it differently, if the Gini index increases by 1%, how much should the mean income increase so that poverty does not increase. An answer to this question can be of value to policymakers to understand how much they should focus on growth and how much they should promote pro-poor policies to reduce inequality. In this context, it is essential to discuss the inequality–growth trade-off index (IGTI) proposed by Kakwani (2000). The proportional change in poverty can be decomposed as

$$\frac{d\theta}{\theta} = \eta_\theta \frac{d\mu}{\mu} + \varepsilon_\theta \frac{dG}{G} \tag{17.7.1}$$

The first term on the right-hand side measures the impact of growth in mean income on poverty. The second term measures the effect of change in the Gini index
on poverty. This equation assumes that the entire Lorenz curve shifts upward or
downward. Equating the proportional change in poverty to zero yields the IGTI:

$$IGTI = \frac{G}{\mu} \frac{\partial \mu}{\partial G} = -\frac{\varepsilon_\theta}{\eta_\theta} \tag{17.7.2}$$

The interpretation of the IGTI follows. If, for example, the IGTI is equal to 3.0, it
means that a 1% increase in the Gini index will require a growth rate of 3% in the
mean income to offset the adverse effect of an increase in inequality. It also means that
following pro-poor policies, if the government can reduce the Gini index by 1%, this
policy is equivalent to a 3% gain in mean income growth. This suggests that the larger
the IGTI, the greater the benefits of pro-poor policies to reduce inequality.

Using equation (17.6.13) on (17.7.2) yields the IGTI:

$$IGTI = \frac{(\mu - z)}{z}, \tag{17.7.3}$$

which on differentiating with respect z yields $\frac{\partial(IGTI)}{\partial z} = -\frac{\mu}{z^2} < 0$, implying that the
lower the poverty line, the larger the IGTI. This leads to an important conclusion that
the pro-poor policies on reducing inequality will significantly impact extreme poverty.
If the government is concerned about lowering severe or ultra-poverty, it should be
more inclined to adopt pro-poor policies.

Equation (17.7.3) also implies that with the poverty line remaining fixed, the IGTI
increases with the mean income μ; therefore, as the country develops, the government should be more inclined to follow the pro-poor policies. This phenomenon has
happened in wealthy industrialized countries, which have increasingly adopted social policies to reduce poverty. The focus on growth policies may be appropriate for
developing countries to reduce poverty.

How does the initial level of inequality affect the choice of policies? From (17.7.3),
it follows that the IGTI is not affected by the initial level of inequality.

17.8 Sectoral Growth and Poverty

Suppose the entire population is divided into K sectors or groups by ethnic, geographical, and other socioeconomic characteristics. A poverty measure θ is said to be additive

decomposable if

$$\theta = \sum_{k=1}^{K} a_k \theta_k \tag{17.8.1}$$

θ_k is the poverty measure of the kth group, and a_k is the proportion of individuals belonging to the kth group such that $\sum_{k=1}^{K} a_k = 1$. The entire class of poverty measures in (17.5.6) are additively decomposable. This section explores how growth in mean income and changes in inequality within groups explain the total poverty in the population.

Differentiating (17.8.1) with respect to the mean income of the kth group gives

$$\overset{*}{\eta}_{\theta_k} = \frac{a_k \theta_k}{\theta} \eta_{\theta k} \tag{17.8.2}$$

where $\eta_{\theta k} = \frac{\partial \theta_k \mu_k}{\partial \mu_k \theta_k}$ is the kth group growth elasticity of poverty, and $\overset{*}{\eta}_{\theta_k} = \frac{\partial \theta \mu_k}{\partial \mu_k \theta}$ is the elasticity of the total poverty with respect to growth in the kth group. This elasticity helps us understand how economic growth in various sectors or groups impacts total poverty. It is easy to show that

$$\eta_\theta = \sum_{k=1}^{K} \frac{a_k \theta_k}{\theta} \eta_{\theta k} = \sum_{k=1}^{K} \overset{*}{\eta}_{\theta_k} \tag{17.8.3}$$

$\eta_\theta = \frac{\partial \theta \mu}{\partial \mu \theta}$ is the elasticity of total poverty with respect to the mean income of the entire population. Equation (17.8.3) shows how the effects of sectoral growth rates on poverty add to poverty's total impact.

Suppose the growth in each sector accompanies a change in the Gini index within sectors, then the growth in poverty in the kth sector can be written as

$$\frac{d\theta_k}{\theta_k} = \eta_{\theta k} \frac{d\mu_k}{\mu_k} + \varepsilon_{\theta k} \frac{dG_k}{G_k} \tag{17.8.4}$$

where $\varepsilon_{\theta k} = \frac{G_k}{\theta_k} \frac{\partial \theta_k}{\partial G_k}$, which on substituting into (17.8.1) gives

$$\frac{d\theta}{\theta} = \sum_{k=1}^{K} \overset{*}{\eta}_{\theta_k} \frac{d\mu_k}{\mu_k} + \sum_{k=1}^{K} \overset{*}{\varepsilon}_{\theta k} \frac{dG_k}{G_k}. \tag{17.8.5}$$

$\overset{*}{\varepsilon}_{\theta k} = \frac{G_k}{\theta} \frac{\partial \theta}{\partial G_k}$ measures the effect of change in the Gini index in the kth sector on total poverty.

Suppose growth rates of mean income in various sectors are known. In that case, the first term on the right-hand side of (17.8.5) measures the proportional change in the total poverty, provided the inequality within various sectors or groups does not change. How realistic is this assumption? According to Kakwani (1993), the answer depends on the nature of the groups or sectors. If the individuals belonging to the

sectors are reasonably homogeneous, this assumption's effect will be negligible. Since
the sectoral growth rates can differ, the population's income inequality may change
due to the changes in between-group inequality. This effect can be significant, which
we can capture by writing the first term on the right-hand side (17.8.5) as

$$\sum_{k=1}^{K} \eta_{\theta_k}^* \frac{d\mu_k}{\mu_k} = \eta_\theta \frac{d\mu}{\mu} + \sum_{k=1}^{K} \eta_{\theta_k}^* [\frac{d\mu_k}{\mu_k} - \frac{d\mu}{\mu}], \qquad (17.8.6)$$

which follows from (17.8.3). The first term on the right-hand side of this equation
is the pure growth effect, which measures the change in the whole population's mean
income on total poverty. The second term measures the effect of change between sector
growth rates caused by different sectoral growth rates in their mean incomes. If every
sector has the same growth rates, the second term will be zero.

   It will be helpful to mention the policy relevance of the decomposition in (17.8.6).
In the 1980s, many developing countries faced a severe economic crisis. In response
to this crisis, several developing countries adopted structural adjustment policies
initiated by the World Bank. These policies had implications for living standards, particularly for the poor. Such policy impact on national poverty can be captured using
the methodology discussed in this section.

   What is needed is the growth rates in various sectors during the adjustment period.
Ideally, these growth rates should be estimated from household surveys, which may
not be possible in the short run because the surveys are not conducted frequently.
But the sectoral growth rates can be approximated by the growth rates in per capita
GDP from the national accounts, which can be available in the short run without con-
ducting a recent household survey. Given these growth rates, it is possible to estimate
the proportional change in total poverty from (17.8.6), provided different groups or
sectors are reasonably homogeneous, implying that changes in sectoral inequalities
will be negligible. If, for instance, an adjustment policy changes trade terms in favor
of specific sectors or shifts resources from one sector to another, the between sector
inequality component in the poverty decomposition in (17.8.6) can capture the effect
of such policy.

17.9 Kakwani's Poverty Decomposition

Section 17.4 presented a poverty decomposition for general poverty measures in
equation (17.4.2) that decomposed the growth in poverty into two components (i) the
impact of economic growth when the distribution of income does not change and
(ii) the effect of income redistribution when the mean income remains unchanged.
This decomposition was derived using the growth and inequality elasticity of poverty.
Section 17.5 derived the growth elasticity for an entire class of utilitarian poverty measures. As pointed out, the derivation of inequality elasticity of poverty was problematic.
The literature does not provide an inequality measure with a one-to-one relationship with any poverty measure. The inequality elasticity can be derived assuming that

the change in inequality occurs only when the entire Lorenz curve shifts upward or downward. This assumption ensures that all poverty measures have a one-to-one relationship with the Gini index. This assumption is rather heroic because, in actual practice, the Lorenz curve can change in an infinite number of ways. Therefore, it is essential to consider the shift in that part of the Lorenz curve that directly impacts the poor. The inequality elasticity derived in Section 17.6 measures the impact of the shift in the entire Lorenz curve on poverty, but not the shift of that part of the Lorenz curve that impacts the poor. This section proposes to resolve this issue by using the poverty decompositions that explain poverty's growth by two components: growth and inequality effects. These decompositions have attracted much attention (Kakwani and Subbarao 1990, Datt and Ravallion 1992, Jain and Tendulkar 1990, Kakwani 2000).

This section elaborates on Kakwani's (2000) poverty decomposition, which explains poverty's growth as the sum of the growth and inequality components. This decomposition satisfies some intuitively natural axioms. It is a discrete-time analog of the poverty decomposition in (17.4.2), and it requires the income distribution for at least two periods. Kraay (2004) also developed a discrete-time decomposition using the Datt and Ravallion (1992) decomposition. It is the sum of three components: growth effect, inequality effect, and a residual term. The residual term in this decomposition is problematic and has no direct meaning to explaining poverty growth. Thus, this decomposition with three components cannot consistently estimate the two growth and inequality components. In contrast, Kakwani's discrete-time decomposition provides a consistent estimate of the continuous decomposition (17.4.2), discussed below.

The general poverty measure $\theta = \theta(z, \mu, L(p))$ depends on the three variables: (i) poverty line, (ii) mean income, and (iii) the Lorenz curve. Following from Kakwani (2000), the growth in poverty between the base year 1 to the terminal year 2 is given by

$$\delta_{12} = \ln\left[\theta\left(z, \mu_2, L_2(p)\right)\right] - \ln\left[\theta\left(z, \mu_1, L_1(p)\right)\right] \qquad (17.9.1)$$

where the mean μ_1 in year 1 changes to the mean income μ_2 in year 2. $L_1(p)$ and $L_2(p)$ are the Lorenz curves in years 1 and 2, respectively. δ_{12} can be decomposed as the sum of the two components η_{12} and ε_{12}:

$$\delta_{12} = \eta_{12} + \varepsilon_{12} \qquad (17.9.2)$$

where η_{12} is the growth effect, measuring the growth in poverty when the mean income μ_1 changes to μ_2, but the Lorenz curve does not change between the two years. ε_{12} is the inequality effect, measuring the effect of change in the Lorenz curve from $L_1(p)$ in year 1 to $L_2(p)$ in year 2, while the mean income does not change between the two years.

In deriving the growth effect, one can fix the Lorenz curve in the base year or the terminal year. Both periods can be equally justified, so the average of the two may be a reasonable compromise. Similarly, in the derivation of the inequality effect, one can fix the mean income either in the base year or the terminal year; one can take the average of the two periods. This issue has an analogy to the construction of the consumer price indices. The Laspeyres price index fixes the base year consumer basket, whereas the Paasche price index fixes the terminal year consumer basket. Fisher's ideal price index takes the average of the two baskets. Kakwani (2000) followed Fisher's idea of constructing growth and inequality effects in poverty.

It is evident from (17.9.1) that $\delta_{12} = -\delta_{21}$, implying that the growth rate of poverty going from the base year to the terminal year is equal to the minus times the poverty growth rate going from the terminal year to the base year. Suppose the incidence of poverty has decreased by 5% between the base and terminal years. Intuitively, the growth in poverty going from the terminal year to the base year must increase poverty by 5%. This symmetry requirement is intuitive and will always be satisfied if $\eta_{12} = -\eta_{21}$ and $\varepsilon_{12} = -\varepsilon_{21}$. Kakwani's (2000) decomposition yields the growth and inequality components as

$$\eta_{12} = \frac{1}{2}[ln\theta\left(z, \mu_2, L_1(p)\right) - ln\theta\left(z, \mu_1, L_1(p)\right) + ln\theta\left(z, \mu_2, L_2(p)\right) \quad (17.9.3)$$
$$- ln\theta(z, \mu_1, L_2(p))]$$

and

$$\varepsilon_{12} = \frac{1}{2}[ln\theta\left(z, \mu_1, L_2(p)\right) - ln\theta\left(z, \mu_1, L_1(p)\right) + ln\theta\left(z, \mu_2, L_2(p)\right) \quad (17.9.4)$$
$$- ln\theta(z, \mu_2, L_1(p))]$$

The relative poverty measures must satisfy the requirement that they are homogeneous with respect to the poverty line and all persons' incomes in the population. That means that if the poverty line and incomes of all persons change by the same proportion, the poverty measures remain the same. This requirement yields

$$\theta\left(z, \mu_2, L_1(p)\right) = \theta\left(\frac{z\mu_1}{\mu_2}, \mu_1, L_1(p)\right) \quad (17.9.5)$$

and

$$\theta\left(z, \mu_1, L_2(p)\right) = \theta\left(\frac{z\mu_2}{\mu_1}, \mu_2, L_2(p)\right) \quad (17.9.6)$$

The distribution in year 1 is characterized by μ_1 and $L_1(p)$. Hence, one can compute $\theta\left(z, \mu_2, L_1(p)\right)$ from the income distribution of year 1 using the poverty line $\frac{z\mu_1}{\mu_2}$. Similarly, one can compute $\theta\left(z, \mu_1, L_2(p)\right)$ from the income distribution in year 2 using the poverty line $\frac{z\mu_2}{\mu_1}$.

Substituting (17.9.5) and (17.9.6) into (17.9.3) and (17.9.4) yields

$$
\eta_{12} = \frac{1}{2}\left[ln\theta\left(\frac{z\mu_1}{\mu_2}, \mu_1, L_1(p)\right) - ln\theta\left(z, \mu_1, L_1(p)\right) + ln\theta\left(z, \mu_2, L_2(p)\right) \right.
$$
$$
\left. - ln\theta\left(\frac{z\mu_2}{\mu_1}, \mu_2, L_2(p)\right)\right] \tag{17.9.7}
$$

and

$$
\varepsilon_{12} = \frac{1}{2}\left[ln\theta\left(\frac{z\mu_2}{\mu_1}, \mu_2, L_2(p)\right) - ln\theta\left(z, \mu_1, L_1(p)\right) + ln\theta\left(z, \mu_2, L_2(p)\right) \right.
$$
$$
\left. - ln\theta\left(\frac{z\mu_1}{\mu_2}, \mu_1, L_1(p)\right)\right] \tag{17.9.8}
$$

If the same year income distribution is used, the increase (decrease) in the poverty line must increase (decrease) poverty measured by any poverty measure. It follows from (17.9.7) that if the mean income increases (decreases) between the base and terminal year, the growth effect η_{12} will always be negative (positive), indicating poverty decreasing (increasing). Thus, a positive (negative) growth rate in the mean income will always reduce (increase) poverty, provided the income distribution does not change. However, the inequality effect ε_{12} can be either negative or positive. If ε_{12} is negative (positive), the growth process redistributes income in favor (against) the poor, meaning that growth is pro-poor (anti-poor). Thus, pro-poor growth achieves a rapid poverty reduction. Whereas anti-poor growth retards the effectiveness of growth in reducing poverty.

A positive economic growth increases poverty if the adverse impact of the increase in inequality offsets economic growth's beneficial effect on poverty reduction. This happens when positive growth results in $\eta_{12} + \varepsilon_{12} > 0$. The available empirical evidence suggests that this is an unlikely outcome. The literature on the linkage between economic growth and poverty has focused on cross-country regressions. This literature has found that the Gini index tends to be relatively stable over time and within countries. This observation has led many economists (also international development organizations) to arrive at the wrong conclusion that growth is good for the poor (e.g., Dollar and Kraay [2002]). It must be emphasized that the Gini index has no one-to-one relationship with any poverty measure unless the entire Lorenz curve shifts upward or downward. The stable Gini index does not necessarily imply that the adverse redistribution impact on poverty does not exist. In the poverty decomposition presented here, the inequality effect ε_{12} has a one-to-one relationship with poverty, making it the most desirable to measure the impact of inequality on poverty. This decomposition informs how much economic growth contributes to poverty and how much the income distribution that accompanies the economic growth impacts poverty. Thus, the decomposition enables calculating the trade-off between growth and inequality effects of poverty.

17.10 A Case Study of China

China had been expanding its output at an unprecedented rate, and it achieved a growth rate in real GDP of over 10% for almost three decades. Sustained economic growth achieves a rapid poverty reduction. If economic growth accompanies the increase in income inequality, economic growth may slow down the rate of poverty reduction. China has also succeeded in attaining an unprecedented poverty reduction. It is exciting to know how much more China could have reduced poverty if inequality had not increased. This question can be answered by the impact of economic growth on poverty if inequality remains the same and the adverse effect of increases in inequality if there is no economic growth. This section approaches this issue utilizing the poverty decomposition discussed in the previous section.

This section's empirical application utilizes five rounds of the Chinese Household Income Project surveys covering 1988–2018. Per capita household income derived from the surveys has been adjusted for spatial prices across rural and urban areas and provinces. Further, the incomes of households have been adjusted to take account of inflation over time. The per capita household incomes are measured in 2013 Beijing prices and are comparable across the country and over time. In this application, the absolute concept of poverty is used, assuming that the price-adjusted (real) line is fixed across regions and over time. In China, the official poverty line is 2,736 yuan per person per month in Beijing's prices in 2013, which is the basis for this case study.

Table 17.2 presents the empirical estimates of mean income and various poverty measures. The table also shows the Gini index estimates—the most widely used measure of inequality. It was unnecessary to present all poverty measures discussed in the chapter, and selected poverty measures that reflect the essential aspects of poverty are presented. The last column in the table shows the annual trend growth rates for the entire period from 1988 to 2018.[3]

The mean income had been growing at an annual rate of 7.08% over the entire period of three decades. This magnitude of economic growth is unprecedented in any country globally for such a long period. The growth rates of the incidence of poverty are even much higher than those of the mean income. The total growth elasticity of poverty presented is defined as the poverty growth rate to the mean income growth rate. This elasticity should be negative but positive for the severity of poverty and Watts measure between 2013 and 2018. The positive growth in mean income has led to increased poverty. These two poverty measures give higher weight to the extremely poor, which implies that economic growth has hurt the ultra-poor more than the poor between 2013 and 2018. This result casts doubt on Dollar and Kraay's (2002) conclusion that "growth is good for the poor." However, the trend growth rates show that economic growth has significantly reduced poverty in China. For instance, the severity of poverty, which gives high weight to the extremely poor, has declined at an annual rate of 11.60% over three decades between 1988 to 2018. Thus, China has achieved an

---

[3] The trend growth rates have been computed using the methodology developed by Kakwani (1997).

Table 17.2 Mean income, the Gini index, and poverty measures, and growth rates and growth elasticity of poverty in China, 1988–2018

	1988	1995	2002	2007	2013	2018	
	Mean income and poverty estimates						
Mean Income	2,732	4,304	5,480	11,074	17,144	20,108	
Gini index	33.77	35.95	38.47	41.01	41.51	42.35	
Percentage of poor	60.65	35.35	26.77	7.76	4.19	3.06	
Poverty gap ratio	23.45	12.01	8.98	2.07	1.31	1.15	
Severity of poverty	11.63	5.73	4.28	0.83	0.63	0.65	
Watts measure	34.04	17.29	12.95	2.77	1.99	2.01	
							Trend growth
	Annual growth rates of mean income and poverty measures						
Mean Income	–	6.5	3.45	14.07	7.29	3.19	7.08
Gini index	–	0.89	0.97	1.28	0.2	0.4	0.87
Percentage of poor	–	−7.71	−3.97	−24.77	−10.26	−6.29	−10.37
Poverty gap ratio	–	−9.56	−4.16	−29.39	−7.56	−2.7	−11.36
Severity of poverty	–	−10.12	−4.17	−32.68	−4.66	0.69	−11.6
Watts measure	–	−9.68	−4.13	−30.85	−5.49	0.15	−11.22
	Total growth–poverty elasticity						
Percentage of poor		−1.19	−1.15	−1.76	−1.41	−1.97	−1.46
Poverty gap ratio		−1.47	−1.21	−2.09	−1.04	−0.85	−1.6
Severity of poverty		−1.56	−1.21	−2.32	−0.64	0.22	−1.64
Watts measure		−1.49	−1.2	−2.19	−0.75	0.05	−1.58

unprecedented poverty reduction. No country in the world has ever achieved such a robust decrease in poverty over such a long period of three decades.

The rate of poverty reduction peaked in the 2002–7 period. In the subsequent years, the rate of poverty reduction has significantly slowed down. The rate of poverty reduction slowed down considerably between 2013 and 2018. In this period, poverty incidence increased for the severity of poverty and Watts measure.

The absolute magnitude of total growth elasticity of poverty significantly exceeds one from 1988 to 2007. This elasticity is called the total elasticity because it measures the combined effect of the mean income growth and the change in income inequality on poverty. It does not inform the separate impact of economic growth on poverty and the separate effect of change in income inequality on poverty. It measures the collective impact of economic growth and change in inequality on poverty. The poverty decomposition discussed in the previous section is utilized to estimate the magnitudes of these two effects separately. Table 17.2 shows the empirical estimates of the two effects.

It is noted from Table 17.2 that the Gini index had been increasing monotonically between 1988 to 2018, and it expanded at an annual rate of 0.87%. The Gini index's

Table 17.3 Poverty decomposition in China, 1988–2018

	1988	1995	2002	2007	2013	2018	Trend growth
		Annual growth in poverty due to growth effect					
Percentage of poor	–	−8.72	−5.54	−12.85	−21.4	−4.71	−10.12
Poverty gap ratio	–	−12.06	−6.8	−15.3	−22.12	−4.58	−12.15
Severity of poverty	–	−14.04	−7.61	−16.9	−21.78	−4.2	−13.28
Watts measure	–	−12.91	−7.11	−15.89	−21.66	−4.24	−12.55
		Annual growth in poverty due to inequality effect					
Percentage of poor	–	1.01	1.56	−11.92	11.14	−1.59	−0.25
Poverty gap ratio	–	2.5	2.63	−14.08	14.55	1.88	0.79
Severity of poverty	–	3.93	3.44	−15.77	17.12	4.89	1.68
Watts measure	–	3.23	2.98	−14.96	16.17	4.39	1.33

expansion does not inform how much poverty increases due to inequality. There exists no one-to-one relationship between poverty and inequality, and the increase in the Gini index may decrease poverty and vice versa. Thus, to measure the effect of inequality on poverty, the Gini index is not suitable.

Table 17.3 presents the empirical estimates of the growth and inequality impacts on poverty. The trend growth effect shows that the head-count measure of poverty declined at an annual rate of 10.12 % over the entire period from 1988 to 2018. This decline is entirely due to the mean income growth when there is no change in income inequality. The actual decline rate in poverty was 10.37 % in the same period, which is the combined effect of growth and inequality. It means that there had been a reduction in the poverty rate of 0.25 % due to decreased income inequality. The severity of poverty, which gives higher weight to the extremely poor, increased at an annual rate of 1.68 % because of increased inequality. Thus, the growth process in China had contributed to the redistribution of income against the ultra-poor. If the redistribution of income had not occurred, the severity of poverty would have decreased at an annual rate of 13.28 % instead of 11.60 %. Thus, the head-count shows a decline in inequality while the severity of poverty increases inequality. Whether the redistribution of income is poverty-reducing or poverty-increasing depends on the poverty measure used. Every poverty measure has a different implicit measure of inequality, and hence, the measure of income redistribution that accompanies the growth process will also be different for various poverty measures.

Between 2002 and 2007 registered a massive reduction in poverty by all poverty measures. For instance, the severity of poverty decreased at an annual rate of 32.68 %. This magnitude of poverty reduction is unprecedented. The mean income increased at an annual rate of 14.07 %, which reduced poverty at a yearly rate of 16.90 %. The growth was accompanied by the redistribution of income in favor of the ultra-poor, reducing the severity of poverty at an annual rate of 15.77 %. Thus, the growth in total poverty was the sum of the growth and inequality effects, adding up to 32.68 %. Interestingly, the Gini index increased at a yearly rate of 1.28 %, but the inequality effect showed a vast poverty reduction. This result indicates that the linkage between poverty and the Gini index is perverse.

In the most recent period between 2013 and 2018, the severity of poverty and Watts measure increased at yearly rates of 0.69 and 0.15, respectively. If the inequality had not increased during the period, these two measures would have declined at an annual rate of 4.20 and 4.25 %, respectively. But the beneficial impacts of growth were offset by the redistribution of income against the poor. The increase in inequality led to increases in poverty by 4.89 and 4.39 %, respectively.

Suppose the poverty alleviation programs benefited the poor relatively more than the non-poor. In that case, income redistribution will favor the poor resulting in poverty reduction due to the inequality effect. Thus, poverty's inequality effect can be a good indicator of assessing efficacy for poverty alleviation programs.

The trend growth rates in Table 17.3 show that economic growth had been the major contributor to the reduction in poverty in China. Although inequality has increased poverty, it had a relatively much smaller impact. The growth had been the dominating factor in achieving the massive reduction in poverty in China.

Table 17.4 presents poverty's growth and inequality elasticity, derived in Sections 17.5 and 17.6, respectively. These are partial elasticities because they measure the impact of economic growth when the inequality does not change or inequality elasticity when there is no economic growth. These elasticities can be calculated from the income distribution survey for one year. The poverty decomposition discussed in the previous section requires distribution data for at least two periods.

The interpretation of these elasticities is as follows. For instance, the Watts measure's growth elasticity in 2007 is −2.80; its interpretation is that if the mean income increases by 1%, poverty measured by the Watts measure reduces by 2.80% when the Lorenz curve does not shift. Similarly, the Watts measure's inequality elasticity for the same year is 8.54%; the interpretation is that if the entire Lorenz curve shifts downward, meaning that if the Gini index increases by 1%, the poverty measure increases 8.54%. It must be emphasized that if the entire Lorenz curve shifts downward or upward, the Gini index has a one-to-one relation with all poverty measures, provided the poverty line is less than the mean income.

The absolute magnitude of growth elasticity of all poverty is significantly greater than unity for all poverty measures presented in the table. Therefore, one can conclude that poverty is highly sensitive to economic growth. Thus, poverty should decrease faster than the economic growth rate, provided the growth process does not accompany an increase in income inequality.

All poverty measures given in Table 17.4 show that poverty is elastic with respect to economic growth. The question then arises whether this result is valid universally. It is impossible to provide a definitive answer to this question unless income distributions are analyzed for many countries. Kakwani (1993) attempted to give a speculative answer by observing the estimated density function. He conjectured that the magnitude of growth elasticity of poverty depends on the density of the people around the poverty line. The density is the highest around the mode of the income distribution. Accordingly, the closer the poverty line to the mode, the larger the growth elasticity's absolute magnitude. It also means that the larger the poverty line's difference from the mode, the smaller the absolute magnitude of poverty's growth elasticity. He supported this conjecture using the empirical estimates using Ivory Coast data. He showed that poverty's growth elasticity became less elastic when the poverty line increased away from the mode. Thus, the effectiveness of economic growth in reducing poverty depends on where the country sets the poverty line.

Economists often engage in heated debates over the effectiveness of economic growth in reducing poverty. These debates generate more heat than light because they try to find universal answers applicable to all countries. All countries set their poverty lines at different income levels in their income distributions to have vastly different growth elasticities of poverty. Thus, the effectiveness of economic growth in reducing poverty will also be vastly different in individual countries. Therefore, it is not feasible to have a one-size-fits-all policy prescription to measure the impact of growth on poverty.

The partial inequality elasticity of the three poverty measures in Table 17.4 is negative in 1988. This result implies that as inequality increases (decreases), the incidence of poverty decreases (increases). This result is counter-intuitive because if a government has a policy that reduces inequality, it has the perverse implication that poverty increases. Section 17.6 theoretically demonstrated that poverty's partial

Table 17.4 Partial growth and inequality elasticity of poverty and IGTI in China, 1988–2018

	1988	1995	2002	2007	2013	2018
	Partial growth elasticity of poverty					
Percentage of poor	−1.218	−0.8513	−1.8398	−1.4105	−2.6106	−2.682
Poverty gap ratio	−1.586	−1.9432	−1.9819	−2.757	−2.1958	−1.67
Severity of poverty	−2.0341	−2.195	−2.1979	−2.9487	−2.1577	−1.5101
Watts measure	−1.7816	−2.0444	−2.0672	−2.8021	−2.1045	−1.525
	Partial inequality elasticity					
Percentage of poor	−0.0019	0.4879	1.8452	4.2982	13.7481	17.0294
Poverty gap ratio	−1.5664	1.1137	1.9876	8.4017	11.5634	10.6037
Severity of poverty	−1.989	1.2581	2.2043	8.9859	11.3628	9.5886
Watts measure	−1.7663	1.1717	2.0732	8.5389	11.0829	9.6833
	Inequality–growth trade-off index					
Percentage of poor	−0.002	0.573	1.003	3.047	5.266	6.349
Poverty gap ratio	−0.988	0.573	1.003	3.047	5.266	6.349
Severity of poverty	−0.978	0.573	1.003	3.047	5.266	6.349
Watts measure	−0.991	0.573	1.003	3.047	5.266	6.349

inequality elasticity is positive for the entire class of utilitarian poverty measures, provided the poverty line is less than the mean income. Thus, the poverty line must be set below the mean income to avoid the perverse conclusion. The per capita mean income in 1988 was 2,732 yuan, while the poverty line was 2,736 yuan, which led to the negative value of partial inequality elasticity. The poverty line was lower than the mean income in other years, giving positive elasticity values.

Table 17.4 also presents the inequality–growth trade-off index (IGTI). This index has the same value for all poverty measures. Its value in 2013 is 5.3, which means that an income growth rate of 5.3 % is required to offset a 1% growth in the Gini index. This suggests that the higher the value of IGTI, the payoff of the inequality reduction strategy will be greater than promoting economic growth. In the past, China has primarily followed a growth-enhancing policy to reduce poverty. The empirical results in Table 17.4 show that the IGTI had increased significantly from 0.573 in 1995 to 6.349 in 2018. Thus, this result's policy implication is that in the future, if China wants to reduce poverty rapidly, it must follow the inequality reduction strategy, which will have a higher payoff than a growth-enhancing policy. Inequality-reducing policies must benefit the poor more than the non-poor, and the extremely poor must receive higher benefits than the poor. China's government must consider how poverty alleviation programs distribute benefits between the poor and the non-poor and between the poor and the extremely poor.

17.11 Concluding Remarks

This chapter has attempted to answer the core question in development economics: whether economic growth is sufficient to eliminate or reduce poverty or whether governments should also focus on poverty alleviation through policies that directly help the poor. Economists have attempted to answer this using cross-country regression models, and this chapter has critically reviewed these models. This review's objective has been to understand whether the literature answers the core question. Unfortunately, the literature on this issue has offered conflicting answers, making an informed policy difficult.

This chapter has made many contributions. First, it has addressed how economic growth should be measured, and it has identified three alternative definitions of economic growth. The most widely used definition is the GDP growth rate, measuring the rate of expansion of the real output, including services produced in the economy. Since the population shares the output so produced, intuitively, per capita GDP growth could be a more appropriate metric of economic growth.

The working population in an economy produces goods and services, which the market economy rewards the people with income. People exchange their income for goods and services produced in the economy. The individuals' actual per capita consumption of goods and services usually measures the population's average standard of living. Poverty and inequality are measured either from per capita income or consumption. The chapter shows no one-to-one relationship between the average standard of living and economic growth measured by the GDP growth rate, implying that economic growth is insufficient to achieve a higher average standard of living.

The poverty and inequality literature uses the three alternative definitions of economic growth interchangeably. Economists have not formed any consensus on which definition is the best for measuring the effect of economic growth on poverty and inequality. Still, the chapter shows that their magnitudes differ across countries and regions in the world. Thus, their impact on the rate of poverty reduction will also be different. That is probably why various studies arrive at conflicting conclusions about the effects of economic growth on poverty.

The growth elasticity of poverty measures the effectiveness of growth on poverty reduction. This elasticity answers the critical question: to what extent does economic growth reduce poverty? The literature mainly estimates growth elasticity from cross-country regressions models. These models specify the regression equations more or less on an ad hoc basis, and they estimate the equations using the cross-section of countries with countries as observations over time. This approach is called a parametric approach because it requires the specification of regression models. This chapter demonstrates that these models estimate the weighted average of poverty's growth elasticity in each country's time spell with weights proportional to their mean expenditure growth rates (income). It is difficult to provide a reasonable justification for this weighting scheme from any welfare functions. Thus, the poverty elasticity estimated from cross-country models is likely to overestimate the poverty growth elasticity in the rapidly growing counties. Therefore, the estimated poverty growth elasticities from the cross-country regression models can result in misleading conclusions about the effectiveness of growth in reducing poverty.

This chapter has followed the non-parametric approach to estimating poverty elasticity for individual countries using household surveys. The chapter has derived the growth and inequality elasticity for several poverty measures estimated from the individual country's household surveys.

Economic growth increases the mean income, which reduces poverty. If economic growth also increases inequality, then poverty may increase. Since economic growth and change in inequality impact poverty, then a relevant question is the trade-off between the two. This question is answered using the inequality–growth trade-off index (IGTI). The interpretation of this index is as follows.

If, for example, the IGTI is equal to 3.0, it means that a 1 % increase in the Gini index will require a growth rate of 3% in the mean income to offset the adverse effect of an increase in inequality. It also means that following pro-poor policies, if the government can reduce the Gini index by 1%, this policy is equivalent to a 3% gain in mean income growth. This suggests that the larger the IGTI, the greater the benefits of pro-poor policies to reduce inequality.

The chapter demonstrates that keeping the mean income constant, the lower the poverty line, the greater the IGTI. This leads to an important conclusion that pro-poor policies that reduce inequality will significantly reduce extreme poverty. If the government is concerned about lowering severe or ultra-poverty, it should be more inclined to adopt pro-poor policies. It is also found that the IGTI increases with the mean income by keeping the poverty line fixed. Therefore, as the country develops, the government should be more inclined to follow pro-poor policies. This phenomenon has happened in wealthy industrialized countries, which increasingly adopted social policies to reduce poverty. This index will be of value to policymakers in assessing how much they should focus on growth and how much they should focus on poverty reduction through poverty alleviation interventions. However, this index is based on a critical assumption that the entire Lorenz shifts upward or downward, which may not be a realistic assumption.

This chapter develops a discrete-time decomposition that explains the growth of poverty as the sum of the growth and inequality components. This decomposition does not require assuming that the entire Lorenz curve shifts upward or downward to capture the inequality effect of poverty. It quantifies the contributions of economic growth and change in inequality on growth in poverty. Thus, this decomposition helps governments understand whether they pursue economic growth first and foremost or, in addition, follow poverty alleviation policies that directly benefit the poor.

The Chinese economy's high economic growth and increasing inequality have been the two main features since the 1970s. The economic growth contributed to a substantial reduction in poverty, and the worsening income distribution contributed to an increase in poverty. This chapter presents a case study for China to understand how much economic growth and inequality have played a role in the unprecedented poverty reduction.

China's growth rate trends in poverty show that economic growth has been the major contributor to poverty reduction in China. Although inequality has increased poverty, it had a relatively much smaller impact. The growth had been the dominating factor in achieving the massive decline in poverty in China. This conclusion emerges from the long-term trend over three decades from 1988 to 2018.

If China wants to reduce poverty rapidly, this study indicates that it must not place entire focus on economic growth and follow the inequality reduction strategy with a higher payoff than the growth-enhancing policies. The inequality-reducing policies must benefit the poor more than the non-poor, and the extremely poor must receive higher benefits than the poor. China's government must consider how poverty alleviation programs distribute benefits between the poor and the non-poor and between the poor and extremely poor.

18

Pro-Poor Growth

18.1 Introduction

The term "pro-poor growth" is relatively new. It evolved in the late 1990s when international development agencies began talking about it. Poverty reduction became a primary concern of their development agenda, spurring interest in pro-poor growth. Rapid and sustained poverty reduction required pro-poor growth. An emerging consensus was that growth alone is a rather blunt tool for poverty reduction. Economic growth always accompanies the redistribution of income across the population. If economic growth redistributes income in favor of the poor, poverty reduction will be accelerated. Pro-poor growth determines how the poor benefit from economic growth.

Pro-poor growth generated a fair amount of policy and academic debate in the new millennium, including from McCulloch and Baulch (1999), Kakwani and Pernia (2000), Dollar and Kraay (2002), Eastwood and Lipton (2001), Ravallion and Chen (2003) and Son (2004). This debate did not lead to consensus on defining or measuring pro-poor growth. This chapter provides a detailed discussion of pro-poor growth and how to measure it.

Poverty reduction depends on two factors. The first factor is the magnitude of the economic growth rate; the larger the growth rate, the greater the poverty reduction. The second factor relates to the distribution of benefits of growth; if the benefits of growth go proportionally more to the poor than to the non-poor, then the poverty reduction will be more considerable. Since two factors impact poverty reduction, maximizing growth alone will not necessarily lead to a maximum poverty reduction. This chapter elaborates on the idea of "poverty equivalent growth rate" (PEGR), proposed by Kakwani and Son (2008), which are the composite indices of the two factors. These indices also satisfy the essential requirement that they increase monotonically with poverty reduction. Thus, maximizing the PEGR indices implies a maximum decrease in poverty. If the goal of policymakers is to achieve rapid and sustainable poverty reduction, they should maximize the PEGR.

Stochastic dominance is a powerful tool used to rank the social welfare of income distributions. Using stochastic dominance, one can rank income distribution without specifying a social welfare function. This chapter has extended this idea of stochastic dominance to determine if a growth process is pro-poor or anti-poor. Two kinds of stochastic dominance are discussed: first-order and second-order.

Economic Inequality and Poverty. Nanak Kakwani and Hyun Son, Oxford University Press.
© Nanak Kakwani and Hyun Son (2022). DOI: 10.1093/oso/9780198852841.003.0018

Household income and expenditure surveys are the data sources used to calculate poverty measures. The chapter provides the method of calculating the PEGR utilizing additive poverty measures. The technique can also offer the PEGR for nonadditive poverty measures—for example, Sen's poverty measure.

Finally, the chapter presents four Asian case studies: South Korea, Thailand, Vietnam, and China. In the late 1990s, the Asian financial crisis hit all Asian countries hard to a varying degree. The case studies analyze how these four Asian countries protected the poor during the crisis.

18.2 What Is Pro-Poor Growth?

The term pro-poor growth is relatively new. Many development practitioners began talking about it in the late 1990s, and they did not have a precise concept of pro-poor growth. International agencies such as the OECD (2001) defined pro-poor growth as benefits to the poor, improving their economic situation. In 1999, the Asian Development Bank produced its Poverty Reduction Strategy, according to which, "growth is pro-poor when it is labor absorbing and accompanied by policies and programs that mitigate inequalities and facilitate income and employment generation for the poor, particularly women other traditionally excluded groups." These definitions are vague and provide little guidance to measuring pro-poor growth.

In the 1950s and 1960s, the dominant development thinking was that economic growth was the main factor in poverty reduction. The rich can invest in the economy to enhance economic growth by increasing productivity. The rich will initially reap higher benefits of growth through their investments, but then in the second round, the poor begin to benefit when the rich start spending their riches. Eventually, the benefits of economic growth will lead to a reduction in poverty. Thus, the governments' strategy for poverty reduction was to promote investments, increase production capabilities, and enhance economic growth. How economic growth distributes benefits among the people was of no concern to the governments. This was known as the trickle-down strategy. It implies a vertical flow from the rich to the poor that happens automatically.

In the 1970s, many economists became disillusioned with the trickle-down strategy. Ahluwalia, Carter and Chenery (1979) and Ahluwalia (1974, 1976) observed that the poor's incomes increased more slowly than the average. Poverty in developing countries remained exceedingly high, mainly due to worsening income distribution. Despite these concerns, the trickle-down development strategy continued until the new millennium. The World Bank economists Dollar and Kraay (2002) concluded that "growth generally does benefit the poor, and that anyone who cares about the poor should favor the growth-enhancing policies of the good rule of law, fiscal discipline, and openness to international trade." This research implied that growth is good for the poor irrespective of the pattern of growth. It also meant that economic growth over four decades had not changed inequality in 80 countries; the proportional benefits of growth going to the poor remained the same as those enjoyed by the non-poor.

The clear message of the World Bank study was that governments need not follow pro-poor growth policies. This development strategy came under fire from Oxfam (2000), who pointed out that the World Bank's new development policy reflected an ideological desire to return to the golden age of free-market economics of the 1980s. This was bad news for poverty reduction.[1]

Although Oxfam's criticism of the World Bank study was rather emotional, the fact remains that the World Bank's research was not convincing. It derived its conclusions from cross-country regression models. It is well-known that concepts and measurement of income and poverty are not consistent across countries; their findings were not robust. Furthermore, cross-country regressions only indicate average trends; individual country experiences can be significantly different (see Chapter 17).

In the new millennium, the focus of development shifted to pro-poor growth. Economists began to define pro-poor growth more precisely. Kakwani and Pernia (2000) described pro-poor growth as growth that "enables the poor to participate in actively and significantly benefit from economic activity." They proposed a precise definition of pro-poor growth: the poor must benefit proportionally more than the non-poor, meaning that growth redistributes income in favor of the poor. When growth is negative, they defined growth as pro-poor if loss from growth is proportionally less for the poor than for the non-poor. This is a relative concept of pro-poor because growth accompanies a reduction in relative inequality. Thus, it is a deliberately biased strategy in favor of the poor.

As noted in Chapter 5, Kolm (1976) introduced the concept of absolute inequality, according to which inequality remains unchanged when everyone's income changes by the same amount. This chapter extends this idea, defining growth as an absolute pro-poor if the poor enjoy greater absolute benefits than the non-poor. When growth is negative, it is absolute pro-poor if the loss from growth is less for the poor than for the non-poor. This requirement is stronger than that of the relative pro-poor growth, and it implies that growth accompanies a reduction in absolute inequality.[2]

Finally, the third definition of pro-poor growth is due to Ravallion and Chen (2003). They defined growth to be pro-poor if it reduces poverty. This definition does not specify how much the poverty reduction should be to classify growth as pro-poor. Under this definition, the poor may receive only a tiny fraction of the total benefits of growth; the growth process will still be pro-poor as long as there is a poverty reduction, however slight. One can imagine scenarios that the economy is enjoying high and sustainable economic growth; still, the individuals with low incomes hardly make gains from this growth. This chapter will show that this definition of pro-poor growth is the weakest when growth is positive. It is the strongest definition when growth is negative, implying that negative growth reduces poverty.

A negative economic growth generally increases poverty. However, there may be a situation when negative growth reduces poverty. This situation can occur if the impact

---

[1] Oxfam commented on Dollar and Kraay's unpublished paper released in 2000, but later published in 2002.
[2] See Chapter 5 for details of absolute inequality.

of inequality reduction on poverty outweighs the adverse effect of negative growth. This growth process may be called "strongly pro-poor."

18.3 Stochastic Dominance and Pro-Poor Growth

One may use stochastic dominance to measure pro-poor growth without specifying a poverty line and a poverty measure. The literature on decision theory has proposed two kinds of stochastic dominance: first-order and second-order. This section extends the idea of stochastic dominance to measure pro-poor growth.

18.3.1 First-Order Stochastic Dominance

Suppose $F(x)$ is the probability distribution function of an individual with income x. It is interpreted as the proportion of persons with income less than or equal to x. It is a monotonic function of x. The change between the base and terminal years is said to be first-order dominance if

$$\Delta F\left(x\right) \leq 0 \text{ for all } x. \tag{18.3.1}$$

This inequality implies that the proportion of persons with income less than or equal to x has declined between the base and terminal years for the entire income range. If x measures the poverty line, then poverty measured by the head-count has fallen between the two periods for all poverty lines.

Suppose $p = F(x)$, which implies that as x increases, p also increases, meaning that there is a monotonic relationship between x and p. Suppose x_p as the income of an individual at the pth percentile, it is derived as

$$x_p = F^{-1}\left(p\right) \tag{18.3.2}$$

where the inverse function $F^{-1}(p)$ is a monotonic function of p. Given this, the first-order dominance in (18.3.1) is equivalent to

$$\Delta x_p \geq 0 \text{ for all } p, \tag{18.3.3}$$

which implies that the income of individuals at all percentiles increases between the two periods. One determines Δx_p for different values of p. The curve can be drawn between Δx_p and p. This curve will be called the absolute growth incidence curve (AGIC).

The inequality in (18.3.3) is also equivalent to

$$\Delta ln(x_p) \geq 0 \ \text{for all } p. \tag{18.3.4}$$

This implies that the growth rate of individuals' income at all percentiles increases between the two periods. Again, one can determine $\Delta ln(x_p)$ for different values of p. Ravallion, and Chen (2003) called this curve a growth incidence curve. This curve will be called a relative growth incidence curve (RGIC), distinguishing it from the proposed AGIC.

The first-order dominance, described in (18.3.3) and (18.3.4), implies that all individuals' income increases between the base and terminal years (or they do not decrease for any p). Therefore, it follows that first-order dominance always reduces poverty measured by any poverty measure.[3]

If the AGIC in (18.3.1) decreases monotonically, it implies that the poor enjoy higher absolute benefits of growth than the non-poor. Thus, one can call such growth absolute pro-poor. If there is no monotonic relationship, one cannot conclude whether growth is pro-poor or not.

Suppose the RGIC in (18.3.4) decreases monotonically. In that case, it means that the poor are receiving proportionally higher benefits than the non-poor, which concludes that growth is relatively pro-poor. If there is no monotonic relationship, one cannot conclude whether growth is pro-poor or not.

18.3.2 Second-Order Stochastic Dominance

Chapter 4 discussed the generalized Lorenz, defined as the product of the mean income μ and the Lorenz function $L(p)$. The curve is given by $\mu L(p)$, which provides the second-order dominance of one distribution over another. The change between the base and terminal years is said to be second-order dominance if

$$\Delta \left[\mu L(p) \right] \geq 0 \ \text{for all } p. \tag{18.3.5}$$

This inequality implies that if the entire generalized Lorenz curve shifts upward, one can say that the terminal year distribution has second-order dominance over the base year. Atkinson (1987) provided a valuable link between second-order dominance and changes in poverty. To show this linkage, consider a general class of additive poverty measures:

$$\theta = \int_0^z \varphi(z, x) f(x) \, dx \tag{18.3.6}$$

---

[3] All poverty measures must satisfy the requirement that if income at all percentiles increases, poverty must decrease.

where $f(x)$ is the density function of income x and z is the poverty line. And

$$\frac{\partial \varphi}{\partial x} < 0, \quad \frac{\partial^2 \varphi}{\partial x^2} > 0, \text{ and } \varphi(z, z) = 0 \qquad (18.3.7)$$

where $\varphi(z, x)$ is a homogeneous function of degree zero in z and x, meaning that if z and x change by the same proportion, $\varphi(z, x)$ does not change. The homogeneity of $\varphi(z, x)$ implies that the poverty measure θ does not change when the poverty line and incomes of all persons change by the same proportion. Such measures are called relative poverty measures.

Using Atkinson's (1987) theorem, one can show that if $\Delta \mu L(p) > 0$ for all p, then $\Delta \theta < 0$ for all poverty lines and the entire class of poverty measures given in (18.3.6), provided restrictions on $\varphi(z, x)$ in (18.3.7) are satisfied. Note if $\varphi(z, x) = 1$, θ equals head-count ratio H, which violates restrictions in (18.3.7), and hence Atkinson's theorem does not apply to the head-count ratio. Thus, the second-order dominance does not ensure a reduction in poverty measured by the head-count ratio. But, the first-order dominance in (18.3.3) ensures that poverty declines by all poverty measures. Thus, the second-order dominance is a weaker requirement and does not ensure that it will reduce poverty by all poverty measures. It also does not necessarily reduce poverty measured by Sen's poverty measure. Sen's poverty measure has many variants, such as Kakwani's (1980) class k-class poverty measures, which may not show a poverty reduction when there is a second-order dominance.

From the definition of the Lorenz curve, one can always write

$$L(p) = \frac{\mu_p p}{\mu} \qquad (18.3.8)$$

where μ_p is the mean income of the bottom p percent of the population, and μ is the mean income of the total population. Taking the logarithm of both sides and taking the first difference of (18.3.8) yields

$$\Delta \ln(\mu_p) = \Delta \ln[\mu L(p)] \text{ for all } p. \qquad (18.3.9)$$

$\Delta \ln(\mu_p)$ is the growth curve of the mean income of the bottom p percent of the population. One can draw the curve $\Delta \ln(\mu_p)$ for different values of p. Son (2004) developed the idea of this curve and called it the poverty growth curve. This curve based on growth rates is the relative poverty growth curve. And therefore, it can be called the relative poverty growth curve (RPGC). Atkinson's theorem and (18.3.9) imply that if the RPGC shifts upward (downward), poverty measured by the entire class of additive poverty measures in (18.3.6) has decreased (increased) between the base and terminal years. It will be helpful to write equation (18.3.9) as

$$\Delta \ln(\mu_p) = \Delta \ln(\mu) + \Delta \ln[L(p)] \qquad (18.3.10)$$

where $\Delta ln(\mu)$ is the growth rate of the mean income of the population. Note that $p=1$, the second term in (18.3.10) is equal to zero, in which case $\Delta ln(\mu_p) = \Delta ln(\mu)$. If $\Delta ln(\mu_p) > \Delta ln(\mu)$ *for all p*, then growth is pro-poor because the proportional benefits enjoyed by the poor will be higher than those by the non-poor. The entire Lorenz curve shifts upward in this scenario, indicating that inequality has reduced unambiguously. If $0 < \Delta ln(\mu_p) < \Delta ln(\mu)$ *for all p*, then, growth reduces poverty but is accompanied by lower proportional benefits to the poor, in which inequality is increasing unambiguously. This situation is characterized as trickle-down growth; growth reduces poverty, but the poor receive proportionally fewer benefits than the non-poor. If $\Delta ln(\mu_p) < 0$ and $\Delta ln(\mu) > 0$ for all p, growth is immiserizing when the positive growth increases poverty (Bhagwati 1988).

The idea of the absolute poverty growth curve (APGC) can now be introduced. Using the definition of the Lorenz curve in (18.3.8), the following relationship is derived:

$$\Delta\mu_p = \Delta\mu - \Delta\left[\frac{\mu(p - L(p))}{p}\right] \qquad (18.3.11)$$

where $\Delta\mu_p$ is the absolute growth in the income of individuals belonging to the bottom p percent of the population, and $\Delta\mu$ is the absolute growth of the mean income of the whole population. Chapter 5 introduced the absolute inequality curve given by

$$\varphi(p) = \frac{\mu\{p - L(p)\}}{p}, \qquad (18.3.12)$$

which has the following property:

$$\lim_{p\to 0}\varphi(p) = \mu, \text{ and } \varphi(1) = 0. \qquad (18.3.13)$$

On differentiating $\varphi(p)$ with respect to p gives

$$\varphi'(p) = \frac{\mu}{p^2}[L(p) - pL'(p)] = \frac{1}{p}[\mu_p - x_p] < 0, \qquad (18.3.14)$$

which shows that $\varphi(p)$ is a monotonically decreasing function p, falling from the maximum value of μ when $p=0$ to the minimum value of 0 when $p=1$. If the entire inequality curve $\varphi(p)$ shifts upward (downward), the absolute income inequality rises (falls). When the entire inequality curve shifts upward (downward), the poor receive lower (higher) absolute benefits from economic growth.

Since $\frac{dln(\mu_p)}{d\mu_p} > 0$ for all p, it means that there is a one-to-one relationship between $ln(\mu_p)$ and μ_p, which also implies a one-to-one relationship between $\Delta ln(\mu_p)$ and $\Delta\mu_p$. From (18.3.9), if we use a class of additive poverty measure, poverty decreases unambiguously. Further, from (18.3.11), it follows that if $\Delta\mu_p > \Delta\mu$ *for all p* the entire absolute inequality curve $\varphi(p)$ shifts downwards, signifying that the poor enjoy higher absolute growth benefits. Thus, the economic growth will be absolute pro-poor. If $0 < \Delta\mu_p < \Delta\mu$ the economic growth reduces poverty but is not absolute pro-poor, the poor receive fewer benefits than the non-poor.

This section has described the curves: (i) growth incidence curve (GIC) and (ii) poverty growth curve (PGC). What are the significant differences between them? First, the GIC is derived from first-order stochastic dominance, while the PGC is derived from second-order stochastic dominance. The GIC results will be stronger because they provide poverty conclusions on all poverty measures proposed in the literature. In contrast, the PGC provides poverty conclusions only on additive poverty measures. They exclude the head-count ratio and Sen's poverty measure based on interdependent welfare function. Thus, GIC results will be stronger than PGC because first-order dominance implies second-order dominance. It means that the second-order dominance requirement is likely to be satisfied more often than the first-order dominance. Thus, the PGC would provide more conclusive results.

The estimation of GIC requires the growth rates of per capita income at each percentile. Estimating growth rates from unit record household surveys will be subject to more errors because the data sources are discrete. However, the discrete data can be made continuous by fitting one of the Lorenz curves proposed in Chapter 3. The accuracy of the results depends on the accuracy of the Lorenz curve's fit. In contrast, the PGC estimation depends on the individuals' mean incomes growth rate up to the pth percentile; they can be directly estimated from unit record data. Therefore, they are subjected to fewer errors because the cumulative means calculate growth rates.

18.4 Relative Poverty Growth Curve for Thailand, 1988–2000

This section illustrates the analysis of the RPGC to determine if growth is poverty-reducing and pro-poor. The RPGC can be calculated from decile shares and the mean income for any two periods (base and terminal years). Son (2004) applied this idea to Thailand, covering 1988–2000. The data source was the Socio-economic Surveys (SES), conducted every two years. These nationwide surveys have a reasonably large sample of more than 17,000. Table 18.1 presents the results.

The RPGC depicts the growth rates of cumulative means and its value when $p=1$ is equal to the growth rate of the mean income of the whole population. Thus, the last row in the table gives the growth rate of the population's mean income.

The table reveals that the RPGC is positive for all values of p varying from 0 to 1 for 1988–90 to 1994–96. Therefore, it is concluded that poverty measured by the entire class of additive poverty measures declined between 1988 and 1996. Unfortunately, the decline in poverty abruptly stopped, mainly caused by the Asian financial crisis. The values of the RPGC became negative for all values of p for the periods 1996–98 to 1998–2000, signifying that the financial crisis led to an unambiguous increase in poverty.

Table 18.1 Relative poverty growth curve in Thailand, 1988–2000

Deciles	1988–1990	1990–92	1992–94	1994–96	1996–98	1998–2000	Trend growth
1st	6.31	2.51	8.89	7.27	−2.55	−4.39	4.68
2nd	6.10	3.21	8.72	7.30	−2.46	−3.11	4.83
3rd	5.84	3.61	9.16	7.14	−2.20	−2.67	4.96
4th	5.85	4.05	9.41	6.99	−2.14	−2.34	5.11
5th	5.89	4.48	9.58	6.81	−2.13	−2.10	5.24
6th	5.95	4.80	9.68	6.72	−2.14	−1.85	5.35
7th	6.00	5.19	9.69	6.59	−2.07	−1.55	5.47
8th	6.05	5.76	9.36	6.54	−1.96	−1.21	5.57
9th	6.29	6.52	8.49	6.48	−1.63	−0.77	5.70
10th	9.06	7.49	7.65	5.75	−1.00	−0.85	6.51

Source: Son (2004).

The pro-poorness of growth is judged if the RPGC is greater than the mean income growth rate for all values p. The mean income's annual growth rate in the 1988–90 period is 9.06%, higher than the cumulative means' growth rates for all value p less than 1. It implies that the growth has not been pro-poor in this period. A similar situation occurs in the following period, 1990–92. In this period, the annual economic growth rate is 7.49% but is not pro-poor; the poor receive proportionally fewer benefits of growth than the non-poor.

The RPGC was uniformly higher than the mean income growth for all values of p less than 1. The growth pattern changed in 1992–94 and 1994–96 when growth became pro-poor. However, the pro-poor growth ceased in the two subsequent periods, 1996–98 and 1998–2000, when the RPGC depicted negative growth rates. Also, the poor suffered a significant decline in their proportional incomes. Thus, first hitting Thailand, the financial crisis contributed to increased poverty and made growth anti-poor. Therefore, the poor got severely hurt by the crisis. The government policies in the post-crisis period did not provide much help to the poor.

18.5 An International Comparison of Pro-Poor Growth

The stochastic dominance curves classify under what conditions growth can be pro-poor or anti-poor without specifying a poverty line and a poverty measure. But, they are partial approaches because they may not always provide conclusive results, and it would be helpful to know how often they provide conclusive or inconclusive results. Son (2004) applied these methods to the data from a large number of countries. She compiled these data from the World Bank's online POVCAL program covering 87 countries with 241 growth spells. Table 18.2 presents a snapshot of the nature of economic growth emerging from the RPGC applied to these growth spells.

Of 241 spells, growth was pro-poor in 95 cases and anti-poor in 94 cases. This finding is surprising because, in almost 50% of cases, economic growth's proportional

Table 18.2 Snapshot of international relative poverty curve

	Positive growth	Negative growth	Total
Pro-poor	84	11	95
Anti-poor	71	23	94
Immiserizing	9	0	9
Inconclusive	35	8	43
Total	199	42	241

benefits did not go to the poor. Growth was immiserizing in nine cases, meaning that positive growth led to increased poverty. Hence, maximizing growth may not be sufficient to achieve a poverty reduction. In 43 spells, it was impossible to conclude whether growth was pro-poor or anti-poor. Thus, in almost 18% of cases, the partial approach did not produce unambiguous conclusions.

The partial approach has two limitations. First, it may not give conclusive results, and second, it does not inform the degree of pro-poorness of a growth process and how much it contributes to poverty reduction. The full approach always gives the compete rankings of growth processes. Unlike the partial approach, a growth process under the full approach is judged from a rate or an index of pro-poor growth, not from a curve.

Implementing the full approach requires a poverty line and a poverty measure, and this demands an inevitable value judgment in choosing the poverty line and a poverty measure. However, an advantage of this approach is that one can test the sensitivity of conclusions for all alternative poverty lines and poverty indices. This chapter's remaining sections are devoted to full approaches, mainly focused on the poverty equivalent growth rate (PEGR) developed by Kakwani and Son (2008).

18.6 Conceptual Framework for Full Approach

The full approach of pro-poor growth requires the specification of a poverty line and a poverty measure. This section provides the framework for a full approach based on a class of additive poverty measures.

The assumption is that the individual income x is a random variable with the density function $f(x)$.[4] Let z denote the poverty line, which measures the society's minimum standard of living. Persons suffer poverty when their income is less than z. If their income is higher than or equal to z, they do not suffer poverty and are identified as non-poor.

This section develops the pro-poor framework using the class of additive separable poverty measures given in (18.3.6) and (18.3.7). The framework is easily extendable to the class of nonadditive separable poverty measures.

---

[4] Instead of income, one can use consumption to measure poverty. Consumption is more widely used than income. The methodology presented in this chapter does not change when we replace income by consumption.

How does economic growth affect poverty reduction? It is essential to measure the factors contributing to poverty reduction to answer this question. Poverty reduction depends on two factors. The first factor is the magnitude of economic growth rate: the larger the growth rate, the greater poverty reduction. Growth generally accompanies changes in inequality; an increase in inequality reduces the impact of growth on poverty reduction.

The relative economic growth is measured by the growth rate of the mean income $\gamma = dln(\mu)$. Differentiating equation (18.3.6) yields the growth rate of poverty measure θ as

$$\delta = dln\,(\theta) = \frac{1}{\theta} \int_0^z \frac{\partial \varphi\,(z,x)}{\partial x} xg\,(x) f\,(x)\,dx \qquad (18.6.1)$$

where $g\,(x) = dln\,(x)$ is the growth rate of income x. Suppose x_p is the income of an individual at the pth percentile where $dp=f(x)dx$, then we can write (18.6.1) as

$$\delta = dln\,(\theta) = \frac{1}{\theta} \int_0^H \frac{\partial \varphi}{\partial x} x_p g\,[x\,(p)]\,dp \qquad (18.6.2)$$

where H is the head-count ratio and $g\,[x_p] = dln\,[x_p]$ is the relative growth rate of the income of individuals at the pth percentile. This section derives the relative and absolute pro-poor indices from this framework.

18.6.1 Relative Pro-Poor Index

$L(p)$ is the Lorenz function, measuring the income share enjoyed by the bottom p percent of the population. The properties of the Lorenz curve discussed in Chapter 3 yields

$$x_p = \mu L'\,(p). \qquad (18.6.3)$$

μ is the mean income of the population and $L'\,(p)$ is the first derivation of the Lorenz function. Taking the logarithm of both sides of (18.6.3) and differentiating yields

$$dln(x_p) = dln(\,\mu) + dln\,[L'\,(p)], \qquad (18.6.4)$$

which immediately gives

$$g\,[x_p] = \gamma + g\,[\,L'\,(p)] \qquad (18.6.5)$$

where $g\,[x_p]$ is the RPGC developed by Son (2004). This equation provides a decomposition of the curve, which is the sum of the growth rate of the mean income γ and the growth rate of the first derivative of the Lorenz curve $g[L'(p)]$. If the Lorenz curve $L(p)$ does not change for all p, the first derivative of $L'(p)$ also does not change, which implies $g[L'(p)] = 0$ *for all p*. This scenario is called the relative inequality-neutral growth process. If the Lorenz curve shifts upward (downward) for all p, the poor benefit proportionally more (less) than the non-poor. That would be equivalent to saying that if $g[L'(p)] > 0$ for all p, the poor will benefit proportionally more than the non-poor, implying that growth will be pro-poor. Similarly, growth will be anti-poor if $g[L'(p)] < 0$.

Now substituting (18.6.5) into (18.6.2) yields the poverty decomposition

$$\delta = \gamma\eta + \zeta \tag{18.6.6}$$

where

$$\eta = \frac{1}{\theta}\int_0^H \frac{\partial\varphi}{\partial x}x_p dp \tag{18.6.7}$$

is the growth elasticity of poverty, discussed in detail in Chapter 17. This elasticity measures the percentage change in poverty when there is a 1% increase in society's mean income and income inequality measured by the Lorenz curve shift does not change. This elasticity will always be negative. The first term on the right-hand side of (18.6.6) is the growth rate of poverty contributed by the growth in the mean income when inequality does not change. This is called the pure growth effect of poverty. The second term in (18.6.6) given by

$$\zeta = \frac{1}{\theta}\int_0^H \frac{\partial\varphi}{\partial x}x_p g[L'(p)]\, dp \tag{18.6.8}$$

measures the growth in poverty contributed by the shift in the Lorenz curve when the mean income does not change. This is called the pure inequality effect of poverty. It informs how poverty changes due to changes in relative inequality that accompany the growth process. In (18.6.8), if $g[L'(p)] > 0$ for all p, $\zeta < 0$, implying an upward shift in the Lorenz curve reduces poverty. But, if $g[L'(p)] < 0$, $\zeta > 0$, meaning that an increase in inequality increases poverty.

The poverty decomposition in (18.6.6) shows that poverty growth is the sum of the pure growth effect and the pure inequality effect. The pure growth effect will always be negative because any positive growth in the mean income must reduce poverty when inequality does not change. The pure inequality effect can be either positive or negative. The inequality effect measures the impact of income redistribution on poverty that accompanies economic growth. When income redistribution reduces poverty, growth favors the poor and is pro-poor. But, if it increases poverty, then growth is against the poor and therefore is anti-poor. The inequality effect measured by ζ in (18.6.8) will be negative (positive) when the redistribution of income reduces (increases) poverty. Thus, the growth is relatively pro-poor (anti-poor) if the inequality effect ζ is negative (positive). Based on this result, Kakwani and Pernia (2000) proposed a relative pro-poor index given by

$$\rho = \frac{\delta}{\gamma \eta}. \tag{18.6.9}$$

This equation informs whether growth is relatively pro-or anti-poor. If the growth rate is positive, $\rho > 1$ ensures that the inequality effect ζ is negative, implying that the poor enjoy higher relative benefits of growth than the non-poor. If the growth rate is negative, the growth is said to be pro-poor if $\rho < 1$, in which case, the loss of income from negative growth is proportionally lower for the poor than for the non-poor. Furthermore, a growth process is neutral in relative distribution if $\rho = 1$, implying that everyone enjoys the same proportional benefits when growth is positive and suffers the same proportional loss when growth is negative.

18.6.2 Absolute Pro-Poor Index

Growth is absolute pro-poor if the poor enjoy the absolute benefits of growth more than the non-poor. Following this definition, absolute inequality falls during growth. Similarly, if absolute growth is negative, meaning that the mean income decreases, the growth is absolutely pro-poor if the poor suffer lower income loss than the non-poor. Using this idea, the absolute pro-poor index is derived as follows:

Using (18.6.3), one can always write

$$x_p = \mu + \mu \left[L'(p) - 1 \right]. \tag{18.6.10}$$

The second term in (18.6.10) is the absolute equality curve. The upward (downward) shift in the curve implies that the distribution has become equal (unequal), favoring the poor (non-poor). Differentiating both sides of (18.6.10) yields

$$d\left[x_p \right] = d\mu + d\left[\mu \{ L'(p) - 1 \} \right], \tag{18.6.11}$$

which immediately gives

$$g_A \left[x_p \right] = \gamma_A + g_A[\mu \{ L'(p) - 1 \}] \tag{18.6.12}$$

where $g_A \left[x_p \right] = d\left[x_p \right]$ is the absolute growth rate of the income of an individual at the pth percentile, $\gamma_A = d\mu$ is the absolute growth rate of the mean income, and $g_A \left[\mu \{ L'(p) - 1 \} \right] = d\left[\mu \{ L'(p) - 1 \} \right]$ is the absolute equality growth curve. If this curve does not shift, $g_A[\mu \{ L'(p) - 1 \}] = 0$ for all p, this scenario is called the absolute equality-neutral growth process, meaning that everyone in society benefits equally from economic growth. If the curve $\mu\{L'(p) - 1\}$ shifts upward (downward) for all p, the poor will enjoy higher (lower) absolute benefits of growth than non-poor. Thus, economic growth will be absolute pro-poor (anti-poor) if $g_A[\mu\{L'(p) - 1\}]$ for all p is greater (smaller) than zero.

Differentiating (18.3.6) yields the growth rate of poverty measure θ as

$$\delta = d\ln(\theta) = \frac{1}{\theta} \int_0^H \frac{\partial P}{\partial x} g_A[x_p]\, dp. \qquad (18.6.13)$$

Now substituting (18.6.12) into (18,6,13) yields

$$\delta = \gamma_A \eta^* + \zeta^* \qquad (18.6.14)$$

where

$$\eta^* = \frac{1}{\theta} \int_0^H \frac{\partial P}{\partial x}\, dp \qquad (18.6.15)$$

is the absolute growth elasticity of poverty. This elasticity measures the percentage change in poverty when everyone receives one income unit. This elasticity will always be negative. When everyone in society gets γ_A income units, the poverty growth rate will be $\gamma_A \eta^*$. Thus, the first term on the right-hand side of (18.6.14) is the poverty growth rate when absolute inequality does not change. This is called the pure absolute growth effect of poverty. The second term in (18.6.14) given by

$$\zeta^* = \frac{1}{\theta} \int_0^H \frac{\partial \varphi}{\partial x} g_A[\mu\{L'(p) - 1\}]dp \qquad (18.6.16)$$

measures the growth in poverty contributed by the change in absolute equality. It informs how poverty changes due to changes in absolute equality that accompany the growth. If $g_A[\mu\{L'(p) - 1\}] > 0$ for all p, $\zeta^* < 0$, implying that a change in inequality reduces poverty. But, if $g[L'(p)] < 0$ for all p, $\zeta^* > 0$, implying that a change in inequality increases poverty.

The poverty decomposition (18.6.14) shows that poverty growth is the sum of the pure absolute growth effect and the absolute inequality effect. The pure absolute growth effect will always be negative because any positive growth in the mean income must reduce poverty when inequality does not change. The pure absolute inequality effect can be either positive or negative. The inequality effect measures the impact of income redistribution on poverty that accompanies economic growth. When income redistribution reduces poverty, growth favors the poor and is pro-poor. But, if it increases poverty, then growth is against the poor and therefore is anti-poor. The inequality effect measured by ζ^* will be negative (positive) when the redistribution of income reduces (increases) poverty. Thus, the growth is absolutely pro-poor (anti-poor) if the inequality effect ζ^* is negative (positive). This immediately leads to an absolute pro-poor index

$$\rho^* = \frac{\Delta}{\gamma_A \eta^*}. \tag{18.6.17}$$

From this, if the growth rate is positive, a growth process is said to be absolute pro-poor if $\rho^* > 1$, implying that the poor enjoy higher absolute benefits of growth than the non-poor. If the growth rate is negative, the growth is said to be pro-poor if $\rho^* < 1$, in which case, the loss of income from negative growth is absolutely lower for the poor than for the non-poor. Furthermore, a growth process is neutral in the absolute sense if $\rho^* = 1$, implying that everyone enjoys the same absolute benefits when growth is positive and suffers the same proportional loss when growth is negative.

18.7 Poverty Equivalent Growth Rate (PEGR)

The previous section developed the two pro-poor growth indices, ρ and ρ^*, which measure how economic growth distributes the benefits from growth across the population. However, they do not inform how effective economic growth reduces poverty. To determine how a growth process affects poverty, both the growth rate in mean income and the distribution of benefits from growth must be considered. Kakwani and Son (2008) developed a poverty equivalent growth rate (PEGR) to address this issue. However, a distinction between the relative and absolute poverty equivalent growth rates must be made.

18.7.1 Relative Poverty Equivalent Growth Rate (RPEGR)

The RPEGR is the growth rate that would result in the same growth in poverty as the actual relative growth rate if the growth process had not accompanied any change in relative inequality. The counterfactual growth rate would occur if everyone received the same proportional benefits. The actual economic growth is γ that results in the poverty growth rate of Δ from a given income distribution. Suppose λ is the distributionally neutral growth rate when inequality does not change, which leads to the growth of poverty equal to $\lambda\eta$, where η defined in (18.6.8) is the inequality-neutral growth elasticity of poverty. This growth rate in poverty must be equal Δ. Thus, solving this equation for λ yields

$$\lambda = \frac{\Delta}{\eta} = \rho\gamma \tag{18.7.1}$$

where ρ defined in (18.6.9) is the relative pro-poor index. λ is the proposed relative poverty equivalent growth rate (RPEGR).

Using (18.6.6) and (18.6.8) into (18.7.1), λ can also be written as

$$\lambda = \frac{\int_0^H \frac{\partial \varphi}{\partial x} x_p g[x_p] \, dp}{\int_0^H \frac{\partial \varphi}{\partial x} x_p \, dp}. \tag{18.7.2}$$

The RPEGR is the weighted average of the relative growth rates of income at each percentile, with the weight depending on the poverty measure used. The RPEGR can be calculated for any poverty measure by specifying $\varphi\ (z, x)$, which for the Foster, Greer, and Thorbecke (1984) class of poverty measures is given by

$$\varphi\ (z, x) = \left[\frac{z - x}{z} \right]^\alpha, \tag{18.7.3}$$

which on substituting in (18.7.2) gives

$$\lambda_\alpha = \frac{\int_0^H \left(\frac{z - x_p}{z} \right)^{\alpha - 1} x_p g\left(x_p\right) \, dp}{\int_0^H \left(\frac{z - x_p}{z} \right)^{\alpha - 1} x_p \, dp} \tag{18.7.4}$$

where $\alpha \geq 1$ is the inequality aversion parameter. Substituting $\alpha = 1$ in (18.7.4) provides the RPEGR with for the poverty gap ratio as

$$\lambda_1 = \frac{\int_0^H x_p g\left(x_p\right) \, dp}{\int_0^H x_p \, dp}. \tag{18.7.5}$$

This shows that each poor person's growth rate gets the weight proportional to the person's income. It means that the PEGR for the poverty gap is entirely insensitive to income distribution among the poor. To make the index sensitive to the income distribution among the poor, $\alpha \geq 2$ must be assumed.

The RPEGR for the Watts measure is obtained by substituting $\varphi\ (z, x) = ln(z) - ln(x)$ in (18.7.4):

$$\lambda_W = \frac{1}{H} \int_0^H g[x_p] \, dp. \tag{18.7.6}$$

Ravallion and Chen (2003) also proposed this index. They derived their index by a different methodology, which applies only to the Watts poverty measure. The index is derived using the general method encompassing all the additive separable poverty measures.

18.7.2 Absolute Poverty Equivalent Growth Rate (APEGR)

The APEGR is the growth rate that would result in the same growth in poverty as the actual absolute growth rate if the growth process had not accompanied any change in absolute inequality. The counterfactual growth rate would occur if everyone received the same absolute benefits or suffered the same absolute income loss. The actual absolute economic growth is γ_A that results in the poverty growth rate of Δ from a given income distribution. Suppose λ^* is the distributionally neutral growth rate when the absolute equality does not change, which leads to the growth of poverty equal to $\lambda^* \eta^*$, where η^* defined in (18.6.15) is the absolute inequality-neutral growth elasticity of poverty. This growth rate in poverty must be equal to Δ. Thus, solving this equation for λ^* yields

$$\lambda^* = \frac{\Delta}{\eta^*} = \rho^* \gamma_A. \tag{18.7.7}$$

where ρ^* defined in (18.6.17) is the absolute pro-poor index. λ^* is the proposed absolute poverty equivalent growth rate (APEGR).

On using (18.6.13) and (18.6.15) into (18.7.7) yields

$$\lambda^* = \frac{\int_0^H \frac{\partial \varphi}{\partial x} g_A \left[x_p \right] dp}{\int_0^H \frac{\partial \varphi}{\partial x} dp}. \tag{18.7.8}$$

The APEGR is the weighted average of the absolute growth rates of income at each percentile, with the weight depending on the poverty measure used. The APEGR can be calculated for any poverty measures by specifying $\varphi (z, x)$. The APEGR for the Foster, Greer, and Thorbecke (1984) class of poverty measures is obtained as

$$\lambda_\alpha^* = \frac{\int_0^H \left(\frac{z-x_p}{z} \right)^{\alpha-1} g_A \left[x_p \right] dp}{\int_0^H \left(\frac{z-x_p}{z} \right)^{\alpha-1} dp} \tag{18.7.9}$$

where $\alpha \geq 1$ is the inequality aversion parameter. Substituting $\alpha = 1$ in (18.7.9) gives the APEGR for the poverty gap ratio as

$$\lambda_1^* = \frac{\int_0^H g_A \left[x_p \right] p}{H}, \tag{18.7.10}$$

which can also be shown to be insensitive to income distribution among the poor. To make the index sensitive to the income distribution among the poor, we need to assume $\alpha \geq 2$.

The PEGR for the Watts measure is obtained by substituting $\varphi (z, x) = ln(z) - ln(x)$ in (18.7.4):

$$\lambda_W^* = \frac{\int_0^H \frac{g(x_p)}{x_p} dp}{\int_0^H \frac{1}{x_p} dp}, \tag{18.7.11}$$

which is different from the RPEGR for the Watts poverty measure.

18.8 Properties of the PEGR

Since $\eta < 0$ implies that λ in (18.7.1) is positive (negative) if Δ is negative (positive), there is a one-to-one negative relationship between the RPEGR and poverty. Hence, the RPEGR is consistent with the direction of the change in poverty; a positive (negative) value of the RPEGR implies a reduction (increase) in poverty. The magnitude of poverty reduction is a monotonically increasing function of the RPEGR; the larger its value, the greater the poverty reduction. Thus, the RPEGR is an effective measure of poverty reduction; the maximization of RPEGR implies a maximum decrease in poverty. This result holds for the APEGR.

To make the message clearer, suppose a country's relative pro-poor index is 2/3, meaning that only 2/3 of growth benefits are going to the poor. Suppose that the country's actual growth rate is 9%, which gives PEGR a 6% value. Thus, poverty reduction's effective growth rate is 3% lower than the actual growth rate because it does not follow pro-poor policies. On the other hand, if the pro-poor index is 1.20, then the country's actual growth rate of 9% will equal the PEGR of 10.8%. Because the country has achieved pro-poor growth, the effective growth rate for poverty reduction is 1.8% higher than the actual growth rate.

To determine the pattern of growth, i.e., whether growth is pro-poor or anti-poor, write

$$\lambda = \gamma + (\rho - 1)\,\gamma. \tag{18.8.1}$$

As noted earlier, growth is pro-poor in a relative sense (the poor receiving proportionally higher benefits) when $\gamma > 0$ and $\rho > 1$. It implies that the second term on the right-hand side of (18.8.1) is positive. Thus, growth will be relatively pro-poor if $\lambda > \gamma$. If the actual growth in mean income is negative, then growth is pro-poor if the poor suffer a proportionally smaller income loss than the non-poor, in which case $\rho < 1$. From (18.8.1), it follows that the growth will be pro-poor if $\lambda > \gamma$, whether the actual growth rate is positive or negative, the pro-poor growth will always result in a growth rate gain. The magnitude of gain in growth rate measures the degree of pro-poorness of growth. Similarly, anti-poor growth will always result in a loss of growth rate.

If $\lambda > \gamma$ and $\gamma > 0$, the positive growth reduces poverty and is pro-poor. If $0 < \lambda < \gamma$ and $\gamma > 0$, the positive growth reduces poverty but is not pro-poor. This scenario refers to trickle-down growth, implying that positive growth reduces poverty, but the poor receive proportionally lower benefits. Suppose $\lambda < 0$ and $\gamma > 0$, the positive growth increases poverty and is also anti-poor. This scenario relates to the immiserizing growth.

If $\gamma < \lambda < 0$ and $\gamma < 0$, the negative growth increases poverty but is pro-poor, meaning that the poor suffer the smaller proportional loss of income. Suppose $\lambda < \gamma$ and $\gamma < 0$, the negative growth increases poverty and is also not pro-poor; if $\lambda > 0$ and $\gamma < 0$, the negative growth reduces poverty and is also pro-poor.

To determine if growth is pro-poor in the absolute sense, write (18.8.1) as

$$\lambda = \gamma \left[1 + (\rho - \rho^*) \right] + (\rho^* - 1)\gamma. \tag{18.8.2}$$

As defined earlier, the growth is pro-poor in the absolute sense if $\gamma > 0$ and $\rho^* > 1$ and $\gamma < 0$ and $\rho^* < 1$. These conditions imply that the second term on the right-hand side of (18.8.2) is positive. Thus, growth will be pro-poor in the absolute sense if $\lambda > \gamma \left[1 + (\rho - \rho^*) \right]$. From (18.6.9) and (18.6.17), it is easy to verify that

$$\frac{\rho}{\rho^*} = \frac{\gamma_A \, \eta^*}{\gamma \, \eta}. \tag{18.8.3}$$

Given that $\gamma_A = \mu\gamma$, from (18.6.8) and (18.6.15), equation (18.6.3) can be written as

$$\frac{\rho}{\rho^*} - 1 = \frac{1}{\theta \eta} \int_0^H \frac{\partial \varphi}{\partial x} \left[\mu - x_p \right] dp. \tag{18.8.4}$$

If the poverty line is less than the mean income, $[\mu - x(p)] > 0$. Given $\frac{\partial \varphi}{\partial x} < 0$ and $\eta < 0$, it follows that $\frac{\rho}{\rho^*} - 1 > 0$, which proves that $\rho > \rho^*$.

Given $\rho > \rho^*$, equation (18.8.2) implies that the pro-poor growth in the absolute sense will always mean pro-poor growth in the relative sense, but not the other way round. Thus, absolute pro-poor growth is a stronger condition than relative pro-poor growth. It means that with the same growth rate in the mean income, the absolute growth pattern will lead to a more rapid reduction in poverty than the relative growth pattern.

Ravallion and Chen's (2003) definition of pro-poor growth is that growth should reduce poverty. According to this definition, growth will be pro-poor if $\lambda > 0$, and if growth rate $\gamma > 0$, then growth is pro-poor if $\lambda > \gamma$, which always implies $\lambda > 0$. Thus, relative pro-poor growth will always reduce poverty, but poverty-reducing growth can be pro-poor or anti-poor. This demonstrates that poverty-reducing growth is a weaker requirement than the relative pro-poor growth when growth is positive.

On the other hand, if growth rate $\gamma < 0$ and $\lambda > 0$, it implies that negative growth reduces poverty, which always means that $\lambda > \gamma$, indicating the poverty-reducing growth rate will always be relatively pro-poor. Thus, the poverty-reducing definition of pro-poor growth is a stronger requirement than the relative pro-poor growth when economic growth is negative. It is straightforward to show from (18.8.2) that the negative growth, if it reduces poverty, is stronger pro-poor growth than even the absolute pro-poor growth.

Inequality is commonly perceived as a relative concept because hardly any study presents the absolute measure of inequality. One can thus expect that there will be a greater consensus on relative inequality. Following this argument, the concept of relative pro-poor growth will be more acceptable. However, the absolute idea of pro-poor growth can also be attractive. Suppose the poor have an income of $10 and the rich have an income of $100. For instance, a policy that gives $2 to the poor and $10 to the rich will readily be accepted as pro-rich because the rich receive five times more benefits. Thus, the policy will intuitively be anti-poor in an absolute sense. The poor receive 20% benefits while the rich receive only 10% benefits, meaning that the policy is pro-poor in a relative sense. This hypothetical example shows that the absolute concept may be appealing to many.

18.9 Operationalizing Pro-Poor Growth Rate

The previous sections presented the ex-ante analysis of poverty growth explained by growth and income redistribution effects. Household income and expenditure surveys are the primary sources of calculating inequality and poverty. As pointed out in Chapter 17, the Lorenz curve can shift in an infinite number of ways; the ex-ante analysis of poverty changes is impossible under general conditions. However, if household surveys are available for at least two periods, one can perform an ex-post analysis of poverty change. This section presents the methodology to estimate the PEGR utilizing the household surveys for two periods.

18.9.1 Estimate of Relative Poverty Equivalent Growth Rate

A general poverty measure is fully characterized by the poverty line z and the income distribution vector $\tilde{x}$:

$$\theta = \theta(z, \tilde{x}) \tag{18.9.1}$$

Suppose the income distributions (adjusted for prices) changes from $\tilde{x}_1$ in the base year, 1, to $\tilde{x}_2$ in the terminal year. Suppose the mean income of $\tilde{x}_1$ is μ_1 and that of $\tilde{x}_2$ is μ_2, then the relative economic growth rate between the base and terminal year γ is estimated as

$$\hat{\gamma} = \ln(\mu_2) - \ln(\mu_1). \tag{18.9.2}$$

The poverty growth rate δ is calculated as

$$\hat{\delta} = \ln[\theta(z, \tilde{x}_2)] - \ln[\theta(z, \tilde{x}_1)]. \tag{18.9.3}$$

The poverty decomposition in (18.6.6) shows that the growth rate of poverty is the sum of the two components: (i) the growth in poverty when the relative inequality does not change, $\gamma\eta$, and (ii) the growth in poverty when the relative inequality changes but the mean income remains the same, ζ.

Using Kakwani's (2000) decomposition discussed in Chapter 17, $\gamma\eta$ is estimated as

$$\widehat{\gamma\eta} = \frac{1}{2}\left[\ln\left\{\theta\left(z, \frac{\mu_2\tilde{x}_1}{\mu_1}\right)\right\} - \ln\left\{\theta\left(z, \tilde{x}_1\right)\right\}\right] + \frac{1}{2}\left[\ln\left\{\theta\left(z, \tilde{x}_2\right)\right\} - \ln\left\{\theta\left(z, \frac{\mu_1\tilde{x}_2}{\mu_2}\right)\right\}\right].$$

$$(18.9.4)$$

The inequality effect ζ is estimated as

$$\hat{\zeta} = \frac{1}{2}\left[\ln\left\{\theta\left(z, \frac{\mu_1\tilde{x}_2}{\mu_2}\right)\right\} - \ln\left\{\theta\left(z, \tilde{x}_1\right)\right\}\right] + \frac{1}{2}\left[\ln\left\{\theta\left(z, \tilde{x}_2\right)\right\} - \ln\left\{\theta\left(z, \frac{\mu_2\tilde{x}_1}{\mu_1}\right)\right\}\right].$$

$$(18.9.5)$$

The estimate of the relative pro-poor index given in (18.6.6) is provided by

$$\hat{\rho} = \frac{\hat{\delta}}{\widehat{\gamma\eta}},$$

$$(18.9.6)$$

which yields an estimate of the RPEGR derived in (18.7.1) as

$$\hat{\lambda} = \hat{\rho}\hat{\gamma}.$$

$$(18.9.7)$$

18.9.2 Estimate of Absolute Poverty Equivalent Growth Rate

The absolute economic growth rate between the base and terminal year γ_A is estimated as

$$\hat{\gamma}_A = \mu_2 - \mu_1.$$

The poverty decomposition in (18.6.14) shows that the growth rate of poverty is the sum of the two components: (i) the growth in poverty when the absolute inequality does not change $\gamma_A\eta^*$ and (ii) the growth in poverty when the absolute inequality changes but the mean income remains the same, ζ. The estimate of $\gamma_A\eta^*$ is obtained as

$$\widehat{\gamma_A\eta^*} = \frac{1}{2}\left[\ln\left\{\theta\left(z, \tilde{x}_1 + \mu_2 - \mu_1\right)\right\} - \ln\left\{\theta\left(z, \tilde{x}_1\right)\right\}\right] + \frac{1}{2}\left[\ln\left\{\theta\left(z, \tilde{x}_2\right)\right\}\right.$$
$$\left. - \ln\left\{\theta\left(z, \tilde{x}_2 - \mu_2 + \mu_1\right)\right\}\right]$$

$$(18.9.8)$$

$$\hat{\zeta}^* = \frac{1}{2}\left[\ln\left\{\theta\left(z, \tilde{x}_2 - \mu_2 + \mu_1\right)\right\} - \ln\left\{\theta\left(z, \tilde{x}_1\right)\right\}\right] + \frac{1}{2}\left[\ln\left\{\theta\left(z, \tilde{x}_2\right)\right\}\right.$$
$$\left. - \ln\left\{\theta\left(z, \tilde{x}_1 + \mu_2 - \mu_1\right)\right\}\right].$$

$$(18.9.8)$$

The estimate of the absolute pro-poor index given in (18.6.17) is provided by

$$\widehat{\rho}^* = \frac{\widehat{\delta}}{\widehat{\gamma}_A \widehat{\eta}^*}, \tag{18.9.6}$$

which yields an estimate of the absolute poverty equivalent growth derived in (18.7.7) as

$$\widehat{\lambda}^* = \widehat{\rho}^* \widehat{\gamma}_A. \tag{18.9.7}$$

18.10 Four Asian Case Studies

This section presents four Asian case studies. The four countries are South Korea, Thailand, Vietnam, and China. These are diverse countries, so understanding how their economic growth pattern differs will be interesting. The case studies are brief, focusing only on how the countries have reduced poverty. The studies use the technique of PEGR developed in the chapter to show to what extent the countries have achieved pro-poor growth. In the late 1990s, the Asian financial crisis hit all countries in Asia hard to a varying degree. The case studies analyze how the four Asian countries managed the crisis in protecting the poor. The empirical results presented here do not go deeper into explaining the complex sets of interactions among policies, institutions, and socio-economic processes that bear the benefits of growth accruing to the poor.

18.10.1 South Korea

The data for South Korea comes from its household survey, the Family Income and Expenditure Survey, conducted every year by the National Statistical Office in South Korea. These household surveys are unit-record data used for this study covering 1990 to 1999. The surveys have a sample size of around 20,000 households in urban areas. The Korean Institute for Health and Social Affairs developed the Minimum Cost of Living basket in 1994, used as the poverty line. However, this poverty line is modified by considering the various living costs between Seoul and other cities. Seoul and other cities' separate consumer price indices update the poverty lines over time.

Table 18.3 presents the estimates of the relative poverty equivalent growth rates for South Korea. In calculating these rates, three poverty measures are utilized: the percentage of poor, the head-count ratio, the poverty gap ratio, and the severity of poverty ratio. These are the most widely used indicators to measure poverty. Economic growth is measured by the annual growth rate of the mean income. Column 2 in the table shows the yearly estimates of economic growth. The last row in the table provides the yearly trend growth rates and the PEGRs.

Table 18.3 Poverty equivalent growth rates in South Korea, 1990–1999

Year	Growth rate of mean income	Poverty equivalent growth rate		
		Percent of poor	Poverty gap ratio	Severity of poverty ratio
1990–91	9.6	10.7	10.4	10
1991–92	4.0	4.1	3.7	3.6
1992–93	4.8	5.8	6.6	6.8
1993–94	7.3	7.2	7.3	7.5
1994–95	8.2	9.7	9.5	8.9
1995–96	5.8	5.1	5	4.6
1996–97	1.8	9	8.3	9.6
1997–98	−7.6	−9	−10	−10.9
1998–99	9.8	9.6	10.5	11.5
Annual trend growth rate	5.78	6.68	6.58	6.51

Until the financial crisis in 1997, the South Korean economy had been perceived as one of the fastest-growing economies in East Asia. Its per capita real GDP growth surpassed an annual rate of more than 5% during 1990–97. South Korea has relatively equal income distribution and full employment, and high economic growth. Until 1997, inequality had declined gradually, while the unemployment rate had been only 2–3%. The financial crisis in 1997 shattered this seemingly good economic outlook.

Table 18.3 reveals that the growth rates of mean income vary substantially over time. However, the trend growth rate showed that the mean income growth rate increased at an annual rate of 5.78%, which is comparable with the per capita GDP growth rates observed in South Korea during the same period. The poverty estimates not presented in the table showed that poverty declined sharply between 1990 and 1997. For instance, the percentage of poor dropped dramatically from 39.6% in 1990 to 8.6% in 1997. This sharp decline in poverty is attributed to two factors. One factor was a high and sustained economic growth rate of over 7%, and the other factor was a steady decline in income inequality.[5]

However, the financial crisis increased the poverty rate to 19 and 13.4% in 1998 and 1999. Thus, the financial crisis had an enormous impact on poverty. The 1998–99 period also saw a remarkable recovery from the financial crisis. Before the financial crisis, the poverty equivalent growth rates were positive and higher than the actual mean income growth rates. Two conclusions emerge from this observation. First, there had been a steady decline in poverty between 1990 and 1997. Secondly, economic growth had been pro-poor in this period, meaning that the poor benefited proportionally more from growth than the non-poor.

After the onset of the crisis between 1997 and 1998, the economic growth became negative equal to −0.7.6%, and the PEGR also became negative for all three poverty measures. Also, their absolute magnitudes were higher than the absolute magnitude of the mean income growth rate. From these results, one can conclude that the crisis

---

[5] The Gini index declined from 0.29 to 0.27 between 1990 and 1997.

led to increased poverty and hurt the poor proportionally more than the non-poor. The ultra-poor were hurt even more than the poor. This result is expected as the poor, more so the ultra-poor, are more vulnerable to such economic shocks. This, in turn, calls for a permanent social safety net system, which can protect vulnerable groups of people in society from economic shocks.

Only one post-crisis observation was available that showed significant recovery from the severe crisis. The PEGR for all three poverty measures became substantially positive, indicating that poverty reduced substantially one year after the crisis. The PEGR for the severity of poverty was 11.5 in 1998–99, which was higher than the economic growth rate of 9.8%. Thus, the ultra-poor benefited proportionally more than the non-poor and the poor. This could have happened because of the South Korean government's prompt response to the crisis. The government introduced many social welfare programs in response to the crisis, including public works and temporary livelihood protection. The public works programs were particularly effective in creating jobs for the extremely poor, who became unemployed and laid-off within the labor market during the economic downturn. Similarly, the temporary likelihood protection program, implemented based on an income means test, helps the desperately poor.

Despite the financial crisis, the annual trend growth rates indicate that the overall growth rate between 1990 and 1998–99 had been pro-poor. The PDGR for all poverty measures exceeds the economic growth. Thus, in South Korea, the overall growth process had been pro-poor. The poor had benefited proportionally more than the non-poor.

18.10.2 Thailand

The data source for Thailand comes from the Socio-economic surveys (SES) covering 1988–2000. These SES data are unit-record household surveys conducted every two years by the National Statistical Office in Thailand. The survey is nationwide and covers all private, non-institutional households. The surveys have a sample of 17,000 households on average between 1988 and 2000. This case study used the official poverty line developed by the authorities in Thailand to estimate poverty.

Unlike in South Korea, overall economic growth in Thailand was not uniformly pro-poor in 1988–2000. Table 18.4 shows that the yearly trend growth rate of the mean income was 6.51%, whereas the annual trend growth rate of the PEGR for the headcount ratio was 4.96%. It means that 1.55% growth was lost annually between 1988 and 2000 because the growth process was not pro-poor. The loss of growth rate was higher for the severity of poverty, giving the extremely poor a higher weight. That means that the growth in Thailand hurt the ultra-poor proportionally more than the poor and the non-poor.

Due to the financial crisis, economic growth in Thailand became negative for the time between 1996–98 and 1998–2000. The per capita income declined at annual rates of 1 in 1996–98, and 0.85% in 1996–98 and 1998–2000. The poor suffered even more

Table 18.4 Poverty equivalent growth rates in Thailand, 1988–2000

Year	Actual growth rate	Poverty equivalent growth rate		
		Head-count ratio	Poverty gap ratio	Severity of poverty ratio
1988–90	9.06	5.5	5.9	6.1
1990–92	7.49	4.3	3.4	3
1992–94	7.65	8.8	8.7	8.8
1994–96	5.75	7.4	7.2	7.2
1996–98	−1	−2.7	−2.5	−2.5
1998–2000	−0.85	−2.3	−3.8	−4.4
Annual Trend growth rate	6.51	4.96	4.76	4.71

during the crisis period 1996–98. The PEGR for the head-count ratio was −2.7, the absolute magnitude of which was much higher than the absolute magnitude of economic growth. The crisis led to the loss of an annual growth rate of 1.57% because the poor suffered proportionally more than the non-poor. The growth continued to hurt the poor in the post-crisis period 1998–2000. Unlike in South Korea, the Thai Government did not respond promptly to protect the poor and more vulnerable ultra-poor. The recovery in Thailand was woefully slow, and it took many years for Thailand to return to the pre-crisis growth.

Although the Thai government provided few social programs constituting social safety nets, the crisis allowed the government to learn how the existing social safety system functions under duress. The crisis revealed that Thailand needed to set up or develop social safety nets.

18.10.3 Vietnam

Data from Vietnam comes from the Vietnamese Living Standard Surveys. This case study could not present trend growth rates because the access to the Vietnamese surveys was minimal. The study could only utilize the two surveys, 1992–93 and 1997–98. While the 1992–93 survey had a sample size of 4,800 households, the 1997–98 survey interviewed 5,999 households. 1997–98 is the crisis year, so growth rates between 1992–93 and 1997–98, although inadequate, measured the impact of the crisis on poverty. It utilized Vietnam's official poverty line to calculate the poverty measures.

Table 18.5 presents the poverty equivalent growth rates for Vietnam. The annual per capita expenditure growth rate was 5.02% for Vietnam. In the urban and rural areas, the growth rates were 5.28 and 4.04%, respectively, which means that Vietnam's growth process increased urban-rural inequality. The PEGR was consistently higher than the economic growth rate. Thus, the growth in Vietnam was pro-poor, benefiting

Table 18.5 Poverty equivalent growth rates in Vietnam, 1992–93 to 1997–98

Measures	Vietnam	Urban	Rural
Economic growth rate	5.02	5.28	4.04
Poverty equivalent growth rates			
Head-count ratio	5.08	6.28	4.61
Poverty gap ratio	5.33	6.46	5.04
Severity of poverty	5.43	6.59	5.19

the poor proportionally more than the non-poor. The PEGR for the severity of poverty is greater than those for the head-count and poverty gap ratios, which means that growth in Vietnam was more beneficial to the ultra-poor than the poor.

Both urban and rural sectors also experienced pro-poor growth. The Gini index for the urban sector fell from 0.351 in 1992–93 to 0.342 in 1997–98, whereas for the rural sector, it declined to 0.264 in 1997–98 from 0.289 in 1992–93. This result is consistent with the declining Gini index in both sectors. Vietnam has not only been a fast-growing economy in East Asia, but it has also maintained pro-poor growth with more signifi-cant benefits flowing to the poor. Kakwani and Son (2003) attribute this success to a series of reforms, known as *doi moi*, launched in the latter part of the 1980s. Reforms began primarily in the agriculture sector, which, at that time, accounted for close to 40% of GDP and 70% of total employment.

Initially, Vietnam focused its reform efforts on the dismantling of collective farms. It carried out land reforms, redistributing land to peasant households through long-term leases, and abolished price control on goods and services. It also eliminated produc-tion and consumption subsidies and streamlined the public sector. Furthermore, the reform efforts included stabilizing inflation and liberalization of trade and investment, as noted by Dollar (2002) from the World Bank. This series of reforms led to spectacu-lar growth and a remarkable decline in poverty. Vietnam became a wholly transformed market economy.

18.10.4 China

Since the 1970s, high economic growth and increasing inequality have been the two main features of the Chinese economy. The economic growth contributed to a sub-stantial reduction in poverty, and the worsening income distribution contributed to an increase in poverty. The two factors' net effect led to a dramatic reduction in poverty during the last 50 years.

The inequality debate in China has mainly focused on the Gini index as a measure of inequality. As pointed out in Chapter 17, the Gini index is not a good vehicle for measuring the impact of inequality on poverty. The Gini index does not have a one-to-one relationship with any poverty measure. While keeping other factors constant, the increase in the Gini index can reduce poverty, or the reduction in the Gini index can increase poverty. Such ambiguity does not happen when the PEGR measures the impact of inequality on poverty. This section analyses the pro-poorness of economic growth in China, covering 1988–2018.

This case study utilizes the Chinese Household Income Project, derived from the more extensive national household surveys conducted by the National Bureau of Statistics. The per capita household incomes are measured in 2013 Beijing prices and are comparable across country regions and over time. China's official poverty line of 2,736 yuan per person per month in Beijing's prices in 2013 is used to calculate poverty measures.

Table 18.6 presents the relative poverty equivalent growth rates along with economic growth rates. The per capita mean income had been growing at an annual rate of 7.08% over the entire period of three decades. No country in the world has achieved such high economic growth sustained over the three decades. The PEGR has a one-to-one relationship with poverty growth. In all periods and poverty measures, the PEGR are all positive, but with one exception. In the period 2013–18, the severity of poverty shows a negative PEGR, even though the economic growth in the period is positive. That happened because the growth had been highly anti-poor, resulting in an annual loss of growth rate of 3.71%.

In the periods 1988–95 and 1995–2002, the PEGR was lower than the actual growth, resulting in a loss of growth rate for all poverty measures. Thus, poverty declined in these periods, but growth was not pro-poor. In the subsequent period 2002–7, the PEGR peaked at exceptionally high values of more than 27% for all poverty measures. The yearly gain of growth rate was around 13%, signifying immensely highly pro-poor growth. In the subsequent periods 2007–13 and 2013–18, the PEGRs fell substantially, meaning that the rate of poverty reduction woefully slowed down. In the period 2013–18, the severity of poverty even increased. Thus, the PEGR followed an inverted U-shaped pattern, growing first and then decreasing. An exceptional period was 2002–7 when China achieved unprecedented pro-poor growth. It would be

Table 18.6 Relative poverty equivalent growth rates in China, 1988–2018

	1988–1995	1995–2002	2002–7	2007–13	2013–18	Trend growth
Economic growth rate	6.50	3.45	14.07	7.29	3.19	7.08
	Relative poverty equivalent growth rate					
Percentage of poor	5.74	2.48	27.12	3.49	4.26	7.26
Poverty gap ratio	5.15	2.11	27.02	2.49	1.88	6.62
Severity of poverty	4.68	1.89	27.20	1.56	−0.52	6.19
	Gain and loss of growth rate					
Percentage of poor	−0.75	−0.97	13.05	−3.79	1.07	0.17
Poverty gap ratio	−1.35	−1.34	12.95	−4.79	−1.31	−0.46
Severity of poverty	−1.82	−1.56	13.13	−5.73	−3.71	−0.90

exciting to explore why this period was exceptional and how the government's policies impacted this extraordinary period.

The trend growth rates for the PEGR for the entire period of 1988–2018 are positive for all poverty measures. Their values are significantly high, varying from 6.19% for the severity of poverty to 7.26% for the head-count ratio. These high values signify that China has achieved an outstanding reduction in poverty as measured by the three main poverty measures. The poverty gap ratio shows an annual growth rate loss of 0.46%. The severity of poverty, which gives higher weight to the extremely poor, shows an even higher yearly loss of growth rate at 0.90%. The overall conclusion emerging from these results is that China has achieved spectacular poverty reduction over three decades, but growth has not been pro-poor. If the growth process had been pro-poor, China would have achieved even higher poverty reduction.

The rising income inequality, especially the enormous urban-rural income disparity, was of much concern to China's policymakers. Thus, the government of China resolved this inequality through public policies. As Kakwani and Luo (2021) point out, the government led by Hu Jintao and Wen Jiabao implemented many social policies to improve the rural population's living conditions. The most critical social policy was improving social insurance programs such as the New Cooperative Medical System and a social pension scheme for rural residents. Simultaneously, the government increased subsidies on agriculture activities[6] nationwide from 51.36 billion yuan in 2007 to 170 billion yuan in 2013. The government also expanded its flagship program of minimum living standard guarantee (Dibao), covering more people and increasing transfers to beneficiaries. Despite all these social programs, it appears from this case study that the overall growth in China has not been favorable to the poor. It would seem that China needs to improve the efficacy of its social policies if it plans to alleviate poverty by 2030.

The empirical analysis presented in this case study also suggests that the Asian financial crisis had little impact on the living conditions of the people in China, unlike other countries in Asia.

18.11   Concluding Remarks

Poverty reduction depends on two factors. The first factor is the magnitude of economic growth, measured by the mean income growth rate. The larger the economic growth, the greater will be the poverty reduction. Economic growth may accompany income redistribution among the poor and the non-poor. The second factor affecting poverty is the inequality effect, which determines the benefits of economic growth between the poor and the non-poor.

This chapter has discussed the development of the poverty equivalent growth rate (PEGR), which is a composite indicator of the two factors: (i) magnitude of economic

---

[6] Subsidies on agriculture activities included subsidy on grain planting, subsidy on adoption of improved seeds, and subsidy on purchasing agriculture machines.

growth and (ii) distribution of benefits of economic growth. The chapter has demonstrated that the magnitude of PEGR determines the growth pattern, whether growth is pro-poor or anti-poor. The PEGR has the attractive feature that it is a monotonically decreasing function of the magnitude of poverty reduction. Hence, if the development objective is to achieve a rapid poverty reduction, policymakers should maximize the poverty equivalent growth rate rather than the actual growth rate.

The chapter has considered three alternative definitions of pro-poor growth: (i) relative pro-poor growth, (ii) absolute pro-poor growth, and (iii) poverty-reducing growth. There is no consensus in the literature on which definition is the most appropriate. All three definitions are essential in understanding the pattern of growth that explains the inter-relationship between economic growth, income inequality, and their impact on poverty. The PEGR provides a unifying conceptual framework encompassing the three alternative definitions of pro-poor growth.

The inequality literature has two approaches to measuring inequality: relative and absolute. This chapter has extended this idea, providing the relative and absolute paths to measuring pro-poor growth. The relative concept arises when growth benefits the poor proportionally more than the non-poor, causing relative inequality to fall. Under this definition, the absolute benefits of growth going to the poor may still be much smaller. That led to absolute pro-poor growth, which gives higher absolute benefits to the poor, causing absolute inequality to fall. The chapter has demonstrated that poverty-reducing growth is the weakest requirement of pro-poor growth when growth is positive. If the growth rate is negative, this definition is the strongest.

This chapter has presented four Asian case studies: South Korea, Thailand, Vietnam, and China. These are diverse countries, and their conclusions revealed how they managed the crisis to protect the poor. While South Korea and Vietnam achieved pro-poor growth in the 1990s, Thailand's economic growth was not pro-poor. Even though China achieved spectacular poverty reduction over three decades, its growth had not been pro-poor. If the growth process had been pro-poor, China would have gained even more significant poverty reduction.

South Korea's government introduced many social welfare programs in response to the crisis, including public works and temporary livelihood protection. The public works programs were particularly effective in creating jobs for the extremely poor, who became unemployed and laid-off within the labor market during the economic downturn. Similarly, the temporary likelihood protection program, implemented based on an income means test, helping the desperately poor.

Although the financial crisis severely impacted the poor in Thailand, unlike in South Korea, the Thai government did not respond promptly to protect the poor and more vulnerable ultra-poor. The recovery in Thailand was woefully slow, and it took many years for Thailand to return to pre-crisis growth. Vietnam introduced a series of reforms before the financial crisis that paved the way for its spectacular economic growth in the 1990s that was pro-poor, contributing to remarkable poverty reduction. The financial crisis had little impact on poverty in Vietnam.

The rising income inequality, especially the enormous urban-rural income dispar-ity, was of much concern to China's policymakers. In response, the government of China evoked many social policies to reduce poverty. Despite all these social pro-grams, the case study of China revealed that the overall growth in China had not been favorable to the poor. It would seem that China needs to improve the efficacy of its social policies if it plans to alleviate poverty by 2030.

The empirical analysis presented in these case studies also suggests that the Asian financial crisis had little impact on the living conditions of the people in China, unlike other countries in Asia.

References

Adams, R. 2004. "Economic Growth, Inequality and Poverty: Estimating the Growth Elasticity of Poverty." *World Development* 32, no. 12, 1989–2014.

Ahluwalia, M. 1974. "Income Inequality: Some Dimensions of the Problem." In H. Chenery M. Ahluwalia, C. Bell, J. Duloy, and R. Jolly, et al. (Eds) *Redistribution with Growth.* London: Oxford University Press.

Ahluwalia, M. 1976. "Income Distribution and Development: Some Stylized Facts." *Papers and Proceedings of the American Economic Association.* Paper presented at the 88th meeting of the American Economic Association, December 28–30, 1975, Dallas, Texas.

Ahluwalia, M., N. Carter, and H. Chenery. 1979. "Growth and Poverty in Developing Countries." *Journal of Development Economics* 6: 299–341.

Aigner, D., and A. Heins. 1967. "A Social Welfare View of the Measurement of Income Equality." *Review of Income and Wealth* 13: 12–25.

Aitchison, J. and J. Brown. 1954. "On Criteria for Description of Income Distribution." *Metroeconomica,* 6: 88–107.

Aitchison, J. and J. Brown. 1957. *The Lognormal Distribution.* Cambridge: Cambridge University Press.

Alkire, S. 2008. "Choosing Dimensions: The Capability Approach, and Multidimensional Poverty." In N. Kakwani and J. Silber (Eds) *The Many Dimensions of Poverty,* New York: Palgrave Macmillan.

Alkire, S. and J. Foster. 2011. "Counting and Multidimensional Poverty Measurement." *Journal of Public Economics* 95: 476–87.

Allen, R. and A. Bowley. 1935. *Family Expenditure.* London: Staples.

Allingham, M. 1972. "The Measurement of Inequality." *Journal of Economic Theory* 5: 63–69.

Amoroso, L. 1925. "Ricerche intorno alla curva dei redditi," *Annali di mathematica pura ed applicata,* Series 4–21, pp 123–59.

Anand, S. and C. Harris. 1994. "Choosing a Welfare Indicator." *American Economic Review* 84, no. 2: 226–31.

Aronson, R., P. Johnson and P. Lambert. 1994. "Redistributive Effects and Unequal Income Tax Treatment." *Economic Journal,* vol. 104, no. 423, pp 262–70.

Arrow, K. 1958. "The Measurement of Price Changes." In *The Relationship of Prices to Economic Stability and Growth,* Joint Economic Committee, US Congress, March 31, 1958.

Atkinson, A. 1970. "On the Measurement of Inequality." *Journal of Economic Theory* 2: 244–63.

Atkinson, A. 1973. "How Progressive Should Income Tax Be?" In *Essays on Modern Economics,* edited by M. Parkin. London: Longman Group.

Atkinson, A. 1974. *Unequal Shares.* UK: Penguin.

Atkinson, A. 1980. "Horizontal Equity and the Distribution of the Tax Burden." In H. Aaron and M. Boskin (Eds) *The Economics of Taxation,* Washington, DC: Brookings Institute.

Atkinson, A. 1987. "On the Measurement of Poverty." *Econometrica* 55: 749–64.

Atkinson, A. 2003. "Multidimensional Deprivation: Contrasting Social Welfare and Counting Approaches." *Journal of Economic Inequality* 1: 51–65.

Atkinson, A. 2015. *Inequality: What Can Be Done?* Cambridge, MA: Harvard University Press.

Atkinson, A. and F. Bourguignon. 1982. "The Comparison of Multidimensional Distributions of Economic Status." *Review of Economic Studies* 49: 183–201.

Barten, A. 1964. "Family Composition, Prices and Expenditure Patterns." In P. Hart, G. Mill, and J. Whittaker (Eds) *Econometric Analysis for National Economic Planning,* London: Butterworth and Company.

Barro, R. 1989. "A Cross-section Study of Growth, Savings and Government." In B. Douglas and J. Showen (Eds) *National Saving, and Economic Performance*, Chicago: Chicago University Press.

Becker, G. 1962. "Investment in Human Capital: A Theoretical Analysis." *Journal of Political Economy* 70: 9–49.

Becker, G. 1967. *Human Capital and the Personal Distribution of Income*. Ann Arbor: University of Michigan Press.

Bentzel, R. 1970. "The Social Significance of Income Distribution Statistics." *Review of Income and Wealth* 16, no. 3 (September): 253–64.

Bergson, A. 1938. "A Reformulation of Certain Aspects of Welfare Economics." *Quarterly Journal of Economics* 52: 310–34.

Berkowitz, J. and J. Jackson. 2005. "Evolution of an Economic and Political Middle Class in Transition Countries." International Poverty Centre Working Paper Series 10.

Berrebi, W. and J. Silber 1985, "Income Inequality Indices and Deprivation: a Generalization", *Quarterly Journal of Economics*, vol. 100, pp 807–810.

Bhagwati, J. 1988. "Poverty and Public Policy." *World Development*, vol. 16 (5), pp 539–654.

Birdsall, N. 2007a. *Do No Harm: Aid, Weak Institutions and Missing Middle in Africa*. Washington, DC: Centre for Global Development.

Birdsall, N. 2007b. "Income Distribution: Effects on Growth and Development." Working Paper no. 118, Washington, DC: Centre for Global Development.

Blackburn, M. and D. Bloom. 1985. "What Is Happening to the Middle Class?" *American Demographics* 7: 18–25.

Blackorby, C., W. Bossert, and D. Donaldson. 1999. "Income Inequality Measurement: The Normative Approach." In J. Silber (Ed) *Handbook of Boston, Income Inequality Measurement*, Boston MA: Kluwer Academic Publishers.

Blinder, A. 1974. *Toward an Economic Theory of Income Distribution*. Cambridge, MA: MIT Press.

Blum, W. 1979. "The Uneasy Case for Progressive Taxation." In C. Campbell (Ed) *Income Redistribution*, Washington, DC: American Enterprise Institute for Public Policy.

Blum, W. and H. Kalven. 1953. *The Uneasy Case for Progressive Taxation*. Chicago: Chicago University Press.

Boltho, A. and A. Glyn. 1995. "Can Macroeconomic Policies Raise Employment?" *International Labour Review* 134: 451–70.

Bonferroni, C. 1930. *Elmenti di statistica generale*. Firenze: Libreria Seber.

Borda, J. 1781. "Memoire sur les Elections an Scrutin." In *Memoires de l'Academic Royale de Science*, Paris.

Bos, D. and B. Felderer. 1989. *Political Economy of Progressive Taxation*. Berlin: Springer Verlag.

Bosmans, K., K. Decancq, and A. Decoster. 2014. "The Relativity of Decreasing Inequality between Countries." *Economica* 81, no. 322: 276–92.

Bossert, W. and A. Pfingsten. 1990. "Intermediate Inequality: Concepts, Indices, and Welfare Implications." *Mathematical Social Sciences* 19: 117–34.

Bourguignon, F. 2015. *The Globalization of Inequality*. Princeton, NJ: Princeton University Press.

Bourguignon, F. and Chakravarty, S. 2003. "The Measurement of Multidimensional Poverty." *Journal of Economic Inequality* 1: 25–49.

Bowles, S. 1969. *Planning Educational Systems for Economic Growth, Harvard Economic studies*, vol. 133, Cambridge, MA: MIT Press.

Braithwait, S. 1980. "Substitution Bias of the Laspeyres Price Index." *American Economic Review*, pp 64–77.

Burr, I. 1942. "Cumulative Frequency Functions." *Annals of Mathematical Statistics* 13: 215–35.

Chakravarty, S. 1997. "On Shorrocks' Reinvestigation of the Sen Poverty Index." *Econometrica* 65, no. 5: 1241–42.

Chakravarty, S. and J. Silber. 2008. "Measuring Multidimensional Poverty: The Axiomatic Approach." In N. Kakwani and J. Silber (Eds) *Quantitative Approaches to Multidimensional Poverty Measurement*. New York: Palgrave Macmillan.

Chakravarty, S. 1983a. "Ethically Flexible Measures of Poverty." *Canadian Journal of Economics* 16: 74–85.

Chakravarty, S. 1983b. "A New Index of Poverty." *Mathematical Social Science* 6, no. 3: 307–13.

Chakravarty, S. 2009. "Inequality, Polarization and Poverty." *Advances in distribution Analysis*, New York: Springer.

Chakravarty, S., and A. Chakraborty. 1984. 'On Indices of Relative Deprivation." *Economic Letters*, vol. 14, pp 283–287.

Chakravarty, S., N. Chattopadhyay, and A. Majumder. 1995, "Income Inequality and Relative Deprivation." *Keio Economic Studies*, vol 32, pp 1–15.

Chakravarty, S. and D. Mukherjee. 1999. "Measures of Deprivation and their Meaning in Terms of Social Satisfaction." *Theory and Decision*, vol. 47, pp 89–100.

Chakravarty, S. and J. Silber. 2008. "Measuring Multidimensional Poverty: Axiomatic Approach." In N. Kakwani and J. Silber (Editors), *Quantitative Approaches to Multidimensional Poverty Measurement*, Palgrave Macmillan.

Champernowne, D. 1952. "The Graduation of Income Distributions." *Econometrica* 20: 591–615.

Champernowne, D. 1953. "A Model of Income Distribution." *Economic Journal* 63: 318–51.

Champernowne, D. 1956. "Discussion on Paper by Hart and Prais." *Journal of the Royal Statistical Society*, part II, 119: 181–83.

Chipman, J. 1974. "The Welfare Ranking of Pareto Distribution." *Journal of Economic Theory* 9: 275–82.

Chiswick, B. 1968. "The Average Level of Schooling and the Intraregional Inequality of Income: A Clarification." *American Economic Review* 58: 495–501.

Chiswick, B. 1971. "Earnings Inequality and Economic Development." *Quarterly Journal of Economics* 85: 21–32.

Chiswick, B. 1974. *Income Inequality: Regional Analysis with a Human-Capital Framework*. New York: National Bureau of Economic Research.

Christensen, L. and M. Manser. 1974. "Cost of Living Indices and Price Indices for US Meat Produce: 1947–1971." National Bureau of Economic Research, Conference in Research in Income and Wealth, vol. 40, Household Behavior and Consumption.

Clark, S., R. Hemming, and D. Ulph. 1981. "On Indices for the Measurement of Poverty." *Economic Journal* 91: 515–26.

Coady D., M. Grosh, and J. Hoddinott. 2004. *Targeting of Transfers in Developing Countries: Review of Lessons and Experience*. Washington, DC: World Bank.

Cowell, F. 1980. "Inequality Decomposition." An Unpublished Note.

Cowell, F. and K. Kuga. 1981. "Additivity and the Entropy Concept: An Axiomatic Approach to Inequality Measurement." *Journal Economic Theory* 25, 131–43.

Crame'r, H. 1946. *Mathematical Methods of Statistics*. Princeton, NJ: Princeton University Press.

Cramer, J. 1964. "Efficient Grouping, Regression, and Correlation in Engel Curve Analysis." *Journal of the American Statistical Association* 59: 233–50.

Dalton, H. 1920. "The Measurement of the Inequality of Incomes." *Economic Journal* 30: 348–61.

Dalton, H. 1920. *Principles of Public Finance*. New York: Frederick A. Praeger.

Dasgupta, P., A. Sen, and D. Starrett. 1973. "Notes on the Measurement of Inequality." *Journal of Economic Theory* 6: 180–87.

Datt, G. and M. Ravallion. 1992. "Growth and Redistribution Components of Changes in Poverty Measures: A Decomposition with Applications to Brazil and India in the 1980s." *Journal of Development Economics* 38: 275–95.

Davis, H. 1941. *Theory of Econometrics*. The Principia Press, INC Bloomington Indiana

Davis, J. and J. Huston. 1992. "The Shrinking Middle Class: A Multivariate Analysis." *Eastern Economic Journal* 18, no. 3: 277–85.

De Wolff, P. and A. Van Slijpe. 1972. *The Relation between Income, Intelligence, Education, and Social Background*. Institute of Actuarial Science and Econometrics, University of Amsterdam.

Deaton, A. 1980. "The Measurement of Welfare." LSMS Working Papers no. 7, Washington, DC: World Bank.

Deaton, A. 1998. "Economies of Scale, Household Size, and the Demand for Food." *Journal of Political Economy* 106: 897–930.

Deaton, A. and J. Muellbauer. 1980. *Economics and Consumer Behavior,* Cambridge: Cambridge University Press.

Deaton, A. and S. Zaidi. 2002. "Guidelines for Constructing Consumption Aggregates for Welfare Analysis." LSMS Working Paper no. 135, Washington, DC: World Bank.

Deutsch, J. and J. Silber. 2005. "Measuring Multidimensional Poverty: An Empirical Comparison of Various Approaches." *Review of Income and Wealth* 51, no 1: 145–74.

Deutsch, J. and J. Silber. 2005. "On the Decomposition of Income Polarization by Population Sub-groups." Unpublished mimeo.

Diamond, P. and D. McFadden. 1974. "Some Uses of Expenditure Function in Public Finance." *Journal of Public Economics* 3: 3–21.

Diewert, W. 1976. "Exact and Superlative Index Numbers." *Journal of Econometrics* 4: 115–45.

Diewert, W. 1983. "The Theory of the Cost of living Index and the Measurement of Welfare Change." In W. Diewert and C. Montmarquette (Eds) *Price Level Measurement.* Ministry of Supply and Services, Canada.

Diewert, W. 1990a. *The Economic Theory of Index Numbers.* Amsterdam: North-Holland.

Diewert, W. 1990b. *Price Level Measurement.* Amsterdam: North-Holland.

Diewert, W. 1993. "Group Cost of Living Indexes: Approximations and Axiomatics." In W. Diewert and A. Nakamura (Eds) *Essays in Index Number Theory.* Amsterdam: North-Holland.

Diewert, W. 1998. "Index Number Issues in the CPI." *Journal of Economic Perspectives* 12: 47–58.

Dollar, D. 2002. "Reform, Growth, and Poverty Reduction in Vietnam." Policy Research Working Paper, no. 2837, Washington, DC: World Bank.

Dollar, D. and A. Kraay. 2002. "Growth is Good for the Poor." *Journal of Economic Growth* 7: 195–225.

Drewnowski, J. 1977. "Poverty: Its Meaning and Measurement." *Development and Change* 8: 183–208.

Donalson, D. and J. Weymark, 1980, "A Single-parameter Generalization of the Gini Index of Inequality." *Journal of Economic Theory*, vol. 22, pp 67–80.

Duclos, J., J. Esteban, and D. Ray. 2004. "Polarization: Concepts, Measurement, Estimation." *Econometrica* 72, no. 6: 1737–72.

Duclos, J., V. Jalbert, and A. Araar. 2003. "Classical Horizontal Inequity and Reranking: An Integrated Approach." *Research on Economic Inequality* 10: 65–100.

Easterly, W. 2001. "The Middle-Class Consensus, and Economic Development." *Journal of Economic Growth* 6, no. 4: 317–35.

Eastwood, R. and M. Lipton. 2001. "Pro-Poor Growth and Pro-Growth Poverty Reduction: Meaning, Evidence, and Policy Implications." *Asian Development Review* 19: 1–37.

Ebert, U. 1988. "Measurement of Inequality: An Attempt at Unification and Generalization." *Social Choice and Welfare* 5: 147–69.

Ebert, U. 2004. "Coherent Inequality Views: Linear Invariant Measures Reconsidered." *Mathematical Social Sciences* 47, no. 1: 1–20.

Ebert, U. 2010. "Inequality Reducing Taxation Reconsidered." In J. Bishop (Ed) *Research on Economic Inequality* 18(18), 131–52.

Ebert, U. and P. Moyes. 2000. "Consistent Income Tax Structures When Households Are Heterogeneous." *Journal of Economic Theory* 90, no. 1: 116–50.

Engel, E. 1957. "Die Produktions- und Consumptionsverhältnisse des Königreichs Sachsen." *Zeitschrift des Statistischen Bureaus des Königlich Sächsischen Ministerium des Innern* 22 (November).

Esteban, J. and D. Ray. 1994. "On the Measurement of Polarization." *Econometrica* 62: 819–52.

Esteban, J., C. Gradin, and D. Ray. 2007. "An Extension of a Measure of Polarization with Application to the Income Distributions of Five OECD Countries." *Journal of Economic Inequality*, vol. 5 (1), 1–19

Fei, J. 1981. "Equity-Oriented Fiscal Programs." *Econometrica* 49: 869–81.

Feldstein, M. 1976. "On the Theory of Tax Reform." *Journal of Public Economics* 6, 77–104.

Fine, B. and K. Fine. 1974. "Social Choice and Individual Ranking." *Review of Economic Studies* 41: 303–22.

Fisk, P. 1961b. "The Graduation of Income Distributions." *Econometrica* 29: 171–85.

Formby, J., T. Seaks, and W. Smith. 1981. "A Comparison of Two New Measures of Tax Progressivity." *Economic Journal* 91: 1015–19.

Forsyth, F. 1960. "The Relationship between Family Size and Family Expenditure." *Journal of the Royal Statistical Society* 123: 367–97.

Foster, J. and M. Wolfson. 1992. "Polarization and Decline of Middle-Class: Canada and the USA." *Journal of Economic Inequality* 8, no. 2: 247–73.

Foster, J. and M. Wolfson. 2009. "Polarization and Decline of Middle-Class: Canada and the USA." OPHI Working Papers, 31, Queen Elizabeth House, Oxford University.

Foster, J. 1984. "On Economic Poverty: A Survey of Aggregate Measures." In R. Baseman and G. Rhodes (Eds) *Advances in Econometrics*, vol. 3, Greenwich: JAI Press.

Foster, J., J. Greer, and E. Thorbecke. 1984. "A Class of Decomposable Poverty Measures." *Econometrica* 52, no. 3: 761–76.

Foster, J. and A. Shorrocks. 1991. "Sub-Group Consistent Poverty Measures." *Econometrica* 59, pp 687–709.

Foster, J. and M. Sze'kely. 2008. "Is Economic Growth Good for the Poor." *International Economic Review*, vol. 49(4), November, pp 1143–1172.

Friedman, M. 1953. "Choice, Chance and Personal Distribution of Income." *Journal of Political Economy* 61: 277–90.

Friedman, M. 1957. *A Theory of the Consumption* Function. Princeton, NJ: Princeton University Press.

Friedman, M. 1962. *Capitalism and Freedom*. Chicago: University of Chicago Press.

Fuchs, V. 1969. "Comment." In L. Soltow (Ed) *Six Papers on the Size Distribution of Income and Wealth*. New York: National Bureau of Economic Research.

Gajdos, T. 2001. "Les fondements axiomatiques de la mesure normative des inégalites." *Revue d'Economie* 5: 683–720.

Gauss, C. 1809. *"Theoria Motus Corporum Coelestium in sectionibus conicis solem ambientium* (Theorie der Bewegung der Himmelskörper, die die Sonne in Kegelschnitten umkreisen)." *Theory of the Motion of Heavenly Bodies Moving about the Sun in Conic Sections* (English translation by C. H. Davis), reprinted in 1963, New York.

Gebeloff, G. and D. Searcey. 2015. "Middle class shrinks further as more fall out instead of climbing up." New York Times.

Gerber, C., A. Klemm, L. Liu, and V. Mylonas. 2019. "Income Tax Progressivity: Trends and Implications." *Oxford Bulletin of Economics and Statistics*. 0305–9049. doi.10.1111/obes.12331.

Gibrat, R. 1931. *Les inégalités économiques*. Paris: Sirely.

Gigliano, C. and K. Mosler, 2009, Constructing Indices of Multivariate Polarization" *Journal of Economic Inequality*, vol. 7, pp 435–460.

Gini, C. 1912. *Variabilita e mutabilita*. Bologna.

Gini, C. 1913–14. "Sulla misura della concentrazione e della variabilita dei caratteri." *Transactions of the Real Instituto Veneto di Scienze, Lettere ed Arti* 53: 1203–12.

Golan, J., T. Sicular, and N. Umapathi. 2017. "Unconditional Cash Transfers in China: Who Benefits from the Rural Minimum Living Standard Guarantee (Dibao) Program?" *World Development* 93, no. 5: 316–36.

Gopalan, S. 1992. "Undernutrition: Measurement and Implications." In S. Osmani (Ed) *Nutrition and Poverty*. Oxford: Clarendon Press.

Green, C. 1966. "Negative Taxes and the Poverty Problem." Conference monograph prepared for the Brookings Institute Studies in Government Finance (June 9–10).

Gustafsson, B., S. Li, and T. Sicular. 2008. *Income Inequality and Public Policy in China Inequality and Public Policy in China*. New York: Cambridge University Press.

Hadar, J. and W. Russell. 1969. "Rules for Ordering Uncertain Prospects." *American Economic Review* 59: 25–34.

Hamada, k. and N. Takayama. 1977. "Censored Income Distribution and Measurement of Poverty." *Bulletin of the International Statistics Institute* 47: 617–632.

Hagenaars, A. 1987. "A Class of Poverty Indices." *International Economic Review* 28: 583–607.

Hanoch, G. and H. Levy. 1969. "The Efficiency Analysis of Choices Involving Risk." *Review of Economic Studies* 36: 334–46.

Hardy, G., J. Littlewood, and G. Polya. 1929. "Some Simple Inequalities Satisfied by Convex Functions." *Messenger of Math* 26: 145–53.

Hardy, G., J. Littlewood, and G. Polya. 1934. *Inequalities.* Cambridge: Cambridge University Press.

Hayakawa, M. 1951. "The Application of Pareto's Law of Income to Japanese Data." *Econometrica* 19: 174–83.

Henderson, A. 1949, The Cost of Children, Population Studies, 3, 130; 4, 267.

Henderson Report. 1975. *Poverty in Australia, Commission of Inquiry into Poverty.* Canberra: Australian Government Publishing Service.

Hey, J. and P. Lambert. 1980. "Relative Deprivation and Gini Coefficient: Comment." *Quarterly Journal of Economics* 94: 567–73.

Hicks, J. 1946. *Value and Capital.* Oxford: Clarendon Press.

Husen, T. 1968. "Ability, Opportunity, and Career: A 26 Year Follow-up." *Education Research* 10: 170–79.

Iman, L. and W. Conover. 1978. "Approximations of the critical region for 's rho with and without ties present." *Communication in Statistics–Simulation and Computation* 7: 269–82.

International Labour Organization. 2005. World Employment 1995/96.

Iyenger, N. 1960. "On a Method of Computing Engel Elasticities from Concentration Curves." *Econometrica* 28: 882–91.

Jakobsson, U. 1976. "On the Measurement of the Degree of Progression." *Journal of Public Economics* 5: 161–68.

Jain, S. 1975. *Size Distribution of Income: A Compilation of Data.* Baltimore: Johns Hopkins University Press.

Jain, L. and S. Tendulkar. 1990. "Role of Growth, and Distribution in the Observed Change of Head-count Ratio Measure of Poverty: A Decomposition Exercise for India." Technical Report No 9004, Delhi: Indian Statistical Institute.

Jenkins, S. 1988. "Empirical Measurement of Horizontal Inequity." *Journal of Public Economics* 37: 305–29.

Jenkins, S. and P. Lambert. 1999. "Horizontal Inequity Measurement: A Basic Reassessment." In J. Silber (Ed) *Handbook of Income Inequality Measurement.* New York: Kluwer Academic Publishers.

Jensen, J. 1906, "Sur less fontions Convexes at les Inegalites Entire les Valeurs Moyennes." *Acta Mathematica,* vol. 30, no. 1, pp 175–193.

Kakwani, N. 1976. "On the Estimation of Income Inequality Measures from Grouped Observations." *Review of Economic Studies* 43: 483–92.

Kakwani, N. 1977a. "Measurement of Poverty and Negative Income Tax." *Australian Economic Papers* 17: 237–48.

Kakwani, N. 1977b. "On the Estimation of Engel Elasticities from Grouped Observations with Application to Indonesian Data." *Journal of Econometrics* 6: 1–17.

Kakwani, N. 1977c. "Applications of Lorenz Curves in Economic Analysis." *Econometrica* 45: 719–27.

Kakwani, N. 1977d. "Measurement of Tax Progressivity: An International Comparison." *Economic Journal* 87: 71–80.

Kakwani, N. 1977e. "Redistributive Effects of Alternative Negative Income Tax Plans." *Public Finance* 32: 77–91.

Kakwani, N. 1977f. "On the Estimation of Consumer Unit Scale." *Review of Economics and Statistics* 59: 507–10.

Kakwani, N. 1980a, *Income Inequality and Poverty: Methods of Estimation and Policy Applications.* New York: Oxford University Press.

Kakwani, N. 1980b. "On a Class of Poverty Measures." *Econometrica* 48: 437–446.

Kakwani, N. 1981a. "Welfare Measures: An International Comparisons." *Journal of Development Economics* 8: 21–45.

Kakwani, N. 1984a. "Issues in Measuring Poverty." In *Economic Inequality: Measurement and Policy: Advances in Econometrics*. Greenwich, CT: JAI Press.

Kakwani, N. 1984b. "Measurement of Tax Progressivity and Redistributions of Taxes with Applications to Horizontal and Vertical Equity." In *Economic Inequality: Measurement and Policy, Advances in Econometrics*. Greenwich, CT: JAI Press.

Kakwani, N. 1984c. "Welfare Ranking of Income Distributions." In *Economic Inequality: Measurement and Policy: Advances in Econometrics*, Greenwich, CT: JAI Press.

Kakwani, N. 1984d. "The Relative Deprivation Curve and Its Applications." *Journal of Business and Economic Statistics* 2, October: 384–94.

Kakwani, N. 1986. *Analyzing Redistribution Policies: A Study Using Australian Data*. Cambridge: Cambridge University Press.

Kakwani, N. 1993. "Poverty and Economic Growth with Application to Cote d' Ivoire." *Review of Income and Wealth* 39: 121–39.

Kakwani, N. 1996. "Income Inequality, Welfare and Poverty in Ukraine." *Development and Change* 27: 663–91.

Kakwani, N. 1997. "Growth Rates of Per Capita Income and Aggregate Welfare: An International Comparison." *Review of Economics and Statistics*, vol. 79, 201–11.

Kakwani, N. 2000a. "Growth and Inequality Components of Change in Poverty with Application to Thailand." *Journal of Quantitative Economics* 16, no. 1: 67–80.

Kakwani, N. 2000b. "Growth and Poverty Reduction." *Asian Development Review* 18, no. 2: 74–84.

Kakwani, N. 2006. "What is Poverty." One Pager, International Poverty Centre, UNDP.

Kakwani, N. 2011. "A New Model of Constructing Poverty Thresholds." In J. Deutsch and J. Silber (Eds) *The Measurement of Individual Well-Being and Group Inequalities*. New York: Routledge.

Kakwani, N. and P. Lambert. 1998. "On Measuring Inequity in Taxation: A New Approach." *European Journal of Political Economy* 14: 369–80.

Kakwani, N. and P. Lambert. 1999. "Measuring Income Tax Discrimination." *Review of Economics and Statistics* 81, no. 1, pp 27–31.

Kakwani, N., S. Li, X. Wang, and M. Zhu. 2019. "Evaluating the Effectiveness of the Rural Minimum Living Standard Guarantee (Dibao) Program in China." *China Economic Review*, vol. 53, pp 1–14.

Kakwani, N. and E. Pernia. 2000. "What is Pro-Poor Growth." *Asian Development Review* 16, no. 1, pp 1–22.

Kakwani, N. and N. Podder. 1973. "On the Estimation of Lorenz Curves from Grouped Observations." *International Economic Review* 14: 278–91.

Kakwani, N. and N. Podder. 1976. "Efficient Estimation of the Lorenz Curve and Associated Inequality Measures from Grouped Observations." *Econometrica* 44: 137–48.

Kakwani, N. and Jacques Siber. 2008. *Many Dimensions of Poverty*. New York: Palgrave Macmillan.

Kakwani, N. and J. Siber. 2008. *Quantitative Approaches to Multidimensional Poverty Measurement*. New York: Palgrave Macmillan.

Kakwani, N. and H. Son. 2003. "Pro-Poor Growth: Concepts and Measurement with Country Case studies." *Distinguished Lectures, Pakistan Development Review* 42(4): 417–44.

Kakwani, N., M. Neri, and H. Son. 2010. "Linkages between pro-poor growth, social programs and labor market: the recent Brazilian experience." *World Development*, 38(6), 881–894.

Kakwani, N. and H. Son. 2008. "Poverty Equivalent Growth Rate." *Review of Income and Wealth* 54, no. 4: 643–55.

Kakwani, N. and H. Son. 2016a. *Social Welfare Functions and Development: Measurement and Policy Applications*. London: Palgrave Macmillan.

Kakwani, N. and H. Son. 2016b. "Global poverty estimates based on 2011 purchasing power parity: where should the new poverty line be drawn?" *Journal of Economic Inequality*, vol. 14, no. 2, 173–184.

Kakwani, N., S. Li, X. Wang, and M. Zhu. 2019. "Evaluating the Effectiveness of the Rural Minimum Living Standard Guarantee (Dibao) Program in China." *China Economic Review*, vol. 53, February, pp 1–14.

Kakwani, N. and H. Son. 2019. *Economic Growth and Poverty*. The International Library of Critical Writings in Economics Series, An Elgar Research Collection, Cheltenham, UK: Edward Elgar Publishing Ltd.

Kakwani, N. and H. Son. 2021, "Normative Measures of Tax Progressivity." *Journal of Economic Inequality*, vol. 19, pp 185–212.

Kakwani, N. and K. Subbarao. 1990. "Rural Poverty, and its Alleviation in India." *Economic and Political Weekly*, vol. 25, A2–A16.

Kakwani, N. and C. Luo. 2021. "How does the Pattern of Growth Impact Poverty Reduction in Rural China?." *Journal of Quantitative Economics*, December.

Kalecki, M. 1945. "On the Gibrat Distribution." *Econometrica* 13: 1961–70.

Kanbur, R. and A. Wagstaff. 2014. "How Useful is Inequality of Opportunity as a Policy Construct." Policy Research Working Paper Series 6980. Washington, DC: World Bank.

Kaplow, L. 1989. "Horizontal Equity: Measures in Search of a Principle." *National Tax Journal* 42, no. 2: 139–54.

Kaplow, L. 2005. "Why Measure Inequality." *Journal of Economic Inequality* 3: 65–79.

Kats, A. 1972. "On the Social Welfare Function and the Parameters of Income Distribution." *Journal of Economic Theory* 5: 90–91.

Khetan, C. and S. Poddar. 1976. "Measurement of Income Tax Progressivity in a Growing Economy: The Canadian Experience." *Canadian Journal of Economics* 9: 613–29.

Kolm, S. 1976a. "Unequal inequalities I." *Journal of Economic Theory* 12: 416–42.

Kolm, S. 1976b. "Unequal inequalities II." *Journal of Economic Theory* 13: 82–111.

Konüs, A. 1924. "The Problem of True Cost of Living." translated in *Econometrica* 7, 1939, 10–29.

Kraay, A. 2004. "When Is Growth Pro-Poor? Cross-Country Evidence." IMF Working Paper no. 47, Washington, DC: International Monetary Fund.

Kundu, A. and T. Smith. 1982. "An Impossible Theorem on Poverty Indices." *International Economic Review* 24: 423–34.

Kuznets, S. 1955. "Economic Growth and Income Inequality." *American Economic Review* 45: 1–28.

Lambert, P. and X. Ramos. 1997. "Horizontal Inequity and Vertical Redistribution." *International Tax and Public Finance* 4, no. 1: 25–37.

Lambert, P. and S. Yitzhaki. 1995. "Equity, Equality and Welfare." *European Economic Review*, vol. 39, pp 674–682

Lampman, R. 1964. "Prognosis for Poverty." In *National Tax Association Proceedings of the 57th Annual Conference*, 71–81. Pittsburgh.

Lampman, R. 1971. *Ends and Means of Reducing Income Poverty*. Chicago: Markham.

Lanjouw, P. and M. Ravallion. 1994. "Poverty and Household Size." Policy Research Working Paper 1332, Washington, DC: World Bank.

Laplace, P. 1812. "*Théorie analytique des probabilités*." Paris First Edition.

Lasso de la Vega, C. and A. Urrutia. 2006. "An Alternative Formulation of Esteban-Gradine-Ray Extended Measure of Polarization." *Journal of Income Distribution*, 15 (Index Issue): pp 42–54.

Lerner, A. 1944. *The Economics of Control*. London: Macmillan.

Levy, P. 1925. *Calculd es probabilities*. Aris: Gauthier-Villars.

Lorenz, M. 1905. "Methods of Measuring the Concentration of Wealth." *Journal of the American Statistical Association*, vol. 9, pp 209–19.

Lucas, R. 1988. "On the Mechanic of Economic Development." *Journal of Monetary Economics*, vol. 22, pp 3–42.

Lustig, N. 2011. "Multidimensional Indices of Achievements and Poverty: What Do We Gain and What Do We Lose? An Introduction to JOEI Forum on Multidimensional Poverty." *Journal of Economic Inequality* 9: 227–34.

Mahalanobis, P. 1960. "A Method of Fractile Graphical Analysis." *Econometrica* 28: 325–51.

Mandelbrot, B. 1960. "The Pareto-Levy Law and the Distribution of Income." *International Economic Review* 1: 79–105.

Manser, M. 1975. "The Translog Utility Function with Changing Tastes." BLS Working Paper 33, January.

Mantovani, D., S. Pellegrino, and A. Vernizzi. 2018. "A Note on the Maximum Value of the Kakwani Index." *Empirical Economics* 24, 1524–26.

Marshall, A. 1930. *Principle of Economics*, 8th edition. London: Macmillan.

Mas-Colell, A., M. Whinston, and J. Green. 1995. *Microeconomic Theory*. Oxford University Press.

McCulloch, N. and B. Baulch. 1999. "Tracking pro-poor growth." ID21 Insights no. 31, Sussex: Institute of Development Studies.

Meade, J. 1976. *The Just Economy*. London: George Allen and Unwin.

Merton, R. 1957. *Social Theory and Social Structure*. Chicago: Chicago University Press.

Milanovic, B. 1992. "Distributional impact of cash and in-kind social transfers in Eastern Europe and Russia." Policy Research Working Papers, no. 1054, Washington, DC: World Bank.

Mincer, J. 1958. "Investment in Human Capital and Personal Income Distribution." *Journal of Political Economy* 66: 281–302.

Moyes, P. 1988. "A Note on Minimally Progressive Taxation and Absolute Income Inequality." *Social Choice and Welfare* 5, no. 2–3: 227–34.

Muellbauer, J. 1974a. "Prices and Inequality: The United Kingdom Experience." *Economic Journal* 84: 32–55.

Muellbauer, J. 1974b. "Household Composition, Engel Curves and Welfare Comparisons between Households." *European Economic Review* 5: 103–22.

Muellbauer, J. 1975b. "Inequality Measures, Prices and Household Composition." *Review of Economic Studies* 41: 493–504.

Muellbauer, J. 1975c. "Identification and Consumer Unit Scale." *Econometrica* 43: 807–9.

Musgrave, R. and T. Thin. 1948. "Income Tax Progression, 1929–48." *Journal of Political Economy* 56: 498–514.

Newbery, D. 1970. "A Theorem on the Measurement of Inequality." *Journal of Economic Theory* 2: 264–66.

Nicholson, J. 1949. "Variation in Working-Class Expenditures." *Journal of the Royal Statistical Society*, series A, 112, pp 359–411.

Nissanov, Z., A. Poggi, and J. Silber. 2011. "Measuring Bi-Polarization and Polarization: A Short Survey." In J. Deutsch and J. Silber (Eds). *The Measurement of Individual Well-being, and Group Inequality: Essays in Memory of Z. M. Berrebi*. London: Routledge.

Nussbaum, M. 2003. "Capabilities as Fundamental Entitlements: Sen and Social Justice." *Feminist Economics* 9, no. 2–3.

Orshansky, M. 1965. "Counting the Poor: An Other Look at the Poverty Profile." *Social Security Bulletin* 28, no. 1: 3–29.

Oxfam. 2000. "Growth with Equity is Good for the Poor." Oxfam Policy Papers, June 27, Oxford, UK.

Padalino, S. and M. Vivarelli. 1997. "The Employment Intensity of Economic Growth in the G-7 Countries." *International Labour Review*. vol. 136, pp 191–213.

Pareto, V. 1897. *Cours d'économique politique*. vol. 2, part I, Chapter 1. Lausanne.

Pattanaik, P. and M. Sengupta, 1995, "An Alternative Axiomatization of Sen's Poverty Measure" *Review of Income and Wealth, Series* 41, Number 1 March pp 73–80.

Paul, S. 1991, "An Index of Relative Deprivation", *Economic Letters*, vol 36, pp 337–341.

Permanyer, I. 2008. "The Measurement of Social Polarization." Memo Institut d'Analistis Economica, Barcelona.

Pfingsten, A. 1987. "Axiomatically Based Local Measures of Tax Progression." *Bulletin of Economic Research* 39, no. 3: 211–23.

Pfingsten, A. 1988. "Progressive Taxation and Redistributive Taxation: Different Labels for the Same Product?" *Social Choice and Welfare* 5, no. 2–3: 235–46.

Pigou, A. 1928. *A Study in Public Finance*. 3rd edition. London: Macmillan.

Pigou, A. 1932. *Economics of Welfare*. London: Macmillan.

Piketty, T. 2014. *Capital in the Twenty-First Century*. Cambridge, MA: Harvard University Press.

Pitman, E. 1937. "Significance Tests That May Be Applied to Samples from any Population: II. The Correlation Coefficient Test." *Journal of Royal Statistical Society* (supplement 4): 225–32.

Plotnick, R. 1981. "A Measure of Horizontal Equity." *Review of Economics and Statistics* 63: 283–88.

Pollak, R. 1971. "Additive Utility Functions and Linear Engel Curves." *Review of Economic Studies* 38, no. 4: 401–14.

Pollak, R. 1980. "Group Cost of Living Indexes." *American Economic Review* 70: 273–78.

Pollak, R. 1981. "The Social Cost of Living Index." *Journal of Public Economics* 15: 311–36.

Pollak, R. 1983. "The Theory of the Cost of living Index." In W. Diewert and C. Montmarquette (Eds) *Price Level Measurement*. Ministry of Supply and Services, Canada.

Pollak, R. 1998. "The Consumer Price Index: A Research Agenda and Three Proposals." *Journal of Economic Perspectives* 12: 69–78.

Prais, S. 1959. "Whose Cost of Living." *Review of Economic Studies* 26: 126–34.

Prais, S. and H. Houthakker. 1955. *The Analysis of Family Budgets*. Cambridge, England: Cambridge University Press.

Pressman, S. 2007. "The Decline of the Middle-Class: An International Perspective." *Journal of Economic Issues*, vol. 41 (1): 181–200.

Ravallion, M. 1998. "Poverty Lines in Theory and Practice." *LSMS Working Paper* No. 133. Washington, DC: World Bank.

Ravallion, M. 1995. "Growth and Poverty: Evidence for Developing Counties in the 1980s." *Economic Letters* 48, 411–17.

Ravallion, M. 1997. "Can High-Inequality Developing Countries Escape Absolute Poverty?" *Economic Letters* 56: 51–57.

Ravallion, M. 1998. "Poverty Lines in Theory and Practice." LSMS Working Paper no. 133, Washington, DC: World Bank.

Ravallion, M. 2001. "Growth, Inequality, and Poverty: Looking Beyond Averages." *World Development*, vol. 29, no. 11, pp 1803–1815.

Ravallion, M. and B. Bidani. 1994. "How Robust Is a Poverty Profile?" *World Bank Economic Review* 8: 75–102.

Ravallion, M. and S. Chen. 1997. "What can New Survey Data tell us about Recent Changes in Distribution and Poverty." *World Bank Economic Review*, vol. 11(2), pp 357–382.

Ravallion, M. and S. Chen. 2003. "Measuring Pro-Poor Growth." *Economics Letters* 78: 93–99.

Ravallion, M. and M. Huppi. 1991. "Measuring Changes in Poverty: A Methodological Case Study of Indonesia During an Adjustment Period." *World Bank Economic Review*, vol. 5 (1), pp 57–82.

Ravallion, M. 2009. "How Relevant Is Targeting to the Success of an Anti-poverty Program." *World Bank Research Observer*, vol. 24 (2), pp 205–231.

Rawls, J. 1971. *A Theory of Justice*. Cambridge, MA: Harvard University Press.

Rodrik, D. 2000. "Growth and Poverty Reduction: What are the Real Questions." Article prepared for publication in *Finance and Development*.

Romer, P. 1994. "The Origin of Endogenous Growth." *Journal of Economic Perspective*, vol. 8 (1), pp 3–22.

Roemer, J. 1998. *Equality of Opportunity*. Cambridge, MA: Harvard University Press.

Rolph, E. 1967. "The Case for a Negative Income Tax Device." *Industrial Relations* 2: 155–65.

Rosen, H. 1978. "An Approach to the Study of Income, Utility, and Horizontal Equity." *Quarterly Journal of Economics* 92: 307–22.

Rothbarth, E. 1943. "Note on a method of determining equivalent income for families of different composition." In C. Madge (Ed) *War-time Pattern of Saving and Spending*. Cambridge: Cambridge University Press.

Rothschild, M. and J. Stiglitz. 1970. "Increasing Risk: A Definition." *Journal of Economic Theory* 2: 225–43.

Rothschild, M. and J. Stiglitz. 1973. "Some Further Results on the Measurement of Inequality." *Journal of Economic Theory* 6: 188–204.

Rowntree, B. 1901. *Poverty: A Study of Town Life*. London: Macmillan.

Roy, J., I. Chakravarty, and R. Laha. 1959. "A Study of Concentration as a Description of Consumption Patterns." In *Studies in Consumer Behavior*. Calcutta: Indian Statistical Institute.

Runciman, W. 1966. *Relative Deprivation and Social Justice: A Study of Attitude to Social Inequality in Twentieth-Century England*. London: Routledge and Kegan Paul.

Rutherford, R. 1955. "Income Distributions: A New Model." *Econometrica* 23: 277–94.

Salem, A. and T. Mount. 1974. "A Convenient Descriptive Model of Income Distribution: The Gamma Density." *Econometrica* 42: 1115–27.

Samuelson, P. 1947. *Foundation of Economic Analysis.* Cambridge, MA: Harvard University Press.

Samuelson, P. and S. Swamy. 1979. "Invariant Economic Index Numbers and Canonical Duality: Survey and Synthesis." *American Economic Review* 64: 566–93.

Sen, A. 1972, "Utilitarianism and Inequality." *Economic and Political Weekly*, vol. 7, pp 54–57.

Sen, A. 1973. *On Economic Inequality.* Oxford: Clarendon Press.

Sen, A. 1976. "Poverty: An Ordinal Approach to Measurement." *Econometrica* 44: 219–31.

Sen, A. 1981. *Poverty, and Famine: An Essay on Entitlement and Deprivation.* New York: Oxford University Press.

Sen, A. K. 1983. "Poor, Relatively Speaking." *Oxford Economic Papers* 35: 153–69.

Sen, A. 1985. *Commodities and Capabilities.* Amsterdam: North-Holland.

Sen, A. 1992. *Inequality Reexamined*, Cambridge, MA: Harvard University Press.

Sen, A. 1997. *On Economic Inequality.* Oxford: Clarendon Press.

Sen, A. 1999. *Development as Freedom.* New York: Alfred A Knopf.

Sen, A. 2004. "Capabilities, Lists, and Public Reason: Continuing the Conversation." *Feminist Economics* 10, no. 3, pp 1–10.

Sen, A. 2006. "Conceptualization and Measuring Poverty." In D. Grusky and R. Kanbur (Eds) *Poverty and Inequality.* Stanford: Stanford University Press.

Shapely, L. 1953. "A Value for n-person games." In H. Kuhn and A. Tucker (Eds) *Contributions to the Theory of Games II.* Princeton, NJ: Princeton University Press.

Sheshinski, E. 1972b. "Relation between a Social Welfare Function and the Gini Index of Inequality." *Journal of Economic Theory* 4: 98–100.

Shirras, G. 1935. "The Pareto Law and the Distribution of Income." *Economic Journal* 45: 663–81.

Shorrocks, A. 1980. "The Class of Additive Decomposable Inequality Measures." *Econometrica* 48, no. 3: 613–26.

Shorrocks, A. 1983. "Ranking of Income Distributions." *Economica* 50: 3–18.

Shorrocks, A., 1988, "Aggregation Issues in Inequality Measurement", In W. Eichhorn (Ed) *Measurement in Economics*, New York: Physica-Verlag.

Shorrocks, A. 1995. "Revisiting Sen's Poverty Index." *Econometrica* 63: pp 1225–1230.

Shorrocks, A. 1988. "Aggregation issues in inequality measurement." In W. Eichhorn (Ed) *Measurement in Economics*, New York: Physica-Verlag.

Shorrocks, A. 2005. "Inequality Values and Unequal Shares." Unpublished Paper UNU-WIDER, Helsinki.

Shorrocks, A. and J. Foster. 1987. "Transfer Sensitive Inequality Measures." *Review of Economic Studies* 54: 487–97.

Singh B., and A. Nagar. 1973. "Determination of Consumer Unit Scales." *Econometrica* 41: 347–56.

Singh, S. and G. Maddala. 1976. "A Function for Size Distribution of Income." *Econometrica*, vol. 44, pp 963–73.

Smith, D. 1965. "A Simplified Approach to Social Welfare." *Canadian Tax Journal* 13: 260–65.

Son, H. 2004. "A Note on Pro-Poor Growth." *Economic Letters* 82: 307–14.

Son, H. 2006. "Assessing the Pro-Poorness of Government Fiscal Policy: The Thailand Case." *Public Finance Review* 34, no. 4: 1–23.

Son, H. 2011. *Equity and Well-Being: Measurement and Policy Practice.* London: Routledge.

Son, H. and N. Kakwani. 2006. "Measuring the Impact of Prices on Inequality with Applications to Thailand and Korea." *Journal of Economic Inequality* 4, no. 2: 181–207.

Son, H. and N. Kakwani. 2008. "Measuring the Impact of Prices Changes on Poverty." *Journal of Economic Inequality* 4: 395–410.

Squire, L. 1993. "Fighting Poverty." *American Economic Review*, vol. 83(2), pp 377–182.

Stern, N. 1991. "Determinants of Growth." *Economic Journal*, vol. 101, issue 404, pp 122–33.

Stiglitz, J. 1969. "Distribution of Income and Wealth among Individuals." *Econometrica* 37: 382–97.

Stiglitz, J. 2012. *The Price of Inequality.* London: Penguin.

Stouffer, S. 1949. *The American Soldier*. Princeton, NJ: Princeton University Press.

Suits, D. 1977. "Measurement of Tax Progressivity." *American Economic Review* 67: 747–52.

Takayama, N. 1979. "Poverty, Income Inequality, and their Measures: Professor Sen's Axiomatic Approach Reconsidered." *Econometrica* 47: pp 747–757.

Theil, H. 1967. *Economics and Information Theory*. Amsterdam: North-Holland.

Thon, D. 1979. "On Measuring Poverty." *Review of Income and Wealth* 25: pp 429–439.

Thon, D. 1983. "A Note on a Troublesome Axiom for Poverty Indices." *Economic Journal* 93: 199–200.

Thorbecke, E. 2008. "Multidimensional Poverty: Concepts and Measurement Issues." In N. Kakwani and J. Silber. (Eds) *The Many Dimensions of Poverty*, New York: Palgrave Macmillan.

Thurow, L. 1984. "Disappearance of Middle Class." New York Times pE2.

Tinbergen, J. 1975. *Income Distribution: Analysis and Policy*. Amsterdam: North-Holland.

Tobin, J. 1965. "Improving the Economic Status of the Negro." *Daedalus* 94: 878–98.

Tsui, K. 2002. "Multidimensional Poverty Indices." *Social Choice and Welfare* 19: 69–93.

Tsuji, M. 1972. "A Note on Professor Stiglitz's Distribution of Income and Wealth." *Econometrica* 40: 947–49.

Urban, I. 2014. "Contributions of Taxes and Benefits to Vertical and Horizontal Effects." *Social Choice and Welfare* 42, no. 3: 619–45.

Urban, I. 2019. "Measuring Redistributive Effects of Taxes and Benefits: Beyond the Proportionality Standard." *FinanzArchiv* 75, no. 4: 413–43. https://doi.org/10.1628/fa-20190008.

United Nations Development Programme. 2020. *Multidimensional poverty index: dimensions, indicators, deprivation cutoffs, and weights*. New York: UNDP.

Watts, H. 1968. "An Economic Definition of Poverty." In D. Moynihan (Ed) *Understanding Poverty*. New York: Basic Books.

Weisskoff, R. 1970. "Income Distribution and Economic Growth in Puerto Rico, Argentina, and Mexico." *Review of Income and Wealth* 16: 303–32.

Wilks, S. 1944. *Mathematical Statistics*. Princeton, NJ: Princeton University Press.

World Bank. 2006. *World Development Report: Equity in Opportunity*. Washington, DC: World Bank.

World Bank. 2015. *The State of Social Safety Net Report*. Washington, DC: World Bank.

Yaari, M. 1988. "A Controversial Proposal Concerning Inequality Measurement." *Journal of Economic Theory* 44, no. 2: 381–97.

Yitzhaki, S. 1979. "Relative Deprivation and the Gini Index." *Quarterly Journal of Economics* 93: 321–24.

Yitzhaki, S. 1983. "On an Extension of the Gini Index." *International Economic Review* 24: 617–28.

Yntema, D. 1933. "Measures of the Inequality in the Personal Distribution of Wealth or Income." *Journal of the American Statistical Association* 28: 423–33.

Zenga, M. 2007. "Inequality Curve, and Inequality Index based on the Ratios of Lower and Upper Arithmetic Means." *Statistics, and Applicazioni* 5, no. 1: 3–27.

Zheng, B. 1993. "An Axiomatic Characterization of Watts Poverty Index." *Economic Letters* 42: 81–86.

Zhang, X. and R. Kanbur. 2001. "What Difference Do Polarization Measures Make? An Application to China." *Journal of Development Studies*, vol. 37 (3), pp 85–98.

Name Index

Hicks, J.R. 21, 384, 406
Hinchliffe, K 4
Hoddinott, J. 19, 355
Huppi, M. 427
Husen, T. 3
Huston, J. 129

Iyenger, N.S. 229 n.2

Jackson, J. 128
Jain, S. 53, 61
Jakobsson, U. 286, 312
Jalbert, V. 317
Jensen, J.L.W.V. 295
Johnson, P. 317

Kalecki, M. 41
Kanbur, R. 14, 133, 263
Kaplow, L. 88
Kats, A. 114
Khetan, C.P. 278
Klemm, A. 301 n.1
Kolm, S. 16, 45, 64, 100, 112, 114, 124, 166, 174,
     281, 303, 304, 319, 452
Konus, A.A. 21, 384
Kraay, A. 25, 439, 442, 451, 451 n.1
Kuga, K. 103 n.3
Kundu, A. 180
Kuznets, S. 4, 59–61, 62, 74–5, 120, 199

Laha, R.G. 230 n.3
Lambert, P.J. 3, 15, 16, 118, 119 n.9, 271, 272,
     288–9, 291–2, 294, 295, 309 n.9, 317
Lampman, R.J. 337
Lanjouw, P. 148
Laplace, P.-S. 30
Lerner, A.P. 89
Levy, P. 3, 37
Lipton, M. 25
Li, S. 20, 356
Littlewood, J.E. 85, 90
Liu, L. 301 n.1
Lorenz, M.O. 4, 44, 73, 95
Lucas, R.E. Jr. 422
Luo, C. 477

McCulloch, N. 25
McFadden, D.L. 386
Maddala, G.S. 39 n.1
Mahalanobis, P.C. 12, 225
Mandelbrot, B. 36–7
Meade, J. 112–13
Merton, R.K. 139 n.1
Mincer, J. 3
Mount, T.D. 42–3

Moyes, P. 277 n.1, 304 n.6
Muellbauer, J. 7, 98, 384
Musgrave, R.A. 271, 275, 276, 285–6, 288, 312
Mylonas, V. 301 n.1

Neri, M.C. 416
Newbery, D. 98, 114, 115
Nussbaum, M. 204

Orshansky, M. 139 n.2

Pareto, V. 3, 27, 30, 33, 39, 42, 81
Pattanaik, P. 170, 173 n.3
Pernia, E.M. 25, 452, 462
Pfingsten, A. 303 n.4
Pigou, A. 79, 271, 275
Pitman, E. 324
Plotnick, R. 307
Poddar, S.N. 278
Podder, N. 4, 44, 52–3
Pollak, R. 21, 303, 319, 384, 385, 389,
     393, 397
Polya, G. 85, 90
Prais, S.J. 21, 384, 387, 389–90
Psacharopoulos, G 4

Ravallion, M. 8, 25, 141, 146–7, 148, 356, 426,
     427, 439, 452, 454, 465, 468
Rawls, J. 366
Ray, D. 7, 99, 128, 132
Rodrik, D. 420
Roemer, J. 14, 263
Rolph, E.R. 18–19, 337
Romer, P.J. 422
Rosen, H. 285, 306
Rothschild, M. 76, 78, 91, 98, 114, 115
Rowntree, B.S. 8, 138, 139
Roy, J. 3, 230 n.3
Runciman, W. 98, 115, 139 n.1
Rutherford, R.S.G. 3, 42

Salem, A.B.Z. 42–3
Samuelson, P.A. 21, 81, 90, 384
Seaks, T. 283, 330
Sen, A.K. 7, 8, 9, 10, 11, 21 n.4, 49, 76, 79, 84–5,
     98, 99, 109, 111, 115, 116–18, 122, 136, 138,
     140, 144, 162, 166, 167, 168–9, 170, 172–5,
     179, 180, 183, 189, 194, 202–3, 204, 211, 215,
     222–3, 239, 306, 366, 385 n.1, 394
Sengupta, M. 170, 173 n.3
Shapely 363
Sheshinsky, E. 98, 114, 115
Shirras, G.F. 33
Shorrocks, A.F. 77, 101, 103, 106, 108, 110, 118,
     177, 179, 194, 195–6

Subject Index